Writer's Northwest Handbook

5th Edition

Writer's Northwest Handbook

5th Edition

Blue Heron Publishing, Inc.
Hillsboro, Oregon

Writer's Northwest Handbook
5th Edition

Copyright © 1993 by Blue Heron Publishing, Inc.

Published by
Media Weavers
Blue Heron Publishing, Inc.
24450 NW Hansen Road
Hillsboro, Oregon 97124
503.621.3911

Editorial and research staff:
Linny Stovall
Dennis Stovall
Mary Jo Schimelpfenig
Christian Seapy
Scholle Sawyer
Daniel Foulkes
Bill Woodall

Advertising sales:
Darlene Fesler
John Johnson
Dennis Stovall

This project is supported in part by grants from the Idaho State Commission on the Arts, the Montana Arts Council, and the Oregon Arts Commission.

Cover art copyright © 1992 by Larry Milam
Design and typography by Dennis Stovall
Printed and bound in the United States of America
at Gilliland Printing, Arkansas City, Kansas.

ISBN 0-936085-56-8
ISSN 0896-7946

Notes on Production

Since the second edition, *Writer's Northwest Handbook* has been designed and typeset electronically. The suite of tools listed below has evolved from the first generation of desktop publishing hardware and software, with each step increasing both the level of automation and the degree of control and precision. We are able to publish a new edition with a minimum lag between updating our data and going to press. Final edits were made less than a week before the printer took over.

While the editorial focus and organization of the essay section requires constant attention, the massive amounts of data in the publisher and resource lists poses special problems. In the past, data-formatting was labor intensive. None of the affordable programs could properly massage and parse the raw data into a state suitable for press. We'd like to acknowledge one tool in particular for changing all of that. Pro-Cite 2.1, marketed as a professional tool for creating lists of citations and other bibliographies in virtually every arcane format, adapted nicely to the exigencies of data base publishing. It not only generated files of consistent, well-formatted text, but it created the indexes that give access to the lists.

Another acknowledgment goes to Gilliland Printing. Their commitment to swift delivery ensures that the data are as fresh as possible — at a cost that allows us to keep the retail price within bounds.

We do our final high resolution output at several reliable service bureaus in turn. This book was handled by L.grafix in Portland, where Andy White and crew marshalled the files through in short order.

Tools used in the production of this book included: Macintosh computers (II, IIcx, IIci, Quadra 700); RasterOps, E-Machines, and Radius monitors; Laserwriter IINT printer and Linotronic imagesetters; HP Scanjet Plus; PageMaker 4.2; Microsoft Word 5.0; FileMaker Pro; Pro-Cite 2.1; Ofoto; Nisus 3.06; Adobe Illustrator 3.0; TypeReader OCR; SuperATM, and other software.

Dedicated to the
teachers.

Contents

SECTION V: ORGANIZATIONS / 75

SECTION VI: PUBLISHING LISTS / 85

Acknowledgments

Support for the 5th edition of *Writer's Northwest Handbook* came from throughout the region's literary community. No project of this scope can continue without the cooperation of many individuals and organizations. We'd especially like to thank for their grants and aid the Oregon Center for the Book, the Idaho Commission on the Arts, the Montana Arts Council, and the Oregon Arts Commission. Their confidence has added to ours.

The writers whose contributions grace the pages that follow were a wonderful bunch to work with. They've offered both a wealth of talent and a bounty of generosity. One of the things that makes the writing and publishing community in the Northwest so vital and productive is the unselfish sharing of ideas and experience.

We thank all of you who used previous editions and provided your suggestions for improvement. Keep those cards and letters coming.

Each edition has a staff that gives the final book its unique character. Those who left their marks are listed on the copyright page. They cannot be thanked enough for their efforts.

Once more, we have Larry Milam to thank for the cover art.

Introduction

Welcome.

For some of you, the 5th edition of *Writer's Northwest Handbook* is an invitation to dip into the deep pool of talent that surrounds us. For others, this completely updated edition is an invitation to dive into that pool and become one with the community it represents.

There are probably as many ways to use this book as there are users. Well, maybe not that many, but a lot. This is the best regional resource for writers, publishers, librarians, booksellers, and teachers of writing, English, and journalism. It's a combination of literary salon, research tool, resource directory, and market guide. It's designed to be useful to beginners and pros. It can be used casually, or it can be a daily reference. The articles may be read for pleasure, or as coursework. Even the directory sections offers their shares of entertainment. Take a cruise through some of the names of publications and you'll see what we mean.

At its heart, *Writer's Northwest Handbook* is an intentional tool for community building. Without pandering to regional chauvinism, we're comfortable in saying that the writers and publishers of the Northwest are exceptionally prolific. But that would be nothing to shout about if the quantity weren't matched by quality. It's the sort of self-reinforcing environment that this book hopes to sustain and enhance. It's our contention that a self-conscious community of the printed word can make it easier for all of us to do more and better work.

You are invited to jump in, to join all of the others who share the wonder of words. It doesn't matter how old you are, if your stories hit their mark. It doesn't matter how much schooling you've had, if you care about the sound, the rhythm, the meaning of the words you commit to paper. It doesn't matter what nationality or religion nurtured your point of view. No one has your vision or your experiences. You read from your own perspective. And, if you write, it's the unique filter of your mind that makes your work special.

Benjamin Hoff Interview

David Pinson

Benjamin Hoff, a Portland resident, is the author of two nonfiction books, The Tao of Pooh *and* The Te of Piglet, *that have enjoyed considerable success. His book,* The Singing Creek Where The Willows Grow, *received a 1988 American Book Award. A Taoist, Hoff is also acquainted with two well-known literary figures, Pooh and Piglet.*

P: What year was *The Tao of Pooh* published?

H: 1982 in hard-cover and 1983 in paperback. One of the unusual things about *The Tao of Pooh* is that it's sold well in paperback. When it came out in paperback it was mentioned on a national public radio show for 90 seconds or so and it went on the *Washington Post* list within a couple of weeks and then onto *The New York Times list.* It was (there) for three months and then it sort of faded out and all of us involved thought: "Well, that was fun." Then about four or five years ago, for some reason, sales started picking up and for the past four or five years it sold more each year than the year previous, and now the US edition alone is selling over 10,000 copies a month, by word of mouth. So something is going on. That has made a big difference financially.

P: Are you surprised?

H: I am, and I'm also surprised at the way *The Te of Piglet* has taken off. Before it was even officially published it was on two or three bestseller lists!

P: I low does that happen?

H: I don't know. If anybody can figure it out, we'd sure like to know. There was one ad in *The New York Times* book review and that was a week after it was officially published, which was Sept. 15, 1992. And that was it as far as the ads go, but something happened. The only thing I can figure out is that the bookstores have been selling *The Tao of Pooh* really well and so they saw this follow-up book come along and they said, "We'll display this and see what happens." It just caught on.

P: When were you first exposed to Taoism?

H: Ever since I was a little kid, I've liked being out in the woods a lot. I grew up outside of Portland. It's now part of a freeway, but there was a woods there and I just loved spending my time out there, mostly watching ants. I love ants. Raccoons, too. Anyway, that's how I started getting interested in the natural world and learning from animals and working with natural laws. Formally, I found out about Taoism, I think, in either high school or college. In college I started buying books like the *Tao Te Ching* and started meeting people involved in Tai Chi, and I then started taking Tai Chi lessons from Chinese people, some of whom had spent years in a Taoist monastery. From them I got more of an official education.

P: Is Taoism a religion or a philosophy?

H: That depends on whom you ask. One school of thought is that it started out as a philosophy and then sort of degenerated into a religion, which is known as Popular Taoism. Another way of looking at it is that Taoism started out as a religion but then became a philosophy, and then later on became sort of a folk religion. It's really a complex situation because Taoism is so old nobody knows exactly how it got started. In China, for at least the last couple thousand years — what there is now, what the Communists haven't gotten rid of — Taoism is both a religion and a philosophy.

P: Do you feel lucky that you've found such a unique idea, this idea of using the Pooh stories to teach Taoism?

H: Yes, the book characters seemed ready-made, universal characters. Once I thought about it, which is sometime after I wrote the book, I wondered why people hadn't done it before. I mean, they are so ready-made, ready for somebody to use for something.

P: When you first had the idea, did you start right away?

H: I let it sit for awhile. Sort of cook, you know, somewhere in the back of my head. I'm not sure how long it took for me to actually start writing notes and things. I started making notes on index cards about ideas that related to the Pooh characters and then started writing, shuffling ideas around and that's when it really got going, I guess.

P: With *The Te of Piglet*, did you write straight through, knowing its form?

H: Basically, yes. Once I did *The Tao of Pooh*, I'd done it, I'd had the experience. It was like swimming or something. Once you've done it, you go away and sort of forget about it until then you try it again and it suddenly comes back to you. In that sense, *The Te of Piglet* was easier, but in another sense it was harder because there were more ideas and it got really complicated.

P: Which character do you identify with the most?

H: I tend to identify with Tigger and Piglet, because I'm like both of them. Emotionally, I am probably more like Piglet, but as far as doing things I'm overactive, I tend to take on more than I can chew, so I'm more like Tigger in that. But there's something in all the Pooh characters I can identify with.

P: What about Pooh?

H: Pooh? He just doesn't let anything bother him. And that's like, to me, Pooh is the ideal. If I can make it through the day without being bothered by something, that's really something! I like Pooh's philosophy on life, which is to take things as they come and live every minute, and appreciate what is happening to you now instead of worrying about what's going to happen later on, but that's a hard thing to live up to. People don't want to let you be Pooh. They want you to be somebody else, like Tigger. Our society is not geared toward Poohs.

P: How can each of us learn from *The Tao of Pooh* and *The Te of Piglet*?

H: *The Tao of Pooh* is a book I wrote to the individual, and how to be happy and not let people get to you too much, just sort of enjoy life. *The Te of Piglet* is more a social and political thing, which is in keeping with Taoism, but is a different side of Taoism than most people are acquainted with even if they read books on Taoism. I think of *The Te of Piglet* as being directed more to current politics and people.

P: Does everybody have a "Te?" And how does one recognize it?

H: That's what we're here for, to discover that virtue, that character, that special something that we've got. And how do we do it? We can, as I tried to make the case for Piglet, by going beyond ourselves and doing something that does somebody some good. But then also you might learn it by being in Tibet and meditating in a cave for all your life. You have to figure out what's good for you.

P: Could your works, then, be thought of as guidebooks?

H: Yes, that's what I tried to make them, and I tried to keep things fun.

P: Why so much humor?

H: It is hard to find anything in philosophy or anything to do with the mind that has a sense of humor. I just like to keep things on a fairly light level. A lot of people think as soon as you interject or apply humor you're debasing something, and that also life isn't funny. *The Tao of Pooh*, for instance, which made fun of desiccated scholars, who are very dry people, and who I and a lot of other Taoists think are ruining Taoism by taking all the life out of it, received a lot of angry reviews from the people it satirized. So with *The Te of Piglet*, I expect a lot of angry reviews from critics.

P: How did you decide which stories from Chinese Taoist writings to use?

H: I just find these things and make mental notes. A couple of those in *The Te of Piglet*, I wrote down from memory because I can't find those stories in English. I have a natural inclination to pick up those things. People ask me about how long it took me to research (both books) and that's really hard to answer because for years and years I've been collecting things. So (the books) were perfect excuses to use some of those stories.

(The books) were more like organization projects than creating projects. I mean there is some creative stuff in there, but it's mostly organizing something I already knew or what somebody else already said, which was fun, but it didn't really involve sitting down and reading. To do the research would have taken me who knows how many years.

P: You quote Thoreau extensively in both books. How does Taoism relate to Early American writings on nature?

H: Thoreau, I particularly like because I like his sarcastic sense of humor and I like the way he organizes things. He'll be writing about fungus or something really minute and scientific, and he'll go from that to a discourse on philosophy, and then he'll go back to the old man who dropped by the other day and left a leaf on his table or something like that. He hop, skips, and jumps from one thing to the other and yet it sort of has this flow to it. Thoreau seemed a natural.

P: What do you hope *The Te of Piglet* readers remember?

H: I would like to think they got some encouragement because in Western society being shy and quiet and introspective is not exactly encouraged. People are made fun of or criticized or even worse — made to feel bad about themselves for being shy, quiet, or intelligent. So I hope I encourage Piglets to take heart and have more courage. I give them an alternative point of view from what they get in school, the workplace or culture, a culture that values people who are colorful, who talk fast, and who shoot people.

P: Any advice for other writers?

H: If you really want to be a writer, you're going to have to endure an awful lot of garbage. People are going to make critical remarks, really snipe at stuff and some of it is going to be direct and some will be sarcastic remarks that just sort of sting. And then there will be all sorts of problems paying the bills, things like that. If I'd known how difficult it was going to be, chances are I wouldn't have done it, so it is just as well that I didn't know. My best advice is not to pay too much attention to other people's advice but just do what you want to do, and just keep working at it.

It's a weird profession. I mean, I've got a book on the best-seller lists right now and I don't know how I did it. I don't know who these people are that are buying the book. I don't know why they like it or dislike it. I hear from quite a few by letter, you know, people talk to me, meet me, whatever. It's just a weird profession.

David Pinson is a fiction writer who lives in Portland. His stories have appeared in ZYZZYVA, Metropolis Monthly, *and* Plazm.

Glyphs

Sandra Alcosser

Sometimes I have worked on countries poetically. Cambodia is an example. In my mind, I had an imaginary Cambodia composed of everything I had read. But, of course, nothing could render the actual experience of going to Cambodia which is something that passes through the body, through the senses, something which happens between Cambodia and me — my encounter with its smell, its space, the colors of the sky. All these different stages are, in reality, the history of a text. And our reading must be a movement capable of following all the stages of this vast journey from one to the other, to me, to you… We have to go to the country of the text and bring back the earth of which the language is made.

          Helene Cixous, Writing Differences

My friend tells me about a cave that he found near the river where we pick blackberries — a cave lined with fur — and when he touched the walls they moved under his fingers. The cave had an odor, not of bear, he said, but of insects, and looking closely he could see that it was not fur at all, but Daddy Long Legs huddled together, sleeping. He touched their bodies and they crawled over the top of each other, a zillion spiders shifting, stirring in their dreams.

When I think of the writing process, the cave of my geologist friend comes to mind. With its attendant mystery and metaphor (dark and firing cavern of the heart, warm cafe of the unconscious), it's a perfect writer's space. The poet's work, writes Denise Levertov, *is not to flood darkness with light so that darkness is destroyed, but to enter into darkness, mystery so that it is experienced.* Mystery — that tactile void flicking with translucent, gray-haired bodies, eight-eyed, nearsighted, smelling of spiders. Even the genre attracts, though I do not read mystery novels. Who would not love a form that through its narrative process, moving from effect to cause, seeking revelation, has the ability to bring a body, or a body's story, back to life?

In *The Perfect Murder*, David Lehman says mystery is always and ever the epistemological riddle, a progression toward truth by questioning our sources of knowledge. Citing Voltaire's *Zadig* (1749) as the first literary exposition of the science of deduction, the story of a holy man whose study of nature enabled him to discern a thousand differences where others saw only uniformity, Lehman explores the way that Zadig turned paleontologist, archaeologist, geologist in his quest for truth. And isn't that the path of the writer as well, following what Wallace Stevens called *the mind in the act of finding what will suffice?*

I think about all this now because I am in the middle of a project that is a bit of a mystery. Last summer I was invited, as one of ten artists, to raft forty-eight miles of the Upper Missouri National Wild and Scenic River in northern Montana from Coal Banks to Judith Landing. The float, organized by the Paris Gibson Museum of Art in Great Falls, Montana, and sponsored by a number of organizations, including the Montana Committee for the Humanities, was to encourage a river dialogue between contemporary artists that would culminate in a catalog, exhibition, and seminar at the museum in February, 1993.

We floated three days over hundreds of millions of years of exposed sea floor, through old marshes, broken tablelands, and wheat stubble, past yellow-faced flannel mullein, shypoke, milk sow thistle. With our rafts and canoes we followed the course of pirogue, bateau, snag boat, keelboat, dugout, mackinaw, bullboat, and steamboat that had come before. We camped one night at Eagle Creek, the next at Slaughter River, where Lewis and Clark slept 187

Mostly the momentary physical world pressed itself upon us. Asteroid fragments and acetylene sparks from Delta Aquari collided overhead as we drank wine around the night's fire.

years earlier, where the Corps of Discovery was commissioned to note the soil and the face of the country, the remains of anything rare or extinct, the minerals and volcanic evidences, the proportion of rainy, cloudy, and clear days, lightning, hail, snow, ice, the coming and going of frost, winds, the dates when plants put forth leaves, flowers, the arrival and departure of birds, reptiles, insects, mammals. *We were now able to penetrate a country at least two thousand miles in width, on which the foot of civilized man had never trodden,* wrote Merriwether Lewis …*I could but esteem this moment of my departure as among the most happy of my life.*

River of trade, of war and resources, of progress and processes of Western development, now government-managed wild and scenic corridor — we crossed the Lewis and Clark Historic Trail in late July, the month that snakes shed their skins, and as we bathed in the green evening river, rattlesnake peelings bobbed beside us, with beaver skulls, syrupy shales, fossil fish, and the detritus of ten thousand years of human habitation. When we searched for evidence of those who had come before, we found petroglyphs rubbed and pecked into sandstone, figures superimposed over each other like palimpsests, what archeologists described as…*a probable right-facing horse ridden by a possible human, best seen in acute angle light, a modern bullet hole appearing at the juncture of throat and jaw, lines fluttering into amorphousness.*

Mostly the momentary physical world pressed itself upon us. Asteroid fragments and acetylene sparks from Delta Aquari collided overhead as we drank wine around the night's fire. Manami Takenchi, a potter from Kumamoto, one of two Japanese artists who accompanied us on the trip, sketched *Naga Re Boshi*, shooting star, in my journal. When someone asked if we planned to leave our mark on the cliffs, in the manner of William Clark, to carve our names into geologic history, I heard the group draw a collective breath. Memory would be our only glyph, incised and in relief, the signature of the expedition.

Mark Twain would have found the Missouri, like the Mississippi, imminently translatable: *the face of the water, in time, became a wonderful book — a book that was a dead language to the uneducated passenger, but which told its mind to me without reserve, delivering its most cherished secrets* as clearly as if it uttered them with a voice. But I knew, as we floated the river's five-mile-an-hour current, that I would not honor my contract until long after we left the water. I thought of Robert Creeley's poem: *There is a world/underneath, or/ on top of/ this one — and /it's here now.* Physicists speculate that the world is only ghostly images, projections from a level of reality beyond our own space and time. I sought an all-inclusive form for the poems that I planned to write, a form similar to that holographic paradigm, slippery as gumbo, full of contradictions, fluid as the migrating shoreline.

Mornings, light broomed our bodies, washed us with cliff colors — lavender to vermilion, rose to ash, opal to gray. And silence. An occasional voice sang over the river to our canoe. One of the photographers told a story that broke into syllabics: *A band of gypsies / crossed the prairie/ a dancing grizzly/ on a chain. /They all drank brandy.* A woman's voice wavered through juniper and limber pine: *In grief we lose the high notes.* Later, the voice of another woman: *When I hear a baby crying, milk pours from my body.*

Lewis and Clark found images of Palladian architecture in the sandstone as they cordelled and catalogued the Missouri Breaks for President Jefferson. *Elegant ranges of freestone buildings having their parapets stocked with statuary, columns of various sculpture, both grooved and plain, long galleries, alcoves, capitals, pedestals, vast pyramids of conic structure.* Prince Maximilian followed almost thirty years later and saw white castles and ancient Gothic chapels in the same shale. We came representing the arts and humanities, seeking the lost voices of the past, and the rock formations we paddled through became catacombs, sloughing cliff faces draped with blue sage, torsos of ghosts huddled together, open-mouthed chalkstone waiting to tell their stories.

Close to knowing, Umberto Eco suggests, is as close as we might ever come to the labyrinth of the world. Eco constructed a best-selling novel in which he intentionally created a mystery for which little was discovered and by which the metaphysical detective was defeated. While Eco's formula might have been the perfect philosophical model for our expedition, the voyages of earlier explorers more closely mirrored the classic mystery novel in which the protagonist assumes that the world is intelligible and that he might gain control over the unknown through logic and deduction.

In the literary construction of mystery, one might take it for granted that nature can be controlled, but of course history proves otherwise. Consider Prince Maximilian who attempted to capture for science the same section of river that we floated. Along with the romantic painter, Karl Bodmer, he studied the Blackfeet, Gros Ventres, and Assiniboine tribes for two months. Together the two men pressed hundreds of plants between pages, collected skins and skeletons of birds, mammals, insects, all of which they tried to haul back to Germany along with two large caged bears and a prairie dog. A storm came up near the Marias River drenching the expedition; the prairie dog drowned, the bears moaned and licked their fur, and the shivering crew came ashore to build fires to dry the Prince's treasures. A wind rose and sent the specimens flying — eagle feathers, butterfly wings, artemesia — now lifeless, lifting and returning home. The buffalo robes and stitched leather dresses blackened with mold. What little the men did save, along with what they picked and dried again, would be destroyed months later when the steamer Assiniboine ran aground outside Saint Louis and its cargo went up in flames.

Mark Twain cautioned that when he had mastered the language of water and *had come to know every trifling feature that bordered the great river as familiarly as (he) knew the letters of the alphabet,* he lost the poetry and grace of his vision, and it could not be restored within his lifetime. Rivers are ambivalent in substance and symbol, marking the edges of civilization, circumnavigating individual intellect. And isn't the writing process itself like the river — fickle, braided, seeking its lost channel, insinuating itself between snags and sawyers, making its soft impression against the walls? The poem, writes Severo Sarduy, is itself perpetual *change, an always unstable substitution, and an always precarious birth of signs at the site of that throbbing between the external and the truth: on the oscillating frontier of the page.*

Sandra Alcosser lives in Florence, Montana. Her poems have appeared in The American Poetry Review, The New Yorker, *and* The Paris Review. A Fish to Feed All Hunger *(Absahta Press '93) was selected by James Tate for the AWP Poetry Award. Alcosser is a professor at San Diego State University.*

*I sought
an all-inclusive
form
for the poems
that I planned
to write,
a form similar to
that holographic
paradigm,
slippery as gumbo,
full of contradictions,
fluid
as the migrating shoreline.*

A Communal Story for the West: An Interview with William Kittredge

Kevin Bezner

Short story writer and essayist William Kittredge turned to memoir with his latest book, Hole in the Sky, *one of the finest books to emerge in recent years from a Western writer. In his story of the MC ranch in the Warner Valley of southeastern Oregon, Kittredge has told of his family's part in the story of the American West, the story of rugged individualism and endless riches that has dominated our nation. Now, Kittredge says, we need a new myth, one told by Westerners who can comprehend the changes that are already occurring in what was once seen as a timeless and endless paradise where anything could, and did, happen.*

Kittredge is the author of two collections of stories, The Van Gogh Field and Other Stories *and* We Are Not in this Together. *He has also published a collection of essays,* Owning it All. *With Annick Smith he edited* The Last Best Place: A Montana Anthology. *Kittredge, who teaches writing at the University of Montana in Missoula, is currently working on a novel.*

KB: How do we live in this landscape and tell stories about it and not degrade ourselves?

WK: The West has been clearly an economic enclave of the East. It's also been an emotional and intellectual enclave. We're really trying to stand up and say, "We're going to define ourselves from now on, thank you." There's a certain hostility or resistance to that. We're doing it with a kind of arrogance that's necessary at the moment because we wouldn't do it at all if we didn't overstate ourselves and get a little cocky. So we're making all kinds of claims about how smart we are and what a cultural renaissance we're in and so on and so forth, which may

not be entirely true but we're headed in that direction.

KB: Do you think part of the problem is that the East still needs this myth of the West as it has been in the past, and I suppose there are Westerners who still need it?

WK: I think so. The world in ways still needs that myth. It's a mythology that tells you there's still some place to go; things are still redeemable; there's still a promised land somewhere; the individual will have a chance; the world is not all paved over with asphalt; there's still a native ecology that exists in working order — the West as an historic safety valve for the East. The only places left now are Australia and Alaska. The West isn't that way anymore. It's clearly all settled. It's all been conquered. What we have to learn to do in the West now is to take care of it and not go on exploiting the things that were found here.

KB: *Hole in the Sky* continually brings up recklessness.

WK: All that heedlessness. It's all there for our amusement. It's all there to be used. There are no limits. Nothing's going to happen to it. We believed that in those days. Doing the work on the ranch, we corralled nature. We ditched and diked. We made nature conform and thought we were doing God's work in that. We intuited we could have it both ways. We could have this heedlessness, this recklessness, in this perfect open place. We could also create this contained pastoral green place, Thomas Jefferson dreamland. White fences and perfect ditches. The whole works. It turned out we couldn't.

KB: There seems to be an aim for balance in *Hole in the Sky*.

WK: I think the kind of adjustments we're going to make in the West are complex. We tend to be simple-minded. We're going to turn it all into buffalo commons. Or natural area. Or we're going to turn it all into agri-business and industrial farming. What we're going to end up with is a very complex mix of both. The ranch where I grew up, the ranch that's talked about in *Hole in the Sky*, narrowly missed being sold recently to the Nature Conservancy. That made me sad. If it had been sold to the Conservancy, a huge area, an area of probably a hundred miles square — not a hundred square miles — with federal land, state

school land, private land, three wildlife refuges, and what would have been a lot of Conservancy land, all would have been mixed up together. They all would have had to figure out some way of proceeding into the future, which would have been more complex than just creating a giant buffalo commons or having it all go private with the sagebrush rebellion. They would have to figure out place by place by place, watershed by watershed by watershed, a kind of sensible way of managing all that expanse of territory, which is going to happen. In the West, we've got to figure out a way to plan things. At the same time, not plan them to death. The first thing that has to happen — we talk about revised mythologies — there has to be a community story in some ways agreed upon and which seems sensible to watersheds, states, all those kind of communal groups. Then we can begin to plan. We've got to figure out some way to proceed that honors individuality and also honors the need of the community to have some control over what things are going to be like in the community. If we just let people go any direction they want to go, pretty soon we've got a mess like we've got on the strip outside Missoula here or endless other strips in the West.

KB: It seems as if *Hole in the Sky* is working towards an understanding of the myth and yet saying let's revise it.

WK: The thing I'm hammering more than anything else is story. The Aristotelian notion is that what stories are for is to help us see. What happens in a story when it works is a moment of recognition, and some implication of the consequences in that recognition. What we do as human beings more than anything else is invent ourselves in a story over and over again all day long. Recognitions, which are understandings of the world, never hold up, really. They work for a while. Then we have to do it over and over and over again. In an individual life or in a society when you lock on some recognition or some version of some mythology and stay with it too long you're bound for disaster.

What's happened in the American West is we're staying with an official mythology that is in the process of being revised, but a lot of people want to hang on to the old version, mostly because they have some economic interest in doing so, and you can't blame them. But they're going to have to change. And they are changing. I don't know many timber fallers in their mid-forties who are advising their sons to get into the timber falling business. It's over. It's the third time it's been over in the United States. It happened in Maine. It happened in the north woods of Michigan and Minnesota. And now it's happening in the Pacific Northwest. It's not like it's a big surprise. The timber companies are not surprised. They knew it was coming, but they didn't tell anyone in Libby, and the people in Libby feel justifiably betrayed and tricked and angry. I don't blame them. I would too.

KB: You're trying to work out some kind of balance between place in the imagination and place as it actually is and how you connect to it?

WK: Place is all mixed up in community. In this whole business of working ourselves through to a new understanding of who we are and how we're going to proceed, one of the prime things we have to recognize in the American West is we have to locate ourselves in a place that we feel is worth taking care of. I'm uncomfortable living in the past, in a mythological place where I don't belong. I went one time to the Cowboy Poetry Gathering in Elko to give a speech as a humanist. I got up at about eight in the morning to speak to an amphitheater of cowboys and I had this kind of humanist message in mind and I looked up and said, "I don't think so." I told anecdotes about grow-

ing up on the ranch, and they all liked it. Basically, I was uncomfortable in that society. They are still deeply into the old world I grew up in. I love that old world, but I don't think trying deliberately as hard as you can to live in the past is a good idea. I know lots of people who take great joy in all that stuff and sometimes get very angry with people like myself who say we've got to change. I appreciate the notion that they're celebrating community, celebrating all these values, but on the other hand I don't think you can live in that past.

KB: You bring up Charlie Russell, the painter, in the book, and how people love that he got it right, how precise he is.

WK: He cared so much.

KB: You seem to be saying that it's wonderful to care but getting it right simply isn't enough.

WK: It isn't. Absolutely, it isn't. Charlie Russell even knew it. He gave that speech to the Great Falls Booster Club. They asked him to speak in 1922 or 3 when he was an old man. They got him up on the stage. I guess he had a few drinks. People gave these long interminable booster speeches. Charlie Russell got up and said something to the effect, "My idea of a pioneer is somebody who turned the grass upside down, built fences, and cheated the Indians out of everything they've got. I wish all of you sons of bitches were back where you came from." Turned around and walked off the stage. Charlie Russell understood a lot more than people give him credit for. But that's right, that same kind of betrayal, that same kind of art which reveres the past, which reveres the present, makes it holy in a way that denies the possibility of change.

Actually, generally, the artist isn't doing that, it's the audience that wants to take the piece, the novel, the sculpture, whatever, and say, "OK, this is how things are supposed to be." That's truly not the way great art functions. Great art somehow tells us to look at ourselves and begin to think about how we're supposed to conduct ourselves in the world, rather than here, this is it, this is how you should be. Great art opens an enquiry. Russell and Remington, they at least had the advantage of being at the beginning. The cowboys and Indians, the western art that's still being done and attracting great prices, it's all looking for the past. It's

nostalgic. It's like country music, although I love a lot of country music — but generally only after I've had about three beers. I don't care for it much sober, but I like it in the right atmosphere. You just can't fix things in time. I get a letter or two every day, it seems, about *Hole in the Sky* from old guys in the West, from all kinds of people. I haven't gotten a single letter berating me yet. I got a letter from a guy in Nevada two or three days ago. This guy said, "People in agriculture face great change. I don't know if they're going to be able to make it or not." There's also some pessimism. In another letter it said, "We thought we were doing the right sorts of things and we didn't really know what we were doing." I was down talking to the Wyoming Outdoor Council. The ranchers like to use the word riparian now. It means streamside, habitat, ecology.

What's happened

in the American West is

we're staying with an official

mythology that is

in the process of being revised,

but a lot of people want to hang

on to the old version, mostly

because they have some

economic interest in doing so,

and you can't blame them.

But they're going to

have to change.

It's a way of not saying, "All the cows tromp the god-damned streambeds. There's always been riparian damage, of course." Driving home, in Idaho into Salmon, looking at some of those stream banks, they're absolutely destroyed. That just can't go on. We can't live in that past where people got to run as many cows as they wanted to, any way they wanted to.

KB: With Gary Snyder and his approach to community, I don't see any difference between what he's doing and what you're doing.

WK: I don't either. I'm pleased I've been invited to go to Miami to be on a panel with Snyder and Terry Tempest Williams. That pleases me enormously, because that's the crowd I'd like to play with. I read Snyder's *The Practice of the Wild* and went, "Yeah." I agree with every bit of it. I think it's absolutely paramount that we start doing something about the environment. I'm also a great admirer of E.O. Wilson. I believe what he says about natural diversity. I believe what he says about how species die out. I think he's right. On the other hand, I still have some sympathy for people who are living through the change and suffering great hardship.

I love going to something like the Wyoming Outdoor Council, which is environmentalists, big-time ruling class ranchers, Native Americans. All those people getting together and beginning to slowly arrive at some kind of communal story about how we're supposed to conduct ourselves. I'm fairly optimistic. I think if we can hang on for another 10 or 15 or 20 years, enormous changes are going to be taking place. I always felt it was my job to just keep bringing these things up and saying them over and over again. I don't think anybody, Snyder or anyone else, really changes society's mind, but if enough people keep saying the same things in various kinds of ways, it's like building a rock wall. You've got a lot of rocks and pretty quick you've got a wall. As a moral purpose, that's good enough.

Kevin Bezner's interviews have appeared in a variety of publications, including American Poetry Review, Denver Quarterly, Mississippi Review, Writer's NW, *and* Sonora Review.

A Deep Craving
David Long

What do I remember from the stories embedded in my reading life? Sometimes, of course, it's the dilemma, the choice suffered through and acted out, especially if it's as stark as the one in Andre Dubus's "A Father's Story," or as morally quirky as that in Ray Carver's "So Much Water, So Close To Home." But other things stick, too. In Dubus, for instance, the father, Luke Ripley, summarizing his life in the opening paragraph. I remember the voice — plain and quietly grieving. But it's the way the story closes that amazes me: with Luke's interrogation of God. And not only because the ideas are powerful, which they are, but because Dubus chose to end with a solo, a riff of astonishing eloquence.

No matter how insanely a writer has tried to unify the story, we remember only fragments, glittering bits, debris. "Aside from whatever cloudy sense of the whole the reader may have held onto," Donald Justice says in an essay, "such pieces are pretty much all that's left to prize, and there need be no Other Life embarrassment in conceding this simple truth." So, this barrage of images. It's easy to understand why some have stuck; they'd stick with any reader. But others remain inexplicably. One of the first things I think of when I think of John Updike is a stray line from "Poker Night": "…when I was a kid there was a field where I can remember the Italians growing runner beans on miles and miles of this heavy brown string."

Why read? The rationales we usually give — for information, for pleasure, for "escape" — aren't nearly illuminating enough. Reading is a deep craving. For most of us, the habit was acquired early and is associated with our most secret selves; but, if anything, it has become a more potent hunger over time. When we're too busy to read, or somehow between books, our lives feel out of whack. If we mean to write, to write *well*, we have to come to terms with the act of reading: What delights us, what dampens

the thrill? "We pay heed so easily," William Gass says in *Fiction and the Figures of Life*.

We are so pathetically eager for this other life, for the sounds of distant cities and the sea; we long, apparently, to pit ourselves against some trying wind, to follow the fortunes of a ship hard beset, to face up to murder and fornication, and the somber results of anger and love; oh, yes, to face up — in books…"

What *is* this otherness? What brings it about, and how can we encourage it in our writing? I'd like to suggest several strategies:

1. We always say too much — too many words, and too many things that don't need saying at all. Have you ever eaten a hamburger, Annie Dillard asks in her brief, solace-filled book, *The Writing Life*. Have you ever taken a commercial airplane flight? Fine. Spare us your report. We live in a late era. We don't need every single thing painted in the way Dickens' readers did (Dickens got paid by the word, remember). I'm not saying prose ought to be stripped down to minimalist word bites; the meagerly imagined is as forgettable as the overfed. And it's irritating when necessary information is missing. We have a right to know who's talking, where people are, when this is all going on. But cut out the stuff people already know. Close your eyes; be there, immerse yourself. What one or two things give the moment its specific gravity? Does light matter? It does if it's oppressive, as in Paul Bowles; or as pale and pure as the light that arrives at the end of Anita Desai's lovely story, "Pigeons at Daybreak." But maybe it *doesn't* matter; if it doesn't, don't talk about it. The same goes for moving people around in a room, and for what they say to each other,

No matter how insanely a writer

has tried to unify the story, we

remember only fragments,

glittering bits, debris.

and for all the back story. Look at the economy of James Salter's opening paragraph in "American Express":

It's hard to think of all the places and nights, Nicola's like a railway car, deep and gleaming, the crowd at the Un Deux Trois, Billy's. Unknown brilliant faces jammed at the bar. The dark, dramatic eye that blazes for a moment and disappears.

How can you tell the difference between vital tissue and filler? Often you can't — at first. But later you see it; your eyes get sick of passing over the dull stuff and, finally, with delicious relief, you jam your finger onto the delete key. A twenty-page story? Cut out two pages of individual words and sentences. Hedging, pointless amplification, baggy constructions, sludgy passive stuff — and anything else readers can be expected to fill in. Am I trying to crimp your style? How do you know what your style *is* until you've brushed away the chips and dust left from composition? What of the larger issues, the moral aspects of storytelling? Bored, sleepy readers think no big thoughts.

2. If we say too much, we also say too little. Our stories need building up. One night, years ago, I found myself playing backgammon against a vastly better player. I couldn't believe the moves he was making; they looked brazen, foolhardy. I got clobbered. Thinking about this afterward, it occurred to me that he wanted the game to become long and decision-rich, since luck might dominate a short game. Lately, I've come to see this as another lesson in getting past What Everybody Already Knows. The more decisions you make in constructing a story, the more likely it is to display unusual symmetries, the more likely it is to become *yours.*

You *do* need luck when you write. You need that amazed feeling every so often: Where did *that* come from? But a story writer's luck — leaps of imagery, plot fixes, sudden awareness of what the work means — is a lot like any problem solver's luck; it visits workers who put in their time.

What, specifically, can you do? Don't be so easily satisfied. Carol Bly's suggestion, in *The Passionate, Accurate Story* is to skip past the first thing you think of. Keep asking what's the *next* thing? Go against the grain some. Assume there's another thing to add that

will shake up or intensify what you've already said. The writer's motto: Crank it another crank. If you're stuck, sneak up on it; come to it in different frames of mind; stick it away until it seems strange to you again.

Keep the company of writers whose work has a richly built-up feel. If you're a fiction writer, read the stories of Alice Munro, William Trevor, Joyce Carol Oates. If

The more decisions you make in constructing a story, the more likely it is to display unusual symmetries, the more likely it is to become yours.

you're after nonfiction, read Diane Ackerman's *A Natural History of the Senses;* Verlyn Klinkenborg's *The Last Fine Time;* Barbara Grizzuti Harrison's *Italian Days.* Locate passages that seem exceptional, then imagine them truncated; imagine the writer stopping too early, not getting to where that wonderful thing gets said. Think of what the word "passage" means. Ask yourself if you want to be a writer who disembarked too soon.

3. I still remember a poem I first read more than a dozen years ago, "The Ten Thousand Things," by Missoula poet Dave Thomas. It amounts to a list of the stuff he worked with building a dam. Boring? Actually, no; it's strangely luminous, a litany of catwalks, carriage bolts, turn-buckles, oakum. The world's full of *stuff.* And stuff — named, examined closely — turns out to be interesting. But why? One reason may be that we ourselves are physical bodies. When we read, our mind's eye (and not just the eye, but the whole inner body) reacts to nouns. Beholds, embraces, shrinks from. Another reason is that naming fosters trust. You may well be making it all up from

scratch, but specifying is a way of insisting that, no, you really were there. Faulkner writes: "There was a wisteria vine blooming for the second time that summer on a wooden trellis before one window, into which sparrows came now and then in random gusts, making a dry vivid dusty sound before going away…" I'm locked down on the scene; when he moves on to emotional truths, I follow.

This applies, as well, to how things are done, especially in the working world. Each of us has insider information. From Bob Shacochis, we learn about the daily life of Caribbean fishermen — what they eat, how they cook it, how they kill time in the evenings. From Ron Hansen, how Nebraskans survived, or didn't, in a blizzard of a hundred years ago. From Margaret Atwood, the fate of sailors on the Franklin Expedition to the North Pole; from Sara Vogan, the legend of the Crane Wife. Too many stories by inexperienced writers aren't about anything. Well, maybe they're *about* something — coming of age or whatever — but there's not enough *in* them. They lack information.

4. As movies are no more and no less than light passing through celluloid, stories are strings of sentences. One after another, each an artifact with its own duration and texture, its own internal drama. That "other life" Gass talked about is strictly illusion, a chain of brief events in the reader's mind, brought about by your choice, over and over, of this word and not that one. We respond to the images before us, but at the same time, we're responding to the intelligence behind the story.

Though progress is nearly impossible to see, up close, writers do get better at making choices over time — sometimes a lot better. Practice creates dexterity. But two

things to do right now: First, as a discrete step in revising, add more interesting words. By "more interesting," I mean: more *exact* (English has an enormous array of near-synonyms — bring the sentences into tight focus); more *unusual* (not glaringly unusual, but words that fall somewhat outside the ring of our most-used words — sometimes you'll want to reach up, or down, for a truly off-the-wall word); and more *saturated with attitude*. In Denis Johnson's "Work," a badly hung over man is helping a friend salvage copper wiring from his flood-ruined house: "I felt weak. I had to vomit in the corner — just a thimbleful of gray bile." Picture the sentence stopping at "corner."

Too many stories

by inexperienced writers

aren't about anything. . . .

They lack information.

Finally, all the good stories hold a few lines that no one has ever written before. How do you know? You *know.* They're the lines you hit with a highlighter. Sometimes they're metaphors — collisions, fireballs of language; other times, simply statements of emotional fact that blind-side you. It's not that a handful of unprecedented lines makes all the difference — *everything* makes all the difference. But they're evidence of how far out on a limb a writer was willing to go. They're not cautious lines. Look at your work-in-progress; ask yourself if you've held back, been timid. It's absurd to sit down with the intention of saying things no one has ever said; yet, they come to you once in a while. Swallow your doubt. Think of Luke Ripley talking to God, think of Dubus letting God answer.

David Long has published two collections of short stories, Home Fires *(1982) and* The Flood of '64 *(1987). Recent stories have appeared in* The New Yorker, Story, Prize Stories 1992: The O. Henry Awards, *and* Best of the West 5. *He lives in Kalispell, Montana.*

Native American Literatures and the Impact of Colonization

Gloria Bird

There is very little that can be applied across the board to the diverse cultures of Native American peoples. Often, writing from my own personal experience of what it means to be "Indian,'" I must provide qualifiers such as, "where I am from." Yet, I have come to realize that the common ground all native peoples share is that we are all the products of colonization.

It seems premature to read the literatures of Native Americans in "post-colonial" context in the same ways that Euro-American literatures are now being discussed in recent literary criticism. The term "post-colonial" itself is problematic. It implies that the time of colonization is past and that we can now comfortably distance our selves from that process. For those of us who are Native American, we see evidence all around us — on the reservations we come from and those of others — of the fact that we are still actively being colonized.

For example, I come from a small community in eastern Washington State, the Spokane Indian reservation. The reservation I know is a mountainous region where there are many lakes and streams. The natural resources that have been depleted there include huge deposits of high-grade uranium and, of course, timber. I remember the trees once grew so thick they over-hung the highway running thorough the reservation. While growing up on the reservation, we were accustomed to seeing uranium and logging trucks go up and down the Canyon road. The last time I visited, the trees had thinned, and the ones left standing grew only for about fifteen feet on each side of the road, a landscape cosmetic. Beyond that point, there weren't any trees to speak of. I associate my growing up on the reservation with these signs of our colonization in the exploitation of our lands. Now it is common knowledge that the old growth is gone, and that we have two open-pit uranium mines like sores upon the land. We are in a situation much like the Navajo living in the Four Corners area: we are living in a tenuous world and our peoples are suffering the consequences of mining/radiation pollution. Back home, an epidemic of various types of cancer is commonplace. Our situation as a tribe is not much different from that of many other tribes. For me, reading Native American literatures in "post-colonial" context makes little sense.

What are the other ways in which we might read contemporary Native American literatures? A novel approach might be to go to the source and ask the Native American writers themselves. Recently, I had the opportunity of attending a reading-lecture series of Native American writers. I was able to hear thirteen Native American writers read their works and speak about writing. Among the issues raised was the roles associated with the position of Native American writers and how our expectations of them burden them as writers. More often than not, these writers disqualified themselves from being representatives for, or spokespersons for, all native experience, saying that they could only speak for themselves as *participants of* a native community. They made the further distinction between their roles as "writers" and that as "storytellers."

As Helen Tiffin reminds us in *Critical Approaches to the New Literatures in English*, "three-fourths of the contemporary world are colonized nations." ("Post-Colonial Literatures and Counter-Discourse," Essen: Verl. Die Blaue Eule, 1989.) The impact of colonization upon our literatures has not as yet been fully explored. Colonization is evident in the ways in which our writing has been shaped by western literary traditions. We have been told throughout history and in the American canon who we are. I am reminded of the writings of James Fenimore Cooper in which I read traces of 15th century philosophies and the used-up paradigms of the Noble and Ignoble Savage that still plague us. Our purpose as Native American writers should be a decolonization of mind and text, a process of deep consciousness-searching, a re-evaluation of where we have come from, and how far we have truly come.

As a native writer, and one who is intimately concerned for the land I call home, I cannot help but feel great urgency for discussion of the situation of the people back home in regard to the land. To believe that our problems are isolated to one small mountain community is presumptuous. The water that has been contaminated in the processing of uranium ore flows from reservation streams into the Spokane River which, in turn, runs through the city of Spokane as well as many outlying non-native communities. The airborne, potentially lethal radioactive particles effect everyone living within a hundred-mile radius of the mines.

The difficulties we face as a consequence of our continued colonization are not confined to a single generation of people. This I believe native writers are aware of and ad-

Our purpose

as Native American writers

should be a decolonization

of mind and text,

a process of deep

consciousness-searching,

a re-evaluation

of where

we have come from,

and how far

we have truly come.

dress. For instance, Modoc writer Michael Dorris's *The Broken Cord* addresses the precariousness of our present situation as well as the future of our peoples in his discussion of fetal alcohol syndrome and its impact upon Native American communities. Likewise, the new manuscript of poetry from Wasco/Warm Springs writer Elizabeth Woody powerfully addresses the waste of land and water in her poem "Inheritance Obscured by Neglect." The "vacuity" of spirit of which she speaks is linked to the breakdown of the relationship between people and land, specifically, in the aftermath of the Alaskan oil spill. As Woody explains, we find ourselves, Native Americans in the late 20th century, still in a place where "we suffocate in the back water of decadence and fragmented contempt." She reminds me that there has always been a distrust of nature, and that we must remember it is America's legacy to have forged a "civilization" in the "taming of the wilderness," a construct of nature that includes the natives as well. This is not simply another revision of romantic Mother Earth Syndrome in which we have been draped.

Only recently has there been a movement of sympathetic and liberal efforts to portray the natives in a "new light" giving us a mediated "truth" of our histories such as the movie *Dances With Wolves.* Yet, in order for these efforts to be accepted the native must possess values that are desirable. What this means in practice is that the image of Native American people that is the most popular is still the one of the dying but noble savage. It identifies for me the long road we have to travel in order to undo what has been handed down to us since the 15th century philosophers constructed this damaging paradigm, which was based on the journals and diaries of missionaries, trappers, and explorers. It is difficult to undo the damage once it has been done; difficult, but not impossible.

Gloria Bird is from the Spokane tribe and is one of the founding members of the Northwest Native American Writers Association based in Oregon. Her book of poetry, Full Moon on the Reservation, *will be published during 1993.*

Toxins in the Mother Tongue: Toward the Clean-up of a Poisoned Spiritual Lexicon

David James Duncan

1. The Truth in Literature

Ever since the advent of the printing press there has been a tendency among readers to slip from enthusiasm for a favorite text into the outright belief that the words in that text embody truth: do not just symbolize it, but literally embody it. An increasingly politicized faction of self-described "conservative Christians" in this country even insists that a single bookful of words *is* Truth. This deification of the written word — in light of every scripture-based Wisdom Tradition in the world, including Christianity's two-thousand-year-old own — is not just naiveté, but idolatry. Words in books can remind us of truth, and occasionally even help awaken us to it. But in themselves, words are just paint, and writers are just painters — Old Testament and Gospel writers, bhakti and Sufi saints, Tibetan lamas and Zen patriarchs included. There are, of course, crucial differences between scripture and *belles lettres*, and between inspired and merely inventive prose. But the authors of both write with human hands, and in human tongues. Let's not overestimate the power of any form of literature.

Let's not underestimate it either. As readers we are asked on page one to lay our hand upon the back of an author's as he or she begins to paint a world. If the author's strokes somehow repel or betray our trust, if our concentration is lax, or if we're biased or closed in some way, then no hand-in-hand magic can occur. But when a great word-painter is read with reciprocally great concentration and trust, an incredible thing happens. First, the painter's hand disappears. Then so does our own. Till there is only the living world of the painting.

This disappearance, this effacement of self in the life of a story is, I believe, the greatest truth in any literature, be it discursive or dramatic, sacred or secular. It is at any rate the greatest *describable* truth — because for the duration of the disappearance we possess no 'I' with which to describe anything outside the text. Like all great truths, literary effacement is simultaneously a sacrifice (of the reader's ego) and a resurrection (of the world, the characters and the ideas in the text). And like all great truths, it is transrational. It is not brought about by any kind of mental computations upon literal meanings of sentences and words. All that's required is a willing immersion of imagination and mind in the dynamic pulse and flow of written language.

2. The "One Sole Morality of Literature"

The most valid case to be made, in light of this great truth, for any form of censorship is for the scrupulous destruction or revision, by the author him (or her) self, of any and all writing that fails to let him vanish into the life of his own story. What writers are morally obligated to censor from their work, in other words, is their own incompetence. Nothing more, nothing less. Simple as it sounds, it keeps most of us more than busy. "Fundamental accuracy of statement," wrote Ezra Pound, "is the one

Let's not overestimate

the power

of any form of literature.

Let's not underestimate it either.

sole morality of literature." If, in other words, a story requires that its writer create a mountain and further requires that this mountain be imposing, the immoral mountain is not the one with the pair of unmarried hikers copulating on a remote slope: it is simply the mountain that fails to be imposing. The "sole morality of literature" demands that an author contemplate his peak till frozen clouds begin to swirl round its summit; till lost Mazama and mountain goat bones appear deep in its crevasses; till its ice and stone mass haunts and daunts us like a cold moon rising not in some safe distance but from the scree at our very feet.

And the same goes — with all due apologies to literary inquisitors everywhere — for the imposing penis. This is not to say that *all* penises are, according to Pound's dictum, moral. Indeed, a gratuitously shocking penis, an extraneous-to-our-story penis, a hey-look-at-me-for-the-sake-of-nothing-but-me penis, however imposing, is literarily "immoral" (that is, incompetent), because by jarring the reader from the narrative or argumentative flow into a mood of "What's this stupid penis doing here?" the author has undermined the greatest truth of his tale: i.e. our ability to immerse ourselves in it. But once the dramatic exigencies of the story itself have requested of its author an imposing penis, it is the one-pointed, apoplectic-veined archetype that has us crossing imaginary legs before we know it (or opening them, as the literary case may be) that is the moral penis, and the church, quasi-religious political cult or government agency that seeks to zip a zipper over it that is immoral.

3. The Amnesiac Questions

"But how could a zippered penis possibly be immoral? Why shouldn't we legislate zippers in order to defend the purity of our children and our culture?" These are the fundamentalist questions, the Jesse Helms Questions — questions the askers of which must pride themselves on their amnesia, considering how recently the likes of the Josephs Stalin and McCarthy and the Ayatollah Khomeini have asked the very same questions. I'll supply both a non-Christian and Christian answer to the questions anyway.

First, the non-Christian:

All Americans possess the Constitu-

tional right to detest the work of any writer or artist they choose to detest, and to criticize that writer or artist, in public and in private, in the most scathing language they are able to devise. I, to cite the handiest possible example, found the few pages of Bret Easton Ellis's *American Psycho* that I was able to read to be as crassly sensationalistic, spiritually bankrupt and literarily incompetent as the average tabloid. To seek to enrich oneself by clumsily holding lit matches up to the wounds of genuine victims is not a literary strategy to which "the one sole morality of literature" would allow most of us to subscribe. But to say that much satisfies me. And it's all the fun the Constitution allows: to carry my detestation further, to try to summon the anger, compose the propaganda, induce the paranoia and generate the political clout that would let me and my ideological clones ban one overpaid hack is not the way people in this tenuously free country long ago agreed to do things.

The old Irish bards, when asked to recite certain stories, would sometimes say to their audience: "'Tis an evil tale for telling. You'd ail if ye heard it, I'd ail if I told it. I cannot make it." And hearing this, the audience would request a different tale. I believe Ellis, and Americans in general, are dying for a dose of this bardic wisdom. Yet sickening stories are an unavoidable by-product of a sick culture, and a crucial diagnostic tool for anyone who seeks a cure. Writers need the freedom to invoke body parts, mayhem and twisted visions for many profound reasons, among them (jumping metaphors) the same reason that chefs need the freedom to invoke curry, garlic, extreme heat, and other things we can't tolerate in straight doses in order to produce a cuisine. There is no mention of jalepeño peppers in the Christian scriptures, and neither the average child nor the average televangelist can handle them. That's no reason to legislate them clean out of our *huevos rancheros*.

Now the Christian answer:

In a book called *An Experiment in Criticism* (Cambridge University Press, 1961) the non-literalistic but doggedly Christian professor of literature, Mr. C.S. Lewis, wrote that our access to a diverse and uncensored literature is spiritually crucial because *we are not content to be Leibnitzian monads. We demand windows. (And) literature… is a series of windows, even of doors… Good reading can be described either as an enlargement or as a temporary annihilation of the self. But that is an old paradox; "he that loseth his life shall save it." We therefore delight to enter into other men's beliefs… even though we think them untrue. And into their passions, though we think them depraved… We become these other selves not only nor chiefly to see what they are like, but in order to see what they see, to occupy, for a while, their seat in the great theatre… Literary experience heals the wound, without undermining the privilege, of individuality… In reading great literature I become a thousand men and yet remain myself… Here, as in worship, in love, in moral action, and in knowing, I transcend myself, and am never more myself than when I do.*

4. Christianity and Christofascism

My intent here is literary, not theological. But my topic is the repeated invasion of literature by a certain kind of theological mind-set. This pattern seems to warrant a look, despite my literary intent (and in defense of it), at the theological motivation of literature's invaders: All of the famous televangelists, all the leaders of the contemporary bible-based political alliances, and most of the recent censors of school libraries, crusaders against homosexuality, and politically-active fundamentalists in general share a conviction that their political and social causes and agendas are approved of, if not inspired by, no less a being than God "Himself." This enviable conviction is less enviably arrived at by accepting on faith, hence as fact, that the Christian bible pared down into American TV English is God's "word" to mankind, that this same bible is "His" only word to mankind, and that the fundamentalist's unprecedentedly literalistic slant on this bible is the one true slant. Possessing little knowledge of and no respect for the world's spiritual and religious traditions, these people have no models of love or compassion but their own, and can therefore honestly, even goodheartedly say that it is out of "Christian" compassion and a sort of "tough love" for others that they seek to impose on these others their own God, bible and slant.

This type of thinking is far from unprecedented. Well-known variations on the same theme include the Crusader's tough love for the Islamic world, the Inquisitor's tough love for heretics, the Conquistador's tough love for Incas, Aztecs, and Mayans, the Puritan's tough love for witches, the white western settler's tough love for Native Americans, and the Nazi Party's tough love for Gypsies and Jews. Every bible-reifying crusader group from the Spanish prototypes to our own Oregon Citizen's Alliance has seen itself as fighting to make its own or some other community more "godly."

This being a literary essay, it's only fair to point out that conservative Christians are book-lovers, too. They just happen to have invested so much brittle love in the one black-covered, cantankerous volume that their ability to comprehend, enjoy or even tolerate other volumes has been drastically curtailed. But a question, both literary and theological, which needs to be asked is: how brittle can one's love become before it ceases to be love at all?

What writers are

morally obligated

to censor from their work,

in other words,

is their own incompetence.

Nothing more,

nothing less.

The Dominican priest and writer, Matthew Fox, answers this question by referring to contemporary evangelical fundamentalism as "christofascism." It's an inflammatory term, certainly. Yet it serves a purpose. To refer to, say, Oral Roberts and St. Francis, Jerry Falwell and Meister Eckhart, Jimmy ("Three K's is Too Obvious") Bakker and Lady Julian of Norwich all as "Christians" stretches the term so far that it is rendered almost meaningless. The word "humanoid" would be as helpful. So, dangerous as the Christian/christofascist distinction may be ("Judge not lest ye be judged"), a distinction needs to be made. A Francis Schaeffer text used to instruct Baptist seminarians all over the United States on the world's cults, doctrinal blunders, and "other religions" defines and illustrates the concept and history of what it calls "mysticism" by analyzing the writings of Henry Miller alone. To refer to this sort of education as "Christian" is to hand the body of that already crucified word over to a pack of quasi-religious zealots. To teach that mysticism equals Henry Miller is not teaching at all. It is textbook christofascism — a cult distinct from Christianity in that it wants no "windows": it is content to read and idolatrize its one book, willfully misread all others, and use the resulting curtailment of comprehension, pleasure, and tolerance as a unifying principle.

The odd, "evangelical" truth of the matter is this: the quasi-Christian political factions need writers, artists, humanists, scientists, believers and nonbelievers of all stripes in a big way. It may not even be going too far to say that they need us for their salvation. As Mark Twain pointed out a century ago, the only really prominent Christian community American fundamentalists have ever managed to establish in any of the worlds is hell.

5. One Mother Earth, One Mother Tongue

There is just one, irreplaceable earth, and it is finite. It can absorb just so many wounds and poisons. And more and more people have recognized that in wounding and poisoning it for decades, we have been steadily wounding and poisoning ourselves. There is also, for each human born on earth, just one mother tongue. And it is much less widely recognized that a given tongue at a given time consists of only so many words, that these words can absorb only so many abuses of meaning before they cease to mean, and that when the meaning of words leaves us and we fail to find replacements, we begin to lose our ability to comprehend both our world and ourselves. When — to cite a crass example — George Bush referred to himself in 1988 as an "environmentalist" and nevertheless won an election, and when dozens of devastating corporations such as Weyerhaeuser and Dow Chemical followed suit by hiring P.R. sophists to help them appropriate the same term, the word "environmentalist" suffered a series of blows from which it hasn't begun to recover.

Our spiritual vocabulary — with its huge defining terms such as "God," "soul," "sacrifice," "mysticism," "faith," "grace" — has endured an even more protracted and hypocritical series of abuses. And creative writers can no more create with toxic or dying language than can painters create with dried-up paints. It's understandable, therefore, that so many American writers and thinkers have tried to escape the damage done to the old Christian lexicon by jettisoning the polluted words and concepts entirely. But the price of this abandonment — complete severance from the riches of early Christian, Celtic, and medieval art and literature, severance from the European mystical and contemplative traditions, even severance from one's ability to think of oneself in native-tongued spiritual terms at all — has been vast. Every time we abandon a word or concept we once valued due to disgust with the way it's been abused, we are granting victory to its abusers and losing, for ourselves, its positive as well as negative potential. Even among non-Christians living in a post-Christian world, the words "God" and "soul" and "grace" can have resonance. For me personally, Meister Eckhart, Julian of Norwich, and the 13th and 14th century mystic/feminists known as "the Beguines" have given these terms so much renewed vitality that I'd feel like a traitor if I surrendered them to the christofascist right. Eckhart defeated such people in debate repeatedly, only to be posthumously excommunicated by them; the Beguines — arguably the most viable, invaluable alliance of feminists in Western history — were destroyed by christofascists, and nearly erased from our memory. To stand up for the "God," "soul," and way of life of these great mystics feels as valid and necessary to this white man as standing up for the gods, rites, and worldview of Black Elk and Chief Joseph might feel to contemporary Native Americans.

Another sizable group has tried to solve the pollution of the Christian lexicon by adopting one or another of the religious traditions and vocabularies of the East. But many of us have found — often after backfiring surrenders to lamas, roshis, sheikhs or gurus — that it is no more difficult for shams and windowless ideologues to skew the search for *nirvana*, *mukti*, or *fana-fillah* than the search for the peace that passeth understanding. No spiritual vocabulary is immune to abuse. It could even be argued that any use of such terms by anyone who has not attained spiritual perfection involves a degree of abuse. We're all involved, all our lives, in learning how to talk. And every writer, reader, and lover of his native tongue owes it to himself, his listeners, his tongue,

As Mark Twain

pointed out a century ago,

the only really prominent

Christian community

American fundamentalists

have ever managed to establish

in any of the worlds

is hell.

and the truth to talk with all the accuracy, integrity, and liveliness that's in him. "Fundamental accuracy of statement is the one sole morality" not only of literature, but of all language.

My mother tongue — the language my parents and grandparents used to draw me from virtual nonbeing into naming and engaging with life — is English. And there are only so many English words with which to describe the eternal verities and the journey of the soul. I've begun to sense that the toxins in our spiritual lexicon are a problem which, like global warming and ozone depletion, cannot be escaped by trading our O.E.D.'s or Webster's in on an Oriental dictionary, or by turning our backs. The God of christofascism, as advertised daily through a variety of mass media, is a supramundane Caucasian male as furious with humanity's failure to live by a few arbitrarily chosen lines from the Book of Leviticus as He is oblivious to His spokespersons' failure to live by the militant compassion of the Gospels. But if this God is in fact God, then the likes of Mahatma Gandhi and Mother Theresa, Leo Tolstoy and Fyodor Dostoevsky, Malcolm X and Martin Luther King, the Alberts Schweitzer and Einstein, Black Elk and Crazy Horse, Rumi and Hafiz, St. John of the Cross and Julian of Norwich, Lao Tzu and Bodhidharma, Kabir and Mira Bai, Shunryu and D.T. Suzuki, Valmiki and Socrates, Dogen and Dante, and (from today's sermon) C.S. Lewis, Matthew Fox and (he said with presumptuous but irresistible pleasure with the company) me, are all heretics, atheists, and infidels — because the Absolute we all worship is an infinitely different sort of Being.

Portland resident David James Duncan is the author of The Brothers K *and* The River Why.

Interview with Chuck Robinson

Jim Bertolino

Chuck Robinson, with his wife Dee, owns and operates one of the most successful independent bookstores in the Northwest. It is located in the Fairhaven district of Bellingham, near the Alaska Ferry Terminal, where it serves as one of the cultural hubs of the region. Besides offering about 50,000 titles, magazines, newspapers, and other publications, Village Books supports an active series of readings and book signings for regional and nationally prominent poets, fiction writers, nonfiction writers, and editors. Chuck also serves as President of the American Booksellers Association, with offices in Tarrytown, New York.

Born in Illinois, Chuck graduated from Sioux Falls College — "a small Christian college for small Christians." Speaking of stature, he resembles a dictionary-sized version of Rob Reiner, and has the affable good nature to match. After graduate school at the University of Missouri, where he got a Masters in Special Education, and following several jobs in Colorado and Illinois, he and Dee remodeled an old motor home and hit the road for a year. New territory, both geographic and professional, had begun to beckon. They got as far as Bellingham and decided selling books would be a great way to make a living. Village Books opened in June of 1980, and expects sales of nearly 1.5 million dollars in 1992.

This interview took place at Village Books on November 13th, 1992.

Jim: We've heard there are a lot of readers in Seattle and Portland — given the number of bookstores per capita, the use of libraries, etc. — does this translate into the Northwest being a particularly good place for writers?

Chuck: A lot of writers think it's a great place to live. Seattle, for its size, is a very literary community — in the broadest sense. A real connection with books of all sorts. That's true of Portland, and it extends throughout a lot of the Northwest. So, for writers, it's a good place. For publishers I'm

not so sure. There have been some fits and starts in Northwest publishing — yet there are certainly some very good publishers out there. I think of Seal Press, for example. Of course we've lost Graywolf to Minneapolis — largely because the literary arts are better supported in Minnesota.

Yet there still are a number of good presses here — mostly smaller ones, like Empty Bowl and Broken Moon, Copper Canyon. People who have tried to start the equivalent to a New York publishing house in Seattle have had some difficulty doing that. Most of the publishing here tends to be regional — books connected to the physical place — but I don't know that that's different from other areas of the country. The centers of publishing still remain New York, and to a smaller degree Chicago and the Bay Area, where there's a mid-size press contingent.

JB: When I was new here it seemed quite provincial, in that only the biggest names made it over the Rockies into the bookstores, to be sold alongside writers from the Northwest. Even books from California presses were hard to find here, much less books from the Midwest, South, and East. Do you think that has changed?

CR: I think it is changing, and not because things are becoming homogenized. Just as economics has become global, publishing is becoming more national and international. Someone who a few years ago would have been totally considered a regional writer — Ivan Doig — is now sold in bookstores coast-to-coast. Now there are writers from Minneapolis and Oxford, Mississippi who you'll find in our store. Some of this change may be due to better communication among booksellers nationally. Some also due to the rise of booksellers who want to offer more than the "bestsellers" and the regional authors.

JB: From a bookseller's point-of-view, and from your work with the American Booksellers Association, do you sense that there is a special Pacific Northwest voice that has become appealing to the mainstream reader across the country?

CR: There's certainly a lot more national interest. To what that's due I'm not exactly sure. Louis Rubin of Algonquin Press once asked, "Did you ever hear anyone call a novel that was set in Manhattan a regional

novel?" His argument is that novels have to be set somewhere, and it's no more regional for them to be set here than in New York. The best writers don't necessarily live within spitting distance of Grand Central Station. On the other hand, I think Northwest writers really do reflect the landscape. We have an astounding landscape — in Ivan Doig's *Sea Runners* it's the fourth character. The parameters of our world are drawn in the language. It affects the way we talk about things.

JB: Do you think multiculturalism in publishing is still growing, or has it become a permanent part of the fabric of American publishing?

CR: Well, I hope the latter is true. Now those books are not just being pulled in from small publishers, but from mainstream publishers. Most people have abandoned the notion of a melting pot and see we're into a cultural mosaic. I think there's a lot more interest in reading fiction and nonfiction from other cultures — we see that all the time in the writers we sell quite well. Toni Morrison and Alice Walker are now considered mainstream — and rightly so. There are still real efforts being made to get other minority writers into the mainstream.

JB: What perspective do you have on the future of information technologies and literature?

CR: Well, I think it's here — I don't think there's any question that computers and CD ROM will be involved in literature. The Modern Library Editions are being done on disk — the Great Works will be available...So, I think that's beyond experi-

Just as economics

has become global,

publishing is becoming

more national

and international.

mental at this point. I just read that even *Reader's Digest* is going to do interactive CDs. We've always said we're booksellers, but part of our mission has always been to provide people with the information they want. Years ago there were booksellers who stood up and said they would not sell paperback books in their stores because they didn't consider them real books. I'm afraid now that booksellers will say CDs are not books, and will cut themselves out of the business. Personally, I have a hard time imagining lying in bed and reading a book on a computer screen, but then people remind me I'm 45 and didn't grow up staring at a screen. So I think it'll be part of the business, but won't replace books as we know them, just as the paperback did not replace the hardcover.

JB: What about book design? These days walking into a good bookstore can be a psychedelic experience with all the flashy covers face-out.

CR: We jokingly said once, when a new book was coming out and someone asked how they could get it noticed, "Make the cover white and put black letters on it. It'll stick out from everything around it!" There's been a sort of snobbishness in the book world, that booksellers have been a part of, but if we're ever going to take the written word to a wider audience, we've got to say reading Danielle Steele is still better than spending X hours in front of the tube. People can discover the joy in reading words and engaging their own imaginations. So, if making books flashy-looking will sell more books, I don't have a problem with that. And some of the new books are

Most people

have abandoned

the notion of a melting pot

and see we're into a

cultural mosaic.

simply beautiful.

JB: Do you think the new administrations, both in the White House and here in Washington State, are going to have a beneficial effect on literature and publishing?

CR: Yes! Barbara Bush was an avid reader, but I don't think George valued books on the same level. When we (the ABA) were at the White House presenting books, one of the booksellers said to Bush, "Perhaps you could carry a book when you go into the helicopter," as a way of promoting reading. Bush said, "Y'know, that would be sort of a gimmick for me, but it would be a natural for her…" as he motioned toward Barbara. It's an attitudinal thing.

JB: As President of the American Booksellers Association, clearly your commitment to books goes far beyond making a living. Is the ABA playing an important role in the U.S.?

CR: We're an association of over 8,000 members, with 4,500 bookstores and bookstore chains represented. This year we worked hard to keep the Pornography Victims Compensation Act from becoming law. Most caring people, when asked if a victim of a crime should be compensated, will say "of course they should." But this legislation would link sex crimes with books the criminal might have read or looked at, and then charge the writer, publisher, and bookseller with crimes, instead of holding the perpetrator of the crime fully responsible.

JB: Have you personally experienced censorship, as a bookseller or reader?

CR: Village Books has remained relatively untouched, but one recent experience involved Bret Easton Ellis's book *American Psycho*. One fellow came into the store and asked that we not carry the book, and I said we would, but that it wasn't our intention to promote or actively display the book. After we'd been carrying it for several months, and interest in it had died away, they did a protest in front of the store. It was rather ironic, because they came and read aloud from the book to people passing by, who had no choice in hearing or not hearing the offensive passages. If their contention was that someone reading the book might go out and commit a sexual crime, it apparently never occurred to them that reading it aloud to people at random might have the very effect they were against. The only com-

plaints we received were from people who were offended that they had no choice in hearing it.

JB: You have a very active program of public readings and book signings. Is it your personal mandate to help build a more vital culture in Bellingham, in your region?

CR: Sure. There's certainly a business aspect to it, and a personal, philosophical commitment to it as well. As my wife Dee and I have told people over and over, this is the community we chose to live in, and we want it to be the kind of place we want to live. I think it's important that books be seen as an integral part of the community. I truly believe a society that values books, that values ideas, is a healthier society.

JB: Seven years from now we'll be leaping (or maybe staggering) into the next millennium. What is your optimistic picture of the year 2,000, and how will you fit in?

CR: There's a lot of anxiety about whether bookstores our size will even exist — I think they will. Multicultural books will be woven into the publishing business, and a very wide range of things will be readily available. The technology for books-on-demand will probably be there. I would hope public encounters with authors will happen even more, and people will find it as exciting as television. It was great last Sunday to be able to pack the store for Denise Levertov and Tim McNulty — to see people here for poetry really enjoying themselves. I get real optimistic when I see that.

Jim Bertolino teaches writing and literature at Western Washington University and Chapman University. New poetry anthologies from Kent State University Press, Carnegie-Mellon University Press, Pig Iron and the Quarterly Review of Literature include selections of his work.

SECTION II

W
R
I
T
I
N
G

T
I
P
S

Deconstructing Audience: In Search of the Montana Society of Explosive Engineers

Greg Keeler

One day in the late seventies, I got back an SASE full of torn up poems from a small magazine in Texas. After piecing them together, I saw that the editor had written WHAT? on the first poem, CRAP! on the second, and then had probably torn them all up without reading the rest. In that same year, I got a personal note from Robert Bly at his *Seventies* asking if I was born in the 1830s. I immediately fired both editors vitriolic letters, but now, over a dozen years later, I'm grateful; for, at the time, I had no concept of audience. I was a poet without a clue — and they clued me in: writers, like it or not, are ultimately responsible to an audience.

Perhaps those two events played a large part in my turning to song writing, an endeavor which demands an immediate concern for the listener. A fan of Tom Lerher, I had accompanied my off-color parodies of popular lyrics on the guitar since I was in my mid-teens and had grown to crave the immediate response from my classmates. Thus, when my career as a fledgling poet was crushed by the aforementioned catastrophes, it was no wonder that I fled to the adolescent security of hearing a guffaw in response to some song of irreverence or sexual innuendo.

Besides, at about the same time, I got unexpected encouragement from X. J. Kennedy. He had seen some of my lyrics in a music issue of Rosemary and Rick Ardinger's *Limberlost Review* and had decided to use them in his college text *Literature*. When the edition came out, I was horrified to see the lyrics next to some from Shakespeare's *Tempest* in a section called "Telling Good from Bad." Dreading once more the stark fist of humiliation, I rushed through the instructor's manual and breathed a sigh of relief to find "These lines by Keeler and Shakespeare seem sufficiently rollicking."

A few years later, Gary Snyder came through town

and, after I strummed some tunes for him, suggested I should release a cassette of my songs through Earth First! I didn't know much about the group, but I liked the sound of Dave Forman's voice on the phone, so soon, my lyrics were being gruffly bellowed from campfire to campfire in America's western wilderness.

All of these minor successes were due to word of mouth. The Ardingers had published my lyrics because a mutual friend had heard me sing them. Snyder had started my cassette career because he liked the way I sang the songs to him. I had tried to determine my poetry's audience by running my finger down the pages of *The International Directory of Little Magazines and Small Presses;* whereas, I had determined my music's audience by sitting in front of people, playing a guitar and singing.

Now, many years, seven cassettes of satirical songs, and two musical comedies later, my audiences are still steering my intentions and ambitions. Even my poetry has gained something of an audience, partially because I started writing verse about fishing and found a slew of angler editors out there and partially because I sneak poems into my tapes and performances.

But still, even after such successes, much of my work bombs when it stares up at its audience from the printed page. Once, after a performance of songs and poems for the International Wildlife Film Festival in Missoula, an assistant editor from *The Smithsonian* rushed up and said "We simply *must* have those poems about duct tape and trash fish for our magazine." I warned her that the power of my work is mostly in its orality, but she assured me I was a shoo-in for an upcoming issue. I, of course, got the poems back from the main editor who snootily implied I was a moron for sending them poetry, not to mention the banal substitute enclosed.

In apprehension of such circumstances, I've of late focused on the oral, for as my tapes circulate and the Vigilante Players tour the Northwest with the musicals, all sorts of groups ask me to perform for their functions. Now I stay relatively busy on the rubber chicken circuit — and each group gives me new ideas for songs. Sometimes it's a challenge to see just how far I can push an audience without totally offending them, though just as often they push back and make me eat my own words.

Once when I performed for the Naropa Institute, I decided to play a song poking fun at my idol, Bob Dylan, since Allen Ginsberg was in the audience. In the song, I pretend that I am Bob Dylan who has become a househusband instead of a folk rock star and in a Dylan whine, sing such lyrics as "And you stay up late at the office, but when I call you're never there,/And the other day cleanin' out from under the bed, I found some Jockey underwear./You know I only wear boxer shorts; come on and give me an excuse./But she was in the kitchen fixin' herself a Bloody Mary, and all she said was 'Bobby, get your butt out here and help me find the tomato juice.'" After the performance, Ginsberg just said, "You have many voices," and walked away. Later I heard that he took serious offense. I was never asked back.

My favorite audiences are usually women who work for men, mainly because I'm a big blond guy and, at least in my personae, sing songs about how stupid and arro-

But soon I found myself,

Jack Daniels in hand,

having a good time among

cowboys, miners,

and a woman who spoke well

of Kurt Vonnegut's work.

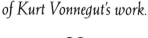

gant I am. One group of female bank tellers invite me back every year to sing songs where women say things to me like, "'Listen buckaroo, I'm splittin' from this scene/'cause last night was just a waste of my time./You might be tall in the saddle but you're short in the jeans.'/Then she turned 'round and flipped me a dime."

In contrast, I recently performed at the annual meeting of the Montana Society of Explosive Engineers. The organizer had called me because he had thought I was someone else, an old cowboy who writes doggerel about outhouses. When I told him I wrote funny songs and poems, he said, "Hell, I guess you'll do in a pinch." I then warned him that my music had been affiliated with Earth First! He said he guessed that was o.k..." but just don't tell anybody since some of these fellows had their operations monkey-wrenched."

As I drove over Homestake Pass to Butte, I felt like I was descending into enemy territory and came close to turning around. These were the guys that we chanted "Burn the dozer!" about out in the woods at whooping, naked eco-terrorist rallies. But soon I found myself, Jack Daniels in hand, having a good time among cowboys, miners, and a woman who spoke well of Kurt Vonnegut's work. In my performance, I steered clear of direct environmental satire and sang songs like *WD-40 Polka, Co-Dependent Cowgirl,* and *White Guy Dancin'.* That is, I got their guard down with a song about spray lubricant then sucker-punched them with songs about inept white guys and irresponsible alcoholics. One Canadian in the crowd really liked a song about Canada that has a subtheme of "I want a Native North American spirit watching over my soul." After my performance, the guy who hired me said (to scare me, I think) "I'm sure glad you didn't play none of them tree huggin' songs."

"Tree huggin'!" blurted the Canadian. "I'd like to dynamite one of them tree huggin' sumbitches."

"Yes," I said, "duct tape a few sticks to his neck and top him like a big Doug Fir!" Everybody laughed. I was a big hit.

Greg Keeler teaches English at Montana State University. His latest book is Epiphany at Goofy's Gas, *his latest tape is* All You Can Eat, *and his latest musical is "Aliens and Canadians."*

Finding a Voice of Your Own

Nancy Henderson

This morning on audio cassette, I heard William Stafford quoted about writing. An actor delivered the quote with stagey inflections, not at all like Stafford's speech. I didn't catch the meaning. The incongruity overwhelmed it.

Your speaking voice is unique like your fingerprints and integral to the impact of what you say. Your writing voice too should be unique and effectual. But problems with voice abound in manuscripts I evaluate for authors.

There are chameleon voices: now brassy, now aloof, now earthy. One-note voices: the angry man posturing. Lifeless voices. Mimic voices. Facile voices that hide their authors behind a polished surface.

A distinctive writing voice is authentic, autonomous, meaningful, courageous, and free. It has integrity, authority, and the fire we call charisma.

Authentic voices are faithful to the truth. They alter reality, not to hide anything, but to reveal more.

When your voice is authentic, you don't watch yourself strutting your stuff in a mental mirror. Nor do you incorporate obfuscations so that, should readers react negatively, you can claim, "That's not what I meant!"

You stand exposed, unprotected, with no place to duck for cover.

Autonomous. Your voice is yours alone, neither an imitation of somebody else nor a product of preconceived notions of how a writer "should" sound.

When you speak with autonomy, you don't serve up images from the conventional larder (dewdrops, roses, stars, and a moonstruck wind) or conventional sentiments (roses are beautiful, stars signal eternity). You've grown your own stock of metaphors from deeply felt experience.

Your autonomous voice isn't the trained monkey of instructors who insist on certain fashions or norms, doesn't hew to your mother's ideas of decorum, isn't lamed by criticism. In fact, it isn't shaped by outside forces at all. It arises from within you, to speak your truth.

Meaningful. A strong voice maximizes itself on strongly felt material, not subjects of only superficial interest to you. If you trust yourself always to have more ideas, you'll be able to discard weak ones. The number of written pieces you will finish in your lifetime is finite…very finite. Here's a tough test for significance: "If I could write only one thing before I died, would I write this?"

Another test: "Can I talk about this subject in a way nobody else can? Is there a special bond between me and this material? Am I the writer for this piece?"

I call the subjects that are yours core material: it bubbles up fiery and substantive from your center.

Courageous. After reading manuscripts for a quarter-century, I have a sixth sense for when an author is dodging core material. If the text turns anecdotal, that's a tip-off. Anecdotes are the antithesis of core material: safe, inoffensive, no teeth. Core material moves both writer and reader. It effects change in feeling or attitude. Change is a sortie into the unknown, and you can't come back. Change is risky.

An authentic, autonomous, meaningful voice demands courage. It will change its owner — toward greater honesty and directness, among other things. Family and friends typically deprecate these changes, which also call the author to new standards of personal conduct. Henry Miller wrote in *The Colossus of Maroussi:* "The mastery of any form of expression should lead inevitably to the final expression — mastery of life."

*Free…*from oppression by the internal

A distinctive writing voice

is authentic,

autonomous, meaningful,

courageous, and free.

censor. Your censor is fixated on safety: you can't reveal such-and-such because people (or God) will isolate you, say terrible things about you, hate you, and punish you in dozens of nameless ways.

Freedom goes hand-in-hand with an authentic voice, unencumbered by self-absorption, self-consciousness, fear of failure, preoccupation with how people will react. This voice speaks the truth of the now without fear of consequence.

Authority, the take-charge characteristic of your voice, requires you to identify your audience so that you can effectively communicate to it.

Your authority allows readers to relax and enjoy the ride, confident that you have matters in hand. You won't make any false moves in characterization. You won't undermine your reader's confidence with an erroneous detail. Like a conductor, you will direct the reader's attention from passage to passage, orchestrating a cohesive experience.

Integrity is wholeness. While autonomy means that you represent emotions that are really yours, integrity asks you to reflect the range of those emotions. Some people's work seems to have been authored by more than one writer. One piece arises from a Pollyanna self, another from an existentially somber soul. Other writers present a one-tone voice without modulation.

A mature writing voice integrates your principal selves. It's the voice of both/and, not either/or. It's honest, sincere, and balanced. A voice with integrity wins readers' trust and respect.

Charisma is the sizzle that comes from strong focus. Readers feel you were compelled to write the piece: you are lifted out of yourself and super-charged by an impulse. This transcendent quality is inherent, not in the subject matter, but in your single-focus commitment.

The enemies of charisma are crossed or

Sample Query Letter
(done only after reading the guidelines of each publisher)

```
Date

Editor's name
 & address

Dear (editor/publisher):

Attract the editor's attention
immediately with your best writing.
Perhaps, lead with the actual lead ¶
of your work. In your style.

Detail your proposed work. Be brief!

Tell why this proposal is
appropriate and why you're the one
to do it. Who? What? When? Where?
Why?
```

false purposes: you want to write the definitive in-depth piece on rain forest ecology and garner your mother's praise and get rich. Writers may state that they want to become wealthy from their writing, or that they're driven to see their names in print, simply because those are accepted motivations, whereas a poet's working for one copy of a publication as pay is considered crazy. Most writers' censors don't like to be called crazy. Yet you can't claim false motivations with impunity.

If your conviction about why you write is firm and unadulterated, you will develop your charisma.

"Having a voice" means power to affect the course of history. As you find a voice of your own — authentic and meaningful, free, courageous and charismatic, a voice with autonomy, authority, and integrity — you'll change your readers. You'll change the human condition at least a little. Most frightening and most thrilling of all, you'll change yourself.

Nancy Henderson has consulted to authors for 20 years. This essay is based on her workshop, "Finding Your Voice." She is the author of two novels and an autobiography published by Doubleday, as well as many articles and interviews. She will appear in The Best New Voices in Poetry *in '93.*

First Clip

Jessica Wade

As a writer looking for my first nonfiction publication, I faced the age-old dilemma: which came first — the freelancer or the clip?

Query letters with snappy leads and well-developed ideas crumbled into wishful thinking when I faced that final paragraph. The one where you display credentials and dazzle the editor with your publication history. I didn't have one.

In order to get published, I needed to be published. What I really needed was a way off the query-go-round.

Help came from a writing instructor who suggested doing a mass mailing to newspapers. What you do, she explained, is sell first rights in each paper's publication area. Newspapers put things in print faster than magazines, and you market the same article to several publications at the same time. What you send is the finished article — no query needed.

Fired with enthusiasm I began searching for a topic with broad appeal. My choice was dandelions; universally recognized as a weed, they are also grown commercially and sold in markets. Written with the food department in mind, the article was accompanied by recipes which could be used with the text or left out.

The instructor recommended the *Gale Directory* as a source of names and addresses. My first rude awakening came when the librarian asked, "Which volume do you want?"

Sitting in front of all three, I pondered my approach. My second rude awakening came with the realization I hadn't a clue as to what a publication area really was.

Looking at the map, state boundaries seemed to be a pretty safe bet, an assumption that would later prove incorrect. Bewildered by sheer numbers, I decided to choose dailies with a circulation of one hundred thousand or more. Larger papers, I reasoned, would have more freelance funds available.

Using this criteria, I arbitrarily compiled a mailing list of fifty-four and also assembled an alternate list that I could use selectively as rejections came in.

I was told to send along a postcard for the editor's reply, but feedback was almost as important as clips. Since I was shooting scattershot in the dark, I wanted to at least gather some information in the process.

Listing what I wanted to know, I devised a form editors could use by checking off their response. I then photocopied this form and the finished manuscript and printed a dual set of labels, with the second set going on the form, to tell me exactly who was replying.

The worst moment came when I arrived at the post office carrying fifty-four envelopes. I felt like a kid with a box full of puppies all needing a good home by sundown.

The first response arrived exactly one week later — a phenomena that almost gave me whiplash. The fact that it was a rejection definitely didn't help. But, the reply form did seem to be working, even if it was telling me stuff I didn't want to hear.

The vast majority of early replies were from editors who indicated they did not accept freelance material. Some wrote this was due to present budget restraints and I should try again "in a few months." Others added they only used local freelancers. Two, *The Providence Journal-Bulletin* and the *Knoxville News-Sentinel*, were kind enough to note the food department did not use freelance material, but the travel section did.

Under the category, "We cannot use this material because..." where a blank space invited comment, most replies also centered around lack of budget. Some stated they used only staff and wire copy. A few noted they only worked with preapproved ideas on as-

signment. One commented they did a similar story last summer, others replied with the well-worn phrase "doesn't fit our needs." Another vague response that popped up regularly was "no space." The food editor from the *San Diego Union* said they were in the midst of a merger — please try again.

The reply form also had a place to indicate writer's guidelines were available. The response here was absolute zero. This may apply to food departments only; I already had a copy of travel freelance guidelines from *The Seattle Times*.

I later added a line to the bottom of the form asking the editor to destroy the manuscript if they could not use it. Some came back with postage due and the entire twelve page manuscript crammed into my business size SASE.

If all this sounds like swimming in a sea of rejection, it wasn't. The first group of articles was mailed January 2. The *Los Angeles Times* replied three weeks later. My article was "under consideration." It appeared in print on January 30.

The *Concord Monitor* accepted the article outright noting it would be printed in April or May. Four others indicated they also had it under consideration and would use it when dandelions were ready to eat in their areas. For the *Anchorage Daily News* that wouldn't be until June.

In the end a total of ninety-four articles were mailed. By March sixty-one had replied. Using the alternate list turned out to be my best move. The *Los Angeles Times* was on "List B."

Along the way, I discovered what a circulation area was — sort of. One rule of thumb is to use a radius of one hundred miles. However, the *Los Angeles Times* covers all southern California while *The Miami Herald* covers the entire state of Florida. *The Boston Globe* includes all six New England states in its circulation area. The *New York Times* and the *Washington Post* do not welcome multiple submissions at all.

So, which came first — the freelancer or the clip? I still couldn't say. But, one thing's certain: next time I ride that query-go-round, I'll have my own brass ring.

Jessica Wade is a Portland writer whose articles have appeared in several newspapers and Oregon Coast *magazine. This article is part of a work-in-progress,* Freelancing to the Nation's Newspapers: A Western Perspective *by Sharon Wood, to be published by Continuing Education Press.*

JESSICA WADE
Address
City, State, Zip
(555) 555-5555

Label with newspaper name and address

Article: "A TASTE OF SUNSHINE"

☐ Accepted
Projected publication date: _____
☐ Under consideration
☐ We cannot use this material because...

☐ Writer's guidelines available upon request
☐ We do not accept freelance material
Signed: _____
Date: _____
Please destroy manuscript if you cannot use it.

Becoming a Business Writer Somewhat Against My Will

Joy Passanante

In the late Fifties, when I was in sixth grade and our *Weekly Readers* focused on Eisenhower's golf scores and UNIVAC, my friend Bonnie and I would sneak into the Girls' Room together every afternoon to talk about books. We were bonded, Bonnie and I, by the simple fact that we preferred Catherine and Heathcliff to the Bobbsey twins. One afternoon, she leaned toward me conspiratorially and confessed that someday she intended to have affairs — a concept she had learned no doubt from reading the same books I had, but which she had obviously comprehended more readily than I. I had certainly been exposed to characters who were having affairs and was duly fascinated by the consequences suffered by the compromised women who had surrendered (or so it had seemed) to male animal desires. But as to the physical realities that having an affair implied, I was in the dark. Bonnie's hushed voice, however, clued me in that this secret was of the highest significance. In exchange for this reckless confession, I whispered back to her the most wildly titillating gem I could conjure up — that I intended to be a writer.

And — lo and behold — it wasn't long after that epiphany that people began to tell me I would become a writer. What no one mentioned was the fact that I would become a business writer.

Even a decade later, when I was about to graduate from college, the idea of being a "business" anything would have seemed not only absurd but anathema. It was, after all, the sixties. After all those years of intense political arguments at coffee houses, after all those rallies for causes, the glow of blazing ROTC buildings still warm on our cheeks, the teargas still pungent in our nostrils, we all had a dream: if not to undermine than at least to circumvent corporate America. I'd taken as much Creative Writing as I could pack into my schedule and no doubt would have called Business Writing, if I had ever heard of the course, an oxymoron.

After four years of ardently exploring the liberal arts, I had such a dim vision of the world of work that launching a career in anything, much less writing, seemed impossible. Since it was 1969, and credentials were less important — and less plentiful — than energy and commitment, I decided to forego an MFA in writing for a quick teaching degree so I could support my husband-to-be; he who was going East and wanted to pack me up with him.

Then we moved to Idaho and I convinced the English department of our state university that I could "teach comp." The university proved a bridge to the business world. It was in fact one of my students who recommended me for my first business writing job. She had graduated and become an assistant in the high school relations department; the university wanted to revamp its high school recruiting pieces and needed a writer to give the program descriptions pizzazz. I almost said no. I was busy enough teaching six sections of writing a year — especially at part-time pay — but something about the situation seemed, well, adventurous. And indeed it was.

This venture unveiled the first in a series of secrets about business writing: writing public relations pieces — recruiting booklets and brochures, cover letters, scripts for slide shows or videos — exercises the same brain cells as writing fiction. Creating an image for a public relations project means using "real-life" material in new ways and choosing only those details to describe, explain, and embellish that further your purpose. Sound familiar?

Second, business writers are guaranteed a wide and often diverse audience. Feedback is immediate. People comment on your work; they have opinions. They pay you. (I now see brochures I write on the desks of staff members, in the book piles of students.) And your successful efforts might even produce "results" (an important business term I picked up in the eighties). Thanks to your skill in fundraising, a children's home might augment its services to more needy teenagers, or an English department might increase the number of its majors. There's a surprisingly pleasurable feeling of closure to this sense of producing results, or of producing anything whatever.

Since our university provides the economic base for our town, news of my newly-retooled writing skills spread to the business community, and organizations in the area began to ask for my services — initially just for writing and editing, but soon for consulting about writing, too. One day an acquaintance asked me to take her place as the presenter of a two day workshop for a nationally known Northwest-based firm. The company's education department had created the workshop; all course materials plus all notes for the presenter were typed like teleprompts on 4 by 6 cards. After I sounded my ignorance of the business world, and catalogued all the reasons I couldn't possibly teach this course, the lure of replacing the shredded cloth covering our living room window with lined drapes that drew open and shut won out. "Yes," I said, sounding as tentative as I felt. But another secret was revealed to me: I could do

And just like

Molly Bloom,

"Yes," I said, "yes."

this stuff — not only do this stuff, but do it well. I was nervous, but the workshop was a success. Presto — I had had experience teaching business writing, and from that germ my repertoire burgeoned. That experience qualified me to teach business writing to college students, and later I was asked to teach in and eventually direct a business writing program through the College of Business and Economics. The more I said "yes," the more I learned and the more frequently I met people who wanted to hire me. Soon people I met through workshops would ask me if I could edit or write marketing materials, computer manuals, river supplies catalogues, grants, applications for bank loans, a TV show on Idaho research. And just like Molly Bloom, "Yes," I said, "yes." Yes.

I was also employed by the College of Business and Economics to give seminars on writing as part of an outreach program to public audiences as well as businesses and organizations. The contacts I made at these workshops brought me more clients than I could serve. I have extracted succinct video scripts from rambling interviews; worked on annual reports, speeches, customer relations letters, company newsletters, brochures; and even written a brief for an attorney. My motley clientele includes banks, a nationally known horse club, seed companies, an orthodontist, a state elderhostel association.

Why do this? One advantage to business writing is that business writers have a wealth of opportunities to sharpen their skills. It's different from classroom teaching, which is such an emotional investment that a writer who teaches writing often feels as if he or she is being siphoned off. Business writers also learn about audiences for their other work; they usually have to please more than one person. And, of course, these bankers and marketing specialists make up a chunk of the book-buying public, and a writer who is agoraphobic about straying far from the comforting click of his or her Mac may not be one who writes something anyone else will want to read.

My experience is that the business world is hungry for people who are at ease with the written word. And I have found I like working with business people. They believe in results and deadlines and the value of honest response; they appreciate a competent person who is dependable and listens well. This appreciation makes my work as a business writer satisfying and fun. After all, many of those people who demonstrated in combat fatigues and linked arms while swaying to "Kumbaya" are now stockbrokers or accountants or administrators — or even presidents. And lots of "businesses" are in fact not-for-profit organizations — hospitals and children's homes and school districts.

Here are some how-to's: Take a business writing class through a local university or a continuing ed program, or buy a professional writing text. (They include not only

the tricks of the trade, but pages of examples.) Do your homework. Business writing does have its own set of prejudices, and you may have to unlearn your hard-won command over the periodic, multi-layered sentence. Find out what writing really goes on in the businesses around your house. Dust off and re-focus your resume to emphasize your writing skills. Pass it out to local organizations. Don't concentrate so much on academic credentials, just on experience. Edit something — a newsletter? an annual report — for an organization. If no one asks you to write anything for profit, volunteer a time or two to get experience. After you complete a project, no matter how small, ask for a letter of recommendation, no matter how brief, from your client. Create a portfolio of your work. Keep a list of the sort of pieces you have worked on. Begin a client list. (Mine, which is about to flow over to page 3, consisted of only one entry for at least a year, but you have to start somewhere.) Give yourself a title (Business Writer? Communication Specialist? Editor to the Stars?) depending on the sort of clients you imagine you want to have. Order a business card that highlights your specialties. As soon as you can, charge for your work. And, most of all, expand your notion about what being a writer means.

My fiction may not be the sort that will keep me in new drapes every other year, but my business writing has already bought me time to write more of the stories I've always wanted to.

And that brings me back to Bonnie. If Bonnie and I were to meet now, I'd take her to the Sawtooths, perch with her on a boulder facing Redfish Lake, and we'd talk about books, gossiping about our old friends, Catherine and Heathcliff, Emma B., and Anna K. She'd tell me about her life as a fundraising research director for a big-city hospital; I'd show her my recent stories, the juiciest scenes marked by brochures I've been paid to write.

Joy Passanante is a lecturer in the English Department at the University of Idaho and is a communications consultant. She has published numerous poems, short stories, and articles and is also a video producer and scriptwriter.

Travel Writers' Press Trip: A Week in the Surreal Lane

Serena Lesley

Journeying on a travel writers' press trip is like a trip in a womb. The cosseting eases, lulls. You never have to jostle for a bus ticket, never have to wait for a restaurant table, never have to hassle with a foreign switchboard to get through to the Minister of Tourism to check your facts.

All is provided. Everybody wants you to love him/his hotel/his country! Sensible, experienced travel writers warned me when I started going on these trips: remember the reader. Remember the couple on a tight budget with two squirmy kids, who wants to fit in a few fine museums as well as frolicking on the paddleboats at the seaside, and who hasn't the faintest idea of how, abroad, to negotiate all that.

How right they were! You have to fight sometimes to hit reality, touch base — i.e., don't just enjoy the private cars, find out the bus schedule. I was blessed for years with travel assignments handed my way as a feature writer on a London newspaper: Mauritius, Zambia, Tunisia, Israel, China, Florida's Gulf Coast…on and on.

The writing was fun, though sometimes the days stretched on for an exhausting 18 hours or more on the trot. Smiles fixed, we toured yet another hotel or museum as we tottered off a plane from London. We writers encountered some brilliant travel press officers and some horrors, for whom any of us could have drawn up ideal game plans. Why didn't anyone ever ask us to?

Like: don't mix two fiercely opposing newspapers on the same trip. That meant, in my case, as I was on *The Daily Telegraph*, please don't make the other woman writer the one from *The Times*. Don't mix people who have had a historic sensational love affair on the last travel outing — and who loathe each other now it's over.

Like: have the writers do something physical and terribly healthy the moment they get off a long plane journey — instead of sending them straight to bed. A brilliant arrival I recall in Sri Lanka sent us straight onto the hotel beach after a tiring flight from London. Freshened by waves and salt and sun, we came off ready for a chat with a government official. By the same token, when we reached Iran our hosts had arranged an instant cocktail party, very formal, very surreal, as we were too weary to make any sense at all to the nice locals who'd gathered to greet us.

The most superbly planned travel writers' trip I ever took was the one to the Indian Ocean island of Mauritius, organized by British Airways. Not just that we covered the island and every aspect of it, including a fire-walking ceremony where we photographed like mad as men walked, apparently painlessly, in a state of ecstasy over blazing coals. No, it was the island leaders who fascinated us. Our PR man brought in a local guest each night to dine with us at our luxury beach hotel. One night it was the leader of the opposition, a fiery and quotable mixture of Indian and French background. Another night, the leader of the Farmers Union. A whole morning was laid on for us with the jovial Prime Minister, especially fruitful as the colony was just about to gain independence from Britain and he had a lot to say. (Should they allow Russian submarines to use their harbors, etc.?)

And thereby hangs another bit of counsel: cycle and re-cycle your notes from such a writing trip. There are bound to be a good half-dozen angles, probably more. The talks in Mauritius, including a magic garden party evening with the Indian community there, yielded me a sturdy political story which was used over an entire (pre-tabloid) page of *The Christian Science Monitor*.

You can turn a look at a crafts market — just another ho-hum on a press trip for some of the writers — into a feature for an American crafts magazine. The food market and its amazing spices, of course, shouts out "write me for *Gourmet*" and on and on.

You never run out. A wonderfully organized press trip can keep a freelancer spinning out stories for a full month on return to the desk. The travel story itself is almost a breeze. Quickly dispatched, it then gets milked for many other angles.

Don't sneer at souvenirs, you world-weary travel writer. Your Christmas and birthday gift lists could be cared for in a trice at some faraway street market, or even better, a government-run crafts center like the one in Tunis where I acquired — and kept for myself — a long rope of carved dark wooden hearts interspersed with pearls, which stops conversation whenever I wear it. Even something that looks mundane to the locals can seem sensational at home, like the quilted, shocking pink silk handbag I got for $8 in China and which took me to Covent Garden opera and to the Paris fashion collections.

Freshened by waves

and salt and sun,

we came off ready for

a chat with a

government official.

Don't forget the comforts. I always traveled with a baby pillow, covered in fine blue linen. Bolsters in some of these faraway lands can be rocky. An immersion heater and handful of tea bags will lift your spirits (check voltage!) and are only unnecessary in China where thermoses of boiling water sit on every night table.

Clothes? Don't worry about weight. Take plenty. Still and yet the most brilliant of women travel journalists was famed for stuffing a week's clothes — chiefly Banana Republic style — into a backpack and walking serenely away to a bus on our return to Heathrow Airport while we hassled with suitcases and cabs.

Consider censorship on your trip and persuade your paper to wait until your return to receive the story. An article I wired from Athens during the reign of the colonels was held up for hours while they pondered whether I was being sarcastic or not. I was. And a travel story on a Madeira cruise which the editor wanted wired from the ship was heavily blue-penciled by the captain, who read every word transmitted from his craft. Hence *The Telegraph* readers never did learn that the ship's closets only held three hangers and that the stewards burst in any old time without knocking!

Sometimes the shifting relationships of the writers' group are every bit as riveting as NASA or whatever else you're seeing. On a Texas trip (hosted by ill-fated Braniff) an English magazine journalist set her sights on the witty, laconic, Dublin political writer. The stalk was on. It took from Houston to Dallas to Galveston, but finally in LBJ ranch country she landed him. General relief from all. It's all very amiable and you feel you are in a family all that intense cocooned week, but it's wise to reflect that there's a gossipy outer world out there and chat wings like first editions. Tempted, over a long, slow dinner and a bottle of wine, people speak vividly, indiscreetly about the horrors of their feature editors, something many of us agree to wholeheartedly. Very soothing, this camaraderie. It can boomerang.

Safest, perhaps, to generalize — like the copy editor who surfaced from an icy swimming pool when we were all hanging about on Reunion Island waiting for Air France to fix the plane: "Whew, it's cold — cold as an editor's handshake!"

Serena Sinclair Lesley left London upon marriage to Earl Lesley and now freelances for anyone who asks — chiefly on restaurants, hotels, travel. She writes the weekly restaurant review in Portland Downtowner, and is also published in Northwest Travel, Architectural Times, Esprit of London, Glasgow Herald, and Daily Telegraph of London.

Cowboy Poetry

Mike Logan

At first glance, the words "cowboy" and "poetry" might seem about as likely to mix as cows and sheep or oil and water. In the cow country of the American West, however, cowboy poetry is as real as a slick fork saddle or the horse you pitch it onto. It can carry the wallop of a forty-five slug or touch you with the velvet smoothness of a night horse nuzzling for a sugar cube.

Cowboy poetry is as old as the cattle drives that flowed north from the cashless cow-rich ranches of post civil war Texas to the beckoning gold of the Kansas railheads. The drovers that pushed the longhorn cows from south of the Red River to the fabled trail towns of Abilene, Wichita, and Dodge didn't carry books. Many of them couldn't have read them if they had. If there was entertainment along the trail, they made their own, and songs, tall tales, and poems were all a part of it.

Cowboy poetry is also as new as the Cowboy Poetry Gathering in Elko, Nevada or some of its exuberant offspring such as the Montana Cowboy Poetry Gathering in Lewistown, Montana.

At its very best, cowboy poetry is on a par with any other genre of poetry. At its worst, it is hackneyed and dull.

In between these two extremes is a poetry that is at once rambunctious and sensitive, humorous and mournful. It is a poetic celebration of a way of life that can be harsh and tedious, but also incredibly beautiful.

Unlike some of its more scholarly cousins, cowboy poetry is almost exclusively intended to be said aloud. Whether the poems are to be said to friends, to a Cattleman's Association banquet, or at a cowboy poetry gathering, cowboy poets spend a lot of their hours ahorseback practicing the poems they recite.

While a lot of the poems are original and from the heart, a great number are old traditional poems. Often these have been memorized because the reciter heard them from a father or a grandfather or read them

and just wants to be able to pass them on to friends. Names like Badger Clark, S. Omar Barker, Bruce Kiskaddon, Curley Fletcher, and Gail Gardner ring down the poetry trails from gathering to gathering.

The first Cowboy Poetry Gathering in Elko, Nevada came about as the result of a bunch of folklorists from the western states looking for a project unique to the West. Everybody thought they were loco. Who would come and just sit and listen to poetry? There surely weren't long lines waiting to get into most poetry readings in the universities or the sitting rooms of America.

It was an explosion.

The first year, 1985, the gathering was relatively small. The ensuing years have seen as many as 14,000 people descend on Elko. Rooms are booked for the next year before most people leave the gathering they are attending. Some drive from as far away as Wells or Battle Mountain each day of the gathering.

It is a love affair.

While Elko remains the Granddaddy of them all, many of the western states and the western provinces in Canada have gone on to have gatherings of their own as a result of the open handed friendliness poets first found there.

One of the first state gatherings, the Montana Cowboy Poetry Gathering, might be typical of a lot of those springing up around the West. Although its birthplace was in Big Timber, Montana, it now takes place in August of each year in Lewistown and is fairly representative of how most gatherings are set up.

During the two days of the gathering, featured poets emcee daytime theme sessions. The hourlong sessions are usually set up so that all of the poets who are signed up, usually six or eight at a session, will re-

At its very best,

cowboy poetry is on a par with

any other genre of poetry.

cite a poem or two the first time around. Then, if there is enough time, they may each have the opportunity to say another. It is the emcee's job to introduce the poets and give them an idea of how much time each has so that things move along quickly and smoothly. Poems are sometimes read rather than said from memory.

The next session starts almost immediately and the biggest problem is usually having enough time to fit all the poets in. As Mike Korn, Montana's former state folklorist, is fond of saying, "If you kick a clump of sage brush in Montana, a jackrabbit will probably jump out one side and a cowboy poet out the other."

Workshops are also frequently held that deal with such themes as the writing, presenting, and publishing of poetry. For those interested in cowboy poetry books and tapes, cowboy art, and cowboy gear there are displays of such trappings for sale.

The evening shows are made up of the featured poets, selected for that gathering, presenting their poetry. For variety, an occasional cowboy singer is mixed into the evening programs.

A cowboy poetry gathering has a language all its own. Sometimes it is a spare, laconic language; at other times it is the wide swinging loop of an old-time spinner of tall tales. Whatever the form, the words come out of the cowboy's work and play. The vocabulary may be as unintelligible to those unfamiliar with cow country lingo as the words of a computer programmer would be to an old puncher who has spent his life riding the high desert or the foothills of the Rockies, but it will be the working language of cow country.

While the words "cowboy" and "poetry" do seem an unlikely combination, they really go together as naturally as boots and spurs or ropes and saddle horns. Someday soon, plan to take advantage of the opportunity to attend a gathering in your area and see just what a smooth team they make. You'll like what you see and hear.

(A longer version of this article appeared in *National Arts Today.*)

Mike Logan of Helena, Montana is the author/photographer of three books of photography and verse, and two books of cowboy poetry. A featured poet and emcee at the national Cowboy Poetry Gathering in Elko, Nevada since 1988, he has recited his poetry all over the western United States and Canada.

The Fabric of Truth

Lauren Kessler

Can fact and fiction peacefully coexist in story-telling? Journalists say no. Journalism tells its story by compiling verifiable fact, documented proof, and attributed comment into real-life narrative. Fiction — in journalistic parlance known as "fabrication of fact" — is a crime punishable by expulsion from the profession. Witness Janet Cooke, the *Washington Post* reporter who lost both her Pulitzer and her job when an editor discovered that the "Jimmy" in her powerful story on youth and drugs was a fabricated composite character, not a "real" boy.

Literary types don't know what to make of the marriage of fact and fiction. A novelist whose work too closely parallels real life is sometimes thought to suffer from a lack of imagination, a dearth of vision. Fiction writers who use fact to help tell stories are considered by many to be less artistic, less creative, less worthy of the term "writer."

Yet human beings have been weaving together fact and fiction to tell powerful, important stories for as long as there have been stories to tell. The long and continuous search for a cultural form best suited to tell the human story has often involved attempts to reconcile fact and fiction into a form that is neither and both.

It may be that the division between fact and fiction is not logical or self-evident, but rather arbitrary, subjective, and highly dependent on context. Fact and fiction may be part of a spectrum, different but complementary colors on the palette of the artist interested in painting a picture of life that is not just true (that is, factual) but True (that is, authentic, meaningful).

Consider the work of the eighteenth century writer Daniel DeFoe, which mixes fact and fiction to create a sharp, meaningful reality. DeFoe was a London penny-a-line reporter in the years before he wrote *Moll Flanders*, and there's evidence to suggest that Moll was a real woman he met during his newspaper days. Certainly the London he describes is real, down to the houses and streets. Does the reality make the book less

of an artistic creation? Does the addition of literary imagination make it any less real?

Consider the works of Mark Twain, Stephen Crane, Walt Whitman, Ernest Hemingway or Tillie Olsen. All freely mixed fact and fiction to tell stories that were both true and True.

Think of John Steinbeck on assignment for a national magazine, gathering information for a series on the dust bowl migration. At some point, he realizes that the material is bigger than the form he is trying to put it in. He scraps the magazine series and instead writes *Grapes of Wrath*. Because he fabricates the name and fictionalizes some details, does that make the Joads any less real?

Steinbeck's book won the Pulitzer prize for fiction, although it was based on just the kind of exhaustive research and documented proof that journalists use to write their stories. Forty years later, Janet Cooke's journalistic Pulitzer was pulled because, in telling a True story, she used literary license. But given the important human stories that need telling and given our national impatience with the written word, don't we sometimes need writers who can invoke both the power of fact and the drama of fiction?

Literary journalists — a relatively new group — say yes. Traditional journalism, they say, is obsessed with verifiable facts, sometimes to the exclusion of truth and often to the exclusion of Truth. Journalistic fact, in fact, is not truth but rather a version of reality dependent on self-interested sources. And at any rate, they say, facts don't necessarily — or even often — lead to understanding. Furthermore, they argue, journalistic objectivity, both as moral philosophy and operational dogma, obscures

Journalistic fact, in fact,

is not truth but rather

a version of reality dependent

on self-interested sources.

truth as often as it clarifies it. On the other hand, literature is not the answer, for literary journalists believe there is a special power derived from the real that is lacking in the imaginative. So what is the answer?

Edna St. Vincent Millay — another Pulitzer winner — alluded to it in yet another form used to tell true stories, the poem:

> *Upon this gifted age, in its dark hour,*
> *Rains from the sky a meteoric shower*
> *Of facts… they lie unquestioned,*
>   *uncombined.*
> *Wisdom enough to leech us of our ill*
> *Is daily spun; but there exists no loom*
> *To weave it into fabric.*

But the loom did and does exist. Throughout the centuries, hybrid writers, from (novelist) DeFoe to (journalist) John McPhee to (essayist) Joan Didion have helped construct it. What they weave is known variously as literary journalism, creative nonfiction, factual fiction and the literature of actuality. A form that allows a writer to both report facts and search for truth/Truth, it blends the empirical eye of the journalist with the moral vision — the I — of the novelist. Today it is found in magazine articles, books, even video documentaries that deal with subjects as prosaic as building a house (Tracy Kidder's *House*) or as profound as what it means to be an American (Jane Kramer's *Last Cowboy*). In between, there are stories about politics, economics, crime, the environment, technology, sports, Hell's Angels, fifth graders, and people who make frozen orange juice. The genre knows no bounds.

Yes, traditional journalism has its place: to signal us that events have or will happen; to alert us to the existence of issues and problems. And of course, traditional literature has its place: to explore timeless themes, to transport us beyond our personal experience. But both a part of and apart from them stands literary journalism. All but orphaned by its nervous journalistic and literary parents who don't know what to make of it, who often wish it would keep quiet and stop asking those embarrassing questions (What is real? What is truth?), literary journalism is a vital, important, dynamic genre. It's time its parents showed some respect.

(First appeared in *Old Oregon Magazine*.)

Lauren Kessler, a social historian and professor at the University of Oregon, is the author of six books. Her seventh, a work of creative nonfiction, follows three generations of a Japanese American Family. The Stubborn Twig (Random House) is due out Fall 1993.

The Changing Face of the Romance Book Business

Jennifer McCord

"Love is an ancient story, yet is ever new." This quote still describes the romance book business, which over the last ten years has not only evolved, but flourished.

Most major houses publish contemporary and historical romances. A contemporary is set in or near the present. A historical can be set in any era prior to World War II. Another area is the romance series or category books. These romances are historical or contemporary books that are published monthly in a paperback edition and are numbered on the spine or cover. Readers know from the name of a line what kind of story they are reading — from the sensual to the sweet. The category series books are only published now by Harlequin, Loveswept, Meteor, and Silhouette, and Zebra's To Love Again.

The romance genre offers a wide spectrum of sub-genres such as Gothic, futuristic, regency, ethnic, time-travel, general historicals, and paranormal. And recently, smaller publishers have ventured into the black romance paperback market.

Romance novels are published in all forms today — paperback, trade, hardcover, and audio tapes. The hardcover and audio marketplace will see an increase in title and author selection during 1993. And all areas have experienced a price increase.

The plot of the romance novel, however, remains the same: the relationship between the man and woman, and their struggle to find love. The theme of love is timeless; as Jung said, the soul cannot exist in peace until it finds its other. Both men and women are waiting for this experience to happen and the romance novel continues to work within this framework.

In romance novels of the past, the hero was often portrayed as the tough, macho super hero who did not show his emotions.

Now there is a broader realm of emotional possibilities for the hero. Super hero types still exist, but a new type of hero is emerging. He has strength, courage, honor, trustworthiness; he can be loving and kind. While the former super macho-man may have possessed some or all of these virtues, the more recent hero talks about his feelings — the man tries to communicate. Above all, he is faithful to the heroine.

If the hero is a contemporary man, he can have all kinds of jobs, including truck driver, detective, rancher, house husband, or school teacher. It is the character of the man that matters. For the historical hero, various roles in history exist, such as pirate, duke, nobleman, lord, Indian, Indian fighter, even an outlaw. The historical hero may remind the reader of an urbane '90s man in another time or place. Again, it is the *character* of the hero that is important. He may enhance the heroine as the reader learns about her through his eyes.

The theme of love

is timeless...

The heroine has evolved from being the young innocent to being the star, the winner (not only because she gets her man, but because almost always she achieves her other goals in the narrative). In the contemporary books, she reflects today's women. She is not necessarily supermom or superwoman. She has broad shoulders, but not broad enough to take on everything and everyone. She works at home, in the corporate world, as a plumber, construction worker, electrician, forester, veterinarian, and so on. In the historicals, the heroine seems to be more and more a '90s woman dressed up in historical garb. But other authors prefer to have more historical accuracy with regard to the role of women in a particular period. This "role of the heroine" is debated in the romance book business, since like any other genre, romance fiction must present characters that appeal to the reader.

Settings for the romance novel continue to include these favorites of readers: the American Civil War, the medieval era, regency England and Scotland, the 18th and 19th centuries, the British Isles, the Viking era, and the old West.

Both historical and contemporary markets continue to address social issues, such as alcoholism, abuse, burnout, homelessness, illiteracy, and so on. Some of these issues are addressed in a less contemporary guise in the historical books.

Cover art has undergone noticeable changes in romance publishing over the last ten years. The covers used to have what was commonly known in slang terms as the vamp-and-clinch — either the hero or heroine would be leaning into the neck — thus the vampire look. The clinch look showed the couple in a passionate embrace. Nowadays, the new pop phrase for the covers is floral historical — a flower, tapestry, or jewel is often on the cover. Both the contemporary and the historical books use the floral historical look. Romance customers can still find the symbol of the hero and heroine together. Some covers have two covers, the first one a floral or tapestry look, the second inner cover showing the couple. When pictures of the couple do appear, they are not always in the traditional vamp-and-clinch. Some illustrations show the couple sitting on a sofa, some have a sensual appeal to them. The category series books have changed their covers in recent years too, by updating their illustrations, changing colors, type, and design.

The new covers are more attractive to the audience. Customers were embarrassed to be seen buying books with the vamp-and-clinch covers. The new look is sophisticated, fun to pick up, and attracts a new group of readers, and sales have expanded because of these changes.

The romance business continues to be a cross-over opportunity for both authors and readers, with series authors writing longer contemporary novels as well as historicals.

And, as the romance novel is usually written for women by women, it always focuses on what is going on in today's culture through the lens of love. And love will remain the focus of the romance genre.

Jennifer McCord began her career in publishing on a dare from her daughter and became a manager for an independent bookstore in Denver, Colorado. She worked for Waldenbooks for over eight years. She was assistant to Waldenbooks Vice-President and a romance specialist, and is now a Seattle based publishing consultant.

Crime With a Political Edge: The Socially Progressive Mystery Novel

Gordon DeMarco

Raymond Chandler and Dashiell Hammett transformed the detective novel, elevating it from the pedestrianism of pulp fiction to serious popular literature. They also took the crime story and gave it a certain political edge. Before them, murder mysteries were either drawing room puzzlers or hard-boiled macho, gunslinging, crime-fighting capers. In both cases they were pure plot, as in crime committed; crime detected; crime solved.

Hammett and Chandler also brought the morality of justice and the suggestion of a class-based society that was out of balance to their stories. Phillip Marlowe roamed the "mean streets" of the city, a *noir* knight errant for the common folk, waging a personal battle to expose the greed and corruption of the rich and powerful. In the course of his travels, the reader learned some of the psychological truths about the human motivations of the political and economic elites.

In their way, Hammett, a communist, and Chandler, a former businessman, gave us a realistic portrait of the big city "where the streets were dark with more than the night." However, their response to the corruption and injustice they wrote about was limited. It was one of cynicism — things can't change, but thank all that's holy there are a few good men who will fight for justice, regardless of the cost. Ross Macdonald with his Lew Archer novels carried this tradition into the next generation.

The progressive impulse in mystery fiction over the past dozen or so years has been to take the lone-wolf white male detective and reinvent him. From Marcia Muller's Sharon McCone and Tony Hillerman's Navajo tribal policemen Jim Chee and Joe Leaphorn to black writer Walt Mosley's Easy Rawlins and Barbara Wilson's lesbian protagonist Pam Nilsson, the genre has been broadened and culturally enlightened on all fronts.

Cultural diversity has been accepted in the mystery community (writers, publishers, and readers) and in a real sense helped rescue the hard-boiled mystery from the anti-communist macho thuggery of Mickey Spillane/Mike Hammer and their numerous imitators of the 1950s and 1960s.

Another, smaller impulse, that has paralleled the rise of the multicultural mystery novel is the mystery that is overtly left-wing. Novels like Nancy Milton's *China Option* and Manuel Montalban's *Murder in the Central Committee* are among the contributions to the politically conscious mystery novel.

The left-wing mystery novel has a much stronger tradition in Europe than in the U.S.

These two, plus two of my own novels, were among the 18 political mysteries published (some were reprints) by Pluto Press in Great Britain between 1984 and 1987. The Pluto Crime Series was a bold attempt by an established left-wing press to publish mysteries that dealt openly with political and social themes. These themes included nuclear waste issues, Euro-communism, post-World War II race relations, and the conflict in Northern Ireland.

Sara Paretsky, Nicholas Freeling, Julian Rathbone, James McClure, and Chris Mullin are authors who have written openly about political subjects from a progressive point of view. It should come as no surprise that of the names mentioned above, only Paretsky is American. The left-wing mystery novel has a much stronger tradition in Europe than in the U.S. Closer to this border, Mexican Paco Taibo II's gritty Marxist mysteries are now making their way into print in this country.

The authors writing political mysteries, as well as some of the multicultural writers, are carrying on the tradition begun by Hammett and Chandler. Like the detectives of the two great trailblazing writers, today's political mystery writers are on a literary excursion that exposes some of the secrets of class society and a system that institutionalizes injustice. However, rather than simply revealing psychological truths about the rich and powerful, today's left-wing mystery writer reveals a truth that is political and tells us, often from a partisan point of view, something about how a particular segment of the social system works.

In this age of Watergate, the Karen Silkwood case, Iran-contra, the Iraq/BNL scandal, and the savings and loan fraud, political exposure of the secrets of government and finance has given the political mystery novel a boost and a relevant national context. It should have come much earlier, for the very form of the mystery novel is so suited to political and social commentary. It is a natural progression from the mainstream mystery, which tracks criminals by unlocking their secrets, to the left-wing mystery, which tracks political criminals by exposing political, social, and cultural secrets.

West Coast Crime is a new publisher of left wing mysteries. It traces its parentage to Hammett, Chandler, Macdonald, the multicultural mystery, and Pluto Press. It is the stated goal of West Coast Crime to publish mysteries that consciously raise and discuss political and social themes and are at the same time entertaining.

The collapse of the Soviet bogeyman and the emergence of the culture from the darkness of the Reagan-Bush era may well liberate a whole host of American writers on the political left from the gag of self-censorship as well as the censorship of the market place. West Coast Crime plans to be one of the literary carpenters which will build a room for the progressive political crime novel in mystery's house.

Gordon DeMarco is the author of four mystery novels, including October Heat *and* The Canvas Prison, *two nonfiction books, and three plays. Special thanks to Carolyn Lane, co-owner of Murder by the Book Bookstores in Portland for her assistance in preparing this article.*

Is This My Story To Tell?

Linda Crew

Standing at my study window one afternoon in the summer of 1980, I watched my farmer husband trying to communicate with a pleasant-looking Asian woman down in the driveway below. Bored with whatever I was supposed to be writing, I took in the little scene with a certain interest — the gesturing of hands, the embarrassed smiles. It was only in looking back several years later, however, that I came to mark this moment as the genesis of my novel, *Children of the River.*

That evening my husband explained that the woman and her family were fairly recent refugees from Cambodia and wanted to work picking raspberries and cherry tomatoes.

Well, fine, we needed the help. And that was all the thought I gave, at the time, to the Reang family.

But our friendship with the family grew over the next couple of summers. They were fast and efficient in their work, and we admired the cheerful good nature and unfailing politeness of their children. Our own small son loved trailing around the farm with their son and three daughters, and often asked us when *his* hair was going to turn black.

Gradually, we learned their story. They had fled their homeland of Cambodia in 1975, just ahead of the Khmer Rouge takeover. Now they were established in Oregon, but still had relatives in Cambodia and strong emotional ties to their homeland. Their tales were heartbreaking, and so far they had not, apparently, told them to many Americans.

Finally, it occurred to me that there might be a book in this. I say finally because, frankly, I'm a bit embarrassed at how long it took me to understand what wonderful material had presented itself to me the day Koh Sam-ou came walking up our driveway.

Somebody ought to write about this, I thought. But was that somebody me? Who was I to presume to tell a story from the point of view of a Cambodian girl?

Fortunately for me, I was unaware at the time of the controversy associated with white writers producing stories featuring characters of other races. If I'd known, I might have been too intimidated to attempt what already seemed a daunting enough task, looking at life through the eyes of another culture. After all, I'd been taught to write what I knew. What on earth did I know about this? And wouldn't telling someone else's story be stealing it, in a way?

In thinking it over, though, it occurred to me that the Cambodians newly arrived in America were too busy just surviving emotionally and economically to make fictionalizing their experiences in an English language novel any kind of a priority. This would not happen for some time to come, and in the meantime, those stories needed to be told, both as an affirmation of the refugee experience, and to enlighten Americans who, like me, hadn't stopped to imagine what life in our culture must be like for newcomers.

I checked around and was surprised to find few books about Southeast Asian refugees for young readers. Those I found described dramatic escapes. The quieter drama of adjustment to life in America had been left largely unexplored. But this was such a powerful story! Surely somebody else, somebody more qualified, must already be hard at work on it. With my background in journalism, I had long before convinced myself that it would be impossible,

Who was I

to presume to tell

a story from the

point of view of

a Cambodian girl?

way out here in Oregon, to be the first to the publishers in New York City with anything.

And yet, the more I thought about it, the more I felt perhaps I was as good a candidate as anyone else to write this book. No, I wasn't well-traveled. I'd never been to Cambodia and wasn't going to have the research budget, as an unpublished novelist, to do so. But since Cambodia was pretty well locked up to Westerners at that point anyway, I was no worse off than the next writer. True, I didn't speak Khmer, which would have been helpful for interviews. But then, only five million people in the whole world do. My deficiencies in this department did not set me apart from other writers here in the States.

What I did have was a friendly relationship with a warm, funny Cambodian woman who seemed willing to share her stories with me. I had a curiosity about her culture that fueled a year of research before I even thought of molding what I'd learned into a novel. And before I was finished, I had a sustaining passion for these people and their lives.

One of the most difficult aspects of writing about a racial group different from my own was my initial reluctance to allow these characters any negative traits. I admired the Cambodians; I didn't want to offend them. And yet, it was only by trusting myself to allow them their full measure and range of attributes that they could become fully human to me and hopefully, to the reader. To deny them this would have been no favor.

Although I thought of these things as I worked on the book, it was only after it was published in 1989 that I became truly self-conscious about being a white writer in a multicultural climate. Now I'm reminded of it when letters from young readers reveal the assumption that I'm Cambodian. I'm reminded when I'm asked to contribute to a multicultural anthology and find myself a bit embarrassed and bewildered as to the filling in of the "ethnic roots" part of the bio form. English? German? Welsh? Do these count?

I wouldn't want to imply for one moment that anyone has given me a hard time about this — far from it. I treasure the letters I've received from young Cambodian girls who strongly identify with Sundara, my protagonist. And the one from the young Cambodian man who begged for the name and address of "the real Sundara." These writers seemed to feel my portrayal of Cambodian culture was convincing, although I know full well that if they felt I'd completely botched the job, they are, by custom, simply too polite to ever tell me so to my face!

Nevertheless, having written this book, I've become attuned to murmurs of controversy surrounding the issue. Who's entitled to write which stories and about whom? One writer friend told me an agent advised her to forget writing about Hispanics, for example, unless her name was Lopez. Publishers want to promote new ethnic voices, and rightly so. They also want the stamp of authenticity that comes from the reassurance that the writer knows what she's talking about.

But where do we draw the line in terms of how far afield from his or her own experience a writer is allowed to go? We don't throw out *Anna Karenina* on the grounds that Tolstoy had no experience actually being a woman. Of course, we've long been conditioned to accept this in terms of gender, so perhaps the closest I can come to understanding those who *do* feel their stories are being stolen is the twinge of possessiveness I've noticed in myself when I hear of the occasional well-known writer visiting the Pacific Northwest to research and write about us. *Well, of all the nerve,* I find myself huffing. *We have plenty of good writers. We can handle this ourselves, thank you very much.* And yet… if the resulting book is well done and rings true, I have no grounds for complaint. Isn't there always the possibility that the outsider will have the clearer perspective? Or at least one that's fresh?

One writer, a young white man whose well-received first novel featured a dynamic black character, told me he feels that writers should write about whatever and whomever they want. Period.

I agree. To my friend's remark I would add the proviso, however, that writers should write about whomever they want as long as their work can be authentic and convincing and as long as they feel they're writing the books they should be writing.

It's been suggested to me, for instance, that I now write about refugees from Central America. And turn out refugee-of-the-year novels, I suppose? The trouble is, while I did not feel overly handicapped by not speaking Khmer, my ignorance of Spanish would put me in the lineup of likely writers far behind all those who could conduct bilingual interviews and better do these stories justice. Furthermore, being fully aware of the hungry market for multicultural stories doesn't necessarily make a person the one best qualified to write them.

My decision to try writing about the Cambodians grew from a certain set of circumstances and a real affection and admiration for a particular family. I did the best I could, through research and imagination, to weave the threads of their individual stories into a tapestry resembling, I hoped, a larger truth. I honestly believe that the passion I felt for the subject sustained me through the years of research, writing, and rejection far better than any sense of the project's marketability ever could have.

My friend's youngest daughter, Putsata, who arrived in Oregon as a baby, now wants to be a writer. She has already won several awards for her work while in high school, and recently began her study of Journalism at the University of Oregon, my alma mater. This pleases me. I'm sure she will soon be writing stories about her cultural heritage full of all the insights and imagery I could never hope to capture. She won't be the only one, either. Someday, I've no doubt, many Cambodian-American writers will keep us spellbound with all the stories we never knew or understood before.

For now, I'm glad I took the risk of telling someone else's story. I'm glad my offering has been welcomed. I'm glad that *Children of the River* seems to be filling a certain need, if only for a time.

Linda Crew is the author of three young adult books: Children of the River, Someday I'll Laugh About This, *and* Nekomah Creek, *and an adult novel,* Ordinary Miracles.

The Cross-Cultural Writer
Claudia Peck

Note: My own cross-cultural writing experience is in African-American and Native American influenced literature and is limited to one novel and one essay. Beyond that I can only claim the knowledge gained through a certain amount of keeping my wits about me and some experience in teaching courses in multiethnic studies. Rather than setting me up as an expert in any sense of the word, the information provided in this article is meant to allow us to think together about this topic. It is not meant as "ten easy ways to become a cross-cultural writer."

The cross-cultural writing scene is opening up in many ways. Though writers wrestle with large questions when they write a work containing cultural references not from their own background, more and more writers are attempting to do so. Writers such as Tony Hillerman, John Nichols, Thomas Berger, and others have been accepted by some of the people they write about, and they have created additional dialogue and understanding among readers. All too often, however, writers still find themselves in a morass of frustration because of certain kinds of response to their work.

There are many ways to run into difficulties when writing about a culture other than your own, or including characters from other cultures in a book predominately about your own ethnic background. While most of the discussion surrounding cross-cultural work has been limited to white writers writing about other lifestyles, it often can be just as difficult to write about people of another ethnic background for an ethnic writer. You should definitely expect to elicit discussion, and not all of the vigorous discussion raised by cross-cultural work is bad. Nonetheless, there are certain ways of approaching this writing that are bound to elicit the sort of discussion you would probably like to avoid.

1. Assuming that you can write without extensive research. In order for cross-cultural characters to ring true, it is important to know something of the history and background that your character may be responding to or rebelling against; therefore, you will need to do more research than you may be accustomed to doing for characters who come from a more familiar heritage. Colloquialisms, music, art, and other specifics must be researched. So must influences from outside that culture that may be perceived differently, for instance, simple things like brand names or slang. While these statements may seem self-evident, time and time again I see evidence of problems in the writing of those who want to write of another society — they haven't done their homework. Your characters and your story will be richer if you take into account the richness of that particular culture.

2. **Assuming that mixed blood characters or writers come from the same cultural backgrounds as characters or writers of full blood.** Historically, mixed blood peoples have had a very difficult time no matter where they derive their heritage from. You can't assume that a Chinese-American has anything like the same attitudes toward Chinese customs that someone born in traditional China has; nor can you assume that someone who was born away from the reservation speaks about the Navaho in the same way someone would who has lived mainly on the reservation. There is no value judgment placed here on who speaks with the most authority or right. The point is simply that the circumstances are different. Publishers traditionally take no note of these differences, but we as writers need to or we will offend those whom we write about.

3. **Assuming that ethnic characters or writers are "representative" of their culture.** It should be self-evident that no one person can represent a culture, and yet time and time again readers and publishers make this mistake. From Maxine Hong Kingston to Louise Erdrich, authors are published as though they are representative of a group. No white person can speak for all white people, just as no black person can speak for all black people. As cross-cultural writers you will constantly struggle with the problem of representation. You will meet it in terms of what readers and editors expect you to do with your fiction and your char-

acters. You will meet it in terms of what sorts of writing are "acceptable" to publishers, and who people expect you to talk about when you mention other writers. Representation is an intense form of stereotyping and it should be avoided as much as possible. Unfortunately, it is difficult to avoid. Even when you do not intend your characters to represent what all _____ people are like, your readers will draw conclusions accordingly, so you need to make sure that your characters are fully rounded, rich characters. And it's possible that you could become a "representative" writer in ways that make no sense at all. For example, publishers often prefer white writers writing about multicultural characters to more controversial people writing within their own ethnic group.

4. **Assuming that if you know something about one culture you understand the concerns and interests of another.** You may know a great deal about what it means to grow up as a Jewish-American in the United States and with an understanding of the history of persecution, but you do not know what it means to grow up as a Japanese-American whose parents went voluntarily to a "relocation" camp during World War II. Though there are common concerns for the many ethnic groups that live in this country, there are many differences that do not translate from one culture to another.

5. **Ignoring large divisions of opinion that exist within the cultural group you are writing about.** There is an enormous amount of controversy surrounding the writing about a culture from within it, no matter which culture you are speaking about. Chinese-Americans have a history of gender splitting that goes far back into the early 1900s and much of it has to do with the U.S. immigration policies toward Asian immigration. For much of the 1900s the bulk of Chinese immigrants were male. If you are writing about the Chinese-American community as a cultural outsider, you need to be aware of this history as you write, just as you need to know about the controversy surrounding who is "Native American" enough to write about "Native American" communities. For example, there are huge controversies about tribal identities, PanIndianism, mixed bloods, reservation-born, and oral and written traditions.

6. **Ignoring the connection between style and content in cross-cultural writing.** There has been a great deal of discussion about the aesthetic quality of works by ethnic writers. It was long claimed by critics that these writers seldom did writing equal to the quality of the classics. Recently, critical standards have begun to change in order to accommodate the differences in approach, style, organization, and subject matter found in ethnic writing, because all of these elements are related to the central concerns of the works. A greater respect has emerged with an approach that considers the writer's purpose. For the cross-cultural writer there are implications as well. It's very

If you are writing

cross-culturally, expect

controversy

and the occasional

weird incident.

difficult to take on the issues and concerns of a particular cultural group without also realizing that these will inevitably affect your writing style (at least for the duration of the project). In particular, the relationship of the novel or fictional work to "voice" is a major stylistic concern.

If you are writing cross-culturally, expect controversy and the occasional weird incident. Writers producing works about their own culture don't escape it, so you won't escape it either. You can expect to be misread, and you can expect to be read more accurately than you might like.

At this point I am sure that you are crying out for examples. Since providing examples can be as hazardous as cross-cultural writing, I'll simply state that the examples I am providing are from writers who have already been well chastised, and the comments I'm making are based on the controversies they provoked.

A white writer, William Styron, ran into difficulties with his *Confessions of Nat Turner* (1967), a fictional recounting of the Nat Turner Rebellion from Turner's perspective. Styron did do research, but his research remained at a certain level of historical knowledge about the character and black/white relations of the time period. He did not consider his black readers and the foment of his own time as well as he might have. Given the fact that he was in constant contact with James Baldwin, a well-beloved black writer, one would think that Styron's novel would have been well received by the black community. He did win high critical acclaim, but his novel soon became the center of a furor. Styron was chastised for not giving Turner a black woman to be connected with, for connecting Turner to a white woman whom he is known to have killed, for presuming to speak from Turner's voice, and for not understanding the core of the black experience. Just as other whites in the sixties, Styron was baffled by the core of anger that exploded in response to white liberal attitudes and he didn't understand what he had done to direct that anger towards his work.

Styron had carefully thought through his fictional choices for the novel. Turner had no history of female contact and his emotional makeup struck Styron, as it did many historians and later writers, as religiously fanatical, a condition that seemed to support the lack of female romantic figures in his life. For this reason Styron never considered connecting Turner with a black female as a partner. On the other hand, Turner hadn't been able to kill anyone during the uprising until near the end of a series of killings on the part of his followers. When he finally did kill someone, it was a white woman named Margaret Whitehead. The killing was brutal. Afterwards, the rebellion seemed to lose steam. Rather than speculating that Turner's actions stemmed from an abhorrence of violence and a sudden excess which then crippled his leadership, Styron chose to assume more personal grounds for his response. There were many objections to this choice, as there were objections to the way that Styron handled Turner's "voice." Since voice is a major issue in ethnic writing, in retrospect the protest should come as no surprise to anyone, though at the time Styron was rocked by the controversy.

The controversies have become quite complicated at this stage of cross-cultural writing, and many of them involve people writing within their own cultures as well as those writing from outside a cultural framework. Maxine Hong Kingston was picked up as the liberal publishing establishment's acclaimed Chinese-American writer for her book *The Woman Warrior: Memoirs of a Girlhood Among Ghosts* (1976). *The Woman Warrior* is a collage filled with the stories of a young Chinese-American girl growing up in California and her perhaps mythical/perhaps not ancestors. In addition to contemporary material, it draws on a series of Chinese tales. Kingston is accused of taking those folktales out of context. But the most interesting part of the controversy rests around the way the book is labeled: autobiography.

Though Kingston herself claims the book is a fictional work, the publishers decided to label the book autobiography because a series of autobiographies of Chinese women had been published in the past. Since this series came from women of "ill repute" who were interviewed by various sorts of religious men, the autobiography had become a controversial form for Chinese writers, particularly women. While it might seem that Kingston could avoid the difficulties of being called a "representative" writer because she selected an autobiographical form, a form that would imply that she is only talking about her own experiences, the choice of labels led to great controversy.

Some of the conflicts come, as I mentioned earlier, from divisions within the community being written about. John Okada's *No-no Boy* (reprinted 1981), acclaimed by some because of its honest portrayal of the difficult life of a Japanese-American conscientious objector during WW II, an anathema among those Japanese-Americans who felt it was honorable to go to concentration camps voluntarily in order to show loyalty to the U.S. For a long while this book was out of print because of the unpopularity of its subject matter until a Chinese writer, Frank Chin, was instrumental in its reprinting.

These three examples are only a handful among many, but I think they illustrate some important points about the care with which you need to proceed and the fact that you cannot anticipate the range of responses you will receive. Styron's novel has continued to be roundly condemned by the black community since its printing date. Kingston is at the center of a twenty year controversy in the Chinese-American writing community. Okada's book was ignored initially for many of the same reasons it is now acclaimed. But proceeding with care can mean that you know more about what you are taking on and you have the opportunity to speak well with culturally literate readers.

There is something further to be considered. While avoiding some of the hidden hazards may save you problems with the culturally literate reader, there is a side effect — publishers may not like or understand the result. In addition, there are labeling difficulties. Publishers like a very clear idea of where your book can be placed for marketing, and books with ethnic concerns have a confused history in that regard, having been placed in everything from speculative fiction to religion to anthropology. There are marketing difficulties for much the same reason. There is no clear bandwagon to "jump onto" if you're interested in the "fad" of multiculturalism.

On the other hand, if your subject matter and your course as a writer compels you, there are many rewards for taking on cross-cultural material. There is no form of writing more stimulating. You will be challenged in all ways: intellectually, emotionally, culturally, and most of all in the realm of your intuitive, deepest self. As you continue to write, you will begin to question many of your assumptions and approaches as a writer and as a human being. You will make tough choices and live with the results of those choices. Because of the fact that you have even less grasp of how your work will be read, you will have to eventually let it go entirely its own way, as you may not have let other projects go. In short, going beyond the level of the monocultural book is well worth the risks.

Claudia Peck is a teacher of Comparative American Cultures at Washington State University, and the author of Spirit Crossings, *a novel from Bantam Doubleday Dell.*

Writing for an Ethnic Newspaper

Susan L. Cassidy

Ethnic newspapers are of critical importance to both the ethnic community they represent and the mainstream community of which they are a part.

Why? Because of the mainstream media.

The face of America is not white, yet television, the papers, and the movies would have you believe differently. Ethnic papers exist to change our perceptions of the American population.

Equally important, given the blanched face of mainstream media, is the need among ethnic Americans to see themselves somewhere. They need to see themselves as three-dimensional people; they need role models and leaders.

The mainstream media has historically included stories about people of color when something sensational has taken place. Such coverage would be beyond reproach if there was balance. Without balance, mainstream and minority Americans get a skewed perception that serves no one.

Ethnic newspapers provide balance, promote role models, and destroy stereotypes. They also exist for a basic journalistic purpose: to inform.

Assunta Ng is the publisher of both the *Northwest Asian Weekly* and the *Seattle Chinese Post*. She started this bilingual paper ten years ago. Assunta, who immigrated from Hong Kong, was an elementary school teacher when she decided to change her life. Unsure of what to do, she recalled the lines of Chinese residents in Seattle's Chinatown waiting to read week-old news about then-President Richard Nixon and the Watergate scandal. The only news available came from San Francisco and was posted on bulletin boards.

With this painful memory in mind, Assunta had her mission, and the *Seattle Chinese Post*, the first of its kind in Seattle since 1927, was born. Today, it's the only surviving bilingual Chinese newspaper in America. The Chinese edition is a primary source of local, national, and international news for those who cannot read the mainstream papers.

This paper is unique because we have a diverse work force. What I mean by that is our Asian paper has a white person for an editor — me. We believe that not only Asian-Americans care about Asian-American issues, civil rights, equal opportunity, glass ceilings, particular cultures, etc. The individual must be hired, not his/her ethnicity. On the staff of the English edition, for instance, the only truly bilingual writer is a Caucasian scholar who speaks fluent Thai.

As a non-Asian, I've found my experience at the *Northwest Asian Weekly* for the past three years to be unique and revealing. At times I've found that I have a distinct perspective as an outsider and view the community without the handicap of personal loyalty. As a fairly watered down Irish, Scottish, German mixture of American, who has moved 28 times in her life as an Air Force brat, I've found it remarkable to be part of so strong an ethnic group. I've also learned what it is to be an outsider, an other.

Working in an environment where everyone other than myself is immigrant Chinese, I've begun to know what it's like to be a minority, if only by day. This is an experience I wish on the entire European-American population, particularly the men.

The advantage I have as a "daytime minority" is that this status is not permanent. One of my most startling experiences was

Working in an environment where everyone other than myself is immigrant Chinese, I've begun to know what it's like to be a minority, if only by day.

attending the Asian-American Journalists Association Convention last year. While I'm probably more accustomed to working with only Asian-Americans than most European-Americans, I'm not accustomed to seeing myself within the context of this environment. One of the convention attendees was a white male, and I couldn't believe how ridiculous and out of place he looked. He simply looked wrong. I wondered, "Is that how I look?"

I walked into the restroom at the convention and was confronted by huge mirrors. I was shocked by how terribly ugly I looked. My hair, skin, and eyes were too pale. My body was all wrong. My own image seemed foreign and disconcertingly odd.

The lesson is, of course, that I felt this way for a three-day convention. People of color battle for a sense of self every day, all day. They constantly combat the images that bombard them, images of what is right to look like, and be. These images are found everywhere from magazines, newspapers, and television to school rooms and books.

It is conveyed to minority Americans daily that they are wrong, even in this time where ethnicity is somewhat more trendy than it has been. We have a long way to go to change this reality. Community newspapers are part of the solution and a great way for writers to get published.

Such ethnic newspapers like ours give voice to a community. Through them, groups that often find themselves disenfranchised speak with one another as well as to the mainstream. Having a voice empowers people.

These newspapers also serve as community advocates and bridge builders. They cannot afford to do otherwise, since by definition they exist for the benefit of a particular community.

Writers interested in publishing in minority newspapers should read the papers and gear their work toward them. The *Northwest Asian Weekly* uses freelance writers and tries to give ethnic writers an opportunity for publication. Your own ethnicity, while not a requirement, could help your chances of publication. We have one writer whose energy is boundless. As a Chinese American woman writer and poet, it seems she writes for practically every community newspaper in Seattle!

Community papers are almost always on shoestring budgets and always understaffed. Having access to writers willing to write for the opportunity for publication, and a small fee, is a blessing. If you prove to be reliable, you'll probably get more work than you wanted. Given limited space, our news must be specifically relevant to the Asian community: of, for, and about the Asian community.

Susan L. Cassidy has a Master of Fine Arts degree from the University of Washington. Her previous work experience has included marketing, technical writing, and editing. Her short story "Blood of the Land" was published in The Written Arts.

Nonsexist Language is Dynamic, Powerful, Easy

Val Dumond

"An apology to women readers:

The masculine personal pronouns he, him *and* his, *as well as references to sir and Mr. are meant to refer to persons of either sex, s/he. I used them to avoid awkward sentence constructions that slow down reading. Thank you for bearing with me, and I apologize if I've given you offense."*

SIGN	MEANING	USED IN A LINE	MARGINAL NOTES
∧	*Insert*	A big dg	a /
#	*Space*	foundout	#/
ℛ	*Delete*	about of	ℛ/
⌢	*Close up*	the con test	⌢/
ℛ	*Delete & close up*	for carnnines	ℛ/
ᴎ	*Transpose*	liked who	ᴎ/
∧	*Semicolon*	to jump	∧/
∧	*Comma*	he'd, unfortunately	∧/
⊙	*Period*	missed it before	⊙/
⊖	*Colon*	They asked for ID	⊖/
∨	*Apostrophe*	his sires middle name	∨/
ᵛ ᵛ	*Quotation marks (open & close)*	and his bark	ᵛ ᵛ
cap	*Capital (≡ under)*	this was	cap /
lc	*Lower-case (/ through)*	not What	lc /
/=/	*Hyphen*	he expect	/=/
1/m	*Dash*	ed the procedure	1/m
ⓧ	*Defective letter (circle)*	seen ed odd.	ⓧ
wf	*Wrong font (circle)*	So he	wf
/	*(Use to separate corrections)*	troted Home	t /lc /
ital	*Italic type (underline)*	without once	ital /
rom	*Roman type (circle)*	wagging his tail.	rom /
sc	*Small caps (= under)*	From an old story	sc /

The above or something like it has appeared in numerous (too numerous) nonfiction, usually how-to, books. Not only is it exceedingly patronizing, it is insulting, offensive, and demeaning to women.

It also says the author is lazy.

This kind of apology screams that the writer is too lazy to take time to clean up the language, to edit in order to present a manuscript that includes both women and men readers.

Any writer worthy of the name ought to be able to handle words well enough to include all readers. It is neither difficult nor time consuming.

Sexism rears its ugly head in three ways: 1) the assumption that the world is male until proven otherwise, 2) demeaning and diminishing language, and 3) stereotyping. Each can be overcome by using simple guidelines.

Women and Men Share the World

Avoid using words like *he, him, his, man* to include women. They don't and never will again. Times and social values are changing to a point this usage is unacceptable to most women.

The only offending pronouns are the third person singular. A simple antidote is to avoid them. Here are quick guidelines.

Write with first or second person pronouns

§ Instead of: A good carpenter cleans his saw regularly.
§ Use: As a good carpenter, I clean my saw regularly.
§ Or Use: As a good carpenter, clean your saw regularly.

Use plurals

§ Instead of: A child can tie his own shoes.

§ Use: Children can tie their own shoes.

Repeat the antecedent noun

§ Instead of: When the doctor arrived to see the patient, he was worried.

§ Use: When the doctor arrived to see the patient, the doctor was worried.

Replace with words like THE, AN, ONE

§ Instead of: A bookkeeper can get used to his detailed work.

§ Use: A bookkeeper can get used to the detailed work.

Omit the pronoun altogether (we use too many anyway)

§ Try: A bookkeeper can get used to detailed work.

Use a passive verb

§ Detailed work can be done by a bookkeeper.

§ Shoes can be tied by children.

Change the subject of the sentence (see above passive verb)

Re-write the sentence to include a defining clause

§ Instead of: If a reader needs a good book, he goes to the library.

§ Use: A reader who needs a good book goes to the library.

Less satisfactory alternative to the above suggestions: use the plural third person with the singular noun

§ Instead of: Each one attending should have his own pencils.

§ Use: Each one attending should have their own pencils.

The word *man* is a perfectly good word

The only offending

pronouns are the

third person singular.

A simple antidote is

to avoid them.

to use when referring to a male person. However, please avoid including women in the term. Choose more accurate terms to reflect your meaning: *humans, citizens, executives, voters, civilians, people, masses, populace, public.*

A good glossary of nonsexist terms will assist in finding just the right word to replace: *salesman, chairman, businessman, man-on-the-street, statesman, sportsman.* You'll want to consider: *sales representative, sales agent, clerk, seller, chair, facilitator, leader, executive, manager, director, street person, people-in-general, diplomat, politician, public leader, hunter, fisher, outdoor enthusiast.*

A half-hearted effort at writing nonsexist language can result in overusing *person.* It can quickly become apparent that a *spokesman* is a man and a *spokesperson* is a woman. Try harder. Make them a *speaker for the company, representative,* or use *spokesperson* to mean both women and men.

Demeaning/Diminishing

Watch the endings of nouns that could indicate male or female when such indications are unnecessary. An actor is an actor, man or woman. A writer is a writer, woman or man.

The endings in question include: *ess, ette, ix* and are found in such words as poetess, bachelorette, aviatrix. These people are poets, singles, aviators, and need not be identified by gender. After all, we do not consider ourselves authorettes, journalistesses, or writeresses.

Demeaning terms for women often carry the connotation that women are things: cooky, squeeze, sweetie, honey, bird, the little woman, the girlfriend. While words like these may be used in fiction, be aware of the implications you are including with the terms.

Which brings us to *girl.* Females over 14 are women and deserve that label. Save the *girl* for the child. To refer to women as girls suggests they are dependent, childish, needful, less than equal.

Stereotyping

Close your eyes and imagine these six people in a room: a bank president, school superintendent, doctor, secretary, teacher, nurse. Were the first three men and the last three women? That's stereotyping. And it flourishes in today's society, much as we wish it would go away. Make it go away in

your writing. Not only select terms that refuse gender identification, but choose careers for your fiction characters that break the stereotypical mold. Women function very well as auto body repairers, telephone lineworkers, neurosurgeons, judges, board chairs. Men function well as nurses, teachers, secretaries, clerks, typists, housekeepers.

Not only select terms

that refuse

gender identification,

but choose careers

for your fiction characters

that break

the stereotypical mold.

Of course all of this fiddling with words plays havoc with computer spell checks. Mine has trouble with the word *nonsexist.* I add the problem words to my word bank as I go along. You can too.

Professional writers find a bonus in using nonsexist language. They discover their writing takes on a strength it didn't have before, an authority. The writing also becomes more accurate.

Add nonsexist words and terminology to your vocabulary and to your way of thinking. Then you won't have to apologize to your readers for being lazy. You'll be using words in a dynamic way.

Val Dumond is a Tacoma, Washington author who writes books on local history and language. Among her published work: Steilacoom's Church, Doin' The Puyallup, Elements of Nonsexist Usage *(1991 Prentice Hall),* and Grammar For Grownups *(1993, HarperCollins).*

A Matter of Individual Concern

Donald E. McQuinn

Anyone engaged in producing fiction is driven by the market. For every thriller born amidst dreams of heart-seizing advances and multi-book contracts, a literary jewel is somewhere being cut and buffed to assure its precise little facets reflect the moment's artistic correctness.

The so-called writer who's immune to the desire to get work published, read, and approved should be clerking yard goods, not despoiling perfectly good paper. Writers produce in the hope we'll impress enough people to earn enough money to support us while we produce another work to impress…ad infinitum. Simultaneously, we present ourselves as the bearers of truth, the cutting edge of culture.

What does that say about words-for-money, or avant-garde lockstep conformity? Is there something wrong with either? Of course — assuming we swallow whole the dictum that fiction is spurred only by the search for truth.

It's not an argument that holds much water.

Unfortunately, writers eat. Most prefer to work indoors, particularly during inclement weather. These things create expense. In a perfect world, artists would be supported by a benevolent, understanding government, rather like dancing bears, or politicians. Struggle is the price of our independence. We engage the world on its terms. We progress at a cost.

Any artist — and every writer is, to one degree or another — is responsible for the survival of the work as well as the body. Parcel out that obligation, and both entities are endangered. Not that support and compromise are evil. We all need financial help sometime. It may come from a government grant, it may come from a loved one. And none of us is always completely right. When our assumed virtue debases our writing to intransigent screed, we deserve the

rejection we get from those outside our circle of fellow fanatics. In these regards, then, it would appear that the writer who pursues the dollar and the writer who pursues the academic laurels are merely taking turns dancing on the tip of the same sword.

So how do we define compromise as opposed to cop out? Where does acceptance of support end, and acknowledgment of obligation begin?

The soul of fiction is the search for truth. Like most souls, it exists in a state of nervous apprehension. Fiction daily confronts an establishment that dictates acceptability. For the commercial author, such fiat originates in the frozen hearts of bean counters. There's more room for experimentation and reach in literary effort, but that work, too, contends with style mavens and critique cliques. On top of that, we're all constantly under examination by twinkies from every point of the socio-political compass, anxious that we haven't been seduced by "them." It makes writing an even more grueling, demanding practice. Those who do it well enough to attract an audience deserve all the gold and glory they can get. Some writers understand that perfectly. As a result, ever more lacy stuff will be sundered to the merry background jingle of colliding coins; literary types will run before winds of juicy-fruit jargon that speak of "resonance" and "non-quotidian concerns." Homage will be rendered.

Damn right. Blessed are the compromisers, for they open the door for the rest of us.

A case can be made that writing, more

…it would appear that the writer who pursues the dollar and the writer who pursues the academic laurels are merely taking turns dancing on the tip of the same sword.

than any other art form, directs its energy to changing society. That's a slow, tedious job. It's one thing to be impatient for improvement. It's dangerously different to be intolerant of someone else's preference for another course. Furthermore, there's an old military axiom that says one spy within the walls is worth more than a division of troops outside. Whenever we read of some glorious proclamation galvanizing the people, we should give a moment of silent praise to the dozens, if not hundreds, of forerunners who quietly, doggedly prepared the ground for acceptance of change.

The hazard, of course, is that the desire to be heard or paid becomes the end in itself. Compromise can become capitulation all too sweetly. For any writer, that is perhaps the ultimate breakdown.

The writer is uniquely responsible for imparting self as part of a transaction. We project a world seen only through our eyes, interpreted solely by our understanding. At our very best, our perceptions and translations create fiction that presents truth so accurately it transcends simple factual data. At the very least, we create small tales that entwine our culture's moral truths into a binding fiber. If we're forced to give a little to get a little, that's a natural thing. The imperative is that we find ways to make ourselves heard, and if the voice is only a whisper, who's to say that's insignificant? It's wrong for any of our fellowship to scorn those who are chipping away at the obstacles confronting all of us. Each in our own way makes room for another, if we have the wit to contend honestly and afford dissent a rightful place. The bigots can only challenge us from without. We can censure ourselves to distraction from within.

The writer's responsibility is to the work, to the self, to the truth, to the public. That's an enormous load. My suggestion is that perhaps there is more. Would it add too much to our burden if we asked of each other the responsibility to be considerate?

Donald McQuinn has published five novels, most of them adventures or dealing with espionage. The last, Warrior, from Del Rey, was a departure into speculative fiction. It was listed in Publishers Weekly *as one of their trade paperback bestsellers in 1991.* Wanderer *follows in 1993.*

How DO Writers Get the Right Agent?

Natasha Kern

I am often asked about the issue of location in determining whether an agency is right for an author and have consistently advised that, although first-time writers often think location matters, it is the least significant criteria for selecting an agency. So what really DOES matter?

The first question to resolve is whether you need an agent at all. If you plan to write an occasional category romance — perhaps for one line like Intrigue or Kismet — or have a very narrow market nonfiction book, say targeted only to slug farmers, it may not be worthwhile to pay a 15% commission to an agent. It might not be worth it to the agent to expend the time and money to represent you either.

If you are the type of person who prefers to do everything for yourself and wants a sense of control, you may want to negotiate your own contract and plan your career unassisted. However, if you hate to argue about money, decipher fine print in legal contracts, market yourself and your work to editors, and have no idea what a long-term career plan looks like, then you probably will feel more comfortable having an agent assist you.

Agents do a lot of things for their clients besides making the sale. If it were an agent's function simply to find a publisher, writers like Robert Ludlum, Danielle Steel or John Grisham would not have one. They have publishers calling them. Agents can help you to get not just a deal, but the best possible deal for you. They can help you to understand publishing as a business. In order to know whether an agent is right for you, you must first understand what we do.

Agenting requires understanding sales and marketing (they are not the same thing); literary law; editing; publishing business practices, industry standards, requirements and protocols; publicity and promotion; counseling and career development;

international and film rights markets; arbitration and a myriad of other things including the rapidly burgeoning opportunities in high-tech publishing.

This leads to the number one concern in selecting an agent: Is he or she competent to represent you? Does the agent know your genre? Has she sold similar books before? Can you see a client list or talk with clients? Can you see a list of recent sales? What is her work history and her relationships with other clients, colleagues, editors, and subagents? Most importantly, how can you find these things out?

A second concern that is of equal importance is: Does the agent like your work? It is not helpful to you to have your manuscript on a shelf in someone else's office for months. If you sent a partial, did the agent really want to see the MS? Has she really read and understood your work and your strengths and problems as a writer? A sense of championship for your work is the most important thing to look for in addition to competence. It is this enthusiasm that keeps the agent positive about you and able to sell your work even when difficulties arise, or she is actually losing money representing you, or nothing has sold in a year or two. You don't want an agent who will drop you if problems arise or one who works hard for

...if you hate to argue about money, decipher fine print in legal contracts, market yourself and your work to editors, and have no idea what a long-term career plan looks like, then you probably will feel more comfortable having an agent assist you.

other writers on her list but not you. Yo want to get what you are paying for, but you also want the concern and support that can only come from someone who believes in you and what you are trying to achieve. Keep in mind that more writing careers develop like Rosamund Pilcher's than Amy Tan's.

A compatible workstyle is also important. Some agents are in frequent contact with clients, make payments promptly, and consult closely about submission strategies. An agent you hear from rarely may be working just as hard for you. The important thing is that you feel comfortable and that your expectations are realistic. Make sure you know if you will receive copies of all correspondence and be informed about progress.

A sense of mutual trust is extremely important. Once this is lost, it is time to consider a frank talk with your agent and if issues are not resolved, changing agents. Agents must trust clients to comply with contract terms, let us know if you cannot make your deadline and tell us about problems. Writers must trust the agent to handle their financial affairs and their careers properly.

The more clearly you understand what you need and want, the easier it will be to assess whether the agent you choose can meet those needs. First develop a list of needs. Then start listing agents that seem to be appropriate, i.e. they represent the genre you write, they have a good track record and are well respected, etc. Request whatever brochures or handouts the agency has available. Talk to other writers. One enterprising writer asked about my agency on an electronic bulletin board and got a surprising number of responses.

You must look at this process as one in which you are hiring someone with expertise to assist you, much as you would hire a doctor, lawyer, or real estate agent.

If the agent expresses interest in you and your work and offers a contract, talk to others who work with the agent. If you already have an editor, ask what your editor thinks of the agent you have selected. I know of more than one case in which the writer was told the editor would not work with a certain agent and lost a contract that had already been offered as a result. Contact local and national writer's groups. This is the time to request any additional information from the agent that will help you to make a decision.

I think it is important to have a written agreement with your agent so that rights and responsibilities are spelled out clearly and you know how to terminate the agreement if you want to.

Is the agency contract acceptable to you? Is there an escape clause? Make sure you will be working with the agent you like and will not be passed on to someone else in the agency either now or in the future. This happens frequently with alarming results.

If the contract is terminated, is it spelled out what happens to works that are sold or are under submission? If you write for a broad market, can the agency represent all of your work? If not, what will happen to your children's books or film scripts?

There are also some basic financial questions you should ask. How much does the agency charge? Will you be billed for expenses? Which ones? Will they be deducted from your income on the sale, billed directly, or credited against an initial deposit? Is there a marketing fee? Does the agency maintain a client trust account? How soon are funds forwarded to clients? Keep in mind some of the less tangible benefits agents offer like availability and reliability. Your agent is working for you and will be with you when editors and even publishers come and go. She can help you with tasks as diverse as rights reversion and reselling your backlist or deciding whether bookmarks or an ad for your book will actually benefit your career. You want an agent you can rely on to help you with all aspects of your career.

Getting an agent is an important step in becoming a professional and taking your writing and your career seriously. Writing books is so difficult and trying to actually earn a living at it so daunting, you should get the help you need in achieving your publishing ambitions.

Natasha Kern is a literary agent in Portland, Oregon.

A Conversation with Sallie Tisdale and her Editor, Channa Taub, at Fishtrap

Fishtrap, Inc.: Writing and the West is an annual Summer Gathering and series of workshops held at Wallowa Lake, Oregon. It now also includes a Winter Gathering, an anthology of workshop writing, and workshops and readings at other times of the year. But the summer show remains at the core of Fishtrap, and the summer audience of writers, editors, publishers, librarians, teachers, and readers sets its tone.

Marketing and the details of publishing have never been the major concerns at Fishtrap. At the Gatherings — and even in the workshops — most of the time is spent talking and thinking about the writing, primarily about the subject matter of the writing.

For instance, at the 1992 Summer Gathering, readings from a historical novelist and a poet were followed by panels about "writing and history." Primus St. John and Rosalie Sorrels read, sang, and talked about issues of "race, class, and gender" in their songs and poems. Sallie Tisdale read from Stepping Westward *and then joined a panel with Missoula Mayor Dan Kemmis to talk about "The Public Good and the Politics of Place."*

Still, there is always a concern about marketing and publishing, and we keep searching for ways to address the concern without losing the flavor of Fishtrap. At some point in the planning of the 1992 Gathering, the idea of having author Sallie Tisdale carry on a conversation with her editor, Channa Taub, in front of the Fishtrap crowd seemed like a way to do this. They did, and it worked.

The conversation was candy for many new writers trying to get a sense of how the business works. It was interesting and useful to veteran professional writers, editors, and publishers as well. And in the end, the dialogue between Sallie Tisdale and Channa Taub has a Fishtrap flavor. It reflects two strong and interesting personalities. It tells us a little about how they work. And in the process it sheds light on how other folks do the same work, and on how we might improve our own.

Rich Wandschneider,
Fishtrap Director

Sallie: My first book was published by McGraw-Hill, and I had a terrible editor there, who can remain nameless. He was terrible because he did nothing. He never called me; he didn't edit. It was my first book and I didn't know what to get from an editor. I didn't know what I had the right to get, what I should demand from an editor, or how to get it.

Although Channa and I had never met, she bought my second and my third book as a package. This suddenly created a long-term relationship with a total stranger. We started to write very long letters back and forth instead of phone calls. We became friends through the mail before we ever worked on a book together.

When she edited my second book, I breathed a sigh of relief because I realized I had gotten myself a really terrific editor.

I've moved to a new publisher. I left Holt. And Channa left at the same time, but not because of me, and was hired by Doubleday, on a contract basis, to edit my book. Basically I said, I don't want a new editor. I want her! I think we have a very unusual relationship, I think it's the way it used to be. She's my only editor, but I'm not her only writer.

Channa: Our relationship is unconventional. The fact that I left a house and am doing Sallie's book contractually is not a typical arrangement. I don't want you to get any ideas that it is typical. I think it's the only one of its kind in town, although I think things like this will start happening more. One of the reasons I did it is because I'm building a family now, and I wanted a way of having more time for my family and having enough time to edit those books that I wanted to work on.

I think people don't know that choosing an editor is going to affect them so drastically. They don't discuss it with their agent; they just tell them what publisher they'd like to go to and rely on the agent to select someone appropriate. There are things you should be asking and looking for in an editor, and you're making a mistake not to look for those things before you sign a contract.

If you don't have a good relationship with your editor, you're probably not serving yourself and your book well. If an agent is hooking you up with an editor, and you're in the other end of the country, at least try a phone call or something.

ST: It took me a long time to not resent being edited. You have a lot of pride in your work and you put everything into it, and then somebody starts screwing around with it, telling you to change things, cut this and so on.

With books, I've come to see that the editor to the writer is a lot like the conductor to the composer. The composer does the work; the editor helps make it something that people can receive. I think a lot of writers tend to devalue the role of the editor and disrespect what their editor can do for them.

What Channa does for me, and she does it better than any other editor I've worked with, is figure out what I skipped. I tend to write skeletal first drafts that are short, and then she starts pointing out to me where all the holes are, and where I have to start putting the flesh on. I'm too close to the material to see it. I think what a writer has to bring to the editor is respect for the third eye that an editor has, and the distance and the objectivity that a writer can't have to her own material. I know Hannah edits me differently than she edits other writers.

CT: An editor has to suit [her] style to the author. In the case of Sallie, I do not change a word. I may query every word, ask numerous questions, but I will not remove a comma on my own.

The conversation

was candy for many

new writers trying

to get a sense of how

the business works.

I have many writers who are professionals in other fields; they're counselors, lawyers, and so on, but they may not be writing professionals. I'll practically rewrite their sentences and they're intensely grateful for that. Not everybody wants a working editor. Some people don't want their writing touched, in which case you'll want a power editor. It's difficult to get both, but not impossible. A power editor is someone with a big title and a big name. A few of them edit, but most pass editing along to assistant editors or other editors in house. That can work perfectly well. You can get very good editing, and you can get the advocacy of the power editor, who has the clout to get you more money, better advertising, and so on. There are many editors who don't line edit and publish perfectly fine books. The copy editors fill in the gaps for them.

Another question you need to ask is: how many books a year does this editor do? A power editor might do thirty books a year. A working editor generally does less.

ST: There's a number of big name writers out there who have gotten too big for their editors. They resist editing. Channa's told me of many books that come out, and the reviews say this book needed an editor. Well somewhere there's an editor who's tearing her hair out, because she tried, and didn't get very far.

CT: One of the things I think you should expect from an editor is responsiveness. If you send them something, and don't hear anything for two weeks, then you're not getting what you deserve. If your editor is not your advocate and not doing battle for you in-house, then you're not getting proper editing. If your editor is not making you feel good about your work, then you're not getting proper editing. If an editor says, "You need to cut two hundred pages," and that's the extent of the guidance, you're not getting proper editing.

There's a tendency now to auction off books to the highest bidder. That leaves you without much choice of publisher or editor. When you speak to agents, keep in mind that if you don't want your book to be auctioned off, you're going to be expected to make a financial sacrifice. That may be a fair trade-off.

ST: I have a new agent this year, and one reason is that my old agent tended to want

me to go the highest bidder a lot of the time. She kept saying that she could get me more money at this other house, and I couldn't convince her that that wasn't what I wanted. My agent now is much more balanced — she wants the right money, the right house, the right editor.

One of the first deals I made with Channa was for every mark she made suggesting a change, she had to find something she liked and mark that. We came up with this little code of symbols. I just had the gumption to negotiate with my editor. I'm surprised by how many writers are timid about that.

CT: In the past, authors stayed with houses for a long time, if not forever. A lot of people back in New York complain that there's no loyalty these days, and that as soon as you make a success of an author, the agent takes them off to the highest bidder. I think this problem is related to the fact that editors jump around so much, and we do it for the same reason authors jump around: to make money. I don't think publishers value their editors enough. They are unwilling to acknowledge that an author stays with a house because of an editor. This is something publishers don't like to acknowledge, because editors do move so much. So many books become inherited books. You sell a book to an editor, and then your editor leaves. There is something called an editor's clause that authors who are important and who command large advances can sometimes get from certain houses that says if their editor leaves, they may leave as well. However, it is a tough clause to get. It is something that authors want who do have clout.

ST: I know writers who have sent in their manuscripts that they received large advances for, and thirty days later their editor hasn't called them. These writers are too timid to call in and say, "Have you read it yet? What's going on?" What shocks me is then when the whole process is over they go into a new contract with the same editor, even though they were very unhappy. Until you have a good experience with an editor, you don't realize how good it can be.

The First and Last Great School of Literary Criticism

William Studebaker

As the proverbial *saw* is turned, every writer worth his or her ink has a stack of rejection slips.

Yes, I know the exception who tries to disprove the rule: "Everything I've written, I've published." Or: "I don't get rejected anymore; everything I write is on demand." Or: "I have a good agent, she places everything I write."

I discount statements like these several ways. A writer might be saving face, or suffering from euphoria after having experienced an "acceptance." A poet may have written, and published, only one poem (as Robert Francis would say, "lucky person"). A writer may not send out experimental regional material, at least not until a former creative writing teacher has read it, friends and agent evaluate it, and all necessary homogenizations are made. No rejection in that process. No sirree. Or, simply, a writer may be lying.

Whatever. Most writers' literary careers are strewn with rejection slips. William Stafford stated once that only ten per cent of his work has been accepted. Judy Steele, a veteran newspaper columnist, still suffers editorial re-writes, cuts-and-pastes. Rejection is a satirical business. It hurts as it helps. But rejection slips are the one constant source of advice for the steady, adventuresome writer.

Once (I can only imagine) all correspondence between writers and editors, even rejection slips, was done by hand. Not only was there a personal touch, but there was a conspicuous opportunity for editorial observation. But not now. This is the age of Styrofoam criticism, throw away rejections — the form letter. Form rejections make the work of the writer more difficult, but still

you must endure to the end, and in so doing glean what guidance you can from the first and last school of literary criticism — the school of rejection, the class of hard knocks.

Consider this rejection from *Outerbridge*: "No. Sorry." The "no" I understand. The "sorry" I'm still working on because I give each word in a rejection equal connotative and denotative attention. I assume editors try to write as well as they expect writers to write. And "sorry" can imply a degree of mutual compassion. But *does* it?

Or consider this diction from *The Georgia Review*: "however…we wish you the best in placing it elsewhere." I understand "wishing," and it is nice to have an editorial staff wishing for me. Or this slip from *The Massachusetts Review*: "hope you will find a place for your work." When I'm depressed, and I usually am after being rejected, the first place that comes to mind may not be *the* place the editor was anticipating. Or this fixed form from *The New England Review* that says: "We're unable to use this work, / but thank you for your interest." "Interest" is not the word I would have chosen if someone asked me why I was submitting to the NER. Because I'm *interested*? But on second thought, I am interested. And this tortured trochaic rejection has its charm, a subtle ambiance. I'm interested.

Then there are those rejections that confer hope: "we are unable to use your manuscript at this time"; "it merely missed what the Editorial Board is looking for at this time"; "it does not meet our editorial needs for the present issue, but *please* keep us in mind *for next year's* issue." Here the negative mind might see litotes; the positive discreet affirmation. Only the most self-flagellating author should opt for being "damned with faint praise" when muffled kudos is inferable.

An overt vote in favor of a work is obviously flattering and instructive, though the net result is still rejection: "made us look twice"; "caught our eye"; "William — your poems are strong…please try us again." From such slight twists of the ball-point, you can sort out a work that the editor liked, study it, compare it, apply your intuition to its appeal, and, like any good craftsman, duplicate the successful elements until they are mastered.

Occasionally, a rejection slip is full of advice, like this one from *The MacGuffin*: "'Unmarking Timber' and 'Running the

Jarbidge River' came closest. The first needs to be tightened a bit and the second needs work on the last stanza." Or this one from Jack Smith at the *Black River Review*:

Thanks for submitting your sketch, "A Good Deal," to Black River Review. *Sorry, we're not going to use it. There's some good color and humor, however. Have you read Mark Twain's "Sketches New and Old"? If not, you might enjoy these. I'm not sure if the people in town actually ever knew any Jews, or would know what to make of a Jewish person if they did (that's an idea you might wish to make clear in the story). The townspeople's stereotyped view of "shrewdness" versus the outcome of Mom's "bargaining," though, seems in Mark Twain's mode of humor.*

After I got over what I took to be an insult, "Have you read Mark Twain," I was able to focus on a flaw in the story, a flaw of exposition, and make what might have been an ethnic slur into genuine humor.

Writers live with rejection. Writing is a business that dictates disapproval if the writer is doing the job: experimenting with ideas, exploiting experiences, and grappling with style. And editors must evaluate, according to their skills and interests, what they read. In a pluralistic society, there is much written and much rejected. And the tendency for writers and editors is to settle on style as the arbitrational value that pasteurizes and homogenizes literature. Rejection is the method by which it is enforced and by which it is fought.

After a writer has written for ten or fifteen years, attended a dozen writing conferences (or earned an MFA), established a voice, ferreted out a compatible genre, and continued writing, rejections slips will also continue. These negative notices, albeit often hard-nosed, are a source of valuable

This is the age of

Styrofoam criticism,

throw away rejections

— the form letter.

criticism. However, to gather the wisdom they harbor, a few simple rules can help:

1. Take rejection as criticism. Trust the editors and readers. Trust that they have read the work and don't like it. There is something wrong.

2. Compare your feelings after receiving the rejection notice with your feelings when you sent it out. Were you completely satisfied then? If there is any doubt, rework the piece. If not, mail it off to another publisher.

3. Compare rejection notices. Has this piece been submitted before? Was it rejected? How many times has it been rejected. Have any "personal" insights been given? Remember when you submit something, you are asking for public approval.

4. Keep a history of each work: where it has been submitted, what "kind" of publishers have read it (national, regional, ethnic, minority), and so on.

5. Learn to see your work as others see it. Understand your sense of place, your voice, your dialect. Categorize your rejections by geographical region.

6. After you have placed a piece, or given up on it, throw the rejections slips away. There is nothing more morbid than a water-closet papered with that type of …stuff.

7. Believe in the process. The editor has rejected your work but not you. Work hard. Try again.

Richard Hugo was wont to say that there are more writers writing today than have lived in the history of the world. If so, it is a tougher business. However, there are more opportunities. More opportunities for experimentation. More opportunities for rejection. The contemporary writer who has a spark of originality will have some work rejected and never graduate from the class of hard knocks — the first and last *great* school of literary criticism.

William Studebaker has published four collections of poetry. His prose book, Backtracking: Ancient Art of Southern Idaho, *is forthcoming from The Idaho Museum of Natural History, and he is co-editing an anthology of essays about Idaho places.*

PR: Doing Your Own

Joel Davis

Congratulations! Your book is finally being published, and this is a great day for you. Maybe your book's in hardback, or perhaps it's a trade or mass market paperback. It may have a national publisher or a local or regional one.

What's important is that it's yours. And your baby's about to be cloned and put on bookstore shelves everywhere!

Well, maybe almost everywhere. Hmmm, maybe a limited press run with limited distribution? Uh-huh. But that's fine. The point is, your book is being published. The next step is to make sure that people know it's published, and what it's about, and where they can buy it. That's where PR comes into play.

And doing PR for your book is something in which you are likely to be involved. Whether your publisher is Random House or In The Basement Press, you're probably going to have to do some of your own post-publishing pushing. Here are some questions you may have about doing your own PR, along with some answers.

Q: What is PR, anyway?

A: PR is public relations; publicity; getting the word out; letting the reading public know that you have a new book published, that it's good, that they all want to go out and buy it. PR is schmoozing. Your book may be the Great American Novel arrived at last, or a deeply moving volume of revolutionary poetry, or the travelogue that makes Jan Morris a has-been. It may be any of these — but if people don't know it exists, they won't look for it. If they don't think it's interesting enough to buy, they'll pass on to the Calvin and Hobbes section. And if booksellers don't think it will sell, they won't stock it. So as crass as it may sound, you're going to have to do a little hustling.

Q: Isn't the publisher supposed to do the PR?

A: In a perfect world, yes. But the last time writers and publishers inhabited a perfect world was…hmmmm…never mind. As a fellow writer once told me: "Publishers have two classes of writers — best-selling writers and mid-list writers. The two things to remember are, most writers are mid-list, and there is no low-list." The big New York publishers will spend plenty of publicity money on their top-line writers. They will do relatively little for the mid-list folks. Regional and local publishers, on the other hand, usually don't have budgets large enough to afford a lot of publicity for any of their writers. They would if they could, but they can't. So, unless you're a best-selling author already, or your book has so captivated a publisher's fancy (and the sales force's fascination), you're going to have to do most of your own publicity.

Q: Well, that sounds a bit depressing…OK, where do I start?

A: Where all good writers begin — at the library. You will have two (and possibly three) targets for your publicity campaign: (1) the news media and (2) booksellers, including distributors. Depending on the type of book you've published, you may also want to target (3) schools. The local library can probably help you find the information you will need.

First, find a copy of *Editor's and Publisher's Yearbook*. This wonderful reference tome lists all the news media outlets in nearly every good-sized city and town in America, including yours and those in your state and region. Copy them out. If you have a computer and a database program, enter them there. Generate your own mailing list of news media outlets, including major newspapers, radio stations, and TV stations.

Next, peruse the Yellow Pages and Business Listings in the phone books for your city and the other large ones in your area. Check the "Bookstore" listings and create a database/mailing list of bookstores and book distributors.

Finally, if you're going to send PR materials to schools, put together a list of the school districts in your area's larger towns and cities. See if you can find the name of the curriculum coordinators, or the school librarians.

Q: Who's more important, booksellers or the news media?

A: As the late, great Casey Stengel might have said, "Yes." They're both important. Booksellers and book distributors need to know about your book's existence, and what it's about. That way they're more likely to stock it. If you stress the "local/regional author" angle, they're even more likely to carry your book. And the news media can be your pipeline to the general public. If you can get the media to mention your book, mention you, or even review the book or get you on the air, so much the better.

Q: Are there some simple and inexpensive ways to do my own PR?

A: Of course, different people have different definitions of "simple" and "inexpensive," so you'll have to apply your own to these suggestions.

Press Releases

Write a short (one page maximum) press release and mail it to the news media outlets on your mailing list. (Don't forget to include writer-, literary- and publishing-oriented publications on your list!) The press release will say "PRESS RELEASE" at its top, have the current date below it, and below that a snappy "slug" or headline. It will mention the name of your publisher, the title, your name, the book's price, and whether it's hard or paperback. It will include a short summary of the book's plot or purpose. It will include some short biographical information about you. And it will include a phone number where you can be contacted. This must look professional, so if you've got a letterhead, use it for the press release. If you don't, get one. You're a professional published writer now, so look the part!

Announcements to Booksellers

Create a one-page flyer about your new book and mail it to booksellers and book distributors. The flyer will have much of the same information that a press release would have. It will also have the book's release date and its ISBN number on it. Booksellers and distributors need this information to order the book. If you're self-publishing, be sure to include your address on the flyer, along with the book's wholesale price. You may also want to "paste" a small reproduction of your book's cover into the flyer. If you've got access to desktop publishing software, this is not difficult to do. And if you've got a scanner, it's really easy. Use colored paper if you like, but don't get too garish.

Follow-up Phone Calls and Letters

Press releases and flyers are great introductions and attention-getters. But it's not enough. About two to four weeks after mail-

ing them out, take some time to make some phone calls. Don't be pushy about it. Just call some of the people on your mailing lists (news media and booksellers), introduce yourself, remind them of your flyer/press release, and ask if they'd like more information. Tell the media you're available for interviews and can send them review copies. Tell the booksellers you'd be happy to do a book signing.

In this vein, remember that the personal touch is always best. So stop by your local newspapers or radio and TV stations. Find

Whether your publisher is Random House or In The Basement Press, you're probably going to have to do some of your own post-publishing pushing.

out who the book reviewers are and make yourself known (not a pest, just known.) Get them review copies. And for heaven's sake, visit your local bookstores! Best-selling author Greg Bear, of Seattle, once told me, "Remember: booksellers are our best friends." Meet the manager and book buyers, and tell them you're always happy to sign copies on the shelves and would love to do book signings.

Bookmarks

And when you visit bookstores, bring along some of your own personal bookmarks. This is something I first learned about from Kathy Tyers, a science fiction writer in Montana. Bookmarks are an easy, inexpensive, and effective way to publicize your book or books. Your bookmark can list your name and the name of your book(s), their publishers and prices. They can be plain or colorful, simple or loaded with graphics. Local printing shops can typeset and print several thousand bookmarks for you at a relatively inexpensive

price. Places like Kinko's can do it even cheaper. Stick some in your car, your luggage, your briefcase, and your pockets when you travel. Most bookstore owners will happily take your bookmarks and pass them out.

Book Signings And Talk Shows

Book signings get you out amongst the book-buying public. Radio talk shows get you onto the ether and into the homes and cars of umpteen numbers of listening folks. Both are good ways to publicize your book. Both can often be hard to pull off. But they're worth trying and being persistent about. I've done signings by myself and with large groups; both are fun. Sometimes few people buy; sometimes the lines are long. It's all part of the game. I've done talk shows by phone to Florida and New York City, and in the studio in Seattle and Spokane. They're fun!

Q: What else can I do?

A: Lots of stuff. Remember, the important rule to follow is to pay attention to what's going on! Consider, for example, your attempts to get onto radio talk shows or to set up a book signing. You're regularly perusing the major book review outlets, right? Plus specialty magazines that may review your book. And when you get a favorable review from *Publisher's Weekly* or *Cat Fancier* magazine, you send out a press release to that effect. And follow it up with phone calls and visits.

Finally, consider getting to know the local or regional book distributor at least as well as you know the booksellers. This is particularly true if your book is a mass market paperback. The book distributor can make or break your sales. Romance writer Theresa Scott of Olympia, Washington has made it a regular policy to visit her local distributor and introduce herself to the drivers of the book delivery trucks. Just an honest smile and a handshake and a good morning. And by golly, her paperbacks always seem to end up in the hot-selling rack spots in supermarkets.

Schmoozing pays off. So schmooze away!

Spokane science writer Joel Davis has six published books. The latest is Journey to the Center of Our Galaxy: A Voyage in Space and Time *from Contemporary Books, Inc. He is working on a book for Random House about science, philosophy, and spirituality, and a book for Birch Lane Press on how the brain learns language.*

First Book

Pete Fromm

The first manuscript I sent to John Daniel and Company came back with a long, admiring critique of my work and an admirably businesslike rejection. John explained that, as a completely unpublished author, it would be economic suicide for him to publish my book. He suggested that I try submitting my stories to the literaries to establish a readership. "Great idea," I thought, adding his rejection to the hundred or so I'd collected from the literaries. But, dangling the carrot, he added that should I find any success in publishing individual stories, I could get back to him and something might be worked out. This was a far cry from a form rejection.

In the next year success started to dribble in with the rejections. A few literaries picked up stories and a link seemed to be building with *Gray's Sporting Journal*, a slick, commercial magazine for highbrow sportsmen. I sent a letter to John, probably making these few sales sound more like a landslide. He bit, and I sent a new manuscript down to California. After a year and half in production, *The Tall Uncut* was published and I began to learn there was no such thing as kicking back and waiting for royalties. The work had just begun.

John's partner, Susan, did an incredible amount of work, sending out review copies to all the big places and searching out anyone else who could possibly be interested. This effort began to pay off with more than fifteen reviews, good reviews, but still, with an unknown name, the publicity wasn't enough.

I began to do signings, and readings, first in the friendly surrounds of my hometown, then home state, but a bigger opportunity came through a friend, Dave Cates, whose novel, *Hunger in America*, published by Simon & Schuster, happened to come out at the same time as my book.

In the few marketplace books I'd read there was always an irritating chapter about making your connections work. I didn't have any connections, and I'd hate to think I'm giving the same advice now.

But Dave set up a tour of the west, the cudgel of Simon & Schuster's influence opening doors to large bookstores like Elliott Bay in Seattle and Powell's in Portland. The bookstores and Dave's sales reps all thought a dual reading was a great idea: his novel, my short stories, hardcover, paperback, twice the draw.

With all but the rarest of first books, there is no tour, no paid publicity. Dave and I went on our own, on the cheap, usually changing from road clothes to reading clothes in the back of my pick-up parked in front of the book store. One night, hoping to catch a few hours sleep in a rest area, Dave wound up wrestling with skunks instead. Nine readings in eleven days, covering 3,800 miles.

> *Dave and I*
>
> *went on our own,*
>
> *on the cheap,*
>
> *usually changing from*
>
> *road clothes*
>
> *to reading clothes*
>
> *in the back of my pick-up*
>
> *parked in front*
>
> *of the book store.*
>
> *One night, hoping to catch*
>
> *a few hours sleep in a rest area,*
>
> *Dave wound up wrestling*
>
> *with skunks instead.*

I seemed to draw the fringe element at the readings; the woman who announced that she'd moved into a teepee to get closer to the earth, who didn't believe in hope or possibilities; the people who asked deeply personal questions after my readings, unable to distinguish personal essay from fiction. But Dave got the deaf family in the Berkeley bookstore, who wandered all around him as he read, unaware they were interrupting anything. And people wondered if we became writers because of the lifestyle.

We sold some books, maybe enough to cover expenses, probably not. But, everywhere we went we read and exposed our books and ourselves to people who most likely never would have heard of us otherwise. Most importantly, we created interest in our books from the owners and staff of the bookstores. And they are the people, more than reviewers and sales representatives, who can really make first books work. Their recommendations and word of mouth sell the numbers that can make first books succeed. Thousands, not tens of thousands or hundreds of thousands.

Those thousands are the springboard to the next book. Since signing on with John Daniel and Company I've sold two more books, entered the New York publishing world, and have just had an offer on a third. But, for a first book, I could not have found better people to work with than John and Susan Daniel, deeply dedicated people despite the size of their company, happy to make profits in hundreds of dollars, delighted if it reaches the thousands. People also happy to send me to bigger publishers, to read through their contracts and offer advice.

The Tall Uncut, six months old, is now in its second printing. Instead of saying that no one has ever heard of me, I can now say with assurance, that *practically* no one has ever heard of me. And that can be the difference in making a manuscript sale and getting the kind of rejection letter John wrote to introduce himself.

Pete Fromm's upcoming books are The Indian Creek Chronicles: A Winter in the Wilderness *(Lyons & Burford) and* Monkey Tag, *a novel, (Scholastic).*

Experiences in Writing, Illustrating, and Publishing: What Makes Danny Run?

Carolyn Erwin

For as long as I can remember I have loved picking up the magical, creative, and imaginative things known as books. My favorite experience in reading was to surround myself by the world and inhabitants of a story. I often wondered if children ever wrote books. One day this question was answered.

When I was in the fourth grade, Elizabeth Haidle (a thirteen year old author) came to our school and explained how her book, *Elmer The Grump*, was published. Landmark Editions Publishing holds a contest called "Written and Illustrated By..." each year. The rules are simple: you write a story, draw the pictures and literally build and bind a book to submit to the contest judges. I thought if Elizabeth Haidle could do it, so could I.

First, I had to think of a story. I had so many in mind. My mother told me to write about what I knew. I remembered an incident that would make a wonderful story: the escape of my pet hamster in an elementary school. From this incident, I created my story, *What Makes Danny Run?* In my story Danny himself described his adventures and I used my pictures to help explain what was happening.

I assembled my story and pictures, bound them into book format, sent the book in, and waited eagerly for any news. Later that year the publishers returned my book. Since I didn't win the contest, the sponsoring publisher wouldn't publish my story. But the contest judges did send me a certificate of Award for Achievement saying that out of 7,500 entries in my age group, my book was in the top 100. Since more than 250,000 students from the United States and Canada had entered the contest, I was very excited about the recognition. My mother thought if my book was in the top 100, it was good enough to be published.

That was when we started researching and talking to other people about how to get the book published ourselves. We first looked into the possibility of another publisher, but we found that they wanted either my manuscript or my illustrations, but not both. Since we wanted the story and illustrations to stay together, we decided to publish it ourselves.

We went to the library to find a book about self-publishing. My mother took a self-publishing course at a community college, since I was too young to take it myself. She joined the Northwest Association of Book Publishers to talk to other people who had published their own books. We learned that there was a lot of work involved.

I had no idea how much work we would have to do, until we sat down and mapped it out. The terms ISBN, Library of Congress number, copyright, ABI, bar code, distributors, typesetters, editors, printers, paper bonds, and many others became part of our vocabulary. Six hard months later, when I was in the sixth grade, we finally published my book *What Makes Danny Run?*.

Now I am in seventh grade at Mt. View Intermediate School. As a result of publishing my book, newspapers printed my picture and articles about my book, and schools invited me to read my book to the students. A local TV cable access show interviewed me, and I participated in an *AM Northwest* TV show about young entrepreneurs. My book is selling in a number of different bookstores and a hospital gift shop. We have donated many books to schools and libraries throughout the United States and foreign countries, as well as to day-care centers, hospitals, and other organizations.

Getting my book published has meant becoming somebody special. I feel good about myself because I know that other people and students are reading and enjoying my book, and I hope and believe that my book will inspire some other young person to want to write a book too.

I am 12 years old and live in Aloha, Oregon. I have a mom, a dad, and a 10 year old brother. I used to have many different kinds of pets, but now I have a special West Highland Terrier (a "Westie") named Brenda and two parakeets. I enjoy tap dancing, playing the violin, acting, drawing, and writing stories and poems.

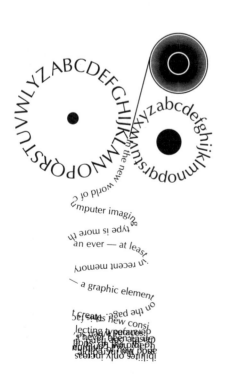

To Young Writers

Sandra Scofield

It may be that the questions you asked seemed simple, and if so, you will wonder how the answers can be so long. Or it may be that you think there is something magical and elusive in inspiration, and I will tell you the secret. In fact most of what I say will not help you at all though I hope it will not be dull. What you must do is find your own way, and all I can do is tell you a little about my own so you will see how eccentric and idiosyncratic art-making is.

I wrote my first poem when I was nine years old and liked a boy a lot who had huge freckles and was always in trouble. I don't remember the poem, but I remember that my teacher said I ought to pick a better subject. After that I wrote essays for school and contests, and my teachers approved. Everything else I kept secret. Usually I tore my writing up when it was done. I was greatly inspired at your age by tales about sad lives. I wrote stories about blinded artists, about a bridge full of people swept away in a flood, about orphans and martyrs. In college I wrote poems for other students to give their girlfriends or boyfriends, and I charged them one dollar each.

Then, for about twenty years, I wrote once or twice a year, in intense sessions of memory and feeling, about events in my own life that seemed to need to be recorded, events that had changed the way I understood my life and the world around me. Some of these stories I saved. The language is very good, but the stories are usually awfully melodramatic.

Now I am visited by voices and dreams, and I listen and watch, and talk back (inside my head) until a shape begins to emerge, and I cannot bear not to start to write.

My ideas come from a single question: WHY? They are embodied in characters made up of one part me, one part sympathy for someone I have known or imagined, and one part sense of crisis or compulsion, which leads to plot. I write a lot before I plan what I will do with my ideas, and then I start all over, even if I have written 400 pages.

I do research to make my writing rich in plausible detail. In my second book, *Beyond Deserving*, which is set in Ashland a few years ago, I had to learn about dogtraining and baton-twirling, about social work and alcoholism, about ballet and pizza, and a little bit about target shooting. I simply go to the library, look up a topic, start browsing, and then reading books, especially older ones that tend to be talkier than new ones. I read until I have enough for my characters to DO things and SAY things, and I watch for quirky details that will make a scene or just a sentence memorable in some small way. I have to look up practically everything, page to page, because I never learned the stuff of day to day life. I don't know weeds or trees for example, but if there's a tree in my book it will be a lodge pole pine or live oak or shedding madrone, and not just some piece of standing wood called a tree.

I want to write a book set in West Texas in the late 1930s, and I will have to learn everything my characters knew. It will probably take me years. I will invent the past out of the memorabilia of history. I can't wait to start.

Now I get to the ADVICE. Some of it I know is right because I was lucky enough to do it by instinct. Some of it I wish I had done and had to start late, and some of it my daughter believed and I can already see how good she is. So here goes.

1. Store the stuff of your experience and your observation in tangible memory. Keep a diary, or a logbook, at least. If you do not feel like feeling when you write, make entries that name the stuff of your life: what fish you ate for dinner (orange roughy or cod?), the price of gum, the stupid thing someone said today. Come to prize the way your words look, the way they lie on the page. Give yourself the gift of your own history.

2. Talk to your cat, to your mirror, to children and to old people. Cherish the stories people tell and the cat's haughtiness. Remember that most unique fiction was once true somewhere.

3. Learn the names of things and how they work. Remember jokes.

4. Read a lot. Sometimes, read very slowly. Sometimes read out loud. Sometimes mimic a sentence you admire, or a paragraph. Read poems you don't understand, as well as those you think you do. Read all the Greek myths, and then read myths from cultures all over the world. This includes Old Testament stories. Memorize a lot of them and write new ones.

5. Visit lots of kinds of churches and go to everything that is free: parades and concerts in the park, galleries and delicatessens, sales, and demonstrations of anything. Learn what other people do to celebrate their birthdays, Christmas, the first hot day of summer.

6. Study the shapes of things, and draw them: people, poems, bridges, books.

7. Tell stories. Maybe to children. To your cat.

8. Insist that your parents and grandparents tell you the stories of their lives. Then ask them to do so again.

9. Imagine other people's lives. This is a very good thing to do in long lines or dentist's offices.

10. Write down your dreams.

11. Love words. Old words, big words, foreign words, funny words.

12. Learn to type.

13. Play hard and spend a lot of time outdoors.

(This article is the text of a speech delivered at Ashland Middle School Honors Night, March 2, 1989.)

Sandra Scofield, a native Texan and long-time resident of Oregon, has been writing fiction and poetry for over twenty years. She has published four novels, and a fifth is due January, 1994 (Villard). Her second novel, Beyond Deserving, was a finalist for the 1991 National Book Award and won an American Book Award in 1992.

Skipping Stones Magazine

Arun Toké

Have you ever felt that you do not really count? Do you sometimes feel that you have no voice? Over the years, as I journeyed through my childhood into youth and beyond, I have come to realize that our society does not validate our youngsters' experience enough. Also, we do not make the best use of our youth: a plentiful and energetic resource.

I came to the United States in August 1971 as a graduate student. It was a plunge into the cold waters of cultural shock. I had spent all of my youth in India, in a totally different environment. Everything was different — culture, climate, religion, geography, economy, lifestyle, and of course, language.

Over the years, I have lived and traveled extensively in Europe, Mexico, Central America, and North America. During my 500-km walk in Central America and 3000-km bicycle trip in Northern Europe, I had numerous cross-cultural experiences that I still cherish. Yet, during the past 20 years, I have also witnessed many situations where cultural insensitivity or racism was displayed, knowingly or unknowingly. Too often, I have observed

I firmly believe that the survival and well being of human societies depends on how well we welcome cultural diversity and ecological richness.

cultural bias and insensitivity against other beings and nature!

Even though I have no formal training in editing, journalism, or publishing, I decided to start *Skipping Stones*. I hoped to offer a forum for communication among children from different lands and backgrounds. I also wanted to help facilitate an awareness of our cultural and ethnic richness, our ecological and natural heritage. I firmly believe that the survival and well being of human societies depends on how well we welcome cultural diversity and ecological richness.

At *Skipping Stones*, we invite children and young adults to share their feelings, thoughts, experiences, and artistic expressions. We especially encourage youth from under-represented populations. We also welcome writings by adults from other cultures to enrich our lives with distinct flavors and insights into human experience. We have published stories, articles, and photos by contributors from rural Mexico to Moscow, from China to inner city New York and Chicago. We welcome writings in *all* languages. We know that *Skipping Stones* must be multilingual, not only to communicate, but to preserve the flavor of the cultures.

As we enter our fifth year of publishing, we continue to broaden our horizons as we attempt to expand those of our young readers.

Skipping Stones is a non-profit children's magazine. We are here to encourage cooperation, creativity, and celebrate cultural and linguistic diversity. We explore and learn stewardship of the ecological web that sustains us. We print on non-glossy, recycled, and recyclable paper using soy-based ink as an expression of our commitment to ecological sustainability.

Features include family, Afro-American heritage, songs from around the world, favorite recipes, substance abuse among young people, adoption, animals, and television. Regular departments that welcome your contributions are: Dear Hanna, Book Reviews, Noteworthy NEWS, Rhymes and Riddles, Networking, Pen Pals, Cultural Collage, and *Skipping Stones* Stew.

Since we are a non-profit publishing house, we need not worry about advertisers or maximizing short-term profits. We are able to attract volunteers for translating, editing, proofing, mailing, and other routine tasks. Our interns do a lot of the daily office work. We have a 72-year old volunteer who has been working with us since day one. She organizes the library. During mailing, she stuffs subscription forms in the magazines or puts on address labels. As other educational and professional journals or publications discover us, they tell their readers about *Skipping Stones*. We have a widely scattered readership from all 50 states and 25 other countries. Our pen pal requests come from Africa to the Ukraine. We believe that hundreds of pen friendships have been established as a result of our work.

My satisfaction comes from receiving letters from the four corners of the globe, some in languages that I can't understand yet, some saying "How I wish a magazine like *Skipping Stones* existed when I was young."

Arun Toké is an electrical engineer turned editor who has co-authored a textbook, Energy, Economics and the Environment *(Prentice-Hall). For information on* Skipping Stones, *write PO Box 3939, Eugene, OR 97403.*

The Claremont Review: Okay, Bob, maybe you don't need a weatherman, but the wind isn't all there is to weather

Terence Young

English teachers have always had their feet in two distinct camps: the camp in which they talk about the writing done by people known as authors, and the camp in which they encourage students to become authors themselves. It is possible to say, of course, as many of us do, that all writing is creative, critical or otherwise, and it is true that I will sometimes enjoy an article on post-structuralism almost as much as I would a short story by Raymond Carver or Alice Munro. I would, however, never confuse the two. Much as I am pleased to follow a student's carefully charted path through the orphan-strewn countryside of Mary Shelley's *Frankenstein*, I would never think it an appropriate submission to *Grand Street* or *The Paris Review*.

It is also true, I think, that in the latter years of high school, teachers — and I include myself — become more concerned with imparting the intricacies of Gustave Freytag's plot paradigm than with helping students use language to give shape to their experiences. The study of English, after all, is not anything so distastefully new age as bibliotherapy, nor is it meant to encourage narcissistic voyages into what is the literary equivalent of finger painting. The mandate of the high school English class is made manifestly clear in the format and content of many final exams, and, while we may complain from time to time about individual questions — I, dullard that I am, had to comb *The Chicago Manual of Style: 12th Edition* for the truth about the titles of paintings and whether or not to italicize — there is no doubt in our minds that we are on this planet to cajole, coerce, intimidate, and sometimes even entice young minds into a thorough understanding of metaphor (one mark for identification, one mark for expla-

nation, and one mark for quality of expression).

Some students, we have noticed, are very sad when they have this subtext revealed to them. In earlier grades, they actually believed English fun. Joyously, they wrote letters to Rascal, molded plaster cast models of *The Island of the Blue Dolphins*, and composed fitting epitaphs for those two wonderful dogs in *Where the Red Fern Grows*. Some even donned Grecian frocks and became Helena pursuing Demetrius through the woods outside ancient Athens. Small wonder they are horrified to discover how deficient their education has been. True, we do allow them the option of writing a story in the essay section of some final exams, but they must realize that writing a story is very, very hard and that English markers do not respond favorably to juvenile forays into the gore-saturated realm of Stephen King. It is better to write what they have been taught to write: clear, precise exposition.

A question remains, however, and a nagging one: if senior English is primarily con-

Some will argue

that writers learn their craft

in the school of life or some such

equally silly nonsense. Writers

learn from other writers…

cerned with the development of analytical skills, what is our responsibility regarding students who demonstrate real talent in the area of poetry and fiction? Literary criticism is to writing what musicology is to music or what art history is to art. Each study has its object of study, but while we offer most high school students an opportunity to explore both art and art history — Western Civilization and Art 12 are good examples of long standing and respected courses — we do little to prepare students for the possibility that they may be writers and not critics. There are creative writing courses across this country just as there are English courses, but we do not encourage students to consider this option. Some will argue that writers learn their craft in the school of life or some such equally silly nonsense. Writers learn from other writers, just as Hemingway learned from Stein or as Canadian writer Jack Hodgins learned from Faulkner. Any writer will tell you it is preferable to study with the living, but the dead will do in a pinch. Creative writing departments are composed of writers, and an aspiring author would be a fool to spurn the help of people like Philip Levine, Mark Strand, or Tillie Olsen. Don't need a weatherman, indeed.

Students enjoy writing fiction and poetry. They clamor for their submissions to be returned as soon as possible to see how their genius has been received. The problem is that teachers are not always eager to read what students have written, especially at the senior levels where the tawdry life of the adolescent — its furtive experiments with sex, its adoration of heavy metal bands, its unabashed admiration for the collected works of Danielle Steele — often fails to inspire a teacher to repeat the "creative experience." A nice lesson on the relevance of the masque in "The Tempest" starts to sound better all the time. And the odd time that something of real merit is submitted, the teacher is often at a loss to offer concrete help with editing. Editing to most English teachers means progress toward greater coherence through the proper use of transitional elements, connectives, subordination. Poetry and fiction generated from such an editorial process will be without exception boring because predictable writing does not engage the imagination. To echo the Talk-

ing Heads, a good editor needs to show a writer how to "stop making sense." Not an easy thing when your whole career has been dedicated to the opposite pursuit. In fact, creative writing teachers at university have expressed to me their dread at the prospect of high school English teachers undertaking to teach students how to write poetry and short stories. They are afraid of having to disabuse whole classes of students of the beauty of duplicating Keats' sonnets or of suffering through entire manuscripts filled with moons and souls and butterflies and the dark despair of an indifferent universe.

I am not suggesting that English teachers generate more creative writing exercises or that they go back to school to learn the art of writing, though both of these ideas have some merit. Occasionally, I will inject writing exercises of a "creative" nature into my English classes to accommodate students who have talent in this area and to assure other jaded students that English can still be fun, but for the most part I haven't the time to pursue fully edited drafts of the caliber I demand in a Writing 12 class. I am really hoping to convince teachers and administrators of the need to introduce writing programs into their schools, writing programs devoted solely to the generation of student writing. I will testify from my own experience that such programs can elicit fierce loyalty and devotion from students, that students learn to abandon the hackneyed story lines of television soaps and to examine their own lives with an artist's eye, that there exists in any town a community of writers who are delighted to

To echo the Talking Heads,

a good editor

needs to show a writer

how to

"stop making sense"

talk about what they do and to give advice on writing, that nothing contributes more to self-esteem than the act of creation and the perfect realization of an idea.

When I started my first writing class two years ago, I did not anticipate the effects such a class would have both in my life and in the lives of my students. The process of writing demands rigorous honesty and fidelity to the truth, and those criteria drastically alter the normal teacher/student relationship. Lecture ceases and modeling becomes the teacher. "Don't tell me, show me" is the guiding rule, and what is revealed is often not pretty. Whatever myths a teacher may maintain about the simplicity of a student's life are quickly shattered, and the only life raft is the stated purpose of the class: to generate art, to transform experience, to "hold up a mirror to nature." The purpose of writing is not therapy, but it just so happens that writing is therapeutic, and that fact allows the teacher to distance himself from the student's experience and deal with the work only. "This is good, but we can make it better, more accurate, more truthful, more you." The result is a cooperative effort in which the student very often takes something that was painful and turns it into something that brings joy or greater understanding and pride instead of shame.

The material generated in the class overwhelmed me, both in its power and in its quantity. Writing classes are a lot of work, believe me. What was produced compelled me to share my results with other teachers, and, during one such session, Bill Stenson, a talented writer himself, suggested collaborating on a student literary review. A year and a half later *The Claremont Review* came into existence, and I don't believe there is any better testimonial to the talents of teenage writers than the poetry and fiction contained between its covers. And not all of it came from writing classes. The opening short story in the first issue as well as several poems came from students who simply love to write. The second issue, September 1992, is even more exciting, especially in its scope. When we started the magazine, we thought the west coast (B.C., Washington and Oregon) would be the perimeter of its appeal. We have expanded to include works from writers in Ontario and Alberta, and receive manuscripts from as far away as Idaho and California. One thing is clear: students across North America are in love with writing and earnestly desire an opportunity to measure the quality of their work beside a larger yardstick than their own high school, their own home town. The father of one girl published recently in *The Claremont Review* wrote for additional copies and confessed that he'd not had high expectations when told his daughter's story was accepted for the magazine. He expected another rainbow-ridden children's publication that concentrated on "happy thoughts." His surprise was considerable when he discovered his daughter's writing had been taken as seriously as she had intended it to be. After all, that's all a young writer wants.

I don't believe it will be hard to convince English teachers to introduce classes where their sole duty will be to work with student writing. There are, in English classrooms everywhere, closet writers who will jump at the chance to occupy themselves with what they love best: writing. There are already many teachers for whom this article is old news, who already know that teaching writing offers untold quantities of vicarious pleasure and success, that the writing process is always a collaboration. This is not, thank goodness, the age of Dryden where we are exhorted to "learn to write well, or not at all." This is the age of Natalie Goldberg and Brenda Ueland where there is risk, certainly, but where there is also encouragement and support. It is my self-destructive hope that all people reading this article will take me up on my request and flood the editor's box of *The Claremont Review* with writing of a quality that will make our first issue look pale in comparison.

Terence Young lives in Victoria B.C., where he teaches English and Writing to high school students, co-edits The Claremont Review, *and steals time to write his own brand of fiction.*

Real Life Writing for Students

Carolyn Coburn Tragesser

Imagine employers instructing workers to have a report, deposition, presentation, or promotional advertisement on their desks by the end of the hour. It must be two pages in length, and only the boss will read it. Because it is practice for the new employee, the company would not use it. Contrast this with an employer who requests a presentation on department expansion for the next board meeting.

Dutiful employees would produce in both cases, but the second scenario offers more incentive for excellence. All too often students are assigned writing as far removed from the reality of their lives as the first situation above is from the real world of work. Having readers and reasons to write beyond the classroom walls offers incentives for students to put their hearts and souls into their writing. The factors are primarily audience and purpose, the cornerstone of Foxfire and of the Northwest Inland Writing Project, affiliated with the National Writing Project.

I offer my eighth grade English students a workshop approach to writing adapted from Nancie Atwell, a pioneer of this method. Students are given nudges in directions, but they have a significant amount of control over their time lines and subjects. Audiences include other students who join us occasionally for oral presentations and evening readings. Students also have writing partners; university students in a teacher education class are paired with us to exchange responses to their writing.

Additionally, several projects have worked well to achieve the goal of making writing important to real-life situations students face. Each spring my students plan an informational packet that we distribute to sixth graders who will attend our junior high the next fall. Students form their own

committees, brainstorm the content, and decide on the time line.

I let students take charge because, frankly, I was on uncharted ground. Teachers' inexperience or lack of knowledge should not prohibit us from providing opportunities for students. Students are resourceful, and giving them a chance offers opportunities for leadership, responsibility, and communication skills development.

I asked the students to think back to what they wanted to know when they were preparing to attend junior high. By giving the students control over their project, the product was more usable than if it had been teacher-directed. For example, I never would have thought of including "hang outs" — areas around the school where different classes of students gather: by the dugout, at the stairwell. Knowing the location of drinking fountains and locker numbers was also important. Showing what their teachers looked like was something students decided to include in the packet, so they snapped pictures of staff.

We noticed students had kept the maps of our building and came to school the first day with them in hand. One year the principal asked permission to replace the map in the student handbook with our more detailed one.

Certainly having students organize projects takes more time — anything done by committee takes time as we know all too well — but the time spent pays off in preparing students for real life. School is to educate students, not only in subject matter content, but for communicating and problem solving. We can't expect those in the work force to make decisions if they have only rarely been given the opportunity.

The Foxfire approach offers validation to my own philosophy of instruction. Core practices include: role of teacher as guide; student action, not passive receipt; emphasis on peer teaching, teamwork; connection between community/real world and classroom; audience beyond the teacher; new activities spiral from previous; reflection on progress; student and teacher evaluation of skills and content.

When a student asked why we hadn't had spelling recently, I reminded him that

The city art committee

asked some of our

student writers

to participate

in poetry

readings

at a

local restaurant.

we had worked on those skills in our letters we were mailing to favorite authors. Jesse Moore agreed, "I like that real writing. It's kinda cool."

Perhaps the most ambitious of all projects I've facilitated is our school literary magazine, *Ursa Major*. Another teacher, Susan Hodgin, and I wrote a grant to the National Writing Project for $1,000 to start a magazine to celebrate student writing. We presented our idea to our student writing club. They bought it and we were off and scrambling to obtain matching funds. We teachers wrote to professional organizations for donations while the students wrote a Foxfire grant. (Foxfire requires that students have an integral part of grant writing to ensure the project arises from students' needs and interests, rather than being teacher-imposed.) Just the act of writing the grant raised the students' self esteem. "I'm only fourteen and I'm writing a grant; I can't believe it," wrote Vern Cantu in her letter to Foxfire. This process entailed planning that proved integral to our success, for we were required to think very carefully about our project: time line, relationship to classroom learning goals, and evaluation. Writing the grant was a learning experience as it provided a real audience and a writing purpose. Writing

Club members learned about sentence structure, word choice, and correct letter form. I was amazed at their dedication: to complete the grant, ten to fifteen members of the group met every day for two weeks during their 30-minute lunch. Students work under schedule constraints: an editorial board in each of two 30 minute lunch periods.

Students say the control they have and the trust we have in them are essential to the success of the endeavor. I have confidence in my students, but I retain "veto power" because of professional responsibility. I have yet to use it. We've been through decisions about using a student's work without obtaining his permission ("he won't find out, he's gone"; "he wouldn't mind, I wouldn't" to "this isn't right, we must contact him"). We learned about using a company's logo. Last year when a well-known national company stated their policy was not to give permission to use their logo but essentially gave us a "green light" by saying we'd probably not hear from them, the editorial board unanimously decided using their logo wasn't worth it. They didn't want a verbal okay; it was written or nothing.

The staff of our literary magazine *Ursa Major* (named for our school mascot) has presented at a regional teachers conference and a university class. We earned an "excellent" rating from the National Council of Teachers of English Program to Recognize Excellence in Student Literary Magazines.

Students organized the sale of the magazine including a promotion to stimulate sales. Area bookstores carry *Ursa Major*, and we are pleased the proceeds from the sales will enable us to publish it again this year when our grants have ended.

There has been a ripple effect. The city art committee asked some of our student writers to participate in poetry readings at a local restaurant. Former *Ursa Major* and regular writing club members have moved to the high school where they have started a writing club.

Gia Trotter, a ninth grade student, was sur-

prised to learn from a survey we conducted of award winning junior high magazines across the country, that only one other junior high publishes a magazine that is entirely student directed. In fact, Gia thinks "...too many teachers limit their kids to writing one subject and only one kind of story. Students need to be allowed to write on what they want to write on. Experience is the key to helping kids — just giving them the chance to write. *Ursa Major* is a good example of this. The students were their own teachers. Sure, we had someone to go to for questions, but primarily it was the students who produced this magazine. Our teachers believe in us and trust our judgment." Like Gia, I appreciate having choices. Real-life writing has a place in the curriculum; just ask my students.

Carolyn Coburn Tragesser teaches at Moscow Junior High School in Idaho, is editor of the Inland Northwest Council of Teachers of English newsletter, and been published in InLand, Hands-On (published by Foxfire), Post Script, and Sports Aviation.

Resources for Young Writers

Scholle Sawyer

Like writing? Want to see your words in print? Opportunities abound for young people with inky fingers. We have here a list of contests, journals, and festivals all for you. This is just a sampling of regional prospects; many more exist locally and nationally. So get those pens, pencils, and computers out and go to it!

Some tips:

- Listings are arranged by state, but be sure to look at more than just your own state. Most of the journals want work from folks throughout the Northwest, and many of the conferences feel the same.
- Don't be shy about submitting your work to the student publications listed here, as well as to other small press journals. High school writers, in particular, aren't really so different from college writers who aren't really so different from older writers. (The editors may not even be able to tell you're "young." They'll just think of you as a writer!)
- Remember to get a sample copy of the publication you're thinking of submitting to, as well as its submission guidelines. Then you'll know if you're sending your poem/story/article to a proper home. If a magazine only prints six-line rhyming poems about frogs in the deserts of Oregon, you wouldn't want to waste a stamp sending in your masterpiece on Aunt Ida's yellow dress.
- Make sure to include an SASE (self-addressed, stamped envelope with the work you send.

Other resources:

- Many newspaper editors are on the lookout for students willing and ready to write about school activities and youth issues. Also, don't forget letters-to-the-editor and community opinion columns. These are for old and young alike!
- Young writers in all states can find out about annual programs, contests, and

conferences sponsored by state affiliates of the National Council of Teachers of English by contacting NCTE, 1111 Kenyon Road, Urbana IL 61801.

- Ask your teachers about national contests like the National Scholastic Writing Awards and PEN student competitions. Also, magazines like *Seventeen, Dirt, Sassy,* and *Cricket* run contests and often pay young writers for their work. For example, *Sassy* pays $300 every month for its "It Happened to Me" column. Aspiring magazine writers may want to check out *Sassy's* annual reader produced issue. The December 1993 issue will be produced by the staff of a teen produced "zine." Winners are flown to New York City for a month, usually July. Watch for the next contest, as guidelines vary from year to year. Deadlines are in January. Write to *Sassy*, 230 Park Ave., NYC, NY 10169.
- Finally, two helpful books are Laurie King and Dennis Stovall's *Classroom Publishing: A Practical Guide to Enhancing Student Literacy.* Hillsboro, OR: Blue Heron Publishing, Inc., 1992; and Kathy Henderson's *Market Guide for Young Writers.* Sandusky, MI: Echo Communications, 1990.

Disclaimer and Request:

In today's turbulent economy, publications, programs, and contests rise and fall more quickly than a two-year reference book can keep up with. We've done everything we can to make these listings current, but we apologize for any inaccuracies. You can help us out and make sure your organization is properly represented by sending brochures and press releases to Young Writers Section, Blue Heron Publishing, Inc., 24450 N.W. Hansen Road, Hillsboro, OR 97124.

Want to see your words in print? Opportunities abound for young people with inky fingers.

ALASKA

- *The Alaska State Writing Consortium* is the Alaskan version of the Writing Project in other states. Its newsletter is aimed primarily at teachers of writing. It announces contests for young writers and lists student newsletters and magazines. Write to the *Consortium* at 801 W. 10th, Ste. 200, Juneau, AK 99801-1894. Or call Judith Entwine at (907) 456-2841.
- *Midnight Sun Writers Conference*, University of Alaska, Fairbanks. This annual young writers summer conference may not run in 1993, but be sure to check. For information contact Dr. Theodore DeCorso at (907) 474-7555.
- *Rainbow Factory: A Very Special Arts Festival* is a week-long festival in spring that focuses on young artists and writers with physical and/or mental disabilities. Workshops change yearly depending on the artists involved and include the visual and performing arts as well as creative writing. Contact Sharon Abbott at Anchorage Museum (907) 343-6187.
- *Musher Monthly* is a publication by and for children of Bethel, AK. Contact Barbara Jones, P.O. Box 900, Bethel, AK 99559. (907) 543-2845.
- *Writings from Alaska Schools* is an annual publication of the Alaska Council of Teachers of English. All Alaskan students are invited to submit samples, which are then judged and edited by the ACTE. Contact Phyllis Rude, 2567 Arlington Drive, Anchorage, AK 99517.
- Students on the Aleutian Islands have their writings published in an annual yearbook organized by the Aleutian School District. Contact Robert Much at (907) 562-2924.

BRITISH COLUMBIA

- *The Claremont Review* showcases the poetry and prose of young writers, grades 8-12. The editors welcome submissions from Canadians and non-Canadians. Write the magazine at: 4980 Wesley Road, Victoria, BC V8Y 1Y9.
- *Chalk Talk Magazine* is written by children for children. Submissions are welcome from writers between the ages of 5 and 14. Contact the magazine at 1550 Mills Rd., RR 2, Sidney, BC V8L 3S1.

- *Red Alder Trunk, The Magazine for Young Writers,* is published every 4 months and seeks submissions from young writers. Produced by parents/homeschoolers/publishers, the magazine is dedicated to encouraging a love of writing. It also runs an annual short story contest. Write the magazine at: 7571 Cresswell Court, Vancouver, BC V5S 3X8.
- *The Vancouver International Writers (& Readers) Festival* takes place in October on Vancouver's Granville Island. Past festivals have sponsored a Young Writers Project in conjunction with *The Vancouver Sun.* Writers in elementary and secondary school submit their work to a panel of professionals. Winners are published over several weeks in the newspaper, and some works are read by their authors at the Festival. Deadlines are usually in September. Contact the Festival for information at 1235 Cartwright Street, Vancouver, BC V6H 4B7. Or call (604) 681-6330.
- Other suggestions for events and publications: Corey Van-Thaaff at the Federation of B.C. Writers. (604) 683-2057; Canada Teachers Union (604) 731-8121; Writers Union of Canada (604) 874-1611; Cultural Services Branch, Canada Council (604) 356-1724.

IDAHO

- *Pathways* is published 3 times a year and seeks new writers, especially children. Magazine prefers "fantasy, animals, essays, humor, travels, historical, children's own ideas." Write to Inky Trails Publication, P.O. Box 345, Middleton, ID 83644 for details.
- Northwest Inland Writing Project publishes *Inland,* a semiannual magazine for English and Language Arts teachers (K-12) that includes student writing. It is co-sponsored by the Inland Northwest Council of Teachers of English and the Idaho Council of Teachers of English. Write Driek Zirinsky, Editor, English De-

partment, Boise State University, Boise, ID 83725. Or leave voice mail for her at (208) 385-1822.
- *The Pilot Knobs Writers Group* runs a mentor program. Young writers in junior and senior high school can work with established writers by mail. Contact Christina Adams, Rt. 1 Box 591, Victor, ID 83455, or call (208) 354-8522.
- Contact Dr. Lynn Meeks at the Idaho State Dept. of Education, (208) 334-2113, for information about the statewide writing contest *WRITE ON! IDAHO.* Winning entries in each district are displayed in the capitol building and then made available for other publications.

MONTANA

- The Office of the Montana Superintendent of Public Instruction will help you find statewide programs and residencies for young writers. Contact Jan Hahn, Education Specialists, Montana OPI, Helena, MT 59620, or call (406) 444-3714.
- *Signatures From Big Sky* was founded by three education groups in 1991. This annual Montana student literary/art publication accepts work in any genre. Deadline is Feb. 1 for spring publication. Contact the magazine c/o Shirley M. Olson, 928 4th Avenue, Laurel, MT 59044.
- The Montana Division of the American Association of University Women sponsors an annual essay contest with prizes, open to all Montana students, grades 10-12. Contact Student Contest Coordinator, 20200 West Dickerson #58, Bozeman, MT 59715.
- The Montana Chapter of the National Council of Teachers of English sponsors a program that recognizes excellence in student literary magazines. Contact Linda Edwards, 301 8th Avenue South, Lewiston MT 59457.
- *The Montana Writing Project* works to inspire young writers and teachers of young writers. Different programs are set

up annually. Contact Dr. Beverly Ann Chin, Director, MWP, Department of English, University of Montana, Missoula, MT 59812, or call her at (406) 243-0211.
- *The Annual Fran McDermott Writing Convention* takes place in spring in different state locations. The conference consists of workshops and readings by guest writers for high school students selected by teachers. For current information contact Corby Skinner or Laila Nelson with the YMCA Writer's Voice, 402 N. 32nd, Billings, MT 59101, or call (406) 248-1685.
- The YMCA Writer's Voice also hosts writing workshops throughout the year, some of which are for young writers. Contact Corby Skinner or Laila Nelson at the number above.

OREGON

- *Skipping Stones* is a quarterly, non-profit children's magazine that seeks artwork, photography, and writing in every language from and for children. Contact the magazine at P.O. Box 3939, Eugene, OR 97403, or call (503) 342-4952.
- Oregon Press Women sponsors a journalism contest for high school students. Categories are features, photography, news, and editorials. Contest is judged by professional journalists. First place winners are entered into the *National Federation of Press Women Contest.* Guidelines are sent to Oregon High Schools. Contact Corky Kirkpatrick at 230 Forest Cove Rd., West Linn, OR 97068, or call (503) 675-6958, extension 2538.
- *The Asterisk,* a newspaper for prize-winning high school journalists, is published by the Oregon Press Women, Inc., P.O. Box 2534, Portland, OR 97225-0354.
- The Oregon Council of Teachers of English and Eastern Oregon State College sponsor the *Oregon Student Magazine Contest.* Open to all student and teacher projects in magazine format. Contact David Axelrod, EOSC, English Department, La Grand, OR 97850.
- The Oregon Students Writing and Art Foundation has published several anthologies of student writing called *Treasures.* High school students are involved in the whole production process. *Treasures III* (spring of 1993) will have stories from

---

The text of articles and essays is set in Weiss.

1 2 3 4 5 6 7 8 9 0 - = a b c d e f g h i j k l m n o p q r s t u v w x y z [ ] \ ; ' , . /
~ ! @ # $ % ^ & * ( ) _ + A B C D E F G H I J K L M N O P Q R S T U V W X Y Z { } | : " < > ?
± — , · ° ‡ fl fi › ¤ ⁄ ¡ ™ £ ¢ ∞ § ¶ • ª º – ≠ Œ Σ ®Ø π " ' « » ' " ∏ ^ ¨ Á ˇ ‰ ´ „
Œ Å Í Î ˜ Ó Ô Ò Ú Å ƒ © ˙ ∆ ° … Æ Ω ≈ Ç √ ʃ µ ≤ ≥ ÷ ¸ ◊ ı ˜ Â ¯ ˘ ¿

Japanese and Oregon students. There will be two editions, one in English, the other in Japanese. Contact Chris Weber for information about future projects at P.O. Box 2100, Portland, OR 97208.

- The Oregon Department of Education and the Oregon Council of Teachers of English sponsor the *Oregon Writing Festival*. This is a one-day spring conference to encourage the efforts of students and teachers to improve writing. It features workshops and guest writers. Students in grades 1-12 are welcome; districts decide which students will attend. Contact the festival c/o Julie Stewart, Gresham High School, 1200 N. Main Street, Gresham, OR 97030.

- LitEruption, Oregon's largest book fair and literary festival held each March in Portland, includes a children's room with young writers as well as adult authors. Contact Lorie Topinka, Artquake Office, 720 S.W. Washington, Ste. 100, Portland, OR 97207 or call (503) 227-2787.

- Physicians for Social Responsibility sponsors an annual writing contest open to Oregon students grades 7–12. Prizes are awarded. For the theme and guidelines, contact PSR, 921 S.W. Morrison, Ste. 500, Portland, OR 97205.

- Willamette Writers sponsors the annual *Kay Snow Writing Contest* which includes a student writer category. Contact the organization at 9045 S.W. Barbur Blvd., Ste. 5A, Portland, OR 97219, or call (503) 452-1592.

- *The Niche, the Bi-weekly High School Open Forum of Free Expression*, is offered free to high schools in the greater Portland area. The magazine accepts all submissions, except "really sicko material," and "hateful, pathological discourses" against any group. Contact *The Niche*, 7950 N. Seward Avenue, Portland, OR 97217.

- *Portland Poetry Festival* holds an annual writing contest which includes categories for primary grades, grades 4–8, and high schoolers. Write the festival for details at P.O. Box 8452, Portland, OR 97207, or call (503) 236-4893.

WASHINGTON

- The Washington State Office of the Superintendent of Public Instruction will send you a statewide bulletin of confer-

ences and programs available for young writers. Request the bulletin from the Supervisor of Reading/Language Arts, Washington OSPI, Old Capital Building, FG11, Olympia, WA 98504-3211.

- The *Campus Journal* is a quarterly magazine for junior and senior high school students in the West. It uses freelance material from students only. Pay is in copies. Accepts student fiction, nonfiction, poetry, biography, reviews, op/ed, artwork, and photography. Student staff works with publisher. Request guidelines from Student Publishing Services, Inc., P.O. Box 3177, Kirkland, WA 98083-3177, or call (206) 889-9762.

- *Lighthouse* is a bimonthly magazine that accepts children's stories and poetry. Write magazine for guidelines at P.O. Box 1377, Auburn, WA 98071-1377.

- *Young Voices* publishes stories, articles, essays, and poems by students, elementary through high school, six times a year. Magazine pays for accepted material. Write to P.O. Box 2321, Olympia, WA 98507 or call (206) 357-4683.

- *The Pacific Northwest Writers Conference* welcomes young writers throughout the Pacific Northwest to the annual *High School Writing Contest and Conference*. The theme for 1993 was "Young Writers Creating New Worlds." Fiction, nonfiction, and poetry deadlines are usually in December. The convention takes place in early Spring. Contact PNWC, 2033 Sixth Avenue, Seattle, WA 98121, or call (206) 443-3807.

- In April, Eastern Washington University sponsors the annual *Young Writers Conference*, a three-state conference for eastern Washington, Oregon, and Idaho writers. There are sections for grade 4–6 and 7–12. In addition, there are workshops for teachers, administrators, and parents. Award-winning authors of children's books are featured at a public reception. Registration forms are sent to schools. Contact Marianne Nelson, EWU, MS-25, Cheney, WA 99004, or call (509) 359-6032.

- In spring, Seattle Pacific University sponsors the annual *Young Authors Conference* for young writers grades 1–8 in western Washington and Oregon. Apply through school beginning in January. Contact

Nancy Johnson, School of Education, SPU, Seattle, WA 98119.

- *Bumbershoot, the Seattle Arts Festival*, takes place every Labor Day weekend and includes readings by winners of the young writers competition. Students in grades 6 through 12 are invited to submit poetry and prose to the Bumbershoot Literary Arts Jury. The Jury selects twelve winners who receive $100 savings bonds and two invitations to the festival. They read their work in the Bookfair Pavilion. Deadline for entries is February. Write to *Bumbershoot Young Writers*, c/o One Reel, P.O. Box 9750, Seattle, WA 98109-0750.

- Washington Poets Association sponsors an annual poetry contest with prizes for young poets. Categories are for grades 6–9 and 9–12. Winners are invited to an awards luncheon and a student reading in Tumwater. Deadlines are usually in April. Contact Betty Fukuyama, 112 Regents Blvd., Apt. 1, Tacoma, WA 98466.

- *Centrum Foundation* in Port Townsend sponsors annual writing workshops for high school students. Two separate week-long residencies are awarded to 40–60 students selected on the basis of manuscript submissions. Apply by December 1. Workshops are held in March and April. Contact the Education Coordinator, *Centrum*, P.O. Box 1158, Port Townsend, WA 98368.

- *The Puget Sound Writing Program for Young Writers* holds an annual week-long workshop for students in grades 5–11. The workshops are usually in the summer. Deadlines are in the spring. Contact Linda Clifton, co-director, PSWP, Department of English, GN-30, University of Washington, Seattle, WA 98195, or call (206) 543-0141.

Scholle Sawyer was just recently a "young writer" herself and had a good time sending away lots of poems to older people in offices who sometimes liked them and gave her money. Now she sends away articles, but doesn't get so much money.

SECTION IV

Make the Most of Your Press Release

Joe Devine

When I first got into publishing, I was uncomfortable with press releases. They seemed so serious, conservative, and responsible. I tried to go along with the crowd by writing a standard press release to announce the birth of my book *Commas Are Our Friends: The Easy, Enjoyable Way to Master Grammar and Punctuation*. The release was so depressingly dull I could not bear to mail it. You'd think I'd get expressions of gratitude from all the editors and producers I didn't send it to, but nary a word of thanks. Ingrates!

Not all books lend themselves to a brief press release. That was certainly true of *Commas Are Our Friends*. It is a whimsical review of the basics of English grammar and punctuation and is composed of three novellas. One tells the story of an archaeologist who sails half way around the world to prove that all the great explorers (Columbus, Magellan, Captain Cook, etc.) used the same water. In another, a young woman replaces the packing in her parachute with popcorn — to play it safe — and then willingly goes aloft clinging to a wing strut. And then there's that tired old plot device of training a gerbil to speak so that he can teach English grammar to school children.

How do you get all that into a press release and still leave the impression that you can be trusted with power tools?

I could not do it and decided to emphasize writing style instead of text. I cooked up a little tongue-in-cheek trifle entitled "The Human Costs of Literary Creation" and sent it to book editors along with a reply card. Many cards were returned and I received many reviews, some of which were real goodies. I tried the same procedure with radio producers and was able to get several interviews. Book sales improved significantly.

"Costs" was reprinted four times, including an appearance in "Publishers' Focus," the Northwest Association of Book Publisher's newsletter. I wound up selling first North American serial rights to Writer's Digest for their *Writer's Life* feature. The combined potential readership for that release was about 500,000. Not bad for a guy who needs written permission to operate a power drill.

The next year I issued another press release entitled "Green Stone Publications Takes Consumer Protection to a New Level." It did not get as much circulation as "Costs" because I was concentrating on other kinds of promotion. They both went out in April, so I call them my spring informals.

I honestly believe that conservative, informational, and responsible press releases are a gamble. They are all pretty much alike, which makes them easy to discard unread. Be creative, be original, and be different. Try for off-the-wall humor. Guarantee a reading by making your press release enjoyably unique. Recipients will appreciate your efforts and be more receptive to your message.

There is, however, a troublesome downside: you may be depriving yourself of the soothing serenity of the power saw.

(Samples of Joe Devine's press releases are reproduced on the following pages.)

Joe Devine is owner of Green Stone Publications in Seattle and a recovering English teacher.

For: Green Stone Publications
P.O. Box 15623
Seattle, WA 98115-0623

Contact: Joe Devine (206) 524-4744

To: Book Editor
For Immediate release

Green Stone Publications takes consumer protection to a new level!!

Our Guarantee: If you are not completely satisfied with *Commas Are Our Friends* by Joe Devine, we will write you the most sympathetic letter you have ever received in your life--and it's free!

Pathos, pity, poignancy--we got 'em all. And we gladly share them with those folks who come first with us, our customers. One of our letters brought tears to the eyes of Idi Amin. Another reduced a motorcycle cop to a blubbering hulk. Still another moved a Midwest banker to wait a whole week before foreclosing on a ninety-three year old invalid who had one payment to go on her thirty year mortgage.

Our carefully selected letter writers were all commiseration majors in college and two of them have match-book M.A.'s in bathos. Each has counseled extensively at half-way houses for fallen TV evangelists, recovering I.R.S. agents and former S&L loan officers. Our people can generate sincere, heart-wrenching compassion on command. Is that customer service, or what?

Each letter is hand delivered by uniformed personnel (via *le rate bulke)*, and every tenth letter is lightly perfumed with our exclusive Parisian scent, *Empathique* (now available to our clients--$3.75 the litre).

We have the field to ourselves on this one because--believe it or not--no other publisher has the courage to match this offer.

Dave Barry, James J. Kilpatrick and Edwin Newman have risked their reputations to endorse *Commas Are Our Friends*. This is your chance to join them. Reply card enclosed.

-30-

For: Green Stone Publications
P.O. Box 15623
Seattle, WA 98115-0623

Contact: Joe Devine (206) 524-4744

To: Book Editor

For Immediate Release

Everybody knows the price of a book, but how many know the cost?

HUMAN COSTS OF LITERARY CREATION FINALLY REVEALED

For the first time ever the human costs of writing have been measured in dollars and cents. The heartaches, the sacrifices, the psychic bruises--they're all there. Herewith the human costs of the 2042 first printing of *Commas Are Our Friends* by Joe Devine:

1.	The agony of creation, the anguish of being a sensitive artist in a harsh and cruel world	$4,415.99
2.	The sting of anonymity, the pain of not being lionized by total strangers	$1,831.35
3.	The aching injustice of not receiving a large advance from greedy, money-mad publishers	$3,965.08
4.	The annoyance of having people insist that the book be published before they pay for it	$2,942.74
5.	The hurt and humiliation of not making even one pre-publication best seller list	$2,627.50
6.	The shock of being snubbed by the Pulitzer Prize Committee	$3,500.00
7.	The misery of receiving a balanced, perceptive and completely honest review	$4,726.13
8.	Fresh, creative, original ideas	$ 3.41
		$24,012.20

There you have it. Figures don't lie. The human costs come to $11.76 per book, but *Commas Are Our Friends* retails for $11.95. That leaves a profit of $.19 a copy, thus honoring Dr. Johnson's dictum: "No man but a blockhead ever wrote except for money."

This book has been praised by James J. Kilpatrick, Edwin Newman and Dave Barry. Reply card enclosed.

Creative Ways To Promote Your Book

Tena Spears

The number of ways to promote books is as infinite as the number of books on the market. There are always crucial elements of a book campaign that must be followed, but in addition to those, there are a few that are frequently ignored, simply because of time limitations. I'd like to share a few special promotion ideas that have proven very effective for me. Here are some of my personal favorites:

I. Seminars/Workshops

If your book lends itself well to the workshop or seminar format, why not offer a free demonstration or participatory/hands-on workshop?

For the past three years, I've organized the *Write Now* handwriting improvement workshop at Portland State University in Portland, Oregon. Since we offer a number of titles appropriate for grades K-adult on this topic, we invite children and adults. Although we do sell handwriting materials at the seminar, the main purpose is to provide information about the program. The selling table is located outside of the auditorium and no one is pressured in any way to buy anything. Last year over 400 people attended and filled the auditorium. The twenty people we had to turn away were given a free copy of one of our lower priced books, articles, and ordering information. Although they may have been initially disappointed, they left knowing that we stood behind our invitation and our program.

Treat people the way you want to be treated. When you invite them to participate in a free event, don't make them feel badly if they don't buy something from you. If you do your job with press releases and announcements and attract the right audience, people will buy your book. They may make the decision later if you provide them with adequate information through your presentation or brochures. This annual workshop has been an enormous success for our program.

Hints/Reminders:

1) Get the word out about the workshop. Newspapers will readily announce free seminars and workshops. Contact any organization you believe might be interested in your program and ask them to include a brief mention of the event in their in-house newsletters. Remember, these people have lead times that vary from two weeks to five months. You can also have fliers printed and ask your local bookstores, coffee shops, and libraries to post them for you.

2) Plan well in advance to provide adequate time for announcing the event — 4 to 5 months.

3) Offer the event free.

4) Don't make buying your book a requirement for attending.

5) Try to have your church, community college, school, parks bureau, etc., sponsor the workshop by allowing you to use its facility. This not only saves you money, but also gives you, in a sense, the organization's endorsement.

6) Provide brochures, worksheets, and hand-outs that can be taken away.

7) Make sure you've got enough people on hand to deal with the attendees — bring friends and relatives to help, if necessary.

8) Have someone else handle selling books so you can concentrate on the workshop.

If you're at a loss

for marketing ideas,

go to your library.

As a group, librarians are

some of the most helpful people

I've ever met.

If your book has an educational message, your local college or university may allow you to offer the seminar on its campus for free. You may need to find a department willing to sponsor you. This type of demonstration/promotion can be applied to almost any subject that has an educational message.

II. The Direct Approach

Mailing lists. If you're going to try to reach people through the mail, you need to have a brochure, flier, or postcard that has been carefully designed with that particular market in mind. Although there are a number of Direct Mail agencies who will rent you their mailing lists, I've found what I call the *Direct Approach* to be much more affordable and very reliable. The *Direct Approach*, essentially means going directly to the original source for mailing lists or labels. The best way to explain this is to give you an example. On a recent campaign for the book, *Getting Funded: A Complete Guide To Proposal Writing*, I found this approach very effective. As you might guess, this particular book has a large audience in social service agencies. Rather than call one of the large list brokers, I instead went to the library to find out if there was an organization that all or most social service agencies belong to. There is. This organization had a directory of all its member organizations throughout the United States. I called these agencies and discovered that the majority of them were willing to *give* me their mailing lists. Those who were unable to give me their lists, often agreed to barter and accepted copies of the book in lieu of paying cash for their lists. Several agreed to send the brochure along free with their next mailing or do a review or brief mention of the book in their newsletter.

Hint: Check the *Encyclopedia of Associations* at your local library.

III. Specialty Catalogs

We all get them. If you have a mailbox, you get specialty catalogs. These catalogs range from the obscure (butterfly catching, orchid growing) to the more common (cat lovers, books on tape). Although I get annoyed by junk mail, I do enjoy trying to figure out where (list broker, mail order house, etc.)

they purchased my name.

The first place to look for appropriate catalogs is your own mailbox. Look at them before you throw them away — you might discover that your book fits in perfectly with their theme. The next thing you'll want to do is go to the library and look for *The Directory of Mail Order Catalogs*. This directory contains literally thousands of catalog companies, their addresses and phone numbers. The product buyer is the person you'll need to contact. Usually, these folks want to see the cover (not the book) along with articles or reviews. Remember, they sell through a catalog — your cover and title are very important to them. Even if the topic is appropriate, they may not buy it simply because the cover isn't what they were looking for.

The book, *Write Now: A Complete Self-Teaching Program for Better Handwriting* is a perfect example of a book well suited for this type of marketing. It now appears in a number of specialty catalogs, including *Fahrney's Pens* (a writing instrument distributor), *Big Books from Small Presses, Cahill & Company*, and several home school supply catalogs (i.e. *God's World, Timberdoodle, Sycamore Tree*).

One final word of encouragement. If you're at a loss for marketing ideas, go to your library. As a group, librarians are some of the most helpful people I've ever met. They truly enjoy sleuthing and have helped me uncover some incredible leads.

For the past seven years, Tena Spears has been publicist for Portland State University's Continuing Education Press. She has been responsible for gaining national recognition for many of the press's titles.

ADOBE CASLON ITALIC SWASH CAPITALS

A B C D E F
G H I J K L
M N O P Q
R S T U V
W X Y Z

In Search of the Elusive Book Review

Scholle Sawyer

You've got a fistful of galleys and stamps on your tongue; what do you do next? Who requires galleys? Who reviews small press titles with some regularity?

Acquiring reviews and other "free media" takes planning far in advance. A little research can save money. You'll find that reviewers demand anything from a copy of the publisher's catalog, to galleys only, to two hardcover copies and author background. Some require galleys as much as four months before publication. Many others accept or prefer finished copies. However, they too want those copies on their desks well before they reach the bookstores.

We hope a look at the variety and specificity of the listed requirements helps you plan your promotion strategy. As you browse, note which reviewers are interested in the subjects or genres in which you specialize. Also some, such as *Hungry Mind Review* and *Voice Literary Supplement*, often review books after their publication date. These publications and others, like *The Bloomsbury Review*, often work with themes and seek books that will fit with certain issues. You'll be one step ahead if you have their editorial schedules in your promotion folder.

Accompany the book with a complete publicity sheet including title, subtitle, author, translator, editor, ISBN, binding information, publication date, pagination, and price. Review media usually welcome any information relevant to the book. Most editors request that publishers do not call to ask if the book has been received or if it has been scheduled for review.

Most of this information was gathered from a survey we sent to reviewers. We also used the Council of Literary Magazines and Presses' *Publicity Basics: A Guide for Literary Magazines and Presses* (1992).

The Bloomsbury Review, 1028 Bannock Street, Denver, CO 80204. (303) 892-0620.

Attn: Tom Auer. Circ: 50,000. Number of reviews per issue: 100. 25 feature-length and 75 bibliography, notices, and lists.

Each issue centers around a theme: "The Whole Person: Psychology, Philosophy, Love," "The American West: History, Art, Literature." Write for editorial schedule. Reviews paperbacks and hardcovers 2–3 months before publication. Send one galley.

Booklist, American Library Association, 50 East Huron, Chicago, IL 60611. Attn: John Mort, Adult Books; Sally Estes, Youth Books; Ilene Cooper, Children's Books. Circ: 31,000. Number of reviews per issue: 300–500.

Covers all areas except narrowly technical or academic. Critical medium for children's books. Reviews paperback and hardcover publications 2–4 months before publication. Send two galleys; if unavailable, send one book.

The Bookwatch, 166 Miramar Avenue, San Francisco, CA 94112. (415) 587-7009. Attn: Diane C. Donovan, Editor. Circ: 50,000. Reviews per issue: 125 capsule.

Specializes in history/culture, art, science fiction, young adult fiction/nonfiction, travel, consumer interest. No novels, plays/drama, poetry, inspirational, religious (unless crossover), romance, or reprints. Publication price/ordering information must be on/with book. Reviews paperback or hardcover originals upon or before publication. Send one copy.

Chicago Tribune Books, 435 N. Michigan Avenue, Chicago, IL 60611. (312) 222-3232. Attn: Clarence Peterson, Paperback Reviewer; Joseph Coates, Reviewer.

Specializes in publications that have "good trade potential." However, no cookbooks, how-to manuals, diet books, or business books. Reviews hardcover and paperbacks before publication. Galleys preferred, but early copy of finished book also acceptable. No photocopies or boxed manuscripts. If review is run, a tear sheet will be sent within five days of the run date. Send one galley.

CHOICE Magazine, 100 Riverview Center, Middletown, CT 06457. (203) 347-6933. Attn: Helen M. MacLam, Publisher Liaison. Circ: 4,700. Number of reviews per issue: 600.

Specializes in academic books appropriate for undergraduate libraries. No fiction, travel, how-to, reprints, foreign language materials. Reviews hardcover books. Paperback OK if there is no hardcover. No galleys. Send one copy as soon as the finished copy is available.

The Coast Book Review Service, P.O. Box 4174, Fullerton, CA 92634. (714) 990-0432. Attn: The Editors, Al Ralston and Don Cannon. Circ: 125 California newspapers, combined circulation of 6.5 million. Reviews per issue: 12–14.

No unsolicited books for review. Catalogs and publication notices will be considered. Reviews paper and hardcover books upon publication.

H.W. Wilson Company, 950 University Avenue, Bronx, NY, 10452. (212) 588-8400. Attn: Nancy Wong, Cumulative Book Index. Circulation of books: monthly and one annual.

Reviews hardcover or paperbacks in all subject areas. Send one copy. No galleys.

The Horn Book Magazine, 14 Beacon Street, Boston, MA 02108-3704. (617) 227-1555. Attn: Anita Silvey.

Published six times a year. Specializes in hardcover books for children and young adults.

The Horn Book Guide, 14 Beacon Street, Boston, MA 02108-3704. (617) 227-1555. Attn: Ann A. Flowers.

Reviews children's books twice a year.

Hungry Mind Review, 1648 Grand Avenue, St. Paul, MN 55105. (612) 699-2610. Attn: Bart Schneider, Editor; Philip Patrick, Associate Editor; Susan Marie Swanson, Children's Book Supplement Editor.

Each quarterly issue centers around a theme. Write or call for editorial schedule. Poetry and fiction included in every issue. Reviews paper and hardcover books before or after publication. Books a year or two old and reprints considered if appropriate. Publishers encouraged to send catalogs and read publication to become familiar with format. Small presses often featured. Send one galley or book 3–4 months before appropriate *Hungry Mind* issue goes to press.

John Barkham Reviews, 27 E. 65th Street, New York, NY 10021. (212) 879-9705. Attn: John Barkham. Circ.: Syndicated to 23 newspapers. Number of reviews per issue: 6–7.

Specializes in general literature for gen-eral readers. Especially concert (not popular) music, good fiction, biography, the arts, history. Prefers hardcover to paperback titles, but occasionally does review them. Send one copy before publication. No galleys.

Kirkus Reviews, 200 Park Avenue S., New York, NY 10003. (212) 777-4554. Attn: Anne Larsen, Fiction Editor; Jeffrey Zaleski, Nonfiction Editor; Joanna Long, Children's Books Editor.

Kliatt, 33 Bay State Road, Wellesley, MA 02181. (617) 237-7577. Attn: Claire Rosser/Paula Rohrlick. Circ: 2300. Number of reviews per issue: 300.

Specializes in young adult and general adult paperbacks. Send one paperback upon publication.

Los Angeles Times Book Review, Times Mirror Square, Los Angeles, CA 90053. (213) 237-5000. Attn: Sonja Bolle, Book Review Editor; Alex Raskin and Georgia Jones-Davis, Assistant Editors.

No travel, cooking, entertainment industry, self-help, how-to, business, or humor. Department prefers to receive 5–6 copies of a publisher's catalog for the season or year as far in advance as is possible. Bound galleys should be sent at least two months in advance of publication. Note if author is from the West. Finished books must be sent once a review is published.

New York Review of Books, 250 W. 57th Street, #1321, New York, NY 10107. (212) 757-8070. Attn: Robert Silvers, Editor; Barbara Epstein, Fiction Editor.

Generally covers university press nonfiction. *NYROB* does cover independent presses from time to time. *Publicity Basics* says there are three top considerations that effect the possibility of getting a review: regular contributors, concurrent events, and the book. It suggests publishers send a galley to both the editor and a regular contributor who has a history of interest in the topic. An artful letter explaining the book's connection with another recent title or current event can also help.

The New York Times Book Review, 229 West 43rd Street, New York, NY 10036. (212) 556-1942. Attn: Rebecca Sinkler, Book Review Editor;

Marvin Siegel, Deputy Editor; Eden Ross Lipson, Editor, Children's Books; Michael Anderson, Nonfiction In Brief.

Specializes in most areas. However, no self-help, how-to, romance, horror fiction, self-published, textbooks, or New Age. Send galleys 3–4 in advance of publication. Send a finished copy as soon as possible as a review will not be published without one. Publishers are also welcome to send catalogs.

Patrician Productions, 145 W. 58th Street, New York, NY 10019. (212) 265-5612. Attn: Vic Kassery. Or: Maureen Crean, John Curtis, Manny Morales. Circ: listeners on radio and TV. Number of reviews: 500/year.

Specializes in nonfiction only. Reviews paper and hardcover upon publication. Send one copy.

Publishers Weekly, 249 W. 17th Street, New York, NY 10011. Fax (212) 463-6631. Attn: Genevieve Stuttaford, Nonfiction (212) 463-6781; Sybil Steinberg, Fiction (212) 463-6780; Diane Roback, Children's (212) 463-6768; Penny Kaganoff, Paperbacks (212) 463-6778; Molly McQuade, Associate Editor and How-To (212) 463-6777; Dulcy Brainard (212) 463-6782, Mystery & Suspense; Sam Baker, Editorial Assistant (212) 463-6782.

PW has a five page guidelines packet with specifics for each book category cited above. Please write for packet as even a summary of it would engulf this section. In brief, the majority of categories require galleys at least three months in advance of publication. However, F&Gs of books with illustrations are generally required 8-12 weeks pre-publication.

Rainbo Electronic Reviews, 8 Duran Court, Pacifica, CA 94044. (415) 359-0221. Attn: Maggie Ramirez. Circ: 500,000. Format: Data-print. Number of reviews per issue: 10.

Specializes in almost any subject. No New Age. Reviews paper and hardcover 3 months before publication. Send one copy.

Reference Book Review, P.O. Box 190954, Dallas, TX 75219. (214) 690-5882. Attn: Cameron Northouse. Circ.: 1,000. Number of reviews per issue: 75-100.

Specializes in references books in all

subject areas. Reviews paper and hardcover publications. No galleys. Send one copy upon publication.

Reference & Research Book News, 5606 N.E. Hassalo Street, Portland, OR 97213-3640. (503) 281-9230. Circ: 1,700.

Specializes in reference and scholarly works of interest to academic, public, and corporate librarians. Reviews hardcover books upon publication. Send one copy.

San Francisco Chronicle Book Review, 275 Fifth Street, San Francisco, CA 94103. (415) 777-7042. Attn: Patricia Holt, Book Editor.

San Francisco Review of Books, 555 De Haro Street, #220, San Francisco, CA 94107. (415) 252-7708. Attn: Donald Paul. Circ.: 10,000. Format: 8 3/8 x 10 7/8. Number of reviews per issue: 40.

Specializes in eclectic and "hopefully unpredictable" subject areas, especially nonfiction and children's titles. Send galleys only as soon as possible. Reviews paperback and hardcover. Prefers information on author and where s/he lives. Send one galley.

School Library Journal, 249 W. 17th Street, New York, NY 10011. (212) 645-0067. Attn: Trevelyn Jones.

Specializes in new children's and young adult general trade books and original paperbacks from established publishers. Also provides coverage of small press books that seem important to library collections, are of national interest, and readily available from national distributors. No reissues, textbooks, books for parents or teachers. Send two copies of the book within or before the month of publication. Galleys accepted, but must be followed by bound books. Send publisher's catalog, two copies, bibliographical information: author, title, binding(s), price(s), publication month and year, ISBN, Library of Congress Catalog Number, and whether or not Cataloging in Publication data will appear in the book.

Small Press, Kymbolde Way, Wakefield, RI. (401) 789-0074. Attn: Wendy Reid Crisp. Circ.: 10,000.

Format: 8 1/2 x 11, 100 pages, four-color cover. Number of reviews per issue: 200–300.

Send self-addressed stamped postcard with galleys or review copies. Book reviewers will return card if they do not review. If they do review, tear sheets will be sent. Reviews paperback and hardcover books upon publication. Send one galley.

Small Press Review, P.O. Box 100, Paradise, CA 95967. (916) 877-6110. Attn: Len Fulton. Circ.: 3,500. Number of reviews per issue: 10-15.

Specializes in publications by small presses only. Reviews paper and hardcover books upon publication. Send one copy.

USA Today, 1000 Wilson Boulevard, Arlington, VA 22229. (703) 276-3400. Attn: Robert Wilson, Book Editor.

Voice Literary Supplement, VV Publishing Corporation, 36 Cooper Square, New York, NY 10003. (212) 475-3300. Attn: Ms. M. Mark, Editor.

Often holds a book until it fits into an issue. Send galleys and finished books.

The Washington Post, 1150 15th Street N.W., Washington, D.C. 20071. (202) 334-7882. Attn: Nina King, Editor.

No self-help, how-to, technical, or scholarly books. Poetry is published every other month. Good record of reviewing small press titles. Send galleys as far ahead of publication as possible. Hardbacks OK. If an original paperback, mark clearly to avoid receiving low priority. Attach publicity information firmly to book. If the book is going to be reviewed, publisher will receive a postcard requesting two finished copies.

Scholle Sawyer is a recent graduate of Oberlin College in Oberlin, Ohio and lives in Portland, Oregon. She currently spends much of her time walking her dog in the rain.

Virtual Publishing

Ivar Nelson

I grew up eagerly awaiting the moment on Christmas morning when my brother, sister, and I raced downstairs to find out what packages awaited under the tree. Part of that anticipation was the knowledge that one of those packages would certainly be a book from Viking Press, where our uncle worked. I can still remember those editions of McCloskey's *Make Way for Ducklings* and *Homer Price*.

In those days, the publishing industry ran along traditional lines: an author had a manuscript that was accepted or rejected by a publishing house and then edited with due care for grammar and content by an in-house editor. The book was designed, produced and printed, often by the publisher, and then marketed and sold by the publisher through house reps to bookstores. A direct relationship existed between author and publisher, although not usually to the degree of involvement or erudition that famous Scribner's editor Maxwell Perkins lavished on his writers.

While that "Algonquian" concept of authorship, editing, and publishing remains one of our most enduring myths in the publishing business, it now barely conceals a system characterized by fragmentation, dispersal, and complexity, where the path to being published is taken through an ever-changing maze.

Consider the case of *The Smithsonian Guide to Historic America* series, of which twelve books have been published covering the different geographical regions of the United States. The books are distributed by Workman; published by Stewart, Tabori & Chang, who owns the copyright; printed in Japan; blessed by the Smithsonian Institution; and created by a staff of twelve editors, designers, cartographers, and data-entry people. And that doesn't cover the funding or the original idea.

Traditional monolithic publishing has disappeared, replaced by a system whose functional parts are like chemical compounds, which can be pulled apart into their separate elements and then reassembled to make a different compound. Remember in Intro Chem in high school putting together the brightly colored balls like so many pop beads to create different molecules? That's the new publishing system, where writers, financiers, editors, designers, printers, and marketing people are popped apart and put back together for each new book. The parts of this many segmented operation, the atoms of the molecule, are the functions needed to make and market the book, whether it is a centennial history for Kendrick, Idaho, or the self-ploitation blockbuster *Madonna* assembled by NYC mega-packager Nicholas Calloway.

The traditional function of the publisher has become pretty much limited by self-definition and corporate management to the roles of financing and marketing, and even the marketing function is being turned over to others. It is no accident that the suits upstairs in the New York skyscrapers are increasing in number while the editors below become fewer. As financing becomes more complex and the stakes larger, the people who understand it become more valuable. It is not uncommon, as happens with a project I'm now doing, that the money comes from a number of sources: two foundations, the staff and support of one university, a publisher at a different university, and guaranteed advanced sales. That the eventual income for many books will never repay the cost often doesn't seem as important as other needs: to provide information, advance careers, or promote another project. Often the book itself is just the nucleus of a complex web of financial deals involving foreign rights, book club editions, magazine excerpts, and movie/television deals. I got my first call for a compact disk version of one of our books last fall.

No longer is the person who has the original idea necessarily the person who writes the book. Where we used to have an author or an occasional ghost writer, we now have a whole smorgasbord of anthologizers, researchers, writing teams, re-writers, and various kinds of editors as writers. It no longer follows that the name on the book jacket in big letters had anything to do with the creative work inside. Closer examination might even reveal an inverse relationship between size of author's name and act of writing.

Publishing houses should board up their front doors; if anyone ever did use them, they rarely do now. This doesn't mean that writers must have agents. It does mean that they need to locate the back doors, of which there are many. In addition to agents, there are friends who know editors, colleagues who went to school with a publisher, sales reps who can send a manuscript in against the marketing flow of books com-

Traditional monolithic

publishing has disappeared,

to be replaced by

a system

whose functional parts

are like

chemical compounds…

ing out, bookstore owners who know acquisition editors from conventions, professors who once worked in the presses' stockroom, and book packagers. I have received ideas or manuscripts for published books from the mother of my daughter's friend, from the parents of a local gemologist, and from casual conversation at a spaghetti feed.

Under increasing pressure to acquire property, editors at larger houses are best approached with a fifteen-second or one-paragraph appeal that mentions similar successful books, favorable popular trends, and a major intellectual or emotional theme. In the search for a publisher, the proposal is a key which needs to be fitted into a large number of locks before finding one that the key will open. That's usually more productive than trying to change the key to fit a particular lock.

That badly edited books are almost literally a dime a dozen can be confirmed by a quick look at any remainder table in the local bookstore. The most ardent computer fanatics have painfully learned that Spell-check is not a substitute for a good editor who will put pen to paper and help with organization, writing, and grammar. It has not only been T.S. Eliot, for whom Ezra Pound edited *The Waste Land*, who has had a good work made into a great one by inspired editing. Publishers have discovered that retaining the organizational and line editing, which is a necessary function in the book-making process, is often cheaper and more easily handled as a free-lance element rather than an in-house function at the publisher. Good copy editors and indexers, much in demand in the industry, can ply their trade sitting at a computer in Martinique as easily as in Milwaukee.

There's always been a tug-a-war between publisher and designer, but with the increasing role of the designer as independent contractor, there is much less interaction between the publishing staff and the designer. The designer becomes someone who conveys the book concept in the design, but is less involved in marketing and content decisions. The involvement of the designer can be as little as doing a cover and the basic page format for a novel, or as much as designing each page for heavily illustrated books and doing marketing materials.

The enormous technological revolution in electronic production methods has hastened the fragmentation of the publishing industry by reducing the need for large production staffs at publishing houses. At their best, the various computerized pagination systems have allowed trained and experienced designers, compositors, and packaging people to set up shop as independents contracting with various publishers. At its worst, these systems have led new people to lose money trying to be publishers before they understood the process. In the excitement over desktop publishing, it is essential to remember that such systems are not publishing systems, but production systems, and that publishing involves much more than production. In the cost of publishing and selling a book, the non-printing production costs are relatively small.

The large number of short-run printers,

mostly located near Ann Arbor, Michigan, and the willingness of their sales and customer service people to deal with all levels of publishing expertise, have made printing more accessible. Their increasing ability to take books on disk, and to forego boards or mechanicals, reduces further the cost of production. The next step will be to bypass the negatives and go directly to plates from the disk. With large, highly-illustrated, color books, the communication revolution has made it as easy to deal with printers in

In the search

for a publisher,

the proposal is a key

which needs to be fitted

into a large number of locks

before finding one

that the key will open.

Singapore, Seoul, or Tokyo as it is with those in Tennessee. Because printing is the major cost of a book, print brokers become another element in making up the publishing molecule. In big houses, the struggle between editing and marketing is over. The salespeople have won, because in the short term, that is where the money is. With some books, control over their destiny has become so much a marketing question that major wholesalers and chain store buyers participate actively in publishing decisions. For many small presses, and some medium-sized ones, the marketing function is done by regional and national distributors, or larger publishers, who get a healthy percent of the income.

The versatility of this new publishing system is enormous, as a sheep-ranching editor in Enterprise, Oregon, can work with a university press in Chicago, or a *House Beautiful* photographer in Los Angeles can shoot Indian artifacts in Spokane, or a packager in Moscow, Idaho, can put together a book on children's play with a writer in Vancouver, British Columbia, a publisher in Boston, and a printer in Ann Arbor.

The dangers are manifest. Consistency of quality and profitability are difficult to maintain when the work is not done under one roof. Without a supporting staff working in one place, the coordinator of the process — the person who puts the molecule together — becomes increasingly important. Whether a publisher, press director, or book packager, the coordinator needs to recognize the vitality of the concept, the talent of the writer, the clarity of the editor, the creativity of the designer, and the salesmanship of the marketers, while simultaneously negotiating the financial support to make the book possible.

Much in the way that a molecule is bonded together by electricity, the often unstable publishing process is held together by the creative energy of the people involved and their mutually recognized desire to make good books. The challenge for all of us is to remain creative in the midst of such continually changing complexity.

So there's this Finnish artist in New York City who wants to do a cultural guide to Finland with a photographer from New York, a writer in Helsinki, and a designer in Marblehead, Massachusetts, while using funding from the Finnish Lottery and a packager in Moscow, Idaho. Go figure!

Ivar Nelson publishes books under the Solstice Press imprint and also produces the Palouse Journal, *a regional magazine for the interior Northwest. As a book packager, he has worked with Harper-Collins, Doubleday, and the University of Washington Press, among others.*

Shaping the Author's Property: What Editors Do

Carol Rosenblum Perry

It's no one's and everyone's fault the term "editor" isn't self-explanatory. Our cultural lexicon is rife with words that, like David Byrne's Big Suit, let us slop around inside. What's worse, trying to explain one sloppy word inevitably invokes others. I should know: I've been an "editor" for over 14 years. But what precisely do I, and others nominally like me, do? And to what end?

Editors are of three types — language editors, content editors, and production editors — though there's considerable overlap among them. You really can't separate words, the province of the language editor, from what they mean, the province of the content editor. And you really can't separate either from the publication process, the province of the production editor.

- **Language editors** manipulate words in the interest of clarity. *Copy editors* operate close to the surface of writing, correcting errors in punctuation, capitalization, spelling, grammar, word usage, and publication format. They flag for the author any organizational problems detected and sometimes proofread. But copy editing has scant benefit if deep structure is unattended. *Substantive editors* (sometimes called *author's editors*) — my type — plumb the depths, reordering to ensure a tight logic flow, eliminating wordiness, checking for consistency, invigorating language, and, where appropriate, minimizing jargon; once the deep work's done, they surface to copy-edit. Sensitive to content, substantive editors flag where key information has been omitted, where speculation outdistances supporting evidence, where tone is wrong for the intended audience.

- **Content editors**, a pot pourri not readily

subcategorized, may evaluate submitted material, decide what gets published, set publication policy, language-edit or write — or some mix of the preceding. *Newspaper* and *magazine editors* head up departments, accept or reject submissions, work with authors to refine conditionally accepted contributions, or write policy or opinion pieces (editorials) generally without a by-line. Mastheads boast editors-in-chief, managing editors, senior editors, associate editors, assistant editors, contributing editors, feature editors, picture editors, book-review editors, and more. *Editors of scientific or technical journals* and *editors of technical books* both are specialists in the field. Journal editors oversee review by technical referees of submitted manuscripts and have ultimate authority to accept or reject; book editors solicit and review chapters from other specialists, then oversee revisions. Both generally publish through an outside press. (The term *technical editor,* sometimes applied to the editor of a technical book, may also apply to a language editor wordsmithing technical material.) *Publishing-house editors* (sometimes called *acquisitions editors*) advise house authors on drafts, confer with production personnel on book design, and may oversee manuscript miscellanea (e. g., securing permissions to reprint from copyright holders, indexing).

- **Production editors** (sometimes called *managing editors*) involve themselves with the physical publication of manuscripts, including copy preparation (typography, artwork, layout, copy editing, proofreading), product quality control, and press and bindery scheduling. However, size

…copyediting

has scant benefit

if deep structure

is unattended.

and type of publishing operation dictate the production editor's actual purview. For example, in a large, more traditional publications shop, where specialized tasks are distributed, the production editor might be responsible for marking the manuscript for typesetting and monitoring it through page proofs. In a desktop-publishing operation, where one or two people may handle everything, the production editor may be language editor, word processor, and designer all rolled into one; here, advances in electronic technology blur the lines between what once were distinct occupations.

Substantive editors

must know when

an author's

had enough,

even though they'd

like to do more…

The editor-author relationship is a sensitive one: whereas editors see themselves as collaborators, authors may see them as annoyances, necessary evils, even adversaries. The balance of power favors whoever has the final say. Authors generally have it over language editors because, ultimately, it's the author's manuscript, something the editor best not forget. Content editors generally have it over authors because, ultimately, it's the content editor's (or publisher's) volume, something the author cannot forget. The situation varies for editors overseeing production, where technological capability, time, and money may be the overriding arbiters.

The relationship I know intimately — that between author and substantive editor — is a ticklish one. Many authors are ambivalent about language editing, resisting

the process while admitting its value. One prickly writer used to arrive at my office door holding his nose, ready to "take my dose of castor oil"; but still, he came. For the substantive editor, who's far more invasive than the copy editor, psychology is 95% of the job because treading on authors' words is treading on their egos. Tact is the watchword. Beyond hands-on know-how, it takes skillful presentation of heavily marked copy to gain an author's trust and build a good working relationship. Substantive editors must know when an author's had enough, even though they'd like to do more; how to communicate what must be done in the guise of "suggestion"; when to insist, retreat, or recommend a third course of action; and how to make needed changes in the author's "style." Style, however defined, is forged, not granted as a birthright. "You've changed my style!" more often than not is the battle cry of those who haven't yet developed one; if style were distinct, no editor would change it. "You've changed my meaning!" more often than not points up muddiness in the original writing; if meaning were clear, no editor would change it. Ultimately, the key to success is a familiar one: compromise and mutual respect. Editors — too often the goat when things go badly and invisible when things go well — want their contributions valued. Authors — too often derided by editors for the writing problems that provide editors their very jobs — want the integrity of their manuscripts preserved.

"The writing process, properly conducted, is a process of selection" which assures that "the contract between writer and reader has been kept." So concludes William Sloane in *The Craft of Writing.* Editors provide the extra sets of eyes to see, the extra sets of ears to hear, what authors no longer can because they're too close to their material. It's to this end — to shape the author's property from what Sloane calls "the totality of his knowledge and his intention" — that editors collaborate with writers on behalf of readers.

As a writer-editor, Carol Rosenblum Perry knows both sides of the coin. Her book The Fine Art of Technical Writing, *which helps writers think their way through their work, grew from her experiences editing publishing scientists.*

How Should One Presume?

Ron McFarland

One evening shortly after the University of Idaho Press published *Idaho's Poetry: A Centennial Anthology* in 1988, I was invited to give a talk on it to a couple dozen UI faculty members and their spouses. From what I could gather, it was a sort of social-intellectual group, literati, virtuosi. At their best, such groups can be stimulating, even invigorating; at their worst, they can be pompous and pretentious. But that night they seemed to be at their best, and the food was good and the wine was excellent. I was proud of the anthology, which represented more than two years of hard work on my part and on that of my coeditor, William Studebaker, who writes and teaches at the College of Southern Idaho in Twin Falls. Moreover, the UI Press had done a fine, professional job with the book. I knew where the flaws were, and I knew they were my fault, but they weren't momentous.

I began by reading a poem or two from each of the five sections: Native Poems, the portion of the anthology I had struggled most with and in which I still have least confidence; The Pioneer Poets (1860-1900), the part I enjoyed doing most, the fruits of scanning microfilms of hundreds of Idaho newspapers in search of nuggets amidst the fool's gold, the doggerel; Poets of a New State (1900-1940), an almost overwhelming task that was made easier by Bess Foster Smith's anthology, *Sunlit Peaks*, which was published in 1931; The Third Generation (1940-1980), a considerable challenge, as the amount of poetry available seemed to be increasing exponentially; The Contemporaries, by definition the riskiest area of the anthology and the section for which Bill and I knew we would take the most flak.

The reading went over pretty well. You can knock out ten poems, including the patter, in about twenty minutes, and an audience that is not accustomed to reading poetry or to poetry readings will generally discover they've been pleasantly surprised, or

at the very least, relieved. Then I launched into a brief ramble on how we assembled each section, emphasizing our method of selection for the 59 poets whose work appears in The Contemporaries. For that, we began by soliciting work from the poets we knew, which were quite a few, as Bill is an Idaho native and edited a literary magazine called *Sawtooth* for several years, while I edited a magazine called *Snapdragon* for ten years and played several editorial roles for *Slackwater Review*. (I've lived in Idaho since 1970.) Then we opened the section for other contributors by announcing the anthology in several newspapers throughout the state. Needless to say, we were deluged. I have a file of more than a hundred letters I wrote to poets, publishers, and Bill, and I have eighty notes and letters Bill wrote to me. Of course there were numerous long distance phone calls as well, and we did not have anything fancy like a grant to help with our expenses. The UI Press, however, did get a grant from the state's centennial commission to assist with publication costs.

When I opened the floor to questions, I had only one, from a woman who was apparently angry. "How do you presume," she asked, "to edit such an anthology?"

Did I think of the anthology as a species just then? The word is from the Greek for "bouquet" or "garland," and records of Greek anthologies go back to the fourth century B.C. The first known anthologizer of poems is Meleager (fl. 80 B.C.), himself a poet, as so many such editors are. Did I think of the renowned Greek Anthology and of the wisdom of that editor, who preserved his ano-

The editors,

who are often

poets and critics themselves,

impose their tastes

on the world . . .

nymity? Or did I think of good old Richard Tottel, the publisher whose "Miscellany" (1557) is often regarded as the first poetry anthology in English? He was once a popular short answer item on doctoral qualifying exams in English. Or did I think of good old Oscar Williams, whose solid little paperback anthology of modern poetry introduced me to the world of Wallace Stevens, William Carlos Williams, Elizabeth Bishop, and Theodore Roethke about thirty years ago? (I remember being amazed at the effrontery of Oscar Williams, to place his own mediocrities beside the poems of the greats.)

Well, no. I did not think any of that just then. What I thought was largely defensive: She's right, who *am* I to presume? The tone of her voice was so much as to say, "How dare you to presume? Who are *you* to presume?" Perhaps I was misinterpreting her inflection, but I don't believe so. And the next thing that popped into my mind was even more defensive: Had she submitted poems that we had rejected?

I do not recall exactly what I said, but I think I proceeded somewhat along the following lines: If not me, then whom? After all, I've devoted the last thirty years of my life to reading, writing, and studying poetry (among other things). I suppose I did burble my experience as a literary magazine editor, and I'm sure I mentioned my earlier anthology, a much simpler compilation entitled *Eight Idaho Poets*, which the university press had published in 1979. Of course I reminded her of my accomplice: after all, it hadn't been a one-man show. She seemed mollified, I guess, but I was not especially happy with my response. It seemed to me that she had touched upon the crux of the matter when it comes to anthologies. The editors, who are often poets and critics themselves, impose their tastes on the world, and even if "the world" is only the million or so prospective book buyers of Idaho, it's a pretty big imposition.

Who *am* I to say what "good poetry" is? I like to tell the students in my poetry writing and modern poetry classes that it's very easy to explain what "good poetry" is. Good poetry is what people who read good poetry *say* is good poetry. Yes, this is a bit tautological, but I think in that teasing statement there is more than a little truth. I hope that definition does not come off as pompous or condescending. I'm not implying that editors like Bill Studebaker and me are a privileged class. *Anyone* can undertake to read good poems, and if they spend a lot of time reading a lot of good poems, they should be able to identify "good poetry." They could all become anthologists, or at least book reviewers. The fact is, of course, that most people do not spend much time reading poems, either good, bad or indifferent, so there is ample opportunity out there for those of us who do.

People depend on anthologists sooner or later, especially when it comes to poetry. The anthology is one way poems become "canonized" as "privileged texts." Those terms at least seem preferable to the phrase "old chestnuts" (*The Best Loved Poems of the American People*). But there is some peril in all this. Take Richard Ellmann and Robert O'Clair's mammoth (nearly two thousand pages) *Norton Anthology of Modern Poetry*, now in its second edition and widely adopted for college-level courses in modern poetry. I have used that anthology off-and-on since the first edition appeared in 1973, and I was among the many consultants who contributed to the 1988 edition. I feel that my comments on the scarcity of poets west of the Mississippi were heeded and certainly some of the poets I suggested were added, though I doubt that my recommendations alone would have been sufficient. Last month, however, as I introduced my modern poetry class to that anthology, I felt obliged to point out, among other things, that I could all too easily list the names of more than forty poets (mostly contemporary) I consider to be "as good as or better than" many who are included. I did not transmit the list to them, but it includes Pulitzer Prize winners Mary Oliver, Henry Taylor, and Carolyn Kizer, Russian-American Nobel Prize winner Joseph Brodsky, and the likes of Robert Hass, William Matthews, Sandra McPherson, and Pattiann Rogers.

But the perils of the anthology go beyond the problems of excluded writers. There's also the problem of selectivity: We see only the best of a poet's output, or at least what the editors claim is the best. Too few students and too few teachers find themselves affording the nine dollars it takes these days to buy a book of poems by a single poet, and as prices increase, that trend will probably continue. Of course the selectivity of the teacher may also enter the calculation: What if I assign only half of the dozen poems by Rita Dove included in the Norton anthology? What if we have time to discuss only three of those? Automatically, it would seem, I have made judgments for my students on top of those already made by the editors. So it is that establishments are contrived and monoliths erected. I like to warn my students: Did you read any poems other than those I assigned? Why not? You don't know me, so why should you trust me? (Some days I don't even trust myself, after all.) For that matter, why should you trust Ellmann and O'Clair? Who are they? Humans, unlike cows for example, are animals that form opinions and judge things and make decisions and act. At the end of the semester, everyone has to either buy or check out of the library a book of poems by a contemporary poet whose work is *not* included in whatever anthology I happen to be using.

And so this apologia for poetry anthologies becomes almost an assault upon them. I believe poetry anthologies are valuable, perhaps even invaluable, and certainly they are useful, handy, practical, economical, despite their perils. Like the skunks in Robert Lowell's poem, they "will not scare," they will not go away. As a teacher, writer, and editor (in that order, I think), I find myself like the speaker in John Donne's "The Prohibition," which begins, "Take heed of loving me," and which ends, "Oh love and hate me too."

Ron McFarland, Director of Creative Writing at the University of Idaho, has recently had a third poetry collection published, The Haunting Familiarity of Things. *He has edited two scholarly collections on James Welch and Norman Maclean for Confluence Press and three poetry anthologies for several academic presses.*

About Some Area Book Publishers

Jerome Gold

Since November of 1991 I have been interviewing independent book publishers in the American Northwest and British Columbia. This project started with the idea of writing an article that would try to define just who, collectively, we book publishers are. I wanted to know this because I had come to the conclusion that, by virtue of being an independent book publisher, I was part of something much larger than any one of us could comprehend, and this something was not going to go away. It seemed to me to be broadening by bounds; I couldn't imagine anything powerful enough to stop it, aside from a plague that would kill instantly anyone whose fingers touched a keyboard or a copy machine.

My original idea was to interview some publishers, find out what personality traits or background they shared, interview others to get a statistically significant sample of the independent publishing universe, and write it up. (My academic training was in anthropology. Does it show?) No names would be used. The numbers, the numbers, ah, the numbers would guide us to such insights about ourselves.

This idea lasted until about halfway through my first interview. I found Paul Doyle, self-publisher of *Mioka: Bride of Bigfoot* to be so introspective, so forthright, that I was seduced into accompanying him on a compact review of his life that may have been more painful for him than for me, but maybe not. I became determined to avoid reducing the experience of life to a list of figures. I was not willing to give up completely on the idea of commonality, however. (I recognize that the conflict between struggling to apprehend the meaning of a human life and reducing that life to something that has no relationship to the experience of the person who lives it is the classic conflict between the humanist and the social scientist or statistician. Beware the humanist who would make social policy. Beware also the administrator of social policy.)

My second interview was such a kick that I was forced to ponder how to catch synergy and humor as they are experienced by the actors, and impress them on the page, much less contain them in a series of statistics. (I do not have a good answer.) By the time we had completed the interview and our latest burst of laughter had abated, I knew that I would be composing a book instead of an article and that the book would emphasize, in the interviews themselves, the publishers as individuals rather than as parts of the mass. I did not have the detachment to reduce my informants to numerical symbols: nor did I want it.

Nevertheless, asked to write an article about my book project (tentatively titled *The Gatekeepers: Interviews with Independent Book Publishers in the American Northwest and British Columbia*), I offer here some of the findings that might have been included in the article I intended originally to do, with the proviso that they are strictly impressionistic. By that, I mean that they are not the results of good science, which I found not to be useful.

I have been impressed with what appears to be the physical vitality of independent publishers, regardless of age. I am not talking about the lack of physical infirmity, but rather of a kind of visceral hunger for something not defined. The single exception among those I have interviewed is a youngish man who seemed to be almost emotionless. But he was in the midst of an obviously painful divorce. (Yet, on the tape of the interview, his lack of affect comes across rather as thoughtfulness, and in fact there are indications of an angry anti-authoritarianism. Makes me wonder about the validity of my impressions. If I were a social scientist, I would approach this from a hermeneutic perspective, focusing on the relationship between interviewer and interviewee. But I have given up social science.)

Not all of the publishers I have interviewed expressed political sentiments, but of those that did, all were left of center. Except, perhaps, for those who identified themselves as anarchists. These have sentiments generally considered leftist — for example, anti-racist, anti-discrimination against gays — but they are also fiercely in-

Where else do you even find the free exchange of ideas in American life now? Nowhere that I know, except among independent publishers.

dividualistic, a characteristic associated by the left with the far right. Of those fierce individualists (whether anarchist or not) I have interviewed, most live in Idaho. I want to point out that the Idaho publishers appear also to have the strongest sense of regionalism I have encountered, though they may define regionalism so narrowly that the definition may include only one middle-size town and its immediate environs.

The Idahoans also have a commitment to helping one another out. If this cooperative activity sounds contradistinctive to our idea of the individual, we need to reexamine our ideas about individualism and cooperation. I must admit to a tremendous admiration for the Idaho publishers. Having lived for many years in the isolation of Montana, I have a special empathy for them.

All but one of the five Canadian publishers I have interviewed get Canada Council (something like our NEA) money. The one who does not is not eligible for it but hopes to be soon. Only one of the eleven U.S. publishers I have interviewed receives grants of any sort. (I do not include awards for books already published or contracted for here.) None of the other ten apply for grants, though a couple have toyed with the idea. None refuse on principle to apply for grants, though one who is also a poet said that the time and energy it would take to apply for a grant is better spent writing poetry. The others said that they do not have the time to spend researching grants and

writing proposals, but none mentioned their own writing. In fact, most publishers do not write for publication, though some did until publishing came to dominate their creative lives. Four American publishers publish themselves as well as other writers. One Canadian publisher I interviewed does this.

I should point out that Canada Council money is available to all publishers who are qualified to receive it. Also, the Canada Council does not require a publisher to have nonprofit status in order to receive federal money. American grant money, on the other hand, is awarded to the winners of competitions between publishers: the losers get nothing. Only nonprofit publishers are eligible to compete.

All of the publishers I have interviewed so far feel passionately about what they do. I have never, until now, come across a category of persons so obsessed with its work, with the mechanics of its work, with the personalities of others in the business, with the ideas behind its product — books, real or proposed. Ideas! Where else do you even find the free exchange of ideas in American life now? Nowhere that I know, except among independent publishers. (Here, too, Canadians may be different from Americans. Rolf Maurer of New Star Books made the point that while Americans are apparently alienated from political discourse, Canadians regard social and political issues as open to public debate.) All, among those I have interviewed, possess this passion for the publishing life. There are no exceptions.

Jerome Gold, publisher of Black Heron Press, is the author of two published novels, The Negligence of Death *and* The Inquisitor; *a third,* The Prisoner's Son, *will be published in 1994. He is currently working on the collection discussed in this essay.*

Becoming Visible: A Brief Profile of Press Gang Publishers

Barbara Kuhne

Press Gang Publishers Ltd. was established in 1970 in Vancouver, B.C. as a community-oriented "leftist" print shop offering printing services to local groups that promoted the liberation of women and an anti-capitalist perspective. It became a women-only collective in 1974 and expanded from printing into publishing in 1976 with the publication of *Women Look at Psychiatry* (Dorothy Smith and Sara David, eds.). At that time Press Gang also began distributing Women's Press (Canada) books in British Columbia, in exchange for having its books distributed in the rest of Canada.

In the early years Press Gang books were released irregularly, as time and money permitted and as local feminist women came forward with manuscripts. Printing remained the primary focus into the 1980s, while the publishing work was done mostly by a volunteer collective. In 1982 the printing and publishing collectives began to work independently, each making its own decisions and handling its own finances. All books continued to be printed by Press Gang Printers and the two groups worked out of shared space. The separation arose because of the very different responsibilities and work schedules involved in publishing and printing: the more immediate nature of a printing job versus the lengthy time commitment required for editing, producing, and selling a book.

The next major turning point in the publishing collective came in 1987 when we dissolved the volunteer component. For several years, one and then two staff women shared all decision-making with a volunteer collective of from four to six women. As the business grew, more and more work fell on the shoulders of the staff people, and the ideal of shared responsibility and an equal voice in all decisions for all collective members became impossible to sustain. The turn-over of women in the volunteer collective was such that each new book was produced by a new group of women, most of whom had no previous publishing experience. While providing skill training for women in the local community had been an important aspect of Press Gang from its inception, it became untenable to continue working with a volunteer collective *and* expand our production as a feminist publisher. After restructuring the volunteer collective several times, it was disbanded.

The staff women committed themselves to increasing the number of books published per year and operating more effectively as a business. One aspect of this decision was that we could no longer afford to

> *We define ourselves as a feminist press that gives priority to Canadian women's writing...*

print all of our books "in house." Press Gang books are now mostly printed out of province (primarily in Quebec and Manitoba) at print shops that specialize in book manufacturing. Press Gang Printers, the only feminist, worker-controlled print shop still in existence in North America, concentrates on posters, booklets, spiral bound materials, catalogues, and brochures.

In 1989 the publishing collective became registered as Press Gang Publishers Feminist Co-operative. Five members, all women, are equal shareholders. The three staff women are the Directors and are responsible for the day-to-day running of the business. As staff, we work collectively in decision-making and all have a voice in what gets published, how, and when. We have always had a commitment to publishing lesbian writers, and over the past several years we have also more consciously adopted an anti-racist editorial policy. This is reflected in some of the outstanding books by Native women Press Gang Publishers has produced in recent years and in plans for forthcoming titles by women of color.

We define ourselves as a feminist press that gives priority to Canadian women's writing aimed at the international women's community. Our list includes fiction, non-fiction covering a wide range of topics, and an occasional poetry book too good to pass up. Best known titles from recent years include *Drawing the Line: Lesbian Sexual Politics on the Wall*, by Kiss and Tell (1991), a postcard book of 40 b&w photos from an art show of the same name which has toured internationally, and *Not Vanishing*, by Chrystos (1988), a remarkable collection of lesbian erotic and political poetry.

We currently publish five books a year and our list is distributed in Canada by the University of Toronto Press; in the U.S. by Inland, Bookpeople, Pacific Pipeline, Moving Books, and other distributors; and in the U.K. and Europe by Turnaround Distribution. The Canadian market alone is too small to sustain a feminist press, and we have therefore worked hard to make our books available in the U.S. Getting Canadian books reviewed in the U.S. press is an on-going challenge. A recent review of *InVersions: Writing by Dykes, Queers and Lesbians* (Betsy Warland, ed.), by Jan Clausen in *The Women's Review of Books*, March 1992, summarized the situation in this way: "[A]s far as the world's concerned, a book by dykes that comes from a Canadian small press might as well have been written in invisible ink."

Mainstream media and chain bookstores may treat us as invisible, but to thousands of readers who have cherished such Press Gang titles as *Daughters of Copper Woman* and *Still Sane* our presence makes a difference. Canadian small press books provide a vital, diverse, and essential addition to the materials produced by our sister publishers in the U.S. At Press Gang Publishers we're proud of our collaborative work with feminist writers and of the quality books we produce.

For a free catalogue of Press Gang Publishers' books write to 603 Powell Street, Vancouver, B.C. V6A 1H2 Canada.

Barbara Kuhne, a graduate of the Communications Department at Simon Fraser University, is a long-time member of Press Gang Publishers, where she is currently managing editor.

Surviving Small

Vi Gale

If you are thinking of starting a small press, doing business with a small press, or just observing from the position of reader and innocent bystander, there are some things I can share with you.

Some time before I founded Prescott Street Press in 1974 I had already moved my writing/teaching activities out of the house and into a low-cost office downtown. The discipline of going to a job is necessary for me. I also found that people respect your time and commitment to work you do outside of your residence. They leave you alone, especially if you don't get an office telephone. My answering machine at home takes messages and book orders just fine until I get to them in the late afternoon. The box at a branch post office a block away holds my incoming mail until I pick it up.

At first I decided that my press would stay small. That I would do everything myself, except for the printing and production which I would job out. Within these limits, I have up-sized, down-sized, right-sized now for almost 20 years. And I have stayed small. I have chosen not to incorporate as a non-profit. Not that one makes a ton of money in this kind of venture, but you can have your own version of the paper reduction act by not having to hassle the payroll deductions and the complicated bookkeeping. Unbelievably, as it is, under an ABN (assumed business name) you are still subject to five different taxes, just for openers.

When I realized that there really wasn't a built-in profit factor in what I was planning, I made a second-next major decision. I'd stay literary by concentrating on poetry, good graphics and art, all of it to come from the Pacific Northwest, or at least from people who were here at the time I accepted the work. Nor has this proved limiting. By working with nationally-known artists and translators who were here at the time, we have presented work from people in Japan and Sweden. In addition, some of the poets in our Prescott

First Book Series have scattered far and wide into prestigious jobs where they have helped bring recognition to us. It still bothers me to have to turn down excellent work from other parts of the country, but it is a matter of self-preservation not to get over extended.

In the beginning and to this day, I have learned to do without a lot of frills. Prescott Street Press does not have a printed catalogue. It relies on *Books in Print*, printed announcements, flyers and brochures. Book signings, carefully chosen advertising, and directory listings also help, but mostly it is that we have good friends who also have good friends. In the end, it is people who help sell books.

We try to be meticulous about credits and permissions. We also send out review copies, and for the most, the reviews have been good. The reviews printed in library publications and small press periodicals have done a lot to bring us orders from jobbers and wholesalers. We welcome these orders particularly because they pay promptly, something that is hard for beleaguered small book stores to do. Currently, cash flow and collections are real problems for everyone.

Sometimes the little economics we practice have their lighter moments. In addition to cutting up cardboard, utilizing brown grocery bags for wrap, and salvaging all manner of boxes, I found that stores would sometimes give me hosiery boxes that were just right for a book of poetry. I'd strip the outside paper from the box, wrap it in brown paper and seal it with the thin-

I have up-sized,

down-sized, right-sized

now for almost 20 years.

And I have

stayed small.

I might also try,

ever so gently,

to sell you a book.

That is the most difficult

and the most important

thing of all.

It is how a press survives.

nest weight of shipping tape. On one occasion, however, I got a phone call from a professor friend of mine who demanded to know why his book was in a container labeled *Barely There*. I now put these single copy orders in a #2 bubble envelope.

In the beginning I did postcard sets. These were very successful until the post office got picky about size, weight, and even the space allotted for message and address. So much for a product known as a "sideline" to the trade, although I still miss them when it comes to paying for binding and cover art. But we learn to be flexible. I now put the poems, which have to be carefully selected for that purpose, on a notecard and package it with a matching envelope in cellophane. Both postcards and notecards certainly got us our money's worth. In some cases they serve as an introduction to poets whose books we then go on to publish. Best of all, it meant some kind of publication for over 50 poets in this way. I once opened an envelope from Florida that had a check in it and said simply: "Send beautiful cards."

But it soon came time to move on to books. Somehow small and first have always seemed related in my mind. Through knowing one of the translators, I was able to publish the first book in the United States by Japan's leading contemporary poet. This was followed by six Prescott

First Books from poets who had their first book publication with the Press. Each of these six books contains work by nationally known artists. More recently we have published the first book in the United States by a well-known Swedish poet. Even if I am not able to take on their succeeding books, I have the feeling that I have helped further their careers. And when I exhibit these books at the American Booksellers Association or the American Library Association shows, it is with a feeling of pride that they have come out of a little regional press. We have even won a couple of distinguished literary awards.

I should mention that I believe wholeheartedly in public aid for the arts. We need to invest in anything that will add to the quality of our lives. And at first I did have some modest amounts of help. The last such money I received came in 1981 and it was $500. About the price of a fair sized ad in a good publication. But by doing one project at a time, then taking time to distribute and recoup, I have managed. All my bills are paid and I am solvent. My next project is in the hopper and the money to pay for it is already set aside. I mention this in all humility for those of you who need to know that it can be done.

There is more, of course. But having taken a solemn vow not to set up as a consultant, since there are already enough of them, I'll stop. But should you catch me at the end of a long day before I head for my other life in the suburbs, I could answer a few questions over a Latté of the Day. But only if I am asked. I might also try, ever so gently, to sell you a book. That is the most difficult and the most important thing of all. It is how a press survives.

Vi Gale has been part of the Pacific Northwest literary scene for over forty years. She was recognized by the Oregon Institute of Literary Arts in 1989 with the C.E.S. Wood Retrospective Award for Lifetime Achievement.

Broken Moon Press

John Ellison

Although it's hard to describe, Broken Moon Press has a personality all its own. From its beginning, Broken Moon has had an energy that we felt instructed and informed us. It has brought together a community of people here in the Northwest who share a similar desire to make books in a region of the country that has supported a fine tradition of small-press publishing for many years. I was asked to write some thoughts on the press's history, which is what I have attempted to do here. But this is just a small part of our history. How does one write about this *work*, this life of Broken Moon Press?

In 1987, Broken Moon Press was "refounded," meaning it was re-created from a small letterpress venture started in 1982 into the small trade house it is today, when Lesley Link and I met each other at Microsoft Corporation. Originally, the press was a vehicle for publishing small chapbooks of poetry and short stories written by my friends. But the little group of college students soon disbanded and I was left with one Chandler & Price printing press, some type, and other printing tools, and a garage that simply wouldn't stop leaking, no matter how much roofing paper and tar I threw on it. With my savings account drained, and with my college studies complete, I focused on my job at the *Morning Tribune* in Tacoma and waited out the winter until I could think of a way to pull the press back together. I put the entire printing studio into storage.

After trying my hand at journalism, mostly writing obituary notices and tide tables, I had the great idea that I should find a job in New York publishing. I didn't seem to be cut out to be a journalist, even after completing college with journalism as my life goal.

This job search was the beginning of the "new" Broken Moon. Late one night I called Les Elliott, the guiding light behind the Elliott Press at Pacific Lutheran University, where I first learned to truly love the art of the book. Les had long since retired from

teaching, but he still knew practically everyone in the publishing business, especially in New York. He was also one of those people anyone could call, at nearly any hour of the day or night and ask a question like "Where do people get jobs in book publishing in New York?" He had several great leads. After a 30-minute conversation about New York literary houses, Les mentioned a local company called Microsoft that hired people interested in publishing to produce the user manuals that come in boxes with software. He implied that a job in computers was about the lowest level one could attain in the publishing food chain. It would be a "last resort."

People ask if we make "a living"

at it —

no, we make a life *of it.*

But the early eighties weren't the best time to find jobs in New York in publishing, as I soon learned. After many letters and many rejections from New York, I found myself at Microsoft. The press's transition from the letterpress world into trade publishing had begun. My plan was to stay at Microsoft just long enough to get some experience for New York where I could find a way into "literature." But then I met Lesley Link, my co-publisher, who had a background in textbook publishing. We learned trade publishing by producing thousands of pages for Microsoft.

Broken Moon was re-created about a year later. Lesley and I *talked* the press into being — we talked all the time about the kind of work we loved, the kind of press we wanted to build. We talked to everyone we could think of. We traveled to meet writers. We took a leap of faith, telling people "Hello, you don't know us, but we're starting a press…" It was as if we couldn't say enough about the need for a new international literary press. Of course, there were many fine small presses in operation in 1987. There still are. But one press in particular didn't survive, the one that we felt was the brightest beacon: North Point Press. Several years later, we were honored to meet its publisher, William Turnbull, at the American Booksellers Association. I still remember when we sent him and North Point fan mail along with our first Broken Moon titles. North Point set such high standards, we only hoped to be as good someday.

Our first goal was to publish the perfect book. We never achieved that and probably never will. But each book has its own character and challenges, making each memorable. Now, three and a half years later, we have 30 titles in print with a publishing schedule that includes 12 titles a year. Broken Moon books have won many prestigious awards, including the American Book Award, the Academy of American Poets Translation Prize, the Western States Book Award, the Bumbershoot/Weyerhaeuser Publication Award, and the Governor's Writers Award.

Broken Moon Press is a community. Our publishing is a partnership between our authors and our staff, and, of course our readers. Our goal is the same today as it was in 1987: to produce beautiful books that make a difference in people's lives. The press has opened up a world to us. People ask if we make "a living" at it — no, we make a *life* of it.

Recently, one of our authors told us a story that once again confirmed our vision. After one of his readings, a woman came up to him to introduce herself. She said she had been so moved by his book that she had one of his poems carved into a piece of wood as a memorial to her late husband, and she placed the carving at the base of a tree in a forest her husband had loved. She said the book helped her better understand death and her husband's passing.

It's stories like these that keep us at our desks late at night making sure the books get off to the printer on time. Stories like this confirm that we are building a life, not just a business or a career.

John Ellison is a senior technical editor at Microsoft Corporation and lives in Seattle. He and Lesley Link published Broken Moon Press' first trade edition in 1989, and he serves as poetry and nonfiction editor.

Brooding Heron Press & Bindery

Sam Green

Eleven years ago my wife, Sally, and I were living in Seattle. Both of us were working at jobs we hated in order to bring in enough money to pay the mounting bills, trapped in a routine from which we could see no escape. Under the imprint of Jawbone Press we had produced 25 books (mostly photo offset poetry pamphlets), but were building a crippling debt. More and more we resented that we didn't have the time to print the sort of books we dreamed about: elegant letterpress editions like those Copper Canyon was then producing, and the early Graywolf books. Kim Stafford had found us a C&P platen press, and Sally had learned the basics of printing from Tree Swenson. I had trained as a bookbinder with Don Guyot of the Colophon Bindery, but the press sat mostly idle, while we grew more desperate and more bitter.

One weekend I pruned the old Gravenstein behind our house, and had an epiphany. Shortly after, I wrote this poem:

Pruning

Whatever doesn't bear fruit,
blocks light, strays
from the center, draws
too much life from the trunk.

With tools I filed myself
I cut these clean from the body,
tie them into bundles to burn
in a fire we kneel before.
How we learn.

I think it was the first time I fully realized how a process could become both a metaphor and *a blueprint for action.* Sally and I set about pruning our lives.

We knew that to do the sort of work we wanted — making the best books of which we were capable — would require a low overhead. Letterpress, with its enormous labor intensity but small cash demands,

seemed perfect. If we lived cheaply, we reasoned, we wouldn't have to make much money. The only problem was where.

Through a series of eerie coincidences (or the unraveling of *karma*), we discovered we could afford to buy 10 acres of raw land on a tiny, isolated island in the San Juans. It took a year to sell our Seattle house, and we got plenty of practice at poverty.

In August of 1982, we loaded our press and everything else we still owned after a dozen garage sales into a U-Haul truck. A ferry and then a private barge carried us to the island where a crowd of neighbors was waiting to help unload the press and wish us well in our new beginning.

Our new house was a 14' x 32' surplus army tent. One end sheltered the press, type cabinet, and binding table. Our 8 year old son, Sally, and I shared the rest of the space with a homemade barrel stove (one of my first projects), a wood range, and assorted furniture. Surprisingly, we were comfortable from the start. When the wind blew, it was like living in a giant lung. Always there was just that thin skin of canvas between us and the weather, and it made us feel more alive than we could remember. So did the lifestyle, though we had less money than ever before.

We lived without electricity or running water (still do), kept chickens, planted fruit trees, kept a garden, and cleared land. Right away we appreciated the *immediacy* of our lives, how everything we did had a measurable, observable effect. We rediscovered our bodies a thousand times a day. It was in this environment that we began to make books again and discovered, to our amazement, that the distinction between "work" and "living" had vanished. The epiphany of the pruning repeated itself over and over: we brought the harmonies and revelations of the garden to the design table when we worked up page layout; we took with us the meticulous nature of doing press makeready and binding measurements as we built the log house we would move into after three years in the tent. From having been oriented toward product and compartmentalization, we followed a different compass into *process* (old wisdom). Recognizing this new, nurturing stance as incompatible with our former one, we changed our name to Brooding Heron, adopting patience as our

Sally and I

think of ourselves

as publishers whose main job

is trying to get work

we believe in — in a form that

we hope does it justice — into

the hands of an appreciative

audience.

watchword.

Today, we live in a two-story log house built with our own hands. One-third of the downstairs holds the shop. In addition to the treadle-operated C&P, we've added a Challenge proof press. The bindery has a huge floor model board shears, and a Peerless Gem paper cutter. A six-foot marble imposing stone rests on a second type cabinet. Sky-lights increase the length of the work day.

Because this lifestyle requires so much time, we're only able to print about three titles a year (17 titles to date). We print only poetry, because that's what we know best, favoring first collections by authors who have been appearing in magazines for years but have never had a book. Still, we are try-ing to publish at least one title a year by a well known author in order to generate in-come beyond bare subsistence. Denise Levertov's *The Double Image* allowed us to drill a well last year and to buy health insurance; a forthcoming book by Gary Snyder will, we hope, pay for additional bindery space and kitchen plumbing. At present we have enough manuscripts to keep us busy for the next three to four years.

We've been lucky with critical re-

sponse to our work. Brooding Heron books have won five awards at the last six Bumber-shoot Bookfairs in Seattle. Increasingly, spe-cial collections librarians have written en-thusiastic letters and backed that enthusi-asm with purchase orders. However, despite the growing tendency to link us with "fine printing," Sally and I think of ourselves as publishers whose main job is trying to get work we believe in — in a form that we hope does it justice — into the hands of an appreciative audience. Except for the spe-cial editions, we keep our prices affordable to people in even our income bracket, and, knowing our own shortcomings, we agree with Edward Grabhorn, who said, "Fine printing? There's no such thing as fine print-ing. It's only a workman who's serious, who takes pride in his work." We do our best.

Sam Green's sixth collection of poems is Communion *(Se-attle: Grey Spider Press, 1992). With his printer wife, Sally, he is co-publisher of Brooding Heron Press.*

Letterpressing the Language of Tribe

Rick Ardinger

"If our concern is the living literature of our tribe, we must be aware that the potential genius and power of contemporary poetry can be frit-tered away by the standardization, marketing im-pulse, and compromise that attend technological advance."

— Clifford Burke, *Printing Poetry*

A while back, the poet Louis Simpson wrote a piece for the *New York Times Book Review* about why he didn't need a computer to write poetry. There was a commitment to the page that was lost on a computer screen, he said. Lines, words can be changed at a whim, tried on for size, as it were, with a computer. Writing poems longhand and typing on a manual typewriter, he said, required of a poet that the poem, each line, each word be vi-sualized with the inspiration of permanence *before* lines were put to paper, as if the vision alone were the foundation upon which important literary work rested. The computer obscures the poet from his voice. The computer further un-focuses the poet's attention to an in-ternal oral tradition. Language be-comes less orally envisioned and, instead, more visual.

On first reading, Simpson's es-say sounds like the argument of an old fogy reluctant to change. It sounds like an argument of a person who's never used a computer. It brings to mind the fear of the medi-eval scribes toward the invention of the printing press. And yet there's a spirit in his thesis I want to embrace when it comes to poetry, where ev-ery word is a chiseled balance of grace and intensity.

To take Simpson's argument a step further, I feel it's even more true when it comes to printing poetry. I'm referring to finely printed, letterpressed editions where the attention of the printer toward paper, type, and design contribute to the delicate force of the poem, where proper presentation of the lines contributes to meaning, and the effort of it all preserves a poem's place in time.

In the summer of 1985, I was scanning the "Miscellaneous" classifieds when I ran across what I was looking for: a Chandler & Price platen printing press for $500. It was a big press, a 12-by-18 platen, weighing nearly a ton. The press was pretty grimy, but the rollers were OK. It had a small motor. I bought the press, a marble composing stone, a cabinet of old worn out type, type sticks and other necessary accoutrements.

It didn't take much handsetting of type to realize the fascinating power of the printed word. "Freedom of the Press" was a Constitutional right fully exercised, not something reserved for the editorial offices of newspapers. In exploiting that right, *what* we printed wasn't as important as *that* we printed. Eventually I landed a modest grant to study for a month with Tom and Barbara Rea of Dooryard Press in Story, Wyoming, where I had a brief hands-on lesson in design, and learned in a few weeks how to layout pages properly, how to do make-ready, and how to appreciate the subtle beauty of consistent impression from page to page.

While in Wyoming, we printed a small collection of poems by Sam Hazo, head of the International Poetry Forum in Pittsburgh. The book was called *The Color of Reluctance*, printed in an edition of 800 copies. I remember once setting two pages, printing the run, and redistributing the type into the cases, only to find a typo after the work was done. I remember the three of us standing there staring at the typo wondering whether we should let it go or whether we should reset. We opted to reset the pages, press again, and order more paper. It was a valuable lesson. Had we let that minor typo stand, it probably would be the only thing we remembered about the book. And as Isaac Bashevis Singer once said, fewer poets die from typhus than from typos.

I returned home to Idaho and my own presses in the winter of 1986, broke and unable to afford paper, but eager to start our first letterpressed book. As our first venture, we decided to publish a small collection of

poems by Bruce Embree, a poet from Inkom, Idaho, near Pocatello. It would be his first book as well as ours. We had enough type to set two pages at a time, press them, redistribute the type in cases, and reset two more pages.

For many reasons that book, called *No Wild Dog Howled*, pressed in an edition of 260 copies, is still my favorite. The press work wasn't all that great, as I struggled with the awkward idiosyncrasies of my worn-out Chandler & Price to attain consistent impression. I learned by doing that book on my own, without the helpful suggestions of

I remember the three of us standing there staring at the typo wondering whether we should let it go or whether we should reset.

Tom and Barb. And I can remember sewing up that first copy in the kitchen, and envisioning more books to come.

Nearly all reviews we receive of our books now comment on the press work — not that it can hold a candle to the work of printers like Clifford Burke, Tree Swenson, Jim Bodeen, Harry Duncan, Tom and Barb Rea, Sam Green, and other masters. But it does receive attention, as the presentation and the poems reflect one intention. The type and design of a letterpressed book should not overshadow or intrude too obviously in a collection of poems. For as Holbrook Jackson states in *The Printing of Books* (1947), "Self-effacement is the etiquette of the book printer."

Letterpress is a subtle art. In no other kind of printing is the concept of "presentation" more acutely palpable than in letterpress printing, where printer sets his metal type to paper in a more physical, active sense. Experiments with type are tempered by tradition. They are physically much more demanding and challenging, and it

shows in the finished product. Choice of type, paper, and design are visualized prior to setting, but the process of mechanical lockup of type forms and that first impression culminates in a magically pleasing moment. Achieving further clarity in impression is like a quest for the right light, even though the masters refer to it as "the black art."

In letterpress the partnership of poet and printer seems so much more vital, perhaps especially these days since letterpress is a choice form of printing and not the standard. I select manuscripts of poems to publish with which I feel I can collaborate with the poet, and I want poets to feel that sense as well. I receive manuscripts daily from poets who have no idea what Limberlost does, poets who blindly submit form-letter queries touting their previous publications and other academic accomplishments in hope of landing another publication. Nearly always I return these submissions quickly.

In the spring of 1987, I met Harry Duncan, master printer and publisher of Abattoir Editions, University of Nebraska, Omaha. He was one of my heroes. Knowing my interest in letterpress, my brother in Omaha sent me a plane ticket to attend one of Duncan's final printing lecture/demonstrations before he retired. Duncan devoted his life to printing the works of now-famous poets, most notably William Carlos Williams. He published a small chapbook by Williams in 1944 entitled *The Wedge*, under his Cummington Press imprint. The book included a poem titled "A Sort of Song," which contained a line that became the inspirational dictum for a generation of poets a few years later — "No ideas but in things."

In his final presentation, Duncan wandered around his presses, demonstrating how they worked and answering questions from the handful of folks who showed up for the lecture. He sipped at a cup of wine, his white mane combed back behind his ears and long over his collar. He preferred non-electric presses, he told me, platens that operated with a sewing machine-like treadle. He didn't like his work to be dependent on any power but himself.

I learned later, listening to a taped interview with Duncan, that even the few copies he'd printed of Williams' *The Wedge* later had to be remaindered in New York City book-stores because they didn't sell. At the time, Duncan himself was broke and living in Up-state New York in a house without heat. The thought of these now-priceless little volumes getting dog-eared and dusty in the remainder bins at the conclusion of World War II is a sad metaphor for contemporary poetry. Passed over, picked over, Williams drove his "wedge" into the "lang-wedge" with Duncan's help, despite the lack of an immediate audience's approval. That deter-mination — by Duncan even more so than good Dr. Williams — gives me hope.

The relationship of poets and publishers has changed a great deal since Duncan pub-lished Williams. That tribal, physical, nearly alchemical process of setting type and etch-ing illustrations with acid washed over metal is nearly a thing of the past. The col-laboration of poet and publisher earned the book — and Williams' voice — a place in time.

A love of letterpress composition is not simply a nostalgic love for the way things used to be printed. It's a love for a pro-cess that deserves the renaissance of interest it's receiving these days by printers of poetry. Though labor intensive, the collaborative effort of poet and publisher is, at bottom, the pur-pose of the process: "preserving the lan-guage of the tribe," as Ezra Pound said. Pres-ervation is

a collaborative effort of poet and publisher, or as James Laughlin, Pound's New Direc-tions publisher, once wrote, "action and thought are/children of one mother."

∾

Working full-time jobs in addition to pub-lishing Limberlost books, my wife Rose-mary and I make it a goal right now to let-terpress two to three poetry chapbooks a year. Limberlost currently receives no grants to support much more of our time than that. Between book projects we pub-lish an on-going series of poetry postcards and broadsides, featuring poems by Nancy Stringfellow, Rosalie Sorrels, William Staf-ford, Charles Bukowski, Allen Ginsberg, Greg Keeler, Charlie Potts, and many oth-ers. We've published chapbooks by Robert Creeley, Ed Dorn, Ray Obermayr, Emily Warn, Gino Sky, William Studebaker, John Clellon Holmes, and others, with chap-books in the works by Margaret Aho, Bruce Embree, and Lawrence Ferlinghetti.

In July of 1992, Limberlost celebrated 16 years of publishing. We held a two-day party, called the "Limberlost Poetry Fandango," that brought poets and artists from all over Idaho and as far off as Boulder, Se-attle, Santa Barbara, El Paso, Salt Lake City, and other

points West. One evening was devoted to a potluck dinner at the mountain cabin of folksinger Rosalie Sorrels, followed by a po-etry reading in the middle of a seven-acre meadow. We used an old wood trailer for a stage, rigged up a microphone and P.A. sys-tem, stretched a Limberlost banner between two poles, and decorated the stage with a spotlight and little white Christmas lights that twinkled like stars as the voices of poets echoed against the mountains around Grimes Creek. As the night wore on, the scene took on a carnival-like atmosphere as poets took their place on stage to read a poem or two. We saw friends we hadn't seen in years, met folks who became friends, and extended the circle of the literary tribe. We said goodbyes in the wee hours of the morn-ing, then later sat around a table with a smaller circle of close friends till nearly dawn, talking, singing, reciting poems, being to-gether.

In the end, how we publish books is not so important as why. In the room below me where I type this now squat several printing presses, flanked by type cabinets, galleys of type to be redistributed, and a foreboding clutter of tools and rags for a new project in the works. Beside them are two large card-board flats of paper recently delivered by the UPS man, marked "Heavy." The process weighs on me like a debt to be paid, work yet to be done. But when I think of Harry Duncan, ink under his fingernails, setting type for a book that would never sell, I find the stuff to carry on. "No ideas/but in things," Williams wrote. "No ideas/but in things," Duncan pressed into paper, into time, into life.

Rick Ardinger is the editor of several antholo-gies and is currently assistant director at the Idaho Humanities Council. A collection of his poems, Goodbye, Magpie, will be published in 1993 by Floating Ink Books.

…you can play with type…you can play with type…you can play with type…you can play with type…you can play with type…you can play with type…you can play with type…you turn it into crazy shapes…you can play with type…you can play with type…you can play with type…

Canadian Publishing: Funding Books & Culture, an Interview with Carl Siegler

Karl Siegler was interviewed in April, 1992. He is a founding member of the British Columbia Association of Book Publishers and the publisher at Talon Books. He serves as President of the Association of Canadian Publishers.

WNH: How did Talon Books get its start?

KS: Talon started as a high school poetry magazine in 1963, went to the University of British Columbia in 1965, then became a book publisher in 1967 when the young writers who had published in the magazine were ready to do their first books. Nobody was going to publish them. Particularly in Toronto, much less in New York and London. All of the interesting presses in Canada were founded between the years 1963 and 1975, particularly those outside of Ontario.

WNH: And this was before the cultural support mechanism was put in place by the Federal government?

KS: Yes, in fact that's what is so gratifying about it. In fact, what this was was not a response to the opening of the public trough, but that people had actually put their lives and their savings and everything else on the line to create this industry. And in fact, I think that the Canadian governments, plural — federal and provincial — would not have taken action otherwise.

WNH: What caused this publishing explosion?

KS: The foundation of these presses in Canada was part of the great social revolution in the '60s in the developed world. One of the overriding factors in that whole revolution was an awareness of and the beginnings of a resistance to the creation of the global village. Mass culture. The cold war had acted as a kind of gigantic distraction

from what the real local issues were.

Since the decline of the cold war, however, these issues of the local community have reemerged. Very powerfully. That's what everybody in the world is talking about.

WNH: This reemergence relates in some way to the market and the culture of Canada?

KS: Yes. Cultural product is by nature market specific. In other words, there is an inverse relationship between the importance of a cultural product to a local community and the ability to export that product to other communities. The more vital and sensitive and important the thing is for here, the less important it is for somebody else. There are significant exceptions to this rule, of course.

So we don't have any illusions about continentalizing the market because we're not doing shoes. We're doing cultural products important to our communities.

WNH: Can you give us the historical context for publishing and the recent funding of publishing in Canada?

KS: Until 1971 Canadian publishing was basically branch plant publishing. And what I mean by that is that the major publishers operating in Canada — with three pretty spectacular exceptions — were foreign owned. In the late '60s and in 1970, these three companies, Canada's largest, most culturally important, publishers either were sold or were for sale to US interests. Pricing and content of Canadian books were largely dictated by the American Anglophone market.

Then the government made a political choice, in 1971, to reduce costs rather than increase the price of incoming products. In order to — to use the current parlance — level the playing field, the government of Canada decided to put in place a program that would subsidize the cost of sales of Canadian books in so far as they were published by Canadian–owned houses, to the point where Canadian–owned publishers could publish Canadian–authored books to achieve a gross margin of roughly 50%.

WNH: What about the erosion of such government support?

KS: It is eroding. Almost every country in the known world is running a deficit. When you're running a deficit what do you

think of doing? You cut in social services of course. Cutting health care is left to the last resort. You cut in cultural programing; it always goes on the block first.

So now they're saying: sorry folks. Things have declined and in the last three years they have gone from giving you enough money to cover slightly over 50% of average reported deficit per book to only 38%. They track all the titles they support. You have to do a revenue statement for every title you do that they support. Literary and belle lettres. They also support nonfiction — social criticism, history, serious writing. Serious nonfiction. Self help, cookbooks, guides, indexes are not eligible.

What this means is that both at the level of the book and at the level of the publisher, the herd is being culled. Since the whole system is funding deficits, only those titles that are more and more popular, not necessarily good, but popular, end up surviving and being funded.

Our fear is that a lot of the serious work is being dropped from lists and the publishers who specialize in very serious work are increasingly financially unhealthy as they carry larger and larger deficits. So clearly we cannot continue in this direction and keep the kind of literature we have created in this country since the '60s.

WNH: Will the government continue to help?

KS: The government of Canada has just introduced a new program which is going to put about 26 million dollars annually into the Canadian owned sector of the industry for the next five years. This money will come from the Goods & Services Tax, which includes a tax on books for the first time in Canadian history. They'll put 10% of what they're collecting under GST back into the industry.

WNH: How does the market look in the future?

KS: I and my colleagues feel that the extent to which we're going to achieve any realistic growth is the extent to which we can penetrate the US and the UK and the Australian and New Zealand markets. And other markets in translation.

The private sector here is saturated, in terms of the financial return per book. It doesn't mean we've reached every interested reader, though, particularly in the public sector.

WNH: What is the strategy for the public sector?

KS: One of the things we lobbied for as part of our public policy was to set up the school library purchase program which would have a system of review of every book published by a B.C. publisher. Those that were suitable in relation to curriculum and resource needs were then bought.

We are in a crisis. There have been five bankruptcies in the last two years and there is a line-up of 13 more. Some very large old houses. This industry is in serious trouble financially.

What we really need are structural measures, some of which are responsible education policy and a responsible library policy, both in terms of selections to make sure the Canadian material is available for readers — cultural concern — and in terms of budgets — fiscal concern.

UPDATE: The new department of communications "Book Industry Development Program" issued its first grants in September, 1992, which has for the moment stabilized the industry. The industry is currently negotiating the shape this program is to take over the next four years.

Contributors to this article: Dennis Stovall, Linny Stovall, and Bill Woodall.

SECTION V

O
R
G
A
N
I
Z
A
T
I
O
N
S

Web-working at Bumbershoot Bookfair

Judith Roche

The Bumbershoot Bookfair was conceived in 1977 when poet Tom Parson was driving down the freeway and heard a call on the radio for literary proposals for Bumbershoot.

That first year about twenty presses showed up with their own tables and set up shop in the Nisqually Room. Someone came, unannounced, in a top hat and tails and acted as a doorman. Someone else walked around with a big sign that said, "Poetry is Dead: Come to the Wake." *Poetry Exchange* came and sold coffee. No records were kept but Tom remembers that Graywolf was there with one title, Barbara Wilson and Rachel da Silva came with Seal Press' first and only title, and Copper Canyon, already a well established press, showed up.

It was a very do-it-yourself venture: no organization, no muss, no fuss, no registration. A spontaneous party with surrealistic overtones and terrific spirit. Tom Parson still glows about it, "Everyone responded with tremendous energy! It confirmed all my feelings about democracy, freedom, and the possibility of successful anarchy. Things can happen without rules — people just get together and do it."

As the person who puts it all together and a natural — if modified by time, life, and the laws of gravity — anarchist, would that it still could be so. But those nascent small presses grew up and so did Bumbershoot Bookfair. Rules were added little by little. The biggest fight came when the jury process was introduced. I was not yet working for Bumbershoot and sat on the other side of that shouting table. People hollered and screamed. Poets slammed down books and walked out of the Elliott Bay Cafe meeting, as Norman Langill, One Reel's president, pointed out that one day there would be more applicants than table space; everything else in Bumbershoot, including the food booths, was juried, and the bookfair was going to be too. Norman, the man who runs the whole bumber show, even though his position prevailed, still talks about that meeting with

something in between awe and respect: "You want to avoid fighting with the writers: they are smart and they can use *words*, unlike some of the other artists." This past year there were over 150 applicants for 78 slots.

Hopefully, the trade-off for all this organization is a more serviceable bookfair for all of us. The literary community is different from any of the other communities Bumbershoot serves. We seem to have a more urgent need to get together to talk and do business with each other than the musicians, crafts people, dancers, and visual artists do. As poet Robert Duncan said, "We are all writing the same poem, adding our own parts." Writers talk to publishers about manuscripts, publishers approach writers. Artistic collaborations are born at the Bookfair.

Several years ago the Bookfair Pavilion Stage was added to the mix, which gives an opportunity to showcase and promote writers' work and new books. Western States Arts Federation brings their four WESTAF award winners to read each year, and this year gave a special program about presenting literature to audiences. Before Columbus Foundation promotes its past and present award winners. Seattle Arts Commission presented five of the writers chosen to appear in its *Image* magazine.

Panel discussions on the Bookfair stage started out aimed at the publishing business, providing information to small publishers, but have since branched out. Recent panels included one on issues of feminist publishing, kids talking about writing, and the Western aesthetic in literature.

Readings on this stage can help promote new books. This year Brenda Peterson, Ray Gonzalez, and Charlotte Watson Sherman read from their new books. Seal Press staged a group reading from *Closer to Home: Bi-Sexuality and Feminism*, its newest anthology. Daily Booksignings help sell the books. Bumbershoot Literary Arts hopes to make the Pavilion Stage part of the community forum that helps us do our web-working. This programming is set in April, so if you are interested in presenting something or have a panel discussion idea, talk to Bumbershoot early.

Expansion plans include becoming more involved in educational programs. Writing workshops for kids are in the planning with the culminating event being young writers reading at Bumbershoot. Using the Bookfair Pavilion Stage for more community needs is also an idea. And if "our" building is turned into the Jimmi Hendrix Museum, we'll certainly have to find another space. As form follows content and vice versa, a new home will inevitably change things. Bigger? More varied? Different criteria and focus? More staged programming? More exhibitions like the Richard Brautigan Library and the Banned Book Exhibit? Nobody knows the answers yet, but there will be new possibilities.

Of course, there are problems with growth. When 150 presses apply for 78 spots there will be a lot of unhappy people. The bigger the bookfair gets, the more there is to solve. And, it's an art fair. A neon art exhibit graced our walls in 1992. It looked great but some press people found the buzzing neon an extreme distraction. That is not a problem to puzzle over as that one won't be repeated.

The feeling that everyone's getting better at what we're doing was borne out in the final figures: bookfair sales were up a big 50 percent from last year, though I know some individual presses did not do as well, probably because we are in a recession. Three days into Festival this past year, I ran into Clifford Burke, the guy who literally *wrote the book* on the small press movement in the sixties, wandering around the Bookfair. "I note a whole new feeling of optimism here," said Clifford. "I haven't come for a few years and the feeling is very different. It used to be that we all felt a little bit apologetic about being small publishers, a little like 'aw shucks, we're just small presses struggling valiantly' but now there's a feeling that we're doing something more successful and making it work and even pay for itself more."

Okay, now that the small press movement that budded in the sixties and seventies has come of age, we still need to keep our event tinged with the spirit of the surrealistic party Tom Parson tells of and remember to have fun with it.

Judith Roche's second book, Myrrh will be published by Black Heron Press, spring, '93. She is currently working on a collection of Alaskan stories and an essay about teaching in the prisons.

Canadian Authors Association: Vancouver, B.C., Branch

Frank Wade

The Canadian Authors Association was formed in 1921 by a group of famous Canadian writers, including the humorist Stephen Leacock, to promote Canadian authorship. A group of Vancouver writers was involved, and the Vancouver Branch has been operating since then.

The aims of the association are to help writers, both beginners and professionals, to develop their writing and marketing skills, promote Canadian writing, and protect their interests. It has a grievance committee that looks into problems members might be having with publishers. A novice writer can always get advice at the local or national level.

The association has sixteen branches across the country with a total of over 800 members. Many fine local writers have been members of the Vancouver branch over the years. The most famous recent one is Raymond Hull, a prolific writer who wrote the world-wide best seller *The Peter Principle*. Roy Minter, a present member, was awarded the Order of Canada for his work and writing on the Yukon. B. Guild Gillespie, another member, has just had her book, *On Stormy Seas, The Triumphs and Torments of Captain George Vancouver*, published to great acclaim.

The association publishes a number of publications: a *National Directory of Members*; the *Canadian Writer's Guide* with 624 pages packed with valuable information on Canadian writing and publishing; and the *Canadian Author* a quarterly magazine (the only one in the country) which is a scaled-down version of *Writer's Guide*. Also it has professionally produced audio tapes on various writing genres. There are also the national and branch newsletters.

The association started the first national literary awards. These were later taken over by the federal government and became the Governor General's Awards. It then started its own prestigious awards: the Vicky Metcalf Award for inspirational writing for Canadian youth ($10,000 cash prize plus a $3,000 and $1,000 award); the Harlequin — Canada's biggest publisher — CAA Awards for fiction, poetry, nonfiction, and drama ($5,000 plus a silver medal); and the Air Canada award for young — under-thirty — writers (free flight for two anywhere in the world).

Canadian writing and publishing is now in a minor renaissance. In the last few years there has been an explosion of Canadian books being produced compared to the past. Until recently, Canadian publishing was dominated by British and American interests.

Our best-selling writers such as Margaret Atwood, Robertson Davies, and Mavis Gallant are now well-known abroad. A new writer, Ondaatje, has just won the prestigious Brooker Award.

Forty years ago a Royal Commission was set up by the federal government to look into the state of the arts in Canada. It was then a sad story. Canadian theater was moribund, English Canada had only published 14 fiction books in a year, and not one of our best composers was able to make a living.

The Commission recommended that a Council be set up to act as a trustee of the country's cultural development to promote and foster the country's artists and writers. As a result, the Canada Council was founded. From then on, the arts in Canada slowly began to flourish.

The financial assistance provided by the Council to Canadian literature is not large, but it has primed the pump. In 1990, the Council awarded about two million dollars to 160 Canadian publishers to promote and publish Canadian writers. Some money was also provided to Canadian periodicals, and about a million given to 120 published Canadian writers for readings, travel, and time to write books.

Only our top writers receive direct assistance, but others receive help indirectly because quite a few of our small publishers receive funding. There are approximately twenty publishers in B.C. publishing about 200 books a year. The association receives some assistance to put on its annual conference.

Recently the Provincial (State) governments have become interested in the arts. The B.C. government provides funds to writers who have published at least two books, and it also underwrites the very successful quarterly magazine *B.C. Bookworld* which promotes the work of B.C. writers and publishers. There are provincial awards for fiction, nonfiction, drama, and poetry. Every little community in B.C. has a writers club, and B.C. has the second largest population of writers in English Canada.

The situation, however, is by no means perfect. Foreign book publishers collect 61% of the value of Canadian book sales. Many have Canadian offices and publish Canadian writers but this amounts to only 22%. There is no tariff on books, so there is a free flow of information into the country. Mel Hurtig, a nationalist publisher calls Canada "Puerto Rico North" with US paperbacks, some not of the highest quality, flooding the market.

Some writers, including some of our own members, do not want government help and would prefer to be on their own. This also applies to some publishers. Nevertheless, there can be no doubt that government assistance has had a beneficial effect on Canadian writing. The main impetus is at the provincial level, but it is important that there be interest at the federal level as well. A national writer's group is needed to ensure that writers from across the country keep in touch.

Frank Wade is President of the CAA Vancouver, B.C., branch. His book, A Midshipman's War, A Young Man in the Mediterranean Naval War 1941 to 1943, *will be published by Cordillera Publishing.*

Pacific Northwest Writers Conference

Mary Sikkema

The Pacific Northwest Writers Conference (PNWC), a non-profit literary organization, came into being in 1956 because a group of writers and business persons decided to create a climate that would do away with the cultural lag in this region. The group also hoped that a writer's conference would be a powerful catalyst in making the Pacific Northwest known for its writers and artists.

Member Ann Rule, our 1990 Achievement Award winner, credits her long association with PNWC as the motivation that kept her writing during the early days of her career. In a May 3, 1991 *Publisher's Weekly* article she said, "Way before I sold anything, I used to go to the PNWC summer conference and sit in the back and think, 'I'm here in this room breathing the same air as writers.'" In an article in the December 1992 *Writers Digest*, interviewer Cheryl Barth said of Ann, "Rule has made a better living off the true crime category than almost any other writer." Ann comes to our events whenever she can and tells aspiring writers, "You can do it. I did. And I was a single mother with five kids."

PNWC continues to offer the opportunities that gave Ann inspiration. Through our programming, writers find hope, motivation, skill development, and enjoy networking with writers of every level of achievement and genre. Opportunities to meet and talk with editors and agents are also provided.

PNWC serves as a conduit for those who succeed to share their expertise and to contribute to the continuing development of this area's reputation as a thriving writing community. For instance, our current Literary Council — composed of Margaret Chittenden, Charles Johnson, John Nance,

Willo Davis Roberts, Ann Rule, and John Saul — makes such a contribution.

Our goals are: (1) to provide educational opportunities for writers, (2) encourage excellence in Pacific Northwest writers, (3) enable the development of new writers, (4) encourage networking between aspiring and published writers, (5) establish and maintain a relationship with the publishing industry, (6) encourage cultural diversity within the Pacific Northwest writing community, and (7) create partnerships with other arts and service organizations.

To achieve these goals we currently have the following annual events.

- **The High School Conference**. Held at Highline Community College, it gives young people an opportunity to meet others smitten by the itch to write and to find encouragement to follow their dreams. The conference offers speakers and workshops that assist students in the development of the kind of writing they may choose to pursue. Students meet and chat with published authors.

- **The High School Contest**. The contest is open to Pacific Northwest high school students. Prizes are awarded at a banquet held in conjunction with the High School Conference. The grand prize winner of the 1989 contest, Jennifer DiMarco, recently had her self-published trilogy picked up by a New York publishing house.

- **The Mid-winter Intensive Workshop Weekend**. The workshops are led by pros who help registrants develop better manuscripts. There are classes such as "Moving from Part to Full Time," "Creating a Safe, Workable Writing Space: Ergonomics," and "Promoting Your Book Through The Media."

- **The Achievement Award Banquet**. The achievement award is given in recognition of professionalism that represents the standards of the PNWC and has enhanced the stature of Northwest literature. This award has been presented to such writers as Lucile McDonald, who helped found PNWC and whose career in journalism forged a path for women in a profession that once closed doors to them.

- **The Adult Literary Contest**. The top ten winners have their manuscripts seen by editors and agents, and the top three winners in each category win generous cash prizes. All entrants receive a critique on the work submitted. Ric Cantrell's novel *Para Ward*, based on Ric's experiences in the paraplegic ward of Madigan Army Hospital in Tacoma, won first place in the 1990 PNWC contest. It also brought him an agent who attended that summer conference. Maureen Goldman from Gibsons, B.C., who won first place in the juvenile novel category in our 1992 contest, received an offer from Delacort for her winning book, *Getting Lincoln's Goat.* *Fantasy and Science Fiction Magazine* bought the short story she entered in PNWC's literary/mainstream category.

- **The Summer Conference.** The three-day conference emphasizes networking. For instance, aspiring writers meet successful ones in Ask-A-Pro, and can make appointments with editors and agents, many of whom come from New York. Also available are critique groups led by noted writers. One attendee of the 1992 conference wrote, "I came expecting help with my writing. But I didn't expect to find good old Southern Hospitality. That was a nice surprise." One editor indicated that the reputation of PNWC among New York editors and agents "is tops now and no one is a close second."

Not only is PNWC overcoming the cultural lag that concerned our founders, we are moving this region into a position of literary prominence. For information, contact Shirley Bishop, Inc., 2033 Sixth Avenue, #804, Seattle, WA 98121.

Mary Sikkema, a freelance writer from Bellevue, WA, writes profiles and biographies. Her latest book is Brehani, A Child Named Light.

```
KAPEL
! $ % & ( ) * , - . / 0 1 2 3 4 5 6 7
8 9 : ; ? A B C D E F G H I J K L M
N O P Q R S T U V W X Y Z [ ] _
` { } Ä Å Ç É Ñ Ö Ü á à â ä ã å ç
é è ê ë í ì î ï ñ ó ò ô ö õ ú ù û ü
° ¢ £ • ß ® © ™ ¨ ≠ Æ Ø ∞ ± ≤
≥ ¥ µ ∂ ∑ ∏ π ∫ ª º Ω ¿ ¡ √ ƒ ≈ ∆
« » … Œ œ – — " " ' ' ÷ ◊ ÿ Ÿ ‹ › fi fl
```

The Walden Residence for Oregon Writers

Diane McDevitt

The Walden Residency program seeks to encourage Oregon writers by providing them the opportunity to pursue their work at a quiet and beautiful mountain farm in southern Oregon. The residency at Walden Farm includes space for one working writer during three residency periods each year. The cabin is ten minutes from Gold Hill and forty minutes from Ashland. There is a phone available nearby, but the essential environment is quiet solitude in a snug room that opens on a meadow surrounded by forest. Utilities and partial board are provided.

Walden residencies are sponsored by a private citizen and have been offered since 1987 to a wide range of writers. A committee selects the recipients on the basis of a project proposal and a writing sample, and typically gives equal consideration to already published writers as well as those who show potential. While there is no expectation that a work be completed during the residency, many of the participants have been able to do just that during this time of concentrated writing. Former recipients include playwrights Sandra de Helen, Carolyn Gage, and Dean Seabrook; poets Sandra Claire Foushee, Oma Miller, and Patricia Mees Armstrong; fiction writers Jerrie Hurd, Scott David Travis, Barbara Ryberg, Simeon Dreyfuss, and Ronald Peterson; essayists Jane Gallin, Sara Miller, and Nancy Yonally; and photographer/writer Jan Bannon.

The application process for the Walden program is coordinated by the Northwest Writing Institute of Lewis and Clark College, and is usually open in the fall with awards announced in December. The three six-week residency periods span early spring through mid-summer. Applicants must be Oregon residents and must agree not to smoke, to do their own cooking, and to keep the cabin in good order.

Diane McDevitt is the program assistant for the Northwest Writing Institute.

Soapstone: A Writing Retreat for Women

Judith Barrington

Soapstone, a Writing Retreat for Women, is a new project undertaken by the women who have organized The Flight of the Mind Writing Workshops for Women since 1984 (Judith Barrington and Ruth Gundle). Through their work with the annual summer writing workshops, they came to understand the enormous need that women writers have for support services.

For nine years, Flight of the Mind has offered workshops by well-known feminist writers. About 500 women, ranging in age from 19 to 88, have taken part. Now the same team is creating a writers' *retreat* at a beautiful location in the Oregon coast range. They are currently engaged in expanding and adapting the existing cabin to accommodate two writers in residence at a time. Much of this work has been done so far by a large pool of volunteers, most of them women and many of them writers.

Although it will probably take at least two more years to complete the new buildings and to install a septic system and bathroom — as the money for them is raised — Barrington has learned that the process of creating this retreat is as important as the ultimate goal. The volunteers have been able to meet other writers, enjoy hardworking days together at a beautiful place, and gradually form a community with a shared vision. The plan for the expansion was made with the help of volunteer architect Tami Beth Katz, and refined and drawn up by a second volunteer architect, Mike McCullough.

Soapstone consists of 24 acres of forest with a beautiful creek running through it. There is alder, fir, cedar, hemlock, and maple on the property, and the creek, which fills to a width of about 25 feet in winter, is a salmon spawning creek.

The purpose of the Soapstone project is to create a place where women writers will be able to work for periods of one week to one month (or possibly more) at a time. The inspiration for this retreat was, in part, a women writers' retreat on Whidbey Island, Cottages at Hedgebrook, on whose selection committee Barrington has served. She believes that supporting women writers in making their work a priority, providing a place where they can go to find peace and inspiration, and making it possible for them to focus exclusively on their work, whether or not they can afford a "getaway," are vitally important to all of us. It is important to the women writers because they deserve to enjoy and exercise their creative talents (in a world which constantly tells them they have other, "more important," obligations), and it is important to the larger community because we need the books that these writers offer, with their wisdom, their political vision, and their testimony about the full range of female experience.

Judith Barrington is executive director of Soapstone and a Portland poet.

ColonyHouse: Oregon Writers Colony

Rae Richen

"It's perfect. How lucky you were to find this house." That's how New York literary agent Meg Ruley expressed her enthusiasm for ColonyHouse during her visit.

Northwest writer Andrea Carlisle spent a week there during which she completed an article for a northwest magazine and 50 pages on her latest book. "ColonyHouse is a wonderful place to write," says Andrea.

In 1988, after seven years of plans and dreams, Oregon Writers Colony established ColonyHouse — a haven by the sea for Northwest writers. Perched on a ridge, at the northern end of the small coastal community of Rockaway Beach, the large two-story log home provides a serene environment for creative growth.

Oregon Writers Colony makes ColonyHouse available for individual writers who need to concentrate on a work in progress. We also sponsor six weekend workshops and at least one week-long conference in the house each year. In the summer of 1993 two week-long conferences on "Writing a Damn Good Novel" with author and teacher Jim Frey are planned. Recent workshops include a weekend with Sharon Wood learning how to write "For Fun and Funds," plus workshops in technical writing, poetry, freelance, theater, photographic articles, and screenplays — support for many types of writing in the warm, communal atmosphere of a log cabin.

Designed by one of the architects of Oregon's celebrated Timberline Lodge, ColonyHouse amenities include: views of the Pacific to the west and wooded Lake Lytle to the east, a spacious living room with a twenty foot high river stone fireplace, four large bedrooms, two baths, and a modern fully equipped kitchen. The rustic interior of hand-hewn logs, carved door handles, and hammered iron fixtures combine with the western sweep of terraced slopes to delight the eye and add to the seaside ambiance.

ColonyHouse has inspired many writers since 1988. One week per month is reserved for three writers to share. Annually, another week is reserved for the winner of the Query Letter contest — a competition for writers who pitch a writing project which would benefit from a week's concentrated work in the ColonyHouse atmosphere.

One query letter contest winner was Linda Lesley who wrote of inheriting a trunkful of poetry and memorabilia from her Mexican grandmother — a woman deeply involved in the Mexican Revolution of 1910. As a contest winner, Linda was able to use her week completing a synopsis of a novel about her grandmother. She went on to outline her book and wrote a chapter-by-chapter description. "Not only that," wrote Linda, "I collated all the poetry and letters into chronological order and translated more of my grandmother's poetry — 30 pages in all." All this during one week at the ColonyHouse.

For more information write Oregon Writers Colony, PO Box 15200, Portland, OR 97215, or call Marlene Howard at 503-771-0428.

Rae Richen is the President of Oregon Writer's Colony.

WEISS
!$%&()*,-./012345678
9:;?ABCDEFGHIJKLM
NOPQRSTUVWXYZ[
]_`{}ÄÅÇÉÑÖÜáàâäã
åçéèêëíìîïñóòôöõúùûü
°¢£•ß®©™¨≠ÆØ∞±≤
≥¥µ∂∑∏∫ªºΩ¿¡√ƒ≈∆«
»…Œœ——""''÷◊ÿŸ‹›fifl

Northern Publishers Conference

Jonathan L. Holland

More than a decade behind the emergence of small presses as an American publishing power, Alaska's publishing houses are now flourishing and proliferating. The situation was amply demonstrated by more than 90 registrants and 150 participants at the Northern Publishers' Conference in October 1992, the first statewide gathering of Alaskan small presses.

Co-sponsored by the University of Alaska Press, Journalism Department, and the Alaska Humanities Forum in Fairbanks, the conference provided a valuable opportunity for Alaskan publishers to meet and exchange ideas. Timed to coincide with the annual Midnight Sun Writers' Conference, it also gave writers and publishers an unprecedented opportunity to network.

The Alaskan publishing boom can be explained, in part, by national publicity surrounding media events like the Iditarod Trail sled dog race, the Exxon Valdez oil spill, record cold spells, and the success of "Northern Exposure." The end result is a nearly insatiable market for books with Alaskan themes.

Frank Soos, director of the writers' conference, believes that combining conferences was a real boon for the writers. "We got to hear the publishers talk and got a lot a lot of good information; like what is a good or not so good manuscript," Soos said. "We also learned a lot about how to present our material to publishers and agents."

The perennially successful writers' conference drew audiences of 100–170 participants to its workshops and readings. "Fairbanks is a very good town for writers," Soos said. Soos also credits the publishers with a certain amount of courage for opening themselves up to a multitude of writers and massed manuscripts. "They put themselves on the line a bit," he said.

The publishers' conference, attended not only by regional publishing houses, but by book sellers, government publishing agents, and every major magazine dealing in Alaskana, covered a broad field of subjects. Panels of Alaskan publishers and buyers discussed marketing, working with authors, agency and educational publishing, and problems unique to small presses in the far north.

Leigh Cohn, president of the Publishers' Marketing Association, held seminars on how to cut overhead and increase profits by mail order marketing and niche or target marketing. "Mail order marketing is one area in which Alaskan publishers enjoy a level playing field," Cohn said. He also participated in the copyright workshop and spoke on quality and integrity in marketing.

Keynote speaker Jennifer Moyer, publisher of *Small Press Magazine,* who was also a guest of the writers' conference, delivered a moving analysis of the role small presses play in support of the First Amendment by providing an alternative to major publishing houses.

Dan Levant, founder of Madrona Publishing of Seattle and now with Levant and Wales Literary Agency, held seminars on working with agents and financial planning in publishing. "What I look for in a writer is a good, strong 'voice.' You can't define it, but you know it when you see it," Levant said. He also participated in the workshop on copyrights and gave an optimistic address on book publishing's future.

At the wrap-up session, the publishers agreed to establish the Consortium of Northern Publishers (CNP) to maintain their new network and to invite Canadian publishers to participate. Consortium members hope to conduct future workshops on the technical and financial aspects of the business. A resource handbook will be published soon to share information about marketing methods, printers, retailers, and to conduct public relations on behalf of the membership.

The next conference is tentatively scheduled for April 24, 1993 in conjunction with Journalism Week in Anchorage and sponsored by the Alaska Press Club. A fall session is planned for Fairbanks. It may not be possible to hold the writing and publishing conferences together next year as funding for future writers' conferences is uncertain. Soos is considering a move from the conference format to a series of guest lecturers.

"Workshops by 'outside' writers are very valuable," Soos said. "I'd like to see an instate writers' exchange with writers traveling to outlying areas like circuit riding preachers."

Regardless of logistical difficulties, Alaska's literary community and small presses are flourishing. Given the hardiness of Alaskans' pioneer spirit, that literary tradition is likely to continue for some time.

Jonathan L. Holland is a freelance writer and student at the University of Alaska in Fairbanks, Alaska. After spending ten years fighting avalanches for the Alaska Department of Transportation, he has embarked on a career as a journalist and author.

OILA Fellowship Recipients

Kay Reid

The winners of Oregon Book Awards each receive $1,000, presented at a public ceremony where the applause of some 400 people provides instant acclaim. Recipients of OILA fellowships, on the other hand, receive their letters of congratulation through the mail, without an audience's admiring applause. The program of Fellowships to Writers and Publishers is at the heart of the work of the Oregon Institute of Literary Arts, and is an area the Board of Trustees is committed to expanding.

From OILA's beginning, founder Brian Booth had in mind an organization that would honor not only completed works and their authors, but also assist writers with works in progress, specific projects, or living expenses. Between 1988 and 1992 OILA gave 36 grants to writers and 18 to publishers, totaling $85,825. Each year applications are solicited from February through June. Out-of-state jurors read submissions through the summer and fall, then make their decisions by telephone conferences. Recipients are announced in December.

Approximately 600 applications for writing grants were submitted during the first five years of the fellowship program. They came from writers doing many different kinds of work — mothers with new babies or five grown children, gas station attendants, farmers, English faculty members, waitresses, retired professionals, ESL tutors, and a couple of men from the Oregon State Penitentiary. The applications are as dramatically diverse as the geography of Oregon.

Applicants are asked to describe their current situations as writers and how they would use the funds. The answers to this question are varied: workshop fees, tuition, research, child care, health care, a Maytag, a Macintosh, special writing equipment for a disability, or plain old bills — rent, food,

debt. *And time.*

Sallie Tisdale, an OILA grant recipient in 1988, speaks for many applicants. "Time is money, if you're in the habit of making money — but to anyone in the habit of making art, money is time. …The check came…just as I'd begun to scan the 'help wanted' ads again. I used it to stay unemployed: paid the rent, kept the electricity on, bought typewriting ribbons, paper, books, kept the door shut and the phone quiet, and gave myself the gift of a really good dictionary." Many recipients also say the grant gave them validation, created an environment of confidence, and led to another award.

Sandra Dorr, who received a grant for fiction in 1991, gave this report to OILA in November 1992: "You might have noticed that I actually didn't cash the check for a while…I wanted to make sure it didn't go straightaway to another bank to pay for our car…or even Christmas toys. But more than that — I looked at it when I sat down to work. I finished writing the novella, "Hold Me Tight."…It has taken me a long time to grow new roots in Oregon and the OILA award shone on my wall as visible proof of the intangible subterranean process that pulled me here to live and write… And the check? You can see it in this Times New Roman fine print. I bought a Gateway 2000 computer, a miraculous jump in technology from my old Kaypro…"

Fiction writer Karen Karbo used a grant to do research in London on a novel in progress, *Chicago May*, based on the life of a turn of the century con woman, who developed her criminal talents in Chicago and made a fortune fleecing the British nobility. Karbo met with a criminologist specializing in female criminals of the 19th century, visited the prison where the protagonist was interred, and bought books unavailable in the United States.

Time and tools for writing and keeping the electricity turned on — you may ask OILA for these things, and you could get them. Oregon residents are eligible to apply for OILA's yearly writing and publishing fellowships. Send an SASE to PO Box 10608, Portland, OR 97210 or call 503-223-3604.

Past recipients of OILA fellowships have been:

1992: Writers: Diana Abu-Jaber, Tim Gillespie, Chang-rae Lee, Ann Packer, Danna Schaeffer, Kathleen Mayer, Sandra Stone, Laurell Swails, and Jane Van Dis. Publishers: *Big Rain*, Blue Heron (for *Left Bank*), *Mississippi Mud*, Mr. Cogito Press, and *Motes — a Poetry Journal*.

1991: Writers: D. Roberts, Judith Barrington, Sandra Dorr, Susan Mach, Anndee Hochman, Andrea Carlisle, Elizabeth Claman, D. Lee Williams, Sandra Scofield, and Sandra Redfield. Publishers: Eighth Mountain Press, Fireweed, and *Silverfish Review*.

1990: Writers: Annie Dawid, John Nance, Sandra Williams, Ehud Havazelet, Penny Allen, Tom Crawford, and Carolyn Gage. Publishers: Blue Heron Publishing, CALYX, and Story Line Press.

1989: Writers: Karen Karbo, Teresa Jordan, Judith Barrington, Floyd Skloot, Philip Metcalfe, Robert Newton, and Dorothy Velasco. Publishers: Arrowood Books and Eighth Mountain Press.

1988: Writers: Gloria Bird, Michele Glazer, Todd Grimson, Sallie Tisdale, Lex Runciman, and Dan Duling. Publishers: CALYX, *Silverfish Review*, and *Mississippi Mud*.

Kay Reid is executive director of OILA.

CASLON

! $ % & ( ) * , - . / 0 1
2 3 4 5 6 7 8 9 : ; ? A
B C D E F G H I J K
L M N O P Q R S T
U V W X Y Z [ ] _ `
{ } Ä Å Ç É Ñ Ö Ü á
à â ä ã å ç é è ê ë í ì î ï
ñ ó ò ô ö õ ú ù û ü ° ¢
£ • ß ® © ™ ¨ ≠ Æ Ø
∞ ± ≤ ≥ ¥ µ ∂ ∑ ∏ π ∫
ª º Ω ¿ ¡ √ ƒ ≈ ∆ « » … Œ
œ – — " " ' ' ÷ ◊ ÿ Ÿ ‹ › fi fl

A Librarian's View

Mary J. Finnegan

Standing behind the curved teal Reference Desk in the newly remodeled Salem Public Library, I realize that I'm in the center of the local literary hustle and bustle. As a reference librarian my job is a varied one. The most visible task is to assist, introduce, instruct, and guide you through the library maze. At times I must calm the frustrated user: "I can't find any current statistics on women in state government"; "Don't you have any books on Salem history?"

Though new technologies such as on-line catalogs and CD ROM indexes have changed libraries, basic services are still the same. Books and information are our business. But there is another part of my job that is perhaps done in a quieter, more subtle way. It is simply the sharing of my love and knowledge of books and literature.

And as writer, as well as a librarian, my job takes on new meaning. Writing has always been a personal activity, something I did alone at home and rarely even talked about. But last year I decided to go public and join the local writer's group SWAP (Salem Writers and Publishers). It's been a natural partnership from the start. The meetings are held in the Salem Public Library. I usually change into comfortable blue jeans and a sweater and become a SWAP member. But throughout the evening my role as librarian slips in. I might mention the new edition of the literary agents directory now on the reference shelf. Or I might hand out a list of the CD ROM resources available. This is also my opportunity to receive input about the library from some frequent library users: "You need more books on the planets"; "Why don't you subscribe to any flying magazines?"

Throughout the week, during regular library hours, familiar faces appear requesting a private lesson with the new CD ROM indexes or a clarification about borrowing books from an-out-of state library. Though writers as library users are no different from business people doing marketing research or college students writing term papers, I must confess a special fondness for writers. These are the individuals who produce the works upon which my industry is based.

I've always felt my job as a librarian makes it easier for me to be a writer. But a far stronger influence is the impact that writing has on my role as a librarian. When I attend a writer's conference such as the Fishtrap Gathering in the Wallowas in Eastern Oregon, I am inspired as a writer. But the librarian in me gains as well. When I get to meet Western regional authors such as Kim Stafford, Terry Tempest Williams, or William Kittredge, I am able to pass my enthusiasm for their work on to library patrons at Salem Public Library. Discovering regional authors and publishers and adding their works to the library enriches our collection.

Books on the bestseller lists provide their own advertising and promotion but regional and small press publications need a little extra help. Library programs are an excellent solution. My library works closely with a local bookstore. When an author comes in for a book signing event, a lecture at the library might be scheduled for that same day. During Salem Public Library's annual Talk to the Expert Day, Portland mystery writer Vince Kohler manned a booth and generously shared writing hints and techniques. During quiet moments he actually used a few items in our library to do research for his next book.

As a librarian, I feel an obligation to give professional input to publishers. I write book reviews for a national library journal and I am not shy about giving an honest review. At library conventions I talk to vendors and publishers about format, pricing, and contents of their books and products.

Writers should have a special relationship with their local library. Here are a few ideas.

Checklist for writers:

- Get to know your librarian. Introduce yourself. Describe your areas of research and interest — briefly. Librarians are trained to act in confidence and we can be on the lookout for new resources for you.

- Give input. Help us build our book collection and improve our services through your recommendations and suggestions. We rely on community input.

- Promote your book or writer's group. Book talks, slide shows, and writing workshops are always welcome ideas for library programs and good advertisement for you.

Writing, like most creative endeavors, requires quiet time. Lost in your own work, you may become isolated. Attending a writer's group or interacting with your library may provide needed inspiration. Hearing about publishing trends or seeing a new magazine on the library shelf may provide some new stimulation which you didn't know you needed.

As a writer I feel I have the ideal job. No, I don't get to read all day, but I do have the pleasure of being surrounded by books, new and old. I watch library users turn bright ideas into successful projects with the help of our resources.

I encourage you to take time this month and stop by your library. Say hello to your librarian. Don't be surprised when you find at least an ally and perhaps a new friend.

Mary Finnegan lives in an old farmhouse outside of Salem, Oregon, with her artist husband Stev Ominski and their two cats, Titanium and Umber. She has worked in libraries for more than twenty years and is currently working on a children's picture book.

OPTIMA

!$%&()*,-./01 23456789:;?A BCDEFGHIJKL MNOPQRSTUV WXYZ[]_`{}ÄÅ ÇÉÑÖÜáàâäãå çéèêëíìîïñóòô öõúùûü°¢£•ß® ©™¨≠ÆØ∞±≤≥ ¥µ∂∑∏π∫ªºΩ¿¡ √ƒ≈∆«»…Œœ—— """''÷◊ÿŸ‹›fifl

A Celebration of Writers & Readers

Kevin Mckeown

The Vancouver International Writers (& *Readers*) Festival each year attracts up to 8,000 avid readers to four venues on Vancouver's Granville Island to hear and take part in over 45 ticketed events. More than 50 writers from across Canada and around the world are featured in five days of readings, seminars, panel discussions and lively audience/author exchanges.

Founded in 1988 by producer Alma Lee, the Festival has grown to be one of Vancouver's major annual cultural events. This is no small achievement in a city known as "the city of festivals."

An extensive program of daytime events geared to younger readers has been well received by the local school districts, and busloads of hundreds of youngsters are welcome guests at each year's Festival. In conjunction with this program, *The Vancouver Sun*, the city's leading daily newspaper, conducts an annual Young Writers Project which sees nearly 2,000 local elementary and secondary students submit their own works to a panel of professionals. A selection of these pieces is published over several weeks in *The Vancouver Sun*, and especially noteworthy works are read by their authors at special events during the Festival. It's a great way to encourage young writers, and Festival organizers look forward to the day that a guest author at the Festival can say that they got their start with the Young Writers Project!

Annual highlights of the Festival include the Annual Poetry Bash, the Literary Cabaret, the Authors' Brunch, and the Duthie Lecture. The Annual Poetry Bash is always a sell-out event and features readings by a dozen or so poets in a cabaret-style setting. It's certainly the largest and best attended poetry event in Vancouver each year and an important boost to "poetry consciousness." The Annual Poetry Bash has become such a popular and widely-known feature that, in response to numerous requests from educators, the 1992 Festival launched a Mini-Poetry Bash, presenting many of the same poets as the main event in a daytime program for students. That too has proven to be an enormous success (sold right out!) and will be a regular highlight of future Festivals.

A unique feature at each year's Vancouver International Writers (& *Readers*) Festival is the Literary Cabaret, which brings together the talents of numerous guest authors, poets, performance artists, and the musical inspirations of Sal Ferreras and his musicians. Ferreras and his team provide musical interludes throughout the evening, but the real fun comes when they improvise background music to the readings. These experiments in multi-disciplinary performance are always interesting, and sometimes so "right on" with the reading that it's hard to believe they weren't carefully rehearsed.

The Sunday morning of Festival week finds Festival staff and volunteers (without whom none of this would ever happen) serving a tasty hot and cold brunch to 150 or so Festival patrons at the Authors Brunch. The authors get to eat too, but are obliged to 'read for their breakfast.' Another highly successful event, the Authors Brunch, offers Festival-goers an opportunity to not only hear some great readings, but also to chat with their favorite writers over coffee and pastries afterwards.

The Annual Duthie Lecture honors the memory of legendary Vancouver bookseller, the late Bill Duthie, whose Duthie Books did much over the years to promote and encourage Canadian literature on the west coast. Speakers at the Duthie Lecture have included Margaret Atwood, Michael Ignatieff, and, this past year, Peter C. Newman.

Festival events run the gamut from the extremely serious to the extremely silly. Readings and discussions touch on every area of literary interest and human concern, including multi-cultural, racial, political, and feminist concerns. And each year's line-up includes a number of different literary genres, from mystery and detection to science fiction, from limericks and doggerel poetry to writing for stage and film.

As well as bringing audiences a wide selection of style and content choices, the Festival also strives to bring together as many national and cultural representations as possible. The 1992 Festival, for example, featured writers with roots in Canada, the U.S., Scotland, Ireland, Australia, Italy, Czechoslovakia, Viet Nam, India, and Trinidad. Also important to the diversity of the Festival's presentations is an annual commitment to bringing First Nations writers and their works to Festival audiences.

The 1993 Vancouver International Writers (& *Readers*) Festival will take place October 20 through 24. For further information please call (604) 681-6330.

Kevin Mckeown is communications and marketing manager for the Festival.

Notes

In the new world of computer imaging, type is more than ever — at least in recent memory — a graphic element on the page. This fact creates new considerations when selecting typefaces. On the one hand, it's necessary to try new combinations that

Introduction to the Directories

Everyone involved in the world of words and ideas requires access to the publishing going on around them, and writers, especially, need to know both where to find information and where to "market" their work. While we have dropped many marginal listings from this edition, we've retained as many as possible, including those who are not interested in submissions. With each new round of surveys, we learn more about the publishers of the NW.

Tips for Writers

Carefully targeting your queries or submissions increases your chances of being published. Study the listings to be sure you're not wasting your time and postage. If a publisher has provided no detailed information, it's best to assume that submissions are unwanted. Sending your work to publishers without first learning their needs ensures rejection. If a publisher with no description happens to be located nearby, you might investigate them. But always make your first approach as economical as possible — and always include a self-addressed, stamped envelope (SASE).

Familiarizing yourself with the editorial requirements, style, and form of a publication helps you prepare your query. Likewise, knowing what books a publisher has previously done is essential. When writers guidelines are available, use them. Samples also are offered by many periodicals for postage or a nominal charge, or you may be able to find them in a library. With book publishers, write for a catalog or look up their titles in *Books In Print*. Remember, most publishers won't change editorial direction to accommodate even the best work that's unrelated to their special focuses.

Unless otherwise indicated, limit your initial approach to a query letter. Sending an entire manuscript or clips of everything you've done is likely superfluous at this stage. Begin by tantalizing the editor or publisher with your idea, letting the query display the quality of your writing and the appropriateness of your ideas. Most editors are always looking for fresh material, so they'll quickly assess from your query whether yours is worth a second look.

Organization of the Directories

This section is divided into three major parts: indexes, publisher listings, and resources.

The Indexes. The primary indexes are divided by major groupings: book publishers, periodicals, and newspapers. These are subdivided by state or province. Following the primary indexes are indexes to special subjects or related groups of subjects.

On the next page, immediately preceding the indexes, is a SUBJECT KEY TO THE INDEXES. The left side of each of these entries is a key word; the right side is an associated key number. In the primary indexes, publishers' names are followed by one or more of these numbers. Having looked up a number for a subject, you can scan the indexes for entries that match. If your subject is among those in the selected indexes, simply look there first. In the directory listings, the numbers are not used; instead, the key words are given a separate line beneath each entry.

You may not find a listing that matches your search. That doesn't mean there are no publishers with that focus. Consider related subjects. It is also a good idea to look under all major categories before giving up. A publisher of both books and periodicals may only be listed under only one of those headings. Of course, scanning the actual listings is an excellent way to familiarize yourself with likely markets or sources.

Listings with unspecified subjects fall into two broad categories: those who told us too little about themselves and those who have general interests. The former are most often tiny publishers and self-publishers; the latter are frequently newspapers.

Index conventions. Indexes and listings are alphabetical within their various heading levels. Cardinal numbers at the beginning of names are before letters. When possible, we've indexed abbreviations according to the whole words they represent, e.g., BC as British Columbia. We weren't always sure if we were dealing with initials, an abbreviation, or an acronym, so if you

SECTION VI

PUBLISHING LISTS

cannot find a title one way, try the other. For the sake of predictable order, we've thrown out the beginning articles "A," "An," and "The" when alphabetizing. If you're looking for a name that begins with one of those, use the next word. A publisher whose name is an individual may be found ordered by either the first name or the last ("Mary Smith Publishing" may also be listed as "Smith Publishing, Mary").

Among the abbreviations that are commonly used are *ASAP* (as soon as possible), *assn* (association), *Ave* (Avenue), *avg* (average), *B&W* (black and white photos), *Bldg* (Building), *Blvd* (Boulevard), *Cdn* (Cana-dian), *col* (column), *ds* (double spaced), *IRC* (International Reply Coupon), *ms(s)* (man-uscript(s)), *pg(s)* (page(s)), *RR* (Rural Route), *Rt* (Route), *S&H* (shipping and han-dling), *SASE* (self-addressed, stamped en-velope), *Ste* (Suite), *Stn* (Station), *sub* (sub-scription), *US* (United States of America), *wd(s)* (word(s)), and *wk(s)* (week(s)).

Updates and Accuracy

Though we regularly clean our lists and resurvey before each edition, we cannot guarantee the current accuracy of the lists. Publishing is a volatile business and there is always much coming and going of publish-ers, publications, and personnel. It's wise to check with a publisher before submitting (see "Tips for Writers" above).

Writer's Northwest Handbook is a commu-nity-building tool. We encourage your sug-gestions and criticisms. And please, inform us of changed or erroneous listings.

Between editions, updates and new list-ings are published quarterly in our tabloid newspaper, *Writer's NW*, which is available by mail for $10 per year in the US and $12 (US) in Canada. *Writer's NW* features news, reviews, interviews, features, and how-to's for the broad community of the printed word.

Subject Key to Primary Indexes

Book Publishers Index

USING THE INDEXES AND DIRECTORY

Primary indexes are divided by Book Publishers, Periodicals, and Newspapers, with each of those categories subdivided by state or province.

Numbers following primary index entries indicate subjects of editorial focus and may be looked up in the subject table at the beginning of this section. Alternately, use the subject table to select numbers for areas of interest, then scan the primary indexes for publishers with those numbers.

Selected subject indexes are groups of several related editorial subject. They do not include the subject numbers but are subdivided by type of publisher.

All directory entries follow the indexes and are organized alphabetically by Book Publishers, Periodicals, and Newspapers. Each entry is followed by the subjects for that listing, which allows scanning of the primary entries for those interested in specific subjects.

Oregon

USING THE INDEXES AND DIRECTORY

Primary indexes are divided by Book Publishers, Periodicals, and Newspapers, with each of those categories subdivided by state or province.

Numbers following primary index entries indicate subjects of editorial focus and may be looked up in the subject table at the beginning of this section. Alternately, use the subject table to select numbers for areas of interest, then scan the primary indexes for publishers with those numbers.

Selected subject indexes are groups of several related editorial subject. They do not include the subject numbers but are subdivided by type of publisher or state.

All directory entries follow the indexes and are organized alphabetically by Book Publishers, Periodicals, and Newspapers. Each entry is followed by the subjects for that listing, which allows scanning of the primary entries for those interested in specific subjects.

Washington

USING THE INDEXES AND DIRECTORY

Primary indexes are divided by Book Publishers, Periodicals, and Newspapers, with each of those categories subdivided by state or province.

Numbers following primary index entries indicate subjects of editorial focus and may be looked up in the subject table at the beginning of this section. Alternately, use the subject table to select numbers for areas of interest, then scan the primary indexes for publishers with those numbers.

Selected subject indexes are groups of several related editorial subject. They do not include the subject numbers but are subdivided by type of publisher or state.

All directory entries follow the indexes and are organized alphabetically by Book Publishers, Periodicals, and Newspapers. Each entry is followed by the subjects for that listing, which allows scanning of the primary entries for those interested in specific subjects.

Periodicals Index

Alaska

USING THE INDEXES AND DIRECTORY

Primary indexes are divided by Book Publishers, Periodicals, and Newspapers, with each of those categories subdivided by state or province.

Numbers following primary index entries indicate subjects of editorial focus and may be looked up in the subject table at the beginning of this section. Alternately, use the subject table to select numbers for areas of interest, then scan the primary indexes for publishers with those numbers.

Selected subject indexes are groups of several related editorial subject. They do not include the subject numbers but are subdivided by type of publisher or state.

All directory entries follow the indexes and are organized alphabetically by Book Publishers, Periodicals, and Newspapers. Each entry is followed by the subjects for that listing, which allows scanning of the primary entries for those interested in specific subjects.

Montana

Oregon

USING THE INDEXES AND DIRECTORY

Primary indexes are divided by Book Publishers, Periodicals, and Newspapers, with each of those categories subdivided by state or province.

Numbers following primary index entries indicate subjects of editorial focus and may be looked up in the subject table at the beginning of this section. Alternately, use the subject table to select numbers for areas of interest, then scan the primary indexes for publishers with those numbers.

Selected subject indexes are groups of several related editorial subject. They do not include the subject numbers but are subdivided by type of publisher or state.

All directory entries follow the indexes and are organized alphabetically by Book Publishers, Periodicals, and Newspapers. Each entry is followed by the subjects for that listing, which allows scanning of the primary entries for those interested in specific subjects.

Washington

Newspapers Index

Newspapers Index

Alaska

Selected Indexes

Agriculture/ Forestry/ Gardening

Book Publishers

Academic Enterprises
Botany Books
Cascade Farm Publishing Company
Dioscorides Press, Inc
Hartley & Marks, Publishers
Juniper Ridge Press
Klamath Falls Publishing
Midgard Press
Offshoot Publications
Oregon Association of Nurserymen
Oregon's Agricultural Progress
Seven Buffaloes Press
Silver Bay Herb Farm
Timber Press, Inc
United States Dept of Ag, Forest Service
University of Oregon Forest Industries Management Ctr
Van Patten Publishing
Whitecap Books

Newspapers

Agri-Times Northwest
Capital Press
Idaho Farm Bureau News
Inland Farmer-Stockman
The Dalles Weekly Reminder
The Sprague Advocate
The Standard-Register
Washington Grange News
Western Livestock Reporter

Periodicals

AcreAGE
AERO Sun-Times
Ag Almanac
Agri Equipment Today
Agri-News
ALKI: The Washington Library Association Journal
American Dry Pea & Lentil Assn Bulletin
American Rhododendron Society Journal

Beef Industry News
BLM News, Oregon &. Washington
Boise Cascade Quarterly
British Columbia Agri Digest
Butter-fat Magazine
Canada Poultryman
Country Roads
Dairyline
Economic Facts/Idaho Agriculture
Farm & Ranch Chronicle
Farm Journal Magazine
Farm Lines
Farm Review
Florist & Grower
Forest Log
Forest Voice
Forest Watch Magazine
Growing Edge Magazine
Herb Market Report
Hi Baller Forest Magazine
Idaho Farmer-Stockman
Idaho Forester
Idaho Grain
Idaho Grange News
Idaho Potato Commission Report
Idaho Thoroughbred Quarterly
Idaho Wheat
Idaho Wool Growers Bulletin
Idahobeef
Idea Productions
Infoletter
IWUA Alert
Journal of Pesticide Reform
Ketch Pen
Land
Line Rider

USING THE INDEXES AND DIRECTORY

Primary indexes are divided by Book Publishers, Periodicals, and Newspapers, with each of those categories subdivided by state or province.

Numbers following primary index entries indicate subjects of editorial focus and may be looked up in the subject table at the beginning of this section. Alternately, use the subject table to select numbers for areas of interest, then scan the primary indexes for publishers with those numbers.

Selected subject indexes are groups of several related editorial subject. They do not include the subject numbers but are subdivided by type of publisher or state.

All directory entries follow the indexes and are organized alphabetically by Book Publishers, Periodicals, and Newspapers. Each entry is followed by the subjects for that listing, which allows scanning of the primary entries for those interested in specific subjects.

Livestock Express
Logging & Sawmill Journal
Marketing Reports & Trade Leads
Master Gardener Notes
Montana Agricultural Statistics Service
Montana Farmer-Stockman
News-Standard
Northern Aquaculture Magazine
Northwest Lookout
Northwest Nurserystock Report
Northwest Seasonal Worker
Nursery Trades BC
Nutrition Notebook
OMGA Northwest Newsletter
Onion World
Oregon Farm Bureau News
Oregon Farmer-Stockman
Oregon Future Farmer
Oregon Grange Bulletin
Oregon Wheat
Ornamentals Northwest
Pacific Coast Nurseryman Magazine
Pea & Lentil News
Permaculture With Native Plants
Pome News
Potato Country
Potato Grower of Idaho
Radiance Herbs & Massage Newsletter
Rancher-Stockman-Farmer
Screef
Small Farmer's Journal
SONCAP News
Sugar Producer
Sustainable Farming Quarterly
The Bread and Butter Chronicles
The Digger
The Extender
The Goodfruit Grower Magazine
The Grange News
The Island Grower RR4
The Smallholder Publishing Collective
The Sproutletter
The Watershed Sentinel
Timber!
Timberbeast
Trout
Washington Cattleman
Washington Farmer Stockman
Washington Water News
Western Cascade Tree Fruit Association Quarterly
Western Farmer-Stockman Magazines
Wheat Life

Arts: Fine/Allied/Applied

Book Publishers

Allegro Publishing
Amadeus Press
Art Gallery of Greater Victoria
Asian Music Publications
At Your Fingertips
Bellevue Art Museum
Braemer Books
Broadsheet Publications
Clark City Press
Crystal Musicworks
Dark Horse Comics, Inc
Four Cedars Productions
Function Industries Press
HearSay Press
Henry Art Gallery
Homestead Book Company
Hughes/Taylor
Inst. for Study of Traditional American Indian Arts
Keyboard Workshop
MatriMedia
Montana Arts Council
Poets. Painters. Composers.
Prescott Street Press
Provincial Archives of British Columbia
Rie Munoz, Ltd
Stonehouse Publications
That Patchwork Place, Inc
The Real Comet Press
University of Washington Press
Urban Design Centre Society
Western Publishing

Newspapers

Bluesnotes
Pike Place Market News
This Week
Willamette Week

Periodicals

ACAPella
Allied Arts Newsletter
Allied Arts of Seattle
Animator
Aristos
Arnazella
Art West Magazine
Arterial

Artist Trust
Artistamp News
Artist's Notes
ArtistSearch/Montana Arts Council
Artoonist
Arts & Crafts News
Arts East/Eastern OR Reg. Arts Council
Arts Washington
Axiom
Beaverton Arts Commission Newsletter
Black Lamb
Bluespaper
Blur
Boulevard Magazine
Brussels Sprout
Colins Magazine
Convictions
Crafts Advocate
CutBank
Designer's Quarterly
Earshot Jazz
Emergency Horse
Encore Arts In Performance Magazine
Eurock
Explorations
Fish Wrap
Gallerie: Women's Art
Heritage Music Review
Historic Preservation League of Oregon Newsletter
Idaho Humanities Council Newsletter
IFCC News
Images
International Art Post
Jeopardy
Journal For Architecture & Design
KBOO Program Guide
Kinesis
KSOR Guide to the Arts
Left Bank
Listening Post - KUOW FM
Metrocenter YMCA
Metropolis
Mid-Valley Arts Council
National Percent for Art Newsletter
Northwest Poets & Artists Calendar
NW Gallery Art Magazine
Old Bottle Magazine/Popular Archaeology
Oregon Arts News
Oregon East Magazine
Oregon Music Educator
Paper Radio
Parallel DisCourse
Passage
Playboard Magazine
Point of View
Portland Live Music Guide

Prism
Puncture
Riffs
Rock Rag
Roseburg Woodsman
Seattle Art Museum Program Guide
Seattle Arts
Skagit Art Magazine
Soul Town Review
Southern Oregon Arts
Southern Oregon Currents
SteppingOut Arts Magazine
Stylus
Tacoma Arts Commission Newsletter
The American Music News
The Arts
The Capilano Review
The Duckbush Journal
The Gilmore Gazette
The Portable Wall/Basement Press
The Printer's Northwest Trader
The Rocket/Murder Inc.
The Signal
The Stranger
The Voice
The Voice
The Wire Harp - Sfcc
Two Louies Magazine
Victory Music Review
Warren Publishing House
Western Living
What's Happening
Yokoi, A. Quarterly Journal of the Arts
SCR
Echo Film Productions

Business/Labor

Book Publishers

Alaska Dept of Labor, Research &. Analysis
Beynch Press Publishing Co.
Bicentennial Era Enterprises
Circa Press
Cleaning Consultant Services, Inc
COMMUNICOM
Consultant Services Northwest, Inc
Entreprenurial Workshops
Global Marketing Intelligence
High Impact Press
Information Press
International Self-Counsel Press, Ltd
Law Forum Press
Lifeworks Press
Management/Marketing Associates, Inc
Maritime Publications
Merril Press
Mind's Ink Publishing
Montana Department of Labor & Industry
Mountain Publishing
New Star Books
Online Press Inc.
Oregon Association of Nurserymen
Oregon Economic Development Department
Pacific Northwest Labor History Assn
Panoply Press, Inc
Pet Owners' Association
Pharmaceutical Technology
Pinstripe Publishing
Price Guide Publishers
Princess Publishing
PSI Research/The Oasis Press
Random Lengths Publications
Self-Counsel Press, Inc
Socialist Party of Canada
Society of Photo-Optical Instrumentation Engineering
Spokane Area Economic Devel. Council
The Tax Tutors
ThunderEgg Publishing
TIPTOE Literary Service
Toy Investments, Inc
Training Associates Ltd.
University of Idaho Ctr for Business Development &
     Research
University of Oregon Forest Industries Management Ctr
Update
Washington Insurance Commissioner
Washington Professional Publications
Western Wood Products Association

Newspapers

Alaska Jrl of Commerce
Big Sky Business Journal
Business Opportunities Journal
Daily Journal of Commerce
Journal of Business
Northwest Computer News
Northwest Labor Press
Pierce County Business Examiner
The Costco Connection
The Stamp Wholesaler
Washington Teamster Newspaper

Periodicals

AcreAGE
Adventures In Subversion
Ag-Pilot International
Agri Equipment Today
Alaska Business Monthly
Alaska Construction and Oil
Alaska Dept of Labor, Research &. Analysis
Alaska Fisherman's Journal/Ocean Leader
Alaska Review of Soc & Econ Conditions
American Contractor
American Dry Pea & Lentil Assn Bulletin
AOI News Digest
Asia Cable
Astrology Night
ATI Newsletter
Auto Glass Journal
Barometer
BC Business Examiner
BC Business Magazine
BC Hotelman
BC Professional Engineer

USING THE INDEXES AND DIRECTORY

Primary indexes are divided by Book Publishers, Periodicals, and Newspapers, with each of those categories subdivided by state or province.

Numbers following primary index entries indicate subjects of editorial focus and may be looked up in the subject table at the beginning of this section. Alternately, use the subject table to select numbers for areas of interest, then scan the primary indexes for publishers with those numbers.

Selected subject indexes are groups of several related editorial subject. They do not include the subject numbers but are subdivided by type of publisher or state.

All directory entries follow the indexes and are organized alphabetically by Book Publishers, Periodicals, and Newspapers. Each entry is followed by the subjects for that listing, which allows scanning of the primary entries for those interested in specific subjects.

Beaverton Business Advocate
Beef Industry News
Boise Business Today
Boise Cascade Quarterly
BookNotes: Resources for Small & Self-Pubs
British Columbia Agri Digest
British Columbia Library Association Newsletter
British Columbia Medical Journal
Brown's Business Reporter
Bulletin of the King Co. Medical Society
Business News
Butter-fat Magazine
Canada Poultryman
Catchline, Ski Business News
CGA Magazine
Changing Homes Magazine
Citizen Action
Cleaning Business Magazine
Commercial Review
Communication Magazine
Construction Data & News
Construction Sightlines
Contacts Influential
Contractors Weekly
Craft Connection
Crafts Report
Creative News n' Views
Current News
Dairyline
Demographics Northwest
Economic Facts/Idaho Agriculture
Em-Kayan
Engineering News-record
Enterprise
Financial Times of Canada Ltd.
Fishing Tackle Trade News
Florist & Grower
Hi Baller Forest Magazine
Home Office Opportunities
Home Source
Home Sweet Home
Hungary International
Idaho
Idaho Business Review
Idaho Council on Economic Ed. Newsletter
Idaho Grain
Idaho Pharmacist
Idaho Potato Commission Report
Idaho Power Bulletin
Idaho Thoroughbred Quarterly
Idaho Voice
Idaho Wheat
Idaho Wool Growers Bulletin
Idahobeef
Idaho's Economy
IEA Reporter

Incredible Idaho
Innkeeping World
Insurance Adjuster
Insurance Week
Intermountain Logging News
IPEA News
IWA Woodworker
Journal of Financial & Quantitative Analysis
Journal of Seattle-King Co. Dental Soc.
Landmark
Livestock Express
Loggers World
Logging & Sawmill Journal
Logistics & Transportation Review
Marketing Index International Pub
Marketing Reports & Trade Leads
Marple's Business Newsletter
Mining Review
Montana Business Quarterly
Montana Farmer-Stockman
National Boycott Newsletter
New Age Retailer
Nike Times
Northern Aquaculture Magazine
Northwest Construction News
Northwest Lookout
Northwest Motor: Journal for Automotive Ind.
Northwest Nurserystock Report
Northwest Oil Report
Nuclear News Bureau
Nursery Trades BC
NW Stylist and Salon
Onion World
Oregon Business Magazine
Oregon Business Review
Oregon Central News
Oregon Contractor
Oregon Freemason
Oregon Independent Grocer
Oregon Masonic News
Oregon Newsletter
Oregon Public Employee
Oregon Public Employees Retirement System
Oregon Publisher
Oregon Realtor
Oregon Restaurateur
Oregon State Trooper
Oregon Teamster
Oregon Vintage Motorcyclist Newsletter
Oregon Wheat
Oregon/Washington Labor Press
Pacific Builder & Engineer
Pacific Coast Nurseryman Magazine
Pacific Fisheries Enhancement
Pacific Fishing
Pacific Marketer

Pacific Network News
Pacific Northwest Executive
Pacific Yachting
Pea & Lentil News
Pet Owners' Tribune
Port Side: The Port of Portland Magazine
Portfolio
Portland News of the Portland Chamber of Commerce
Potato Country
Potato Grower of Idaho
Potlatch Times
Puget Sound Business Journal
Random Lengths
Review of Social & Economic Conditions
R.N. Idaho
RNABC News
Screef
Seafood Leader
Skies America
Snow Action
Spokes
Stat
SteppingOut Arts Magazine
Sugar Producer
The Adjusting Entry
The American Music News
The Business Journal
The Competitive Advantage
The Digger
The Exhibit Review
The Fisherman's News
The Fraser Institute
The Gated Wye
The Golden Eagle
The Goodfruit Grower Magazine
The Journal of the Oregon Dental Assn
The Printer's Northwest Trader
The Rose
The Washington Horse
The Willamette Writer
Timber/West Magazine
T.I.P.S. Employment Guide
TOWERS Club, USA Newsletter
Transport Electronic News
Truck Logger
Truck World
Vernon Publications
Washington Business
Washington Cattleman
Washington CEO
Washington Farmer Stockman
Washington Food Dealer Magazine
Washington Newspaper
Washington Stylist and Salon
Western Banker Magazine
Western Business

Western Cascade Tree Fruit Association Quarterly
Western Fisheries
Western Investor
Western Mills Today
Western Remodeler Magazine
Women's Work
Women's Yellow Pages

Children/Family

Book Publishers

Alaska Council of Teachers of English
Bear Creek Publications
Beautiful America Publishing Company
Beyond Words Publishing Inc.
Blue Heron Press
Blue Heron Publishing, Inc
Bob Books Publications
Bonnie Scherer Publications
Bright Ring Publishing
Browndeer Press
Callan and Brooks Publishing Company
Castalia Publishing Company
Centerplace Publishing Company
Childbirth Education Association
Coalition For Child Advocacy
Creative Children
Dolan Press
Edmonds Arts Commission Books
Energeia Publishing, Inc
Estrada Publications and Photography
Grapevine Publications, Inc
Graphic Arts Center Publishing Company
Havin' Fun, Inc
Home Education Press
Hug-a-book Publications
Incline Press Book Publisher
Insight Passage
Legacy House, Inc
Legendary Publishing Co.
Markins Enterprises
Merrill Court Press
MicNik Publications
National Seafood Educators
Nerve Press
Newport Bay Publishing Ltd
Nobility Press
Northwest Parent Publishing
Northwest Parent Publishing
Orca Book Publishers
Pacific Edge Publishing and Media Services Ltd.
Pacific Educational Press
Pandora's Treasures
Parenting Press, Inc
Paws IV Publishing Co.
Peel Productions
Pennypress, Inc
Planned Parenthood Association of Idaho
Price Productions
Printery Farm
Puppet Concepts Publishing
Purna Press

Questar Publishers, Inc
Rae Publications
Ramalo Publication
Roger Pond & Associates
Sagebrush Books
Saturday's Child
Steppingstone Press
SwanMark Books
TGNW Press
The Charles Franklin Press
The Pedersens
Unique Press
Upper Case Publications
Wheel Press
Wilander Publishing Co.

Newspapers

The Asterisk

Periodicals

Adopted Child
After the Wedding
Caronn's Town & Country w The Crib Sheet
Chalk Talk
Chanticleer
Christian Parenting Today
Coeur d'Alene Homes Messenger
Enfantaisie
First Alternative Thymes
Ghost Town Quarterly
Grandparents Journal
Home Education Magazine
Images
Kid Care Magazine

USING THE INDEXES AND DIRECTORY

Primary indexes are divided by Book Publishers, Periodicals, and Newspapers, with each of those categories subdivided by state or province.

Numbers following primary index entries indicate subjects of editorial focus and may be looked up in the subject table at the beginning of this section. Alternately, use the subject table to select numbers for areas of interest, then scan the primary indexes for publishers with those numbers.

Selected subject indexes are groups of several related editorial subject. They do not include the subject numbers but are subdivided by type of publisher or state.

All directory entries follow the indexes and are organized alphabetically by Book Publishers, Periodicals, and Newspapers. Each entry is followed by the subjects for that listing, which allows scanning of the primary entries for those interested in specific subjects.

Lighthouse
Listen: Promoting Positive Choices
LUNO: Learning Unlimited Network of Oregon
Musher Monthly
Northwest Parent Publishing
Oregon Council on Alcoholism & Drug Abuse Newsletter
Our Little Friend
Pathways
Pen Pals Northwest
Phinney Ridge Review
Portland Family Calendar
Portland Parent
Primary Treasure
P.R.O. Newsletter of Oregon
Ruralite
Seattle's Child/Eastside Project
Signatures from Big Sky
Skipping Stones
Street Times
Teaching Home
Teaching Research Infant and Child Center News
The Book Shop/Children's Newsletter
The Mirror
The Ovulation Method Newsletter
The Vancouver Child
Totline
Warren Publishing House
Young Voices

Fiction

Book Publishers

Alki
Angst World Library
Anvil Press
Arrowood Books, Inc
Arsenal, Pulp Press , Ltd.
Barlow Press
Bear Grass Press
Bellowing Ark Press
Black Heron Press
Blue Heron Publishing, Inc
Blue Scarab Press
Blue Unicorn Press
Broken Moon Press
Cacanadadada Press Ltd.
Castle Peak Editions
Charles Seluzicki, Fine Press Series
Clark City Press
Council for Indian Education
Current
Edprint, Inc
Empty Bowl Press
Fall Creek Press
Fjord Press
Floating Ink Books
Globe Publishing Co.
Harbour Publishing
Intertext
Keepsake Publications
LetterPress
Maverick Publications
Montana Arts Council
Mother of Ashes Press
Nerve Press
New Dawn Books Inc.
Oolichan Books
Owl Creek Press
PSI Research/The Oasis Press
Pulphouse Publishing
Questar Publishers, Inc
Quiet Lion Press
Ramalo Publication
Repository Press
Ritz Publishing
Ruth Edwins-Conley, Publishing
Sagebrush Books
Seven Buffaloes Press
Signpost Press, Inc
Silverleaf Press
StarLance Publications
Strawberry Hill Press
Studio 0403

SwanMark Books
Tabula Rasa Press
Talent House Press
Talonbooks
The Caitlin Press
The Quartz Press
Theytus Books
Trace Editions
Trout Creek Press
Turman Publishing Company
Vagabond Press
West Coast Crime
Wheel Press
Writer's Publishing Service Company

Periodicals

Adventure in Hell
Alchemy
Beacon
Bellowing Ark
BikeReport
Boredom Magazine
Box Dog
British Columbia Monthly
Cacanadadada Review
Caronn's Town & Country w The Crib Sheet
Catalyst
Chalk Talk
Chanticleer
Crab Creek Review
CutBank
Dalmo'ma
Denali
Dog River Review
Edprint, Inc
Elixir of Oregon Wordworks
Ellensburg Anthology
Encounters Magazine
ERGO! Bumbershoot's Literary Magazine
Essence
Event
Exhibition
Explorations
Fantasy and Terror
Fantasy Macabre
Figment: Tales from the Imagination
Fine Madness
FINESSE Magazine for the Washington Woman
Glimmer Train Press, Inc
Grassroots Oracle
Inky Trails Publications
Jeopardy
Kinnikinnik
Lighthouse
Literary Creations

Matrix
Mississippi Mud
Montana Review
(m)Other Tongues
Northwest Passage
Northwest Review
NRG Magazine
Oregon English Journal
Outlaw Newsletter
Pen Names
Perceptions
Permafrost
Plant's Review of Books
Poetic Space
Poetry Exchange
Poptart
PRISM International
Pulphouse: A Fiction Magazine
Puzzle Mystery Magazine
Rain
Rain City Review
Realms
Rhapsody!
Rocky Mountain Poetry Magazine
Room of One's Own
Sign of the Times-a Chronicle of Decadence
Silverfish Review
Slightly West
Snake River Reflections
Spindrift
sub-TERRAIN
Testmarketed Downpour
The Bellingham Review
The Claremont Review
The Duckbush Journal
The Eclectic Muse
The Eloquent Umbrella
The Jason
The Malahat Review
The Pacific Review
The Pointed Circle
The Seattle Review
The Silver Apple Branch
The Valley Magazine
The Village Idiot
The Written ARTS
Tickled by Thunder
Tidewater
Trestle Creek Review
University of Portland Review
Vintage Northwest
Warner Pacific College Art & Literature Magazine
West Coast Review
West Wind Review
Westwind
Willow Springs

Writers' Open Forum
Writing Magazine
Young Voices

Gay/Lesbian/ Sexuality

Book Publishers

Judy Ford & Company
Land Mark Publishing
Pacific Coast Centre of Sexology
Playful Wisdom Press
Press Gang Publishers
Purna Press
Silverleaf Press
The Eighth Mountain Press
The Seal Press

Newspapers

Guide Magazine
Womyn's Press

Periodicals

Alternative Connection
Catalyst
Diversity: The Lesbian Rag
In Common
Island Men
Just Out
Lesbian Contradiction:
Northwest Gay and Lesbian Reader
Oregon Gay News
Seattle Gay News
The City Open Press

USING THE INDEXES AND DIRECTORY

Primary indexes are divided by Book Publishers, Periodicals, and Newspapers, with each of those categories subdivided by state or province.

Numbers following primary index entries indicate subjects of editorial focus and may be looked up in the subject table at the beginning of this section. Alternately, use the subject table to select numbers for areas of interest, then scan the primary indexes for publishers with those numbers.

Selected subject indexes are groups of several related editorial subject. They do not include the subject numbers but are subdivided by type of publisher or state.

All directory entries follow the indexes and are organized alphabetically by Book Publishers, Periodicals, and Newspapers. Each entry is followed by the subjects for that listing, which allows scanning of the primary entries for those interested in specific subjects.

History/ Biography

Book Publishers

Alaska Pacific University Press
Alberni District Historical Society
Allegro Publishing
Arthur H Clark Co
Backeddy Books
Bayless Enterprises Inc.
Bear Grass Press
Bellevue Art Museum
Best Editions
Binford & Mort Publishing
Boise State U. Western Writers Series
Bonanza Publishing
Bowen Island Historians
Broken Moon Press
Calapooia Publications
Canadian West Magazine
Center for Pacific Northwest Studies
Deep Well Publishing Company
Douglas & McIntyre Publishers
Douglas Geidt
Eastern Washington State Historical Soc
Edmonds Arts Commission Books
Edprint, Inc
Elephant Mountain Arts
Falcon Press Publishing Co., Inc
Far Corner Books
Fjord Press
Footprint Publishing Company
Frontier Publishing
Great Eagle Publishing, Inc
Hancock House Publishers Ltd.
Haralson Enterprises
Harriet U. Fish
Historical Society of Seattle & King Co.
Horsdal & Schubart Publishers Ltd.
Idaho State Historical Society
Institute for Judaic Studies
Jordan Valley Heritage House
Kamloops Museum & Archives
Lambrecht Publications
Land Mark Publishing
Latah County Historical Society
Legacy House, Inc
Legendary Publishing Co.
Leo F. Vogel
LetterPress
Lincoln County Historical Society
LPD Publishing
Lumby Historians

Madison County History Association
Montana Historical Society Press
Montevista Press
Mountain Press Publishing Company
Museum of History & Industry
Nanaimo Historical Society
Nor 'West Publishing
Norjak Project
Nugget Enterprises
Old Harbor Press
Olympic Publishing, Inc
Oolichan Books
Open Hand Publishing, Inc
Orca Book Publishers
Orcas Publishing Company
Oregon Historical Society Press
Pacific Northwest Labor History Assn
Pictorial Histories Publishing Company
Pika Press
Pioneer Press Books
Portland Chess Press
Powell River Heritage Research Assn.
Printery Farm
Provincial Archives of British Columbia
Publication in History
Pumpkin Ridge Productions
Questar Publishers, Inc
Rainy Day Press
Red Apple Publishing
Ritz Publishing
Rose Wind Press
Sagebrush Heritage
Sagittarius Press
Sandhill Publishing
SCW Publications
Skagit County Historical Society
Skookum Publications
Sky House Publishers
Solstice Press
Sono Nis Press
Sourdough Enterprises
Southern Oregon Historical Society
Spencer Butte Press
Spirit Mountain Press
Springfield Historical Commission
Strawberry Hill Press
Sunfire Publications Ltd.
TABA Publishing, Inc
Tabula Rasa Press
Tahlkie Books
Tamarack Books
The Bear Wallow Publishing Co.
The Boag Foundation Ltd.
The Caxton Printers, Ltd
The Georgian Press Company
The Pedersens

The Touchstone Press
Trail City Archives
Turman Publishing Company
University of British Columbia Press
University of Idaho Press
University of Washington Press
Vanessapress
Washington State Historical Society
Washington State University Press
Western Horizons Books
Whitecap Books
Wilson Publications
Woodford Memorial Editions, Inc
Ye Galleon Press

Newspapers

Baker Democrat-Herald
Cowlitz County Advocate
Hardball Northwest Baseball
Spectrum
The Dalles Weekly Reminder
The Frontiersman

Periodicals

Adventure in Hell
Alaska History
American Indian Basketry Magazine
Art West Magazine
BC Historical News Magazine
Boots
Callboard
Cascades East
Columbia The Magazine Of Northwest History
Crook County Historical Society Newsletter
Cumtux
Curry County Echoes
Edprint, Inc
Famous Faces Magazine
FINNAM Newsletter
Ghost Town Quarterly
Heritage Quest
Historic Preservation League of Oregon Newsletter
Historical Gazette
Historical Perspectives
Idaho Yesterdays
Idahoan
Inland Country
Journal of Everett & Snohomish Co. Hist.
La Posta: A Journal of American Postal History
Land
Landmarks
Latah Legacy
Montana, The Magazine of Western History
Mountain Light

Musings
Northwest Discovery
Northwest Passages Hist. Newsletter
Old Stuff
Oregon Focus
Oregon Historical Quarterly
Oregon Historical Society News
Oregon Humanities
Owyhee Outpost
Pacific Northwest Forum
Patchwork
Pioneer Trails
Rocking Chair Studio
Sherman County For The Record
Snake River Echoes
The Bridge
The Golden Age
The Montana Journal
The Portland Alliance
The Quarterdeck Review
The Senior Messenger
The Table Rock Sentinel
The Trainmaster
The Trolley Park News
The Washboard
This Is Just to Say
Timberbeast
Trail Breakers
Trainsheet
Umatilla County Historical Society News
Umpqua Trapper
Upper Snake River Valley Historical Society
Vancouver History
We Proceeded On
Western Genesis
Western Journal of Black Studies

Literary/Poetry

Book Publishers

Alaska Pacific University Press
Alberni District Historical Society
Allegro Publishing
Arthur H Clark Co
Backeddy Books
Bayless Enterprises Inc.
Bear Grass Press
Bellevue Art Museum
Best Editions
Binford & Mort Publishing
Boise State U. Western Writers Series
Bonanza Publishing
Bowen Island Historians
Broken Moon Press
Calapooia Publications
Canadian West Magazine
Center for Pacific Northwest Studies
Deep Well Publishing Company
Douglas & McIntyre Publishers
Douglas Geidt
Eastern Washington State Historical Soc
Edmonds Arts Commission Books
Edprint, Inc
Elephant Mountain Arts
Falcon Press Publishing Co., Inc
Far Corner Books
Fjord Press
Footprint Publishing Company
Frontier Publishing
Great Eagle Publishing, Inc
Hancock House Publishers Ltd.
Haralson Enterprises
Harriet U. Fish
Historical Society of Seattle & King Co.
Horsdal & Schubart Publishers Ltd.
Idaho State Historical Society
Institute for Judaic Studies
Jordan Valley Heritage House
Kamloops Museum & Archives
Lambrecht Publications
Land Mark Publishing
Latah County Historical Society
Legacy House, Inc
Legendary Publishing Co.
Leo F. Vogel
LetterPress
Lincoln County Historical Society
LPD Publishing
Lumby Historians
Madison County History Association
Montana Historical Society Press

Montevista Press
Mountain Press Publishing Company
Museum of History & Industry
Nanaimo Historical Society
Nor 'West Publishing
Norjak Project
Nugget Enterprises
Old Harbor Press
Olympic Publishing, Inc
Oolichan Books
Open Hand Publishing, Inc
Orca Book Publishers
Orcas Publishing Company
Oregon Historical Society Press
Pacific Northwest Labor History Assn
Pictorial Histories Publishing Company
Pika Press
Pioneer Press Books
Portland Chess Press
Powell River Heritage Research Assn.
Printery Farm
Provincial Archives of British Columbia
Publication in History
Pumpkin Ridge Productions
Questar Publishers, Inc
Rainy Day Press
Red Apple Publishing
Ritz Publishing
Rose Wind Press
Sagebrush Heritage
Sagittarius Press
Sandhill Publishing
SCW Publications
Skagit County Historical Society
Skookum Publications
Sky House Publishers

USING THE INDEXES AND DIRECTORY

Primary indexes are divided by Book Publishers, Periodicals, and Newspapers, with each of those categories subdivided by state or province.

Numbers following primary index entries indicate subjects of editorial focus and may be looked up in the subject table at the beginning of this section. Alternately, use the subject table to select numbers for areas of interest, then scan the primary indexes for publishers with those numbers.

Selected subject indexes are groups of several related editorial subject. They do not include the subject numbers but are subdivided by type of publisher or state.

All directory entries follow the indexes and are organized alphabetically by Book Publishers, Periodicals, and Newspapers. Each entry is followed by the subjects for that listing, which allows scanning of the primary entries for those interested in specific subjects.

Solstice Press
Sono Nis Press
Sourdough Enterprises
Southern Oregon Historical Society
Spencer Butte Press
Spirit Mountain Press
Springfield Historical Commission
Strawberry Hill Press
Sunfire Publications Ltd.
TABA Publishing, Inc
Tabula Rasa Press
Tahlkie Books
Tamarack Books
The Bear Wallow Publishing Co.
The Boag Foundation Ltd.
The Caxton Printers, Ltd
The Georgian Press Company
The Pedersens
The Touchstone Press
Trail City Archives
Turman Publishing Company
University of British Columbia Press
University of Idaho Press
University of Washington Press
Vanessapress
Washington State Historical Society
Washington State University Press
Western Horizons Books
Whitecap Books
Wilson Publications
Woodford Memorial Editions, Inc
Ye Galleon Press

Newspapers

Baker Democrat-Herald
Cowlitz County Advocate
Hardball Northwest Baseball
Spectrum
The Dalles Weekly Reminder
The Frontiersman

Periodicals

Adventure in Hell
Alaska History
American Indian Basketry Magazine
Art West Magazine
BC Historical News Magazine
Boots
Callboard
Cascades East
Columbia The Magazine Of Northwest History
Crook County Historical Society Newsletter
Cumtux
Curry County Echoes

Edprint, Inc
Famous Faces Magazine
FINNAM Newsletter
Ghost Town Quarterly
Heritage Quest
Historic Preservation League of Oregon Newsletter
Historical Gazette
Historical Perspectives
Idaho Yesterdays
Idahoan
Inland Country
Journal of Everett & Snohomish Co. Hist.
La Posta: A Journal of American Postal History
Land
Landmarks
Latah Legacy
Montana, The Magazine of Western History
Mountain Light
Musings
Northwest Discovery
Northwest Passages Hist. Newsletter
Old Stuff
Oregon Focus
Oregon Historical Quarterly
Oregon Historical Society News
Oregon Humanities
Owyhee Outpost
Pacific Northwest Forum
Patchwork
Pioneer Trails
Rocking Chair Studio
Sherman County For The Record
Snake River Echoes
The Bridge
The Golden Age
The Montana Journal
The Portland Alliance
The Quarterdeck Review
The Senior Messenger
The Table Rock Sentinel
The Trainmaster
The Trolley Park News
The Washboard
This Is Just to Say
Timberbeast
Trail Breakers
Trainsheet
Umatilla County Historical Society News
Umpqua Trapper
Upper Snake River Valley Historical Society
Vancouver History
We Proceeded On
Western Genesis
Western Journal of Black Studies

Minority/Ethnic

Book Publishers

Alaska Pacific University Press
American Institute for Yemeni Studies
American-Nepal Education Foundation
Bear Tribe Publishing
Blue Water Publishing
Council for Indian Education
Cross Cultural Press
Elephant Mountain Arts
Finnish American Literary Heritage Found
G.M. White
Gros Ventre Treaty Committee
Hancock House Publishers Ltd.
Haralson Enterprises
Insight Passage
Inst. for Study of Traditional American Indian Arts
Institute for Judaic Studies
Lillooet Tribal Council Press
Mountain Press Publishing Company
National Book Company
Newport Bay Publishing Ltd
Press Gang Publishers
Spencer Butte Press
Storypole Press
The Denali Press
Theytus Books
University of British Columbia Press
University of Idaho Press
University of Washington Press
Washington State University Press
Welcome Press
Write-On Press

Newspapers

Guide Magazine
Seattle Chinese Post
Spilyay Tymoo
The Hispanic News
The Hispanic News
Tundra Times
Yakima Nation Review

Periodicals

Aguelarre
American Indian Basketry Magazine
ANC News
BC Business Examiner
Before Columbus Review
Chinatown News Magazine
Community Digest Magazine

Council for Human Rights in Latin Amer Nwsltr
Environmental Law
FINNAM Newsletter
Finnish Connection
Health News and Notes
Il Centro, Newletter of Italian Canadian Community
International Examiner
Just Out
La Lucha Solidaria
LaVoz de Idaho
LaVoz Newsmagazine
North American Post
Northwest Anthropological Research Notes
Northwest Arctic NUNA
Northwest Ethnic News
Northwest Indian Fisheries Commission
Northwest Nikkei
Northwest Seasonal Worker
Oregon Chinese News
Outlook
Oyate Wo'wapi
Rainbow News
Salud de la Familia News
Skipping Stones
Swedish Press
The Bridge
The Golden Age
The Journal of Ethnic Studies
The Oregon Witness
The Raven Chronicles
Washington State Migrant Ed News
Wildfire

Psychology/New Age/Religion/Spiritual

Book Publishers

Abbott Loop Christian Center
Aglow Publications
Apostolic Book Publishers
Arrow Point Press
Autodidactic Press
Barclay Press
Beginning Press
Ben-Simon Publications
Bible Temple Publications
Blue Water Publishing
Caber Press
Castalia Publishing Company
Centerplace Publishing Company
Christian Zion Advocate
Dimi Press
Earth View, Inc
Earth-Love Publishing House
Expansions Publishing Company, Inc
Future Science Research Publishing Co.
Glen Abbey Books, Inc
Good Times Publishing Co.
Gospel Tract Distributors
Hartley & Marks, Publishers
Harvest House Publishers
Inner Growth Books
Inspirational Publisher
Jennifer James, Inc
Jesuit Books
Lifeworks Press
Medic Publishing Company
Metamorphous Press
Nobility Press
Oakbridge University Press
Oregon Catholic Press
Pacific Press Publishing Association
Pacific Publishers
Pallas Communications
Playful Wisdom Press
Pleneurethic International
Princess Publishing
Progress Publishing Co.
Purna Press
Robert Briggs Associates
Shiloh Publishing House
Special Child Publications
St. Nectarios Press
Sunburst Press

Sweet Forever Publishing
The Christ Foundation
Truth on Fire (Hallelujah) Publishing
Upword Press
Vision Books
Void Press
White Plume Press
Wise Owl Books & Music
Wood Lake Books, Inc
Zen 'n' Ink

Newspapers

Catholic Sentinel
Great Falls Montana Catholic Register
Jewish Transcript
Journey Press
The New Times
The Voice

Periodicals

ACAPella
Aglow Magazine
Alaska Metaphysical Council N/L
Bridges
Christian Parenting Today
Coeur d'Alene Homes Messenger
Hallelujah!
Inland Register
Insight Northwest
Island Men
Listen: Promoting Positive Choices
Mentor
METAlink
Mustard Seed Faith, Inc

USING THE INDEXES AND DIRECTORY

Primary indexes are divided by Book Publishers, Periodicals, and Newspapers, with each of those categories subdivided by state or province.

Numbers following primary index entries indicate subjects of editorial focus and may be looked up in the subject table at the beginning of this section. Alternately, use the subject table to select numbers for areas of interest, then scan the primary indexes for publishers with those numbers.

Selected subject indexes are groups of several related editorial subject. They do not include the subject numbers but are subdivided by type of publisher or state.

All directory entries follow the indexes and are organized alphabetically by Book Publishers, Periodicals, and Newspapers. Each entry is followed by the subjects for that listing, which allows scanning of the primary entries for those interested in specific subjects.

NAPRA Trade Journal
New Age Retailer
Oregon Assn of Christian Writers Nwslttr
Oregon Episcopal Churchman
Our Little Friend
Panegyria
Portland Magazine
Primary Treasure
Recovery Life
Renewal
Shalom, Oregon
Signs of the Times
Smoke Signals
Teaching Home
The Jewish Review
The Montana Catholic
Transformation Times
Truth on Fire (Hallelujah)
Virtue
Westgate Press
White Ribbon Review
Whole Self
Writers Information Network

Women/Feminist

Book Publishers

Aglow Publications
All About Us Books
Cacanadadada Press Ltd.
Calyx Books
Deep Well Publishing Company
Douglas & McIntyre Publishers
Lifeworks Press
MatriMedia
Moonstone Press
New Sage Press
New Star Books
Pennypress, Inc
Press Gang Publishers
Red Cedar Press
Silverleaf Press
Swan Raven Company
The Charles Franklin Press
The Eighth Mountain Press
The Seal Press
Trabarni Productions
User-Friendly Press
Vanessapress
Womanshare Books
Wood Lake Books, Inc
Write-On Press

Newspapers

Blue Stocking
Womyn's Press

Periodicals

Aglow Magazine
Alaska Women
Alaskan Women
Apropos
Bridges
Calyx, A. Journal of Art & Literature by Women
CSWS Review
Diversity: The Lesbian Rag
Feminist Broadcast Quarterly of Oregon
FINESSE Magazine for the Washington Woman
Focus on Women Magazine
Freedom Socialist
Gallerie: Women's Art
Herspectives
Kinesis
Lesbian Contradiction:
Midwifery Today
Network News

Northwest Gay and Lesbian Reader
Panegyria
Perceptions
Portland Pen
Progressive Woman
Talking Leaves
The Beltane Papers: A Journal of Women's Mysteries
The Ovulation Method Newsletter
The Rude Girl Press
Virtue
Washington Clubwoman
White Ribbon Review
Woman To Woman Magazine
Women's Work
Women's Yellow Pages

Writing/ Publishing/ Language/ Libraries

Book Publishers

ABZ Books
Accord Communications Ltd
Alaska Council of Teachers of English
Alaska Native Language Center
Alcove Publishing Co.
Barbarian Press
Blue Heron Publishing, Inc
Cain-Lockhart Press
Cherry Tree Press
Civetta Press
Copyright Information Services
Elk Ridge Publishing
Elmer E. Rasmuson Library
Features Northwest
Finnish American Literary Heritage Found
Idaho State University Press
Information Press
Laing Communications
National Book Company
Old Violin-Art Publishing
Orca Book Publishers
Orcas Publishing Company
Overland West Press
Pacific Edge Publishing and Media Services Ltd.
Pandemic International
Parlie Publications
Price Productions
Pulphouse Publishing
Resolution Business Press
Sakura Press
Second Language Publications
Snohomish Publishing Company
Star Valley Publications
The Denali Press
Washington State Library
Word Power, Inc
World Without War Council
Yinka Dene Language Institute

Newspapers

BC BookWorld
The Hispanic News
The Hispanic News
Writer's NW

Periodicals

ACRL Newsletter
American Accents
Amphora
Before Columbus Review
Book Dealers World
BookNotes: Resources for Small & Self-Pubs
British Columbia Library Association Newsletter
CCLAM Chowder
Colonygram
Comparative Literature
CVAS
Editors Roundtable
Emergency Librarian
Enfantaisie
Et Cetera
Fairbanks Arts
Finnish Connection
Footnotes
Grassroots Oracle
Haiku Zasshi Zo
Hands On
Hortus Northwest
Idaho Foxfire Network
Idaho Librarian
Inland
Inscriptions
Journal of B.C. English Teachers' Association
LaVoz de Idaho
LaVoz Newsmagazine
Letter to Libraries
Life Scribes
Line
Literary Creations
Literary Markets
Modern Language Quarterly
Montana Author
Montana English Journal
Montana Library Association Focus
Montana Newsletter
NAPRA Trade Journal
Network News
North American Post
Northwest Inland Writing Project Newsletter
Northwest Notes
Northword: Alaska State Writing Consortium Newsletter
OCTE Chalkboard Newsletter
Oregon Assn of Christian Writers Nwslttr
Oregon Authors
Oregon Humanities
Oregon Library News
Plant's Review of Books
PNLA Quarterly
Poetry Exchange
Portland Pen

Pulphouse: A Fiction Magazine
Reference & Research Book News
Rendezvous
Satellite Guide
Scitech Book News
Sesame
Shaping the Landscape
Signatures from Big Sky
Snake River Reflections
Spokes
The Burnside Review
The Canadian Writer's Journal
The Desktop Publishing Journal
The Montana Poet
The Northwest Review of Books
The Printer's Devil
The Printer's Northwest Trader
The Sourdough
The Willamette Writer
TOWERS Club, USA Newsletter
University of Portland Writers
Upstream
Washington Library News
Washington Newspaper
Watermark
WLA Highlights
Word Works
Wordworks
Writers
Writers Information Network
Writers' Open Forum
Writing Magazine
Yinka Dene Language Institute

USING THE INDEXES AND DIRECTORY

Primary indexes are divided by Book Publishers, Periodicals, and Newspapers, with each of those categories subdivided by state or province.

Numbers following primary index entries indicate subjects of editorial focus and may be looked up in the subject table at the beginning of this section. Alternately, use the subject table to select numbers for areas of interest, then scan the primary indexes for publishers with those numbers.

Selected subject indexes are groups of several related editorial subject. They do not include the subject numbers but are subdivided by type of publisher or state.

All directory entries follow the indexes and are organized alphabetically by Book Publishers, Periodicals, and Newspapers. Each entry is followed by the subjects for that listing, which allows scanning of the primary entries for those interested in specific subjects.

Book Publishers

123 studio, 123 S. Turner St., Victoria, BC V8V 2J9. Poetry.
POETRY

3 S Fitness Group Ltd., Box 5510, Station B, Victoria, BC V8R 6S4. 604-598-1426. Contact: Gord Stewart. Publishes health, fitness, and sports-related books. No unsolicited manuscripts.
HEALTH

Abbott Loop Christian Center, 2626 Abbott Rd., Anchorage, AK 99507. Publisher of Christian books.
RELIGION

Abraxas Publishing, PO Box 1522, Bellevue, WA 98009-1522.
UNSPECIFIED

ABZ Books, PO Box 1404, Vancouver, BC V6C 2P7. 604-263-0014. Contact: Jackson House. Publisher of hard- & softcover books. Topics: literature, reference, sports. No unsolicited submissions. Catalog.
LITERATURE, REFERENCE/LIBRARY, SPORTS

Academic Enterprises, PO Box 666, Pullman, WA 99163-0666. 509-334-4826. Self-publisher of books on agriculture, biology, and biography. Founded 1983. Not a freelance market.
AGRICULTURE/FARMING, BIOLOGY, SCIENCE

Accord Communications Ltd., 18002 15th Ave N.E. Ste. B, Seattle, WA 98155. 206-368-8157. Contact: Karen Duncan. Publisher of hard- & softcover books. Accepts unsolicited submissions. Pays money, copies. Submit query letter, SASE, outline, sample chapters, or synopsis. Photocopies, dot matrix, simultaneous submissions OK. Responds 2 mos; publishes 2 yrs. Accepts fiction and nonfiction. "Strong bias towards N.W. writers in our startup mystery publishing program. Also broker printing services."
MYSTERY, PUBLISHING/PRINTING

Ad-Dee Publishers Inc., 2736 Lincoln St., Eugene, OR 97405.
UNSPECIFIED

Adrienne Lee Press, PO Box 309, Monmouth, OR 97316. 503-838-6292. Editor: Thomas Ferte. Publishes books of poetry irregularly. Query with 5 samples plus SASE. Report within 4-6 wks; publishes in 1 yr. If its not exceptional and different, forget it.
POETRY

Aerie Publishing, Deep Bay, Vancouver Island, RR1, Bowser, BC V0R 1G0. Contact: John C. Whelan.
UNSPECIFIED

Agarikon Press, PO Box 2233, Olympia, WA 98507.
UNSPECIFIED

Aglow Publications, PO Box 1548, Lynnwood, WA 98046-1557. 206-775-7282. Publisher of 12 softcover originals per yr. Print run: 10,000. Payment: Royalties. Rights purchased: 1st and reprint. Query with sample chapters, SASE. Photocopies OK. Reports in 6 wks. Publishes in 6-12 mos. Nonfiction. Look for Christian solutions to problems faced by today's women. To 50,000 wds. Guidelines; catalog.
RELIGION, WOMEN

Ahsahta Press, 1910 University Dr., Boise, ID 83725. 208-385-1999. Contact: Tom Trusky. Publishes 3 softcover books per yr. Print run: 500. Pays copies for 1st & 2nd printing; 25% royalties commence with 3rd printing. Acquires 1st rights. Reads samplers only (15 poems) sent Jan-Mar w/SASE. Reports in 2 mos. Accepts: poetry of the American West only. Guidelines included in catalog. Sample: $7.95 ppd.
POETRY

AK Sea Grant, 138 Irving #11, Fairbanks, AK 99775.
ALASKA, BIOLOGY, ENVIRONMENT/RESOURCES

AKHT Publishing, 2420 Parkview Dr., Kamloops, BC V2B 7J1.
UNSPECIFIED

Aladdin Publishing, PO Box 364, Palmer, AK 99645. 602-347-5115. Editor: Marilyn Carter. Self-publisher of books. Not a freelance market. Catalog.
UNSPECIFIED

Alaska Angler Publications, PO Box 83550, Fairbanks, AK 99708. 907-455-8000. Editor: Chris Batin. Book publisher and monthly newsletter. Subs. $49/yr. Uses freelance material. Byline given, pays money on acceptance, acquires all rights. Query w/SASE. Responds in 1 mo. Accepts nonfiction, news items, interviews, articles. Catalog; sample $8.50.
ALASKA, FISHING, RECREATION

Alaska Council of Teachers of English, PO Box 3184, Kodiak, AK 99615. Editor: Kate O'Dell.
CHILDREN (BY/ABOUT), EDUCATION, ENGLISH

Alaska Dept of Labor Research &. Analysis, PO Box 25501, Juneau, AK 99802-5501. 907-465-4500. Editor: J. P. Goforth. Publisher of softcover books. Query w/ SASE. All pubs free. Freelance material accepted. Pays on publication. Responds in 4-6 wks; publishing time varies. Accepts nonfiction. Catalog.
ALASKA, ECONOMICS, LABOR/WORK

Alaska Geological Society, PO Box 101288, Anchorage, AK 99510.
GEOLOGY/GEOGRAPHY, SCIENCE

Alaska Illustrated, 4341 MacAlister Dr., Anchorage, AK 99515. 907-243-1286. Editor: Kevin Cassity. 1-3 softcover Alaska, travel books a yr. Accepts freelance submissions. Payment terms vary. Submit query w/SASE. Dot matrix, photocopied, simultaneous OK. Reports in 4-6 wks. Publishing time varies. Accepts nonfiction and photos.
ALASKA, TRAVEL

Alaska Native Language Center, PO Box 900111, University of Alaska, Fairbanks, AK 99775-0120. 907-474-7874. Publishes softcover books. No unsolicited mss. Scholarly publishing in and about Alaska's Native languages. Reporting time and payment vary. Catalog.
ALASKA, LANGUAGE(S), SCHOLARLY/ACADEMIC

Alaska Natural History Association, 605 W. 4th Ave. #120, Anchorage, AK 99501-2231.
ALASKA, NATURAL HISTORY

Alaska Northwest Publishing Company, 2208 N.W. Market St., Ste. 300, Seattle, WA 98107. 206-784-5071; Fax 206-784-5316. Contact: Marlene Blessing. An imprint of Graphic Arts Center Publishing. Print runs: 2,000-10,000. Publishes 12-20 hard- & softcover originals & reprints per yr. Accepts unsolicited mss. Pays royalties on publication; sometimes gives an advance. Acquires all rights. Query letter, SASE, outline, sample chapters, synopsis. Photocopy OK. Responds in 1-3 months; publishes in 1-2 years. Accepts nonfiction, children's nonfiction & regional fiction. "Our region is Alaska and the Northwest, and our primary subjects are: nature/environment; northern adventure, travel, and recreation; Native heritage; cooking and gardening; essays of place." Guidelines; brochure.
ALASKA, NATURAL HISTORY, NORTHWEST

Alaska Pacific University Press, 4101 University Dr., Anchorage, AK 99508. 907-564-8304; Fax: 907-562-4276. Publisher of 1 hard- or soft book a yr. Accepts unsolicited submissions. Pays royalties & copies on publication. Acquires all rights. Submit ms, SASE, outline, sample chapters. Reports in 3 mos. Publishes in 1 yr. Accepts nonfiction, fiction, and poetry with focus on Alaskan people, places, and history. Book length determined by topic and information presented.
ALASKA, AMERICAN HISTORY, NATIVE AMERICAN

Alaska Viking Press, PO Box 11-3231, Anchorage, AK 99511. 907-345-0451. Editor: Gunnar S. Pedersen. Self-publisher of books on fishing. Does not accept unsolicited submissions.
FISHING

Alberni District Historical Society, P. O. Box 284, Port Alberni, BC V9Y 7M7. 604-723-3006. Publisher of occasional softcover books. Canadian history and biography. Not a freelance market.
BIOGRAPHY, CANADA, COMMUNITY

Alcove Publishing Co., 6385 N.E. Barclay, West Linn, OR 97068. 503-655-5564. Editor: Bruce Taylor. Publisher of softcover, nonfiction books on English usage, writing, and editing. Accepts unsolicited freelance material. Pays royalties; acquires all rights. Submit query letter. Dot matrix, simultaneous subs OK. Responds in 2 wks; publishes in 6 mos. Catalog.
COLLEGE/UNIVERSITY, ENGLISH, WRITING

Alioth Press, PO Box 1554, Beaverton, OR 97075. 503-644-0983. Editor: Mark Dominik. Publishes hardcover reprints. Does not accept unsolicited submissions.
UNSPECIFIED

Alki, 2819 First Ave, Ste 240, Seattle, WA 98121. Publisher of fiction.
FICTION

All About Us Books, RR #3 Yellow Point Rd., Ladysmith, BC V0R 2E0. 604-722-3349. Contact: Seymour Trieger. Unsolicited submissions not accepted. Pays copies & royalties. Query letter, SASE, outline, sample chapters. Responds in up to 3 months; publishes in 8 months.
EDUCATION, SENIOR CITIZENS, WOMEN

Allegro Publishing, 1075 N.W. Murray Rd., Ste 266, Portland, OR 97229-5501. 503-690-7726. Editor: Phillip Bride. Publisher of softcover books. Accepts unsolicited submissions. Query by letter or phone OK. Submit sample chapters, photocopy, disk, ms OK. Pays advance: 50% at acceptance, 50% on publication; acquires first rights. Accepts fiction, poetry, biography, nonfiction.
ARTS, BIOGRAPHY, MUSIC

Altitude Medical Publishing Company, 5624 Admiral Way, Seattle, WA 98116. Book publisher health & medical subjects.
HEALTH, MEDICAL

Amadeus Press, 9999 S.W. Wilshire, Ste. 124, Portland, OR 97225-9962. 503-292-0961. Editor: Reinhard Pauly. 20 music-related hard- & softcover books/yr. Accepts unsolicited submissions. Acquires all rights. Submit query w/clips. Dot matrix, photocopied OK. Reports in 3-4 wks.
MUSIC

Amateur Brewer Information, PO Box 546, Portland, OR 97207. 503-289-7596. Contact: Fred Eckhardt. Publisher of books on beermaking.
CRAFTS/HOBBIES, FOOD/COOKING

American Geographic Publishing, PO Box 5630, Helena, MT 59604. 406-443-2842. Editor: Mark Thompson. Publishes regional photo books with text. Accepts unsolicited submissions. Pays royalties/advance. Submit query, sample chapters, SASE. Photocopy OK. Responds in 2 wks to queries, 4-6 wks to mss. Publishes in 9 mos.
GEOLOGY/GEOGRAPHY, OUTDOOR, PHOTOGRAPHY

American Institute for Yemeni Studies, Portland State U., History Dept, PO Box 751, Portland, OR 97207. 503-725-3983. Contact: Dr. John Mandaville.
COLLEGE/UNIVERSITY, MINORITIES/ETHNIC

American-Nepal Education Foundation, 2790 Cape Meares Loop, Tillamook, OR 97141. Contact: Hugh B Wood.
EDUCATION, MINORITIES/ETHNIC

Amity Publications, 78688 Sears Rd., Cottage Grove, OR 97424.
UNSPECIFIED

Ampersand Publishing, 3609 Mukilteo Blvd., Mukilteo, WA 98203-1249.
UNSPECIFIED

Ananse Press, PO Box 22565, Seattle, WA 98122.
UNSPECIFIED

Anchor Publishing, PO Box 30, Homer, AK 99603. 907-235-6188. Contact: Ted Gerken. Self-publisher. Not a freelance market.
UNSPECIFIED

Angst World Library, PO Box 593, Selma, OR 97538-0593. Book publisher of fiction.
AVANT-GARDE/EXPERIMENTAL, FICTION

The Antique Doorknob Publishing Company, PO Box 2609, Woodinville, WA 98072-2609. 206-483-5848. Editor: Maud L. Eastwood. Self-publisher & publisher of softcover books. Query letter, SASE. Responds in 30 days. Accepts material on door hardware. Catalog.
ANTIQUES, COLLECTING, TECHNICAL

Antonson Publishing Ltd., 1615 Venable St., Vancouver, BC V5L 2H1.
UNSPECIFIED

Anvil Press, PO Box 1575, Station A, Vancouver, BC V6C 2P7. 604-876-8710. Brian Kaufman, Publisher. Founded 1988. Publishes fiction, nonfiction, plays, poetry by new writers. Send query letter w/ sample chapters or synopsis. Responds in 2 months. Publishes in 4-6 months. Publishes sub-TERRAIN magazine and sponsors the International 3-Day Novel Writing Contest. Catalog.
FICTION, POETRY

Aphra Behn Press, 13625 S.W. 23rd, Beaverton, OR 97005. 503-646-0471. Contact: Suzanne Graham. Publisher of 1-2 nonfiction, softcover originals a yr. Press run: 500-5,000. Accepts freelance submissions. Payment: 8-12% royalties, on retail minimum price, with average advance. Reports in 2 wks. Publishes in less than 1 yr. Query w/SASE. Dot matrix, photocopies and simultaneous submissions OK. Mss from 60,000-100,000 wds on popular science technology — prefer medical, biological, engineering, cosmological, philosophical. Informative, with self-help orientation, socio-economic commentary or philosophy of science.
HEALTH, MEDICAL, SCIENCE

Apostolic Book Publishers, 9643 N. Lombard, Portland, OR 97203.
RELIGION

Apple Books, 1370 E. Georgia, Vancouver, BC V5L 2A8.
UNSPECIFIED

Apple Press, 5536 S.E. Harlow, Milwaukie, OR 97222. 503-659-2475. Editor: Judith Majors. Publishes health sugar-free cookbooks, and travel related softcover books. Does not accept unsolicited submissions. Submit query w/SASE. Dot matrix, photocopied, simultaneous, electronic, computer disk OK. Reports in 4 wks; publishes within 1 yr.
FOOD/COOKING, HEALTH, TRAVEL

Applegate Computer Enterprises, 4039 Oakman St. S., Salem, OR 97302-2730. 503-846-6742. Self-publisher of 1 softcover book a yr on personal computers. Print run: 2,000. Not a freelance market. Catalog.
COMPUTERS

Applied Therapeutics Inc., PO Box 5077, Vancouver, WA 98668-5077. 206-253-7123. Contact: Caren Haldeman. Books on medical subjects.
HEALTH, MEDICAL

Arbutus Publications Ltd., PO Box 35070, Sta. E., Vancouver, BC V6M 4G1.
BIOLOGY, UNSPECIFIED

The Archive Press, 2101 192nd Ave. S.E., Issaquah, WA 98027.
UNSPECIFIED

Arctic Environmental Info & Data Center, University of Alaska, 707 A St., Anchorage, AK 99501.
ALASKA, NATURAL HISTORY, SCIENCE

Ariel Publications, 14417 S.E. 19th Pl., Bellevue, WA 98007. 206-641-0518. Editor: Lenore B. Aken. Self-publisher of softcover books.
TRAVEL

Arrow Point Press, 605 S.E. 15th Ave, Portland, OR 97214. 503-236-7359. Publisher of softcover books. Accepts unsolicited submissions. Pays royalties. Submit query letter or query by phone. Responds 1 mo. Publishes nonfiction. Focus: seeds, permaculture, ecological restoration, intentional communities, indigenous culture, earth spirituality and bioregionalism.
ENVIRONMENT/RESOURCES, COMMUNITY, NEW AGE

Arrowood Books Inc., PO Box 2100, Corvallis, OR 97339. 503-753-9539. Editor: Lex Runciman. Founded 1985. Publisher of 1-2 hard- & softcover books per year of general literary interest. Unspecified payment schedule. Query w/SASE before submitting. Responds in 3 months, publishes in one year. Accepts nonfiction, fiction, poetry, plays. Guidelines w/ SASE.
FICTION, LITERATURE, POETRY

Arsenal Pulp Press, Ltd, 100-1062 Homer St., Vancouver, BC V6B 2W9. 604-687-4233. Contact: Brian Lam. Pays royalties. Query w/SASE (Intl. reply coupon if from USA) outline, sample chapters. Dot matrix, photocopied subs OK. Reports in 2 months; publishes in 1 year. Accepts nonfiction, fiction, poetry, plays. Guidelines w/ SASE
BRITISH COLUMBIA, ENVIRONMENT/RESOURCES, FICTION

Art Gallery of Greater Victoria, 1040 Moss St., Victoria, BC V8V 4P1. Nonfiction. Guidelines.
ARTS

Artdog Press, 252 Memorial Crescent, Victoria, BC V8S 3J2.
UNSPECIFIED

Arthur H. Clark Co., PO Box 14707, Spokane, WA 99214. 509-928-9540. Contact: Robert Clark. Publisher of hardcover, nonfiction originals on history and Americana. Also subsidy publisher. No unsolicited submissions. Query with synopsis/outline/SASE.
AMERICANA, AMERICAN HISTORY

ASA Publications, 7005 132nd Pl. S.E., Renton, WA 98056-9236.
UNSPECIFIED

Asian Music Publications, School of Music, University of Washington, Seattle, WA 98105.
ASIA, COLLEGE/UNIVERSITY, MUSIC

At Your Fingertips, 7260 N. Mercer Way, Mercer Island, WA 98040-2132. 206-443-3220. Contact: Kathleen Dickenson. Publisher of art books.
ARTS, VISUAL ARTS

Autodidactic Press, PO Box 872749, Wasilla, AK 99687-2749. 907-376-2932. Editor: Charles Hayes. Self-publisher of books. Does not accept unsolicited submissions.
EDUCATION, HOW-TO, PSYCHOLOGY

Azure Press, PO Box 2164, 2417 Beacon Ave #3, Sidney, BC V8L 3S6.
UNSPECIFIED

Backeddy Books, PO Box 301, Cambridge, ID 83610. Old West.
OLD WEST, UNSPECIFIED

Barbarian Press, 12375 Ainsworth Rd., R.R. #5, Mission, BC V2V 5X4. 604-826-8089. Editors: Jan & Crispin Elsted. Publisher of limited edition books. Unsolicited submissions OK. Pays in copies on publication. Submit query w/clips, ms, SASE. Dot matrix, photocopied OK. Reports in 6 wks; publishing time varies. Accepts nonfiction, poetry, translations. Topics: Block printing, especially wood engraving, emphasis is on quality of production & text. Photos, suitable graphic media for letterpress.
LITERATURE, POETRY, PUBLISHING/PRINTING

Barclay Press, 600 E. 3rd St., Newberg, OR 97132. 503-538-7345; FAX: 503-538-7033. Submit query letter, outline, sample chapters, SASE. Photocopy OK. Responds in 1 mo. Topics: spiritual, compatible with the convictions of the Friends (Quaker) Church. Catalog.
PEACE, RELIGION

Bardavon Books, PO Box 1378, Ashland, OR 97520. 503-773-7035. Contact: James L. Rodgers. Assignment only, does not accept unsolicited mss. Query w/SASE. Topics: Elizabethan (primarily Shakespearean) literature.
DRAMA, LITERATURE

Barleycorn Books, 290 S.W. Tualatin Loop, West Linn, OR 97068.
UNSPECIFIED

Barlow Press, PO Box 5403, Helena, MT 59604. 406-449-7310. Editor: Russell B. Hill. Does not accept unsolicited mss. Pays by arrangement. Submit query w/SASE. Dot matrix, photocopies, simultaneous, computer disk OK. Reports in 2 mos. Publishes by arrangement. Accepts nonfiction, fiction, poetry. Topics: traditional fiction set in the modern or historic Northwest; also interested in nonfiction compilations of letters, diaries, clippings, journals, etc. from the Northwest.
BOOK ARTS/BOOKS, FICTION, MONTANA

Bassett & Brush, W. 4108 Francis Ave., Spokane, WA 99205.
UNSPECIFIED

Bauhinea Press, 7756 Lawrence Dr., Burnaby, BC V5A 3M9. 604-420-1578. Contact: Benjamin Ho.
UNSPECIFIED

Baum Publications, 831 Helmcken, Vancouver, BC V6B 2E6.
UNSPECIFIED

Bay Press, 115 W. Denny Way, Seattle, WA 98119. 206-284-5913; Fax: 206-286-1335. Editor: Thatcher Bailey. Publishes 4 art and cultural criticism books per yr. Press run 5,000. Pays 5% cover/advance and payments twice yearly. Reports in 4 wks. Publishes within 1 yr. Submit query, SASE. Dot matrix, photocopied OK. Accepts nonfiction only. Catalog.
CULTURE

Bayless Enterprises Inc., 501 S.W. 7th St., Renton, WA 98055-2918. 206-622-6395. Contact: George Bayless. Self-publisher of two softcover maritime books per yr. Print run 7,500. Not a freelance market.
NW/REGIONAL HISTORY, RECREATION

BCS Educational Aids Inc., PO Box 100, Bothell, WA 98206.
EDUCATION

Beach Holme Publishers Ltd., 4252 Commerce Circle, Victoria, BC V8Z 4M2. 604-727-6522. Contact: Guy Chadsey. Publishes softcover trade books. Accepts freelance material. Pays royalties, advance negotiable. Acquires all rights. Submit query letter, outline, sample chapters, SASE. Simultaneous OK. Reports in 3-4 mos; publishes in 1-2 mos. Accepts science fiction, poetry. We publish Canadian authors only. Guidelines, catalog.
BRITISH COLUMBIA, FANTASY/SCI FI, POETRY

Bear Creek Publications, 2507 Minor Ave. E., Seattle, WA 98102. Editor: Kathy Shea. Publisher of 1-2 nonfic-

tion, softcover originals per year for parents/expectant parents. Press run: 2,000. Accepts freelance material. Query with outline, sample chapters, SASE. Photocopies, simultaneous subs OK. Reports in 1 month. Publishes in 6 mos. Payment and rights negotiable.
FAMILY, HOW-TO

Bear Grass Press, Box 211, Robson, BC V0G 1X0. 604-365-6549. Contact: Kathy Armstrong. Publishes hard- & softcover, subsidy books. Accepts unsolicited submissions. Pays copies, royalties. Acquires 1st rights. Submit query letter, outline, sample chapters, SASE, phone. Dot matrix, photocopied, simultaneous, disk (Mac) subs OK. Responds in 2 mos; publishes in 12-18 mos. Accepts fiction, poetry, biography, nonfiction, memoirs. SASE for catalog.
BIOGRAPHY, FICTION, POETRY

Bear Tribe Publishing, PO Box 9176, Spokane, WA 99209. 509-326-6561. Contact: Matt Ryan. Publisher of books on environment, Native American philosophy. 3-6 titles per yr. Query w/SASE.
ENVIRONMENT/RESOURCES, NATIVE AMERICAN

The Bear Wallow Publishing Co., 57919 High Valley Rd., Union, OR 97883. 503-562-5687. Contact: Jerry Gildemeister. Publisher of hardcover books. Query by phone or letter before sending ms. Pays money, royalties, & copies. Responds promptly to queries; publishing time variable. "Primarily for self-publishing projects, but also assist other self-publishers."
AMERICANA, HISTORY, NW/REGIONAL, OLD WEST

Beartooth Networks Inc., Box 1742, Billings, MT 59103. Editor: Lee Lemke.
UNSPECIFIED

Beautiful America Publishing Company, PO Box 646, Wilsonville, OR 97070. 503-682-0173. Editor: Andrea Tronslin. Ads: Larry Miller. Publisher of hard- & softcover books. No unsolicited mss. Pays copies, royalties, advance on acceptance. Acquires 1st rights. Submit query letter, outline, SASE. Accepts nonfiction, children's, photos. Catalog.
CHILDREN, NORTHWEST, TRAVEL

Beaver Publications, 15605 N.W. Cornell Rd., Beaverton, OR 97006.
UNSPECIFIED

Beginning Press, 5418 S. Brandon St., Seattle, WA 98118-2525. 206-723-6300. Publishes 3 softcover original books a year. Press run: average 6,000. Does not accept unsolicited submissions.
CONSUMER, HEALTH, RELIGION

Bellevue Art Museum, Bellevue Square, 3rd Floor, Bellevue, WA 98004.
ARTS, GENERAL HISTORY

Bellowing Ark Press, PO Box 45637, Seattle, WA 98145. 206-545-8302. Editor: Robert R Ward. Publishes softcover original books. Does not accept unsolicited submissions. Pays royalties. Publishes fiction, poetry. Catalog.
FICTION, POETRY

Bench Press, 3100 Evergreen Point Rd., Bellevue, WA 98004.
UNSPECIFIED

Ben-Simon Publications, PO Box 318, Brentwood Bay, BC V0S 1A0. 604-652-6332. Address in U.S.: PO Box 2124, Port Angeles, WA 98362. Editor: B. Bach. Accepts unsolicited submissions. Submit query, sample chapters; SASE. Dot matrix, photocopies OK. Reports ASAP. Accepts nonfiction. Topics: Judaica. Catalog.
RELIGION

Berry Patch Press, 3350 N.W. Luray Terrace, Portland, OR 97210.
UNSPECIFIED

Best Editions, 7841 Leary Way, Redmond, WA 98052. 206-883-6588. Contact: David Grant Best. Self-publisher

of hard & soft cover books. No unsolicited submissions. Publishes a semi-annual newsletter. Circ. 300. Does not accept freelance material. Back issues $2 each. "Newsletter published for friends, collectors, and those interested in the career and special editions of photographer/writer David Grant Best."
PHOTOGRAPHY, SOCIOLOGY, HISTORY, GENERAL

Beynch Press Publishing Co., 1928 S.E. Ladd Ave., Portland, OR 97214. 503-232-0433. Contact: Alyce Cornyn-Selby. Self-publisher, not a freelance market.
BUSINESS, HUMOR

Beyond Basals Inc., 586 University Dr., Pocatello, ID 83201. 208-233-9717. Editor: Gale Sherman. Self-publisher of materials for teachers. Not a freelance market.
EDUCATION

Beyond Words Publishing Inc., 13950 Pumpkin Ridge Rd., Hillsboro, OR 97123. 503-647-5109. Editor: Cynthia Black. Ads: Richard Cohn. Publishes 5-10 hard- & softcover books a yr. Accepts unsolicited submissions in areas of interest. Payment negotiated, on publication. Acquires all rights. Submit query w/clips, SASE, phone. Mac computer disk OK. Reports in 3 mos. Publishes in 1-2 years. Accepts nonfiction, fiction, & photos. "Three areas of interest: photography w/text, healthy self-help, and children's books with illustrations." Guidelines, catalog.
HEALTH, PHOTOGRAPHY, CHILDREN/TEEN

Bible Temple Publications, 7545 N.E. Glisan St., Portland, OR 97213.
RELIGION

Bicentennial Era Enterprises, PO Box 1148, Scappoose, OR 97056. 503-684-3937. Self-publisher of softcover books. Not a freelance market.
ECONOMICS, GOVERNMENT, POLITICS

Bigoni Books, 4121 N.E. Highland, Portland, OR 97211.
UNSPECIFIED

Binford & Mort Publishing, 1202 N.W. 17th Ave., PO Box 42368, Portland, OR 97242. 503-221-0866. Contact: Paula Gardenier. Publisher of 10-12 hard- & softcover books and reprints per year on themes of Western Americana, history, biography, travel, recreation and reference. Does some subsidy publishing. Payment: variable advance to established authors; 10% royalties. Query w/SASE. Dot matrix OK. Reports in 2-4 mos. Publishes in 1 yr. Nonfiction: on above themes, with emphasis on N.W./Pacific Coast. Fiction: only if heavily historical.
BIOGRAPHY, NW/REGIONAL HISTORY, RECREATION

Bippity-Boppity Books, W. 915 12th, Spokane, WA 99204.
UNSPECIFIED

Birds' Meadow Publishing Company Inc., 1050 E. Center St., Pocatello, ID 83201. Contact: Margaret Stucki, Director.
UNSPECIFIED

Black Current Press, Gutenberg Dump, PO Box 1149, Haines, AK 99827. Book Publisher, poetry.
POETRY

Black Heron Press, PO Box 95676, Seattle, WA 98145. 206-363-5210. Contact: Jerry Gold. Publisher of 4 hard- & softcover fiction books/yr. Accepts unsolicited mss. Pays royalties. Submit ms w/SASE. Dot matrix, photocopies, simultaneous subs OK. Reports in 2-4 mos. Publishes in 18 mos. Accepts nonfiction, fiction. "Intellectually stimulating and/or emotionally moving without being sentimental." Catalog with SASE.
FICTION, LITERATURE, MILITARY/VETS

Black Sheep Newsletter, 25455 N.W. Dixie Mountain Rd., Scappoose, OR 97056. 503-621-3063. Editor: Peggy Lundquist. Quarterly newsletter, books. Circ. 1,500. Sub $12/yr US. Uses freelance material. Pays copies on publication. Acquires all or 1st rights. Byline given. Query/SASE.

Photocopy, disk OK. Responds quarterly; publishes quarterly. Accepts nonfiction, poetry, news items, interviews, articles, reviews, photos (B&W & color; good contrast). Topics: animal fiber raising and use of animal fibers. Sample, back issues $2.50-$3.00. Guidelines & index of back issues.
ANIMALS, CRAFTS/HOBBIES

Blackfish Books, 1851 Moore Ave., Burnaby, BC.
UNSPECIFIED

Blue Begonia Press, 225 S. 15th Ave., Yakima, WA 98902. 509-575-3308. Editor: Jim Bodeen. A fine hand letterpress publisher/printer of poetry originals. Press run: 250-300. Accepts poetry for two books per yr. We don't encourage submissions. There's too much to do as it is. "We're not interested in adding another book to a poet's resume A manuscript needs to be important enough for one person working nights to want to do it by hand." Pays in copies on publication. Query w/SASE. Catalog, samples.
POETRY

Blue Heron Press, PO Box 5182, Bellingham, WA 98227. 206-671-1155. Contact: Mitch Lesoing/Carol Anderson. Publisher of softcover books. No unsolicited mss. Query with clips, SASE. Reports in 6-8 wks. Publishes in 6-12 mos. Accepts nonfiction, fiction, photos. Topics: computer education materials, children's books, outdoor recreation (boating, hiking, fishing). Stock photos & graphics sometimes purchased at standard rates.
CHILDREN/TEEN, COMPUTERS, RECREATION

Blue Heron Publishing Inc., 24450 N.W. Hansen Rd., Hillsboro, OR 97124. 503-621-3911. Contact: Dennis Stovall/Linny Stovall. Publishes 1-2 writing- or publishing-related books. Media Weavers imprint (*Writer's Northwest Handbook* and *Writer's N.W.*, a quarterly newspaper). Publishes 1-2 young adult novels, reprints/originals per year. Publishes the book series Left Bank, biannual thematic collections. Will consider queries with outlines, sample chapters, and SASE for books aimed at publishers, writers, editors, and teachers of writing, English, and journalism.
CHILDREN/TEEN, FICTION, WRITING

Blue Nun Press, Site 346, C-14, Port Alberni, BC V9Y 7L7. 604-723-8085.
UNSPECIFIED

Blue Scarab Press, 243 S. 8th Ave., Pocatello, ID 83201. Editor: Harald Wyndham. Publisher of softcover books of poetry and fiction. No unsolicited submissions. Acquires no rights. Query letter w/SASE, photocopy OK, responds in 4 weeks.
FICTION, LITERARY, POETRY

Blue Unicorn Press, PO Box 40300, Portland, OR 97240-0300. 503-238-4766. Contact: Wanda Z. Larson. Publisher of books of prose, poetry and literary chapbooks. Not accepting queries or submissions at this time. Catalog/SASE.
FICTION, POETRY

Blue Water Publishing, PO Box 230893, Tigard, OR 97224. 503-684-9749. Editor: Brian Crissey. Ads: Pam Meyer. Publishes original books. Accepts unsolicited submissions. Submit query letter, phone, outline, sample chapters or ms/SASE. Dot matrix, photocopies, simultaneous, electronic/modem, computer disk OK. Reports in 4 wks; publishes in 1 yr. Accepts nonfiction, fiction, poetry. Topics: New Age and UFOs.
ASTROLOGY/SPIRITUAL, NATIVE AMERICAN, NEW AGE

The Boag Foundation Ltd., 576 Keith Rd., West Vancouver, BC V7T 1L7. Publishes socialist books on social and historical topics. Query w/SASE.
GENERAL HISTORY, SOCIALIST/RADICAL

Bob Books Publications, PO Box 633, West Linn, OR 97068. 503-657-1833. Editor: Bobby Lynn Maslen. Publisher of illustrated books for very young readers. No submissions, please.
CHILDREN/TEEN

Boise State U. Western Writers Series, Department of English, BSU, 1910 University Dr., Boise, ID 83725. 208-385-1246. Contact: James H. Maguire. Publisher of books of critical introductions to the lives and works of authors who have made a significant contribution to the literature of the American West. Print run: 1,000. Those who write for us are usually members of the Western Literature Association or read the association's journal, Western American Literature. No pay. Rights purchased: All. Query w/SASE. Photocopies OK. Reports in 1 month. Publishes in 5-10 yrs. Guidelines, catalog.
BIOGRAPHY, COLLEGE/UNIVERSITY, LITERARY

Bold Brass Studios & Publications, PO Box 77101, Vancouver, BC V5R 5T4.
UNSPECIFIED

Bonanza Publishing, 203320 Wainwright Rd., Prineville, OR 97754. Editor: Rick Steber. Book publisher, hard- & softcover on the old west history. Press run: 5,000-10,000. Does not accept unsolicited submissions.
OLD WEST, AMERICAN HISTORY, NW/REGIONAL HISTORY

Bonnie Scherer Publications, 1021 Alderson, Billings, MT 59102. 406-245-7289. Editor: Mary Roberts. Self-publisher only of books about children. Not a freelance market.
CHILDREN (BY/ABOUT)

Botany Books, 1518 Hayward Ave., Bremerton, WA 98310. 206-377-6489. Self-publisher of softcover books, how-to and gardening. Accepts no mss.
GARDENING, HOW-TO

Bowen Island Historians, R.R. 1, Bowen Island, BC V0N 1G0.
CANADIAN HISTORY

Box Dog Press, PO Box 9609, Seattle, WA 98109. Editor: Craig Joyce. Publishes softcover books. Accepts unsolicited submissions. Byline given; pays copies. Submit query letter, outline, SASE. Responds in 1 month; publishing time varies. Accepts fiction, poetry, photos, cartoons. Catalog.
AVANT-GARDE/EXPERIMENTAL, FILM/VIDEO, LITERATURE

Braemar Books Ltd., PO Box 4142 Station A, Victoria, BC V8X 3X4.
UNSPECIFIED

Braemer Books, PO Box 25296, Portland, OR 97225. 503-292-4226. Contact: Craig Patillo. Self-publisher of 1 softcover book per year for record collectors, music stores, radio stations. Print run: 500. Not a freelance market.
COLLECTING, LITERATURE, MUSIC

Briarwood Publishing Ltd., 7411 Ash St., Richmond, BC V6Y 2R9. 604-278-8108. Contact: Sharon MacGougan. No unsolicited manuscripts.
UNSPECIFIED

Brighouse Press, Box 33798, Sta. D, Vancouver, BC V6J 4L6. 604-731-9994. Contact: Terri Wershler or Elizabeth Wilson. Publisher of 5 softcover regional nonfiction originals per yr. Accepts unsolicited mss. Query w/clips, SASE. Pays royalties, advance on publication. Dot matrix, photocopied subs OK. Reports in 6 weeks.
NORTHWEST

Bright Ring Publishing, PO Box 5768, Bellingham, WA 98227. 206-734-1601. Contact: Mary Ann Kohl. Publisher of 1 softcover children's book per yr. Pays royalties, copies. Query with letter, sample chapters, ms, SASE, phone. Dot matrix, photocopies, simultaneous submissions, electronic OK. Reports in 2-4 wks; publishes in 1 yr. Accepts nonfiction. Topics: creative activity ideas for children. Guidelines, catalog.
CRAFTS/HOBBIES, EDUCATION, FAMILY

British Columbia Genealogical Society, PO Box 94371, Richmond, BC V6Y 2A8. 604-325-0374. Publishes softcover books, quarterly journal, bimonthly newsletter, and conducts educational programs for members only. Journal sub/$30. No unsolicited submissions, no freel-

ance material. Back issues of journal $3.25, newsletter $5.25.
BRITISH COLUMBIA, GENEALOGY

Broadsheet Publications, 620 Arthur, McMinnville, OR 97128. 503-472-5524. Contact: Wilma Grand Chalmers. Self-publisher of 1 softcover book per year for adult music listeners. Not a freelance market.
ENTERTAINMENT, MUSIC

Broken Moon Press, PO Box 24585, Seattle, WA 98124-0585. 206-548-1340. Contact: John Ellison or Lesley Link. Ads: Tina Metzger. Publishes books. Catalog.
BIOGRAPHY, FICTION, POETRY

Brooding Heron Press, Bookmonger Rd., Waldron Island, WA 98297. Contact: Sam Green/Sally Green. Founded 1984. Literary publisher of hard & softcover books. No unsolicited submissions. Pays copies on publication. Acquires 1st rights. Publishes poetry. Send SASE business-size for catalog.
POETRY

Browndeer Press, PO Box 80160, Portland, OR 97280. 503-452-1795. Publishes picture books, mid-grade fiction, nonfiction and some young adult works. Accepts unsolicited material. Send query letter & resume with sample chapters.
CHILDREN/TEEN

Bruce Gould Publications, PO Box 16, Seattle, WA 98111.
UNSPECIFIED

Caber Press, 1417 N.W. Everett, Portland, OR 97209. Book publisher. Self-help, motivational.
PSYCHOLOGY

Cacanadadada Press Ltd., 3350 W. 21st Ave, Vancouver, BC V6S 1G7. 604-738-1195. Contact: J. Michael Yates. Ads: Margaret Fridel. Publishes 8-10 softcover books per yr. Press run: 1,000. Accepts unsolicited submissions. Pays copies, royalties on publication. Submit ms. Dot matrix, computer disk subs OK. Reports in 4 mos. Publishes in 6 mos. Accepts nonfiction, fiction, poetry, plays. Topics: Literature, women. Catalog.
FICTION, POETRY, WOMEN

Cain-Lockhart Press, PO Box 1129, 19510 S.E. 51st St., Issaquah, WA 98027. 206-392-0508. Self-publisher of travel books and audio tapes. Not a freelance market.
ASIA, LANGUAGE(S), TRAVEL

The Caitlin Press, Box 2387, Sta B, Prince George, BC V2N 2S6. 604-964-4953. Editor: Cynthia Wilson. Publishes hard & softcover books. Pays royalties, acquires no rights. Submit query letter, SASE, sample chapters, complete ms, synopsis. Responds in 6-8 wks; publishes in 1 to 1 1/2 yrs. Accepts fiction, poetry, memoirs, biography, cartoons, nonfiction. "Specializes in northern BC. Submissions from other areas not accepted." Catalog.
FICTION, LITERATURE, POETRY

Calapooia Publications, PO Box 160, Brownsville, OR 97327. 503-369-2439; 503-926-0350. Contact: Margaret Standish Carey, Patricia Hoy Hainline. Publishers of regional histories. Not presently accepting mss. Query w/SASE. Catalog.
NW/REGIONAL HISTORY

Callan and Brooks Publishing Company, 550 S.W. 5th St., Corvallis, OR 97333. 503-754-1439. Contact: Caron Klopping. Publishes hard & softcover originals. Fiction: children and young adult. Nonfiction: angling, regional, technical. Photocopies, 3 1/2" disk OK. Invites appropriate artwork portfolios. Query or ms with SASE.
CHILDREN/TEEN, FISHING, TECHNICAL

Calyx Books, Calyx, Inc., PO Box B, Corvallis, OR 97339. 503-753-9384; FAX: 503-753-0515. Editor/Ads: Margarita Donnelly. Publishes hard- & softcover original books by women. Accepts unsolicited submissions Jan 1st to March

15th each yr. Pays royalties. Dot matrix, photocopies, computer disk OK. Reports in 1 yr; publishes in 1-2 yrs. Accepts fiction, poetry, art. Topics: fine literature & art by women. SASE for book submission guidelines; catalog.
LITERATURE, POETRY, WOMEN

Camp Denali Publishing, PO Box 67, McKinley Park, AK 99755.
ALASKA, OUTDOOR

Canadian West Magazine, Sunfire Publications Ltd., P. O. Box 3399, Langley, BC V3A 4R7. 604-534-9378. Editor: Garnet Basque. Publisher of hard- & softcover books & quarterly magazine. Sub $15/yr. Circ. 9,000. Use freelance material. Pays money on publication. Acquires 1st rights. Byline given. Submit query letter, outline, complete ms, SASE, phone. Dot matrix, photocopied subs OK. Accepts nonfiction, biography. Topics: pioneer history of BC, Alberta and the Yukon; historical-ghost towns, mining, lost treasure, Indians, shipwrecks, rocks, gems & bottles, robberies, battles, etc. Articles should be accompanied by suitable artwork/photos. Factual accuracy required. Guidelines; sample $4.
BRITISH COLUMBIA, CANADIAN HISTORY, NW/REGIONAL HISTORY

Canho Publishers, 229 Greenwood Dr., Penticton, BC V2A 7P9. 604-493-7964. Publishes softcover, original, educational, historical dramas. Query. Catalog.
DRAMA, EDUCATION, NORTHWEST

CAREsource Program Development Inc., 505 Seattle Tower, 1218 Third Ave., Seattle, WA 98101-3021. 800-448-5213; 206-625-9128. Contact: Elizabeth Hendricks. Publisher of materials for the long term care industry, with special emphasis on regulatory compliance, resident activity programs, family support, quality assurance, and staff development.
HEALTH

Carnot Press, PO Box 1544, Lake Oswego, OR 97034.
UNSPECIFIED

Cascade Automotive Resources, 125 S.W. Wright Court, Troutdale, OR 97060.
UNSPECIFIED

Cascade Farm Publishing Company, 21594 S. Springwater Rd., Estacada, OR 97023.
AGRICULTURE/FARMING, GARDENING, UNSPECIFIED

Castalia Publishing Company, PO Box 1587, Eugene, OR 97440. 503-343-4433. Contact: Scot Patterson. Publisher of 2-3 hard- & softcover books a year. Print run 2,000-5,000. No unsolicited mss. Pays royalties, advance. Rights purchased: All. Reports in 3 mos. Publishes in 1 yr. Psychology textbooks & books on childrearing issues for parents. Materials are research-based. Catalog.
FAMILY, PSYCHOLOGY, SCHOLARLY/ACADEMIC

Castle Peak Editions, 1670 E. 27th Ave, Eugene, OR 97403. 503-342-2975; 503-846-6322. Contact: Jim Hall or Judith Shears. Publisher of books poetry, fiction, and texts (grammar and lit anthologies). Accepts submissions of collections of poetry or short stories of extraordinary quality. Query w/SASE. Reports in 1-2 mos; publication time varies.
FICTION, POETRY, TEXTBOOKS

Catalytic Publications, 2711 E. Beaver Lake Dr. S.E., Issaquah, WA 98027. 206-392-2723. Self-publisher of educational materials. Not a freelance market.
EDUCATION

The Caxton Printers Ltd., 312 Main St., Caldwell, ID 83605. 208-459-7421. Editor: Pam Hardenbrook. Publishes nonfiction, hard- & softcover originas. Unsolicited submissions OK. Pays advance, royalties. Query letter, outline, sample chapters, SASE. Photocopy OK. Responds in 1-3 mos; publishes in 8-12 mos. Accepts nonfiction, biography, memoirs, photos. Topics: history, travel biog-

raphy, lifestyle, Western Americana. Guidelines, catalog.
AMERICANA, NW/REGIONAL HISTORY, OLD WEST

CEcom Publishing, Box 3059, Homer, AK 99603. 206-299-1465; 907-235-6378. Publisher of books on health, allergies, environmental illness. Sample $11.95
HEALTH

Cedar Island Press, PO Box 113, West Linn, OR 97068. 503-636-7914. Contact: Helen Garcia. Self-publisher of 1 softcover original per year on cooking. Not a freelance market.
FOOD/COOKING

Celestial Gems, 404 State St., Centralia, WA 98531. Contact: Gypsy Al Coolidge.
UNSPECIFIED

Center for East Asian Studies, Western Washington University, Bellingham, WA 98225-9056. 206-676-3041. Editor: Henry G. Schwarz. Publisher of hard & soft cover books. Founded in 1971. Accepts unsolicited mss. Pays copies. Submit query letter, outline, sample chapters, complete ms, SASE. Photocopies, dot matrix subs OK. Responds in 2 wks; publishes in 1 yr. Accepts nonfiction, biography, poetry, fiction, monographs, memoirs. Guidelines, catalog.
ASIA, COLLEGE/UNIVERSITY

Center for Pacific Northwest Studies, Western Washington University, Bellingham, WA 98225. 206-647-4776; 206-676-3125. Contact: Dr. James W. Scott. Publishes softcover original books. Does not accept freelance material. Topics: academic works on the Pacific N.W., usually by resident faculty and graduate students. Catalog.
BIOGRAPHY, AMERICAN HISTORY

Center for Urban Education, 2710 N.E. 14th, Portland, OR 97212-3299. 503-249-2857. Contact: Karen Quitt or Rod Barrows. Publisher of Oregon Media Guide, media directory & educational materials for non-profit groups. Book publisher. Phone or query w/SASE.
EDUCATION, LITERATURE, MEDIA/COMMUNICATIONS

The Center Press, 14902 33rd Ave. N.W., Gig Harbor, WA 98335. 206-858-3064.
UNSPECIFIED

Centerplace Publishing Company, P. O. Box 901, Lake Oswego, OR 97034. 503-636-8710. Editor: Paul J. Lyons. Publisher of softcover parenting related/children's books. Accepts unsolicited mss. Pays on publication. Acquires 1st rights. Query w/clips. Dot matrix, computer disk subs OK. Reports in 2 wks; publishes in 3 mos. Does all design/coordinate illustrations. We focus on practical, how-to information for parents and children on self-improvement and improvement of relationships.
CHILDREN/TEEN, FAMILY, PSYCHOLOGY

Chalet Publishing Co., 18186 S. Chalet Dr., Oregon City, OR 97045. 503-631-3247. Contact: Doris Charriere.
UNSPECIFIED

The Charles Franklin Press, 7821 175th Street S.W., Edmonds, WA 98020. 206-774-6979. Contact: Linda Meyer or Denelle Peaker. Publisher of 3 nonfiction, hard- & softcover, originals per year; self-help and booklets for national organizations. "We specialize in children's books which teach safety and common sense, especially sexual assault and abduction prevention skills. Most of our books are 25 to 40 pages. They must be written in a non-threatening style. We rely heavily on an organization's existing network to distribute our books." Print run: 5,000. Accepts freelance material. Payment: Money, 8% without split, 5 or 6% with split, or negotiable. Rights purchased: all. Query with sample chapters of complete ms and SASE. Photocopies OK. Reports in 1 month. Publishes in 6 months. Author should indicate the market its extent as well as organizations that might be interested in the book. Catalog.
CHILDREN/TEEN, FAMILY, WOMEN

Charles Seluzicki Fine Press Series, Fine and Rare Books, 3733 N.E. 24th Ave., Portland, OR 97212. 503-284-4749. Contact: Charles Seluzicki. Publisher of 2-4 hard- & softcover originals, reprints a year. Print run: 50-300. Accepts freelance material with strict qualifications. Payment: copies, small cash payments at times. Acquires first rights. Submit ms, SASE. Photocopies OK. Reports in 1 month. Publishes in 6-24 months. Book arts, fiction, poetry, plays. "Interested in the best possible writing for fine press formats. Such publishing requires materials that suggest strong graphic and tactile expression. Mss are primarily solicited. Our authors have included Ted Hughes, William Stafford, Tess Gallagher, Seamus Heaney, and Charles Simic." Catalog.
BOOK ARTS/BOOKS, FICTION, POETRY

Cherry Tree Press, Box 5113, Sta B, Victoria, BC V8R 6N3. Self-publisher of writer's books.
BRITISH COLUMBIA, WRITING

Childbirth Education Association, 10021 Holman Rd. N.W., Seattle, WA 98177-4920.
CHILDREN/TEEN, EDUCATION, FAMILY

The Christ Foundation, PO Box 10, Port Angeles, WA 98362. 206-452-5249. Self publisher. Not a freelance market. Query w/SASE.
NEW AGE

Christian Zion Advocate, PO Box 971, Port Angeles, WA 98362.
RELIGION

Cinnabar Press Ltd., Box 392, Nanaimo, BC V9R 5L3. 604-754-9887.
UNSPECIFIED

Circa Press, PO Box 482, Lake Oswego, OR 97034. 503-636-7241. Editor: Robert Brooks. Publishes hard- & softcover original nonfiction books. Accepts unsolicited submissions. Pays royalties. Acquires all rights. Submit query letter, SASE. Dot matrix, photocopies OK. Reports in 3-6 wks; publishes in 6-9 mos. Catalog.
ECONOMICS, POLITICS, SCIENCE

Circinatum Press, Box 99309, Tacoma, WA 98499.
UNSPECIFIED

CIRI-BETH Publishing Company, 4638 E. C St., Tacoma, WA 98404-1309.
UNSPECIFIED

Civetta Press, PO Box 1043, Portland, OR 97207-1043. 503-228-6649. Editor: Charlotte Digregorio. Book publisher: crafts, how-to, writing. Accepts unsolicited submissions. Pays royalties. Submit query letter, SASE. Responds in 2 wks; publishes in 6 mos. Accepts nonfiction. No phone calls on queries.
WRITING

Clark City Press, PO Box 1358, 109 West Callendar, Livingston, MT 59047. 406-222-7412. Contact: Russ Chatham. Book publisher of nonfiction. Print run: 7,500 to 12,500. No unsolicited submissions. Pays advance, royalties; rights acquired vary. Not accepting submissions. Catalog.
ARTS, FICTION, POETRY

Classics Unlimited Inc., 2121 Arlington Ave., Caldwell, ID 83605.
UNSPECIFIED

Cleaning Center Books, PO Box 39, Pocatello, ID 83204-0039. 208-232-6212.
UNSPECIFIED

Cleaning Consultant Services Inc., PO Box 1273, Seattle, WA 98111. 206-682-9748; FAX: 206-622-6876. Contact: William R. Griffin. Publisher of soft- & hardcover originals. Accepts unsolicited submissions. Pays money, royalties on publication. Acquires 1st/all rights. Complete ms, query w/SASE. Disk/modem sub OK. Responds in 1

mo; publishes in 6 mos. Accepts nonfiction: references, directories, how-to and textbooks on cleaning and maintenance, health and self-employment, and entrepreneurship. Also seeking poetry, cartoons, photos, and illustrations on the same subjects. Catalog free.
BUSINESS, EDUCATION, LABOR/WORK

Cloudburst Press, Hartley & Marks, PO Box 147, Point Roberts, WA 97281. 206-945-2017. Imprint of Hartley & Marks.
HEALTH, HOW-TO, SENIOR CITIZENS

Coalition For Child Advocacy, 314 E. Holly St. #200, Bellingham, WA 98225-4736. 206-734-5121.
CHILDREN/TEEN, FAMILY, HEALTH

Coast Publishing, PO Box 3399, Coos Bay, OR 97420. 503-271-3418. Contact: W. J. Howard. Strictly self-publishing books on science and math simplified for the layman. Information available with SASE.
SCIENCE

Coastal Press, 1205 N.W. 191, Richmond Beach, WA 98177.
UNSPECIFIED

cold-drill Books, Department of English, Boise State University, Boise, ID 83725. 208-385-1246. Contact: Tom Trusky. Publisher of 1 softcover original book a year. Print run: 500. No unsolicited mss. Pays copies on publication; acquires 1st rights. Assignment only. Dot matrix, photocopies, simultaneous subs OK. Accepts nonfiction, fiction, poetry, photos, plays, cartoons, other. Catalog.
AVANT-GARDE/EXPERIMENTAL, COLLEGE/UNIVERSITY, LITERATURE

COMMUNICOM, 19300 N.W. Sauvie Island Rd., Portland, OR 97231. 503-621-3049. Contact: Donna Matrazzo. Publisher of softcover books for film/video/multi-image professionals. Not a freelance market. Catalog.
BUSINESS, HOW-TO, MEDIA/COMMUNICATIONS

Comprehensive Health Educ. Found., 22323 Pacific Hwy. South, Seattle, WA 98198. 206-824-2907. Contact: Robynn Rockstad or Steven Goldenberg. Publisher of books, videos, and health education curricula used in schools. No unsolicited submissions. Catalog.
EDUCATION, HEALTH

Confluence Press Inc., Lewis-Clark State College, 8th Ave. & 6th St., Lewiston, ID 83501. 208-799-2336. Contact: James R. Hepworth. Publisher of 5 hard- & softcover original books a yr. Press run 5,000. Accepts unsolicited submissions. Pays royalties, advance, on publication. Rights acquired: All. Submit query w/clips, SASE. Photocopies OK. Reports in 6-8 wks; publishes in 12-18 mos. Accepts nonfiction, fiction, poetry. "We're looking for the best writing in the Northwest. We have excellent national distribution." Catalog with SASE.
LITERATURE, NORTHWEST, POETRY

Conscious Living Foundation, PO Box 9, Drain, OR 97435. 503-836-2358. Editor: Dr. Tim Lowenstein. Publishes 1-6 softcover books a yr. Accepts unsolicited submissions. Submit query w/clips. Dot matrix, photocopied, simultaneous, electronic subs OK. Reports in 3 wks. Publishes in 8 mos. Accepts nonfiction. Catalog.
UNSPECIFIED

Constant Society, 4244 University Way N.E., PO Box 45513, Seattle, WA 98105.
UNSPECIFIED

Consultant Services Northwest Inc., 839 N.E. 96th St., Seattle, WA 98115. 206-524-1950. Editor: Charna Klein. Publishes 1 softcover book a yr. Does not accept unsolicited submissions.
BUSINESS, COMPUTERS

Contemporary Issues Clearinghouse, 1410 S. Second, Pocatello, ID 83201.
UNSPECIFIED

Continuing Education Press, PO Box 1491, 1633 S.W. Park, Portland, OR 97207. 503-725-4846. Contact: Tony Midson. Hard- & softcover books for individuals with a desire for self-improvement or development of professional skills. Pays royalties. Submit query letter, SASE. "We're looking for materials for educators, students or professionals, especially items with a continuing education function or for self-instruction and improvement. Should be appropriate for academic review before acceptance. Writers should be established authorities, or have special insight."
EDUCATION

Copper Canyon Press, Box 271, Port Townsend, WA 98368. 206-385-4925. Editor: Sam Hamill. Publishes hard- & softcover originals, reprints; poetry and poetry in translation. Accepts no unsolicited material. Query w/SASE. Reports in 1 mo; publishes in 2 yrs. Acquires all rights. Catalog.
POETRY, LITERARY

Copyright Information Services, Div. of Harbor View Publications Group, PO Box 1460-A, Friday Harbor, WA 98250-1460. 206-378-5128. Contact: Jerome K. Miller. Publisher of 5 hardcover original books a yr. about USA copyright law. Accepts unsolicited submissions. Pays 15% net royalties. Submit query w/clips, SASE. Dot matrix, computer disk OK. Reports in 6 wks. Publishes promptly. Accepts nonfiction. Catalog.
LAW, WRITING

Coriolis Publishing Company, 425 S.E. 3rd, Portland, OR 97214.
UNSPECIFIED

Council for Indian Education, 517 Rimrock Rd., Billings, MT 59102. 406-252-7451. Editor: Hap Gilliland. Ads: Sue Clague. Publishes 6 softcover books a yr. Accepts unsolicited mss & freelance material. Byline given. Pays royalties & copies on publication. Acquires first rights. Send query w/ SASE, sample chapters, complete ms, synopsis. Photocopy, dot matrix, simultaneous sub, OK. Responds in 3 mos, publishes in 18 mos. Accepts fiction, poetry, biography, nonfiction, photos. "...only material related to American Indian life and culture." Guidelines, catalog.
NATIVE AMERICAN, FICTION, CULTURE

Cowles Publishing Company, 927 Riverside, Spokane, WA 99210.
UNSPECIFIED

Crabtree Publishing, PO Box 3451, Federal Way, WA 98063. 206-927-3777. Contact: Catherine Crabtree. Publisher of 2 hard- & softcover originals a year on cooking, home design, health/fitness, entertainment/restaurant guides. Print run: 5,000. Accepts freelance material with permission. Send request letter stating type of material. Include SASE. Rights purchased: All. Guidelines, catalog.
ENTERTAINMENT, FOOD/COOKING, HEALTH

Creative Children, c/o Keith McAlear, 811 15TH AVE. E., Polson, MT 59860.
CHILDREN/TEEN

Crompton Books, 142A - West 15th St., N. Vancouver, BC V7M 1E8. 604-986-0987. Contact: Dr. John Matsen.
UNSPECIFIED

Crook Publishing, 1680 Cornell Ave., Coquitlam, BC V3J 3A1.
UNSPECIFIED

Cross Cultural Press, 1166 S. 42nd St., Springfield, OR 97478. 503-746-7401. Editor: Ken Fenter. Publishes hard- & softcover original, subsidy books. No unsolicited mss. Query w/SASE. Dot matrix, photocopies, computer disk OK. Reports in 1-4 wks; publishes within 1 yr. Topics: Japanese-American experiences, Asian-American experiences.
ASIA, ASIAN AMERICAN, CULTURE

Crow Publications Inc., PO Box 25749, Portland, OR 97225. 503-646-8075.
UNSPECIFIED

Crystal Musicworks, 2235 Willida Lane, Sedro Woolley, WA 98284.
MUSIC

Culinary Arts Ltd., PO Box 2157, Lake Oswego, OR 97035. 503-639-4549; Fax 503-620-4933. Editor: Cheryl Long. Softcover books. Does not accept unsolicited submissions. Pays royalties. Query w/clips, SASE, phone.
FOOD/COOKING

Current, PO Box 247, Walla Walla, WA 99362. Contact: Dave Hiatt. "Currently seeking exciting literary manuscripts — poetry and prose."
FICTION, POETRY

Current Lit Publications Inc., 1513 E. St., Bellingham, WA. 98225. 206/671-6664.
COMMUNITY, MEDIA/COMMUNICATIONS

Cybele Society, W. 1603 9th Ave., Spokane, WA 99204-3406. Book publisher. Query with SASE.
UNSPECIFIED

Daniel W. Giboney, PO Box 5432, Spokane, WA 99205. 509-326-3602. Self-publisher of a book on divorce. Not a freelance market.
LAW

Dark Horse Comics Inc., 10956 S.E. Main, Milwaukie, OR 97222. 503-652-8815. Contact: Submissions Department. Publishers of softcover and comic books. Most comic books appear monthly. Publishes 30 titles a month, plus special projects. Unsolicited submissions OK. Do not send originals. Payment is negotiable; frequently gives advances. Two types of rights; creator-owned projects and those owned by the business. Query by phone. Accepts cartoons. Call the submissions hotline ext. 479 for a detailed recording of an outline for both writers and artists. Catalog.
ARTS, FANTASY/SCI FI, FISHING

Darvill Outdoor Publications, 1819 Hickox Rd., Mt. Vernon, WA 98273.
OUTDOOR

Dee Publishing Company, 774 Cottage N.E., Salem, OR 97301.
UNSPECIFIED

Deep Well Publishing Company, 1371 Peace St. S.E. #12, Salem, OR 97302-2572. 503-581-6339. Editor: Jim Martin. Publisher of softcover books. No material accepted at this time.
BIOGRAPHY, HISTORY NW/REGIONAL, WOMEN

The Denali Press, PO Box 021535, Juneau, AK 99802. 907-586-6014. Editor: Alan Schorr. Publishes softcover originals. Unsolicited submissions OK. Pays royalties. Submit query w/clips, outline, sample chapters, synopsis. Photocopies OK. Reports in 3 wks; publishes in 9-14 mos. Accepts nonfiction and biography. Topics: primarily reference books, but also travel guides and Alaskana, Hispanic, refugees, immigrants, cultural diversity. Catalog.
ALASKA, MINORITIES/ETHNIC, REFERENCE/LIBRARY

Devils Thumb Press, Box 1136, Petersburg, AK 99833.
UNSPECIFIED

Dewdney Publishing, PO Box 231, Cranbrook, BC V1C 4H7.
UNSPECIFIED

Dimi Press, 3820 Oak Hollow Lane S.E., Salem, OR 97302. 503-364-7698; Fax: 503-364-9727. Publisher of softcover books and cassettes. Unsolicited submissions OK. Pays royalties on publication. Query w/SASE. Simultaneous submission OK. Reports in 4 wks. Topics: relaxation and other psychological self-help. "Know your market." Also helps writers self-publish. Guidelines, catalog.
HEALTH, HOW-TO, PSYCHOLOGY

Dioscorides Press Inc., 9999 S. W. Wilshire, Ste. 124, Portland, OR 97225. 503-292-0745. Contact: Dale Johnson, Acquisitions Editor.
GARDENING, SCIENCE, SCHOLARLY/ACADEMIC

DNR Geologic Publications, PO Box 47007, Olympia, WA 98504-7007. 206-459-6372. Publishes softcover books & an irregular newsletter. Uses freelance material on assignment. Query letter, SASE.
GEOLOGY/GEOGRAPHY, NATURAL HISTORY, SCIENCE

Dolan Press, 3308 - 22nd Pl., Apt 1, Forest Grove, OR 97116. 503-359-0431. Contact: Eileen Dolan Savage. Self-publisher of hard- & softcover books.
CHILDREN, HEALTH

Doorway Publishers, 703 N.E. Hostmark St. A #13, Poulsbo, WA 98370-8709. 206-297-7952. Editors: Doris Moore, Connie Lord. Publisher of softcover books. Does not accept unsolicited submissions. Submit query/SASE. Responds in 2-3 wks. Accepts nonfiction. Topics: how-to, crafts/hobbies.
CRAFTS/HOBBIES, HOW-TO

Doral Publishing, 32025 Village Crest Lane, Wilsonville, OR 97070. 503-694-5707. Editor: Dr. Alvin Grossman. Publishes hard- & softcover books. Accepts unsolicited submissions. Submit sample chapters, SASE. Simultaneous submissions, photocopies OK. Responds in 3 wks; publishes in 1 yr. Topics: dog books. Catalog.
ANIMALS

Douglas & McIntyre Publishers, 1615 Venables St., Vancouver, BC V5L 2H1. 604-254-7191. Contact: Shaun Oakey. Publisher of hard and softcover originals and paperbacks, primarily by Canadian writers. Also contact Rob Sanders, head of Greystone Books, an imprint of this company. It features natural history, outdoor, guidebooks, and prairie titles. Payment: Advances average $500; royalties 8-15%. Query or mss w/SASE. Nonfiction, fiction. Topics: biography, ethnic, experimental, historical, and women's literary fiction. Catalog.
BIOGRAPHY, CANADIAN HISTORY, WOMEN

Douglas Geidt, Box 246, Union Bay, BC V0R 3B0. 604-335-1042. Self-publisher
CANADIAN HISTORY

Doves Publishing Company, PO Box 821, Newport, OR 97365.
UNSPECIFIED

Dream Research, PO Box 107, Grapeview, WA 98546-0107. Editor: Adrienne Quinn.
UNSPECIFIED

Drelwood Publications, PO Box 10605, Portland, OR 97210.
UNSPECIFIED

Drift Creek Press, PO Box 511, Philomath, OR 97370. 503-754-6303; 800-338-0136. Editor: Craig J. Battrick. Publishes books and irregular newsletter. Publishes 3 titles yearly. Negotiable payment. Copyrights for authors. Query w/SASE, outline, sample chapter, or by phone. Photocopied, disk, dot matrix subs OK. Reports in 1 mo; publishes in 1 yr. Subjects: nonfiction, cookbooks, N.W. regional.
FOOD/COOKING, POETRY, NORTHWEST

Duane Shinn Publications, 5090 Dobrot, Central Point, OR 97501.
UNSPECIFIED

Eagle Signs, 1015 Hutson Rd., Hood River, OR 97031.
UNSPECIFIED

Earth View Inc., 6514 18th Ave. N.E., Seattle, WA 98115. 206-527-3168. Contact: Bryan Brewer. Self-publisher only of computer, health, and new age books.
COMPUTERS, HEALTH, NEW AGE

Earth-Love Publishing House, 302 Torbett #100, Richland, WA 99352. 509-943-9567. Publisher of new age and metaphysical books.
NEW AGE

Eastern Washington State Historical Soc., W. 2316 1st Ave., Spokane, WA 99204.
NW/REGIONAL HISTORY

Eastland Press, 119 1st Ave. S., #400, Seattle, WA 98104. 206-587-6013. Editor: John O'Connor. Ads: Patricia O'Connor. Three hardcover orig. books a yr. Unsolicited mss OK. Pays royalties; plus advance against royalties. Rights purchased: All. Submit: ms. Dot matrix, photocopy, computer disk OK. Reports in 1 month; publishes in 1 year. Accepts alternative medical nonfiction. "We publish only medical books, principally Oriental medicine and manual medicine (bodywork)." Guidelines, catalog.
HEALTH, MEDICAL, TEXTBOOKS

Eastside a la Carte, 4231 135th Pl. S.E., Bellevue, WA 98006.
UNSPECIFIED

Eclectic Press Inc., PO Box 14462, Portland, OR 97214. 503-286-4018. Contact: Barbara Cogan Neidig. Reprint and copublish books for the gift trade floral crafts, gardening. Not a freelance market. No submissions please.
CRAFTS/HOBBIES

Ecotope Group, 2812 E. Madison, Seattle, WA 98112.
UNSPECIFIED

Edmonds Arts Commission Books, 700 Main St., Edmonds, WA 98020. 206-775-2525. Self-publisher. Assignment only. Pays money, copies on acceptance. Rights purchased: First. Byline given. Dot matrix, photocopy OK. Reports in 1-2 mos. Publishes in 2-3 mos. Accepts nonfiction, fiction, poetry, cartoons, line drawings. Publication projects vary with contest subject. 500 word max. Contest awards plus free copies. Sample $7.95+ hand.
FAMILY, NW/REGIONAL HISTORY, HUMOR

Edprint Inc., 17936 Woodinville-Snohomish Rd., Woodinville, WA 98072. 206-483-0606. Hard- & softcover books. Also book distributor. Accepts unsolicited submissions, freelance material. Byline given. Pays copies, royalties on publication. Responds 1-2 mos. Accepts fiction, nonfiction, poetry, photos, cartoons, memoirs, biography.
BIOGRAPHY, FICTION, POETRY

Educare Press, PO Box 31511, Seattle, WA 98103. 206-781-2665. Editor: Shane O'Mahony. Self-publisher.
EDUCATION

Edward-Lynn Jones & Associates, 5517 17th Ave. N.E., Seattle, WA 98105.
UNSPECIFIED

Edwards Publishing Company, PO Box 998, Milton, WA 98354. 206-927-8409. Editor & Ads: Barbara Manies. Publisher of softcover books & an animal breeders directory. Circ. 1500. Founded 1983. No unsolicited submissions. Query by phone. Acquires all rights.
ANIMALS

The Eighth Mountain Press, 624 S.E. 29th, Portland, OR 97214. 503-233-3936. Editor: Ruth Gundle. Publishes soft & hard cover original books by women. Accepts unsolicited submissions. Pays advance & royalties. Query w/ sample chapters, letter, & SASE. Reports in 1-2 months. Publishes in 1-2 years. Accepts fiction, memoirs, poetry, essays, and nonfiction. Biennial poetry prize (see Contests). Send SASE for guidelines; 52 cents postage for catalog.
FEMINISM, GAY/LESBIAN, WOMEN

Ekstasis Editions, Box 8474, Main Postal Station, Victoria, BC V8W 3S1. 604-385-3378. Editor: Richard Olafson. Ads: Carol Ann Sokolaff. Publishers of hard- & softcover books, journal. Accepts unsolicited submissions. Pays 20% of run, royalties on publication. Submit query letter, complete ms, SASE. Photocopies, simultaneous subs OK. Responds in 8-10 wks; publishes in 1 yr. Accepts fiction, nonfiction, poetry, photos, plays. Catalog.
BOOK ARTS/BOOKS, BRITISH COLUMBIA, POETRY

Elephant Mountain Arts, PO Box 1304, Hood River, or 97040. 503-233-9841. Contact: Chuck Williams. Self-publisher of hard- & softcover books. Not a freelance market.
ENVIRONMENT/RESOURCES, NW/REGIONAL HISTORY, NATIVE AMERICAN

Elk Ridge Publishing, PO Box 633, Manzanita, OR 97130-0633. 503-368-5584. Contact: Mark Beach. Publishes trade references and resources for printers, publishers, and buyers of such services.
COMPUTERS, PUBLISHING/PRINTING

Elliott & Fairweather Inc., PO Box 1524, Mercer Island, WA 98040-1524. 206-236-9008. Editor: Priscilla Johnston. Publishes softcover books. Unsolicited submissions accepted. Submit query letter, outline, sample chapters, phone. Responds in 30 days. Topics: city guidebooks.
NORTHWEST, RECREATION, TRAVEL

Elmer E. Rasmuson Library, University of Alaska, Fairbanks, AK 99701. University of Alaska Library, Elmer E. Rasmuson Library, Fairbanks, AK 99701.
COLLEGE/UNIVERSITY, REFERENCE/LIBRARY

Empty Bowl Press, PO Box 646, Port Townsend, WA 98368. 206-385-6132. Contact: Jerry Gorsline. Small press publisher of nonfiction, fiction, poetry and other material.
FICTION, POETRY

Enchantment Publishing Of Oregon, Rt. 1 Box 28H, Enterprise, OR 97828. Editor: Irene Barklow.
UNSPECIFIED

Energeia Publishing Inc., PO Box 985, Salem, OR 97308-0985. 503-588-2926. Contact: Laureal Williams. Softcover books. Unsolicited mss OK. Pays in copies. Send query letter w/ SASE. Responds in 4-6 weeks, Publishes in 8-12 months. Publishes cartoons under the imprint of Doggerel Press, children's under Frog-Head Press, and nonfiction under Energeia Publishing. No guidelines.
CHILDREN (BY/ABOUT), HOW-TO, HUMOR, EDUCATION

English Literature Studies Monograph Series, Dept of English, U. of Victoria, PO Box 1700, Victoria, BC V8W 2Y2.
COLLEGE/UNIVERSITY, EDUCATION, LITERARY

Ensemble Publications Inc., 3972 S.W. Dolph Ct., Portland, OR 97219-3659.
UNSPECIFIED

Entertainment Publications Inc., 15115 S.W. Sequoia Pkwy. #170, Portland, OR. 97224-7131.
ENTERTAINMENT

Entrepreneurial Workshops, 6722 Park Point Way N.E., Seattle, WA 98115-7805. Editor: Fred Klein. Publisher of books on building businesses and entrepreneurship.
BUSINESS

Epicenter Press Inc., 18821 64th Ave. N.E., Seattle, WA 98155. (206) 485-6822. Editor: Kent Sturgis. Also: Box 60529, Fairbanks, AK 99706. 907-474-4969. Publishes hard & softcover originals. Accepts unsolicited submissions w/SASE. Pays royalties. Acquires all rights. Submit ms, SASE, query letter, outline, sample chapters. Dot matrix, simultaneous sub, photocopy OK. Responds in a maximum of 8 weeks. Publishes in a maximum of two years. Accepts nonfiction and biography. Catalog, guidelines.
ALASKA, NORTHWEST, TRAVEL

ERIC Clearinghouse on Educational Mgmt., 1787 Agate St., Eugene, OR 97403. 503-686-5043. Contact: Stuart C. Smith. Softcover books on educational research. The Educational Resources Information Center (ERIC) is a decentralized nationwide network, sponsored by the National Institute of Education, and designed to collect educational documents and to make them available to teachers, administrators, researchers, students. Query w/SASE. Photocopies OK. Education research. Guidelines, catalog.
EDUCATION

Estrada Publications and Photography, 5228 Rambler Rd., Victoria, BC V8Y 2H5. 604-658-8870. Self-publisher. Not a freelance market.
CHILDREN/TEEN, HOW-TO, SPORTS

Estrela Press, 2318 2nd Ave., Box 23, Seattle, WA 98121.
UNSPECIFIED

Evergreen Pacific Publishing, 18002 15th Ave. N.E. Ste. #B, Seattle, WA 98155-3838. 206-368-8158. Editor: Larry Reynolds. Publishes hard & soft cover books. Query w/SASE. Responds in 4 weeks, publishes in 18 months. Accepts nonfiction. Topics: charts, guides and logbooks for boating, fishing and scuba diving.
BOATING, FISHING, RECREATION

Evergreen Publishing, PO Box 17090, Seattle, WA 98107-0790.
UNSPECIFIED

Ex Libris, Box 225, Sun Valley, ID 83353.
UNSPECIFIED

Expanducators Publishing, 135 N. Howard Ave., Burnaby, BC V5B 1J6. Expanducators Publishing, 135 N. Howard Ave, Burnaby, BC V5B 1J6. Contact: Mrs. Fraser. Book publisher. No unsolicited manuscripts
UNSPECIFIED

Expansions Publishing Company Inc., PO Box 1360, Ellensburg, WA 98926. 509-968-4714. Editor: Janet Spath. Self-publisher only.
ASTROLOGY/SPIRITUAL, PHILOSOPHY, NEW AGE

Fade in Publications, 312 S. 6th, Bozeman, MT 59715.
UNSPECIFIED

Fairhaven Communications, 810 N. State St., Bellingham, WA 98225.
UNSPECIFIED

Falcon Press Publishing Co. Inc., 48 N. Last Chance Gulch, PO Box 1718, Helena, MT 59624. 406-442-6597. Editor: Chris Canble. Publishes 50 hard- & softcover books per yr. Unsolicited submissions OK. Payment & rights vary. Submit query, outline, sample chapters, complete ms, SASE, phone. Photocopied, simultaneous subs OK. Reports in 2-3 mos; publishes in 6-12 mos. Nonfiction, biography, memoirs, photos. Topics: hiking and nature guides, gift books, Western history. Guidelines, catalog.
NW/REGIONAL HISTORY, MONTANA, OLD WEST

Fall Creek Press, PO Box 1127, Fall Creek, OR 97438. 503-744-0938. Contact: Helen Wirth. Publisher of hard- and softcover books. "Do not send manuscripts w/out first requesting a copy of the Authors' Guide, SASE. With request, state where you learned about Fall Creek Press." Pays in royalties, advance, copies. All rights acquired. Responds in 4 wks. Accepts short stories t of 9,000 words.
FICTION

Family Tree Pony Farm, Publications Division, 1708 Burwell, Bremerton, WA 98310.
UNSPECIFIED

Far Corner Books, PO Box 82157, Portland, OR 97282. 503-230-1900. Contact: Tom Booth & Megan Holden. Publishes hard and softcover books. No unsolicited manuscripts accepted in 1993-94. Pays advance and royalties. Accepts fiction, nonfiction, biography, poetry, memoirs. Catalog.
HISTORY NW/REGIONAL, LITERATURE, NORTHWEST

Fax Collector's Editions Inc., PO Box 851, Mercer Island, WA 98040.
UNSPECIFIED

Features Northwest, 5132 126th Pl. N.E., Marysville, WA 98270. 206-659-7559. Contact: John & Roberta Wolcott. Self-publishers, not a freelance market.
WRITING, UNSPECIFIED

The Fernglen Press, 473 Sixth St., Lake Oswego, OR 97034. 503-635-4719. Contact: Eila S. Chisholm. Self-publisher softcover book on hiking trails, Hawaii, nature.
NATURAL HISTORY, OUTDOOR, TRAVEL

Findhorn Publications, PO Box 57, Clinton, WA 98236.
UNSPECIFIED

Finnish American Literary Heritage Found, PO Box 1838, Portland, OR 97207.
GENEALOGY, LANGUAGE(S), MINORITIES/ETHNIC

Firsthand Press, 137 Sixth St., Juneau, AK 99801.
UNSPECIFIED

Fjord Press, PO Box 16501, Seattle, WA 98116. 206-625-9363. Editor: Steve Murray. Adv: Nete Leth. Publishes hard- & softcover books. Unsolicited submissions OK. Pays royalties, copies on publication. Query, SASE. Photocopied, simultaneous subs OK. Reports in 1-12 wks; publishes 18-24 mos. Accepts translations (include sample of original language text); fiction & nonfiction from western US writers, "preferably published ones, but will consider first-timers if high literary quality." Catalog.
FICTION, NW/REGIONAL HISTORY, LITERARY

Flight Press, 3630 W. Broadway, No. 2, Vancouver, BC V6R 2B7. Publisher of nonfiction books.
UNSPECIFIED

Floating Ink Books, 211 W. State, Boise, ID 83702. 208-344-4642. Contact: Alan Minskoff. Publisher of 1-3 literary hard & soft cover books yearly, a division of Idaho Annual, Inc. No unsolicited submissions. Pays on money & copies on publication. Query by letter w/ SASE. Responds in 1 month. "We are a very small book publishing company which focuses on Idaho."
FICTION, POETRY, PEACE

The Florian Group, 5620 S.W. Riverside Ln. #8, Portland, OR 97201. 503-638-1972. Editor: F. Michael Sisavic. Publishes hard- & softcover nonfiction travel books. Press run: 5,000-10,000. Unsolicited submissions, dot matrix, photocopied OK.
TRAVEL

Flying Pencil Publications, 33126 Callahan Rd., Scappoose, OR 97056. 503-543-7171. Editors: Madelynne Diness Sheehan. Publishes softcover reprints and originals. Accepts unsolicited submissions. Pays royalties. Query letter, SASE, phone, outline, sample chapters. Responds in 60 days. "Specializes in fishing and outdoor guidebooks; will consider travel literature, and fiction or humor with a fishing or outdoor focus. Save yourself postage and do not send complete ms unless requested."
FISHING, RECREATION

Flying-W Publishing Co., PO Box 3118, Courtenay, BC V9N 5N3. Contact: Gordon Wagner.
UNSPECIFIED

Footprint Publishing Company, PO Box 1830, Revelstoke, BC V0E 2S0. 604-837-3337. Published 5 hardcover original books in last 5 yrs. Does not accept unsolicited submissions.
BRITISH COLUMBIA, CANADIAN HISTORY

Forrest-Park Publishers, 5163 Ranchos Rd., Bellingham, WA 98226. 206-398-8915. Editor: Dan and Janet Homel. Publishes 2-3 softcover books per yr. Press run 2,000-4,000. Subjects: N.W. regional outdoor recreation - particularly fishing and fly fishing. Query w/SASE; clear, concise, well written submissions with high quality illustrations and/or photographs considered.
FISHING, NORTHWEST, OUTDOOR

Foundation House Publications, Box 9, 100 Mile House, BC V0K 2E0. Contact: Norman Smookler.
UNSPECIFIED

Fountain Books, 2475 W. 37th Ave., Vancouver, BC V6M 1P4. Publisher of softcover books for lawyers and legal secretaries. Accepts unsolicited queries. Pays royalties on publication. Query by letter, send sample chapters. Responds in two weeks, publishes in 3 months.
LAW

Fountain Publications, 3728 N.W. Thurman St., Portland, OR 97210.
UNSPECIFIED

Four Cedars Productions, Box 464, Harrison Hot Springs, B.C. V0M 1K0. Publishes art books.
ARTS.

Four Rivers Press, 19996 S. Sweetbriar Rd., West Linn, OR 97068. 503-650-5344. Contact: Scott Richmond. Not a freelance market.
OUTDOOR

Four Winds Publishing, PO Box 19033, Portland, OR 97219. 503-246-9424. Contact: Barbara Brewster or Judy Estes.
UNSPECIFIED

The Fox Hunt, 506 W. Crockett, Seattle, WA 98119.
UNSPECIFIED

Fox Publishing Company, 320 S.W. Stark St., #519, Portland, OR 97204. 503-223-0051. Editor: Susan Monti. Ads: Lindsey McGrath. Publisher of annual directory. Sub $11/copy. Circ. 18,500. Uses freelance material. Byline given. Pays money, copies on acceptance. Acquires 1st rights. Submit query letter, SASE, assignment only. Responds in 1-2 wks. Accepts articles, reviews, photos. Sample $7.50.
TRAVEL

Fox Reading Research Company, 2975 E. Packsaddle Dr., Coeur d'Alene, ID 83814-9533.
UNSPECIFIED

Frank Amato Publications, PO Box 02112, Portland, OR 97202. 503-653-8108. Publishes hard- & softcover originals, reprints; also 2 fishing magazines. Accepts unsolicited submissions. Query w/clips, ms, SASE. Interested in nonfiction book proposals most subjects. Catalog.
FISHING

Fredrickson/Kloepfel Publishing Company, 7748 17th S.W., Seattle, WA 98106. 206-767-4915. Contact: J. Fred Blair. Publishes softcover books. Accepts unsolicited submissions. Payment by profit-share. Rights revert to author. Submit query, SASE. Photocopy, simultaneous OK. Responds in 1 wk. Accepts fiction, poetry, nonfiction, cartoons, articles. Topics: anthologies on specific subjects announced through national newsletter grapevine.
CULTURE, PHILOSOPHY, POETRY

Friendly Press, 2744 Friendly St., Eugene, OR 97405.
UNSPECIFIED

Friends of Wells Gray Park Society, Box 1386, Kamloops, BC V2C 6L7. Self-publisher only. Not a freelance market.
UNSPECIFIED

Friendship Publications Inc., PO Box 1472, Spokane, WA 99210.
UNSPECIFIED

Frontier Publishing, PO Box 441, Seaside, OR 97138. 503-738-8489; 1-800-821-3252. Editor: Jerry Russell. Publishes 4 books a yr. Press run: 3,000. Accepts unsolicited submissions. Pays royalties. Submit query. Reports in 1 mo. Publishes in 1 yr. Guidelines.
NW/REGIONAL HISTORY, HOW-TO, NORTHWEST.

Function Industries Press, PO Box 9915, Seattle, WA 98109. 206-784-7685. Contact: Tom Grothus. Self-publisher.
HUMOR, VISUAL ARTS

Future Science Research Publishing Co., PO Box 86372, Portland, OR 97286. 503-235-1971. Self-publisher of books on environment, new age science. Not a freelance market. Catalog.
ENVIRONMENT/RESOURCES, SCIENCE, NEW AGE

Gadfly Press, 8925 S.W. Homewood St., Portland, OR 97225. 503-292-8890. Self-publisher only. Topic: weather forecasting.
SCIENCE

Gaff Press, 114 S.W. Willow Lane, PO Box 1024, Astoria,

OR 97103. 503-325-8288. Contact: John Paul Barrett. Publisher of hardcover books; distributor, manufacturer. Unsolicited manuscripts OK. Bylines given. Pays money, copies. First rights acquired. Submit query, SASE, photocopy OK, clips, complete ms, simultaneous sub OK. Reports in 1 week. Publishing time varies. Accepts poetry, fiction, nonfiction, biography, and sea stories. Guidelines.
ADVENTURE, HUMOR, POETRY

Gahmken Press, PO Box 1467, Newport, OR 97365. 503-265-2965. Contact: Range D. Bayer. Publishes softcover books. Accepts unsolicited submissions. Pays 4 copies. Acquires 1st rights. Submit ms, SASE. Dot matrix, photocopies, computer disk OK. Reports in 3 wks; publishes in 6 mos. Accepts nonfiction, monograph-length mss dealing with detailed studies of OR ornithology or ornithologists. Guidelines, samples.
NATURAL HISTORY, OREGON, SCHOLARLY/ACADEMIC

Galloway Publications Inc., 2940 N.W. Circle Blvd., Corvallis, OR 97330.
UNSPECIFIED

Gardyloo Press, 2620 S.W. De Armond Dr., Corvallis, OR 97333. Poetry books.
POETRY

Garren Publishing, 01008 S.W. Comus, Portland, OR 97219. 503-636-3506. Contact: John H. Garren. Self-publisher of books on whitewater rivers. Not a freelance market.
OUTDOOR

Gasworks Press, 16292 37th N.E., Seattle, WA 98155.
UNSPECIFIED

Gemaia Press, 209 Wilcox Lane, Sequim, WA 98382.
UNSPECIFIED

Geophysical Institute, University of Alaska, 903 Koyukuk Ave., Fairbanks, AK 99701.
ALASKA, NATURAL HISTORY, SCIENCE

The Georgian Press Company, 2620 S.W. Georgian Pl., Portland, OR 97201. Contact: E. K. MacColl. Publisher of Portland histories. Not a freelance market.
NW/REGIONAL HISTORY, OREGON

Getting Together Publications, 3214 24th Ave. S., Seattle, WA 98144-6512.
UNSPECIFIED

Glacier Natural History Assn Inc., Glacier National Park, West Glacier, MT 59936. 406-888-5756. Publisher, educational organization. Does not accept unsolicited submissions. Catalog.
NATURAL HISTORY

Glen Abbey Books Inc., 735 N. Northlake Way, Seattle, WA 98103. 206-548-9360. Editor: Bill Pittman. Publishes softcover original books. Unsolicited manuscripts OK. Pays royalties. Acquires all rights. Submit query, outline, sample chapters, synopsis, or complete ms with SASE. No photocopies. Computer disk OK (IBM). Reports in 2 mos; publishes in 6-12 mos. Accepts nonfiction only. Topics: 12-step recovery groups (from alcohol, drugs, etc.). Guidelines, catalog.
HEALTH, PSYCHOLOGY

Global Fishing Publications, 2442 N.W. Market St. #113, Seattle, WA 98107. 206-789-8405. Contact: Donal Driscoll. Ads: C. Mahoney. Self-publisher. Not a freelance market.
FISHING

Global Marketing Intelligence, PO Box 91396, Portland, OR 97291-0396. 690-9175. Contact: Sonal Shah. Publisher of softcover books. No unsolicited submissions; freelance material OK. No byline. Pays on publication. Pays in royalties, no rights acquired.
BUSINESS

Globe Publishing Co., 3625 Greenwood N., Seattle, WA

98103. Publishes poetry and prose on love. No submissions info. Query w/SASE.
FICTION, POETRY

Glover Publications, PO Box 21745, Seattle, WA 98111.
UNSPECIFIED

Gluten Intolerance Group of NA, PO Box 23053, Seattle, WA 98102.
HEALTH

G.M. White, PO Box 365, Ronan, MT 59864. 406-676-3766. Self-publisher of softcover Indian and Eskimo culture and history books. Not a freelance market.
CRAFTS/HOBBIES, NATIVE AMERICAN, NORTHWEST

Golden Horizons Inc., 5238 Pullman Ave. N.E., Seattle, WA 98105. 206-525-8160. Self-publisher only.
SENIOR CITIZENS

Golf Sports Publishing, 1813 Mark St. N.E., Olympia, WA 98506-3833. Contact: Craig Foster. Self-publisher of 1 softcover book a yr. for golfers. Print run: 10,000. Not a freelance market.
SPORTS

Goliards Press, 19 Mill St., Friday Harbor, WA 98250-9545.
UNSPECIFIED

Good Times Publishing Co., PO Box 8071-107, Blaine, WA 98230. 604-736-1045. Editor: Dorothy Miller. Nonfiction self-help books, particularly nutrition and psychology. Reports in 2 months. Pays 2-4%. 2 titles in 1991.
FOOD/COOKING, PSYCHOLOGY

Gordon Soules Book Publishers Ltd., 1352-B Marine Dr., West Vancouver, BC V7T 1B5. 604-922-6588. Editor: Gordon Soules. Publishes softcover nonfiction books. Accepts unsolicited high-quality submissions. Topics: biography, guide books, medicine, sports. Query w/clips, SASE. Submit outline, sample chapters, complete ms. Photocopy, dot matrix, simultaneous subs, phone queries OK. Responds in 1 month; publishes in 6 months. Catalog.
BRITISH COLUMBIA, MEDICAL, RECREATION

Gospel Tract Distributors, 8036 N. Interstate Ave., Portland, OR 97217. 503-283-5985. Contact: President.
RELIGION

Grapevine Publications Inc., PO Box 2449, 626 N.W. 4th St., Corvallis, OR 97339-2449. 503-754-0583. Contact: Chris Coffin. Ads: Soraya Simons. Publishes hard & softcover books. Accepts unsolicited submissions. Pays royalties; acquires all rights. Query letter, outline, sample chapters. Photocopy, dot matrix, simultaneous subs all OK. Responds in 3 weeks if interested. "Due to volume we cannot reply to items we are not interested in." Publishes in 6-12 months. Accepts fiction, poetry, cartoons, nonfiction. "We're looking for quality writing and illustrating for children and adults; instruction in math/science technology & consumer products." Guidelines, catalog.
CHILDREN (BY/ABOUT), COMPUTERS, SCIENCE

Graphic Arts Center Publishing Company, 3019 N.W. Yeon Ave., PO Box 10306, Portland, OR 97210. 503-226-2402. Editor: Jean Andrews. Publishes hard- & softcover books. Does not accept unsolicited submissions. Pays money, copies, royalties, advance. Acquires all rights. Submit query letter, SASE. Responds in 3 mos; publishes in 6 mos. Accepts nonfiction. Guidelines, catalog.
CHILDREN/TEEN, NORTHWEST, OUTDOOR

Gray Spider Press, 3317 18th Ave. S., Seattle, WA 98144.
UNSPECIFIED

Grayfellows Inc., 20294 Murphy Rd., Bend, OR 97702-2612. Contact: Linda Gray.
UNSPECIFIED

Great Eagle Publishing Inc., 3020 Issaquah-Pine Lake. Rd. S.E., STE. 481, Issaquah, WA 98027-7255. 206-392-9136; FAX 206-391-7812. Contact: Donald M. Hines. Self-

publisher of hard & softcover books.
ANTHROPOLOGY/ARCHAEOLOGY, HISTORY, NW/REGIONAL

Great Northwest Pub. & Dist. Company PO Box 103902, Anchorage, AK 99510.
ALASKA, UNSPECIFIED

Green Stone Publications, 5612 56th N.E., Seattle, WA 98105. 206-524-4744. Editor: Joe Devine. Publishes hard- & softcover books on English education. Self-publisher only. Does not accept unsolicited submissions.
EDUCATION

Greer Gardens, 1280 Goodpasture Island Rd., Eugene, OR 97401. 503-686-8266. Editor: Harold Greer. Self-publisher.
UNSPECIFIED

Greycliff Publishing Co., Box 1273, Helena, MT 59624. Publisher of hard- & softcover books on fishing. Query letter, SASE.
FISHING, MONTANA

The Griffin Press, PO Box 85, Netarts, OR 97143. 503-842-2356.
UNSPECIFIED

Griggs Printing & Publishing, 426 1st Ave., Box 1351, Havre, MT 59526.
UNSPECIFIED

Gros Ventre Treaty Committee, R.R. #1, Box 66, Harlem, MT 59526-9706.
NATIVE AMERICAN

Gryphon West Publishers, PO Box 12096, Seattle, WA 98102. Publisher of 1 hard- & softcover original a yr. Query w/SASE.
UNSPECIFIED

Haiku, 6944 S.E. 33rd, Mercer Island, WA 98040-3324. 206-232-3239. Contact: Francine Porad. Publishes chapbook collections of haiku.
POETRY

Haker Books, 2707 1st Ave. N., Great Falls, MT 59401.
UNSPECIFIED

Hancock House Publishers Ltd., 1431 Harrison Ave., Box X-1, Surrey, BC V3S 5J9. 604-538-1114. Editor: David Hancock. Ads: Penny Deming. Publisher of hard & soft cover books. Accepts unsolicited submissions. Pays advance, royalties. Acquires all rights. Submit query letter, outline, sample chapters, SASE. Accepts nonfiction, biography. Topics: guidebooks, Native American. Academic standards. Catalog.
BIOGRAPHY, NW/REGIONAL HISTORY, NATIVE AMERICAN

Hands Off, PO Box 68, Tacoma, WA 98401.
UNSPECIFIED

Hapi Press, 512 S.W. Maplecrest Dr., Portland, OR 97219. 503-246-9632. Contact: Joe E. Pierce. Self-publisher of textbooks for university classes or reference books. Does not accept unsolicited submissions. Pays royalties. Acquires all rights. Submit query letter, outline, sample chapters, synopsis, SASE. Dot matrix, simultaneous photocopied subs OK. Reports in 2 mos; publishes in 1 yr. Accepts nonfiction. Catalog.
LITERATURE, TEXTBOOKS

Haralson Enterprises, PO Box 31, Yarrow, BC V0X 2A0. 604-823-4654. Self-publisher of softcover nonfiction & fiction books. Not a freelance market.
CANADA, CANADIAN HISTORY, NATIVE AMERICAN

Harbor Features, PO Box 1061, Olympia, WA 98507.
UNSPECIFIED

Harbor Press Inc., PO Box 919, Gig Harbor, WA 98335-0920. 206-851-5190. Hard- & softcover books. Founded 1985. Accepts unsolicited submissions. Pays royalties. Acquires 1st, 2nd rights. Submit sample chapters, SASE. Responds in 4 mos. Accepts nonfiction. Topics: longevity,

rejuvenation, natural healing, alternative health.
HEALTH

Harbour Publishing, Box 219, Madeira Park, BC V0N 2H0. 604-883-2730. Book publisher. Contact: Howard White. Poetry, environment, fiction.
ENVIRONMENT/RESOURCES, FICTION, POETRY

Harriet U. Fish, PO Box 908, Carlsborg, WA 98324. 206-542-9195. Self-publisher of 1 softcover book, reprint a yr. on local history. Print run: 1,000. Not a freelance market. Catalog.
NW/REGIONAL HISTORY

Hartley & Marks Publishers, PO Box 147, Point Roberts, WA 98281. 206-945-2017. Editor: Susanne Tauber. Publishes hard- & softcover books. Accepts unsolicited submissions. Pays royalties on publication. Acquires all rights. Submit query letter, sample chapters, outline, SASE. Reports in 6 weeks. Publishes in 9 months. Accepts nonfiction. "We publish holistic health and environmentally conscious books, if based on solid research." Catalog.
AGRICULTURE/FARMING, HOW-TO, PSYCHOLOGY

Harvest House Publishers, 1075 Arrowsmith, Eugene, OR 97402. 503-343-0123. Editorial Coordinator: LaRae Weikert. Publishes 80 hard- & softcover originals, reprints books a yr. Unsolicited manuscripts OK. Pays royalties on publication. Submit query w/clips, ms, SASE. Photocopied, simultaneous OK. Reports in 28 wks. Accepts nonfiction, fiction. Topics: "…we have a specialty — books that 'help the hurts of people.' We publish books and fiction with a Christian theme or message consistent with Scripture." Catalog with SASE`.
RELIGION

Havin' Fun Inc., PO Box 70468, Eugene, OR 97401. 503-344-6207. Publishes softcover original books for children. Does not accept unsolicited submissions. Catalog.
CHILDREN/TEEN

HearSay Press, PO Box 3877, Eugene, OR 97403-0877. 503-233-2637. Contact: Cliff Martin. Publisher of 4-6 hard- & softcover, originals, reprints a yr. on: social sciences, especially oral history, sociology, anthropology; music, criticism, reference works, contemporary themes/subjects; literature, esp. local (Pacific N.W. themes and authors). Print run: 2,000-5,000. Accepts freelance material. Payment: Advance, royalties. Rights purchased: All. Query, outline, table of contents w/SASE. Dot matrix, photocopies, simultaneous submissions OK. Reports in 2 wks. Publishes in 6-12 mos. Accepts nonfiction, fiction.
LITERARY, MUSIC, SOCIOLOGY

Helstrom Publications, 3121 S.E. 167th Ave., Portland, OR 97236.
UNSPECIFIED

Hemingway Western Studies Series, Boise State University, 1910 University Dr., Boise, ID 83725. 208-385-1999. Contact: Tom Trusky. Publisher of multiple editions artists books relating to the Intermountain West, its cultures, the environment, politics, arts, social issues and history. Accepts freelance material. Payment: Copies; royalties after expenses met. Acquires 1st rights. Query with outline, SASE. Simultaneous submissions OK. Reports in 6 mos. Publishes in 1 yr. Catalog.
COLLEGE/UNIVERSITY, CULTURE, NORTHWEST

Henry Art Gallery, DE-15, University of Washington, Seattle, WA 98195.
ARTS, COLLEGE/UNIVERSITY

Henry Philips Publishing, 19316 3rd Ave. N.W., Seattle, WA 98177.
UNSPECIFIED

Herbi Gray Handweaver, PO Box 2343, Olympia, WA 98507. 206-491-4138. Self-publisher of softcover originals on handweaving. Accepts no submissions. Catalog.
CRAFTS/HOBBIES, HOW-TO

Heritage House Publishing Co., Box 1228, Sta. A, Surrey, BC V3S 2B3. Contact: Art Downs.
BRITISH COLUMBIA, UNSPECIFIED

The Heron Press, 2427 Panorama Dr., North Vancouver, BC V7G 1V4. Contact: Frankie Smith.
UNSPECIFIED

Heron's Quill, 10511 S.E. Crystal Lake Lane, Milwaukie, OR 97222.
UNSPECIFIED

High & Leslie Press, 490 Leslie St. S.E., Salem, OR 97301. 503-363-7220. Publishes softcover original books. Does not accept unsolicited submissions.
UNSPECIFIED

High Impact Press, PO Box 262, Cheney, WA 99004. 509-235-8916. Contact: Marvin Oliver. Subsidy self-publisher of softcover books. Educational organization. Unsolicited submissions accepted. Pays money/copies on publication. All rights acquired. Query w/SASE, sample chapter, outline, photocopy and simultaneous sub OK. Responds in 2 wks, publishes in 2-3 mos. Accepts nonfiction.
EDUCATION, SCHOLARLY/ACADEMIC, BUSINESS

Highland Press Ltd., PO Box 689, Tonasket, WA 98855. Contact: Lael Duncan.
UNSPECIFIED

Highway Milemarker Guide Co. (HMG Co.) 525 East Bridge St., Blackfoot, ID 83221-2806. 208-785-5125. Contact: John Aulik. Publishes and packages books on travel in Idaho. Query w/SASE and outline. Payment varies. Report time is 60-90 days.
IDAHO, TRAVEL

Historical Society of Seattle & King Co., 2161 E. Hamlin St., Seattle, WA 98112.
NW/REGIONAL HISTORY

Holden Pacific Inc., 814 35th Ave., Seattle, WA 98122. 206-325-4324. Self-publisher of 1 wine/travel book a yr. Not a freelance market.
FOOD/COOKING, TRAVEL

Holtz-Carter Publications, 4326 Dyes Inlet Road N.W., Bremerton, WA 98312. 206-377-2432. Contact: Nancy Holtz-Carter. Publisher of 1 softcover book a yr. on cottage crafts for consumers and crafters. Print run: 5,000. Accepts freelance material. Unspecified payment schedule. Query w/SASE. Photocopies OK. Nonfiction, poetry, photos. Guidelines.
CRAFTS/HOBBIES, POETRY

Home Education Press, PO Box 1083, Tonasket, WA 98855. Editor: Helen Hegener. Self-publisher of softcover books relating to home schooling or alternative education. Submit query, SASE. Dot matrix, photocopied, simultaneous, electronic/modem, computer disk OK. Catalog.
CHILDREN (BY/ABOUT), EDUCATION, FAMILY

Homestead Book Company, P. O. Box 31608, Seattle, WA 98103. 206-782-4532. Editor: David Tatelman. Publisher of 2-3 softcover, original books a yr. Accepts unsolicited submissions. Pays royalties. Rights acquired: All. Byline given. Query w/clips, SASE. Dot matrix, photocopies OK. Reports in 3 mos. Publishes in 6 mos. Accepts nonfiction, cartoons. Topics: restaurants, drugs, music, food, counter-culture.
FOOD/COOKING, MUSIC

Hoogan House Publishing, PO Box 14823, Portland, OR 97214. 503-231-4320. Contact: Carolyn Steiger. Texts on midwifery. Not accepting submissions. Catalog.
HEALTH, MEDICAL

Horsdal & Schubart Publishers Ltd., 4252, Commerce Circle, Victoria, BC V82 4M2. 604-360-2031. Contact: Marlyn Horsdal. Publisher of 15 hard & softcover originals and reprints. Does not accept unsolicited mss. Query w/SASE first. Reports in 2-4 weeks; publishes in 6-9 months.

Accepts nonfiction, Canadian histories, and biographies. Catalog.
BIOGRAPHY, CANADA, NW/REGIONAL HISTORY

Horsemanship, 105 Old Oak Circle, Grants Pass, OR 97526. 503-476-8902. Editor: L.W. Lefler. Self-publisher of 1 hardcover book a year for horse owners. Print run: 1,000. Not a freelance market.
ANIMALS

Hot Off The Press, 1250 N.W. 3, Canby, OR 97013. Publisher of 60 craft books per year. "Accepts submissions from designers who would work with in-house editors if their work is accepted." Query by phone or send sample. Interested in all crafts. Guidelines.
CRAFTS/HOBBIES

Hound Dog Press, 10705 Woodland Ave., Puyallup, WA 98373. 206-845-8039. Self-publisher of 1 hardcover book on bloodhounds for search & rescue work. Not a freelance market.
ANIMALS

House By The Sea Publishing Company, 8610 Hwy. 101, Waldport, OR 97394.
UNSPECIFIED

House Of Charles, 4833 N.E. 238th Ave., Vancouver, WA 98662.
UNSPECIFIED

House Of Humor, PO Box 7302, Salem, OR 97303. 503-585-6030. Editor: Paul Everett.
HUMOR

The Howe Street Press, 212 E. Howe St., Seattle, WA 98102.
UNSPECIFIED

Howlet Press, 2741 S.W. Fairview, Portland, OR 97201. 503-227-6919. Contact: Doris Avshalomov. Fine letterpress self-publisher of limited editions of poetry and other literary works. Query w/SASE. I will publish chapbooks (letterpress) or print full-length books for self-publishing (upon acceptance).
LITERATURE, POETRY

Hth Publishers, PO Box 460, Freeland, WA 98249.
UNSPECIFIED

Hug-a-book Publications, 390 West A St., Lebanon, OR 97355. Contact: Cindy Butherus. Publishes books for children.
CHILDREN/TEEN

Hughes/Taylor, PO Box 12550, Portland, OR 97212. 503-287-0412. Contact: Barb Hughes. Self-publisher of softcover books and audio production. Does not accept unsolicited submissions. Free brochure.
MUSCI, HUMOR, ENTERTAINMENT

Hulogos'i Cooperative Publishers, Box 1188, Eugene, OR 97440. 503-343-0606. Eight softcover originals a year on N.W. region, environment, political activism, co-operatives and New Age consciousness. Print run: 5,000. Freelance material OK. Payment: 8-10 % of retail, every 6 mos. Rights purchased: first; can be individually negotiated. Submit ms, SASE. Dot matrix, photocopies, simultaneous submissions, electronic OK. Reports in 1 month. Publishes in 6-12 mos. Uses nonfiction, poetry, photos, cartoons.
ENVIRONMENT/RESOURCES, NORTHWEST, SOCIALIST/ RADICAL

Hundman Publishing, 5115 Montecello Dr., Edmonds, WA 98037. 206-743-2607. Editor: Cathy Hundman Lee.
UNSPECIFIED

I Can See Clearly Now, 262 W. Beach Lane, Coupeville, WA 98239.
UNSPECIFIED

Idaho State Historical Society, 450 N. 4th St., Boise, ID 83702. 208-334-3428. Editor: Judith Austin. Publishes hard- & softcover books. Accepts unsolicited submissions.

Pays royalties, copies. Submit query letter, outline, sample chapters, synopsis, complete ms, SASE, phone. Photocopy OK. Responds in 1 mo; publishing time varies. Accepts nonfiction, biography, memoirs. Topics: Idaho history. Catalog (Univ. of Idaho Press).
NW/REGIONAL HISTORY, IDAHO

Idaho State University Press, c/o University Bookstore, Box 8013, Pocatello, ID 83209.
COLLEGE/UNIVERSITY, PUBLISHING/PRINTING

Image Imprints, PO Box 370, Junction City, OR 97448-0370. Contact: Marje Blood.
UNSPECIFIED

Image West Press, PO Box 5511, Eugene, OR 97405.
UNSPECIFIED

Incline Press Book Publisher, PO Box 913, Enumclaw, WA 98022. 206-825-1989. Contact: Bernard Winn. Self-publisher, subsidy books. Topics: European railway guides.
CHILDREN/TEEN, RECREATION, TRAVEL

Incunabula Press, 310 N.W. Brynwood Lane, Portland, OR 97229.
UNSPECIFIED

Indian Feather Publishing, 7218 S.W. Oak, Portland, OR 97223.
UNSPECIFIED

Info Alternatives, 19031 33rd Ave. W. #301, Lynnwood, WA 98036.
UNSPECIFIED

Information Center, Northwest Regional Educational Lab, 101 S.W. Main St., Portland, OR 97204. 503-275-9555. Editor: M. Margaret Rogers.
EDUCATION

Information Press, Box 1422, Eugene, OR 97440. 503-689-0188. Contact: Richard Yates. Publishes hard- & softcover reference books related to government, business. Not a freelance market.
BUSINESS, GOVERNMENT, REFERENCE/LIBRARY

Inner Growth Books, PO Box 520, Chiloquin, OR 97624. Self-publisher of 2 softcover original books.
PHILOSOPHY, PSYCHOLOGY, RELIGION

Insight Passage, PO Box 587, Glenn Allen, AK 99588. 907-822-3911. Contact: Christopher Wright. Self-publisher of softcover originals. No unsolicited submissions. Pays copies & royalties; acquires all rights. Query letter, synopsis. Dot matrix & simultaneous subs OK. Responds in 1 month. Topics: mental health, social services from the perspective of front-line providers and recipients in isolated and multi-cultural areas, extreme environments.
CHILDREN (BY/ABOUT), CULTURE, NATIVE AMERICAN

Inspirational Publisher, 2500 S. 370th St., Ste. 134, Federal Way, WA 98003. 206-874-2310. Nonfiction self publisher. 1 title 1990. Press run 1M.
RELIGION

Inst. for Study of Traditional American Indian Arts, PO Box 66124, Portland, OR 97266.
ARTS, NATIVE AMERICAN

Institute for Judaic Studies, PO Box 751, Portland, OR 97207. Soft- and hardcover books on Judaic history.
GENERAL HISTORY, MINORITIES/ETHNIC

Institute for Quality in Human Life, 6335 N. Delaware Ave., Portland, OR 97217.
UNSPECIFIED

Integrity Publications, PO Box 9, 100 Mile House, Yarrow, BC V0K 2E0. Contact: Chris Foster.
UNSPECIFIED

International Bicycle Fund, 4887 Columbia Dr. S., Seattle, WA 98108-1919. 206-628-9314. Books on bicycle travel, especially trips sensitive to the environments and cultures of the hosts.
BICYCLING, TRAVEL

International Communication Center, School of Communications DS-40, University of Washington, Seattle, WA 98195.
COLLEGE/UNIVERSITY, MEDIA/COMMUNICATIONS

International Self-Counsel Press Ltd, 1481 Charlotte Rd., N. Vancouver, BC V7J 1H1. Contact: Diana Douglas. Publisher of softcover original, nonfiction. Book publisher. Query w/SASE. Guidelines, catalog. Also see Self-Counsel Press Inc.
BUSINESS, HOW-TO

Intertext, 2633 E. 17th Ave., Anchorage, AK 99508. Contact: Sharon Ann Jaeger. Publishes hard- & softcover books. Accepts freelance material. Payment: 10% royalty after costs of production, promotion, and distribution. Acquires 1st rights; option on second printing. Submit query letter, sample chapters, SASE. No simultaneous ms submissions. Reports in 3-6 mos; publishes in 1-2 yrs. Accepts poetry and translations. Query first, poets send 3-5 poems with SASE and by first-class mail. Vivid use of imagery and strong, alchemical use of language are essential; poetry collections should be powerful, sustained groups of 48-80 poems. Not considering unsolicited poetry mss until 1996. No longer publish unsolicited fiction. Guidelines with SASE.
FICTION, LITERARY, POETRY

The Interwest Applied Research, 4875 S.W. Griffith Dr., Beaverton, OR 97005. 503-641-2100. Editor: Mary L. Lewis. Hard- & softcover education materials & videos, 30-60 topics per yr in 2-4 subject areas. Pay: Money, on acceptance or by assignment. Rights acquired: All. Byline depends on extent of contribution. Phone query, computer disk OK. Reports in 1 mo. Publishes in 3-12 mos. Actively soliciting writers for development of textbooks, study guides, examination questions, and video scripts for production/distribution as college-level course materials. Topics: math, music, geography, law, child development, philosophy, and others. Call for Writer Information Form describing current needs and soliciting information on writer's qualifications. Writers are interviewed based on this form.
EDUCATION, SCHOLARLY/ACADEMIC, TEXTBOOKS

ISBS Inc., 5602 N.E. Hassalo St., Portland, OR 97213. 503-287-3093. Editor: Jeanette Bokma.
UNSPECIFIED

Island Books, 3089 Gibbons Rd., Duncan, BC V9L 1E9.
UNSPECIFIED

Island Publishers, Box 201, Anacortes, WA 98221-0201. 206-293-3285. Publisher of poetry and nonfiction.
POETRY, UNSPECIFIED

Island Spring, PO Box 747, Vashon, WA 98070.
UNSPECIFIED

J. Larsen Publishing, PO Box 586, Deer Lodge, MT 59722.
RECREATION

Jackson Mountain Press, Box 2652, Renton, WA 98056. 206-255-6635. Contact: Carole Goodsett. Accepts freelance material. Acquires 1st rights. Query letter, outline, SASE. Dot matrix, photocopies OK. Reports in 1 mo; publishes in 6-12 mos. Accepts nonfiction. Topics: geology: state field guides, 48-200 pgs.; general popular geology subjects up to 100 pgs. Food: local interest cookbooks, to 100 pgs.; guides to best of area, best of type, to 200 pgs. "Our expertise is in marketing local guides to specific areas, i.e., a specific city, half a state, or N.W." Catalog.
FOOD/COOKING, GEOLOGY/GEOGRAPHY, NORTHWEST

Jalapeno Press, PO Box 12345, Portland, OR 97212-0345.
UNSPECIFIED

Jaleo Press International, 2453 Heights Dr., Ferndale, WA 98248. Contact: Jonni Dolan.
UNSPECIFIED

Janes Publishing, 25671 Fleck Rd., Veneta, OR 97487-9510. 503-343-2408. Contact: Bobbi Corcoran.
UNSPECIFIED

Janice McClure Hindman Books, PO Box 208, Durke, OR 97905.
UNSPECIFIED

Janus Press, PO Box 1050, Rogue River, OR 97537.
UNSPECIFIED

Jean's Oregon Collections, 3486 Wood Ave., Eugene, OR 97402-2184.
OREGON, UNSPECIFIED

Jennifer James Inc., 9250 45th Ave S.W., Seattle, WA 98136-2633.
PSYCHOLOGY

Jesuit Books, Seattle University, Seattle, WA 98122.
RELIGION

Jewell-Johnson & Company Inc., 502 Benton St., Port Townsend, WA 98368.
UNSPECIFIED

Joan Keil Enterprises, PO Box 205, Medina, WA 98039.
UNSPECIFIED

John and Dottie Blake Assn Inc., Box 785, White Salmon, WA 98672. 509-493-2820. Self-publisher only. Not a freelance market.
UNSPECIFIED

Joint Development Trading Company Ltd., R.R. 3, 1970 Nicholas Pl., Victoria, BC V8X 3X1.
UNSPECIFIED

Jomac Publishing, PO Box 1420, Beaverton, OR 97075. 503-646-9660. Editor: Jo Ann Lippert. Book publisher. Does not accept unsolicited submissions. Query with SASE.
UNSPECIFIED

Jordan Valley Heritage House, 43592 Hwy 226, Stayton, OR 97383. 503-859-3144.
NW/REGIONAL HISTORY, UNSPECIFIED

Judy Ford & Company, 11530 84th Ave. N.E., Kirkland, WA 98034. 206-823-4421. Editor: Judy Ford.
SEX

Judy Lindahl Unlimited, 3211 N.E. Siskiyou St., Portland, OR 97212. 503-288-0772. Self-publisher only.
UNSPECIFIED

Junior League of Eugene Publishers, 2839 Willamette St., Eugene, OR 97405.
FOOD/COOKING

Juniper Ridge Press, PO Box 1278, Olympia, WA 98507. 206-705-1328. Editor: Rosana Hart. Publisher of 1-3 softcover original, and 1-2 videotapes, a yr; for llama owners. Print run 2,000. Accepts no unsolicited mss. Pays copies, royalties. Dot matrix, photocopies, simultaneous OK. Accepts: Nonfiction primarily related to llamas. Will consider submissions from writers knowledgeable about the animals. Most of our products are created in house. Catalog.
AGRICULTURE/FARMING, ANIMALS, RECREATION

Jupiter Publications, 7527 Lake City Way N.E., Seattle, WA 98115.
UNSPECIFIED

Just in Time Publishing, 401 Olson Rd., Longview, WA 98632.
UNSPECIFIED

Kabalarian Philosophy, 908 W. 7th Ave., Vancouver, BC V5Z 1C3.
PHILOSOPHY

Kamloops Museum & Archives, 207 Seymour St., Kamloops, BC V2C 2E7. 604-828-3576. Contact: Elisabeth Duckworth. Book publisher Canadian (esp. BC) history and natural history. Does not accept unsolicited submissions. Submit query letter w/SASE, or phone.
BRITISH COLUMBIA, CANADIAN HISTORY, NATURAL HISTORY

Karwyn Enterprises, 17227 17th Ave. W., Lynnwood, WA 98036.
UNSPECIFIED

Keepsake Publications, PO Box 362-W, West Linn, OR 97068. Seeks poems; fiction, nonfiction and family short stories for special book series.
POETRY, FICTION

Keyboard Workshop, P. O. Box 700, Medford, OR 97501. 503-664-6751. Self-publisher of 50 new cassettes, videos or softcover original books a yr. No freelance material.
HOW-TO, MUSIC

Ki2 Enterprises, PO Box 13322, Portland, OR 97213. Editor: K. Canniff. Publisher of 2 originals per yr; totally unique nonfiction about OR/WA. Average print run 5,000. Accepts freelance material. Payment negotiated at time of purchase. Rights purchased: All. Submit outline, sample chapter, SASE. Tell me why readers need this book too. Dot matrix, photocopies, simultaneous OK. Reports in 4-6 wks. Publishes in 1 yr. Accepts nonfiction, 80-160 pgs.; B&W artwork and photos. "We don't do coffee table books."
NORTHWEST, TRAVEL

KID Broadcasting Corporation, PO Box 2008, Idaho Falls, ID 83401.
MEDIA/COMMUNICATIONS

Kimberlite Publishing Co., 4033 S.E. 64th Ave, Portland, OR 97206. 503-775-0500. Publisher of hardcover books. Self-publisher only. Not a freelance market.
UNSPECIFIED

King Books, 817 S. 265th St., Kent, WA 98032.
UNSPECIFIED

Klamath Falls Publishing, PO Box 788, Klamath Falls, OR 97801. 503-883-4000. Contact: Dennis Taylor. Publishes Cascade Cattleman, Cascade Horseman, Polled Hereford Journal. Uses freelance features focusing on people in the trades. Include photos.
AGRICULTURE/FARMING, ANIMALS

Klassen & Foster Publications, PO Box 18, Barriere, BC V0E 1E0.
UNSPECIFIED

KMG Publications, 290 E. Ashland Lane, PO Box 1055, Ashland, OR 97520.
UNSPECIFIED

Krause House Inc., PO Box 880, Oregon City, OR 97045.
UNSPECIFIED

Lacon Publishers, Route 1, PO Box 15, Harrison, ID 83833.
UNSPECIFIED

Laing Communications, 16250 N.E. 80th St., Redmond, WA 98052. 206-869-6313. Contact: Norman Bolitin or Christine Laing. Publisher of studies and monographs on publishing. Book packager. We acquire books & regularly contract w/writers/authors for projects on behalf of our publishing clients. Subjects: biography, business, economics, computers, history, travel, how-to. Submit query w/credentials and brief synopsis.
MEDIA/COMMUNICATIONS, PUBLISHING/PRINTING, REFERENCE/LIBRARY

Lambrecht Publications, 1763 Maple Bay Rd., Duncan, BC V9L 4T6. 604-748-8722. Contact: Helga Lambrecht. Self-publisher. Not a freelance market.
BRITISH COLUMBIA, FOOD/COOKING, HISTORY

Lance Publications, PO Box 61189, Seattle, WA 98121. 206-442-4613. Cookbooks. Book publisher. Query w/SASE before submitting.
FOOD/COOKING

Land Mark Publishing, PO Box 776, Pocatello, ID 83204. 208-233-0075. Publishes softcover books. Topics: education, sex education, and biography.
BIOGRAPHY, EDUCATION, SEX

Larry Langdon Publications, 17314 S.W. Loma Vista St., Aloha, OR 97007-5791.
UNSPECIFIED

Larsen Publishing Co., 9243 Shaw Square, Aumsville, OR 97325. Contact: Lee Larsen.
UNSPECIFIED

Latah County Historical Society, 327 East 2nd, Moscow, ID 83843. 208-882-1004. Editor: Bert Cross. Publisher of hard & soft cover books on local and regional history. Also publishes a journal, Circ. 700, $4/yearly. No unsolicited submissions, no freelance material accepted.
NW/REGIONAL HISTORY

Laughing Dog Press, 12509 S.W. Cove Rd., Vashon, WA 98070. 206-463-3153. Handmade books, both cloth and paper bound, of nature poetry. Pays in copies. Acquires 1st rights. Dot matrix, photocopies OK. Reports in 6 mos; publishes in 1-2 yrs. No unsolicited submissions.
CONSERVATION, ENVIRONMENT/RESOURCES, POETRY

Law Forum Press, 2318 Second Ave., Seattle, WA 98121. 206-622-8240. Editor: Don Berry. Publishes softcover how-to guides for small business owners, 50 pgs. Accepts unsolicited submissions, phone query. Pays 10% gross revenue royalties. Dot matrix, photocopied, simultaneous, electronic subs OK. Reports in 4 wks. Publishes in 3 mos.
BUSINESS

Lazara Press, Box 2269 MPO, Vancouver, BC V6B 3W2. Contact: Penny Goldsmith.
UNSPECIFIED

Lazy Mountain Press, PO Box 2650, Palmer, AK 99645. Contact: Kathy Hunter. Books on Alaska. Self-publisher.
ALASKA

Legacy House Inc., PO Box 786, 139 Johnson Ave., Orofino, ID 83544. 208-476-5632. Self-publisher of 4 hard- & softcover original books a year for animal lovers, children, history buffs. Print run: 1,000. Not a freelance market.
ANIMALS, CHILDREN/TEEN, AMERICAN HISTORY

Legendary Publishing Co., PO Box 7706, Boise, ID 83707-1706. 208-342-7929.
US HISTORY, FAMILY, HEALTH

Leo F. Vogel, 2526 Dilling Rd., Connell, WA 99326. 509-234-5112. Self-publisher of hard- & softcover original books. Print run: 2,000. Not a freelance market.
NW/REGIONAL HISTORY, HUMOR

L'Epervier Press, 5419 Kensington Pl. N., Seattle, WA 98103. 503-547-8306.
UNSPECIFIED

LetterPress, 6606 Soundview Dr., Gig Harbor, WA 98335. 206-851-5158. Garrett Boge, Director. Small literary press specializing in contemporary N.W. writers. Fiction.
FICTION, HISTORY, NW/REGIONAL, LITERATURE

Life Messengers Inc., PO Box 1967, Seattle, WA 98111-1967.
UNSPECIFIED

Lifeworks Press, PO Box 19476, Portland, OR 97280. 503-299-6565; 800-488-4163. Contact: Marti Chaney or Vicki Thayer. Ads: Marti Chaney. Self-publisher of softcover books. No unsolicited submissions.
WOMEN, BUSINESS, PSYCHOLOGY

Light-House Publications, 1721 Wallace, Vancouver, BC V6R 4J7.
BRITISH COLUMBIA, UNSPECIFIED

Lightship Press Ltd., 109-1418 Newport, Victoria, BC V8S 5E9.
UNSPECIFIED

Lillooet Tribal Council Press, PO Box 1420, Lillooet, BC V0K 1V0. Publishes Native-American books.
NATIVE AMERICAN

Limberlost Press, HC 33 Box 1113, Boise, ID 83706. 208-344-2120. Contact: Richard Ardinger. Query/SASE. Nonfiction, poetry.
CULTURE, LITERARY, POETRY

Lincoln County Historical Society, 545 S.W. 9th St., Newport, OR 97365.
NW/REGIONAL HISTORY

Link International, PO Box 899, Ashland, OR 97520. 503-488-5465. Contact: Dustine Davidson. Publisher of softcover books. No unsolicited ms. Pays on publication. Pays advances, money, and royalties. Acquires first rights. Query by letter w/ SASE, photocopy OK, simultaneous sub OK. Responds in 3 weeks, publishes in 6 months. Accepts nonfiction related to travel or the environment.
TRAVEL, OUTDOOR, RECREATION

Little Red Hen Inc., PO Box 4260, Pocatello, ID 83201.
UNSPECIFIED

Little Wooden Books, 1890 Road 24 S.W., Matawa, WA 99344. 509-932-4729.
UNSPECIFIED

The Lockhart Press, Box 1207, Port Townsend, WA 98368. 206-385-6412. Contact: Russell A. Lockhart, Ph.D. Publishes handmade books of poetry. Accepts unsolicited submissions. Pays money, copies, royalties. Acquires all rights. Submit complete ms, SASE. Photocopy, dot matrix, disk/modem, simultaneous subs OK. Responds in 2-3 mos.
POETRY

Log House Publishing Company Ltd., Box 1205, Prince George, BC V2L 4V3. Publisher of nonfiction books on modern log building construction.
HOW-TO, TEXTBOOKS

London Northwest, 929 S. Bay Rd., Olympia, WA 98506.
UNSPECIFIED

Lone Star Press, PO Box 165, LaConner, WA 98257.
UNSPECIFIED

Long House Printcrafters & Publishers, 680 Spring St. #216, Friday Harbor, WA 98250-8058.
UNSPECIFIED

Longanecker Books, PO Box 127, Brewster, WA 98812.
UNSPECIFIED

Loompanics Unlimited, PO Box 1197, Port Townsend, WA 98368. Contact: Michael Hoy. Publishes soft- & hardcover books. Accepts unsolicited submissions. Pays advance, copies, royalties. Acquires all rights. Submit query letter, outline, sample chapters, SASE. Photocopy, disk/modem OK. Responds in 6 wks; publishes in 6 mos. Accepts nonfiction, must be out-of-the-ordinary. Guidelines; catalog $3.
HOW-TO

Lord Byron Stamps, PO Box 4586, Portland, OR 97208. 503-254-7093. Editor: Tom Current. Self-publisher of softcover books on British philately. Query w/SASE.
COLLECTING, CRAFTS/HOBBIES

Louis Foundation, Main St., PO Box 210, Eastsound, WA 98245.
UNSPECIFIED

Love Line Books, 790 Commercial Ave., Coos Bay, OR 97420.
UNSPECIFIED

Low Fat Lifeline Associates, PO Box 1889, Port Townsend, WA 98368. 206-379-9724.
HEALTH

The Lowell Press, 1760 E. 27th Ave., Eugene, OR 97403. 503-345-4594.
UNSPECIFIED

LPD Publishing, 7143 Dumfries St., Vancouver, BC V5P 3C3. 604-324-4870. Contact: Don Lewis. No unsolicited manuscripts. Send query letter with SASE. Publisher of

books on railways and locomotives.
HISTORY, GENERAL

Lumby Historians, c/o Rosemary Deuling, R.R. 2, Lumby, BC V0E 2G0.
CANADIAN HISTORY

Lyceum Press, 2442 N.W. Market St. #51, Seattle, WA 98107. 206-547-6651. Editor: David D. Horowitz. Publishes one softcover original book of poetry every 1-2 yrs. Not accepting unsolicited submissions.
POETRY

The M Kimberly Press, 3331 279th Ave., N.E., Redmond, WA 98053. 206-880-6235. Contact: Mare Blocker. Artist books/handmade books/limited editions. Poetry, literature, and illustrations. No submissions accepted. Info available.
BOOK ARTS/BOOKS

MacManiman Inc., 3023 362nd S.E., Fall City, WA 98024.
UNSPECIFIED

Madison County History Association, PO Box 228, 207 Mill St., Sheridan, MT 59749.
NW/REGIONAL HISTORY, MONTANA

Madison Park Press, 3816 E. Madison St., Seattle, WA 98112.
UNSPECIFIED

Magnifica Books of Oregon, 1000 Marjean Ln. #M-4, Grants Pass, OR 97526-7005. 503-474-0139.
UNSPECIFIED

Magnolia House Publishing, 1820 Dartmouth W., Seattle, WA 98199.
UNSPECIFIED

MAIA Publishing Ltd., 302 E. 6th St., Vancouver, BC V7L 1P6. 604-988-5887. Contact: Maggie Paquet. Publishes books on outdoor education and recreation, environment, forestry, park and wilderness, and sustainable development. No unsolicited manuscripts. Send query letter w/ SASE.
OUTDOOR, CONSERVATION

Management/Marketing Associates Inc., 707 S.W. Washington St., Bank of California Tower, Portland, OR 97205. Self-publisher of books. "We publish our own reports & material."
BUSINESS

Manna Publications Inc., PO Box 1111, Camas, WA 98607.
UNSPECIFIED

Maritime Publications, 3560 Alm Rd., Everson, WA 98247-9273. Self-publisher. Not a freelance market.
BUSINESS

Mark West Publishers, PO Box 1914, Sandpoint, ID 83864.
UNSPECIFIED

Markins Enterprises, 2039 S.E. 45th, Portland, OR 97215. 503-235-1036. Contact: Myrna Perkins. Self-publisher of 4 softcover childrens picture books per year educational, science oriented, entertaining. Press run: 500.
CHILDREN/TEEN, ENTERTAINMENT, SCIENCE

Marlene Y. Bastian, PO Box 66117, Portland, OR 97290. 503-698-2335. Self-publisher. Not a freelance market.
CONSUMER, HOW-TO

Mary Anne Bauer Productions, PO Box 82467, Portland, OR 97282. 503-777-0373.
RECREATION

The Mason Clinic, 1100 9th Ave., PO Box 900, Seattle, WA 98111.
UNSPECIFIED

Master Press, PO Box 432, Dayton, OR 97114.
UNSPECIFIED

Math Counseling Institute Press, 4518 Corliss Ave N., Seattle, WA 98103.
EDUCATION

MatriMedia, PO Box 6957, Portland, OR 97228. Contact: Ellen Nichols. Softcover books on women and art. Pays on publication; acquires all rights. Query w/SASE. Responds in 2-3 mos. Uses nonfiction, photos, interviews.
ARTS, NORTHWEST, WOMEN

Maverick Publications, Drawer 5007, Bend, OR 97708. 503-382-6978. Contact: Ken Asher. Publisher of 10 hard- & softcover originals per year for the general trade. Print run: 2,000. Accepts freelance material. Payment: Money. Rights acquired: Book rights plus 50% of subsidiary. Query w/outline, sample chapters, SASE. Dot matrix, photocopies, simultaneous submissions, electronic OK. Reports in 6 wks. Publishes in 6 mos. Nonfiction, fiction. Catalog.
DRAMA, FICTION, NORTHWEST

MCSA-Medical Cttee & Service Assn, 10223 N.E. 58th St., Kirkland, WA 98033.
HEALTH, MEDICAL

Mediaor Company, Box 631, Prineville, OR 97754.
UNSPECIFIED

Medic Publishing Company, PO Box 89, Redmond, WA 98073. 206-881-2883. Editor: Murray Swanson. Booklet publisher. Accepts unsolicited submissions. Pays royalties. Query letter, SASE. Dot matrix, photocopies OK. Reports in 1 mo. Topics: bereavement, medical patient instruction. All are booklets, typically 24 pgs., 9,000 wds. We are the country's leading publisher of grief literature, with some titles exceeding 1 million copies. Catalog.
HEALTH, MEDICAL, PSYCHOLOGY

Merle Osgood Productions, 455 S. 156 St., Apt. 201, Seattle, WA 98148-1234.
UNSPECIFIED

Merril Press, PO Box 1682, Bellevue, WA 98009. 206-454-7009. Editor: Ron Arnold. Ads: Julie Versnel. Publishes 4-6 hard- & softcover originals, reprints, subsidy books/yr. Unsolicited mss OK. Pays money, royalties. Acquires all rights. Prefers phone query. Dot matrix, photocopies, simultaneous, electronic/modem, computer disk OK. Publishes in 3-6 mos. Accepts nonfiction: how-to, politics, special interest, hobby material, economics.
CRAFTS/HOBBIES, ECONOMICS, HOW-TO

Merrill Court Press, PO Box 85785, Seattle, WA 98145-1785. 206-325-5785. Editor: Pleasant DeSpain. Softcover books. No unsolicited submissions. Accepts Childrens & storytellers. Catalog available. "We are a new & small press focusing on quality books for children and storytellers. We have more than enough stories to publish at present."
CHILDREN (BY/ABOUT)

Metamorphous Press, PO Box 10616, Portland, OR 97210-0616. 503-228-4972. Contact: Nancy Wyatt-Kelsey. Founded 1982. Orders 800-937-7771, Fax 503-223-9117. Publishes hard- & softcover books. Accepts unsolicited submissions. Submit query w/clips, outline, sample chapters, SASE. Dot matrix, photocopied, disk/modem, simultaneous subs OK. Reports in 3-6 mos; publishes in 1 yr. Accepts nonfiction. Topics: self-help, psychology, health & fitness, business and sales, education, and children. Guidelines, catalog.
EDUCATION, HEALTH, PSYCHOLOGY

Michael Yaeger, PO Box 4304, Pioneer Square, Seattle, WA 98104. 206-624-9102. Self-publisher. Not a freelance market.
AVANT-GARDE/EXPERIMENTAL, HUMOR, NORTHWEST

MicNik Publications, PO Box 3041, Kirkland, WA 98083. 206-881-6476. Editor: Michelle O'Brien-Palmer. Self-publisher of children's book. Does not accept manuscripts.
CHILDREN/TEEN

Microsoft Corp., PO Box 97017, Redmond, WA 98073-9717. Contact: Salley Oberlin. Publisher of 50-100 hard- & softcover nonfiction books per yr on software, science, and math, aimed at people interested in computers, science, and people. Query, w/ms, outline, sample chapters, SASE. Dot matrix, photocopies, simultaneous submissions, electronic OK. Publishes submissions in 6-9 mos. Catalog.
COMPUTERS

Midgard Press, 4214 Midway Ave., Grants Pass, OR 97527. 503-476-3603. Contact: Signe M. Carlson. Self-publisher of hard- & softcover books. Not a freelance market. Topics: dairy goat owners, Northern Scandinavia.
AGRICULTURE/FARMING, ANIMALS, LITERATURE

Milco Publishing, 18910 37th S., Seattle, WA 98188. 206-244-8387. Contact: A. Miller. Self-publisher only.
HOW-TO

Milestone Publications, 3284 Heather St., Vancouver, BC V5Z 3K5. 604-251-7675; 604-875-0611. Contact: Anne Werry.
ENVIRONMENT/RESOURCES

Mind's Ink Publishing, PO Box 2701, Eugene, OR 97402. 503-689-4785. Editor: Phillip Hennin. Publishes 10 softcover books/yr. Accepts unsolicited mss. Submit query w/clips, SASE. Dot matrix, photocopied, simultaneous, electronic, computer disk (IBM) OK. Reports in 6 wks. Business, success stories, business resource material. Photos: graphics preferred, price negotiable. Also accepts articles for inclusion in The Gold Book series a series of established business books for Oregon, by assignment only. Write for guidelines.
BUSINESS, CALENDAR/EVENTS, HOW-TO

Mineral Land Publications, PO Box 1186, Boise, ID 83701.
UNSPECIFIED

MIR Publication Society, PO Box 730, Grand Forks, BC V0H 1H0.
UNSPECIFIED

Miscellania Unlimited Press, 5014-D Roosevelt Way N.E., Seattle, WA 98105. 206-525-0632. Contact: Edd Vick.
UNSPECIFIED

Mole Publishing Company, Route 1, Box 618, Bonners Ferry, ID 83805.
UNSPECIFIED

Montana Arts Council, 316 N. Park Ave., Helena, MT 59620. 406-444-6430. Editor: Martha Sprague. Publishes 1 softcover book a yr. Accepts unsolicited submissions. Submit query w/clips, SASE. Dot matrix, photocopied, simultaneous, electronic subs OK. Accepts fiction, poetry, other. Guidelines.
ARTS, FICTION, POETRY

Montana Department of Labor & Industry, PO Box 1728, Helena, MT 59604.
BUSINESS, LABOR/WORK, MONTANA

Montana Historical Society Press, PO Box 201201, 225 N. Roberts St., Helena, MT 59620-1201. 406-444-4708. Editor: Marilyn Grant. Educational organization and publisher of a quarterly newsletter. Circ. 9000. Sub/$20. Freelance material not accepted. No byline given. Clips. Accepts news items. Back issues free, send cost of shipping.
NW/REGIONAL HISTORY, MONTANA, SCHOLARLY/ACADEMIC

Montevista Press, 5041 Meridian Rd., Bellingham, WA 98226. 206-734-4279. Editor: J. Burkhart. Publisher of 1 hard- & softcover book a yr. Freelance material not accepted. Catalog.
ANIMALS, AMERICAN HISTORY, NW/REGIONAL HISTORY

Moonstone Press, 7620 S.E. Hwy 160, Port Orchard, WA 98366. 206-746-9201. Editor: Gayle Vogel Thomsen.

Publisher of poetry, prose and mythological illustrations about the Goddess and other literary, amusing, and mystical subjects. No submissions info. Query w/SASE.
ASTROLOGY/SPIRITUAL, ENTERTAINMENT, FEMINISM

Mosaic Enterprises Ltd, 1420 St. Paul St., Kelowna, BC V1Y 2E6.
UNSPECIFIED

Mother of Ashes Press, PO Box 66, Harrison, ID 83833-0066. 208-689-3738. Contact: Joe M. Singer. Small publisher. Does not accept unsolicited submissions. Query letter, SASE, assignment only. Catalog.
FICTION, POETRY

Mount Vernon Press, 1750 112th N.E. #C-247, Bellevue, WA 98004.
UNSPECIFIED

Mountain Meadow Press, PO Box 1170, Wrangell, AK 99929. 907-874-2565. Editor: Borg Hendrickson. Book publisher. Accepts unsolicited ms with SASE. 4-8 wk. response time. Softcover. Subsidy publisher.
MONTANA, TRAVEL, RECREATION

Mountain Press Publishing Company, PO Box 2399, Missoula, MT 59806. 406-728-1900. History/General Editor: Daniel Greer. Natural History Editor: Kathleen Ort. Publisher of hard- & softcover books. No unsolicited mss. Submit query letter w/SASE, outline, sample chapters or synopsis. Photocopies, dot matrix OK. Titles/yr: 1-2. Guidelines, catalog.
NW/REGIONAL HISTORY, NATIVE AMERICAN, NATURAL HISTORY

Mountain Publishing, 16175 S.W. Holly Hill Rd., Hillsboro, OR 97123. 503-628-3995; 800-879-8719. Editor: J. K. Basco. Book publisher. Does not accept unsolicited submissions. Submit query letter, SASE. Responds in 3 wks. Topics: business, entrepreneurs.
BUSINESS

Mountain View Publishing, 5451 Eastside Hwy., Florence, MT 59833. 406-273-6837. Contact: Brent Sisson. Self-publisher. Accepts unsolicited submissions. Pays copies on publication. Submit query letter, SASE, outline, sample chapters, synopsis, or query by phone. Dot matrix, photocopies, disk/modem OK (MAC). Responds 30 days. Publishes 6-12 mos. Guidelines.
EDUCATION, LAW

The Mountaineers Books, 1011 S.W. Klickitat Way, #107, Seattle, WA 98134. 206-223-6303. Editor: Margaret Foster. Ads: Patrick Lanfear. Publishes hard- & softcover books. Accepts unsolicited submissions. Pays royalties, advance. Acquires 1st rights. Submit query letter w/clips, outline, sample chapters, SASE. Dot matrix, photocopies, simultaneous subs OK. Reports in 2-3 months; publishes in 1 yr. plus. Accepts nonfiction: how-to's, guides and adventure narratives for non-motorized, non-competitive outdoor sports (skiing, biking, hiking, climbing, mountaineering, kayaking, walking, etc.; also, nature, conservation, history. Guidelines, catalog. "Include competing titles and marketing info w/ submission. Ms should be printed w/ dark ribbon, ds. Request catalog to see if book fits with our line."
NATURAL HISTORY, OUTDOOR, RECREATION

Mr. Cogito Press, Pacific University, Humanities PO Box 627, Forest Grove, OR 97116. 503-226-4135. Editors: Robert Davies, John Gogol. Publishes softcover books. Does not accept unsolicited submissions. Publishes in 6-12 mos. Poetry: translations and English. "We are a very small press, highly selective; our magazine submissions are our source for selecting authors." Catalog.
POETRY

M/T/M Publishing Company, PO Box 245, Washougal, WA 98671.
UNSPECIFIED

Murray Publishing Company, 2312 3rd Ave., Seattle, WA 98121. Contact: John Murray. Publisher of textbooks and other nonfiction.
TEXTBOOKS

Museum of History & Industry, 2700 24th Ave. E., Seattle, WA 98112. 206-324-1125.
GENERAL HISTORY, NW/REGIONAL HISTORY

Nanaimo Historical Society, PO Box 933, Nanaimo, BC V9R 5N2. 604-758-2828. Contact: Mrs. Mar. Self-publisher of historical hard- & softcover original books. Not a freelance market.
BRITISH COLUMBIA, GENEALOGY, CANADIAN HISTORY

National Book Company, P. O. Box 8795, Portland, OR 97207. 503-228-6345. Hard- & softcover books. Unsolicited submissions OK. Reports in 1-2 mos; publishes in 6-12 mos. Accepts nonfiction. Query, outline, sample chapters, complete ms, SASE. Dot matrix, photocopy, disk/modem subs OK. Topics: textbooks, multimedia instructional programs and computer software in Jr. High-Jr. College range; library and business references, educational policy studies, ethnic issues, computer software. Catalog.
MINORITIES/ETHNIC, REFERENCE/LIBRARY, TEXTBOOKS

National Seafood Educators, PO Box 60006, Richmond Beach, WA 98160. 206-546-6410. Editors: Evie Hansen, Janis Harsila. Publishes softcover books. Accepts unsolicited submissions. Submit query letter, outline, sample chapters, complete ms, SASE. Topics: cartoons, children's books, marine historical.
CHILDREN (BY/ABOUT), FISHING

Natural World Press, 47227 Good Pasture Rd., Vida, OR 97488. 896-0263. Contact: Russ & Blithe Carpenter. Publisher of softcover books and laminated cards. No unsolicited submissions. Pays in royalties, all rights acquired. Query by letter. Accepts nonfiction. "We specialize in the natural history of the Pacific Coast, Northwest and Hawaii."
NATURAL HISTORY

Navillus Press, 1958 Onyx St., Eugene, OR 97403. Editor: William L. Sullivan. Self-publisher. Accepts no submissions.
OREGON, OUTDOOR

NBS West, PO Box 1039, Vashon, WA 98070.
UNSPECIFIED

The Neo Vatikan Press, c/o The Bush School, 405 36th St. E., Seattle, WA 98112. 206-284-9498. Contact: Carmine Chickadel. Fine letterpress publisher of broadsides and other mixed media projects.
LITERARY, POETRY

Nerve Press, 5875 Elm St., Vancouver, BC V6N 1A6. Publisher of childrens fiction & sci-fi.
CHILDREN/TEEN, FANTASY/SCI FI, FICTION

Nesbitt Enterprises, 7421 Tennessee Ln., Vancouver, WA 98664-1442.
UNSPECIFIED

New Capernaum Works, 4615 N.E. Emerson St., Portland, OR 97218.
UNSPECIFIED

New Dawn Books Inc., Box 242, 439-4800 Kingsway, Burnaby, BC V5H 4J8. 604-431-7517. Contact: J. Andrews. Quality adult fiction. No unsolicited manuscripts.
FICTION

New Riders Publishing, Division of Que Corporation, 3731 130th Ave N.E., Bellevue, WA 98005. Contact: Jesse Berst. Twenty softcover original books per yr. Accepts query letters only; include outline, bio, writing sample, statistics about target market. Technical expertise required. Pays advance, royalties. Dot matrix, computer disk subs OK. Topics: computer books on leading edge topics graphics, desktop publishing, CAD, networking, and others. Catalog.
COMPUTERS, TECHNICAL

New Sage Press, 825 N.E. 20th Ave., Ste. 150, Portland, OR 97232. 503-232-6794; Fax 503-232-6891. Contact: Maureen Michelson. Publisher of hard & softcover books. Accepts unsolicited submissions. Pays royalties; acquires first rights. Queries should include a sample of text and color/B&W prints of photos or reproductions of photos or artwork. Responds in 3-6 months; publishes in 1-2 years. Accepts nonfiction, specializing in photo essays. "No fiction, please. Photo essay projects on multicultural and socially relevant issues. Must be of high quality." Catalog.
SOCIOLOGY, PHOTOGRAPHY, WOMEN

New Society Publishers, PO Box 189, Gabriola, BC V0R 1X0. 604-247-9737. Contact: Judith or Chris Plant. Nonfiction hard- & softcover books. No unsolicited submissions. Query w/SASE. Pays royalties, advance. Responds ASAP. Guidelines.
ENVIRONMENT/RESOURCES

New Star Books, 2504 York Ave., Vancouver, BC V6K 1E3. 604-738-9429. Contact: Rolf Maurer. Publisher of 8 nonfiction softcover originals a year for left-wing readers. Query, manuscript, outline, sample chapters w/SASE. Responds 6 mos. Publishes in 1 year. Nonfiction: labor, social history, feminism, gay liberation, ethnic studies. Catalog.
FEMINISM, LABOR/WORK, SOCIALIST/RADICAL

Newport Bay Publishing Ltd, 356 Cyril Owen Pl., RR 3, Victoria, BC V8X 3X1. Native titles.
BRITISH COLUMBIA, CHILDREN (BY/ABOUT), NATIVE AMERICAN

Nexus Press, 13032 N.E. 73rd, Kirkland, WA 98033.
UNSPECIFIED

N.H. Fieldstone Publishing PO Box 22, Medina, WA 98039.
UNSPECIFIED

Niagara Publications, 35960 N. Santiam Hwy., Gates, OR 97346. 503-897-2675. Contact: David or Lisa Barnhardt. Thus far a self-publisher of mysteries set in the Cascades. Open to book queries along those lines. Enclose an SASE with your letter.
UNSPECIFIED

Nobility Press, 811 N.W. 20th, Ste 103, Portland, OR 97209. 503-221-4243. Editor: Kelly Osmont. Book publisher. Grieving. Self-publisher only.
FAMILY, PSYCHOLOGY

Noetic Press, PO Box 10851, Eugene, OR 97440. 503-937-3437; 937-2314 Fax. Contact: Jan Sellon. Publishes hard- and softcover books highly original with a firm intellectual base on the subjects of creativity, ethics, and evolution. We strive to be thoroughly scientific in our mysticism and thoroughly mystical in our science. Accepts poetry and nonfiction. No unsolicited submissions. Gives byline and acquires all rights. Pays all costs of publication; gives no advances, shares profits with author. Material must relate to backlog and backlist. Responds in 3 wks; publishes in 2 yrs. Query first. Guidelines, catalog.
EDUCATION, PHILOSOPHY, SCIENCE

Nor 'West Publishing, Box 379, Sechelt, BC VON 3A0. 604-885-5272. Contact: Susan Jackson. Publisher of regional history. No unsolicited manuscripts.
HISTORY NW/REGIONAL

Norjak Project, 6059 Tollgate, Sisters, OR 97759-3006. 503-655-3675. Editor: Tom Worcester.
NW/REGIONAL HISTORY

North Country Publishing, 112 W. 4th, PO Box 9223, Moscow, ID 83843. 208-882-0888. Editor: Ivar Nelson. Hard- and softcover books. Uses freelance material. Pays money on publication. Acquires all rights. Byline given. Query, complete ms, SASE, phone. Reports in 3 wks; publishes in 2 mos. Accepts biography, photos (on request), interviews, op/ed, articles, reviews. Topics: local history,

natural history, politics, environment issues, sports, food, science, business, regional travel, recreation, arts, people, must be of interest to interior Northwest readers. Guidelines, catalog send SASE. Solstice Press is an imprint of North Country and handles book packaging projects.
NORTHWEST, RECREATION, TRAVEL

North Pacific Publishers, PO Box 13255, Portland, OR 97213. Publisher of physics books.
SCIENCE

North Publishing, 4217 W. Bertona St., Seattle, WA 98199-1840.
UNSPECIFIED

Northland Publications, PO Box 12157, Seattle, WA 98102.
UNSPECIFIED

Northwest Bed & Breakfast Travel Unltd, 610 S.W. Broadway, Ste. 609, Portland, OR 97205. 503-243-7616. Self-publisher, bed & breakfast directory. Not a freelance market.
CALENDAR/EVENTS, NORTHWEST, TRAVEL

Northwest Botanicals Inc., 1305 Vista Dr., Grants Pass, OR 97527. 503-476-5588. Contact: Richard Alan Miller
HEALTH

Northwest Interpretive Association, 83 S. King St., Ste. 212, Seattle, WA 98104. 206-553-7958. Book publisher. Not a freelance market.
CONSERVATION, NORTHWEST, OUTDOOR

Northwest Parent Publishing, 2107 Elliot Ave #303, Seattle, WA 98121. 206-441-0191. Contact: Ann Bergman. Publisher of 12 softcover nonfiction originals and magazine for/by Children. Submit query letter w/SASE, manuscript, outline, sample chapters. Dot matrix, photocopies OK. Reports in 3 mos. Publishes in 6-12 mos. Accepts nonfiction, interviews and reviews. Issues relevant to parent, educators, professionals working with children 12 or under. Guidelines, sample ($1.50).
CHILDREN/TEEN

Northwest Silver Press, 88 Cascade Key, Bellevue, WA 98006.
UNSPECIFIED

Nosado Press, 203 E. 4th Ave., Ste. 318, PO Box 634, Olympia, WA 98507-0634. 206-754-0152. Editor: L. B. Arender. Publishes softcover books. Accepts unsolicited submissions. Submit query letter, outline, sample chapters, SASE. Photocopy, dot matrix, simultaneous subs OK. Responds in 10 days. Accepts nonfiction.
NORTHWEST, OUTDOOR

Nugget Enterprises, PO Box 184, Enumclaw, WA 98022. 206-825-3855. Contact: Roy F. Mayo. Self-publisher of 1-2 softcover originals on gold and gold mining. Print run: 1,000. Not a freelance market. Catalog.
GEOLOGY/GEOGRAPHY, NW/REGIONAL HISTORY, RECREATION

Oak Lodge Publishing, 3320 S.E. Pinehurst, Milwaukie, OR 97267. 503-653-9046. Contact: Janet Higginson.
UNSPECIFIED

Oakbridge University Press, 6716 Eastside Dr. N.E., Ste. 50, Tacoma, WA 98422. 206-952-3285. Contact: Judi or Thomas Coates. Publisher of metaphysical and New Age books. Query w/SASE. Accepts, poetry, fiction and nonfiction.
NEW AGE

Ocotillo Press, 215 N. 51st St., Seattle, WA 98103.
UNSPECIFIED

Offshoot Publications, 1280 Goodpasture Island Rd., Eugene, OR 97401-1794. 503-686-8266. Self-publisher of 1 hard- & softcover book a yr.
GARDENING

Old Harbor Press, PO Box 97, Sitka, AK 99835. 907-

747-3584. Publisher of 1 hard- & softcover original, reprint a year. Press run: 3,000. Does not accept unsolicited submissions.
ALASKA, FOOD/COOKING, NW/REGIONAL HISTORY

Old Time Bottle Publishing, 611 Lancaster Dr. N.E., Salem, OR 97301.
COLLECTING, CRAFTS/HOBBIES

Old Violin-Art Publishing, Box 500, 225 S. Cooke, Helena, MT 59624-0500.
PUBLISHING/PRINTING

Olympic Publishing Inc., PO Box 353, Port Ludlow, WA 98365. 206-437-2277. Publisher of 2 nonfiction books a year: local history/travel, boating, other. Query, outline, sample chapters w/SASE. Reports in 2 mos. Catalog.
BOATING, NW/REGIONAL HISTORY, TRAVEL

Omega Publications, PO Box 4130, Medford, OR 97501.
UNSPECIFIED

Online Press Inc., 14320 N.E. 21st, Ste 18, Bellevue, WA 98007. 206-641-3434. Contact: Sally B. Oberlin. Publisher of 6 softcover books per year on computers, technology, and software streamlined instruction for professional and business users (Quick Course Series). Query w/SASE.
BUSINESS, COMPUTERS, TECHNICAL

Onset Publications, 692 Elkader St., Ashland, OR 97520.
UNSPECIFIED

Oolichan Books, PO Box 10, Lantzville, BC V0R 2H0. 604-390-4839. Editor: Ron Smith, Rhonda Bailey. Ads: R. Smith. Circ. 1,000. Publishes hard- & softcover original books. Accepts unsolicited submissions. Pays 10% royalties, copies on publication. Query w/SASE. Reports in 2 mos. Publishes within 1 yr. Accepts nonfiction, fiction, poetry. Topics: literary press, primarily interested in high quality fiction and poetry; also BC history and a few general titles of specific interest to western Canadians. Length can vary from 48 pgs. for poetry title to 448 pgs. for regional history. Catalog with SASE.
FICTION, CANADIAN HISTORY, POETRY

Open Hand Publishing Inc., PO Box 22048, Seattle, WA 98122. 206-447-0597. Editor: P. Anna Johnson. Publishes hard- & softcover originals. Does not accept unsolicited mss. Pays royalties on publication. All rights acquired. Submit query, outline, SASE. Dot matrix, photocopied OK. Accepts nonfiction. Topics: Afro-American issues, bilingual childrens books. Guidelines, catalog.
BLACK, LITERATURE, AMERICAN HISTORY

Open Path Publishing, Box 3064, Boise, ID 83703-0064.
UNSPECIFIED

Open Road Publishers, 3316 West 8th Ave., Vancouver, BC V6R 1YA. 604-736-0070. Contact: Russell Jennings. Self-publisher, softcover. Not a freelance market.
TRAVEL

ORC Enterprises Ltd., 7031 Westminster Hwy., Ste. 305, Richmond, BC V6X 1A3.
UNSPECIFIED

Orca Book Publishers, PO Box 5626, Sta. B, Victoria, BC V8R 6S4. 604-380-1229; FAX: 604-380-1892. Editor: R. J. Tyrrell. Publishes soft- & hardcover originals. Pays advance, royalties. Query letter, outline, sample chapters, SASE. Reports in 6-8 wks; publishes in 6-18 mos. Accepts nonfiction, fiction, biography. Publishes Canadian authors only. Topics: regional history, geology, guidebooks, children's. Catalog with SASE.
CHILDREN/TEEN, CANADIAN HISTORY, PUBLISHING/
PRINTING

Orcas Publishing Company, Rt. 1 Box 104, Eastsound, WA 98245. Publisher of books on history and language. Does not accept unsolicited submissions.
NW/REGIONAL HISTORY, LANGUAGE(S)

Oregon Association of Nurserymen, 2780 S.E. Harrison, Milwaukie, OR 97222.
AGRICULTURE/FARMING, BUSINESS

Oregon Catholic Press, PO Box 18030, Portland, OR 97218.
RELIGION

Oregon Economic Development Department, International Trade Division, 595 Cottage Street N.E., Salem, OR 97310.
BUSINESS, ECONOMICS, OREGON

Oregon Health Sciences University, Center Foundation, 3181 S.W. Sam Jackson Park, Portland, OR 97201.
COLLEGE/UNIVERSITY, HEALTH, SCIENCE

Oregon Historical Society Press, 1200 S.W. Park, Portland, OR 97205. 503-222-1741. Editor: Bruce Taylor Hamilton. Publishes hard- & softcover originals. Accepts unsolicited mss. Acquires all rights; negotiable on all contracts. Submit query w/outline, sample chapters, SASE. Photocopies OK. Reports in 2-6 wks; publishes in 1-3 yrs. Accepts nonfiction, fiction, photos. Topics: Pacific N.W. history and allied subjects. Firm scholarship or experience. Will review article-length (for Oregon Historical Quarterly) to book length mss. Material must be new or new interpretation. Guidelines, catalog.
NW/REGIONAL HISTORY, NATURAL HISTORY, NORTHWEST

Oregon Scholastic Press, 201 Allen Hall, University of Oregon, Eugene, OR 97403.
EDUCATION, TEXTBOOKS

Oregon State University Press, 101 Waldo Hall, Corvallis, OR 97331-6407. 503-737-3166. Editor: Jo Alexander. Founded 1965. Publishes nonfiction, hard- & softcover original & reprint books. Accepts unsolicited submissions. Pays royalties. Rights purchased: negotiable. Submit query, ms, SASE. Dot matrix, photocopies OK. Reports in 1 mo. Publishes in approx 1 yr. Accepts scholarly book-length manuscripts. Topics: a limited range of disciplines, with a special emphasis on the Pacific Northwest. Query with sample chapter & table of contents. Acceptance process is lengthy & involves outside reviews & editorial board. Catalog.
ENVIRONMENT/RESOURCES, NORTHWEST, SCHOLARLY/
ACADEMIC

Oregon's Agricultural Progress, AdS 416, Oregon State University, Corvallis, OR 97331. 503-737-3379. Editor: Andy Duncan. Quarterly magazine. Uses freelance material. Byline given. Submit query letter, clips, SASE. Responds in 2-4 wks; publishes in 3-8 mos. Accepts nonfiction.
AGRICULTURE/FARMING, CONSUMER, GARDENING

Oriel Press, 2020 S.W. Kanan St., Portland, OR 97201-2039. Book publisher. Not a freelance market.
UNSPECIFIED

Osprey Press, PO Box 32, Sedro Woolley, WA 98284. 206-755-0941.
UNSPECIFIED

Outdoor Empire Publishing Inc., 511 Eastlake Ave. E., Seattle, WA 98109. 206-624-3845. Editor: Fay Ainsworth. Publisher of biweekly Fishing and Hunting News newspaper plus educational book publisher. Newspaper Circ. 135,000; sub $39.95/yr. Accepts unsolicited submissions, freelance material. Byline Given. Payment in copies on publication. All rights acquired. Submit query letter, clips, SASE, outline or sample chapters. Dot matrix, photocopies OK. Responds 6 wks.
BOATING, FISHING, RECREATION

Outdoor Pictures, PO Box 277, Anacortes, WA 98221.
OUTDOOR, PHOTOGRAPHY

Overland West Press, PO Box 17507, Portland, OR 97217.
PUBLISHING/PRINTING

O.W. Frost Publisher, 2141 Lord Baranof Dr., Anchorage, AK 99503.
UNSPECIFIED

Owl Creek Press, 1620 N. 45th St., Seattle, WA 98103. 206-633-5929. Contact: Rich Ives. Publisher of 6-10 hard- & softcover and mass market, originals and reprints a year. Print run: 1,000. Accepts freelance material. Payment: 10% in copies to 20% in cash. Rights purchased: All. Sample chapters w/SASE. Dot matrix, photocopies OK. Reports in 2-12 wks. Nonfiction, fiction, poetry. Catalog.
FICTION, LITERARY, POETRY

The Oz Press, PO Box 33088, Seattle, WA 98133.
UNSPECIFIED

Pacific Coast Centre of Sexology, Sta. C, Box 24400, Vancouver, BC V5T 4M5. Sexual education books.
EDUCATION, SEX

Pacific Edge Publishing and Media Services Ltd., R.R. #2, Site 21, Gabriola Island, BC V0R 1X0. 604-247-8806. Contact: Ron Mumford. "Prefer a letter of inquiry but will accept manuscripts for children's material suitable for marketing as educational resources."
EDUCATION, CHILDREN/TEEN, PUBLISHING/PRINTING

Pacific Educational Press, Univ. of B.C., Faculty of Education, 2173 West Mall, Vancouver, BC V6T 1Z4. 604-822-5385. Editor: Catherine Edwards. Publishes 12 quarterly journals and 5 hard- & softcover original books a year. Accepts unsolicited submissions. Pays royalties/advance on publication. Rights acquired vary. Submit query w/SASE, manuscript, outline or sample chapters. Photocopies OK. Reports in 3-6 mo. Publishes 1 yr. Accepts educational & academic nonfiction. "We do not publish trade books unless they have school potential." Pays royalties on publication. Catalog, sample.
EDUCATION, TEXTBOOKS, CHILDREN/TEEN

Pacific Fast Mail, PO Box 57, Edmonds, WA 98020. Contact: Donald Drew.
UNSPECIFIED

Pacific House Enterprises, 65 W. 26th Ave., Eugene, OR 97405. 503-344-0395.
UNSPECIFIED

Pacific International Publishing Company, PO Box 1596, Friday Harbor, WA 98250-1596.
UNSPECIFIED

Pacific Meridian Publishing, 13540 39th Ave N.E., Seattle, WA 98125-3808.
UNSPECIFIED

Pacific Northwest Labor History Assn, PO Box 75048, Seattle, WA 98125. 206-524-0346. Contact: Ross Reider.
BUSINESS, NW/REGIONAL HISTORY, LABOR/WORK

Pacific Press Publishing Association, Seventh-Day Adventist Church, PO Box 7000, Boise, ID 83707. 208-467-7400. Publisher of 50 books a year. Query w/SASE.
RELIGION

Pacific Publishers, 515 W. Pender, Vancouver, BC V6B 1V5.
RELIGION

Pacific Rim Press, 5615 N. Burrage Ave., Portland, OR 97217-4131. Self-publisher only. Not a freelance market.
FOOD/COOKING, TRAVEL

Pacific Soccer School, 1721 22nd Ave., Forest Grove, OR 97116.
RECREATION, SPORTS

Paddlewheel Press, 15100 S.W. 109th Ave., Tigard, OR 97224. 503-639-5637. Contact: Marge Davenport.
UNSPECIFIED

Painted Smiles Inc., 1105 West Idaho St., Boise, ID 83702.
UNSPECIFIED

Pair-o'-Dice Press, 525 S.E. 16th Ave., Portland, OR 97214.
UNSPECIFIED

Paisley Publishing, PO Box 201853, Anchorage, AK 99520-1853. 907-346-2789. Editors: Betsy Arehart, Anne Marie Holen. Self-publisher. Not a freelance market.
UNSPECIFIED

Pallas Communications, 4226 N.E. 23rd Ave., Portland, OR 97211. 503-284-2848. Editor: Douglas Bloch. Publisher of 2-3 New Age, softcover, original books per year. Unsolicited submissions OK. Pays royalties. Submit query, sample chapter, outline w/SASE. Dot matrix, photocopied, simultaneous, computer disk OK. Reports in 4-6 wks. Publishes within 1 yr. Accepts nonfiction. Topics: self-help, psychology, astrology, metaphysics, holistic health, women's spirituality, and inspirational writing; any path that leads to personal or planetary transformation. Catalog.
NEW AGE, ASTROLOGY/SPIRITUAL, HEALTH

Palmer Press, #23-659 Clyde Ave., West Vancouver, BC V7T 1C8. 604-922-3624. Contact: P. M. Coles. Publisher of hardcover and softcover books. No unsolicited manuscripts.
UNSPECIFIED

Palmer-pletsch Associates, PO Box 12046, Portland, OR 97212.
UNSPECIFIED

Panda Press Publications, Richards Rd., Roberts Creek, BC V0N 2W0. 604-885-3985. Contact: L. R. Davidson. Publisher of 1 softcover original a year. Print run: 300. Accepts freelance material. Payment: Copies. Rights purchased: First. Query, sample chapters w/SASE. Photocopies, simultaneous submissions OK. Reports in 3-4 wks. Publishes in 1-3 yrs. Fiction: Stories of any kind with excellent, three-dimensional characters interacting with each other and the plot in a logical and interesting way.
AVANT-GARDE/EXPERIMENTAL, FANTASY/SCI FI, SATIRE

Pandemic International, PO Box 61849, Vancouver, WA 98666. Editor: Deborah Horan. Publisher of soft/hardcover books. Accepts unsolicited submissions. Pays upon publication. Submit with query litter, SASE, query by phone, outline, sample chapters, photocopy OK. Reports in 2 weeks +. Publishes in 9 months. Accepts nonfiction and Language Phrase books.
LANGUAGE(S)

Pandora's Treasures, 1609 Eastover Terrace, Boise, ID 83706. Dr. R. Dwayne Moulton.
CHILDREN/TEEN

Panoply Press Inc., PO Box 1885, Lake Oswego, OR 97035. 503-620-7239. Heather Kibby. Publisher of 2-5 softcover original books a year. Accepts unsolicited queries. Pays royalties. Submit query w/clips, SASE. Dot matrix, photocopied OK. Nonfiction. Topic: real estate.
BUSINESS

Paradise Publications, 8110 S.W. Wareham, Portland, OR 97223. 503-246-1555. Publisher of softcover books & quarterly newsletter on travel; sub $6/yr. Circ. 2,000. Founded in 1983. Accepts unsolicited book submissions. Pays royalties. Submit query letter, outline, SASE. Photocopy, simultaneous subs OK. Responds in 1 mo; publishes in 6-12 mos. Catalog; newsletter sample $1.50.
TRAVEL

Parenting Press Inc., 11065 5th Ave. N.E. #F, Seattle, WA 98125. 206-364-2900. Editor: Elizabeth Crary. Publishes hard- & softcover books. Accepts unsolicited submissions. Pays royalties. Submit query letter, SASE. Dot matrix, photocopied, simultaneous subs OK. Reports in 2-3 mos; publishes in 1-2 yrs. Accepts nonfiction. Topics: child guidance/parenting, social skills building books for children. Write for submission guidelines before submitting material. Catalog.
CHILDREN (BY/ABOUT), EDUCATION, FAMILY

Parkside Press, 2026 Parkside Court, West Linn, OR 97068.
UNSPECIFIED

Parlie Publications, 15525 S.W. 114th Court, Ste. 31, Tigard, OR 97224-3310. 503-639-2694. Contact: Alice Pohl. Publisher of books on parliamentary procedure.
REFERENCE/LIBRARY

The Patriot, Runaway Publications, Box 1172, Ashland, OR 97520-0040. 503-482-2578. Editor: James Berkman. Self-publisher only. Annual issue + special editions. Sub $10. Circ. 100. Not a freelance market. Catalog.
AMERICANA, POETRY

Paws IV Publishing Co., PO Box 2364, Homer, AK 99603. 907-235-7697. Contact: Shelley Gill. Publisher of 2 hard- & softcover originals a year. Accepts unsolicited submissions. Submit ms, SASE. Photocopied, simultaneous OK. Reports in 1 mo. Accepts nonfiction, fiction. Topics: Alaska, childrens.
ADVENTURE, ALASKA, CHILDREN/TEEN

Peanut Butter Publishing, 200 2nd Ave W., Seattle, WA 98119-4204. 206-628-6200. Publisher of 40 hard- & softcover, original, reprints, subsidy books a year. Print run: 5-10,000. Accepts freelance material. Rights purchased: First, all. Outline, sample chapters, ms w/SASE. Dot matrix, photocopies OK. Nonfiction: Food cooking, dining. Catalog.
ENTERTAINMENT, FOOD/COOKING, RECREATION

Peavine Publications, PO Box 1264, McMinnville, OR 97128-1264. 503-472-1933. Editor: W. P. Lowry. Publishes softcover books. Accepts unsolicited mss. Pays royalties. Submit query letter, outline, sample chapters, SASE. Photocopy, dot matrix subs OK. Reports in 1 mo; publishes in 6-12 mos. Accepts nonfiction. Topics: ecological, balanced analyses with mild advocacy preferred.
ENVIRONMENT/RESOURCES, SCIENCE, TEXTBOOKS

The Pedersens, PO Box 128, Sterling, AK 99672. Self-publisher. Not a freelance market.
ALASKA, CHILDREN/TEEN, AMERICAN HISTORY

Peel Productions, PO Box 185, Molalla, OR 97038-0185. 503-829-6849. Contact: Susan Joyce. Hard- & softcover original books. Does not accept unsolicited mss. Pays in copies, royalties on publication. Acquires first rights. Submit query letter. Photocopies OK. Reports in 5-6 wks. Publishes in 1 yr. Accepts nonfiction, fiction. Topics: illustrated childrens books and how-to-draw books. Catalog.
CHILDREN/TEEN, CRAFTS/HOBBIES, HOW-TO

Pen Print Inc., 230 E. 1st St. #A, Port Angeles, WA 98362.
UNSPECIFIED

Pennypress Inc., 1100 23rd Ave. E., Seattle, WA 98112. 206-324-1419. Contact: Penny Simkin. Publisher of 1 nonfiction, softcover original a year. Print run: 3,000. Rarely accepts freelance material. Query w/SASE. Dot matrix, photocopies, simultaneous submissions, electronic OK. Reports in 1-5 mos. Publishes in up to 2 yrs. Our publications deal with controversial issues in childbearing and topics of interest to young families. They are accurate, up-to-date and encourage decision making by informed consumers in matters relating to maternity care and parenting. I am very selective and usually invite authors to write for Pennypress. Write w/query and ask for guidelines; they vary according to audience targeted. Catalog.
FAMILY, HEALTH, WOMEN

People's Law Books, Juvenile Rights Project, 123 N.E. 3rd Ave., #310, Portland, OR 97232-2970.
EDUCATION, LAW

Personal Power Press Int., Box V-49, R.R. #1, Bowen Island, BC V0N 1G0. 604-947-2739; Fax 604-947-0706. Contact: Lorna Lyons. Publisher of educational and self-directed learning books. No unsolicited manuscripts. Send query letter w/SASE
EDUCATION

Pet Owners' Association, PO Box 2807, Portland, OR 97208. 503-297-7530. Editor: Joan Dahlberg. Publishes softcover books, videotapes, bimonthly magazine. Very limited acceptance of freelance material, assignment only. Byline given. Pays money on acceptance.
ANIMALS, BUSINESS, TRADE/ASSOCIATIONS

Petarade Press, Box 65746 Station F, Vancouver, BC V5N 5N7. 604-873-2703. Contact: Gordon Murray. Publishes 3 softcover, original performance texts per yr: novels, short stories, poetry. Query w/SASE, but not encouraged unless specifically performance oriented. Pay varies.
DRAMA, LITERARY, POETRY

Pharmaceutical Technology, 859 Willamette St., PO Box 10460, Springfield, OR 97440. 503-343-1200.
BUSINESS, SCIENCE

Phelps Enterprises, 3838 Kendra, Eugene, OR 97404.
UNSPECIFIED

Philam Books Inc., 2101-2077 Nelson St., Vancouver, BC V6G 2Y2.
UNSPECIFIED

Phoenix Publishing Company, PO Box 10, Custer, WA 98240.
UNSPECIFIED

Photography at Open-Space, 510 Fort St., Victoria, BC V8W 1E6.
PHOTOGRAPHY

Pickle Point Publishing, PO Box 4107, 1020 108th Ave. N.E., Bellevue, WA 98009. 206-462-6105. Contact: Bonnie Stewart Mickelson.
UNSPECIFIED

Pictorial Histories Publishing Company, 713 S. 3rd, Missoula, MT 59801. 406-549-8488. Contact: Stan Cohen. Publishes 1-2 hard- & softcover books/yr. No unsolicited ms accepted. All rights acquired. Query w/SASE. Catalog.
GENERAL HISTORY, MILITARY/VETS, PHOTOGRAPHY

Pika Press, PO Box 457, Enterprise, OR 97828. 503-426-3623. Publishes 3-5 hard- & softcover originals, reprints a year. Press run: 1,500-3,000. Pays royalties. Submit query w/clips, phone. Accepts books of special interest to the inland Northwest. "Chances for an outside manuscript now are very slim. A year from now we should be better able to evaluate manuscripts."
NW/REGIONAL HISTORY, NORTHWEST, OUTDOOR

Pill Enterprises, N. 22790, Hwy. 101, Shelton, WA 98584. 206-877-5825. Self-publisher only. Not a freelance market.
FOOD/COOKING

Pinstripe Publishing, PO Box 711, Sedro-Woolley, WA 98284. 206-855-1416. Editor: Helen Gregory. Publishes 1-2 softcover original books/yr. Query only w/outline & SASE. How-to, small business & crafts. Booklist.
BUSINESS, CRAFTS/HOBBIES, HOW-TO

Pioneer Press Books, 37 S. Palouse, Walla Walla, WA 99362. 509-522-2075. Editor: Robert A. Bennett. Publisher of 3-5 hard- & softcover, books/yr. Pays royalties. Query, SASE. Report time varies. Nonfiction: Western history.
NW/REGIONAL HISTORY, NORTHWEST, OLD WEST

Pioneer Publishing Company, Box 190, Big Timber, MT 59011.
UNSPECIFIED

Planned Parenthood Association of Idaho, 4301 Franklin Rd., Boise, ID 83705.
EDUCATION, FAMILY

Playful Wisdom Press, PO Box 834, Kirkland, WA 98083-0834. 206-823-4421. Editor: William Ashoka Ross. Publishes softcover, original books. Accepts unsolicited submissions. Charges a reading free of $250. Submit query letter, sample chapters, SASE before the whole ms. Topics: "Playfully instructive insights about the human condition.

Our books are for and by grownups who delight in childlike enthusiasm and celebrate being alive. We love love.
HUMOR, RELIGION, SEX

Pleneurethic International, Earth Light Bookstore, 113 E. Main, Walla Walla, WA 99362. New Age books.
NEW AGE

Poeticus Obscurirant Publications, PO Box 85817, Seattle, WA 98145. Contact: Patrick McCabe.
POETRY

Poets. Painters. Composers, 10254 35th Ave. S.W., Seattle, WA 98146. 206-937-8155. Contact: Joseph Keppler. Publisher of Poets. Painters. Composers, an arts journal; Colins Magazine, a review of contemporary culture & technology; and various poetry books and broadsides. Accepts freelance material. Pays copies (negotiable). Query w/ms, SASE. Photocopies OK. Reports immediately. Publishes in 3 mos. Poetry, art, music, essays; experimental, short works, original in concept and design, provocative, ingenious, knowledgeable, beautiful.
ARTS, MUSIC, POETRY

Polestar Press, Box 69382, Sta. K, Vancouver, BC V5K 4W6. Contact: Michelle Benjamin. Publisher of hard- & softcover books. Accepts unsolicited submissions. Pays advance; acquires all rights. Submit outline, sample chapters, synopsis w/SASE. Photocopies, simultaneous submissions OK. Responds 3-6 mos; publishes 1 yr. Accepts fiction and poetry. Catalog.
BRITISH COLUMBIA, SPORTS, LITERARY

Poltergeist Press, 706 S. Morain St., Kennewick, WA 99336.
UNSPECIFIED

Ponderosa Publishers, 2037 Airport Rd., Saint Ignatius, MT 59865-9602. 406-745-4455. Editor: E. V. Hamel. Publishes hard & softcover books. No unsolicited submissions. Pays money and advances. Rights acquisition is negotiable. Query w/SASE, outline, sample chapters. Dot matrix and photocopy OK. Responds in 2 mos; publishing time varies.
UNSPECIFIED

Pooka Press, 150 Mt. Olympus Dr. N.W., Issaquah, WA 98027-3019. 206-392-6674. Contact: Robert A. Fletcher. Self-publisher of hand-made books. Not a freelance market.
AVANT-GARDE/EXPERIMENTAL

Poppies Publishing, PO Box 33, Ester, AK 99725. Publisher of photo history books about Alaska.
PHOTOGRAPHY, ALASKA

Portland Chess Press, 6051 S.E. Stark #1, Portland, OR 97215. 503-236-0042. Contact: Casey Bush. Self-publisher of softcover books.
BIOGRAPHY, HISTORY NW/REGIONAL, SPORTS

Port/Manhattan Publishers, 6406 N. Maryland Ave., Portland, OR 97217.
UNSPECIFIED

Post Point Press, PO Box 4393, Bellingham, WA 98227. 206-676-9531. Editor: Jack W Bazhaw.
ANTHROPOLOGY/ARCHAEOLOGY

Poverty Bay Publishing Company, 529 S.W. 294th St., Federal Way, WA 98003.
UNSPECIFIED

Poverty Hill Press, PO Box 519, Leavenworth, WA 98826.
UNSPECIFIED

Powell River Heritage Research Assn., 7155 Hazelton St., Powell River, BC V8A 1P9. 604-485-5537. Editors: Karen Southern, Peggy Bird. Publishes hard- & softcover books on N.W. regional history. Does not accept unsolicited submissions. Submit query letter, outline, sample chapters, SASE. Responds in 2 months. Publishes nonfiction with photos.
NW/REGIONAL HISTORY

Prasad Press, PO Box 11804, Eugene, OR 97440. 503-741-3992. Contact: Richard Reed.
UNSPECIFIED

Prescott Street Press, PO Box 40312, Portland, OR 97240-0312. 503-254-2922. Publisher of hard- & softcover originals. Accepts freelance submissions. Payment negotiated. Rights purchased: first, all. Reports in 1 mo. Submit query letter, SASE. Publishing time varies. Topics: poetry, art. PSP arranges artwork and pays artist.
ARTS, POETRY

Press Gang Publishers, 603 Powell St., Vancouver, BC V6A 1H2. 604-253-2537. Editor: Della McCreary. Softcover originals. Unsolicited submissions OK. Pays royalties. Acquires all rights. Query w/clips, SASE. Dot matrix, photocopied, computer disk OK. Reports in 2-4 mos; publishes in 1-2 mos. Accepts nonfiction, fiction, priority to Canadian women's writing. Seeking submissions by Native women. "We are a feminist collective interested in publishing fiction and nonfiction that challenges traditional assumptions about women and provides a feminist framework for understanding our experience. We look for work that is not homophobic, racist, classist or sexist." Catalog.
FEMINISM, GAY/LESBIAN, NATIVE AMERICAN

Preston & Betts, c/o Camosun College, Victoria, BC V8P 5J2.
COLLEGE/UNIVERSITY

Price Guide Publishers, PO Box 525, Kenmore, WA 98028.
BUSINESS, CONSUMER

Price Productions, 373 Altadena, Astoria, OR 97103. 503-325-3733. Contact: Juanita B. Price. Publishes a bibliography of authors and illustrators of children's books in Oregon. SASE for flyer.
CHILDREN (BY/ABOUT), REFERENCE/LIBRARY, WRITING

Primavera Productions, PO Box 669, Union, OR 97883.
UNSPECIFIED

Princess Publishing, PO Box 25406, Portland, OR 97225. Editor: Cheryl Matschek. Publishes hard- & softcover originals. Accepts unsolicited submissions. Submit query letter, outline, sample chapters, complete ms, SASE. Reports in 2 wks; publishes in 3 mos. Accepts nonfiction. Topics: self-help, new age, sales, management, business.
ASTROLOGY/SPIRITUAL, BUSINESS, PSYCHOLOGY

Printery Farm, 153 Benson Rd., Port Angeles, WA 98362. 206-457-0248. Self-publisher. Not a freelance market.
BIOGRAPHY, FAMILY

Professional Business Communications, 11830 S.W. Kerr Pkwy, Ste. 350, Lake Oswego, OR 97035. 503-293-1163. Contact: Marian Woodall. Publisher softcover books on public speaking and communications skills. Not a market.
HOW-TO

Progress Publishing Co., PO Box 13025, Spokane, WA 99213-3025. 509-238-6196. Contact: Jerry Marlin. Publishes hardcover books. Unsolicited and freelance submissions accepted. Payment on publication. Acquires all rights. Query by letter. Send complete manuscript, photocopy and dot matrix OK. Responds in 2-5 weeks; publishes in 5 months. Accepts new age material. Guidelines; no catalog.
NEW AGE

Provincial Archives of British Columbia, Sound and Moving Image Division, Victoria, BC V8V 1X4.
BRITISH COLUMBIA, CANADIAN HISTORY, VISUAL ARTS

PSI Research/The Oasis Press, 300 N. Valley Dr., Grants Pass, OR 97526. 503-479-9464. Contact: Virginia Groso. Publisher of hard- & softcover originals and reprints. Pays money, royalties in advance, upon publication. Acquires all rights. Byline given author's name on book cover. Submit ms w/SASE or query by phone. Dot matrix, photocopies OK. Reports in 2 wks. Publishing time

varies, but 1 yr at most. Accepts fiction. Topics: wide variety of business subjects; especially sales, management, decision-making, customer service, interviewing, leadership. Guidelines.
BUSINESS, FICTION

Ptarmigan Press, 1372 Island Hwy., Campbell River, BC V9W 2E1. 604-286-0878. Contact: Bryan Wiley. Publisher of hard- & softcover books. Submit query letter, sample chapters. Photocopies OK. Responds 4-6 wks. Accepts nonfiction biography and cooking-related material. Note: limited capacity. We are also a printing company and do vanity press on a frequent basis.
UNSPECIFIED

Publication in History, University of Montana, Missoula, MT 59812.
AMERICAN HISTORY, NW/REGIONAL HISTORY, MONTANA

Publishers' Press, 1935 S.E. 59th Ave., Portland, OR 97215.
UNSPECIFIED

Puffin Press, 151 Wallace Way N.E., Bainbridge Island, WA 98110.
UNSPECIFIED

Pulphouse Publishing, Box 1227, Eugene, OR 97440. 503-935-6322. Editor: Dean Wesley Smith. Publisher of hard- & softcover books (including Axolotl Press Series and Writer's Notebook Press) and five periodicals. Uses freelance material. Byline given. Pays money, advance, royalties. Acquires 1st or anthology rights. Submit query letter, complete ms. Responds in 2 mos; publishes in 8 mos. Accepts fiction, cartoons, photos. Topics: science fiction, fantasy. Guidelines, catalog.
FANTASY/SCI FI, FICTION, WRITING

Pumpkin Ridge Productions, PO Box 33, North Plains, OR 97133. 503-647-0021. Contact: Jim Long. Publisher of a newsletter and softcover books. Newsletter irregularly published. Unsolicited submissions occasionally accepted. Acquires other rights. Query by phone. Interested in news items, nonfiction, and op/ed. Back issues $24.95.
OREGON, HISTORY NW/REGIONAL

Puppet Concepts Publishing, PO Box 15203, Portland, OR 97215. 503-236-4034. Self-publisher only. Contact: Susan Barthel or Bruce Chess. Books/video on puppetry and puppet construction by and for children. Not accepting mss.
DRAMA, EDUCATION/CHILDREN, ENTERTAINMENT, FILM/VIDEO

Purna Press, 12756 103rd Pl. N.E., Kirkland, WA 98034. 206-821-2552. Contact: Henry Borys. Self-publisher only. Softcover books. No unsolicited submissions. Catalog.
FAMILY, PSYCHOLOGY, SEX

Quality Paperbacks, PO Box 7, Boring, OR 97009. 503-663-3428. Contact: Mabel Johnson.
UNSPECIFIED

Quality Publications, 12180 S.W. 127th, Tigard, OR 97223. Self-publisher.
UNSPECIFIED

The Quartz Press, 392 Taylor St., Ashland, OR 97520-3058. 503-482-8119. Publisher of 2 softcover books a year. Print run: 100. Accepts freelance material. Payment: Royalties negotiated. Dot matrix, photocopies OK. Reports in 6 mos. Publishes in 1-2 yrs. Nonfiction, fiction, poetry, plays. We seek revolutionary material with no known market, and hence not publishable commercially.
CULTURE, FICTION, POETRY

Quest Northwest, PO Box 200, Salkum, WA 98582. 206-985-2999. Contact: Dean Marshall.
UNSPECIFIED

Questar Publishers Inc., 210 S. Elm St., Box 1720, Sisters, OR 97759. 503-549-1144; 800-933-7526. Editor: Thomas Hale Womack. Ads: Brenda Jacobson. Publishes

hard & softcover books. Accepts unsolicited submissions. Pays royalties; acquires all rights. Submit query letter, outline, sample chapters, SASE. Photocopied, dot matrix subs OK. Responds in 1 month; publishes in 6-18 months. Fiction, nonfiction, biography.
BIOGRAPHY, CHILDREN/TEEN, FICTION

Quicksilver Productions, Box 340, Ashland, OR 97520. 503-482-5343. Contact: Jim Maynard. Publisher of 4 books a year.
UNSPECIFIED

Quiet Lion Press, 7215 S.W. LaView Dr., Portland, OR 972219. 503-771-1907. Editor: Brian Christopher Hamilton. Publisher of softcover books. Founded 1992. Unsolicited submissions not accepted. Pays copies & royalties on publication. Acquires first or second rights. Query by letter or phone. Accepts fiction, poetry.
POETRY, FICTION

Quimper Press, c/o Port Townsend Publishing, PO Box 552, Port Townsend, WA 98368-0552.
UNSPECIFIED

R & M Press, 917 Pacific Ave #216, Tacoma, WA 98402. 206-272-1609. Editors: Ann Roush, Jon Martin. Publishes hard- & softcover books. Unsolicited submissions OK. Pays royalties. Submit query letter, outline, sample chapters, SASE. Responds in 4 wks; publishes in 9 mos. Accepts nonfiction. Topics: textbooks, how-to. Guidelines, catalog.
FOOD/COOKING, TEXTBOOKS

R & P Publishing, PO Box 2265, Homer, AK 99603. Contact: Keith Iverson.
UNSPECIFIED

R. C. Publications, 1828 N.E. Stanton, Portland, OR 97212. 503-287-1009. Self-publisher. Not a freelance market. Catalog.
CRAFTS/HOBBIES, HOW-TO

R. J. Watts & Associates, 4010 Bayridge Crescent, W. Vancouver, BC V7V 3K4. Contact: Reg Watts.
UNSPECIFIED

Rae Publications, PO Box 731, Brush Prairie, WA 98606-0731. 206-687-3767. Contact: Pat Redjou. Self-publisher only. Not a freelance market.
HEALTH, ENTERTAINMENT, CHILDREN/TEEN

Railway Milepost Books, 4398 Valencia Ave., North Vancouver, BC V7N 4B1.
UNSPECIFIED

Rain Belt Publications Inc., 18806 40th Ave. W., Lynnwood, WA 98036.
UNSPECIFIED

Raincoast Books, 112 E. 3rd Ave., Vancouver, BC V5T 1C8.
BRITISH COLUMBIA, OUTDOOR

Rainforest Publishing, PO Box 101251, Anchorage, AK 99510. 907-274-8687. Editor: Duncan Frazier. Publishes 13 softcover books a year. Press run 3,000. Payment negotiated. Acquires 1st rights. Submit query. Photocopied, simultaneous OK. Reports in 1 mo. Publishes in 6 mos. Accepts nonfiction on any Alaska-related topic. Catalog.
ALASKA

Rainy Day Press, PO Box 3035, Eugene, OR 97403. 503-484-4626. Contact: Mike Helm. Publishes books of N.W. folklore, history, poetry. Has not published for others yet, but would "listen to a good idea."
NW/REGIONAL HISTORY, NORTHWEST, POETRY

Rainy Day Publishing, 13222 S.E. 57th St., Bellevue, WA 98006. 206-746-0802. Contact: Renae R Knapp.
UNSPECIFIED

Ralmar Press, 3623 S.W. Nevada St., Portland, OR 97219.
UNSPECIFIED

Ramalo Publication, 2107 N. Spokane St., Post Falls, ID 83854. 208-773-9416. Editor: Marie Fish. Book pub-

lisher. Not accepting mss at this time. Topics: family-oriented
FAMILY, FICTION, POETRY

Random Lengths Publications, PO Box 867, Eugene, OR 97440-0867. 503-686-9925. Self-publisher weekly, biweekly newsletters, 3 hard- & softcover books/yr. Not a freelance market.
BUSINESS

Randy Stapilus Ridenbaugh Press, 1429 Shenandoah Dr., Boise, ID 83712-6658.
UNSPECIFIED

Raven Press, PO Box 135, Lake Oswego, OR 97034. Editor: Richard W Helbock.
UNSPECIFIED

RDM Enterprises, PO BOX 1067, Columbia Falls, MT 59912. 406-892-3942. Contact: Ronald D. Mohn. Self publisher of softcover books. No unsolicited submissions accepted. Subjects include hunting, fishing, and the outdoors.
OUTDOOR, FISHING

The Real Comet Press, 1463 E. Republican St. #126, Seattle, WA 98112-4517. 206-328-1801. Publishes hard- & softcover books. Editor: Catherine Hillenbrand. Topics: contemporary culture, especially where art, humor and social commentary intertwine. No longer publishing new titles. Catalog.
ARTS, CULTURE, HUMOR

Red Apple Publishing, PO Box 101, Gig Harbor, WA 98335. 206-265-6595. Publisher: Peggy J. Meyer. Subsidy publisher.
SENIOR CITIZENS, GENERAL HISTORY, BIOGRAPHY

Red Cedar Press, 606 First St., Nanaimo, BC V9R 1Y9. 604-753-8417. Editor: W. & A. Baker. Ads: A. Baker. Publishes 2 softcover books/yr. Press run 500-1,000. Does not accept unsolicited submissions at the present time.
FEMINISM, HUMOR, LITERARY

Red Lyon Publications, 2123 Marlow, Eugene, OR 97401-6431.
UNSPECIFIED

Reference West, 2450 Central Ave., Victoria, BC V8S 2S8. Newsletter editors: Charles Lillard and Robin Skelton. Publishes limited edition chapbooks of the Hawthorne Society, limited edition literary chapbooks and the Poetry Newsletter. Newsletter appears monthly and is open to submissions. Topics: N.W. poets and their poetry and books. Queries welcome w/SASE. Responds 2 wks; publishes 8 wks. Pays in copies. Rights vary.
LITERARY

Reflections Publishing, Box 178, Gabriola, BC V0R 1X0. 604-247-8685. Contact: Neil Aitken. Publisher of books on ecology, human rights, and Native American issues. Press runs of 2,000-2,500. Acquires 1st rights. Pays royalties. Responds in 3 wks; publishes within a year. Query w/SASE (CDN) or IRC (US), including outline, sample chapter, and authors qualifications/previous credits. Photocopied OK. Catalog.
BRITISH COLUMBIA, ENVIRONMENT/RESOURCES, PUBLIC AFFAIRS

Reliant Marketing & Publishing, PO Box 17456, Portland, OR 97217. Contact: Florence K. Riddle. Publisher softcover original books. Accepts freelance material. Query letter, outline, SASE. Dot matrix, photocopies OK. Reports in 3 wks. Accepts nonfiction. Topics: how-to, self-help, money making. Guidelines.
CRAFTS/HOBBIES, HEALTH, HOW-TO

Repository Press, RR #7, Site 29, Comp. 8, Prince George, BC V2N 2J5. 604-562-7074. Contact: John Harris. Publishes softcover books. Accepts unsolicited manuscripts for travel books only. Submit query letter. Responds 3 mos. Catalog.
FICTION, POETRY, TRAVEL

Researcher Publications Inc., 18806 40th Ave. W., Lynnwood, WA 98036.
UNSPECIFIED

Resolution Business Press, 11101 N.E. 8th St., Ste. 208, Bellevue, WA 98004. 206-455-4611. Editor: John Spilker. Unsolicited submissions OK. Acquires all rights. Submit query, clips, SASE. Responds in 3-5 wks; publishes in 6-12 mos. Accepts nonfiction, interviews, articles. Topics: computer and business-related. Guidelines.
COMPUTERS, REFERENCE/LIBRARY, TECHNICAL

Revolution Books, Banner Press, 5519-A University Way N.E., Seattle, WA 98105. 206-527-8558. Radical and socialist books.
COMPUTERS, LAW, SOCIALIST/RADICAL

Reynard House, 5706 30th N.E., Seattle, WA 98105.
UNSPECIFIED

Rhino Press, PO Box 5207, Sta. B, Victoria, BC V8R 6N4.
UNSPECIFIED

Richard Stine Publishing, 8100 Hidden Cove Rd., Bainbridge Island, WA 98110. 206-842-8077. Contact: Richard Stine. Humor publisher.
HUMOR

Rie Munoz Ltd, 233 S. Franklin St., Juneau, AK 99801-1323. 907-586-3037. Contact: Adele Henry. Self-publisher. Does not accept unsolicited submissions.
ARTS

Right White Line, 531 N. Inlet, Lincoln City, OR 97367.
UNSPECIFIED

Ritz Publishing, 202 W. Fifth Ave, Ritzville, WA 99169. 509-659-4336. Publisher: Star Andersen. Contact: David Andersen. Alternative press for Vietnam War literature. Trade paperbacks and semiannual journal (Adventures in Hell). Vietnam War-related poetry, fiction, 1st person historical narratives. Length open. Reports in 1 mo; publishing time varies. Query/SASE. No dot matrix. Typed ms, or laser (suitable for scanning). "I believe wholeheartedly that this writing helps in the healing process of a war wound of the nation, as well as helping new authors get established."
FICTION, AMERICAN HISTORY, MILITARY/VETS

River West Books, 663 S. 11th St., Coos Bay, OR 97420. 503-269-1363. Contact: Nathan Douthit.
UNSPECIFIED

Robert Briggs Associates, 400 Second Street #108, Lake Oswego, OR 97034. 503-635-0435. Editor: Robert Briggs. Publishes new age books and pamphlets. No unsolicited submissions accepted, all rights acquired. Query with letter and SASE. Reports in 5-7 weeks. Publishes in 1-8 months. Nonfiction material accepted.
NEW AGE

Robinson Publishing Company Inc., 207 S.W. 150th, Seattle, WA 98166.
UNSPECIFIED

Rockland Publishing, PO Box 1597, Kalispell, MT 59901. 406-756-9079. Contact: Judy Overbeek. Publishes original softcover advanced computer books. Pays royalties. Query w/clips. Dot matrix, electronic/modem, computer disk submissions OK. Reports in 3-4 weeks. Publishes within 1 yr.
COMPUTERS, HOW-TO, TECHNICAL

Roger Pond & Associates, PO Box 289, Goldendale, WA 98620-0289. 509-773-4718. Contact: Roger Pond. Publishers of books on rural life.
FAMILY

Rose Press, 6531 S.E. Ivon St., Portland, OR 97206.
UNSPECIFIED

Rose Wind Press, 2110 S.E. 105th Ct., Vancouver, WA 98664. 206-693-7742. Contact: Mary Rose. Publisher of hard & softcover literary books. Send query letter & outline /sample chapters before sending ms. Pays royalties/other

on publication. Acquires first/other rights. Dot matrix or photocopy OK. Responds in 3-4 months; publishes in 1-2 years. Accepts nonfiction, biography, memoirs. "Small, quality press concentrating on subjects of general appeal to Northwest audience."
BIOGRAPHY, HISTORY NW/REGIONAL, MILITARY/VETS

Royal British Columbia Museum, 675 Belleville St., Victoria, BC V8V 1X4. 604-387-6357. Contact: Gerry Truscott.
SCHOLARLY/ACADEMIC

Ruth Edwins-Conley Publishing, 495 Aeneas Valley Rd., Tonasket, WA 98855. 206-659-1229. Contact: Ruth Edwins-Conley. Self-publisher of 1-2 softcover subsidy books a yr; poems, fiction, diaries of literary merit, translations. Press run: 100. Not a freelance market.
FICTION, POETRY

Ryder Press, 424 N.W. 14th, Portland, OR 97209.
UNSPECIFIED

Sachett Publications, 100 Waverly Dr., Grants Pass, OR 97526. 503-476-6404. Self-publisher of 1 softcover original book a year. Print run: 1,000-2,500. Not a freelance market. Catalog.
COLLECTING, EDUCATION, TRAVEL

Sagebrush Books, 25 N.W. Irving Ave, Bend, OR 97701. 503-385-7025; 1-800-779-7025. Contact: Carey Vendrame. Ads: Carla Wigle. Publisher of hard- and softcover children's and young adult books. Unsolicited submissions OK. Payment negotiable. Acquires first rights. Ms/SASE, photocopy OK. Responds in 4-6 weeks; publishes in 1 yr. Fiction, nonfiction, juvenile. "We want to publish children's stories with a regional 'feel'. We are not interested in stories that are cute or condescending. Northwest authors and illustrators only." Brochure.
CHILDREN/TEEN, FICTION

Sagebrush Heritage, 368 N.E. 19th Ave., Hillsboro, OR 97124. 503-648-4587. Contact: Robert J. White. Self-publisher of books on Oregon history and the Seabees of WWII.
NW/REGIONAL HISTORY, MILITARY/VETS

Sagittarius Press, 930 Taylor, Port Townsend, WA 98368. 206-385-0277.
CRAFTS/HOBBIES, NW/REGIONAL HISTORY

Sakura Press, 36787 Sakura Lane, Pleasant Hill, OR 97455-9727. 503-747-5817. Self-publisher of 1-3 softcover originals a year and tapes & cards. Print run: 500. Not a freelance market. Assignment only.
ASIA, LANGUAGE(S)

Salmonberry Publishing Company, PO Box 479, Skagway, AK 99840. 907-983-2674. Editor: Cindy Roland. Publishes softcover books. Accepts unsolicited submissions. Submit query/SASE. Responds in 1 mo; publishes in 1 yr. Accepts fiction, nonfiction, biography, photos, interviews, memoirs must relate to Alaska.
ALASKA

San Juan Naturals, PO Box 642, Friday Harbor, WA 98250. 206-378-2648. Contact: Lee Sturdivant. Self-publisher of softcover books.
UNSPECIFIED

Sandhill Publishing, Box 197 Sta A, Kelowna, BC V1Y 7N5. 604-763-1406. Editor: Nancy Wise. Publisher of books on BC history and outdoor recreation.
BIOGRAPHY, BRITISH COLUMBIA, SPORTS

Sandpiper Press, PO Box 286, Brookings, OR 97415. 503-469-5588. Contact: Marilyn Riddle. Publisher of softcover books for vision-impaired (18 pt. large print books). No unsolicited submissions. Submit query, SASE. Photocopies, dot matrix, simultaneous subs OK. Reports in 2 mos. Accepts nonfiction, fiction, poetry, cartoons. Topics: save the planet, peace, brotherhood, one God seen from many angles and our constant companion, verified Native American legends, healing plants, first-person experiences

of rising above physical handicaps to find what we CAN do instead of settling for what we can't (no bragging or preaching). Rod Serling type short stories; no horror; want irony, moral, and surprise ending. Guidelines, catalog.
FANTASY/SCI FI, PEACE, DISABLED

Santiam Books, 744 Mader Ave. S.E., Salem, OR 97302.
UNSPECIFIED

Saratoga Publishers, 1581 W. Links Way, Oak Harbor, WA 98277. 206-675-9592. Contact: Laura Moore & Deborah Skinner. Self publisher only.
FOOD/COOKING

Sasquatch Publishing Company, 1931 2nd Ave., Seattle, WA 98101. Contact: David Brewster. 6-8 hard- & softcover nonfiction originals per yr, mostly guidebooks and reprints of *Weekly* material. Pays royalties. Query with outline, sample chapters, SASE. Nonfiction: travel in the N.W. and other nonfiction for and about the N.W. "Most of our books are produced totally by in-house staff of writers and researchers, though we have purchased material from other writers on occasion." Catalog.
NORTHWEST, TRAVEL

Saturday's Child, PO Box 148, Cloverdale, OR 97112. Self-publisher.
CHILDREN/TEEN, FAMILY

Sauvie Island Press, 14745 N.W. Gillihand Rd., Portland, OR 97231.
UNSPECIFIED

SCW Publications, 1011 Boren Ave. #155, Seattle, WA 98104. 206-682-1268. Publisher: Jack R. Evans. Histories of cities in Washington State.
HISTORY NW/REGIONAL

Sea Grant Program, University of Alaska, 303 Tanaka Dr., Bunnell Bldg. Rm. 3, Fairbanks, AK 99701.
COLLEGE/UNIVERSITY, NATURAL HISTORY, SCIENCE

Sea Pen Press & Paper Mill, 2228 N.E. 46th St., Seattle, WA 98105.
UNSPECIFIED

Seablom Design Books, 2106 2nd Ave. N., Seattle, WA 98109.
UNSPECIFIED

Seagull Publishing, 2628 W. Crockett, Seattle, WA 98199.
UNSPECIFIED

The Seal Press, 3131 Western Ave., #410, Seattle, WA 98121. 206-283-7844. Editors: Faith Conlon and Barbara Wilson. Publishes 10 softcover originals, reprints, a year. Press run 4,000-10,000. Query w/clips, SASE. Dot matrix, photocopied OK. Reports in 4-8 wks. Accepts nonfiction, fiction. "We are a feminist publisher specializing in works by women writers." Catalog.
FEMINISM, GAY/LESBIAN, WOMEN

Searchers Publications, 4314 Island Crest Way, Mercer Island, WA 98040.
UNSPECIFIED

Seattle Airplane Press, 6727 Glen Echo Lane, Tacoma, WA 98499.
UNSPECIFIED

Seattle Audubon Society, 8028 35th Ave. N.E., Seattle, WA 98115. 206-523-4483. Educational/environmental publisher of hard- & softcover books. Query w/SASE, outline. Photocopies, simultaneous subs OK. Responds 15 days. "This is an active environmental organization. It helps to understand the audience." Guidelines.
WASHINGTON, NORTHWEST, CONSERVATION

Seattle Group Theatre, PO Box 45430, Seattle, WA 98145-0430. 206-685-4969. Contact: Nancy Griffiths, Dramaturg/Lit. Mgr. Submit synopsis, sample dialogue, SASE. Responds 4-6 months. Production 3-4 months.
DRAMA

Second Amendment Foundation, James Madison Bldg., 12500 N.E. 10th Pl., Bellevue, WA 98005.
UNSPECIFIED

Second Language Publications, PO Box 1700, Blaine, WA 98230.
LANGUAGE(S)

Self-Counsel Press Inc., 1704 N. State St., Bellingham, WA 98225. 206-676-4530. Publisher of softcover original books, legal and business self-help. Query w/SASE. Guidelines, catalog.
BUSINESS, HOW-TO

Seven Buffaloes Press, PO Box 249, Big Timber, MT 59011. Contact: Art Cuelho. Publisher of a newsletter series, poetry, fiction, essays; devoted to the rural heritage, farmers, workers, the land, and to regionalism. "The role of the small press is at best the seedbed of this country's best potential writers and poets. You can pick up 50 to over 100 magazines in this country and find the same poets in all of them. You don't see that in magazines or presses where strong focus is on regionalism." Query/SASE. Catalog.
AGRICULTURE/FARMING, FICTION, POETRY

Shane Press, 4719 S.E. Woodstock, Portland, OR 97206.
UNSPECIFIED

Shaun Higgins Publisher, W. 428 27th Ave., Spokane, WA 99203.
UNSPECIFIED

Shiloh Publishing House, 1490 Greenview Ct., Woodburn, OR 97071. 503-981-4328. Editor: Jerry Robeson. Self-publisher. Not a freelance market. Catalog.
RELIGION

Shorey Publications, 110 Union St., PO Box 21626, Seattle, WA 98111.
UNSPECIFIED

Signmaker Press, PO Box 967, Ashland, OR 97520.
UNSPECIFIED

Signpost Books, 8912 192nd S.W., Edmonds, WA 98026. 206-776-0370. Contact: Cliff Cameron. Softcover originals on N.W. outdoor recreation, with emphasis on hiking, bicycling, canoeing/kayaking, and cross country skiing. Accepts freelance material. Pay negotiated. Query, sample chapters, SASE. Dot matrix, photocopies, simultaneous submissions, electronic (call first) OK. Reports in 3-4 wks. Accepts nonfiction. Topics: self-propelled outdoor recreation activities in the Pacific N.W. Length 100-250 published pgs, including text, photos, maps. "In addition to showing knowledge of a subject, it is impressive when the author shows that he/she has considered the whole book, including artwork, appendices, promotional material for covers, potential markets, and other details of the finished book."
BICYCLING, OUTDOOR, RECREATION

Signpost Press Inc., 1007 Queen St., Bellingham, WA 98226. 206-734-9781. Softcover books and semiannual magazine (see Bellingham Review). Book, mag editor: Knute Skinner. Sub $5/yr. Circ. 600. Uses freelance material. Byline given. Submit query for books, complete ms for magazine, w/SASE. Accepts fiction, poetry, plays. Tip: submission period is from Sept 1 to March 1. Guidelines for magazine; sample $2.50.
DRAMA, FICTION, POETRY

Silver Bay Herb Farm, 9151 Tracyton Blvd., Bremerton, WA 98310. 206-692-1340. Contact: Mary Preus.
GARDENING

The Silver Creek Press, PO Box 925, Hailey, ID 83333. Contact: Jan Roddy or Joan Nelson.
UNSPECIFIED

Silver Fox Connections, 3614 Larchmont Ave. N.E., Tacoma, WA 98422-2235. Contact: Emilie Johnson.
UNSPECIFIED

Silver Pennies Press, 1365 E. 30th Ave., Eugene, OR 97405.
UNSPECIFIED

Silver Seal Books, PO Box 106, Fox Island, WA 98333.
UNSPECIFIED

Silverleaf Press, PO Box 70189, Seattle, WA 98107. Editor: Ann E. Larson. Publishes softcover original books. Accepts unsolicited submissions. Pays royalties on publication. Submit ms, SASE. Dot matrix, photocopied OK. Reports in 1-3 mos; publishes in 6-12 mos. Accepts fiction, cartoons. Topics: feminist writing, does not have to be political, but should contain strong women (including lesbian) characters. Currently accepting novels and short story collections. Catalog.
FICTION, GAY/LESBIAN, WOMEN

Skagit County Historical Society, PO Box 818, LaConner, WA 98257-0818.
NW/REGIONAL HISTORY, WASHINGTON

Skein Publications, PO Box 5326, Eugene, OR 97405. Contact: Nancy A. Hoskins. Self publisher of softcover books. No unsolicited submissions.
UNSPECIFIED

Skookum Publications, Site 176, Comp. 4, 1275 Riddle Rd., Penticton, BC V2A 6J6. 604-492-3228. Editor: Doug Cox. Publisher of 2-3 softcover books a year. Does not accept freelance submissions.
BRITISH COLUMBIA, NW/REGIONAL HISTORY

Skribent Press, 9700 S.W. Lakeside Dr., Tigard, OR 97223.
UNSPECIFIED

Sky House Publishers, PO Box 1718, 318 N. Last Chance Gulch, Helena, MT 59624. 406-442-6597. Contact: Rick Newby. Ads: Beth Uda Massman. An imprint of Falcon Press Publishing Co Inc.
NW/REGIONAL HISTORY, MONTANA, OLD WEST

SL Publishers, Box F110-223, Blaine, WA 98230.
UNSPECIFIED

Slug Press, 128 E. 23rd Ave., Vancouver, BC V5V 1X2.
UNSPECIFIED

Small Pleasures Press, 88 Virginia Street #29, Seattle, WA 98101.
UNSPECIFIED

Smith Smith &. Smith Publishing Company, 17515 S.W. Blue Heron Rd., Lake Oswego, OR 97034. 503-636-2979. Contact: Harriet Smith.
UNSPECIFIED

Smith-Western Inc., 1133 N.W. Glisan St., Portland, OR 97209.
UNSPECIFIED

Snohomish Publishing Company, PO Box 499, Snohomish, WA 98290. 206-568-4121. Contact: David Mach. Publisher of 50 softcover, reprint books a year. Accepts freelance material. Rights purchased: First. Query with outline, SASE. Photocopies, electronic OK. Nonfiction, fiction, poetry, photos, plays, cartoons. Guidelines.
LITERATURE, MEDIA/COMMUNICATIONS, PUBLISHING/PRINTING

Socialist Party of Canada, Box 4280, Vancouver, CANADA V8X 3X8. Contact: Steve Szalai. Publisher of quarterly journal. Accepts freelance material: articles, op/ed. Byline given. Sample $1.
POLITICS, SOCIALIST/RADICAL, ECONOMICS

Society of Photo-Optical Instrumentation Engineering, PO Box 10, 1022 19th St., Bellingham, WA 98227-0010. 206-676-3290; Fax 206-647-1445. Contact: Eric Pepper, Senior Editor. Book and newspaper publisher. Newspaper accepts material relevant to optical and optoelectronic engineering. Contact Rich Donelly, Managing Editor. Circ. 30,000 (members only). Submit query letter, outline, sample chapters, synopsis. Dot matrix, photocopies, simultaneous subs OK. Pays in copies. Photo specs: B&W.
BUSINESS, SCIENCE, TECHNICAL

Solstice Press, Box 9223, Moscow, ID 83843. 208-882-0888. Contact: Ivar Nelson. Publisher and packager of hard- and softcover nonfiction books of national and/or regional interest. Accepts unsolicited submissions. Query w/SASE/outline/sample chapters. Photocopied and simultaneous subs OK. Pays royalties. Responds in 2 weeks; publishes in 2 months.
NW/REGIONAL HISTORY, NORTHWEST, TRAVEL

Solstice Press, Box 111272, Anchorage, AK 99511.
ALASKA, UNSPECIFIED

Sono Nis Press, 1745 Blanshard St., Victoria, BC V8W 2J8. 604-382-1024. Editor: Patricia M. Sloan. Publishes 10 hard- & softcover originals per yr. Accepts unsolicited submissions. Pays royalties. Submit query w/clips, SASE. Dot matrix, photocopied, simultaneous OK. Reports in 3 wks. Accepts nonfiction, poetry, humor.
BRITISH COLUMBIA, NW/REGIONAL HISTORY, POETRY

Sonotek Publishing Ltd, PO Box 1752, Merritt, BC V0K 2B0. 604-378-5930. Contact: Murphy O. Shewchuk. Small, one-man publishing house specializing in BC interior nonfiction books. Eight titles since 1989. No unsolicited mss. Send query letter w/SASE, outline.
UNSPECIFIED

Source Publishing, 5820 S.E. 20th Ave., Portland, OR 97202-5226. Contact: Jan Kennedy.
UNSPECIFIED

Sourdough Enterprises, 16401 3rd Ave. S.W., Seattle, WA 98166. 206-244-8115. Contact: Howard Clifford. Publisher of 2-3 softcover originals, reprints a year for an audience of travel, history, rail fans. Press run: 500-20,000. Accepts freelance material. Rights purchased: First. Query w/SASE. Photocopies, simultaneous submissions OK. Reports in 2-3 wks. Nonfiction.
ALASKA, GENERAL HISTORY, TRAVEL

Southern Oregon Historical Society, 106 N. Central Ave., Medford, OR 97501-5926. 503-773-6536. Bimonthly magazine founded in 1946. Editor: Catherine Noah. Ads: Joy Dunn. Membership/Circ. 3,000. Uses freelance material. Byline given. Pays money, copies on acceptance. Acquires 1st rights. Submit query letter, complete ms, SASE, phone. Photocopy, simultaneous subs OK. Responds in 2-3 mo; publishing time varies. Accepts biography, interviews, memoirs, oral history, photos (B&W, $10-50). Topics: regional history, thoroughly documented, accurate. Guidelines; sample $2.50.
AMERICAN HISTORY, NW/REGIONAL HISTORY, OREGON

Southwestern Oregon Publishing Co., 350 Commercial, Coos Bay, OR 97420. 503-269-1222.
UNSPECIFIED

Sovereign Press, 326 Harris Rd., Rochester, WA 98579. Publisher of 5 books a year.
UNSPECIFIED

Special Child Publications, J.B. Preston, Editor & Publisher, PO Box 33548, Seattle, WA 98133. 206-771-5711. Editor & Publisher: J. B. Preston. Publisher of 5-10 softcover originals, subsidy (rarely) books a year. Print run: 500-2,000. Rarely accepts freelance material. Payment: 10% of cash received, payable 6 mos after close of royalty period. Rights purchased: All. Query with outline, SASE. Photocopies OK. Reports in 1 mo. Publishes in 1-3 yrs. Professional books, college texts, curriculum guides, assessment instruments. Mss must be neatly typed, following Chicago Manual. Authorial style should approximate Psychology Today or Omni. Guidelines, catalog.
EDUCATION, PSYCHOLOGY, TEXTBOOKS

Special Interest Publications, 202-1132 Hamilton St., Vancouver, BC V6B 2S2.
UNSPECIFIED

Spencer Butte Press, 84889 Harry Taylor Rd., Eugene, OR 97405. 503-345-3962. Editor: Lois Barton. Self-publisher of softcover books. Not a freelance market.
NW/REGIONAL HISTORY, NATIVE AMERICAN, POETRY

Spice West Publishing Company, PO Box 2044, Pocatello, ID 83201.
UNSPECIFIED

Spirit Mountain Press, PO Box 1214, Fairbanks, AK 99707. 907-452-7585. Contact: Larry Laraby. Self-publisher of 3-6 softcover books about AK. Print run: 1,500. Accepts freelance material. Rights purchased: First. Submit ms, SASE. Dot matrix, photocopies OK. Reports in 1-6 mos. Publishes in 6-12 mos. Nonfiction, fiction, poetry. We are looking for material from or about Alaska primarily. Catalog.
ALASKA, BIOGRAPHY, POETRY

Spokane Area Economic Devel. Council, PO Box 203, Spokane, WA 99210. 509-624-9285. Contact: Meri Berberet. Private nonprofit book publisher & newsletter. Sub $14/yr. Circ. 2,000. Not a freelance market. Sample $3.50.
ECONOMICS, WASHINGTON

Spokane House Enterprises, 2904 W. Garland Ave., Spokane, WA 99205-2336.
UNSPECIFIED

Springfield Historical Commission, Planning Department, Springfield City Hall, Springfield, OR 97477.
NW/REGIONAL HISTORY, OREGON

ST 02 Publishing, 203 Si Town Rd., Castle Rock, WA 98611.
UNSPECIFIED

St. Nectarios Press, 10300 Ashworth Ave. N., Seattle, WA 98133-9410. 206-522-4471. Self-publisher of 3-4 softcover originals, reprints a year for Eastern Orthodox Christian audience. Print run: 2,000. Not a freelance market. Catalog.
RELIGION

St. Paul's Press, PO Box 100, Sandy, OR 97055.
UNSPECIFIED

Stan Jones Publishing Inc., 3421 E. Mercer St., Seattle, WA 98112. 206-323-3970. Editor: Stan Jones. Self-publisher of 12 softcover fishing, outdoor-oriented books a yr. Average print run 15,000. Not a freelance market. Catalog.
FISHING, FOOD/COOKING, NORTHWEST

Star Press, Box 835, Friday Harbor, WA 98250.
UNSPECIFIED

Star System Press, PO Box 15202, Wedgewood Station, Seattle, WA 98115.
UNSPECIFIED

Star Valley Publications, PO Box 421, Noti, OR 97461. 503-935-3032. Contact: Greg Williams. Publisher of hard- & softcover books, newsletter.
HEALTH, WRITING, HOW-TO

Starbright Books, 1611 E. Dow Rd., Freeland, WA 98249.
UNSPECIFIED

StarLance Publications, 50 Basin Dr., Mesa, WA 99343. 509-269-4497. Publishes 4-6 titles per year; collections of fantasy & sf illustrations, cartoons, graphic novels, and illustrated fantasy & sf short fiction. Reports in 2-4 wks. Payment: negotiable. No further submission info; query w/SASE.
FANTASY/SCI FI, FICTION

Starmont House, PO Box 851, Mercer Island, WA 98040. Contact: Ted Dikty.
UNSPECIFIED

Stay Away Joe Publishers, Box 2054, Great Falls, MT 59401.
UNSPECIFIED

Stay Smart Shoppers, 2729 S. Marylhurst Dr., West Linn, OR 97068.
CONSUMER

Stephens Press, Drawer 1441, Spokane, WA 99210.
UNSPECIFIED

Steppingstone Press, 3113 Falling Brook Ln., Boise, ID 83706. 208-384-1577. Editors: Martha Miller, Dorris Murdock.
CHILDREN/TEEN

Sternwheeler Press, 19500 Hidden Springs Rd., #25, West Linn, OR 97068. 503-636-7580. Contact: S.A. Carrigan. No unsolicited submissions. Submit query letter, SASE. Responds in 3 mos; publishes in 1 year. Accepts nonfiction. Topics: all aspects of personal computers written specifically for non-technical computer users cookbooks and menu books for singles and small families.
COMPUTERS, FOOD/COOKING

The Stoma Press, 13231 42nd Ave. N.E., Seattle, WA 98125.
UNSPECIFIED

Stonechild Press, PO Box 1612, Havre, MT 59501. 406-265-2005. Editor: Paul Russette. Greeting cards, and subsidy books. Pays money, copies, royalties, advance. Acquires 1st, 2nd rights. Submit query letter, complete ms, synopsis, sample chapters, SASE. Photocopy OK. Responds in 2 wks; publishes in 3 mos. Accepts greeting card poetry, fiction, nonfiction, cartoons, biography.
POETRY

Stonehouse Publications, Timber Butte Rd., Box 390, Sweet, ID 83670. Self-publisher only. No submissions.
ARCHITECTURE, HOW-TO

Stoneydale Press Publishing Company, 274 Cap de Villa, Lolo, MT 59847.
UNSPECIFIED

Story Line Press, 3 Oaks Farm, Brownsville, OR 97327-9718. 503-466-5352. Contact: Joseph Bednarik. Publisher of 13 hard & softcover fiction and poetry books per year. Unsolicited submissions accepted. Pays advance; royalties on publication. Acquires all rights. Query letter, SASE, outline, sample chapters. Photocopy OK. Responds in 2 weeks to 2 months; publishes in one year. Accepts fiction and poetry. Guidelines with SASE. Also see listing for Nicholas Roerich Contest in Resources.
LITERARY, POETRY

Storypole Press, 11015 Bingham Ave. E., Tacoma, WA 98446. Publishes out-of-print books on N.W. Indians and legends. Acquires all rights. Query w/SASE. Responds in 3 mos; publishes in 1 yr.
NATIVE AMERICAN

Storyteller Guidebook Series, 10 S. Kenneway Dr., Medford, OR 97504. Contact: Barbara Budge Griffin.
EDUCATION, HOW-TO, TEXTBOOKS

Straub Printing & Publishing Company, PO Box 1230, Everett, WA 98206.
UNSPECIFIED

Strawberry Hill Press, 3848 S.E. Division St., Portland, OR 97202. 503-235-5989. Editor: Jean-Louis Brindamour. Publisher of softcover and hardcover books. World-wide circulation. Submissions accepted. Pays money, copies and royalties. All rights acquired. Submissions accepted with letter, SASE, outline, sample chapter, photocopy OK. Response in 4-8 weeks. Publication time 18-24 months. Accepts fiction, biographies, nonfiction.
FICTION, BIOGRAPHY

Studio 0403, PO Box 70672, Seattle, WA 98107-0672. Book publisher: fiction, photos, cartoons, other.
FICTION, HUMOR, PHOTOGRAPHY

Studio Solstone, PO Box 4304, Pioneer Sq. Station, Seattle, WA 98110. 206-624-9102. Contact: Michael Yaeger. Self-publisher of 2 softcover books a year. Print run: 5,000.
UNSPECIFIED

Subterranean Company, PO Box 168, Monroe, OR 97456-0168.
UNSPECIFIED

Sumner House Press, 2527 W. Kennewick Ave., Ste. 190, Kennewick, WA 99336. 509-783-7800. Editor: R F. Hill.
UNSPECIFIED

Sun King Publishing Company, 12024 26th Ave S., Seattle, WA 98168-2402.
UNSPECIFIED

Sun Magic, 911 N.E. 45th, Seattle, WA 98105.
UNSPECIFIED

Sunburst, 1322 Coral Dr. W., Tacoma, WA 98466-5832.
UNSPECIFIED

Sunburst Press, PO Box 14205, Portland, OR 97214. Editor: Johnny Baranski. Ads: Grace Jewett. Self-publisher of 1 softcover original book a year. Press run: 300-1,000. Not a freelance market. Catalog.
PEACE, POETRY, RELIGION

Sundance Publishing Company, 1270 Colgan Court S.E., Salem, OR 97302.
UNSPECIFIED

Sundial Press, 2168 Lancaster Dr. N.E., Salem, OR 97305. 503-362-7250. Contact: Lyndon McGill. Ads: Micki Manthe. Self-publisher only. Not a freelance market.
UNSPECIFIED

Sunfire Publications Ltd., PO Box 3399, Langley, BC V3A 4R7. 604-576-6561. Contact: Garnet Basque. Pard- & softcover originals, reprints on historical subjects from British Columbia, Alberta and the Yukon. Catalog.
BRITISH COLUMBIA, CANADIAN HISTORY, OLD WEST

Sunrise Publishing, 109 Highland Ave., Hope, ID 83836.
UNSPECIFIED

Sunrise Tortoise Books, 109 Highland Ave., Hope, ID 83836-9721.
UNSPECIFIED

Survival Education Association, 9035 Golden Givens Rd., Tacoma, WA 98445.
UNSPECIFIED

Swan Raven Company, 1427 N.W. 23rd Ave., Ste. 8, Portland, OR 97210. 503-1274-1337. Contact: David T. Kyle. Publishes softcover books. Unsolicited submissions accepted. Pays royalties. Query letter, sample chapters, complete ms, synopsis. Photocopies, electronic, phone queries OK. Responds in 1 month; publishes in 1 year. Accepts fiction, nonfiction. Catalog.
ASTROLOGY/SPIRITUAL, HEALTH, WOMEN

SwanMark Books, PO Box 2056, Valdez, AK 99686. 907-835-4385. Contact: Harry Swan. Publisher of books about Alaska by Alaskans. Childrens' stories, animal stories, short stories for young adults, stories about Alaskan Native life, works in the humanities for all ages.
ALASKA, CHILDREN/TEEN, FICTION

Sweet Forever Publishing, PO Box 1000, Eastsound, WA 98245. Book publisher of New Age subjects.
NEW AGE

Synesis Press, PO Box 1843-N, Bend, OR 97709. 503-382-6517. Contact: Juliana Panchura. Publishes 6 softcover originals per year. Accepts unsolicited submissions w/SASE. Pays royalties on publication. Query by phone OK. Dot matrix photocopied, computer disk subs OK. Reports in 3 wks. Topics: nonfiction, health/fitness, diet/nutrition, food/cooking, exercise/training, self-help/how-to.
FOOD/COOKING, HEALTH, SPORTS

Syringa Publishing, 1340 Eldorado, #D, Boise, ID 83704. Editor: Susan A. Lewis.
UNSPECIFIED

TABA Publishing Inc., 24103 S.E. 384th St., Enumclaw, WA 98022. 206-825-9709. Contact: Eugene E. Bauer. Publisher of books on the history of the aircraft industry.
AVIATION, GENERAL HISTORY

Tabula Rasa Press, 621 Western Ave., Seattle, WA 98104. 206-682-5185. Editor: John P. Lathourakis. Hard- & softcover books. Unsolicited mss OK. Royalties, copies on publication. Query, complete ms, or by phone. Photocopy, disk/modem subs OK. Responds in 1 mo; publishes in 6 mos-1 yr. Accepts fiction, poetry, biography, nonfiction, articles, short stories (1,000-5,000 wds). Catalog.
BIOGRAPHY, FICTION

Tadalex Books, 10843 Dixon Dr. S., Seattle, WA 98178-2719. Editor: Larry G. Carlson. Ads: LaDonna Brown. Accepts unsolicited submissions. Pays royalties/copies, acquires all rights. Submit ms, query/SASE. Responds in 8 wks; publishes in 6 mos. Accepts science fiction for science education only. No excessive violence, language, sex. Guidelines.
EDUCATION, ENTERTAINMENT, FANTASY/SCI FI

Tag Books, PO Box 111, Independence, OR 97351.
UNSPECIFIED

Tahlkie Books, 2912 N.W. Logan St., Camas, WA 98607. Contact: Jim Attwell. Books on regional and Columbia Gorge history and peoples.
NW/REGIONAL HISTORY

Tai Chi School, PO Box 2424, Bellingham, WA 98227.
SPORTS

Talent House Press, 1306 Talent Ave., Talent, OR 97540. Contact: Paul Hadella. Book Publisher. "Queries are welcome, but keep in mind that our next few projects are already lined up." No unsolicited submissions accepted.
FICTION, LITERARY POETRY

Talonbooks, 201-1019 E. Cordova St., Vancouver, BC V6A 1M8. 604-253-5261. Editor: Michael Barnholden. Book publisher. No unsolicited ms. Query letter w/SASE, outline, sample chapters. Dot matrix, photocopies, simultaneous submissions OK. Unsolicited ms reviewed only twice a yr. Pays royalties. Acquires all rights. Publishes 2x/yr. Concentrates on Canadian authors. Accepts drama (must have been professionally produced), fiction, poetry, nonfiction, photography. Tip: make it new. Catalog.
DRAMA, FICTION, POETRY

Tamarack Books, PO Box 190313, Boise, ID 83719-0313. 208-362-1543. Contact: Kathy Gaudry. Unsolicited submissions accepted w/SASE. Pays royalties. Acquires all rights. Responds 1-3 mos; publishes 12 mos.
US HISTORY, TRAVEL, OLD WEST

Tantalus Research, PO Box 34248, 2405 Pine St., Vancouver, BC V6J 4N8. Contact: David Hardwick. Books on geographical management. No unsolicited manuscripts.
GEOGRAPHY/GEOLOGY

Tantrum Press, 1862 Parker St., Vancouver, BC V5L 2L1. Editor: Charles Watts.
UNSPECIFIED

Tao of Wing Chun Do, 11023 N.E. 131st, Kirkland, WA 98034.
UNSPECIFIED

Target Seattle, 909 4th Ave., Seattle, WA 98104.
UNSPECIFIED

Tari Book Publishers, 2840 Ferry St., Eugene, OR 97405-3634. Contact: Becky or Matt Dravich.
UNSPECIFIED

TASH (The Assn. for Persons with Severe Handicaps), 11201 Greenwood Ave. N., Seattle, WA 98133.
DISABLED

The Tax Tutors, 506 7th Ave., Oregon City, OR 97045. 503-657-9521. Contact: Janis E. Salisbury. Books on taxes.
CONSUMER, ECONOMICS, HOW-TO

Temporal Acuity Press, 1535 121st Ave. S.E., Bellevue, WA 98005.
UNSPECIFIED

Terragraphics, PO Box 1025, Eugene, OR 97440. 503-343-7115. Editor: Peter Powers. Self-publisher. Not a freelance market.
BICYCLING, RECREATION, TRAVEL

TGNW Press, 2429 E. Aloha, Seattle, WA 98112. 206-328-9656. Editor: Roger Herz. Self-publisher. Does not accept unsolicited submissions. Submit query letter, SASE. Dot matrix, simultaneous subs OK. Topics: juvenile.
CHILDREN/TEEN, HUMOR, SPORTS

That Patchwork Place Inc., 18502 142nd Ave. N.E., Woodinville, WA 98072. 206-483-3313. Contact: Nancy Martin. Publisher of 2-5 softcover books a year on quilting, creative sewing. Print run: 12,500. Accepts freelance material. Rights purchased: All. Pay: varies. Query w/outline, SASE. Dot matrix, photocopies OK. Reports in 1 month. Quilting techniques or quilt history; new techniques or speed techniques for patchwork; creative sewing especially that related to folk art, quilting, Christmas and other holidays. Guidelines, catalog.
CRAFTS/HOBBIES, VISUAL ARTS

Theytus Books, Box 218, Penticton, BC V2A 6K3. Editor: Jeff Smith. Book publisher: poetry, fiction, photos, nonfiction.
FICTION, NATIVE AMERICAN, POETRY

Thin Power, 2519 First Ave. #709, Seattle, WA 98121.
HEALTH, UNSPECIFIED

Third Age Press, 1075 N.W. Murray Rd., Ste 277, Portland, OR 97229. 503-690-3251. Contact: Florence Tauber. Publisher of books on aging and health. Accepts unsolicited submissions. Submit query letter.
HEALTH, SENIOR CITIZENS

Thorn Creek Press, 220 N. Van Buren, Moscow, ID 83843.
UNSPECIFIED

Thunderchief Corporation, 18460 S.E. Stephens St., Portland, OR 97233-5537.
UNSPECIFIED

ThunderEgg Publishing, 3929 Overland Rd., Ste 773, Boise, ID 83705. 208-887-4964. Contact: Jana Pewitt. Books on computers and business. No unsolicited mss. Query w/SASE and experience/clips. Responds in 1 mo; publishing time varies. Payment varies.
BUSINESS, COMPUTERS

Timber Press Inc., 9999 S.W. Wilshire, Portland, OR 97225. 503-292-0745. Editor (acquisitions): Dale Johnson. Ads: Michael Fox. Publicity: Debby Garmon. Publishes 45 hard & softcover books in horticulture, fine gardening and forestry, plus selected N.W. regional per yr. Accepts unsolicited submissions. Acquires all rights. Submit query letter, SASE. Dot matrix, photocopied subs OK. Reports in 3-4 wks. Accepts nonfiction: horticulture, landscape design, garden history, botany & other plant sciences, agriculture, farming, forestry, ecology. Catalog.
AGRICULTURE/FARMING, FORESTRY, GARDENING

Timberline Press, PO Box 70071, Eugene, OR 97401. Self-publisher. Not a freelance market.
UNSPECIFIED

The Times Journal Publishing Co., PO Box 73504, Puyallup, WA 98373-0504. Contact: Darlene E. Brown. Book publisher. Does not accept unsolicited submissions. Submit query letter, SASE. Responds in 1 mo. Accepts nonfiction, fiction, biography, photos.
UNSPECIFIED

Tin Man Press, Box 219, Stanwood, WA 98292.
UNSPECIFIED

TIPTOE Literary Service, 110 Wildwood Dr., PO Box 206-H, Naselle, WA 98638-0206. 206-484-7722. Contact: A. Grimm-Richardson. Self-publisher of educational pamphlets. Uses freelance material. Query letter, SASE or phone query. "We use 1,200 to 1,400 words of explicit information as 'Keys to Success' in a variety of fields. We welcome your expertise and use your byline." Catalog.
EDUCATION, HOW-TO, BUSINESS

Tolemac Inc., PO Box 418, Ashland, OR 97520.
UNSPECIFIED

Tops Learning Systems, 10978 S. Mulino Rd., Canby, OR 97013.
EDUCATION

Touch the Heart Press, PO Box 210, Eastsound, WA 98245.
UNSPECIFIED

The Touchstone Press, PO Box 81, Beaverton, OR 97075. 503-646-8081. Contact: Tracy. Publisher of 2-3 softcover originals a year for outdoor people. Print run: 3,000. Accepts freelance material. Payment: Royalties. Rights purchased: All. Query, sample chapters w/SASE. Photocopies OK. Reports in 15-45 days. Publishes in 1 year. Trail guides, wildflower books, wilderness guides, local history (OR, WA, CA, ID, MT, NV). Catalog.
NW/REGIONAL HISTORY, NATURAL HISTORY, OUTDOOR

Town Forum Inc., Cerro Gordo Ranch, PO Box 569, Cottage Grove, OR 97424.
UNSPECIFIED

Townson Publishing Co. Ltd, Box 8023, Blaine, WA 98230. 604-263-0014. Book Publisher. Does not accept unsolicited submissions.
UNSPECIFIED

Toy Investments Inc., 6529 S. 216th St., Kent, WA 98032-2301.
BUSINESS, CRAFTS/HOBBIES, UNSPECIFIED

Trabarni Productions, Box 64026-555 Clarke Rd., Coquitlam, BC V3J 7V6. Contact: Gail D. Whitter. Publisher of softcover original books. No unsolicited submissions. Acquires 1st rights. Book subjects: poetry, mythology, nonfiction, West Coast.
ASTROLOGY/SPIRITUAL, POETRY, WOMEN

Trace Editions, Fine and Rare Books, 3733 N.E. 24th Ave., Portland, OR 97212. 503-284-4749. Contact: Charles Seluzicki. Publisher of 2 hard- & softcover books a year. Print run: 500. Accepts freelance material. Payment: Copies; small cash payment at times. Rights purchased: First. Submit ms, SASE. Photocopies OK. Reports in 1 month. Publishes in 6-12 mos. Nonfiction, fiction, poetry, plays. "Quality writing in well designed offset formats produced to high standards. Primarily mss are solicited. Our authors include Sandra McPherson, Vasko Popa, Charles Wright, Charles Simic and Z Herbert." Catalog.
BOOK ARTS/BOOKS, FICTION, POETRY

Trail City Archives, 1394 Pine Ave., Trail, BC V1R 4E6. 604-364-1262. Contact: Jamie Forbes. Publishes softcover books. Does not accept unsolicited submissions. Query letter, SASE, phone. Responds in 1 wk. Accepts nonfiction, photos, articles. Topics: history.
BRITISH COLUMBIA, CANADIAN HISTORY

Training Associates Ltd., 1701 W. 3rd, Vancouver, BC V6J 1K7. 604-263-7091. Contact: Peter Renner. Publisher of 2 softcover, how-to books a year. Print run: 2,500. Accepts freelance material. Pays biannually; 10-18%; advance to be negotiated. Negotiates rights purchased. Outline, sample chapters w/SASE. Dot matrix, photocopies OK. Reports in 4 wks. Publishes in 6 mos. Nonfiction: how-to, business and training. Catalog.
BUSINESS, EDUCATION, HOW-TO

Trask House Press, 2754 S.E. 27th, Portland, OR 97202. 503-235-1898. Contact: Carlos Reyes. Irregular publisher of poetry books. Print run: 500. Accepts freelance material. Query w/SASE. Reports in 30-60 days. Poetry.
POETRY

Traveler's Companion Press, 16200 S.W. Pacific Hwy., Ste. 175, Tigard, OR 97224.
TRAVEL

Traveller's Bed & Breakfast, PO Box 492, Mercer Island, WA 98040.
TRAVEL

Tremaine Publishing, 2727 Front St., Klamath Falls, OR 97601.
UNSPECIFIED

Tri County Special Services, 48 E. 1st North, St. Anthony, ID 83445.
UNSPECIFIED

Trilogy Books, 4316 Riverside Rd. S., Salem, OR 97306. 503-362-3300. Contact: Kay L. McDonald. Book publisher. Self-publisher only.
UNSPECIFIED

Trout Creek Press, 5976 Billings Rd., Parkdale, OR 97041. 503-352-6494. Contact: Laurence F. Hawkins. Publishes a semi-annual literary magazine. Founded 1982. Circ. 300. Sub/$7. Freelance material accepted; byline given. Pays copies on publication. Acquires first rights. Query letter, SASE. Photocopy, Mac disk, simultaneous subs, dot matrix, OK. Responds in 1-3 months; publishes in 6 months to a year. Accepts fiction, poetry, nonfiction, interviews, articles, plays, reviews, memoirs. Guidelines, catalog, back issues. Send SASE.
FICTION, POETRY, AVANT-GARDE/EXPERIMENTAL

Truth on Fire (Hallelujah) Publishing, The Bible Holiness Movement, PO Box 223, Postal Sta. A, Vancouver, BC V6C 2M3. 604-498-3895. Contact: Wesley H. Wakefield. Publishes 2-3 softcover assigned originals, reprints a year. Submit query letter, outline, sample chapters or synopsis. Dot matrix, photocopies, simultaneous subs OK. Pays royalties. Responds 6 wks. Accepts nonfiction, biography with evangelical Christian bent.
RELIGION

Turman Publishing Company, 1319 Dexter Ave. N., Seattle, WA 98109-3519. 206-282-6900. Softcover book publisher. Accepts unsolicited submissions. Pays money on acceptance. Acquires all rights. Submit query letter, outline, sample chapters, synopsis, SASE. Disk (Word 4) OK. Responds in 6 wks; publishes in 4 mos. Accepts nonfiction, fiction, biography. Topics: for young adult low readers. Guidelines, catalog.
BIOGRAPHY, FICTION

Turock Fitness Publishers, 6206 114th Ave. N.E., Kirkland, WA 98033-7203.
HEALTH

Twin Peaks Press, PO Box 129, Vancouver, WA 98666. 206-694-2462. Contact: Helen Hecker. Publishes hard- & softcover reprints. Accepts unsolicited submissions. Submit query, SASE. Pays on publication. Dot matrix, photocopied, simultaneous OK. Accepts nonfiction.
MEDICAL, TRAVEL, HOW-TO

Two Magpie Press, PO Box 177, Kendrick, ID 83537. 208-276-4130. Not a freelance market. Query w/SASE.
UNSPECIFIED

Two Rivers Press, 28070 S. Meridian Rd., Aurora, OR 97002.
UNSPECIFIED

Umbrella Books, Harbor View Publications Group, 440 Tucker Ave., PO Box 1460-A, Friday Harbor, WA 98250-1460. 206-378-5128. Editor: Jerome K. Miller. Publishes 4 softcover original books a year. Accepts unsolicited submissions. Pays 10% royalty plus payment for photos. Submit query w/clips, SASE. Dot matrix, computer disk OK. Reports in 6 wks. Publishes very promptly. Accepts nonfiction. Topics: tour guides to the Pacific Northwest. Guidelines.

NORTHWEST, TRAVEL

Unicornucopia, 1824 S.W. Market St., #H, Portland, OR 97201-2481.

UNSPECIFIED

Unique Press, 917 Pacific Ave. #216, Tacoma, WA 98402-4421. 206-272-1609. Editors: Ann Roush, Jon Martin. Subsidy publishing imprint of R & M Press. Accepts nonfiction, memoirs, poetry, biography, and photos.

CHILDREN (BY/ABOUT), POETRY, UNSPECIFIED

University of Alaska Institute of Marine Science, University of Alaska, Fairbanks, AK 99775-1080. Contact: Helen Stockholm.

COLLEGE/UNIVERSITY, NATURAL HISTORY, SCIENCE

University of Alaska Museum, 907 Yukon Dr., Fairbanks, AK 99775. 907-474-6939. Publisher of softcover books & annual newsletter. Free. Circ. 50,000. Query w/ SASE. Catalog, sample.

ALASKA, ANTHROPOLOGY/ARCHAEOLOGY, NATURAL HISTORY

University of Alaska Press, Gruening Bldg., 1st Floor, University of Alaska, Fairbanks, AK 99775-1580. 907-474-6389. Managing Editor: Carla Helfferich. Acquisitions: Pam Odom. Ads: Debbie Van Stone. Publishes hard- & softcover original, reprint books. Accepts unsolicited submissions. Submit ms, SASE. Nonfiction: emphasis on scholarly and nonfiction works related to Alaska, the circumpolar north, and the North Pacific rim. Guidelines, catalog.

ALASKA, COLLEGE/UNIVERSITY, SCHOLARLY/ACADEMIC

University of British Columbia Press, 6344 Memorial Rd., Vancouver, BC V6T 1Z2. 604-822-3259. Editor: Jean Wilson. Ads: Berit Kraus. Publishes hard- & softcover originals, reprints, subsidy books. Accepts unsolicited submissions. Pays royalties. Acquires all rights. Submit query w/outline, sample chapters. Disk, photocopies OK. Accepts nonfiction. Topics: humanities and social sciences: monographs and upper level textbooks. Catalog, guidelines.

SCHOLARLY/ACADEMIC, NATIVE AMERICAN, CANADIAN HISTORY

University of Idaho Ctr for Business Development & Research, College of Business & Economics, University of Idaho, Moscow, ID 83843.

BUSINESS, ECONOMICS, IDAHO

University of Idaho Press, The University of Idaho, Moscow, ID 83843. 208-885-7564; 208-885-6245. Editor: James J. Heaney. Ads: Mitzi Boyd, 208-885-6245. Publishes hard- & softcover, original, reprint, subsidy books. Accepts unsolicited submissions. Pays 8-12% net royalties, advance on publication. Acquires all, 2nd rights. Submit query letter, outline sample chapters, SASE. Photocopied, dot matrix disk/modem subs OK. Reports in 3 mo; publishes in 12 mos. Accepts nonfiction, fiction: scholarly and regional, including Native American studies, resource and policy studies, Pacific Northwest history and natural history, literature and criticism. Ms between 25,000-100,000 wds. Catalog.

NW/REGIONAL HISTORY, NATIVE AMERICAN, SCHOLARLY/ ACADEMIC

University of Oregon Bureau of Governmental Research/Service, University of Oregon, PO Box 3177, Eugene, OR 97403.

PUBLIC AFFAIRS

University of Oregon Center for Educational Policy & Management, College of Education, University of Oregon, Eugene, OR 97403.

EDUCATION

University of Oregon Ctr of Leisure Studies, Department of Recreation/Parks, Rm. 138, Eugene, OR 97403.

RECREATION

University of Oregon Forest Industries Management Ctr, College of Business Administration, University of Oregon, Eugene, OR 97405.

BUSINESS, FORESTRY, NATURAL HISTORY

University of Washington Press, Box 50096, Seattle, WA 98105. 206-543-4050. Contact: Naomi Pascal. General publisher of trade and academic books, biographies, arts, travel, Native American, history. Catalog.

ARTS, NW/REGIONAL HISTORY, NATIVE AMERICAN

University Press of the Pacific, Box 66129, Seattle, WA 98166. Not a freelance market.

UNSPECIFIED

Update, B.C. Teachers' Federation, 2235 Burrard St., Vancouver, BC V6T 3H9.

BRITISH COLUMBIA, EDUCATION, LABOR/WORK

Upper Case Publications, 1018 Oliphant Ave., Victoria, BC V8V 2V1. 604-380-0349. Editor: Eileen Marrett. Ads: John Marrett. Self-publisher of softcover books. Unsolicited submissions not accepted. Publisher of titles related to travel, family.

TRAVEL, ENTERTAINMENT, FAMILY.

Upword Press, PO Box 1106, Yelm, WA 98597. 206-458-3619. Editor: Lyn Evans. Ads: Warren Evans. Hard- & softcover originals. Unsolicited mss OK. Submit query w/ clips, ms, SASE. Dot matrix, photocopied OK. Reports in 6 wks. Nonfiction, fiction: New Age, metaphysical.

ASTROLOGY/SPIRITUAL, AVANT-GARDE/EXPERIMENTAL, NEW AGE

Urban Design Centre Society, 1630 E. Georgia St., Vancouver, BC V5L 2B2. Book publisher. Query w/SASE.

ARCHITECTURE, CULTURE

U.S. Department of Ag Forest Service, Pacific N.W. & Range Experiment Sta., PO Box 3890, Portland, OR 97208.

AGRICULTURE/FARMING, CONSERVATION, NATURAL HISTORY

User-Friendly Press, 6552 Lakeway Dr., Anchorage, AK 99502-1949. 907-243-5589. Contact: Ann Chandonnet. Self-publisher of 1 or fewer softcover books a year on Alaskan history or poetry. Does not accept unsolicited submissions. Back list for $7.95.

ALASKA, POETRY, FEMINISM

Vagabond Press, 605 E. 5th Ave., Ellensburg, WA 98926-3201. 509-962-8471. Editor: John Bennett. Publishes 3 softcover books/yr. Press run 1,000. Accepts unsolicited submissions. Pays on publication. Acquires 1st rights. Submit query, SASE. Photocopies OK. Reports in 1 mo. Accepts nonfiction, fiction. Catalog.

FICTION

Vail Publishing, 8285 S.W. Brookridge, Portland, OR 97225. 503-292-9964. Self-publisher of 1 softcover book a year. Print run: 2,000. Not a freelance market. Catalog.

EDUCATION, TEXTBOOKS

Valley View Blueberry Press, 21717 N.E. 68th St., Vancouver, WA 98662.

UNSPECIFIED

Van Dahl Publications, PO Box 10, Albany, OR 97321. 503-928-3569. Editor: Ken Palke. Publisher of 1-2 books per year for stamp collectors. Does not accept unsolicited submissions.

COLLECTING, CRAFTS/HOBBIES

Van Patten Publishing, 4204 S.E. Ogdon St., Portland, OR 97206. 503-775-3815. Editor: George Van Patten. Publisher of hard & softcover books. Accepts unsolicited submissions. Pays copies on publication. Acquires all rights. Submit query letter, outline, SASE—no phone queries

please. Photocopies, simultaneous subs OK. Reports 4-8 wks, publishing time 1 yr. Accepts nonfiction, photos (covers $100-300). Topic: organic gardening. Catalog.

GARDENING

Vandina Press, PO Box 1551, Mercer Island, WA 98040. 206-232-3239. Editor: Francine Porad. Publishes 1-2 softcover poetry chapbooks a year. Also publishes a poetry journal, Brussels Sprout, 3 times a year.

POETRY

Vanessapress, PO Box 81335, Fairbanks, AK 99708. Alaska's only feminist press.

NW/REGIONAL HISTORY, WOMEN

Vardaman Press, 2720 E. 176th St., Tacoma, WA 98445.

UNSPECIFIED

Velosport Press, 1100 E. Pike, Seattle, WA 98122. 206-329-2453. Contact: Denise de la Rosa. Publisher of 1 softcover book a year on cycling. Print run: 6,000. Accepts freelance material. Pay negotiable. Sample chapters w/ SASE. Photocopies OK. Reports in 1 month. Publication time varies.

BICYCLING

Vernier Software, 2920 S.W. 89th St., Portland, OR 97225. 503-297-5317. Editor: Chris Vernier.

COMPUTERS

Vernon Printing & Publishing, 1701 Hwy 83 N., Seely Lake, MT 59868. 406-754-2369. Contact: Suzanne Vernon. Publisher of softcover books. Averages 1-2 titles/yr; print runs less than 3,000. Topics: outdoor and hiking.

OUTDOOR, RECREATION

Vidiot Enterprises, 501 N. M St., Tacoma, WA 98403.

UNSPECIFIED

Vision Books, 790 Commercial Ave., Coos Bay, OR 97420. Publisher of books on philosophy, peace, and nuclear disarmament.

PEACE, PHILOSOPHY, PSYCHOLOGY

Void Press, PO Box 15, Ellensburg, WA 98926-0015. 509-925-1339. Editor: John Stehman. Publisher of softcover books and journal. Accepts unsolicited and freelance material. Byline given. Pays in money, copies on publication. First rights acquired. Submit query letter w/SASE. Photocopies OK. Responds 2 wks. Publishes poetry, nonfiction articles, photos, interviews. Main emphasis on modern shamanism, personal experience, spirit guides, earth energy work, the path of power. Catalog $1.

ASTROLOGY/SPIRITUAL, HOW-TO, NEW AGE

Walking Bird Publishing, 340 N. Grand St., Eugene, OR 97402.

UNSPECIFIED

Washington Cookbook, PO Box 923, Spokane, WA 99210. Cookbook publisher.

CRAFTS/HOBBIES, WASHINGTON

Washington Insurance Commissioner, Insurance Bldg., Olympia, WA 98504.

BUSINESS, CONSUMER, WASHINGTON

Washington Professional Publications, PO Box 1147, Bellevue, WA 98009. 206-643-3147. Self-publisher of real estate books. Not a freelance market.

BUSINESS, CONSUMER, WASHINGTON

Washington Sea Grant Program, University of Washington, 3716 Brooklyn Ave. N.E., Seattle, WA 98105. 206-543-6600. Contact: Louie Echols.

NATURAL HISTORY, SCIENCE

Washington State Historical Society, 315 N. Stadium Way, Tacoma, WA 98403. 206-597-4227. Publisher of hard- and softcover books, plus quarterly mag. Editor: Christina Orange. Accepts nonfiction photos, articles and biography. Query w/SASE. Responds 3-4 wks; pub 1-2 yrs. Magazine Circ. 3,000; sub free w/$30 membership.

NW/REGIONAL HISTORY, WASHINGTON

Washington State Library, Washington/Northwest Room, PO Box 42475, Olympia, WA 98504. 206-753-4024. Contact: Ellen Levesque. Publishes 1 softcover list of Washington-author books per year. Not a freelance market.
REFERENCE/LIBRARY, WASHINGTON, WRITING

Washington State University Press, Cooper Publications Building, Pullman, WA 99164-5910. 509-335-3518. Director: Thomas H. Sanders. Hard- & softcover originals, reprints. Unsolicited mss OK. Pays copies, royalties. Rights acquired vary. Query letter, complete ms, SASE. Dot matrix subs OK. Reports in 1 mo; publishes in 2 yrs. Accepts nonfiction. Topics: regional studies (history, political science, literature, science); Western Americana; Asian American, Black, Women's Studies; Pacific N.W. art, natural sciences. Publishes 5 scholarly journals: *Poe Studies; ESQ: A Journal of the American Renaissance; Northwest Science; Western Journal of Black Studies; Journal of International Education Administrator.* Catalog, guidelines.
NW/REGIONAL HISTORY, MINORITIES/ETHNIC

Waterfront Press Company, 1115 N.W. 45th, Seattle, WA 98107.
UNSPECIFIED

Watermark Press, 6909 58th N.E., Seattle, WA 98115.
UNSPECIFIED

Weather Workbook Company, 827 N.W. 31st St., Corvallis, OR 97330. 503-753-7271. Contact: Charlotte E. Decker.
UNSPECIFIED

Weatherly Press, Division Robert Hale & Co., Inc., 1803-132nd Ave. N.E., #4, Bellevue, WA 98005. 206-881-5212. Editor: Robert Hale.
UNSPECIFIED

Welcome Press, 2701 Queen Anne N., Seattle, WA 98109. 206-282-5336. Self-publisher of 1-2 softcover originals, reprint books of Scandinavian interest. Print run: 2,500. Not a freelance market.
CULTURE, MINORITIES/ETHNIC

Wells & West Publishers, 1166 Winsor St., North Bend, OR 97459.
UNSPECIFIED

West Coast Crime, PO Box 82352, Portland, OR 97282. 503-641-0901. Publisher of hard- & softcover books. Accepts unsolicited submissions. Pays royalties. Acquires all rights. Submit query letter w/SASE, synopsis, outline, sample chapters (max 50 pages). Dot matrix, photocopies, simultaneous subs OK. Responds 2-4 mos; publishes 12-18 mos. Fiction: "Looking for left/progressive mystery novels from West Coast authors."
POLITICS, FICTION

Western Geographical Series, Dept of Geography, U. of Victoria, PO Box 3050, Victoria, BC V8W 3P5. 604-721-7331. Contact: Dr. Harold D. Foster. Book and educational journal publisher. Journal circ. 500-1,000. Query w/SASE. Responds 1 mo; publishes 1 yr. Accepts nonfiction on geology/geography. Sample.
COLLEGE/UNIVERSITY, GEOLOGY/GEOGRAPHY

Western Horizons Books, PO Box 4068, Helena, MT 59604. 406-442-7795. Softcover originas. No unsolicited submissions. Query w/SASE. Photocopied OK. Accepts nonfiction, fiction. Topics: sports boxing, historical Montana, Upper Rocky Mountain Region, Southwest.
NW/REGIONAL HISTORY, MONTANA, SPORTS

Western Horizons Press, 15890 S.E. Wallace Rd., Milwaukie, OR 97222. 503-654-1626.
UNSPECIFIED

Western Publishing, PO Box 61031, Seattle, WA 98121. Contact: Robert D. Ewbank. Periodical. Accepts freelance material. Query w/SASE. Topics: Music, performing arts, poetry, painting.
ARTS, MUSIC, POETRY

Western Traveller Press, 205-2170 W. 1st Ave., Vancouver, BC V6K 1E8. 604-738-8592. Contact: Chris Huddlestay. Publishes guidebooks and travel books. No unsolicited manuscripts.
TRAVEL

Western Wood Products Association, 1500 Yeon Building, Portland, OR 97204.
BUSINESS

Westridge Press Ltd, 1090 Southridge Pl. S., Salem, OR 97302. Contact: Bill Mainwaring. Book publisher. No unsolicited submissions.
OREGON, TRAVEL

Westwind Publishing, 2505 Davis St., Boise, ID 83702.
UNSPECIFIED

W.H. 1, 21349 N.W. St. Helens Rd., Portland, OR 97231.
UNSPECIFIED

Wheatherstone Press, 20 Wheatherstone, Lake Oswego, OR 97034.
UNSPECIFIED

Wheel Press, 9203 S.E. Mitchell St., Portland, OR 97266. 503-777-6659. Contact: Arthur Honeyman. Self-publisher of 2 softcover, original, reprint, subsidy books a year. Audience: Students, educators, sensitive readers of all ages interested in social issues with emphasis on (but not limited to) handicapped people. Print run: 500. Sometimes accepts freelance material. Submit ms, SASE. Reports in 1 month. Nonfiction, fiction, poetry, plays, cartoons. No photographs or multi-colored pictures. Topics: Almost any subject. Catalog.
CHILDREN/TEEN, FICTION, DISABLED

Whistle Punk Books, 2035 Stanley Ave., Victoria, BC V8R 3X7.
UNSPECIFIED

Whistler Publishing, Box 3641, Courtenay, BC V9N 6Z8. 604-334-2852. Contact: K. Ben Buss. Publisher of 10 nonfiction, softcover originals per year to outdoor recreation enthusiasts, environmentally aware. Accepts freelance material. Payment: Money, royalties. Ms outline, sample chapters w/SASE. Nonfiction: Any material applicable to the outdoors from handicrafts to hiking and from cottage industries to flora & fauna. Should be of a practical nature easily illustrated or photographed.
ENVIRONMENT/RESOURCES, OUTDOOR, RECREATION

White Mammoth, 2183 Nottingham Dr., Fairbanks, AK 99709. 907-479-6034. Contact: M. L. Guthrie. Publishes softcover books. Not a freelance market.
ALASKA, NATURAL HISTORY

White Plume Press, 2701 Calif. Ave S.W., Ste. 221, Seattle, WA 98116. 206-343-8399. Contact: Gene Nelson. Publisher of softcover books. Not a freelance market.
GOVERNMENT, POETRY, RELIGION

Whitecap Books, 1086 W. 3rd. St., N. Vancouver, BC V7P 3J6. 604-980-9852. Publisher: Colleen MacMillan. Ads: Robert McCullough. Publishes hard- & softcover books. Accepts unsolicited submissions. Pays advance, royalties. Acquires all rights. Submit query letter, outline, sample chapters, SASE. Photocopy OK. Responds in 3 mos; publishes in 12-18 mos. Accepts nonfiction, photos. Topics: gardening, natural history, history, colour scenic, regional guides plus children's nonfiction.
GARDENING, GENERAL HISTORY, NATURAL HISTORY

Whitman College Press, Office of Publications, Whitman College, Walla Walla, WA 99362.
COLLEGE/UNIVERSITY, EDUCATION

Wilander Publishing Co., 17934 N.W. CheSta.ut Lane, Portland, OR 97231. 503-621-3964. Contact: Jodi L. Fisher. Self-publisher of children's book. Not accepting freelance submissions.
CHILDREN/TEEN

Wilderness House, 11129 Caves Hwy., Cave Junction, OR 97523.
UNSPECIFIED

Wildlife-Wildlands Institute, 5200 Upper Miller Creek Rd., Missoula, MT 59803.
ANIMALS, CONSERVATION, NATURAL HISTORY

Wildwood Press, 209 S.W. Wildwood Ave., Grants Pass, OR 97526. 503-479-3434. Self-publisher of 1 softcover original book. Does not accept unsolicited submissions.
ADVENTURE, OUTDOOR

Willamette Kayak & Canoe Club, PO Box 1062, Corvallis, OR 97339. Book publisher. Query w/SASE.
RECREATION, SPORTS

Willamette River Books, PO Box 605, Troutdale, OR 97060. Contact: Evelyn Sharenov, Douglas Allen Conner. Publishes softcover books. Accepts unsolicited submissions if query with samples, SASE. Pays on acceptance in money, copies. Submit sample chapters. Photocopy, dot matrix, simultaneous subs OK. Reports in 3 mo. Publishes in 9 mo. "We run a competition once or twice yearly, announced in Poets & Writers; we publish chapbooks & collections of poetry." No guidelines or catalog. Samples on request.
POETRY

William & Allen, PO Box 6147, Olympia, WA 98502.
UNSPECIFIED

Willoughby Wessington Publishing Company, 7820 79th Ave. S.E., Mercer Island, WA 98040-5525.
UNSPECIFIED

Wilson Publications, PO Box 712, Yakima, WA 98907. 509-457-8275. Self-publisher. Not a freelance market.
AMERICAN HISTORY, TRAVEL

Wind Vein Press/White Clouds Revue, PO Box 462, Ketchum, ID 83340. 208-788-3704. Contact: Scott Preston. Self-publisher of high quality limited editions. All of the books published by Wind Vein will be privately arranged. Not a freelance market.
BOOK ARTS/BOOKS, IDAHO, POETRY

Windows Watcher Newsletter, CompuTh!nk Inc., 3731 130th Ave. N.E., Bellevue, WA 98005-1353. 206-881-7345. Editor: Jesse Berst. Softcover books, monthly newsletter. Sub $195. Unsolicited mss OK. Query w/SASE.
COMPUTERS, HOW-TO, TECHNICAL

Windyridge Press, PO Box 327, Medford, OR 97501.
UNSPECIFIED

Winn Book Publishers, PO Box 80096, Seattle, WA 98108. 206-763-9544. Contact: Larry Winn. Book publisher. Not a freelance market at this time.

Winterholm Press, PO Box 101251, Anchorage, AK 99510.
UNSPECIFIED

Wise Owl Books & Music, PO Box 621, Kirkland, WA 98083. 206-822-9699. Contact: Mark Ortman. Self-publisher only. Not a freelance market.
PHILOSOPHY, PSYCHOLOGY

Wistaria Press, 4373 N.E. Wistaria Dr., Portland, OR 97213.
UNSPECIFIED

Wizard Works, PO Box 1125, Homer, AK 99603. Contact: Jan O'Meara.
ALASKA, UNSPECIFIED

Wolfdog Publications, PO Box 142506, Dept. R, Anchorage, AK 99514-2506.
UNSPECIFIED

Womanshare Books, PO Box 681, Grants Pass, OR 97526.
WOMEN

Wood Lake Books Inc., Box 700, Winfield, BC V0H 2C0. 604-766-2778. Editor: Ralph Milton. Book and magazine publisher. Uses freelance material. Query w/SASE. Dot matrix, photocopies OK. Responds 4 mos; publishes 1-2 years (books). Subjects: "We publish material for the liberal mainline Christian market in Canada."
RELIGION, FEMINISM, BOOK ARTS/BOOKS

Woodford Memorial Editions Inc., PO Box 55085, Seattle, WA 98155. 206-364-4167. Contact: Jess E. Stewart. Publisher presently accepting only information or mss on Jack Woodford from those who knew him personally. Otherwise concerned mainly with the person and career of Mr. Woodford (Josiah Pitts Woodford) and his ability to inspire people to write books in one's own style. Catalog.
BIOGRAPHY

Word Power Inc., PO Box 17034, Seattle, WA 98107.
LANGUAGE(S)

Words & Pictures Unlimited, 37112 Moss Rock Dr., Corvallis, OR 97330.
UNSPECIFIED

Words Press, 8787 S.W. Becker Dr., Portland, OR 97223. 503-246-9709. Contact: George J. Eicher.
UNSPECIFIED

Wordware, PO Box 14300, Seattle, WA 98114. 206-328-9393. Contact: Marguerite Russell.
UNSPECIFIED

World Wide Publishing Corporation, PO Box 105, Ashland, OR 97520. 503-482-3800. Contact: Hans J. Schneider. Not a freelance market.
ADVENTURE, HOME, TRAVEL

World Without War Council, 2929 N.E. Blakeley St., Seattle, WA 98105. 206-523-4755. Contact: Holf Ruffin. Self-publisher of books.
PEACE, PUBLIC AFFAIRS, REFERENCE/LIBRARY

Write-On Press, Box 86606, N. Vancouver, BC V7L 4L2. 604-858-7739. Editor: Dennis Maracle. Softcover books. Accepts unsolicited submissions. Pays copies, royalties. Acquires all rights. Submit query letter, complete ms, SASE. Photocopy OK. Responds in 2-6 wks. Accepts fiction, poetry, biography, nonfiction, photos, plays. Catalog.
NATIVE AMERICAN, WOMEN

Writer's Publishing Service Company, 1512 Western Ave., Seattle, WA 98101. 206-284-9954; Fax 206-622-6876. Contact: William Griffin, Publisher, or Thomas Aaron, Associate Publisher and Production Manager. Publishes hard- & softcover originals, reprints, subsidy books. Accepts unsolicited submissions. Pays money, copies on publication. Rights acquired depend on the project. Submit query w/clips, ms, SASE or query by phone. Photocopies OK. Reports in 1-2 mos; publishes in 6-12 mos. Accepts nonfiction, fiction, poetry, cartoons, other. "...we do purchase or co-publish 3-5 projects a year." Brochure.
FICTION, GENEALOGY, POETRY

Ye Galleon Press, 103 E. Main, PO Box 287, Fairfield, WA 99012. 509-283-2422; 1-800-488-8928 (book orders only). Contact: Glen Adams. Publisher of hard- & softcover originals, reprints. Accepts freelance material. Acquires 1st rights. Submit query, SASE. Reports in 1 mo. Accepts nonfiction, poetry, biography, memoirs, Northwest Coast voyage books; I publish (at my expense) Pacific N.W. and rare western US history. Modern books with living authors are nearly all paid for by authors, but editions are sometimes split. Catalog.
AMERICANA, AMERICAN HISTORY, NW/REGIONAL HISTORY

Yellow Hat Press, PO Box 34337, Sta. D, Vancouver, BC V6J 4P3. Editor: Beverly D. Chiu.
UNSPECIFIED

Yellow Jacket Press, Rt. 4 Box 7464, Twin Falls, ID 83301. Editor: Bill Studebaker.
LITERATURE

Yinka Dene Language Institute, PO Bag 7000, Vanderhoof, BC V0J 3A0. 604-567-9236. Contact: Linden A. Pinay. Self-publisher of hard and softcover books. Educational organization. Freelance material and unsolicited submissions not accepted. Query by letter or phone. Responds in 7 days. Accepts fiction biography, nonfiction, photos, interviews, and memoirs. Catalog free.
LANGUAGE(S)

Young Pine Press, c/o International Examiner, 622 S. Washington St., Seattle, WA 98104-2720.
UNSPECIFIED

Zen 'n' Ink, PO Box 11714, Winslow, WA 98110. 206-842-4224. Contact: John T. Wood. Founded in 1990, publishes philosophy and psychology softcover books. Not a freelance market.
PHILOSOPHY, PSYCHOLOGY

Notes

Periodicals

1000 Friends of Oregon Newsletter, 534 S.W. 3rd Ave., Ste. 300, Portland, OR 97204. Quarterly newsletter. Byline given. Query w/SASE. Accepts news items, photos (color and B&W, $50-200), interviews, op/ed, articles. Topics: issues of Oregon land use, development and environment. Sample $1.50.
ENVIRONMENT/RESOURCES, CONSERVATION

ACAPella, PO Box 11, Days Creek, OR 97429. 503-825-3647. Editor: Eleanor Davis. Quarterly. Circ. 300. Sub $10. No one receives any remuneration for the publication in ACAPella of their original gospel music or poetry. Accepts nonfiction, poetry. Purpose of our organization is to assist and encourage members in the writing of gospel music and poetry, and provide timely articles about the state of the art. Sample $1.
MUSIC, POETRY, RELIGION

AcreAGE, PO Box 130, Ontario, OR 97914. 503-889-5387; Fax 503-889-3347. Editor: Larry Hurrle. Ads: Linda Warren. Circ. 24,200. Founded 1978. Monthly tabloid distributed free to rural residents of Oregon and Idaho and related agri-business firms of the region. "We're interested in anything agriculturally oriented that will help our readers farm or ranch better, or entertain them." Pays money on publication. Query w/SASE. Reports in 2 wks. Publishes in 1-2 mos. Accepts nonfiction, photos (B&W glossy, 5X7, good quality). "AcreAGE is a very localized magazine and mainly accepts items related to ranchers in Eastern Oregon and Southwest Idaho."
AGRICULTURE/FARMING, BUSINESS, ENTERTAINMENT

ACRL Newsletter, Washington State University, Owen Science & Engineering Lib, Pullman, WA 99164-3200. Periodical for academic and research librarians.
REFERENCE/LIBRARY, SCHOLARLY/ACADEMIC, SCIENCE

The Active Pacifist, 454 Willamette, Eugene, OR 97402. Editor: Gary Kutcher. Monthly periodical devoted to the struggle for peace through non-violence.
PEACE

Ad Lib, University of Idaho Law Library, Moscow, ID 83843. Contact: Trish Cervenka. Irregularly published law periodical.
LAW

The Adjusting Entry, PO Box 2896, Boise, ID 83702. 208-344-6261. Editor: Joyce Kasper. Ads: same. Quarterly aimed at CPAs. Circ. 1,500. Sub by membership. No pay. Byline given. Phone query, dot matrix, and photocopies OK. Reporting time varies. Technical information.
BUSINESS, ECONOMICS

Adopted Child, PO Box 9362, Moscow, ID 83843. 208-882-1181. Editor: Lois Melina. Monthly. Subs $22. Circ. 3,500.
CHILDREN (BY/ABOUT), FAMILY, SOCIOLOGY

Adventure in Hell, Ritz Publishing, 202 W. Fifth Ave, Ritzville, WA 99169-1722. 509-659-4336. Publisher: Star Andersen. Contact: David Andersen. Alternative semiannual book/journal for Vietnam War literature. Seeking Vietnam War related material poetry, fiction, or 1st person historical narratives. Length open. Reports in 1 mo; publishing time varies. Query W/SASE. No dot matrix. Typed ms, or laser (suitable for scanning). "I believe wholeheartedly that this writing helps in the healing process of a war wound of the nation, as well as helping new authors get established."
FICTION, AMERICAN HISTORY, MILITARY/VETS

Adventure Northwest Magazine, 2521 D Pacific Hwy E., Tacoma, WA 98424. 206-922-2080; Fax 206-922-2153. Editor: Kerry Ordway. Ads: Patricia DeLaney. Monthly on

N.W. travel for upper middle class audience about 45 yrs old. Circ. 75,000. Buys 75 mss/yr. Payment: Money on publication. Byline given. Rights purchased: 1st. Query with mss, SASE. Dot matrix OK. Simultaneous submissions OK to non-competing markets. Publishes submissions in 2-6 mos. Nonfiction: 800-1,000 wds, $25. Guidelines; sample.
TRAVEL

Adventures, Sheldon Jackson College, 801 Lincoln, Sitka, AK 99835.
COLLEGE/UNIVERSITY

Adventures In Subversion, PO Box 11492, Eugene, OR 97440. 503-344-3119; 503-345-1147. Contact: John Zerzan, Dan Todd. Self-publisher of occasional flyers and papers which present a critical contestation of contemporary capitalism and its spurious opposition. Not a freelance market.
LABOR/WORK, SATIRE, SOCIALIST/RADICAL

The Advocate, Vancouver Bar Association, 4765 Pilot House Rd., West Vancouver, BC V7W 1J2. 604-925-2122. Editor: David Roberts, QC. Ads: Gillian Roberts. Bimonthly journal of the bar association. Circ. 8,500. Subs $20/yr (CDN) plus 7% GST where applicable. Founded 1943. Accepts freelance material. Byline given. Usually does not pay. Send query letter w/ SASE. Some back issues, $4.00 CDN plus 7% GST.
LAW

The Advocate, Idaho State Bar, PO Box 895, Boise, ID 83701. 208-342-8958. Editor/Ads: Linda Watkins. Monthly. Sub $30/yr. Circ. 3,000. Byline given. Submit query letter, outline. Photocopies and phone queries OK. Reports in 2 mos. Nonfiction, articles, reviews. Topics: law-related. Max 6 pgs, typed, ds. Guidelines; sample $3.
IDAHO, LAW

AERO Sun-Times, 44 N. Last Chance Gulch #9, Helena, MT 59601. 406-443-7272. Editor: Wilbur Wood. Quarterly magazine. Sub $15/yr. Circ. 1,000. Accepts nonfiction, poetry, photos, cartoons, interviews, news items, articles, reviews, other. Topics: renewable energy, sustainable agriculture, economic development. Reporting time varies. Sample $2.50.
AGRICULTURE/FARMING, ENVIRONMENT/RESOURCES, POETRY

After the Wedding, 7000 S.W. Hampton, Ste. 218, Portland, OR 97223. 503-684-0437. Editor: Kathy Chretien. Bi-monthly. Free sub. Circ. 180,000. Accepts unsolicited submissions. Freelance material accepted. Pays upon publication. No rights acquired. Submit with query letter, query by phone. Reports in 2 weeks. Publishes in 60 days. Accepts poetry, cartoons, interviews, articles. $35 photo session, $12/photo. Seeks articles on quality relationships in marriage and submissions on how to and what makes great marriages today. Guidelines; back issues.
FAMILY

Ag Almanac, PO Box 2604, 510 1st Ave. N. Rm. 110, Great Falls, MT 59403. 800-426-2196; 406-727-7244.
AGRICULTURE/FARMING

Agent West Weekly, 2225 Inglewood, West Vancouver, BC. 604-922-2241. Editor: Douglas W. Keough. Periodical.
UNSPECIFIED

Aglow Magazine, PO Box 1548, Lynnwood, WA 98046-1557. 206-775-7282. Editor: Gloria Chisholm. Bimonthly magazine for charismatic Christian women. Circ. 36,000. Sub $10.97/yr. Uses freelance material. Pays money on acceptance, byline given, acquires 1st and reprint rights. Submit query w/SASE. Photocopies OK. Reports in 6 wks; publishes within 1 yr. Accepts nonfiction, interviews, articles. Guidelines/sample with SASE.
RELIGION, WOMEN

Ag-Pilot International, PO Box.1607, Mt. Vernon, WA 98273. 206-336-9737. Contact: Tom Wood. Monthly

magazine for crop dusters. Circ. 8,500. Sub $29.95. Acquires all rights to nonfiction related to the industry and those engaged in it. Query w/ms. Uses color or B&W photos. Accepts poetry, short humor, articles, news items. Guidelines; back issues $2.
AVIATION, BUSINESS

Agri Equipment Today, PO Box 1467, Yakima, WA 98907. 509-248-2457. Monthly on farm implements.
AGRICULTURE/FARMING, BUSINESS

Agri-News, PO Box 30755, Billings, MT 59107-0755. 406-259-4589. Editor: Rebecca Tescher. Weekly agricultural tabloid also interested in cottage industry. Circ. 17,000. Writers must have expertise in agriculture. Pays money. Query w/SASE. Phone query OK. Nonfiction: 750 wds for $20-35 on Montana & Wyoming ag-related stories/profiles. Fillers: 500-1,000 wds for $15-25 on farm taxes, ag-related business, gardening, & crafts. Photos: B&W, good quality, $5, as used. "Must be useful to Montana & Wyoming agrarians." Guidelines; sample.
AGRICULTURE/FARMING, CRAFTS/HOBBIES, MONTANA

Aguelarre, C/O Box 65535 St. F, Vancouver, BC V5N 5K6. 604-251-6678 or 604-253-5109. Contact: Margarita Sewerin. Ads: Deborah Mcinnes. Quarterly magazine. Circ. 2,000. Sub $12/yr; USA $17/yr. Uses freelance material. Byline given, pays copies. Query w/ SASE, outline, photocopy OK, disk/modem OK, synopsis, dot matrix OK. Reports in 3 months; publishing time varies. Accepts fiction, poetry, cartoons, news items, biographies, nonfiction, photos, interviews, op/ed, articles and reviews. 1500 words max. Bilingual, Spanish/English editions avail. Back issues available $2.
CULTURE, MINORITIES/ETHNIC

Alaska Airlines Magazine, 2701 1st Ave. #250, Seattle, WA 98121. 206-441-5871. Editor: Paul Frichtl. Inflight monthly magazine for West Coast travelers. Freelance material accepted; byline given. Pays money on publication; acquires first rights. Send a single page query letter and clips. Responds in 4-6 weeks; publishes in 3 months. Accepts articles about travel/entertainment on the west coast. "Read the magazine first. Focus the query to one section of the magazine."
ALASKA, ENTERTAINMENT, TRAVEL

Alaska Business Monthly, PO Box 241288, Anchorage, AK 99524-1288. Editor: Paul Laird. As the name says.
ALASKA, BUSINESS

Alaska Construction and Oil, 3000 Northrup Way #200, Bellevue, WA 98004-1407. 206-285-2050. Monthly.
ALASKA, BUSINESS, ENVIRONMENT/RESOURCES

Alaska Dept. of Fish & Game, PO Box 3-2000, Juneau, AK 99802-2000. 907-465-4112. Editor: Sheila Nickerson. Bimonthly magazine. Sub $12. Circ. 10,000. Occasionally takes freelance material. Pays money/copies on publication; acquires 1st rights. Byline given. Submit ms, SASE, phone. Dot matrix, photocopies, simultaneous subs OK. Reports in 4-6 wks; publishes in 6 mos. Accepts nonfiction on Alaska-related outdoors only. Photos: B&W $10-25; color $15-35; cover $100, back $50. Guidelines; sample $3.
ALASKA, FISHING, OUTDOOR

Alaska Dept of Labor Research &. Analysis, PO Box 25501, Juneau, AK 99802-5501. 907-465-4500. Editor: J. P. Goforth. Publisher of monthly journal. Query w/ SASE. All pubs free. Freelance material accepted. Pays on publication. Responds in 4-6 wks; publishing time varies. Accepts nonfiction. Sample.
ALASKA, ECONOMICS, LABOR/WORK

Alaska Fisherman's Journal/Ocean Leader, 1115 N.W. 46th St., Seattle, WA 98107. 206-789-6506; Fax 206-789-9193. Editor: John van Amerongen. Ads: Laurie Munnis. Monthly tabloid newspaper serving the North Pacific commercial fishing industry. Circ. 13,000. Free to

licensed commercial fishermen, sub/$18. Founded 1977.
ALASKA, BUSINESS, FISHING

Alaska Geographic, Alaska Geographic Society, PO Box 93370, Anchorage, AK 99509-3370. 907-562-0164; FAX: 907-562-0479. Editor: Penny Rennick. Quarterly manual covering Alaska, northern and western Canada, and the Pacific and polar rims. Circ. 13,000. Sub $39 for membership in Alaska Geographic Society. Pays money (approx $100/printed page) on publication; byline given; acquires 1st rights. Query w/SASE. Photocopies and simultaneous submission OK. Reports in 1 month. Accepts nonfiction, photos. Mss are lengthy with finished issues ranging from 100-300 pages. Topics include geography/natural resources in the broadest sense. Photos: 35mm color, $300 cover, $100 full pg, $50 half pg; good captions with photos. Has guidelines and will answer letters promptly.
ALASKA, NATURAL HISTORY, TRAVEL

Alaska History, Alaska Historical Society, PO Box 100299, Anchorage, AK 99510. 907-276-1596. Editor: James H. Ducker. Subs $10/yr. Circ. 800. Publishes 2 softcover journals a yr. Uses 3 freelance mss per issue. Pays copies; acquires 1st rights. Byline given. Submit ms w/ SASE. Dot matrix, photocopied subs OK. Reports in 3 mos; publishes in 8 mos. Accepts nonfiction. Tip: Photos and maps desired. Sample $5.
ALASKA, AMERICAN HISTORY

Alaska Magazine, 808 E. St., Ste. 200, Anchorage, AK 99501. 907-272-6070. Editor: Tobin Morrison. Published 10x yearly. Magazine concerning natural resources and non-urban life in Alaska/Western Canada. Circ. 230,000 to college educated readers, 35 and older. Pays money on acceptance. Byline given. Buys 1st rights. Submit ms w/ SASE. Dot matrix, electronic subs OK. Responds in 6 weeks; publication time varies. Accepts biography, travel, history, adventure. "Must have a strong Alaska connection." Photos: send color slides. Pays $300 per page. Back issues.
ALASKA

Alaska Medicine, 4107 Laurel St., Anchorage, AK 99504. 907-562-2928. Editor: William Bowers, MD. Periodical.
ALASKA, HEALTH, MEDICAL

Alaska Metaphysical Council N/L, 3701 Eureka St., #21C, Anchorage, AK 99503. Monthly newsletter of metaphysical organizations, services, and calendar events. Sub $12/yr.
NEW AGE

Alaska Nurse, Alaskan Nurses Association, 237 E. 3rd, Anchorage, AK 99501. Periodical.
ALASKA, HEALTH, MEDICAL

Alaska Outdoors, 1013 E. Dimond Blvd. #290, Anchorage, AK 99519-2099. 907-276-2672. Editor: Christopher M. Batin. Periodical. Uses freelance material. Byline given, pays money on acceptance, acquires all rights. Query w/ SASE. Responds in 1 mo. Accepts nonfiction, news items, interviews, articles. Query w/SASE.
ALASKA, OUTDOOR, RECREATION

Alaska Quarterly Review, College of Arts & Sciences, U. of Alaska, 3221 Providence Dr., Anchorage, AK 99508. 907-786-1731. Contact: Ronald Spatz or James Liszka. Quarterly review of literature and philosophy. Circ. 1,000. Acquires 1st rights. Pay varies on publication according to available funds. Seeks criticism, reviews, fiction, poetry, essays. Accepts unsolicited mss.
LITERARY, PHILOSOPHY, POETRY

Alaska Review of Social & Economic Conditions, University of Alaska, 707 A. St., Anchorage, AK 99501. 907-278-4621. Editor: Ronald Crowe. Periodical.
ALASKA, ECONOMICS, SOCIOLOGY

Alaska Today, Department of Journalism, University of Alaska/Fairbanks, Fairbanks, AK 99701. Periodical.
ALASKA, COLLEGE/UNIVERSITY, PUBLIC AFFAIRS

Alaska Women, Alaskan Viewpoint Publishing Co., HCR 64, Box 453, Seward, AK 99664. 907-288-3168. Editor: L. B. Leary. Quarterly journal. Subs $30/yr. Uses freelance material. Byline given. Submit ms, query letter, SASE. Responds in 2 wks; publishing time varies. Accepts nonfiction, photos. Topics: "this is a living history journal featuring women throughout Alaska involved in a variety of endeavors." Guidelines; sample.
ALASKA, WOMEN

Alaskan Bowhunter, PO Box 870, Kasilof, AK 99610. 907-262-9191. Editor: Dave Hopkins. Quarterly magazine. Subs $10/yr. Circ. 1,000. Uses freelance material. Byline given, no pay. Submit query, ms, SASE. Dot matrix, disk subs OK. Accepts nonfiction, op/ed, articles, prefers B&W photos. Topics: hunting, bowhunting, archery. Sample $1.50.
ALASKA, ANIMALS, SPORTS

Alaskan Byways, PO Box 211356, Anchorage, AK 99521. Editor: Lisa M. Short. Periodical.
ALASKA, TRAVEL

Alaskan Women, HCR 64 Box 453, Seward, AK 99664. 907-288-3168. Contact: Lory B. Leary. Quarterly magazine. Circ. 50,000. Interested in freelance writing, photos, cartoons, poetry by Alaskan women. Pays byline, title page listing, and subscription. Submit query, mss, and SASE. Reports in 1 month.
ALASKA, POETRY, WOMEN

Alchemy, Portland Community College, 12000 S.W. 49th Ave., Portland, OR 97219. College literary magazine. Editor could change yearly. SASE for guidelines.
COLLEGE/UNIVERSITY, FICTION, LITERARY

Aldrich Entomology Club Newsletter, University of Idaho, Division of Entomology, Moscow, ID 83843. Irregular periodical devoted to insects.
BIOLOGY, COLLEGE/UNIVERSITY, SCIENCE

ALKI: The Washington Library Association Journal, 1232 143rd Ave. S.E., Bellevue, WA 98007. 206-747-6917. Editor: Regan Robinson. Quarterly journal. Sub $14. Circ. 1,200. Uses freelance material. Pays copies on publication. Byline given. Submit query w/clips, ms, or phone. Dot matrix, photocopied, simultaneous, electronic/modem subs OK. Accepts nonfiction, photos, cartoons. Topics: libraries and all related issues for people concerned with libraries. Photos: B&W glossy w/captions. Guidelines; sample.
BOOK ARTS/BOOKS, FORESTRY

Allied Arts Newsletter, PO Box 2584, Bellingham, WA 98227. 206-676-8548. Editor: Miriam Barnett. Circ. 500+. Sub $15. Monthly newsletter. Accepts unsolicited, freelance mss. No pay. Phone query OK. Photocopy OK. Reports on 15th of the month. Accepts poetry, photos, cartoons. Will print anything related to visual, performing, or literary arts.
ARTS, MUSIC, VISUAL ARTS

Allied Arts of Seattle, 107 S. Main, Room 201, Seattle, WA 98104. 206-624-0432. Publishes a newsletter 6 times a yr. We are not publishers but we have published a few titles such as Art Deco, Impressions of Imagination: Terra Cotta Seattle, and Access to the Arts.
ARTS

Alternative Connection, PO Box 2039, Portland, OR 97208. 503-236-3055. Editor & Ads: Inga Swanson. Monthly publication. Circ. 25,000. Sub/$18. Freelance material accepted, byline given, pays money & advance. Acquires no rights. Accepts news stories on the gay/lesbian community. Back issues 50 cents.
GAY/LESBIAN, COMMUNITY

American Accents, PO Box 1305, Lake Oswego, OR 97035. 503-656-2618. Contact: Robert L. Hamm. Magazine published semi-annually. Circ. 500, Sub/$10. Freelance material accepted, byline given. Pays on publication

in copies. First rights acquired. Send complete manuscript, photocopy OK, dot matrix and simultaneous subs OK. Responds in 1-2 months, publishes in 6 months. "Topics are American authors and literary works. Not to be restricted only to literature of the U.S., but Canada, Mexico, Central America, and South America. However, emphasis is on U.S. literature." Back issues/$4.
LITERATURE, ENGLISH

American Contractor, Who's Who Publishing, PO Box 3165, Portland, OR 97208-3165. 503-226-1331; 503-280-9000. Editor: Cardice Crossley. Ads: Bruce Broussard at 503-280-9000. Weekly trade publication. Subs. $100/yr. Circ. 20,000. Uses freelance material. Byline given; pays on acceptance. Submit clips, query by phone, assignment only. Computer disk subs OK. Guidelines; sample.
BUSINESS, TRADE/ASSOCIATIONS

American Dry Pea & Lentil Assn Bulletin, PO Box 8566, Moscow, ID 83843. Editor: Harold Blain. Trade monthly. Circ. 350.
AGRICULTURE/FARMING, BUSINESS

American Indian Basketry Magazine, PO Box 66124, Portland, OR 97266. 503-233-8131. Editor: John M. Gogol. Quarterly of photo-essays on Native American basketry and crafts. Interested in history, biography, artistic methods and materials used. Heavily dependent on quality photos. "Thorough understanding of Native American arts and crafts is important."
CRAFTS/HOBBIES, GENERAL HISTORY, NATIVE AMERICAN

The American Music News, 4450 Fremont Ave. N., Seattle, WA 98103. 206-633-1774; 206-633-1419. Editor: Shannon Celli. Circ. 36,800. Founded 1979. Quarterly four-color magazine focusing on musical equipment and the Northwest music industry.
MUSIC, BUSINESS

American Rhododendron Society Journal, 201-A S. State St., Bellingham, WA 98225. Editor: Sonja Nelson. Quarterly sent with membership in American Rhododendron Society. Subs $25/membership. Circ. 6,000. Uses several freelance mss per issue. Byline given, no pay. Submit ms w/SASE. Phone query, dot matrix, photocopies, computer disk OK. Reports in 2-4 wks. Publishes usually within 1 yr. Topic: rhododendrons & azaleas. Guidelines; sample $4.
GARDENING

Americas Focus, 2000 S.W. 5th Ave., Portland, OR 97201. Editor: Donald Bassist. Periodical.
UNSPECIFIED

Amphora, The Alcuin Society, PO Box 3216, Vancouver, BC V6B 3X8. 604-872-2326. Quarterly newsletter. Sub $35/yr (CDN). Circ. 300+. Accepts freelance material. No pay. Acquires 1st rights. Byline given. Submit ms w/SASE. Dot matrix, photocopied OK. Publishes 1st issue w/available space. Accepts nonfiction, photos. Topics: book arts, calligraphy, book collecting, book binding, etc. Sample $5(CDN).
BOOK ARTS/BOOKS, PUBLISHING/PRINTING

Analysis and Outlook, PO Box 1167, Port Townsend, WA 98368. Editor: R. W. Bradford. Monthly.
UNSPECIFIED

ANC News, Alaska Native Coalition, C/O 310 K. St., Ste. 708, Anchorage, AK 99501. Periodical.
NATIVE AMERICAN

The Anchovy Review, 4223 Fremont Ave. N., Seattle, WA 98103. Contact: Mark Briggs. Periodical published irregularly. Accepts prose, photos, artwork, poetry, journalism, humor, and letters.
LITERARY

Animal Aid, 408 S.W. 2nd, Rm 318, Portland, OR 97204. Periodical.
ANIMALS

Animator, Northwest Film & Video Center, 1219 S.W. Park Ave., Portland, OR 97205. 503-221-1156. Editor/Ads: Kathy Clark. Quarterly on film, video, public relations, media. Circ. 2,000. Sub $6 individual, $10 institution. Payment: Copies on acceptance. Byline given. Submit ms w/ SASE. Nonfiction, photos, cartoons. Sample.
ARTS, FILM/VIDEO, VISUAL ARTS

AOI News Digest, Associated Oregon Industries, 1149 Court N.E., Salem, OR 97301. 503-588-0050. Editor: Jack Zimmerman. Ads: Mediamerica, 503-223-0304. Bimonthly newsletter. Does not use freelance material.
BUSINESS, OREGON

APA-EROS, Sylvia, c/o Correspan, PO Box 759, Veneta, OR 97487. Contact: Sylvia. Bimonthly periodical. Accepts freelance material. Submit query w/clips, SASE. Accepts nonfiction, fiction, poetry, other. Sample $2.
CULTURE, ENTERTAINMENT, MEN

Appaloosa Journal, Appaloosa Horse Club, PO Box 8403, Moscow, ID 83843. 208-882-5578. Editor: Debbie Pitner Moors. Ads: Tim Devaney. Sub $15. Circ. 14,000. Monthly. Accepts unsolicited mss on spec. Uses 2 freelance mss per issue. Pays money, copies on publication. Byline given. Submit query w/clips & SASE. Dot matrix, photocopies OK. Accepts nonfiction, photos (5x7 or larger B&W glossies/color prints/color transparencies). Pays $50-$300 depending on length, content, & presentation, illustrations & photos, and whether or not is audience-specific (relating to Appaloosa horses and their owner/trainers). Accepts training, breeding, health and management, human interest and personality profiles as they relate to the Appaloosa breed. Guidelines/sample: $2.50+$1 post.
ANIMALS, RECREATION

Apropos, 339 Telegraph Rd., Bellingham, WA 98226. Monthly of health, beauty, fashions for women. Sub $5/yr.
CONSUMER, FASHION, WOMEN

Arabian Horse Country, 4346 S.E. Division, Portland, OR 97206. Monthly.
ANIMALS, CRAFTS/HOBBIES, RECREATION

Arches, Office of Public Relations, University of Puget Sound, Tacoma, WA 98416. Editor: Gregory W. Brewis. Periodical.
COLLEGE/UNIVERSITY

Aristos, PO Box 7272, Tacoma, WA 98407-0272. Contact: Penny Lynn Dunn, Editor. Quarterly publication of a nonprofit organization dedicated to enhancing appreciation of Washington artists on a national and international level.
ARTS

Arnazella, Bellevue Community College, 3000 Landerholm Circle S.E., Bellevue, WA 98007. Annual literary magazine. Circ. 400. Founded 1976. Submit query, ms, w/ SASE. Up to 1 yr response time. Accepts fiction, nonfiction, poetry, cartoons, photos (8x10 B&W), plays, artfixed charcoal, pen & ink, calligraphy, photography of sculpture and pottery. Limited to entries from Northwest states. Guidelines; sample $5.
ARTS, COLLEGE/UNIVERSITY, LITERARY

Art West Magazine, PO Box 310, Bozeman, MT 59771. 406-586-5411. Contact: Henori M. Graff. Bimonthly of wildlife and Western & American realism, aimed at collectors. Interested in historical as well as contemporary pieces. Uses photo essays and profiles of artists, galleries, and museums. Nonfiction, photos. Query w/SASE. Guidelines, sample.
ARTS, COLLECTING, AMERICAN HISTORY

Arterial, 1202 E. Pike St., #697, Seattle, WA 98122. 206-285-7182. Contact: Sheila Jolley. Ads: David Fair.
LITERARY, ARTS, POETRY

Artist Trust, 512 Jones Building, 1331 Third Ave., Seattle, WA 98101. 206-467-8734. Director: David Mendoza.

Editor: Loch Adamson. Nonprofit foundation, quarterly journal of information by, for, and about individual artists in all media in Washington State. Sub/$10. Circ. 15,000. Uses freelance material; byline given. Pays money for solicited material. Submit ms, query, clips, SASE. Dot matrix OK. Responds in 2 weeks; publishes in 12 months. Accepts nonfiction, interviews, B&W prints. Sample.

ARTS, CULTURE, VISUAL ARTS

Artistamp News, Banana Productions, PO Box 3655, Vancouver, BC V6B 3Y8. 604-876-6764. Editor: Anna Banana. Circ. 300; subs $12/3 issues. "News, reviews, artist profile...everything and anything about stamps artists. Also info on Mail Art shows and projects." Freelance material relating to theme accepted. Byline given, pays copies, acquires first rights. Send SASE, phone, or invitation. "Nothing usual in our way of operation." Accepts articles and reviews "related only to stamps by artists. Our interests range to all non-postal stamp productions by individuals ...not fund raisers or commercial promotional materials." Back issues $3.

ARTS, COLLECTING, VISUAL ARTS

Artist's Notes, Lane Regional Arts Council, 411 High St., Eugene, OR 97401. 503-485-2278. Editors: K. Wagner/ D. Beauchamp. Monthly periodical. Sub $20-29. Query w/ SASE.

ARTS, LITERARY

ArtistSearch/Montana Arts Council, New York Block, 48 North Last Chance Gulch, Helena, MT 59620. 406-444-6430. Editor: Julie Smith. Monthly arts publication. Circ. 2,000. This is a newsletter that includes space for artists to communicate with other artists. Very little poetry, fiction or essay publication.

ARTS, MONTANA

Artoonist, 2325 N.E. 42nd Ave., Portland, OR 97213. Periodical. Articles, cartoons.

ARTS, HUMOR

The Arts, King County Arts Commission, 506 2nd Ave. #1115, Seattle, WA 98104. 206-344-7580. Editor/Ads: Joan Mann. Monthly newsletter of the King County Arts Commission. We welcome articles, photographs, drawings, but such material must be accompanied by a SASE.

ARTS, CULTURE, WASHINGTON

Arts & Crafts News, Burnaby Arts Council, 6528 Deer Lake Ave., Burnaby, BC V3B 1E7. 604-294-7322. Editor: Margaret Franz. Quarterly newsletter. Circ. 10,000. Uses freelance material. Byline given, no pay. Submit query letter. Responds in 2 mos; publishes in 6 mos. Dot matrix, simultaneous submissions OK. Accepts: nonfiction, fiction, poetry, cartoons, news, photos, interviews, reviews, memoirs. Topics: arts, craft making and marketing. Sample $2.50.

ARTS, CRAFTS/HOBBIES, CULTURE

Arts East/Eastern OR Reg. Arts Council, EOSC: Loso 220, 1410 L Ave., LaGrande, OR 97850-2899. 1-800-452-8639; 503-962-3624. Editor: Anne Bell. Uses freelance material. No pay. Byline given. Submit query letter, SASE. Dot matrix, photocopy OK. Accepts fiction, poetry, photos, interviews. Topics: art-related events, programs and profiles in Eastern Oregon, S.E. Washington and West Idaho.

ARTS, COLLEGE/UNIVERSITY, LITERARY

Arts Washington, PO Box 42675, Olympia, WA 98504-2675. 206-753-3860. Editor: Mark Wallace. Quarterly newsletter. Circ. 5500. Free. Freelance material accepted. Byline given, no pay. Submit query letter or phone. Responds in days, publishes in up to three months. Accepts news items, nonfiction, B&W photos, and interviews. Back issues.

ARTS, CALENDAR/EVENTS, WASHINGTON

Asia Cable, 1248 S.W. Larch, Lake Oswego, OR 97034. Editor: John Vezmar. Periodical.

ASIA, BUSINESS

Astrology Night, Oregon Astrological Association, PO Box 6771, Portland, OR 97228. Periodical.

ASTROLOGY/SPIRITUAL, BUSINESS

ATI Newsletter, Associated Taxpayers of Idaho, PO Box 1665, Boise, ID 83701. Editor: Randy Nelson. Irregular periodical. Circ. 1,500.

ECONOMICS, IDAHO, PUBLIC AFFAIRS

Auto Glass Journal, PO Box 12099, Seattle, WA 98102-0099. 206-322-5120. Editor: Burton Winters. Monthly trade magazine for the auto glass replacement industry. Uses how-to articles, history, profiles, trends, news. Query w/ SASE.

BUSINESS

Auto Trader, PO Box 23369, Tigard, OR 97223. 503-244-2886. Weekly periodical. Does not use freelance material.

CONSUMER

Automotive News of the Pacific Northwest, 14789 S.E. 82nd Dr., Clackamas, OR 97015-9624. Editor: Bradley Boyer. Monthly periodical.

CONSUMER

Aviation News, ODOT Public Affairs, 140 Transportation Building, Salem, OR 97310. 503-378-4880. Editor: Ed Schoaps. Quarterly newsletter. Limited use of freelance material. Byline given, no pay. Submit query, SASE, phone. Disk sub OK. Responds in 2 wks; publishing time varies. Accepts news items, interviews, articles related to Oregon pilots, aviation. Guidelines; sample.

AVIATION, GOVERNMENT, OREGON

Axiom, Triangle Circle Productions, 1101 S.W. Washington, Ste. 119, Portland, OR 97205. 503-236-3165. Contact: Nathan Marcel. Literary/graphic arts publication. Accepts fiction, poetry, comics, reviews, editorials, art.

LITERARY, VISUAL ARTS

Back Door Travel, 120 4th Ave. N., Edmonds, WA 98020. 206-771-8303. Editor: Mike McGregor. Quarterly on budget travel, helping people to travel as temporary locals. Interested in personal accounts about meeting people, traveling on a budget, discovering new places. Circ. 6,000. Sub free. Uses 2-3 mss per issue. Payment: Copies. Byline given. Rights purchased: 1st, 2nd, 3rd. Query with ms, SASE. Dot matrix, photocopies, simultaneous submissions OK. Nonfiction, poetry, photos, cartoons. Articles should be practical, how-to, destination-oriented travel pieces. Our readers range from just planning a first trip to just returning from the tenth trip. Information about alternate modes of travel (bicycle, trekking) are welcome. Sample Free.

TRAVEL

Backbone, PO Box 95315, Seattle, WA 98145. Contact: Lauren Fortune

UNSPECIFIED

Bad Haircut, 1055 Adams S.E., #4, Olympia, WA 98501. Editors: Kim & Ray Goforth. Irregular journal. Founded 1987. Subs $14/4 issues. Circ. 1,000. Uses freelance material. Pays copies & money on publication; acquires 1st rights. Byline given. Submit ms/SASE, biographical cover letter. Reports in 12 mos; publishes in 28 mos. Accepts: fiction, nonfiction, poetry, news items, biography, interviews, photos, cartoons. Topics: politics, human rights and environmental issues. Poems in batches of 5; prefers fiction of 2,000 words, 5,000 max. Guidelines with SASE. Sample $4.

PEACE, POLITICS

Barometer, Western Wood Products Association, 1500 Yeon Bldg., Portland, OR 97204. Weekly which publishes statistical reports. Not a freelance market.

BUSINESS

Basement Press, 215 Burlington, Billings, MT 59101. 406-256-3588. Contact: Dan Struckman. Semiannual magazine. Sub $10/4 issues. Circ. 200. Freelance material accepted. Query with complete ms and SASE. Photocopies

and dot matrix submissions OK. Responds in 30 days; publishes within 1 year. Buys 1st rights. Gives byline; pays in copies on publication. Uses fiction, poetry, cartoons, interviews, op/ed, articles, reviews, and memoirs. Back issues $5.

HUMOR, MONTANA, POETRY

BC Business Examiner, 112-2465 Beta Ave., Burnaby, BC V5C 5N1. 604-291-1320. Editor & publisher: Bert Walker. Business periodical published 10x yearly. Pays money. If looking for a particular article, the publisher approaches a writer. Occasionally uses new writers. Focus is usually business information, such as managing cash flow.

ASIAN AMERICAN, BUSINESS

BC Business Magazine, 401-4180 Lougheed Hwy., Vancouver, BC V5C 6A7. 604-299-7311. Editor: Bonnie Irving. Monthly magazine owned by Canada Wide, which owns 12 magazines. Uses freelance material for about 75% of each issue. Request guidelines first. Pays 35 cents per word. Accepts business features and photos. Most of the smaller pieces and columns are done in-house.

BRITISH COLUMBIA, BUSINESS

BC Historical News Magazine, PO Box 105, Wasa, BC V0B 2K0. Quarterly. Submit ms w/SASE. Accepts nonfiction: articles of no more than 2,500 wds, accompanied by photos if available, substantiated with footnotes if possible. Quarterly deadlines are Feb 15, May 15, Aug 15, and Nov 15. Topics: any facet of BC history.

BRITISH COLUMBIA, CANADIAN HISTORY, NW/REGIONAL HISTORY

BC Hotelman, 124 W. 8th St., North Vancouver, BC V7M 3H2. 604-985-8711. Editor: Vivian Rudd. Periodical.

BRITISH COLUMBIA, BUSINESS

BC Outdoors, 202-1132 Hamilton St., Vancouver, BC V6B 2S2. 604-687-1581. Editor: George Will. Ads: Mark White. Magazine, 8X/yr. Subs $25.63 CDN/yr. Circ. 35,000. Uses freelance material. Byline given; pays money on publication; acquires 1st rights. Submit query letter. Responds in 2 wks; publishes in 3 mos. Accepts nonfiction, news items, cartoons, reviews photos (color slides, B&W glossy). Topics: Hunting, fishing, conservation and other outdoor recreation in British Columbia. Tip: read the mag before submitting material. Guidelines; back issues $2.

BRITISH COLUMBIA, FISHING, OUTDOOR

BC Professional Engineer, 210-6400 Roberts St., Burnaby, BC V5G 4C9. 604-929-6733. Editor: Colleen Chen. Ads: Gillian Cobban. Periodical published 10X/yr. Circ. 15,000; subs $25 Canadian/yr.

BRITISH COLUMBIA, BUSINESS, TRADE/ASSOCIATIONS

BC Sport Fishing Magazine, 1161 Melville, Vancouver, BC V6E 2X7. As the title suggests.

BRITISH COLUMBIA, FISHING, RECREATION

B.C. Studies University of British Columbia, 218-2029 West Mall, Vancouver, BC V6T 1Z2. 604-822-3727. Editor: Prof. Allan Smith. Business Mgr.: Henny Winterton. Quarterly journal. Sub $25 indiv, $30 inst/yr. Circ. 800. Uses freelance material. Pays copies. Submit complete ms. Dot matrix OK. Reports in 1-3 mos. Publishes up to 1 yr. Accepts nonfiction: scholarly articles on any aspect of human history in BC. Catalog, guidelines, sample.

BRITISH COLUMBIA, SCHOLARLY/ACADEMIC, SOCIOLOGY

B.C. Teacher, 2235 Burrard St., Vancouver, BC V6J 3H9. 604-731-8121. Editor: Larry Kuehn. Periodical.

BRITISH COLUMBIA, EDUCATION

Beacon, Southwest Oregon Community College, Coos Bay, OR 97420. 503-888-2525 ext. 304. College literary magazine. Published twice yearly. Editor could change yearly. SASE for guidelines. Accepts fiction, poetry, and photos. Photos must be black & white.

COLLEGE/UNIVERSITY, FICTION, OREGON, FICTION, PHOTOGRAPHY

The Bear Facts, The Citizens' Utility Board of Oregon, 921 S.W. Morrison #550, Portland, OR 97205-2734. 503-227-1984. Consumer affairs periodical.
CONSUMER, OREGON

Beautiful British Columbia, 929 Ellery St., Victoria, BC V9A 7B4. 604-384-5456. Editor: Bryan McGill. Quarterly magazine. Accepts freelance material only from BC writers. Pays money on acceptance. Acquires first rights. Query by phone, or send photos w/ manuscript. Accepts nonfiction, articles, photos. "We only expect submissions from freelancers living in BC who constantly travel here. No photographs, no story." Guidelines & back issues ($5).
BRITISH COLUMBIA, PHOTOGRAPHY, TRAVEL

Beaver Briefs, Willamette Valley Genealogical Soc., PO Box 2083, Salem, OR 97308. Quarterly.
GENEALOGY, OREGON

Beaverton Arts Commission Newsletter, PO Box 4755, Beaverton, OR 97075. 503-644-2191.
ARTS

Beaverton Business Advocate, Beaverton Area Chamber of Commerce, 4800 S.W. Griffith Dr. #100, Beaverton, OR 97005. 503-644-0123. Editor: Jerri Doctor. Periodical.
BUSINESS

Beef Industry News, Oregon Cattlemen's Association, 729 N.E. Oregon St., Portland, OR 97232-2107. 503-281-3811. Periodical.
AGRICULTURE/FARMING, BUSINESS, OREGON

Before Columbus Review, American Ethnic Studies, GN-80, University of Washington, Seattle, WA 98195. 206-543-4264. Contact: Shawn Wong. Promotes the efforts of minority and multicultural writers and topics. Seeking book reviews, articles, and critical comments about multicultural literature. Query w/SASE.
LITERATURE, MINORITIES/ETHNIC, WRITING

The Bellingham Review, Signpost Press, Inc., 1007 Queen St., Bellingham, WA 98226. 206-734-9781. Editor: Knute Skinner. Semiannual magazine of poetry, drama, art, fiction. Sub $5/yr. Circ. 600. Pays 1 copy + sub on publication. Byline given, acquires 1st rights. Submit complete ms, SASE. Photocopy, simultaneous submission OK. Reports in 3 mos; publishes in 12 mos. Accepts fiction, poetry, photos, plays. Guidelines; sample $2.50. "Submission period is from Sept. 1 to March 1."
DRAMA, FICTION, POETRY

Bellowing Ark, PO Box 45637, Seattle, WA 98145. 206-545-8302. Editor: Robert R. Ward. Bimonthly journal. Sub $15/yr. Circ. 1,000. Uses about 30 mss per issue. Pays in copies, byline given acquires all rights. Submit ms, SASE. Responds in 2-6 wks; publishes in 1-3 mos. Accepts nonfiction, fiction poetry, photos (B&W), memoirs. Topics: literary works in the American Romantic tradition, think of Roethke, Whittier, Emerson, Lindsay. Mostly poetry, fiction and serializations but other forms sometimes used (plays, essays). Some short autobiography used for Literal Lives section. We do not hesitate to publish newcomers if the work is right. Sample $3 + 1.25 postage. Guidelines, catalog; sample $3.
FICTION, POETRY

The Beltane Papers: A Journal of Women's Mysteries, PO Box 8, Clear Lake, WA 98235. Co-editors: Waverly Fitzgerald and Helen Farias. Ads: Shirley Dawson-Meyers. Biannual magazine of pagan women's spirituality. Sub address: 1333 Lincoln St., #240, Bellingham, WA 98226. Sub in US/$13, outside US $24. Prefer submissions on disk, include SASE. Artwork must be crisp, black, camera-ready, include SASE.
WOMEN, ASTROLOGY/SPIRITUAL

The Bicycle Paper, 4710 University Way N.E. #214, Seattle, WA 98105. Editor: Dave Shaw. Ads: Paul Clark. Monthly tabloid. Sub $8/yr. Circ. 7,500. Uses freelance material. Byline given, pays money on publication, acquires 1st rights. Submit query letter, ms, SASE. Photocopied subs and phone queries OK. Responds in 1-4 wks; publishes in 1-3 mos. Accepts news, articles, interviews, photos (B&W, $15/photo printed). Topic: bicycling. "Readership is sophisticated and knowledgeable about bicycling; articles must reflect same level of sophistication." Guidelines.
BICYCLING, SPORTS

BikeReport, PO Box 8308, Missoula, MT 59807. 406-721-1776. Editor: Daniel D'Ambrosio. Published 9 times a year for touring bicyclists. Circ. 18,000. Sub/$22. Uses 9 mss per issue. Pays money, copies on publication. Byline given. Acquires 1st rights. Query with ms, SASE. Dot matrix, photocopies OK. Nonfiction, fiction, cartoons. We like imaginative pieces that use cycling as a starting point to investigate or reveal other topics. They could include anything relating to tours in the USA, foreign countries, or any essay with cycling as a theme. Guidelines; sample $1.
BICYCLING, FICTION, TRAVEL

Bingo Today, Dart Publishing, Inc., 1550 140th Ave. N.E. #201, Bellevue, WA 98005-4500. 206-232-6071. Editor: Rim Miksys. Semimonthly for bingo players/managers. Sub $9/6 mos. Circ. 20,000. Not a freelance market. Sample $1.
ENTERTAINMENT, RECREATION

Bioenergy Bulletin, Bonneville Power Administration, PO Box 3621, Portland, OR 97208-3621. Editor: Tom White. Bimonthly periodical.
GOVERNMENT

Black Lamb, PO Box 4531, Portland, OR 97208-4531. Contact: Terry Ross. Biweekly magazine covering international and local arts, politics, and sports. Considers unsolicited manuscript only if accompanied by a stamped return envelope.
ARTS, POLITICS, SPORTS

Black Powder Times, PO Box 842, Mount Vernon, WA 98273. 206-336-2969. For black powder firearms enthusiasts.
CRAFTS/HOBBIES, RECREATION, SPORTS

BLM News Oregon &. Washington, Bureau of Land Management, PO Box 2965, Portland, OR 97208. 503-280-7031. US Government agency periodical. Not a freelance market.
FORESTRY, GOVERNMENT, PUBLIC AFFAIRS

The Bloodletter, Friends of Mystery, PO Box 8251, Portland, OR 97207. Editor: Debbara Hendrix. Newsletter published 3-5 times a yr. Circ. 1000. Accepts unsolicited freelance material. Byline given. Photocopied OK. Accepts nonfiction, reviews, cartoons. Topics: any aspect of mystery. Sample.
LITERARY

Bluespaper, 3438 S.E. Caruthers St., Portland, OR 97214. 503-231-5605. Editor: Mark Goldfarb. Quarterly. Sub free. Circ. 10,000.
MUSIC, NORTHWEST

Blur, 1245 Liberty St., Salem, OR 97302. 503-375-7626. Quarterly magazine. Sub $28. Accepts freelance material. Byline given. Responds to queries 1 wk. Publishes fiction, poetry, photos, interviews, art. Sample $7.
ARTS, CULTURE, MUSIC

Boat World Magazine, 750 Pacific Blvd. S., Box 33, Plaza of Nations, Vancouver, BC V6B 5E7. 604-669-8554; Fax 604-669-8564. Editor: Gerry Kidd. Ads: Jason Rhodes. Monthly magazine on boating. Circ. 13,500. About 50% of articles in each issues are written by freelancers. Wants to use more freelance material. Pays money; acquires one time North Canada rights. Query by phone. Accepts photos, interviews, articles. Interested only in BC coast. Two subdivisions: sailing and power boats. Topics: offshore cruising, technical info, engines, repairs.
BOATING

Boating News, 26 Coal Harbour Wharf, 566 Cardero St., Vancouver, BC V6G 2W6. Periodical.
BOATING, OUTDOOR, RECREATION

Boise Business Today, Boise Chamber of Commerce, PO Box 2368, Boise, ID 83701. Editor: Lee Campbell. Monthly devoted to issues of interest to the Boise area business community.
BUSINESS, IDAHO

Boise Cascade Quarterly, Boise Cascade Corporation, One Jefferson Square, Boise, ID 83728. Editor: Don Hicks. Corporate quarterly. Circ. 100,000.
BUSINESS, FORESTRY

Boise Senior Center Newsletter, 690 Robbins Rd., Boise, ID 83702. 208-345-9921.
SENIOR CITIZENS

Book Dealers World, North American Bookdealers Exchange, PO Box 606, Cottage Grove, OR 97424. 503-942-7455. Contact: Al Galasso. Quarterly magazine for mail order book promotion. Circ. 20,000. Subs: $25 US, $30 CDN per year for nonmembers. Freelance material accepted, byline given, pays on publication. Query by letter with SASE, outline, dot matrix OK. Responds in 4 weeks; publishes in 3 to 6 months. Accepts articles, interviews, news items.
BOOK ARTS/BOOKS, PUBLISHING/PRINTING

The Book Shop/Children's Newsletter, The Book Shop, 908 Main St., Boise, ID 83702. 208-342-2659. Editor/Ads: Lori Benton. Biannual newsletter reviewing new children's titles, mostly read by parents, teachers, and librarians. Circ. 250. Sub free. Uses 2 mss per issue. Byline given. Query with ms, SASE. Phone queries, photocopies OK. We are interested in book reviews only. Copy should be limited to seven paragraphs. Guidelines, sample.
CHILDREN/TEEN, LITERARY

Bookletter Newsletter, Bookloft, 107 E. Main St., Enterprise, OR 97828.
BOOK ARTS/BOOKS

Bookmark, Library, University of Idaho, Moscow, ID 83843. 208-885-6584. Editors: Richard Beck and Gail Eckwright. Semiannual newsletter free to UI Faculty. Circ. 1,000. Not a freelance market.
BOOK ARTS/BOOKS, LITERARY, LITERATURE

BookNotes: Resources for Small & Self-Pubs, PO Box 3877, Eugene, OR 97403. 503-655-5010. Editor: Cliff Martin. Quarterly provides marketing help for small publishers, self-publishers. Not a freelance market. Sample $5.
BUSINESS, PUBLISHING/PRINTING, WRITING

Boots, Summerhouse Press, PO Box 770, Challis, ID 83226-0770. 208-879-4475; 208-879-4300. Editor: Ethie Corrigan. Publishes softcover books and semi-annual magazine. Circ. 3000. Sub $8.50. Freelance material accepted and byline given. Pays copies upon publication. Submit SASE, photocopy OK, disk/modem OK (Mac). Publishes in 2-3 months. Accepts poetry, cartoons, biography, nonfiction, photos, interviews, reviews, memoirs. Photos: B&W. Sample $4.25
POETRY, BIOGRAPHY

Boredom Magazine, PO Box 85817, Seattle, WA 98145. 206-525-7947. Editor: Patrick McCabe. Magazine of poetry, art, fiction, nonfiction, cartoons, criticism, reviews, novel excerpts, plays, news, etc. Uses photos. Pays in copies. Query w/SASE.
FICTION, LITERARY, POETRY

Boulevard Magazine, Bay Publishing, 1183 Fort St., Victoria, BC V8V 3L1. 604-386-1443. Contact: Vivian Sinclair. Quarterly magazine founded in 1989. Circ. 20,000. Sub/free in Victoria, $18 CDN all others. Freelance material accepted; byline given. Pays money 30 days after publication. Acquires 1st rights. Query letter, SASE, clips. Photocopy OK. Responds in 4 weeks; publishes in 3 months.

Accepts nonfiction: visual arts in Victoria, architecture & design, profiles of young artists. Submissions must be Victoria-oriented, from area writers.
ARCHITECTURE, VISUAL ARTS, CULTURE

Box Dog, PO Box 9609, Seattle, WA 98109. Editor: Craig Joyce, Ads: Peter Wick. Quarterly magazine. Subs. $8/yr. Circ. 500. Accepts unsolicited submissions with $10 reading fee. Freelance material accepted, byline given, pays copies. Catalog; sample $2.
AVANT-GARDE/EXPERIMENTAL, FILM/VIDEO, LITERATURE

The Bread and Butter Chronicles, Seven Buffaloes Press, PO Box 249, Big Timber, MT 59011. Editor: Art Cuelho. Semiannual with essays and columns on contemporary American farmers and ranchers. Sub $2.50. Query w/SASE. Sample: $1 w/SASE.
AGRICULTURE/FARMING, MONTANA, NORTHWEST

Bricolage, c/o Creative Writing Office, UW, Dept of English, GN-30, Seattle, WA 98195. Periodical.
COLLEGE/UNIVERSITY, LITERARY

The Bridal Connection, 7000 S.W. Hampton Ste 218, Tigard, OR 97223. 503-684-0437. Editor: Kathy Chretien. Published bimonthly. Circ. 180,000 in Oregon; 240,000 in Seattle. Free sub. Byline given. Pays $.12 a word upon publication. No rights acquired. Guidelines and back issues. Profiles, relationships, self-help in marriage preparation.
CONSUMER

The Bridge, Danish-American Heritage Society, 29681 Dane Lane, Junction City, OR 97448. Editor: Egan Bodtker. Semiannual periodical. Sub $15/yr. Uses freelance material. Byline given. Submit query letter, complete ms, SASE. Responds in 1 mo; publishes in 1 yr. Accepts biography, nonfiction, articles, reviews, memoirs.
AMERICAN HISTORY, CANADIAN HISTORY, MINORITIES/ETHNIC

Bridge Tender, 9070 S.W. Rambler Lane, Portland, OR 97223. Quarterly.
UNSPECIFIED

Bridges, PO Box 18437, Seattle, WA 98118. 206-721-5008. Editor: Clare Kinberg. Semiannual journal. Subs $15/yr. Circ. 3,000. Uses freelance material. Byline given, pays copies. Submit ms/SASE. Photocopy OK. Responds in 3 mos; publishes in 6 mos. Accepts: fiction, poetry, cartoons, nonfiction, photos, interviews, biography, op/ed, reviews, memoirs. Topics: Jewish, feminism, politics. Guidelines, sample.
RELIGION, WOMEN

British Columbia Agri Digest, DoMac Publications Ltd, #810 207 W. Hastings St., Vancouver, BC V6B 1J8. 604-684-8255. Editor: Edna Mackey. Ads: Lloyd Mackey. Glossy tabloid published 9 times a yr, with thematic issues for segments of BCs ag industry: dairy, growers, swine & poultry, farm business, and horse. Circ. varies with theme. Does not use freelance material. Pays money.
AGRICULTURE/FARMING, BRITISH COLUMBIA, BUSINESS

British Columbia Library Association Newsletter, 110-6545 Bonsor, Vancouver, BC. 604-430-9633.
REFERENCE/LIBRARY, TRADE/ASSOCIATIONS

British Columbia Medical Journal, B.C. Medical Association, 115-1665 West Broadway, Vancouver, BC V6J 5A4. 604-736-5551. Editor: W. Alan Dodd, MD. Ads: Doug Davison. Monthly professional journal. Sub $50 CDN, $65 Foreign. Circ. 7,100. Freelance ms accepted. No pay. Byline given. Submit ms. Computer disk OK. Accepts medical/medically-related/scientific articles 2,500 wds. Photos: 5x7 B&W glossy. Guidelines; back issues. Sample $5.50.
MEDICAL, TRADE/ASSOCIATIONS

British Columbia Monthly, Box 48884, Bentall Station, Vancouver, BC V7X 1A8. Monthly literary publication.
AVANT-GARDE/EXPERIMENTAL, FICTION, LITERARY

British Columbia Report Weekly News Magazine, 103-1161 Melville, Vancouver, BC V6E 2X7.
BRITISH COLUMBIA, UNSPECIFIED

Brown's Business Reporter, P. O. Box 1376, Eugene, OR 97440. 503-345-8665. Editor: Dennis Hunt. Weekly newsletter. Sub $45. Circ. 1,300. Uses 0-1 freelance mss per issue. No pay. Byline given. Dot matrix, photocopied, simultaneous, electronic, computer disk OK. Publishes in 2-3 wks. Accepts business briefs, 150-300 wds. Sample, SASE.
BUSINESS

Brussels Sprout, Vandina Press, P. O. Box 1551, Mercer Island, WA 98040. 206-232-3239. Editor: Francine Porad. Haiku poetry journal 3 times/yr. Subs $14. Uses freelance material. Byline given, cash ($10) awards, acquires 1st rights. Submit ms w/SASE. Dot matrix, photocopy OK. Reports in 3-5 wks; publishes in 3-5 mos. Accepts haiku, senryu. Guidelines; sample $6.50.
ARTS, POETRY

BSU Focus, Boise State University, 1910 University Dr., Boise, ID 83725. 208-385-1577. Editor: Larry Burke. Quarterly magazine. Circ. 43,000. Accepts unsolicited/freelance mss. Pays money on publication. Rights purchased: 1st. Byline given. Query w/clips. Dot matrix, photocopy, simultaneous, etc. OK. Reports in 1 wk. Publishes in 3-4 mos. Accepts nonfiction, many topics. Sample.
COLLEGE/UNIVERSITY

BSU/Search, Boise State University, 1910 University Dr., Boise, ID 83725. Editor: Larry Burke. Semiannual. Circ. 1,000.
COLLEGE/UNIVERSITY

Buckman Voice, Buckman Community Association, 3534 S.E. Main, Portland, OR 97214. Periodical.
COMMUNITY

Bugle, Rocky Mt. Elk Foundation, PO Box 8249, Missoula, MT 59807. 406-523-4568. Editor: Dan Crockett. Ads: Eric Elander. Quarterly magazine. Sub/$12.50. Freelance material accepted, byline given, pays on publication. Acquires 1st rights. Query letter, SASE, query by phone, disk/modem OK, complete ms. Responds in 30 days; publishing time varies. Accepts fiction, nonfiction, articles. Photo payment varies, send prints or slides. Guidelines; back issues $3.95.
ANIMALS, CONSERVATION, OUTDOOR

Bulletin, Genealogical Forum of Portland, Inc., 1410 S.W. Morrison, Ste. 812, Portland, OR 97205. 503-227-2398. Editor: Ruth C. Bishop. Ads: Wilfred Burrell. Quarterly periodical. Sub $15/mbr. Circ. 900. Uses freelance material. Submit ms, SASE. Reports in 8 wks. Accepts nonfiction, poetry, other. Sample $1/SASE.
GENEALOGY

Bulletin of the King Co. Medical Society, PO Box 10249, Bainbridge Island, WA 98110. 206-682-7813. Professional publication, 11 times per yr.
BUSINESS, HEALTH, MEDICAL

The Burnside Review, 1005 W. Burnside St., Portland, OR 97209. 503-228-4651. Editor: Bob Durand. Periodical. Published by Powell's Books. This publication will be about books and more. We provide a behind the scenes look at Powell's Books itself, including how and why we choose the used books we do, and offer tips on selling us your own used books.
BOOK ARTS/BOOKS, LITERARY, PUBLISHING/PRINTING

The Business Journal, PO Box 14490, Portland, OR 97214. 503-274-8733; Fax 503-227-2650. Editor: Steve Jones. Ads: Candace Clement. Founded 1984. Subs/$48. Weekly periodical covering business in the greater Portland area. Circ. 15,00. Freelance market, buys 2-4 mss per issue. Payment: Money on publication. Query w/SASE. Phone query, dot matrix OK. Reports in 1-2 wks. Publishes in 2-6 wks. Nonfiction: 800-1,200 wds at $3 per published

column inch on local business. Guidelines with SASE; sample $1.
BUSINESS

Business News, 220 Cottage N.E., Salem, OR 97301. 503-581-1466. Editor: Jeff Marcoe. Biweekly periodical. Sub $6. Circ. 1,350. Uses freelance material. Byline given. Submit by phone. Photocopied OK. Accepts nonfiction. Sample.
BUSINESS, ECONOMICS, PUBLIC AFFAIRS

Butter-fat Magazine, Fraser Valley Milk Producers Co-Op Assoc., Box 9100, Vancouver, BC V6B 4G4. 604-420-6611. Editor: Grace Chadsey. Ads: Karen Redkwich. Quarterly magazine for dairy industry. Sub $8/yr. Circ. 2,500. Accepts freelance material by assignment only. Byline given. Query by letter or phone. Accepts fiction, nonfiction. Guidelines.
AGRICULTURE/FARMING, BUSINESS, TRADE/ASSOCIATIONS

Cacanadadada Review, PO Box 1283, Pt Angeles, WA 98362. Contact: Jack Estes. Twice yearly magazine. We like unusual work, anything risk-taking, iconoclastic, satirical, parodic, challenging or irreverent. Accepts submissions w/SASE. Reports in 3-4 wks. Accepts short stories, poetry, essays, reviews, letters, artwork, cartoons. Pays copies. Sample issues $5.
FICTION, LITERARY, POETRY

CADalyst Publications Ltd., 1727 West Broadway, 4th Fl., Vancouver, BC V6J 4W6. 604-737-1088; Fax 604-736-7169. Editor: Colleen McLaughlin. Circ. 40,000. Sub $59/yr. Monthly magazine. Freelance material accepted; byline given. Pays money and copies upon publication. First rights acquired. Submit query letter, query by phone, outline, disk/modem preferred, synopsis. Responds in 2 weeks. Publication time 4-6 months. Accepts cartoons news items, nonfiction, photos(color), interviews, op/ed, articles. Publications relating to autocad systems. Sample $5.50.
COMPUTERS, TECHNICAL

Calapooya Collage, PO Box 309, Monmouth, OR 97316. 503-838-6292. Editor: Thomas L. Ferte. Annual literary journal. Circulated nationally. Published Aug; deadline May 1. Accepts freelance material. Pays in copies. "All submissions must be typed ds, and accompanied by a SASE." Nonfiction, fiction: 1,700 wds. Poetry: any type, length. Sponsor of the annual $1000 Carolyn Kizer Poetry Awards. Sample $5.
COLLEGE/UNIVERSITY, LITERARY, POETRY

Callboard, Box 114, Victoria, BC V8W 2M1. Annual. Accepts freelance material. Byline given. Rights purchased: All. Submit ms w/SASE. Dot matrix, photocopies OK. Nonfiction, photos w/article. Sample.
NW/REGIONAL HISTORY

Calyx A. Journal of Art & Literature by Women, Calyx, Inc., PO Box B, Corvallis, OR 97339. 503-753-9384; FAX: 503-753-0515. Ed Coordinator: Beverly McFarland. Editor/Ads: Margarita Donnelly. Semiannual magazine. Sub $18/3 issues. Circ. 3,000. Most articles by freelance writers. Pays copies on publication, money when grants allow. Byline given. Submit ms, query letter w/SASE. Dot matrix, photocopies, simultaneous submissions OK. Reports in up to 6 mos; publishes in 6-9 mos. Accepts fiction, poetry, photos, art, book reviews, essays, interviews; work by women fine literature and art. Guidelines with SASE; sample $8.00 + $1.25 S&H.
LITERATURE, POETRY, WOMEN

Campus Magazine, W. 827 25th Ave., Spokane, WA 99203. Free periodical.
COLLEGE/UNIVERSITY

Canada Poultryman, 105A-9547 152nd St., Surrey, BC V3R 5Y5. 604-526-8525. Editor: Anthony Greaves. Trade periodical.
AGRICULTURE/FARMING, ANIMALS, BUSINESS

The Canadian Biker, Box 4122, Station A, Victoria, BC

V8X 3X4. 604-384-0333. Contact: W. L. Creed. Periodical published 8 times yearly. Sub/$19.95 for 12 issues. Circ. 20,000. Query with SASE. Guidelines; sample $3.
SPORTS

Canadian Human Rights Reporter Inc., 3683 W. 4th, Vancouver, BC V6R 1P2. Periodical.
PUBLIC AFFAIRS

Canadian Literature, 2029 West Mall, Room 223, University of British Columbia, Vancouver, BC V6T 1Z2. 604-822-2780. Editor: W H. New. Ads: B. Westbrook. Quarterly journal. Circ. 2,250. Rarely accepts unsolicited submissions. Pays in money, copies on publication. Acquires 1st rights. Query w/clips, SASE. Reports in 1 wk. Publishes in up to 2 yrs. Accepts poetry, criticism. For Canadian writers and writing; average 10 printed pages. $5 per printed page, $5 poems. Sample cost varies.
COLLEGE/UNIVERSITY, LITERARY, POETRY

The Canadian Press, 1445 W. 43rd Ave., Vancouver, BC V6H 1C2.
UNSPECIFIED

The Canadian Writer's Journal, Gordon M. Smart Publications, Box 6618-Depot 1, Victoria, BC V8P 5N7. 604-477-8807. Editor/ads: Gordon M. Smart. Quarterly magazine. Sub $15/yr. Circ. 250. Uses freelance material. Byline given, pays money/exchange on publication. Acquires 1st rights. Submit ms, SASE. Photocopy, dot matrix OK. Responds in 2-6 wks; publishes in 2-12 mos. Accepts occasional fiction and biography, poetry related to writing, articles, reviews. Topics: how-to for writers, but avoid overworked subjects such as overcoming writer's block and dealing with rejections. Guidelines; sample $4.
HOW-TO, LITERARY, WRITING

Canoe Magazine, 10526 N.E. 68th, Kirkland, WA 98083. 206-827-6363. Editor: Les Johnson. Ads: Glen Bernard. Bimonthly. Sub $18/6 issues. Circ. 65,000. Uses freelance material. Byline given. Pays money on publication. Acquires all rights. Submit query, SASE. Reports in 6 wks; publishes in 1 mo. Accepts nonfiction, interviews, reviews, photos (slides). Guidelines; sample $3.
OUTDOOR, RECREATION

Capilano Courier, Capilano College, 2055 Purcell Way, North Vancouver, BC V7H 3H5. 604-986-1911; 604-980-7367. Contact: News Coordinator. Ads: Imtiaz Popat. Biweekly. Circ. 2,000. Accepts freelance material. Byline given. No pay. Query w/SASE. Photocopies OK. Nonfiction, fiction, poetry, photos, cartoons. Topics: Education, student related issues. Guidelines, sample.
COLLEGE/UNIVERSITY, EDUCATION, POETRY

The Capilano Review, 2055 Purcell Way, North Vancouver, BC V7J 3H5. 604-986-1911. Editor: Dorothy Jantzen. Quarterly literary and visual arts magazine, publishing only what its editors consider to be the very best work being produced. Circ. 1,000. Sub/$12. Accepts freelance material. Payment: $40 maximum/$10 minimum and copies on publication. Byline given. Submit ms w/SASE. Photocopies, electronic OK. Reports in 6 mos. Fiction, poetry, photos, plays. We are most interested in publishing artists whose work has not yet received the attention it deserves. We are not interested in imitative, derivative, or unfinished work. We have no format exclusions. Guidelines; sample $5.
AVANT-GARDE/EXPERIMENTAL, LITERARY, VISUAL ARTS

Caronn's Town & Country with The Crib Sheet, 1518 S.E. 115th Ct, Vancouver, WA 98664-5443. 206-892-3037. Editor: Karen LaClergue. 206-892-3037. Monthly. Circ. 200. Sub $10. Uses 1-5 mss per issue. Payment: Money and copies on publication. $5/500 wds and up; $2.50/below 500 wds. Photos & mss: $7.50. $2.50 inside cover. $5 cover photo. Byline given. Submit ms, SASE. Dot matrix, photocopies, simultaneous submissions, electronic OK. Reports in 5-6 wks. Nonfiction, fiction, poetry, photos,

plays, cartoons. For Town & Country portion: garden/plant tips & photos; decorating ideas & photos; remodeling ideas & photos. Crib Sheet portion: articles pertaining to childrearing. Also adult and juvenile fiction. Guidelines; sample $2.
FAMILY, FICTION, PHOTOGRAPHY

Cascades East, PO Box 5784, 716 N.E. 4th St., Bend, OR 97708. 503-382-0127. Editors: Geoff Hill, Jan Siegrist. Ads: Geoff Hill. Quarterly magazine. Sub $12/yr. Circ. 10,000. Uses freelance material. Byline given. Pays 3-10 wd on publication. Acquires 1st rights. Submit ms, SASE. Photocopies OK. Reports in 6-8 wks; publishes in 6-12 mos. Accepts nonfiction (1,000-2,000 wds) photos (B&W glossy/color prints or transparencies, $8 to $50). Topics: recreation, general interest in Central Oregon. Guidelines; sample $4.
COMMUNITY, NW/REGIONAL HISTORY, OUTDOOR

Catalyst, PO Box 20518, Seattle, WA 98102. 205-523-4480. Editors: M. & Kathleen Kettner. Literature magazine published 2-3 times a year; special issues of erotica. Subscription: $7 for 3 issues. 75% of each issue is freelance. Submit ms w/SASE. Buys one time rights. Byline given. Pays in copies. Accepts fiction, poetry, photos, cartoons and B&W art. Open to all types of material, lean toward modern/experimental. Translations welcome. No length limits on poetry. Prose up to 10,000 wds. Samples available: 2nd Erotica, $2, & Mary Jane, $3.
FICTION, POETRY, SEX

Catchline Ski Business News, Drawer 5007, Bend, OR 97708. Trade periodical.
BUSINESS, SPORTS

CBA Bulletin, Citizen's Bar Association, PO Box 935, Medford, OR 97501. 503-779-7709. Conservative tabloid on opposition to government oppression.
LAW, POLITICS

CCLAM Chowder, Shoreline Community College Library, 16101 Greenwood Ave. N., Seattle, WA 98133. 206-546-4556. Contact: John Backes. Librarian newsletter.
COLLEGE/UNIVERSITY, REFERENCE/LIBRARY

CGA Magazine, 1176 West Georgia, Ste. 740, Vancouver, BC V6E 4A2. 604-669-3555. Editor: Lesley Wood. Ads: Bryan Cousineau. Sub $30/yr. CDN, $45 elsewhere. Circ. 40,000. Monthly for accountants. Uses some freelance material. Byline given, pays money on acceptance. Submit outline, query, SASE. Responds in 1 mo; publishes in 3-4 mos. Accepts nonfiction articles related to accounting. Guidelines.
BUSINESS, TRADE/ASSOCIATIONS

Chalk Talk, 1550 Mills Rd., RR 2, Sidney, BC V8L 3S1. 604-656-1858. Editor: Virginia Lee. Monthly magazine. Circ. 3,600; sub/$16.95. Pays copies; acquires 1st rights. Accepts (from children only): fiction, nonfiction, poetry, cartoons, news items, interviews, reviews. "Written by children for children 5-14 years." Guidelines; sample $1.50.
CHILDREN (BY/ABOUT), FICTION, POETRY

Challenge Alaska, 720 W. 58th Ave., Unit J, Anchorage, AK 99518. Newsletter for the disabled.
ALASKA, DISABLED

Changing Homes Magazine, 510 S.W. Third Ave, Portland, OR 97204. 503-635-7642; 800-289-3746. Contact: Lavonne or Clark Schenkenberger. Ads: Mike Maloney. Circ. 92,000. Founded 1989. A quarterly targeted to people moving in Oregon and Washington. Two regional editions featuring articles on financing, taxes, moving tips, remodeling, home security.
BUSINESS, CONSUMER, NORTHWEST

Chanticleer, 11700 Palfrey Dr., Vernon, BC V1B 1A8. Contact: Michael Galloway/Francis Hill. Published 10 times a year. Circ. 300. Sub/$5. Accepts freelance material. Pays in copies. Submit ms, SASE. Dot matrix, photocopies, simultaneous submissions, electronic OK. Reports in 4 wks.

Nonfiction, fiction, poetry. Topics: General, good taste, suitable for family reading. Contemporary as well as material of traditional nature. Max 2,000 wds. Sample with SASE.
FAMILY, FICTION, POETRY

Chinatown News Magazine, 459 E. Hastings, Vancouver, BC Canada. Chinese community publication.
ASIA, COMMUNITY, MINORITIES/ETHNIC

Christian Parenting Today, PO Box 3850, Sisters, OR 97759-9981. 503-549-8269. Contact: Janett Alvarez. Circ. 175,000. Bimonthly magazine of evangelical Christian parenting of children from birth through teen years. Accepts nonfiction, poetry, photos, fillers. Pay varies. Length varies. Pays acceptance for 1st or second serial rights. Sample with 8x11 SASE ($1.45). Guidelines free.
CHILDREN/TEEN, FAMILY, RELIGION

Circle, Box 176, Portland, OR 97207. Poetry.
POETRY

Citizen Action, Oregon Public Employees Union, PO Box 12159, Salem, OR 97309-0159. Bimonthly union publication.
LABOR/WORK

The City Open Press, Opus 2 Publications, 6332 S.E. Division St., Portland, OR 97206. 503-777-6121. Editor: T. C. Distel. Monthly tabloid for Portland's progressive gay people. "We want to provide an outlet for the creative individuals among us. This includes poets, prose writers, artists, photographers. We are instituting a quarterly feature called Creatively Ours! which will highlight the best of each item submitted to us. A prize will be offered."
GAY/LESBIAN PHOTOGRAPHY, POETRY

The Claremont Review, 4980 Wesley Rd., Victoria, BC V8Y 1Y9. 604-658-5221. Contact: Bill Stenson or Terence Young. Semi-annual literary journal. Sub/$10, Circ. 1000. Freelance material accepted. Byline given. Pays in copies & money. Acquires first rights. Query by SASE, photocopy or disk OK. Send complete manuscript. Responds in 2-6 weeks. Publishes in 1 to 6 months. Accepts fiction, poetry, or plays. "Restricted to students grades 8-12. We are looking for first class, edited fiction and poetry both modern and traditional, but not couch potato fuzz." Guidelines; back issues $5.
FICTION, POETRY, LITERATURE

Classical Assn of the Pacific NW Bulletin, University of Idaho, Moscow, ID 83843. Editor: C. A. E. Luschnig. Semiannual scholarly publication.
COLLEGE/UNIVERSITY, SCHOLARLY/ACADEMIC

Claustrophobia: Life-Expansion News, 1402 S.W. Upland Dr., Portland, OR 97221-2649. 503-245-4763. Periodical.
HEALTH

Cleaning Business Magazine, 1512 Western Ave., Seattle, WA 98101. 206-622-4241; FAX: 206-622-6876. Editor: Jim Saunders. Ads: Betty Saunders. Quarterly magazine. Circ. 5,000; sub $20/yr. Uses freelance 5-10 freelance mss per issue. Requires knowledge of the cleaning industry, or good research ability. Pays $10-90 for up to 2,500 wds on publication. Acquires 1st or all rights. Byline given. Submit query w/clips, ms w/SASE, or phone query. Good dot matrix, photocopied or computer disk OK. Accepts nonfiction, photos, cartoons. Topics: exposes, cleaning and maintenance for self-employed professionals in this field, interviews with successful cleaning business operators, business, fact-based management advice geared to on-site cleaning. Prefers solid technical articles, positive slant, helpful, friendly. Polished ms only. Photos B&W or color, not over 5x7; $5 per photo used. Guidelines for SASE. Sample $3.
BUSINESS, LABOR/WORK, TECHNICAL

Clients Council News, PO Box 342, Eugene, OR 97440. 503-342-5167. Contact: Susan Stern
UNSPECIFIED

Cloudline, PO Box 462, Ketchum, ID 83340. 208-788-3704. Editor: Scott Preston. Biannual exploring various themes relating to the conflict/impact of mans presence in the wilderness and natural environment. Circ. 300. Sub/ $6. Rarely accepts freelance material, but we are open. Payment: Copies on publication. Byline given. Rights purchased: First. Reports in 2-4 wks. Fiction, poetry, B&W graphics. Guidelines with SASE.
ENVIRONMENT/RESOURCES, OUTDOOR, POETRY

Coast Tidings, The News Guard, PO Box 848, Lincoln City, OR 97367. 503-994-2178. Editor: Duane C. Honsowetz. Periodical.
COMMUNITY, RECREATION

Coeur d'Alene Homes Messenger, 704 W. Walnut, Coeur d'Alene, ID 83814. Quarterly directed to residents of local homes for the aged and their families. Circ. 4,000.
FAMILY, PSYCHOLOGY, SENIOR CITIZENS

cold-drill Magazine, Department of English, Boise State University, Boise, ID 83725. 208-385-1999. Contact: Tom Trusky. Annual magazine. Sub/$10. Circ. 500. Uses 30 freelance mss per issues. Pays copies on publication; byline given. Acquires 1st rights. Submit ms, SASE. Dot matrix, photocopies, simultaneous subs OK. Nonfiction, fiction, poetry, photos, plays, cartoons, other. "Know the magazine; we're not your average literary magazine…Our format is boxed loose-leaf, which means we do 3-D comics, scratch'n sniff poems, accordion-fold extravaganzas — plus traditional literary publishing (poems, short stories, plays, etc.)." Guidelines; sample $10.
AVANT-GARDE/EXPERIMENTAL, COLLEGE/UNIVERSITY, IDAHO

Colins Magazine, 10254 35th Ave. S.W., Seattle, WA 98146. 206-937-8155. Editors: Carl Diltz, Joe Keppler. Quarterly. Uses freelance material. Pays copies on publication. Acquires all rights. Query, complete ms, SASE. Responds immediately, publishes in 3 mos. Accepts poetry, photos, interviews, op/ed, articles, plays, reviews. Topics: computer technology and the literary arts; design; art publications; poetry. A review of contemporary culture & technology. (See Poets. Painters. Composers.) Sample $7.
COMPUTERS, LITERARY, MUSIC

Collegian, Willamette University, 900 State St., Salem, OR 97301. 503-370-6053. Periodical.
COLLEGE/UNIVERSITY

Collegiate, City University, 16661 Northrup Way, Bellevue, WA 98008. 206-643-2000. Quarterly newsletter. Circ. 90,000. Founded 1973. Does not accept freelance material, produced in-house. "If you have an article idea, please submit a press release."
COLLEGE/UNIVERSITY

Colonygram, PO Box 15200, Portland, OR 97214. Contact: Rae Richen. Circ. 1,000. Sub w/membership/$15. One or two short pieces per issue. Published by N.W. writers for N.W. writers. Payment: Copies on publication. Byline given. Submit ms w/SASE. Dot matrix, photocopies, simultaneous submissions, electronic OK. Nonfiction only, except December, special fiction issue. Short pieces on marketing your writing: 250 wds, free copies on request. Book review on books about writing: 500 wds, $5. Strong interview with a published writer: 500-1,000 wds, query first, $10. Tip: Read Colonygram first. Do you have something to contribute to other writers? Sample/SASE.
BOOK ARTS/BOOKS, PUBLISHING/PRINTING, WRITING

Columbia Communicator, 4628 S. W. 49TH, Portland, OR 97221. 503-236-7377. Editor: Donna Snyder. Monthly.
UNSPECIFIED

Columbia The Magazine Of Northwest History, Washington State Historical Society, 315 N. Stadium Way, Tacoma, WA 98403. 206-593-2830. Editor: David L. Nicandri. Quarterly magazine. Sub/$5. Circ. 2,600. Uses freelance material. Pyas $25 and copies on publication.

Acquires 1st rights; byline given. Submit query w/ clips, ms, SASE. Reports in 2-4 weeks; publishes in 9 months. Nonfiction, biography, op/ed, articles, photos. Topics: N.W. history; preferred length 3,000 wds or less. Guidelines, sample.
NW/REGIONAL HISTORY, LITERARY, WASHINGTON

Columbiana, Chesaw Rt. Box 83F, Oroville, WA 98844. 509-485-3844. Editor: J. Payton. Ads: R. Gillespie. Quarterly bio-regional journal. Sub $7.50. Circ. 4,000. Uses 10 freelance mss per issue. Pays money/copies on publication. Acquires 1st rights. Byline given. Query w/clips, SASE. Dot matrix, computer disk OK. Reports in 1 mo. Publishes in 16 mos. Accepts nonfiction, fiction, photos, cartoons. Topics: progressive, relevant to inland Northwest, Columbia River Drainage. Prefers features of 1,000 wds with accompanying illustrations. Pays 1/word plus 6 mos subscription. Photos: B&W prints only, $5+. Guidelines; sample $2.
ENVIRONMENT/RESOURCES, NORTHWEST, RECREATION

Columns Magazine, University of Washington Alumni Assoc., 1415 N.E. 45th, Seattle, WA 98105. 206-543-0540; Fax 206-685-0611. Editor: Tom Griffin. Ads: Mike Nienaber. Quarterly magazine. Circ. 160,000. Founded 1908. Accepts freelance material. Pays money on publication. Byline given. Acquires 1st rights. Submit query, SASE. Reports in 1 mo; publishes in 3-6 mos. Accepts nonfiction, interviews. No manuscripts, query only, must be related to UW.
COLLEGE/UNIVERSITY, WASHINGTON

The Comics Journal, Fantagraphics Books, 7563 Lake City Way, Seattle, WA 98115. 206-524-1967. Contact: Carole Sobocinski. Monthly magazine on comic book industry. Circ. 10,000. Freelance material accepted. Send for guidelines first. Pays on publication. Acquires 1st rights. Responds in 6-8 weeks. Accepts nonfiction and reviews. Query w/clips & SASE. Guidelines, back issues.
CULTURE, LITERARY

The Coming Revolution, Box A, Livingston, MT 59047. 406-222-8300. Periodical.
UNSPECIFIED

Commercial Review, 1725 N.W. 24, Portland, OR 97210-2507. Weekly periodical on Portland business and commerce. Not a freelance market.
BUSINESS

Common Ground, Box 34090, Station D, Vancouver, BC V6J 4M1. 604-733-2215. Editor: Joseph Roberts. Ads: Nick Walker. Quarterly celebrating the art of living. Circ. 100,000. Sub $17. Uses 6 mss per issue. Payment: $0-100, copies on publication. Byline given. Query w/ms, SASE. Nonfiction, fiction, photos, cartoons. Book reviews: 250-300 wds; interviews: 500-1,500 wds; topic article: 750-2,000 wds. Photos: B&W inside, $25-75; color cover only $25-100. Lots of highlights work best. Lots of mid-tone and good contrast. "We touch on a lot of subjects and are always looking for good editorials." Guidelines/sample, send $2.
ENTERTAINMENT, HUMOR, PHOTOGRAPHY

Communication Magazine, 1133 Melville St., 6th Floor, Vancouver, BC V6J 2K1. 604-681-3264. Editor: Penelope Noble. Ads: Kirsty Gladwell. Monthly magazine for Institute of Chartered Accountants of British Columbia. Circ. 6,500. Freelance material accepted. No pay. Byline given. Submit query by letter or phone. Reports in 1 wk, publishes in 2-3 mos. Accepts articles relating to accounting. Generally written by accountants. Situations in the US may be of interest. Guidelines, samples.
BUSINESS, TRADE/ASSOCIATIONS, UNSPECIFIED

Communicator, SFCC - MS 3050, W. 3410 Ft. Geo. Wright Dr., Spokane, WA 99204. 509-459-3602. Editor: Klaus Scherler. Biweekly periodical. Circ. 3,000. Uses freelance material. Byline given. Accepts news items, interviews, articles, photos (B&W).
COLLEGE/UNIVERSITY

Community Digest Magazine, 216-1755 Robson St., Ste. 216, Vancouver, BC V6G 3B7. 604-875-8313. Editor: S. M. Bowell. Ads: N. Ebrahim. Weekly magazine. Sub $25/ yr. Circ. 25,000. Uses freelance material. No pay. Submit query letter, complete ms, SASE, phone. Dot matrix, photocopies OK. Accepts nonfiction, news items, photos. Topics: for an ethnic audience, stress Indian (East), African, South Asian.
COMMUNITY, CULTURE, MINORITIES/ETHNIC

Comparative Literature, 223 Friendly Hall, University of Oregon, Eugene, OR 97403. Quarterly academic publication. Not a freelance market.
COLLEGE/UNIVERSITY, ENGLISH, LITERARY

The Competitive Advantage, PO Box 10091, Portland, OR 97210. 503-274-2953. Editor: Jim Moran. Monthly periodical on sales and marketing. Sub $96. Circ. 10,000. Uses 1-2 freelance mss per issue. No pay. Byline given. Submit ms, phone. Dot matrix, photocopied OK. Accepts nonfiction, cartoons.
BUSINESS

Computer Education News, Box 5182, Bellingham, WA 98227. 206-676-3954. Editor: Carol Anderson. Newsletter devoted to computer education in schools & industry. Includes product reviews, computer industry developments, training ideas, etc. Sub/$36.
EDUCATION, COMPUTERS

The Computing Teacher, University of Oregon, 1787 Agate St., Eugene, OR 97403-1923. 503-686-4414; Fax 503-346-5890. Editor: Anita Best. Ads: Lynda Ferguson. Publishes 8 times a year. Circ. 12,000. Sub $52. Uses 11-13 mss per issue. Writers must be well versed in computer education. Submissions are reviewed anonymously by at least three qualified reviewers. TCT emphasizes teaching about computers, teaching using computer curriculum, teacher education, computer software programs and the general impact of computers in education today. Pays copies on publication. Query w/ms, SASE. Dot matrix, simultaneous submissions, electronic OK. Reports in 16 wks. Nonfiction, photos. Approx. 600-3,000 wds. Guidelines; free sample.
COMPUTERS, EDUCATION

Conscience, 4534 1/2 University Way N.E., Seattle, WA 98105. Editors: Vivien Sharples & Geov Parrish. Quarterly newsletter of the Conscience & Military Tax Campaign. Circ. 2500. Founded 1979. Sub/$10. Freelance material accepted, byline given. No payment.
PEACE, PUBLIC AFFAIRS

Construction Data & News, PO Box 3165, Seattle, WA 98114. Periodical.
BUSINESS, TRADE/ASSOCIATIONS

Construction Sightlines, 124 W. 8th St., North Vancouver, BC V7M 3H2. 604-985-8711. Editor: Tom R. Tevlin. Quarterly trade magazine. Uses freelance material. Byline given. Submit outline, SASE. Dot matrix sub OK. Accepts articles.
TRADE/ASSOCIATIONS

Consumer Resource N.W., 5215 W. Clearwater #107-25 B, Kennewick, WA 99336. 509-783-3337. Editor: Jo Hollier. Ads: Deb Layman. Monthly magazine. Circ. 41,000. Uses 1-2 freelance mss per issue. Pays copies. Rights acquired: First. Byline given. Submit mss, SASE. Reports in 1 mo. Accepts nonfiction, poetry, photos. Topics: Mature, retirement; 100-150 wds. PMTs on photos.
CONSUMER, PUBLIC AFFAIRS, SENIOR CITIZENS

Contacts Influential, 1630 S.W. Morrison St., #100, Portland, OR 97205-1815. 503-227-1900. Monthly newsletter. Sub $150. Circ. 400. Not a freelance market.
BUSINESS

Contractors Weekly, 1213 Valley, Seattle, WA 98109. 206-622-7053. Trade periodical.
BUSINESS, TRADE/ASSOCIATIONS

Controversy in Review, PO Box 11408, Portland, OR 97211. 503-282-0381. Editor: Richard E. Geis. Bimonthly periodical. Sub $9. Circ. 1,000. Uses 1 freelance ms per issue. Pays copies on publication. Byline given. Submit ms, phone. Dot matrix, photocopied, simultaneous OK. Reports in 1-2 wks. Accepts nonfiction, cartoons.
LITERARY, POLITICS

Convictions, PO Box 1749, Corvallis, OR 97339-1749. 503-754-1564. Quarterly by and for prisoners. Sub: prisoner $8, Indiv. $10. Accepts ms w SASE. All topics except religious disputation. Poems of confession/repentance not generally. Sample $4.00.
FICTION, POETRY, PRISON

Council for Human Rights in Latin America Newsletter, 3835 S.W. Kelly Ave., Portland, OR 97201-4312.
MINORITIES/ETHNIC, POLITICS

Country Roads, DoMac Publications Ltd, #810 207 W. Hastings St., Vancouver, BC V6B 1J8. 604-684-8255. Editor: Barb Schmidt. Ads: Fran Kay. Free distribution in Frazer Valley community newspapers. Circ. 25,000. Bimonthly tabloid serving the Fraser Valley's independent and small scale farmers. News, features, and articles for and about people and events in rural BC. No submission into.
AGRICULTURE/FARMING, BRITISH COLUMBIA

Cowlitz-Wahkiakum Senior News, PO Box 2129, Longview, WA 98632. Monthly periodical.
COMMUNITY, SENIOR CITIZENS

Crab Creek Review, 4462 Whitman Ave. N., Seattle, WA 98103. 206-633-1090. Editor: Linda Clifton/Carol Orlock, fiction. Literary magazine of poetry/fiction published 2 times a yr. Sub rate $8. Circ. 350-500. All articles freelance. Pays copies on publication. Rights purchased: First. Byline given. Submit ms, SASE. Dot matrix, photocopies OK. No simultaneous submissions. Reports in 6-8 wks. Publishes in 2-24 mos. Accepts fiction: up to 3,500 wds, strong voice, imagery; nonfiction: up to 3,500 wds; poetry: under 40 lines (free or formal, clear imagery, wit, voice that is interesting and energetic, accessible to the general reader rather than full of very private imagery and obscure literary allusion); art: B&W, pen or brushwork. "Translations accepted. Please accompany with copy of the work in the original language. Accepting work only by invitation." Guidelines. Sample $3.
FICTION, POETRY

Craft Connection, PO Box 40035, Bellevue, WA 98005-4035. Editor: Friedda Kimball. Sub $12/yr. Circ. 40,000. Published bimonthly. Uses freelance material. Byline given. No pay, acquires 1st rights. Photocopies, computer disk OK. Reports in 1 mo. Accepts nonfiction, photos (B&W), cartoons, graphics. Topics: craft how-to's; general interest business, how to start, wholesale, marketing; history or topical stories about handcrafts or local artist. Sample $2.
BUSINESS, CRAFTS/HOBBIES, HOW-TO

Crafts Advocate, 950 Fish Hatchery Rd., Grants Pass, OR 97527. Bimonthly periodical featuring listings of Oregon craft fairs & festivals and evaluations of them by readers. Not a freelance market. Back issues available only to subscribers.
ARTS, CRAFTS/HOBBIES, OREGON

Crafts Report, 87 Wall St., Seattle, WA 98121. 206-441-3102. Editor: Christine Yarrow. Ads: Sheila Haynes. Monthly tabloid. Sub/$19.25. Circ. 20,000. Uses freelance material. Business subjects for crafts professionals. Pays on publication. Byline given. Send photo with submission. Query w/SASE. Guidelines; sample $2.50.
BUSINESS, CRAFTS/HOBBIES

Creative News n' Views, C.E.D.F., PO Box 1001, Tualatin, OR 97062. 503-624-0131(V); 503-624-0351 (TDD). Editor: Paula Reuter-Dymeck. Ads: Don Carbone. Monthly newsletter for membership.
LABOR/WORK, DISABLED

Crook County Historical Society Newsletter, 246 N. Main, Prineville, OR 97754. Irregular periodical.
NW/REGIONAL HISTORY

Cryptogram Detective, 8137 S.E. Ash, Portland, OR 97215. 503-256-2393. Editor: Joan Barton. Bimonthly periodical/membership. Uses 1-9 freelance mss per issue. Pays copies on publication. Byline given. Submit ms, SASE. Dot matrix, photocopied, simultaneous OK. Reports in 6 mos. Accepts fiction. Sample $1.25.
ENTERTAINMENT

CSWS Review, Center for the Study of Women in Society, University of Oregon, Eugene, OR 97403. 503-346-5015. Annual educational publication. Articles by assignment only. Topics: feminism.
COLLEGE/UNIVERSITY, WOMEN

Cumtux, Clatsop County Historical Society, 1618 Exchange St., Astoria, OR 97103. 503-325-2203. Editor: Lisa Penner. Quarterly journal. Circ. 1000, founded 1980. Sub/$25. Freelance material accepted, byline given. Pays in copies. Acquires first rights. Query by letter or phone. Send outline, complete ms. Dot matrix, photocopy OK. Responds in one month, time to publication varies. Accepts biography, nonfiction, photos, interviews, articles, and memoirs. Guidelines; back issues $5.
NW/REGIONAL HISTORY

The Current, KMUN-FM, PO Box 269, Astoria, OR 97103. Contact: Polly Buckingham or Doug Sweet. Ads: Polly Buckingham. Monthly newsletter of North Coast community radio. Sub $25/yr. Circ. 2,500. Not a freelance market.
COMMUNITY

Current Concepts-Oral/Maxillofacial Surgery, 101 E. 8th St. #120, Vancouver, WA 98660-3294. 206-254-8540. Editor: Dr. Jack Stecher. 206-254-8540. Monthly. Also publishes Current Concepts in Orthodontics and Current Concepts in Clinical Pathology a Physicians Newsletter. Circ. 12,000. Not a freelance market.
MEDICAL

Current News, Idaho Power Company, PO Box 70, Boise, ID 83707. Editor: Nikki B. Stilwell. Published 8 times a yr. Circ. 3,200.
BUSINESS, CONSUMER, PUBLIC AFFAIRS

Curry County Echoes, Curry County Historical Society, 920 S. Ellensburg Ave., Gold Beach, OR 97444. 503-247-6113. Editor: Virginia Fendrick. Monthly on local history. Sub w/membership in historical society, $5. Not a freelance market.
NW/REGIONAL HISTORY

CutBank, c/o English Department, University of Montana, Missoula, MT 59812. 406-243-5231. Editor: Judy Blunt. Semiannual literary journal. Sub $12. Circ. 600. Uses freelance material. Pays 2 copies on publication. Byline given. Submit query w/ms & SASE. Photocopied, disk/modem, simultaneous subs OK. Reports in 2-3 mos. Publishes in 2-4 mos. Accepts fiction (to 40 ds pages), poetry (3-5), photos, interviews, plays, reviews, art (1-5 slides). Send B&W slides of artwork labeled with name, title, medium, and date of work. Most visual arts reproduced in B&W. Work must be of high quality to be considered. No stylistic limitations. Staff reads from August 15 to Feb. 1. Guidelines. Sample $4.50.
VISUAL ARTS, FICTION, POETRY

CVAS, Bellingham Pub. Lib., Fairhaven Branch, Bellingham, WA 98227. Periodical.
REFERENCE/LIBRARY

Dairyline, United Dairymen of Idaho, 1365 N. Orchard, Boise, ID 83760. Bimonthly. Circ. 3,000.
AGRICULTURE/FARMING, BUSINESS

Dalmo'ma, Empty Bowl, PO Box 646, Port Townsend, WA 98368. 206-385-4943. Editor: Michael Daley. Circ. 1,500. Sub $7/issue. Irregularly published anthology of

literature and responsibility, and regional/rural quality of life, by N.W. writers. Accepts freelance submissions on themes. Nonfiction, fiction, poetry, photos, plays, cartoons almost anything serious considered. Past edition included a record. Rights revert to author. Pays in copies on publication. Reports in 2 mos. Query w/SASE. Dot matrix, photocopies and simultaneous submission OK. Guidelines; sample/$7.
CULTURE, FICTION, POETRY

Deals & Wheels, 11717 N.E. 50th AVE. #1, Vancouver, WA 98682. Editor: Shelly Wilson. Periodical.
UNSPECIFIED

Demographics Northwest, 317 S.W. Alder, Ste. 1285, Portland, OR 97204. 503-222-5412. Contact: John Ettinger. Monthly newsletter. Sub $63/yr. Byline given, pays money, copies on publication, acquires all rights. Submit query letter, outline, synopsis, SASE. Response time varies, publishes in 1 mo. Accepts nonfiction, news items. Topics: trends, trend tracking in the N.W., news of research, surveys, studies.
BUSINESS, ECONOMICS, MEDIA/COMMUNICATIONS

Denali, Lane Community College, 4000 E. 30th Ave., Eugene, OR 97405. 503-747-45012830. Editor: Karen Loche. College literary magazine. Editors could change yearly. SASE for guidelines.
COLLEGE/UNIVERSITY, FICTION, OREGON

Desert Trail Association, PO Box 537, Burns, OR 97720. 503-281-8891; 503-636-1323. Editor: Ross Edginton. Quarterly newsletter. Circ. 1200, founded 1972. Sub/$10. No freelance material accepted. Byline given. Query by letter w/ SASE, phone. Accepts news items, Bd&W photos, articles, reviews. Back issues.
UNSPECIFIED

Designer's Quarterly, PO Box 19876, Portland, OR 97219. 503-245-8127. Query editor: Kirt Dye.
ARTS

The Desktop Publishing Journal, 4027-C Rucker Ave, Ste. 821, Everett, WA 98201. 206-568-2950. Editor: Linda Hanson. Ads: Jared Hays. Circ. 50,000. Sub $10.99. Monthly journal. Uses 25 freelance mss per issue. Some technical expertise needed to write for us. Pays money on publication: $200 for feature articles of 4,000-7,000 wds; $100 for articles 1,000-4,000 wds; $25 for cartoons. Likes to trade articles for 1/4 page ads. Graphic reqs: 85-line screen. Rights purchased: First. Reprints OK. Byline given. Query w/clips, SASE. All forms of submission, OK. Reports in 2 mos. Publishes in 2 mos. Accepts nonfiction, photos, cartoons. We need articles written for all levels, but prefer beginners level. How-to articles are preferred, but print anything and everything related to DTP. Guidelines. Sample $1.50.
COMPUTERS, PUBLISHING/PRINTING, TECHNICAL

Dialogue - Thoughtprints, Center Press, 14902 33rd Ave. N.W., Gig Harbor, WA 98335-9215. 206-858-3964. Editor: E. J. Featherstone. Quarterly of poetry with inspirational (nonreligious) humorous philosophical message. Circ. 2,000-3,000. Pays on publication. Byline given. Query w/ms, SASE. Dot matrix, simultaneous submissions OK. Publishes submissions in 3-12 mos. Nonfiction: on poetry and poetry markets, 250 wds, no pay. Poetry: 2-4 lines; pays in prizes/subs. Short rhymed humor: pays $1. "No sensational morbid themes. Good imagery — meter will be edited if poem merits publication. Mankind's needs addressed, looking for upbeat material — no heavy religious or Pollyanna."
PHILOSOPHY, POETRY

The Digger, Oregon Association of Nurserymen, 2780 S.E. Harrison, Ste. 102, Milwaukie, OR 97222. 503-653-8733. Editor: Miles McCoy. Monthly agricultural trade magazine. Circ. 4,500. Uses freelance material. Byline given. Pays money on publication. Acquires all rights.

Submit query letter, SASE, phone. Responds in 3-4 wks; publishes in 1-6 mos. Accepts nonfiction, news items, interviews, photos. Topics: plant nursery business. Sample.
AGRICULTURE/FARMING, BUSINESS, GARDENING

Discovery, 1908 Second St., Tillamook, OR 97141. 503-842-7535. Periodical.
UNSPECIFIED

Diver Magazine, Seagraphic Publications Ltd., #295-10991 Shellbridge Way, Richmond, BC V6X 3C6. 604-273-4333. Editor: Peter Vassilopoulos. Magazine published 9X/yr. Circ. 20,000. Uses freelance material. Byline given. Pays money, copies on publication. Query letter, complete ms, SASE. Dot matrix, disk/modem OK. Accepts nonfiction, fiction, news items, reviews, photos. Topics: subjects of interest to divers. Guidelines; sample $3.
OUTDOOR, RECREATION, TRAVEL

Diversity: The Lesbian Rag, PO Box 66106, Sta. F, Vancouver, BC V5N 5L4. 604-872-3026. Editor: Evie Mandel. Ads: Jo'anne Lambert. Bimonthly magazine. Circ. 2,000, subs. $18/yr US. Uses freelance material. Byline given; pays copies. Submit ms, query/SASE (Canadian stamps), phone. Photocopied sub OK. Responds in 1-6 mos. Accepts fiction, nonfiction, poetry, cartoons, articles, art, news items. Material by and for lesbians, include bio for publication with work. Guidelines, sample $2.
GAY/LESBIAN, SEX, WOMEN

Dog River Review, PO Box 125, Parkdale, OR 97041-0125. 503-352-6494. Editor: Laurence F. Hawkins, Jr. Semiannual of fiction, poetry, art. Circ. 200. Sub $6. Accepts freelance material. Payment: Copies on publication. Rights purchased: First. Submit ms, SASE. Dot matrix, photocopies OK. Reports in 1-3 mos. Fiction: to 2,500 wds. Poetry: prefer verse to 30 lines but will consider longer, all forms. Also accepts plays, B&W art. No pornography; eroticism OK. No sermonizing, self-indulgent material. No religious verse. Guidelines; sample $2.
CRAFTS/HOBBIES, FICTION, POETRY

Doll Mall, Paddlewheel Press, PO Box 230220, Tigard, OR 97223. 503-292-8460. Quarterly.
UNSPECIFIED

The Downtowner, 621 S.W. Morrison St., Ste 140, Portland, OR 97205. 503-243-2600. Editor: Maggi White. Ads: Kathleen Doherty. Founded 1973. Weekly focusing on Portland, entertainment, culture. Sub $26/yr. Circ. 26,000. Uses freelance material. Byline given. Pays money on publication. Query letter, SASE, clips. Responds in 30 days; publishes in 60 days. Nonfiction, cartoons, interviews, op-ed, articles. Upbeat, lively, not investigative. Free sample.
CULTURE, ENTERTAINMENT, HUMOR

Dragonfly, 4102 N.E. 130th Pl., Portland, OR 97230. Editor: L.E. Harr. Quarterly haiku journal.
POETRY

The Duckabush Journal, PO Box 390, Hansville, WA 98340-0390. 206-683-0647. Editor: Ken Crump. Literary regional periodical published 3 times a yr. Sub $12. A creative insight to the Olympic Peninsula and adjacent areas. Pays copies on publication. Submit ms, query w/SASE. Accepts poetry, short stories, historical studies, character sketches, other nonfiction, B&W art, photographs. Prose should have a tone or feeling of Olympic Peninsula. Guidelines. Sample $4.50.
FICTION, POETRY, VISUAL ARTS

dVoid, Fraser Valley College, RR No 2, Abbotsford, BC V2S 4N2. Magazine of poetry and translations. Submit ms w/SASE.
LITERARY, POETRY

Dwelling Portably, PO Box 190-MW, Philomath, OR 97370. Editor: Holly Davis. Newsletter published 3X/yr. Sub $1/issue. Circ. 1,000. Uses freelance material. Pays subscription or ad on acceptance. Submit ms, no-return copies preferred. Dot matrix, photocopied, simultaneous, subs

OK. Accepts nonfiction. Topics: information related to camping for long periods or living in tipis, vans, trailers, boats, remote cabins, etc. No photos, line drawings & screens only. "Want candid reports from those doing what they are writing about. Polish not important." Guidelines; sample $1.
HOW-TO, OUTDOOR

Early Warning, Ste. 1, EMU, Eugene, OR 97403. Periodical.
UNSPECIFIED

Earshot Jazz, 3429 Fremont Pl. #308, Seattle, WA 98103. 206-547-6763; 206-624-1451. Editor: Andrew Freund. Ads: Ernie Saylor. Monthly newsletter. Founded 1986. Sub $20/yr. Circ. 7,000. Uses freelance material. Byline given. Pays money on publication. SASE. Photocopy, dot matrix, disk/modem OK. Reports in 1 month. Accepts nonfiction, news items, interviews, reviews, articles, poetry, cartoons, biography, photos (5x7 print $15-25). "Jazz articles, reviews, and related material. We focus on the N.W. jazz scene. Back issues $1.
MUSIC

Earthwatch Oregon, 2637 S.W. Water, Portland, OR 97201. 503-222-1963. Editor/ads: Heath Lynn Silberfeld. Quarterly on environmental issues of concern to Oregonians. Circ. 2,000. Sub $25. Accepts freelance material. No pay. Byline given. Phone query, dot matrix, photocopies OK. Uses nonfiction, photos. Environmental issues reporting/opinion pieces of 1-10 typewritten pages, with emphasis on legislative activity, lobbying, and enforcement of environmental law, statutes, rules. Photos: B&W prints. Sample.
ENVIRONMENT/RESOURCES, OREGON, POLITICS

East is East, PO Box 95247, Seattle, WA 98145-2247. 206-522-1551. Periodical.
UNSPECIFIED

The Eastern Beacon, Eastern Oregon State College, Hoke College Center, La Grande, OR 97850. 503-962-3526. Editor: Jennie Beyerl. Ads: Artie Peterson. Bimonthly to college students, professors, staff and community. Circ. 1,800. Accepts freelance material. No pay. Byline given. Dot matrix, photocopies, simultaneous subs OK. Uses nonfiction, fiction, poetry, photos, cartoons. Sample with SASE.
COLLEGE/UNIVERSITY, ENTERTAINMENT, SPORTS

Echo Digest, 10300 S.W. Greenburg Rd., #280, Portland, OR 97223. Editor: Owen R. Brown. Periodical.
UNSPECIFIED

The Eclectic Muse, 340 W. 3rd St. #107, N. Vancouver, BC V7M 1G4. 604-984-7834. Editor: Joe M. Ruggier. Ads: Bill Marles. Magazine published 3x yearly. Sub $20. Circ. 200. Uses freelance material; byline given. Pyas copies on publication. Submit query letter, SASE. Photocopy, dot matrix, simultaneous subs OK. Responds in 4 months; publishing time varies. Accepts fiction, poetry, articles, interviews, reviews. "Can you write in free form like the Authors of Scripture?" Guidelines; sample $7.
FICTION, POETRY

Economic Facts/Idaho Agriculture, University of Idaho Extension Service, College of Agriculture, Moscow, ID 83843. Editor: Neil Meyer. Quarterly.
AGRICULTURE/FARMING, BUSINESS, IDAHO

Editors Roundtable, E. 1419 Marietta Ave., Spokane, WA 99207. 509-487-3383. Editor: Elinor Nuxoll. Quarterly newsletter. $4/sub. Circ. 100. Uses freelance material from newsletter editors. Byline given. Pays in copies, subscriptions, acquires first rights. Send query letter, complete ms, SASE. Dot matrix, photocopy, simultaneous sub OK. Publishes in 2 months. Guidelines; back issues $1.
MEDIA, PUBLISHING, WRITING

Edprint Inc., 17936 Woodinville-Snohomish Rd., Woodinville, WA 98072. 206-483-0606. Publisher of

magazine and newsletter. Accepts unsolicited submissions, freelance material. Byline given. Pays copies, royalties on publication. Responds 1-2 mos. Accepts fiction, nonfiction, poetry, photos, cartoons, memoirs, biography.
BIOGRAPHY, FICTION, POETRY

Educational Digest, The Riggs Institute, 4185 S.W. 102nd Ave., Beaverton, OR 97005. 503-646-9459. Periodical.
EDUCATION

El Centinela, Pacific Press Publishing Association, 1350 Kings Rd., Nampa, ID 83651. Editor: Tulio Peverini. Monthly. Circ. 113,000.
UNSPECIFIED

Elixir of Oregon Wordworks, PO Box 514, Manzanita, OR 97130. 503-368-7017. Editor: Cathleen Thomsen. Quarterly magazine. Circ. 5,000. Uses freelance material. Byline given. Pays copies. Submit query letter, complete ms. Photocopy, simultaneous subs OK. Responds in 2 wks; publishes in 3 mos. Accepts fiction, nonfiction, poetry, cartoons, photos.
FICTION, POETRY, UNSPECIFIED

Ellensburg Anthology, Four Winds Bookstore, 202 E. 4th, Ellensburg, WA 98926. 206-754-1708. Editor: Tom Lineham. Periodical of poetry and prose for emerging N.W. writers. Circ. 200-300. Sub $3.50 + post. Uses 5 mss per issue. Payment: Copies. Byline given. Rights purchased: First. Submit ms, SASE. Dot matrix, photocopies, simultaneous submission, electronic OK. Reports in 2-4 mos. Fiction (2,000 wds), poetry (100 lines), plays (sections only), illustrations. We are looking especially for new talent. Deadline: July 31 each yr. Guidelines; sample $3.50 with SASE.
DRAMA, FICTION, POETRY

The Eloquent Umbrella, English Dept., LBCC, 6500 Pacific Blvd. S.W., Albany, OR 97321-3799. 503-928-2361x208. Contact: Linda Smith. Annual literary journal. Accepts freelance material. Query w/SASE.
FICTION, LITERARY, POETRY

Emergency Horse, 1430 Willamette, #271, Eugene, OR 97401. Editor: Howard Libes. Avant Garde periodical of arts, literature, and commentary.
ARTS, LITERARY

Emergency Librarian, PO Box C34069, Dept. 284, Seattle, WA 98124-1069. 604-734-0255. Also PO Box 46258, Sta. G, Vancouver, BC V6R 4G6. Editor: Ken Haycock. Ads: Dana Sheehan. Circ. 10,000. Sub $40 prepaid. Publishes magazine 5 times a yr. Uses 3 freelance mss per issue. Request guidelines before writing. Pays money on publication. Rights purchased: All. Byline given. Query w/clips. Dot matrix, photocopy OK. Reports in 6 wks. Publishes within 1 yr. Accepts: Nonfiction, cartoons. Guidelines.
BOOK ARTS/BOOKS, EDUCATION, REFERENCE/LIBRARY

Em-Kayan, Morrison-Knudsen Corporation, PO Box 73, Boise, ID 83707. Editor: Vern Nelson. Monthly for employees, stockholders and customers of M-K.
BUSINESS

The Emshock Letter, Randall Flat Rd., PO Box 411, Troy, ID 83871. 208-835-4902. Editor: Steven E. Erickson. Newsletter published irregularly. Sub $25/yr, Circ. 17. Submissions accepted only from subscribers. Topics: philosophical, metaphysical.
ASTROLOGY/SPIRITUAL, CULTURE, HUMOR

Encore Arts In Performance Magazine, 1987 S.W. Montgomery Pl., Portland, OR 97201-2446. 503-226-1468. Editor: Philbrook Heppner. Ads: Tom Brown. Published 60 times a season. Circ. 986,000. Not a freelance market. Sample: 73 cents.
ARTS, DRAMA, MUSIC

Encounters Magazine, Black Matrix Press, PO Box 5737, Grants Pass, OR 97527. 503-476-7039. Editor: Guy Kenyon. Sub $6. Circ. 500. Uses 5-8 mss an issue. Pays in

3 copies (additional copies at 1/2 price) on publication. First rights acquired. Byline given. Submit mss with SASE. Accepts dot matrix, photocopies. Uses fiction, cartoons, B&W art work both for cover and interior. Send portfolio of at least 6 images. Maximum length 5,000 wds. Any material not accompanied by SASE cannot be returned. We accept SF, horror, fantasy and humor. There is no particular slant to the type of fiction we need, just tell us a good story, and if we like it we will try to fit it into our printing schedule.

FANTASY/SCI FI, FICTION, HUMOR

Enfantaisie, 2603 S.E. 32nd Ave., Portland, OR 97202. 503-235-5304. Editor: Michael Gould. Published bimonthly for children learning French. Circ. 2,000. Not accepting submissions at this time. We do not guarantee return of any unsolicited material.

CHILDREN (BY/ABOUT), CHILDREN/TEEN, LANGUAGE(S)

Engineering Geology/Soils Engineering Symposium, Idaho Transportation Department, PO Box 7129, Boise, ID 83707. Annual periodical. Circ. 500.

IDAHO, SCIENCE

Engineering News-record, 6040 Fifth N.E., Seattle, WA 98115. 206-525-0433. Periodical.

BUSINESS

Enterprise, c/o B. C. Central Credit Union, 1441 Creekside Dr., Vancouver, BC V6B 3R9. Editor: David Morton. Bimonthly concerning credit unions in BC, aimed at managers and directors. Circ. 2,000. Payment: $200-300 on publication. Query w/SASE. Phone query, dot matrix OK. Publishes submissions in 1-2 mos. Nonfiction: 1,000-2,000 wds about credit unions and cooperatives. Photos: contact sheet and negatives w/article. Guidelines, sample.

BUSINESS

Environmental Law, Northwestern School of Law, 10015 S.W. Terwilliger Blvd., Portland, OR 97219. 503-768-6700. Contact: Managing Editor. Sub $24. Publishes quarterly journal on environmental law and natural resources only. Circ. 1200. Accepts freelance material. No pay. Submit ms w/SASE. Photocopy OK. Reports in 1 month, publishes in 6 months. Accepts nonfiction & environmental law subjects. Sample or back issues $10.

ENVIRONMENT/RESOURCES, LAW

ERGO! Bumbershoot's Literary Magazine, PO Box 9750, Seattle, WA 98109-0750. 206-448-5233. Editor/ads: Louise DiLenge. Annual of works by Bumbershoot literary arts program participants, book reviews, bookfair participant directory, articles of literary interest. Circ. 3,000. Accepts freelance material. Payment: Copies. Byline given. Query w/SASE. Phone query, dot matrix, photocopies, simultaneous submission, electronic OK. Uses nonfiction, fiction, poetry, photos, plays, cartoons. Photos: B&W glossy, no smaller than 3x5. "Reviews should be for small press publications. Articles should be of particular interest to the literary community. Make contact between the months of Feb./May." Sample: $1.

FICTION, LITERARY, POETRY

ESQ, Washington State University Press, Pullman, WA 99164-5910. 509-335-3518. Quarterly. Sub $15.

COLLEGE/UNIVERSITY, SCHOLARLY/ACADEMIC

Esquimalt Lookout, CFB, Esquimalt FMO, Victoria, BC V0S 1B0. 604-385-0313. Editor: A. C. Tassic. Periodical.

UNSPECIFIED

Essence, Central Oregon Community College, N.W. College Way, Bend, OR 97701. 503-382-6112x304. Editor: Bob Shotwol. College literary magazine. Editors could change yearly. SASE for guidelines.

COLLEGE/UNIVERSITY, FICTION, OREGON

Et Cetera, King County Library System, 300 - 8th Ave. N., Seattle, WA 98109. Contact: Public Information Officer. Periodical.

REFERENCE/LIBRARY

Ethos, Campus Box 8841, Idaho State University, Pocatello, ID 83209. Editor: Mary Beitia.

COLLEGE/UNIVERSITY

Eurock, PO Box 13718, Portland, OR 97213. 503-281-0247. Editor: Archie Patterson. Quarterly of new music by experimental musicians from around the world. Circ. 700. No pay. Byline given. Phone queries. Interested in features, interviews, LP reviews. Knowledge necessary in this very specialized area of music. Familiarity with the publications concept is necessary. Pre-arrangement of artist's material suggested. Sample: $1.

MUSIC

Europe Through The Back Door Travel Newsletter, 120 4th Ave. N., Edmonds, WA 98020. 206-771-8303. Editor: Eileen Owen. Sub free. Circ. 12,000. Uses 2 freelance mss per issue. Pays copies on publication. Rights acquired: None. Byline given. Submit ms, SASE. Dot matrix, photocopies, simultaneous OK. Reports in 1 mo. Publishes within 1 yr. Accepts nonfiction, poetry, photos, cartoons. Budget European travel tips, unusual places, how-to, personal experiences, specific tips, keep it light, 500-700 wds. B&W photos, camera-ready. Guidelines. Sample free.

TRAVEL

Event, Kwantlen College, Box 9030, Surrey, BC V3T 5H8. Semiannual periodical. Not a freelance market.

COLLEGE/UNIVERSITY

Event, Douglas College, PO Box 2503, New Westminster, BC V3L 5B2. 604-527-5293. Editor: Dale Zieroth. Managing editor: Bonnie Bauder. Literary journal published 3X/yr. Sub $15/yr, $25/2 yrs. Circ. 1,000. Uses freelance material. Pays money, copies on publication. Acquires 1st rights. Byline given. Submit ms, SASE. Photocopied OK. Reports in 4-5 mos; publishes 1 yr. Accepts fiction, poetry, photos; nonfiction for creative nonfiction contest only. "Readers are sophisticated, open-minded; invite involvement and present experiences." Usual fiction about 5,000 wds. Prefer 5X7 glossy B&W prints. Guidelines. Sample $4.

FICTION, LITERARY, POETRY

The Exhibit Review, 3800 S.W. Cedar Hills Blvd. #241, Beaverton, OR 97005. 503-643-2783. Editor: Mary K. Bucknell. Ads: Jim Sleeper. Quarterly directory. Sub $50/yr. Circ. 40,000. Uses freelance material. Pays copies, acquires all rights. Query letter, SASE. Responds in 6 wks; publishes in 4 mos. Accepts nonfiction, news items, interviews, reviews. Topics: international trade shows & exhibits.

BUSINESS, CALENDAR/EVENTS

Exhibition, Bainbridge Island Arts Council, 261 Madison Ave. S., Bainbridge Island, WA 98110. 206-842-7901. Editor: Mary Guterson. Bi-annual magazine. Sub $15/yr. Circ. 1,000. Uses freelance material. Byline given, pays copies on publication. Submit ms w/SASE, short bio. Photocopied sub OK, no simultaneous. Reports in 3 mos. Accepts nonfiction, fiction (2,000 wds), poetry, cartoons, photos, B&W art, some half tones. Sample $3.

FICTION, POETRY

Explorations, U. of AK, Dept. of English, 11120 Glacier Hwy., Juneau, AK 99801. 907-789-4418. Contact: Art Petersen. Annual literary publication. Circ. 500. Accepts poetry, fiction, fine arts. Pays prize money to winners of annual competition. Subject matter less important than quality. Best for submitters to purchase a copy first. Send SASE for guidelines. Sample: $2.50.

ARTS, FICTION, POETRY

The Extender, Jackson County Extension Service, 1301 Maple Grove Dr., Medford, OR 97501. 503-776-7371. Periodical.

AGRICULTURE/FARMING, GOVERNMENT

Fairbanks Arts, Fairbanks Arts Association, PO Box 72786, Fairbanks, AK 99707. 907-456-6485. Editor: Al Geist. Bimonthly magazine. Circ. 1200. Sub/$15. Founded 1990. Freelance material accepted; byline given. Pays copies on publication. Acquires no rights. Query by letter w/SASE, clips, complete ms. Photocopy, simultaneous subs OK. Responds in 3 weeks; publishes in 4 months. Accepts fiction, poetry, news items, nonfiction, photos (35 mm slides, color or B&W prints), interviews, articles. Guidelines; back issues $3.00.

LITERARY, POETRY, WRITING

Famous Faces Magazine, 139 Water, Vancouver, BC V6B 1A7. Periodical.

BIOGRAPHY, CONSUMER

Fantasy and Terror, PO Box 20610, Seattle, WA 98102. Editor: Jessica A. Salmonson. An octavo format magazine, payment in copies, uses macabre poems-in prose, themes covering ghosts and graves, morosity and fear, somewhat experimental, highly refined, dark, cruel, evil, jaded, darkly romantic. Not for everyone. Queries w/SASE.

FANTASY/SCI FI, FICTION, POETRY

Fantasy Football, 18411 60th Pl. N.E., Seattle, WA 98155. 206-525-6928. Editor: Bruce Taylor. Annual magazine. Newsstand $3.95. Circ. 37,000. Will use 3-4 freelance mss per issue. Pays copies. Byline given. Interested in columnist material on pro football, offensive play photographs, cartoons. Football expertise and wit is important.

SPORTS

Fantasy Macabre, Box 20610, Seattle, WA 98102. Editor: Jessica A. Salmonson. Periodical. Payment: 1 per wd; copies. Queries w/SASE. Fiction: under 3,000 wds, supernatural literature with a slant towards translations from European authors. Translators always welcome. Lyric poetry (nothing experimental, no free verse).

FANTASY/SCI FI, FICTION, POETRY

Farm & Ranch Chronicle, Box 157, Cottonwood, ID 83522. 208-962-3851. Monthly. Query/SASE.

AGRICULTURE/FARMING

Farm Journal Magazine, S. 2517 Greenferry Rd., Coeur d'Alene, ID 83814. 208-664-9324. Contact: Nita Effertz.

AGRICULTURE/FARMING

Farm Lines, PO Box 190, Burley, ID 83318. 208-678-2201. Contact: Mike Call.

AGRICULTURE/FARMING

Farm Review, PO Box 153, Lynden, WA 98264. 206-354-4444. Monthly.

AGRICULTURE/FARMING

Fathoms, 763 N.W. 10th St., Corvallis, OR 97330. Literary journal. Prefers short manuscripts and appreciates writing that is rich in concrete imagery and expresses the musicality of language.

LITERARY

Fedora, PO Box 577, Siletz, OR 97380. Editor: John E. Hawkes. Periodical.

UNSPECIFIED

Feminist Broadcast Quarterly of Oregon, PO Box 19946, Portland, OR 97280. 503-220-6413. Editor: Mimi Yahn. Quarterly magazine. Circ. 2,000. Sub $8/yr, Canada $10/yr. Freelance material accepted, byline given. Acquires no rights. Query w/SASE or send complete manuscript. Photo copy and dot matrix OK. Responds in 1-3 months. Accepts fiction, poetry, cartoons, news, biography, nonfiction, photos, interviews, op/ed, articles, short plays, reviews, memoirs, and satire/songs. Query for photo requirements. Pays money, copies on end of fiscal year. "Multicultural, multi-racial magazine for, by and about women; predominantly women of color."

FEMINISM, WOMEN

Ferry Travel Guide, Olympic Publishing, Inc., 7450 Oak Bay Rd., Port Ludlow, WA 98365. 206-437-2277. Editor: Dan Youra. Ads: Tom McKinnon. Founded 1984. Published

3X a year. Sub $6/yr. Circ. 110,000. Byline given. Pays money on publication. Query letter, SASE. Simultaneous submissions OK. Accepts nonfiction, articles, news items, photos. Sample $2.

NORTHWEST, TRAVEL, WASHINGTON

Figment: Tales from the Imagination, PO Box 3128, Moscow, ID 83843. 208-882-8201. Editors: J. C. & Barb Hendee. Ads: J. C. Hendee. Quarterly magazine founded in 1989 for fiction, nonfiction, and poetry in the genres of SF, fantasy, and SF/F related horror. Sub $14.50/yr. Circ. 500. No unsolicited submissions. Accepts freelance material. Pays money, copies on acceptance. Byline given. Acquires 1st North American serial rights. Query SASE for guidelines before submitting. Photocopy, dot matrix OK. Reports in 8 wks; publishes in 12 mos. Accepts fiction, poetry, cartoons, nonfiction, interviews, and articles. Accepts photos only if available w/interview. Sample $4. Some back issues.

FANTASY/SCI FI, FICTION, POETRY

Financial Times of Canada Ltd., 960-789 W. Pender St., Vancouver, BC V6C 1H2. 604-683-4349. Vancouver Bureau Chief: Allan Bayless. Circ. 107,265. Sub $26.75. Weekly business publication. Freelance material accepted. Byline given; pays money on publication. Query by phone. Responds instantly; publishes in one month. Accepts photos. Main office: Attn: Managing Editor, 440 Front St. W., Toronto M5V 3E6, Ontario. 416-585-5555.

BUSINESS, CANADA, ECONOMICS

Fine Madness, Box 31138, Seattle, WA 98103. Semiannual journal of poetry, fiction reviews, essays. Circ. 800, sub $9/yr. Byline given, pays copies on publication, acquires 1st rights. Accepts freelance mss. Submit typewritten w/SASE only. Reports in 2 months; publishes in 1 yr. or less. Accepts fiction, poetry. Poetry, 10 poems max; fiction, 20 pages max. Annual awards for best of volume. Guidelines. Sample $4.

FICTION, LITERARY, POETRY

FINESSE Magazine for the Washington Woman, 14346 Burke Ave. N., Seattle, WA 98133. 206-259-4377. Contact: Barb Bond. Bimonthly, offers the Fiction (1000 wd limit)/Poetry (12 line limit) Contest open to all WA women.

FICTION, POETRY, WOMEN

FINNAM Newsletter, Finnish-American Historical Soc. of West, PO Box 5522, Portland, OR 97208. 503-654-0448. Editor: Gene A. Knapp. Quarterly, membership. Circ. 400. Uses freelance material. Byline given. Pays copies. Submit query letter, ms, SASE, phone. Dot matrix, PC disk, photocopied OK. Accepts nonfiction, photos, monographs. Guidelines, sample.

NW/REGIONAL HISTORY, MINORITIES/ETHNIC

Finnish Connection, PO Box 1531, Vancouver, WA 98668. 206-254-8936. Editor/ads: Eugene Messer. Sub Assoc. $10/yr. Circ. 5,500. Published 6 times per yr. Accepts 2-3 freelance mss per issue pertaining to Scandinavians and Finns in the US and Canada: nonfiction, fiction, poetry and photos (B&W/color glossies) w/articles. Query w/clips, ms, SASE. Phone queries, photocopied & simultaneous submissions OK. Reports promptly. Gives byline and pays $20-$50 on publication. Guidelines; sample $1.

CULTURE, LANGUAGE(S), MINORITIES/ETHNIC

Fireweed: Poetry of Western Oregon, 1330 E. 25th Ave., Eugene, OR 97403. 503-344-1053. Contact: E. Muller. Quarterly journal. Sub $10/yr. Circ. 250. Uses freelance material. Byline given. Pays copy on publication. Acquires 1st rights. Submit complete ms, short bio, SASE. Dot matrix, simultaneous subs OK. Responds in 8 wks; publishes in 2-5 mos. Accepts poetry written by western Oregon poets; no subject, length or style limitations. Sample $2.50.

OREGON, POETRY

First Alternative Thymes, 1007 S.E. 3rd St., Corvallis, OR 97333. 503-929-4167. Editor: Christine Peterson.

Monthly. Sub $6. Circ. 1,000. Uses 10 freelance mss per issue. Pays in copies. Submit query w/clips, ms, phone, SASE. Dot matrix, photocopied, simultaneous OK. Reports in 1-2 wks. Accepts nonfiction, photos, cartoons. Sample.

ADVENTURE, CHILDREN (BY/ABOUT), ENTERTAINMENT

Fish Wrap, 921 1/2 24th Ave, Seattle, WA 98122. 206-323-6779. Editor: Jim Maloney. Literary magazine irregularly published 1-3 times yearly. Circ. 3,000. Founded 1990. Accepts freelance material. Byline given. Pays copies on publication. Acquires first rights. Query w/SASE, by phone, send complete ms. Dot matrix and simultaneous sub OK. Responds in 3-4 months. Accepts short fiction, poetry, B&W art & photos. Send B&W copies of photos. Back issues $1.

ARTS, LITERATURE, POETRY

The Fisherman's News, C-3 Building, Rm. 110, Seattle, WA 98119. Bimonthly.

BUSINESS

The Fishermen's News, 4005 20th Ave. W., Ste. 110, Seattle, WA 98199-1291. 206-282-7545. Editor: John Fiorillo. Ads: Sherry Kisner. Monthly magazine. Circ. 15,000. Sub/$14 yearly. Freelance material accepted. Byline given. Payment on publication. First rights acquired. Query by phone or letter w/SASE. Send clips. Responds in 2-4 weeks, publishes in 2-6 weeks. Accepts cartoons, news items, biography, nonfiction, photos, interviews, articles. Guidelines, back issues.

FISHING

Fishing And Hunting News, Box C-19000, 511 Eastlake E., Seattle, WA 98109. 206-624-3845; Fax 206-340-9816. Editor: David Ellithorpe. Ads: Brian Thurston. Founded 1954. Circ. 39,000. Sub/$49.95. Biweekly tabloid newspaper with local fishing, hunting, camping, and boating news.

OUTDOOR, RECREATION, SPORTS

Fishing Tackle Trade News, PO Box 2669, Vancouver, WA 98668-2669. 206-693-4721. Editor: John Kirk. Ads: Robert Vickers. Published 12 times a yr. for retailers of fishing tackle, hunting gear, camping gear, marine equipment. Circ. 23,000. Sub $45. Accepts freelance material. Payment: Money on acceptance. Byline given. Queries w/ SASE. Phone queries, dot matrix, photocopies OK. Uses nonfiction, photos, cartoons, illustrations. Stories cover management, merchandising, business topics, species slants (how retailers can use info on particular species to assist their selling efforts). Photos: B&W, verticals, $25; $50 color transparencies.

BUSINESS

Florist & Grower, 686 Honeysuckle N., Salem, OR 97301. 503-390-0766. Editor: Donald H. Johnson. Monthly.

AGRICULTURE/FARMING, BUSINESS

The Flyfisher, PO Box 1387, Idaho Falls, ID 83403-1387. 208-523-7300. Editor: Dennis G. Bitton. Quarterly journal of the Federation of Fly Fishers. Circ. 10,000. Accepts nonfiction/fiction, to 2,000 wds, on flyfishing. Buys photos w/ articles. Pays various rates on publication. Query w/SASE. Guidelines; samples $3 from Federation of Fly Fishers, PO Box 1088, West Yellowstone, MT 59758.

CRAFTS/HOBBIES, FISHING, SPORTS

Flyfishing, Frank Amato Publications, PO Box 02112, Portland, OR 97202. 503-653-8108. Editor: Marty Sherman. Ads: Joyce Sherman. Magazine published 5 times a yr. Uses 15 freelance mss per issue. Pays money on publication. Acquires 1st rights. Byline given. Submit query w/ clips, ms, SASE. Reports in 2 wks. Accepts nonfiction articles (approx 1,500 wds) related to all aspects of flyfishing location, water management, equipment, etc. buys ONLY stories which are accompanied by color transparencies, B&W glossies and/or original art work. Guidelines.

FISHING, OUTDOOR

Flyfishing News Views &. Reviews, 1387 Cambridge Dr., Idaho Falls, ID 83401. 208-523-7300. Editor: Dennis

G. Bitton. Ads: Mae Farrow. Semimonthly. Sub $15/yr. Circ. 5,000. Uses freelance material. Byline given. Pays money ($50-150), copies on publication. Acquires 1st rights. Query letter, outline, complete ms, SASE, or phone. Reports in 2 wks; publishes in 6-24 mos. Accepts fiction, nonfiction, cartoons, news items, biography, essays, op/ ed, interviews, and reviews. Length: 500-3,500 wds. Photos: B&W and color slides w/article. Topics: must deal with flyfishing. Guidelines; sample $2.

FISHING, OUTDOOR, RECREATION

Focus on Women Magazine, 1218 Langley St., Victoria, BC V8W 1W2. 604-388-7231. Contact: Maggie Kerr-Southin. Ads: Pat Montgomery. Monthly magazine publisher. Circ. of 30,000. Subs: $20. Freelance material accepted. Byline given. Payment on publication. Pays in money. First right acquired. Query w/ SASE, disk/modem okay, send complete manuscript, features by assignment only. Responds in 2 months, publishes in 6 months. Accepts fiction, nonfiction, interviews, op-ed, local profiles, and articles. Guidelines; back issues $2. "No recipes, no fashion. Think of content for six months down the road."

BRITISH COLUMBIA, FEMINISM, WOMEN

Footnotes, Pacific Northwest Booksellers Assoc., 5903 SE 19th, Portland, OR 97202. 503-282-7515. Bonny B. McKenney. Monthly. Circ. 500. Uses freelance material. Dot matrix, photocopied OK.

BOOK ARTS/BOOKS, PUBLISHING/PRINTING

Forest Log, Department of Forestry, 2600 State St., Salem, OR 97310. 503-378-8645. Editor: Brian Ballou. Bimonthly, free. Does not use freelance material.

AGRICULTURE/FARMING, FORESTRY, GOVERNMENT

Forest Perspectives, World Forestry Center, 4033 S.W. Canyon Rd., Portland, OR 97221. Periodical on forestry, forest practices, and related topics.

ENVIRONMENT/RESOURCES, LUMBER, NATURAL HISTORY

Forest Voice, Native Forest Council, PO Box 2171, Eugene, OR 97402. Editors: Timothy Hermach & Harold Lonsdale. Sub $25/yr, free to contributors and members. Nonprofit educational newsletter devoted to preservation of publicly owned forests. Contributions welcomed with SASE. Sample.

CONSERVATION, ENVIRONMENT/RESOURCES, FORESTRY

Forest Watch Magazine, 14417 S.E. Laurie, Oak Grove, OR 97267. 503-652-7049. Monthly magazine. Sub $25/ yr. Not a freelance market. Sample $2.

ENVIRONMENT/RESOURCES, FORESTRY

The Foreword, 15455 65th Ave. S., Tukwila, WA 98188. Monthly periodical.

UNSPECIFIED

The Fount, c/o The Northland Letterpress Co. Ltd., 1340 East Pender St., Vancouver, BC V5L 1V8.

UNSPECIFIED

Foxtalk, Pinnacle Publishing Inc., PO Box 1088, Kent, WA 98035-1088. Contact: David M. Johnson. Monthly newsletter. Accepts freelance material. Byline given. Pays money on publication. Acquires all rights. Submit complete ms. Publishes in 6 weeks. Pinnacle publishes technical journals for users of software, including FoxPro, Clipper, Q & A, and Alpha Four. "All submissions are reviewed by technical editors for accuracy and quality." Guidelines; sample $10.

COMPUTERS

The Fraser Institute, 626 Bute St., 2nd Fl., Vancouver, BC V6E 3M1. 604-688-0221. Contact: Sally Pipes. Publisher of trade books and journal (sub $48-95/yr. Circ. 4,500; not a freelance market). Topics: religion, social sciences, business, social issues. Catalog; SASE/IRC for guidelines.

BUSINESS, ECONOMICS, SCHOLARLY/ACADEMIC

Free! Newsletter of Free Materials/Services, Department 284, Box C34069, Seattle, WA 98124-1069. Published 5 time a yr. Lists free materials which have been evaluated by professionals and are readily available. Short descriptions. Sub $18. No submissions info. Query w/ SASE.
CONSUMER, EDUCATION

Freedom Socialist, New Freeway Hall, 5018 Ranier Ave. S., Seattle, WA 98118. 206-722-2453. Political tabloid.
FEMINISM, POLITICS, SOCIALIST/RADICAL

Freighter Travel News, 3524 Harts Lake Rd., Roy, WA 98580. Editor: Leland Pledger. Monthly newsletter with first-hand reports of freighter voyages. Sub $18. Freelance mss accepted. Pays copies. Byline given. Submit ms, SASE. Dot matrix, photocopies OK. Reports in 15 days. Publishes in 6 mos. Nonfiction. Wants articles on recent travel experience aboard freighters, barges, or other unique water craft. Sample $1.50
TRAVEL

Front Lines, Real Good Food Store, 2375 N.W. Thurman, Portland, OR 97210. 503-222-5658. Editor: Rachel O'Neal. Bimonthly newsletter. Circ. 3000. Free sub. Freelance material accepted. Pays on publications, byline given. Pays $15 to $25. Acquires first rights. Send query letter. Usually assignment only. Responds in 2 moths, publishes in 6 months. Accepts nonfiction and articles. "We are a very specialized publication with limited resources for paying contributors. We welcome writers who have a passionate interest in natural foods and related issues, and who don't need money."
ENVIRONMENT/RESOURCES, FOOD/COOKING, HEALTH

Fryingpan, 7378 S.W. Pacific Coast Hwy., Waldport, OR 97394. Editors: Carol Alice/John Fry. Monthly magazine.
UNSPECIFIED

Fugue: Literary Digest of the University of Idaho, Brink Hall, Room 200, University of Idaho, Moscow, ID 83843. 208-882-8201. Editor: J. C. Hendee. Ads: Leiloni Reed. Tri-annual magazine. Sub $11/yr. Circ. 200+. Accepts submissions by U of I or Lewis Clark State College students only. Byline given. Pays copies on publication. Submit complete ms, SASE. Photocopied, dot matrix subs OK. Reports in 3-12 wks; publishes in 3-6 mos. Accepts nonfiction, fiction, poetry, plays, B&W photos. Guidelines.
COLLEGE/UNIVERSITY, LITERARY

Fur Bearers, 2235 Commercial Dr., Vancouver, BC V5N 4B6. Periodical.
UNSPECIFIED

FVCC Literary Review, Flathead Valley C.C., 777 Grandview, Kalispell, MT 59901. Editor: Ed Hanley.
COLLEGE/UNIVERSITY, LITERARY

Gallerie: Women's Art, 2901 Panorama Dr., North Vancouver, BC V7G 2A4. 604-929-7129. Editor: Caffyn Kelley. Quarterly journal. Sub $20/yr. Circ. 1,500. Uses freelance material. Submit query w/clips. Reports in 1-2 mos. Accepts photos and mss from women artists and philosophical articles by writers on women's art. All articles include B&W photos. Guidelines; sample $6.
ARTS, VISUAL ARTS, WOMEN

The Gated Wye, Office of State Fire Marshall, 3000 Market Street N.E. #534, Salem, OR 97310. 503-378-4464. Editor: Nancy Campbell. Monthly of timely items and important features for the fire service. Sub $10. Circ. 1,150. Uses freelance mss. Pays copies on publication. Byline given. Query w/SASE. Phone queries, dot matrix, photocopies OK. Reports in 2 mos. Publishes in 2 mos. Accepts nonfiction, poetry; fire service related, training and education. Sample free.
GOVERNMENT, LABOR/WORK, PUBLIC AFFAIRS

Geist, 100-1062 Homer St., Vancouver, BC V6B 2W9. Literary arts journal.
LITERARY

Gem State Geological Review, Idaho Geological Survey, c/o University of Idaho, Moscow, ID 83843. Editor: Roger C. Stewart. Annual periodical.
GEOLOGY/GEOGRAPHY, IDAHO, SCIENCE

Genealogical Forum of Portland Bulletin, Rm. 812, 1410 S.W. Morrison, Portland, OR 97205. Monthly.
GENEALOGY

General Aviation News & Flyer, PO Box 98786, Tacoma, WA 98498-0786. 206-588-1743. Editor: Dave Sclair. Biweekly tabloid devoted to general aviation. Circ. 35,000. Rights purchased: One time rights, 1st or 2nd. Query w/SASE on longer pieces; send ms or phone on breaking news. Dot matrix, simultaneous submissions OK. Reports in 2-3 wks. Publishes in 2-3 mos. Nonfiction: 500-2,000 wds on sport and general aviation news, safety, pilot reports, people, airports, destinations, etc. Review back issues for hints on departments, columns, fillers. Photos: B&W prints $10, color slides or prints $2550. Guidelines with #10 SASE; sample $2.
AVIATION, RECREATION, SPORTS

Geo-Heat Center Bulletin, Oregon Institute of Technology, 3201 Campus Dr., Klamath Falls, OR 97603. 503-885-1750. Editor: Paul S. Lienau. Quarterly, free. Circ. 2,000. Uses freelance material. No pay. Query letter, SASE, phone. Photocopied, dot matrix, disk/modem subs OK. Nonfiction topics: technical, geothermal heat. Sample free.
COLLEGE/UNIVERSITY, ENVIRONMENT/RESOURCES, TECHNICAL

The Georgia Straight, 1235 W. Pender St., 2nd Fl., Vancouver, BC V6E 2V6. 604-681-2000. Contact: Charles Campbell. Weekly entertainment guide. Sub $25/yr CDN, $40/yr US. Unsolicited mss, photographs and graphics must be accompanied by SASE & Canadian stamp. Payment at approved rates will be made 30 days after publication, upon presentation of invoice.
BRITISH COLUMBIA, ENTERTAINMENT

Ghost Town Quarterly, PO Box 714, Philipsburg, MT 59858. 406-859-3736. Editor/Ads: Donna McLean. Quarterly magazine. Sub $8. Circ. 5,000-7,000. Uses freelance material. Pays 5/word on publication. Acquires first rights. Byline given. Submit ms, SASE. Dot matrix, photocopied OK. Reports in 2-3 mos. Publishes 1-12 mos. Accepts nonfiction, fiction, poetry, photos, cartoons, historical documents (letters, diary pages). Features a "Student's Corner" for K-12 writers. Topics: traditions, history & heritage of ghost towns in North America; events of a historical nature; unique places to visit; unusual museums. "Use extreme care with factual information." Guidelines. Sample $3.50.
CHILDREN (BY/ABOUT), OLD WEST, TRAVEL

Gilgal Publications, PO Box 3386, Sunriver, OR 97707. 503-593-8639. Editor: Judy Osgood. Periodical.
UNSPECIFIED

The Gilmore Gazette, 113 N.W. Coast, #1, Newport, OR 97365. 503-265-5029. Contact: Ed Cameron. Tri-quarterly. Circ. 2,000. Founded 1981. Accepts freelance cartoons & comics only. Byline given; pays in copies. Acquires 1st rights. SASE. Responds in 1 mo.; publishes in 6 mos. "We solicit comic strips & cartoons only. Clean photocopies best."
HUMOR, VISUAL ARTS

Glimmer Train Press Inc., 812 S.W. Washington St., Ste. 1205, Portland, OR 97205-9907. 503-221-0836. Editors: Susan Burmeister, Linda Davies. Ads: Susan Burmeister, Linda Davies. Quarterly fiction magazine. Sub $29/ 1 yr. Single issue $9. Accepts freelance material in January, April, July, October. Pays $300 per story on acceptance, if chosen for anthology $300 more, copies. Byline given. Acquires first and anthology rights. Submit ms/ SASE, dot matrix or photocopy OK. Reports in 12 weeks; publishes in 3-6 months. Accepts fiction. Guidelines.
FICTION

The Globe & Mail, 920-1200 Burrard St., Vancouver, BC V6Z 2C7. Periodical.
BRITISH COLUMBIA, UNSPECIFIED

The Golden Age, Nez Perce Historical Society, 0306 3rd St., Lewiston, ID 83501-1860. 208-743-2535. Editor: Ladd Hamilton. Semiannual. Circ. 200. Sub/$20. Accepts freelance material. Byline given. Query by letter, phone. Photocopy OK. Accepts biography, nonfiction, photos, interviews, articles, and memoirs. Back issues $3.
NW/REGIONAL HISTORY, NATIVE AMERICAN

Golden Eagle, Audubon Society, PO Box 8261, Boise, ID 83707. Editor: Scott Tuthill. Monthly.
CONSERVATION, NATURAL HISTORY, OUTDOOR

The Golden Eagle, Oregon Autobody Craftsman Association, 4370 N.E. Halsey, Portland, OR 97213. 503-284-7762. Editor: John Yoswick. Monthly trade magazine. Circ. 3,500. Uses freelance material. Byline given. Submit query letter, clips, complete ms, SASE. Photocopied, dot matrix subs OK. Responds in 3 wks; publishes in 1-3 mos. Accepts cartoons, news items, biography, photos, interviews, op/ed, articles. Sample $1.
TRADE/ASSOCIATIONS

Golden Messenger, 3025 Lombard, Everett, WA 98201. Monthly.
UNSPECIFIED

The Goodfruit Grower Magazine, PO Box 9219, Yakima, WA 98909. 509-457-8188. Editor: Phil Shelton. Ads: Randy Morrison. Sub/$18. Circ. 13,000. Trade magazine published 21 times a year. Uses 4-6 freelance mss per issue. Pays $2 column inch, $5 pictures, more for color or cover material; on publication. Acquires 1st rights; byline given. Submit query w/clips. Phone queries, dot matrix OK. Reports in 4 weeks; publishes in 4-12 weeks. Accepts nonfiction, photos, the official trade publication of the Washington State tree fruit industry, but circulates far beyond the boundaries of the state and is a respected source of information for orchardists everywhere, including overseas. Subject matter includes growing and marketing of commercial tree fruit. Grower profiles, too.
AGRICULTURE/FARMING, BUSINESS

The Gorge Current, 4594 Woodworth Rd., Mount Hood Parkdale, OR 97041-9746. 503-386-6223. Editor: Mike Worral. Weekly magazine. Sub $24/summer season. Circ. 7,000. Uses freelance material. Byline given. May pays money on publication. Submit query letter, outline, SASE, phone. Dot matrix, simultaneous, disk/modem subs OK. Responds in 2-4 wks, publishes in 1-6 wks. Accepts nonfiction, cartoons, news items, biography, interviews, op/ ed, reviews, photos (B&W, color print, $10). Topics: Columbia Gorge, Portland to Arlington, Oregon and Washington: recreation, land use, environment; timely info most desirable. Guidelines; sample 50 cents.
NORTHWEST, RECREATION, SPORTS

Grandparents Journal, E. 1419 Marietta Ave., Spokane, WA 99207. 509-487-3383. Editor: Elinor Nuxoll. Quarterly newsletter. Sub $6. Circ. 700+. Uses freelance material from grandparents. Byline given, pays copies, prizes, acquires 1st rights. Submit clips, ms, SASE. Dot matrix, photocopied, simultaneous subs OK. Reports in 2-3 mos. "Wants news clips for 'grandparents in the news.'" Guidelines; sample $1.
CHILDREN/TEEN, FAMILY, SENIOR CITIZENS

The Grange News, PO Box 1186, Olympia, WA 98507-1186. 206-943-9911; Fax 206-357-3548. Editor: Pat Nikula. Monthly for rural WA audience on agricultural news/ information about the Grange. Circ. 49,000. Subs $2.40 grange members; $4.75 to non-members. Payment: Money on acceptance. Byline given. Query w/SASE. Publishes submissions in 1 month. Nonfiction: 600-800 wds on agriculture, personal finances, home economics.
AGRICULTURE/FARMING, WASHINGTON

Grassroots Oracle, 29581 Fraser Hwy., Aldergrove, BC V0X 1A0. Contact: Arthur Joyce. Publication of writers' group.
FICTION, POETRY, WRITING

Gray Power, 16901 S.E. Division St. #111, Portland, OR 97236-1487. Semiannual.
SENIOR CITIZENS

Group 1 Journal, 45 W. Broadway, Ste. 205, Eugene, OR. 97401. 503/344-7813.
UNSPECIFIED

Growing Edge Magazine, New Moon Publishing Co., PO Box 90, Corvallis, OR 97339. 503-757-8477. Editor: Don Parker. Ads: Jane DeHart. Quarterly. Sub $24.95/yr. Circ. 40,000. Uses freelance material. Byline given. Pays $.10/wd on publication. Acquires first, reprint rights. Query letter, outline, synopsis, SASE, or phone. Photocopy, dot matrix, disk/modem, simultaneous subs OK. Responds in 2-3 wks; publishes in 3 mos. Accepts nonfiction, news items, biography, interviews, op/ed, reviews, photos (B&W-color, $550). Topics: high-tech gardening techniques, people using them use. Guidelines; sample $6.50.
AGRICULTURE/FARMING, GARDENING, TECHNICAL

Haiku Zasshi Zo, 325 N. 125th St., Seattle, WA 98133. 206-524-9692. Editor: George Klacsanzky. Semiannual. Sub $6. Accept 1-2 freelance mss an issue. No pay. No byline. Submit 15-20 haiku with SASE. Dot matrix, photocopies, simultaneous subs OK. Reports in 1-3 mos. Publishes in 1-4 wks. Accepts haiku poetry, reviews of haiku books, essays on haiku composition, or other artforms and practices that influence the writing of haiku, poetic diaries incorporating haiku. May be from 3-21 syllables long. Also line drawings in B&W. Guidelines, samples.
LITERARY, POETRY, WRITING

Hallelujah!, The Bible Holiness Movement, PO Box 223, Sta. A, Vancouver, BC V6C 2M3. 604-498-3895. Bimonthly evangelical magazine. Sub $5. Circ. 1,000-10,000. Accepts freelance material. Byline given. Pays money on acceptance. Acquires all rights. Submit query letter, clips. Photocopies, dot matrix, simultaneous subs OK. Responds 6 wks. Accepts nonfiction, articles, photos, news items, biography. Biblically oriented to evangelical and Wesleyan viewpoint. Topics: peace, anti-nuclear, racial equality and justice, religious liberty, etc. "Prefer action or solution-oriented articles; must understand evangelical viewpoint and life style." Guidelines, sample.
RELIGION

Hands On, Bitterroot Teachers' Network, S-22385 Cave Bay Dr., Worley, ID 83876. 208-686-1444. Coordinator: Reva Luvaas-Hess. Editor & Ads: Susan Walker. Quarterly education journal written by teachers and students using the Foxfire approach to learning. Sub $15/yr. Does not accept freelance material. Sample $5.
COMMUNITY, EDUCATION, PUBLISHING/PRINTING

Hard Row to Hoe, Seven Buffaloes Press, PO Box 249, Big Timber, MT 59011. Editor: Art Cuelho. Published 3 times a yr. Mostly regional reviews of rural America that librarians, individuals, and the general public can use as a guide to purchasing books and mags about the common people who still work the land. Sub $3. Query w/SASE. Sample/$1 SASE.
LITERARY

HDTV, 753 E. Fall Creek Rd., Alsea, OR 97324-9504. Newsletter with articles relating to video conferencing, production, and interviews.
MEDIA/COMMUNICATIONS

Health Education League of Portland, 9242 S.W. Terwilliger Blvd., Portland, OR 97219. Periodical.
HEALTH

Health News and Notes, N.W. Portland Area Indian Health Board, 520 S.W. Harrison, #440, Portland, OR 97201-5258. Editor: Sheila Weinmann. Quarterly.
HEALTH, NATIVE AMERICAN

Heartland Magazine, Fairbanks News Miner, PO BOX 710, Fairbanks, AK 99701. Editor: Dave Stark. Weekly.
ALASKA

Herb Market Report, O.A.K., Inc., 1305 Vista Dr., Grants Pass, OR 97527. 503-476-5588. Editor: Richard Alan Miller. Ads: Iona Miller. Monthly newsletter. Sub $12/yr. Circ. 2,000+. Uses freelance material. Pays money. Acquires all rights. Query by phone. Disk/modem subs OK. Reports in 2 wks; publishes in 1 mo. Accepts nonfiction, news items, interviews, photos. Topics: alternative agriculture, herbs & spices, marketing, cottage industry, rural economic development, processing, small farming, foraging, secondary timber products. 2,000-4,000 wds. Artwork. Sample $1.50.
AGRICULTURE/FARMING, FORESTRY, HOW-TO

Heritage Music Review, 4217 Fremont N., Apt. 5, Seattle, WA 98103. Periodical review of music.
CULTURE, MUSIC

Heritage Quest, PO Box 40, Orting, WA 98360. 206-893-2029. Editor: Leland K. Meitzler. Bimonthly on genealogy and local history, all geared toward helping researchers. Sub rate $30. Circ. 10,000. Uses 8 freelance mss per issue from historians or genealogists. Pays from 75 cents to $1.25 per column inch, on publication. Byline given. Rights purchased: All. Submit ms, SASE. Reports in 1 mo. Publishes in 2-6 mos. Guidelines; sample $6.
GENEALOGY, AMERICAN HISTORY, GENERAL HISTORY

Herspectives, Box 2047, Squamish, BC V0N 3G0. 604-892-5723. Editor: Mary E. Billy. Quarterly newsletter. Sub $22/yr. Circ. 50. Uses freelance material. Byline given, pays copies on publication. Submit query, SASE. Simultaneous sub OK. Responds in 2 wks; publishes in 1-3 mos. Accepts nonfiction, poetry, cartoons, biography, interviews, op/ed, reviews, memoirs. Topics: feminist perspective; no racist, sexist, homophobic mss accepted. Guidelines; sample $5.
FEMINISM, POETRY, WOMEN

Hewitt Research Foundation, PO Box 9, Washougal, WA 98671-009. Periodical.
UNSPECIFIED

Hi Baller Forest Magazine, 117-543 Seymour St., North Vancouver, BC V6B 3H6. 604-669-7833. Editor: Paul Young. Periodical.
BRITISH COLUMBIA, TRADE/ASSOCIATIONS, FORESTRY

Highway Information, Idaho Transportation Department, PO Box 7129, Boise, ID 83707. Editor: Pat Youngblood. Bimonthly. Circ. 1,200.
IDAHO, PUBLIC AFFAIRS

Historic Preservation League of Oregon Newsletter, PO Box 40053, Portland, OR 97240. Quarterly.
ARCHITECTURE, NW/REGIONAL HISTORY, OREGON

Historical Gazette, PO Box 527, Vashon, WA 98070. 206-463-5656. Editor: Roger Snowden. Ads: Don King. Monthly. Sub $10. Circ. 10,000. Uses freelance material. Pays money on publication. Byline given. Submit query w/ clips, ms, phone. Dot matrix, photocopied OK. Accepts nonfiction, photos, other. Guidelines; sample 50 cents.
NW/REGIONAL HISTORY

Historical Perspectives, Oregon State Archives, 1005 Broadway N.E., Salem, OR 97310. 503-378-4241. Editor: Elizabeth Uhlig. Free semiannual newsletter. Circ. 1,700. No freelance mss accepted. Sample.
GENEALOGY, GOVERNMENT, NW/REGIONAL HISTORY

Holistic Resources, PO Box 25450, Seattle, WA 98125. 206-523-2101. Editor: Susan James. Periodical.
HEALTH

Home Education Magazine, PO Box 1083, Tonasket, WA 98855. Editor/Ads: Helen Hegener. Bimonthly magazine. Sub $24/yr. Circ. 5,200. Uses freelance material. Pays money, copies (about $10 per 750 wds) on publication. Byline given. Submit query letter, ms, SASE. Dot matrix, photocopied, simultaneous, electronic, computer disk subs OK. Accepts nonfiction, photos, cartoons, artwork. Photos: clear B&W, rates negotiable. Writers must know home schooling or alternative education. Guidelines, catalog; sample $4.50.
CHILDREN (BY/ABOUT), EDUCATION, FAMILY

Home Office Opportunities, Page One Press, 9330-D Bridgeport Way S.W. #40, Tacoma, WA 98499. 206-582-1757. Editor: Kay Kennedy. Quarterly newsletter. Sub $12/yr. Uses freelance material. Pays copies on publication. Submit query letter, complete ms, SASE. Photocopied, dot matrix subs OK. Responds in 1 mo; publishes in 3-6 mos. Accepts nonfiction, interviews, reviews, photos (B&W). Topics: how-to, informative, personal experience about owning and operating a home-based business. 600 words or less, business software reviews. Guidelines. Sample $3.
BUSINESS, HOW-TO

Home Source, PO Box 50596, Idaho Falls, ID 83405-0596. 208-338-1561. Contact: Mark Russell. Circ. 200,000. Biannual magazine of regional and national real estate info for home buyers and sellers. Pays on acceptance for 1st or 2nd serial rights for nonfiction features, how-to pieces, etc. from 800 to 1,800 wds. Uses photos. SASE for guidelines. Sample free.
BUSINESS, CONSUMER

Home Sweet Home, E. 201 Bourgault Rd., Shelton, WA 98584-9737. 206-922-5941. Editors: Mark & Laurie Sleeper. Quarterly magazine. Sub $20/yr. Circ. 700. Uses freelance material. Byline given. Pays money, copies on publication. Acquires 1st rights. Submit complete ms, SASE. Disk/modem, dot matrix, simultaneous subs OK. Responds in 4 mos; publishes in 6 mos. Accepts interviews, articles, reviews, poetry. Guidelines; sample $6.
BUSINESS, HOME, HOW-TO

Homes & Land Magazine, 3606 Main St. #205, Vancouver, WA 98663. Editor: Alicia Ord. Periodical.
BRITISH COLUMBIA, HOME

Honeybrook Press, PO Box 883, Rexburg, ID 83440. 208-356-5133. Editor: Donnell Hunter. Publishes 3 books a yr; poetry chapbooks, and some subsidy printing. Accepts unsolicited mss only on a subsidy basis. Reports in 2 wks. Publishes in 2 mos. Except for subsidy printing, I publish only those authors I am interested in who are already established.
POETRY

Horizons Sf, Student Union Bldg., Box 75, UBC, Vancouver, BC V6T 1W5. Biannual science fiction & fact publication which showcases unpublished Canadian writers. Query w/SASE.
COLLEGE/UNIVERSITY, FANTASY/SCI FI, SCIENCE

Horse & Rider, PO Box 8, Stevensville, MT 59870. Editor: Tom Bryant. Quarterly. Sub $4.
ANIMALS, RECREATION

Horse Times, PO Box 351, Star, ID 83669. Editor: Jo O'Connor. Periodical.
ANIMALS, RECREATION

Hortus Northwest, PO Box 955, Canby, OR 97013. 503-266-7968. Editor: Dale Shank. Annual directory-journal, commercial sources for PNW native plants. Circ. 700. Uses freelance material. Byline given. Pays money on publication. Acquires 1st rights. Submit query letter, outline, synopsis, SASE. Photocopy, dot matrix subs OK. Responds in 3 mos; publishes within 1 yr. Accepts nonfiction, articles. Topics: Pacific Northwest native plants. Guidelines.
ENVIRONMENT/RESOURCES, REFERENCE/LIBRARY

Hot Springs Gazette, 12 S. Benton, Helena, MT 59601-6219. 406-482-5766. Editor: Suzanne Hackett. Periodical. Sub $12. Circ. 1,000. Uses 12 freelance mss per issue.

Pays copies on publication. Acquires 1st rights. Byline given. Submit ms. Dot matrix, photocopied OK. Reports in 2 mos. Accepts nonfiction, fiction, poetry, cartoons. Guidelines; sample $4.

ENTERTAINMENT, HOME, LITERARY

How To Travel Inexpensively, Nomadic Books, 1911 N. 45th St., Seattle, WA 98103-6804. Periodical.

CONSUMER, TRAVEL

Hubbub A. Poetry Magazine, Reed College, 5344 S.E. 38th Ave, Portland, OR 97202. 503-775-0370. Editor: Lisa M. Steinman. Nationally circulated biannual of poetry. No editorial strictures. Circ. 350. Sub/$5. Submit 3-5 poems w/SASE. Pays in copies. Guidelines; sample $3.85.

POETRY

The Humanist Newsletter, PO Box 3936, Portland, OR 97208.

PHILOSOPHY

Hungary International, 4416 134th Pl. S.E., Bellevue, WA 98006. 206-643-1023. Editor: Helen Szablya. Monthly newsletter for American business people about trade with Hungary. Circ. 3500. Founded 1990. Sub/$47 Ind., $197 Corporate, $97 Nonprofit. Accepts relevant freelance material. Byline given. Rights acquired and pay vary. Query w/ SASE or by phone. Responds within 2 weeks, publishes in 1-2 months. Accepts business news items, nonfiction, photos, interviews, business op/ed. Guidelines; back issues $10. Free sample for writers.

BUSINESS, LAW, TRADE/ASSOCIATION

Hunt Magazine, Timberline-B, Inc., PO Box 58069, Renton, WA 98058. 206-226-4534. Editor: Bill Boylon. Bimonthly. Sub $19.97/yr. Circ. 100,000. Uses freelance material. Acquires 1st rights. Submit complete ms, SASE. Responds in 1-2 mos; publishes in 1 yr. Accepts articles, cartoons, photos w/ms. Sample $3.50.

COMMERCE, OUTDOOR

The Hyacinth Poetry Review, Daffodil Press, 6426 198th St. East, Spanaway, WA 98387. 206-847-4892. Editor: Sandra VanOrman. Quarterly newsletter. Sub $12/yr. Uses freelance material. Pays copies on publication. Acquires 1st rights. Submit complete ms, SASE. Photocopy, dot matrix OK. Responds in 2-3 wks. Accepts poetry (1-24 lines, no longer than one page), cartoons. Guidelines.

POETRY

Hydrazine, Northwest Science Fiction Society, PO Box 24207, Seattle, WA 98124. Periodical.

FANTASY/SCI FI

Iconoclast, Foundation of Human Understanding, PO Box 1009, Grants Pass, OR 97526. Monthly.

UNSPECIFIED

Idaho, Boise State University, College of Business, Dept of Economics, Boise, ID 83725. Editor: Charles L. Skoro. Quarterly.

BUSINESS, COLLEGE/UNIVERSITY, IDAHO

Idaho Archaeologist, Idaho Archaeological Society, PO Box 7532, Boise, ID 83707. Editor: Mark G. Plew. Semiannual. Circ. 100.

ANTHROPOLOGY/ARCHAEOLOGY, IDAHO

Idaho Business Review, 4218 Emerald St., Ste. B, Boise, ID 83706. Editor: Carl A. Miller. Weekly periodical. Circ. 2,000.

BUSINESS, IDAHO

Idaho Cities, Association of Idaho Cities, 3314 Grace St., Boise, ID 83707. Editor: Ray Holly. Monthly. Circ. 2,200.

IDAHO, PUBLIC AFFAIRS

Idaho Clean Water, Division of Environment/IDHW, 450 West State St., Boise, ID 83720. 208-334-5867. Editor: Tom Aucutt. Quarterly focusing on improving Idahos water quality. Circ. 2,000. Sub free. Query w/SASE. Guidelines; free sample.

CONSERVATION, ENVIRONMENT/RESOURCES, IDAHO

Idaho Conservation League Newsletter, PO Box 844, Boise, ID 83701. 208-345-6933. Editor: Lisa Krepel. Monthly. Circ. 2,500. Founded 1973. Sub/$25. Accepts freelance material, byline given, no payment, no rights acquired. Photocopy OK. Accepts nonfiction, new items, interviews, and articles.

CONSERVATION, IDAHO, ENVIRONMENT/RESOURCES

Idaho Council on Economic Ed. Newsletter, 1910 University Dr., Boise, ID 83725. Editor: Dr. Gerald Drayer. Semiannual periodical. Circ. 7,000.

ECONOMICS, EDUCATION, IDAHO

Idaho Currents, Idaho Department of Water Resources, Statehouse, Boise, ID 83720. Monthly. Circ. 9,000. Query with/SASE.

CONSERVATION, ENVIRONMENT/RESOURCES, IDAHO

Idaho Farmer-Stockman, PO Box 2160, Spokane, WA 99210. Contact: Thomas D. Henry. Biweekly agricultural periodical. Circ. 18,000. Uses news and farmer profiles. Guidelines with SASE.

AGRICULTURE/FARMING, IDAHO

Idaho Forester, College of Forestry/Wildlife/Range Sc., University of Idaho, Moscow, ID 83843. Idaho Forester, College of Forestry/Wildlife/Range Science, University of Idaho, Moscow, ID 83843. Annual. Circ. 1,200.

AGRICULTURE/FARMING, FORESTRY, IDAHO

Idaho Foxfire Network, c/o Reva Luvaas, S. 22385 Cave Bay Dr., Worley, ID 83873. 208-752-6978. Periodical.

EDUCATION, WRITING

Idaho Genealogical Society Quarterly, Idaho Genealogical Society, 325 W. State, Boise, ID 83702. 208-384-0542. Editor: Jane Walls Golden. Sub $10/yr. Circ. 450. Publisher of hard- & softcover books and quarterly magazine. Uses freelance material. Byline given. Pays money on acceptance. Submit query letter, SASE. Responds in 3 wks; publishes in 3 mos.

GENEALOGY

Idaho Grain, Peak Media, PO Box 925, Hailey, ID 83333. 208-726-9494. Owned by Peak Media. Bimonthly magazine. Sub $10/yr. Circ. 16,000. Uses freelance material. Pays money on publication. Acquires 1st rights. Byline given. Submit query , complete ms, SASE, phone. Reports in 3 wks; publishes in 2 mos. Accepts biography, photos (on request), interviews, op/ed, articles, reviews. Topics of interest to Idaho grain producers and related industries. Study sample before querying. Guidelines; sample $2.

AGRICULTURE/FARMING, BUSINESS, IDAHO

Idaho Grange News, PO Box 367, Meridian, ID 83642. 208-888-4495. Idaho Grange News, PO Box 367, Meridian, ID 83642. Editor/ads: Glen Deweese. 208-888-4495. Bimonthly of agriculture and fraternal news. Circ. 8,000. Sub w/membership. Not a freelance market.

AGRICULTURE/FARMING, IDAHO

Idaho Humanities Council Newsletter, Len B. Jordan Bldg., 650 W. State St., Room 300, Boise, ID 83720. 208-345-5346. Editor: Sharron Bittich. Circ. 5,200.

IDAHO, ARTS

Idaho Law Review, University of Idaho, College of Law, Moscow, ID 83843. Editor: Nancy M. Morris. Published 3 times a year. Circ. 1,000. No submission info

IDAHO, LAW

Idaho Librarian, Library, University of Idaho, Moscow, ID 83843. Editor: Mary K. Bolin. Quarterly. Circ. 600.

BOOK ARTS/BOOKS, IDAHO, REFERENCE/LIBRARY

Idaho Motorist, Idaho Automobile Association, PO Box 15240, Boise, ID 83715. Editor: Grant C. Jones. Irregular periodical.

CONSUMER, IDAHO, TRAVEL

Idaho Museum Of Natural History, PO Box 8183, Idaho State University, Pocatello, ID 83209. 208-236-3717. Editor: B. Robert Butler. Periodical of primitive pottery/ceramics. Circ. 250. Uses 2-5 mss per issue. Byline given. Submit ms w/SASE. Phone query, photocopies OK. Notes on replication of experiments in primitive pottery manufacture, processes, techniques, etc. Observations, discoveries, tips, materials, techniques, especially as they relate to prehistoric or folk pottery, but also as they can be applied to contemporary ceramics. Photos: glossy. Good, straight forward writing; first person, present tense.

ANTHROPOLOGY/ARCHAEOLOGY, IDAHO, NATURAL HISTORY

Idaho Outdoor Digest, PO Box 454, Rupert, ID 83350. Contact: Ed Mitchell, editor. Ads: Vickie Higgins. Monthly magazine. Sub $12/yr. Circ. 1525,000. Uses 15-18 freelance mss per issue. Pays money on publication. Acquires first rights. Byline given. Query by phone or w/SASE. Dot matrix, photocopies, simultaneous, modem, disk subs OK. Accepts nonfiction, photos, cartoons. Topics: adventure, bicycling, boating, environment, fishing, how-to, Idaho, Montana, outdoor recreation. Guidelines and sample.

HOW-TO, OUTDOOR, RECREATION

Idaho Pharmacist, Idaho State Pharmaceutical Association, 1365 N. Orchard, Rm 316, Boise, ID 83706-2250. Editor: JoAn Condie. Monthly. Circ. 350.

BUSINESS, HEALTH, IDAHO

Idaho Potato Commission Report, Idaho Potato Commission, PO Box 1068, Boise, ID 83701. Bimonthly.

AGRICULTURE/FARMING, BUSINESS, IDAHO

Idaho Power Bulletin, Idaho Power Company, PO Box 70, Boise, ID 83707. Editor: Jim Taney. Quarterly. Circ. 60,000.

BUSINESS

Idaho Senior News, PO Box 6662, Boise, ID 83707. Editor: Owen Krahn. Monthly.

SENIOR CITIZENS

Idaho Soccer Net, PO Box 6662, Boise, ID 83707. 208-336-6707. Contact: Owen Krahn.

SPORTS

Idaho The University, Office of University Communications, University of Idaho, Moscow, ID 83843. 208-885-8973. Editor: Stephen Lyons. Ads: Terry Maurer. Quarterly magazine. Free. Circ. 60,000. Uses freelance material. Byline given, pays money/copies on publication. Submit query letter w/SASE. Dot matrix, simultaneous subs OK. Responds in 1 mo; publishes in 2 mos. Accepts nonfiction, photos, interviews, articles. Photos: B&W, color slides, pays $50-100. "All stories must have a Univ. of Idaho link. Our standards are high. We are not the usual university magazine." Guidelines and samples, free.

COLLEGE/UNIVERSITY, IDAHO, NORTHWEST

Idaho Thoroughbred Quarterly, 5000 Chinden Blvd. #B, Boise, ID 83714.

AGRICULTURE/FARMING, ANIMALS, BUSINESS

Idaho Voice, Idaho Fair Share, Inc., PO Box 1927, Boise, ID 83701. 208-343-1432. Editor: Ralph Blount. Quarterly to members of Idaho Fair Share. Circ. 10,000. Sub $15. 90% freelance material. Byline given. Uses nonfiction, poetry, photos, cartoons. Photos: B&W, 3x5 preferred.

CONSUMER, ECONOMICS, POLITICS

Idaho Wheat, Idaho Wheat Growers Assn., Ste. M, Owyhee Plaza, Boise, ID 83702. Editor: Vicki Higgins. Bimonthly. Circ. 13,850.

AGRICULTURE/FARMING, BUSINESS, IDAHO

Idaho Wildlife, Idaho Department of Fish & Game, P. O. Box 25, Boise, ID 83707. 208-334-3748. Editor: Diane Ronayne. Bimonthly magazine with widespread readership interested in fishing, hunting, and wildlife watching in Idaho. Other topics include fish and wildlife behavior, conservation, and management. Sub $10/yr. Circ. 30,000. Accepts photographs only. "Photographers with substantial files of subjects photographed in Idaho are placed on the want list mailing list." Submit sample sleeve of 20 slides. Pays $40 per photo for 1 time rights, cover, $80; plus copies and byline. Response time 3 wks. Guidelines; sample $1.50.

BIOLOGY, CONSERVATION, OUTDOOR

Idaho Wool Growers Bulletin, Idaho Wool Growers Association, PO Box 2596, Boise, ID 83701. Editor: Stan Boyd. Monthly. Circ. 1,800.

AGRICULTURE/FARMING, BUSINESS, IDAHO

Idaho Yesterdays, Idaho Historical Society, 450 N. 4th St., Boise, ID 83702. 208-334-3428. Editor: Judith Austin. Quarterly. Sub $15/yr. Circ. 1,200. Uses freelance material. Pays copies. Query letter, complete ms, SASE, phone. Photocopy OK. Responds in 2 wks; publishing time varies. Topics: Idaho history (nonfiction). Sample $1.50-3.75.

NW/REGIONAL HISTORY, IDAHO

Idahoan, National Railroad Historical Society, PO Box 8795, Boise, ID 83707. Editor: Milt Sorensen. Monthly. Circ. 60.

CRAFTS/HOBBIES, AMERICAN HISTORY, NW/REGIONAL HISTORY

Idahobeef, Idaho Cattle Association, 2120 Airport, Boise, ID 83705. Editor: Tom Hovenden. Monthly. Circ. 900.

AGRICULTURE/FARMING, BUSINESS, IDAHO

Idaho's Economy, College of Business, Boise State University, Boise, ID 83725. 208-385-1158. Editor: C. Skoro. Quarterly magazine. Sub free. Circ. 4,500. Uses freelance material. Pays in copies. Byline given. Submit ms, SASE. Dot matrix, photocopied, computer disk. Reports in 2 mos; publishes in 6 mos. Accepts nonfiction. Sample.

BUSINESS, ECONOMICS, IDAHO

Idea Productions, PO Box 516, Royal City, WA 99357. 509-346-9456. Semi-monthly agricultural trade magazine. Circ. 5000. Free. Freelance material accepted. Pays in money, on publication. Acquires first rights. Query letter, clips, complete ms. Responds in 2 wks. Accepts news items, interviews, and articles.

AGRICULTURE/FARMING

IEA Reporter, Idaho Educational Association, PO Box 2638, Boise, ID 83701. Editor: Gayle Moore. Monthly. Circ. 9,000.

EDUCATION, IDAHO, LABOR/WORK

IFCC News, 5340 N. Interstate Ave., Portland, OR 97217. 503-243-7930. Periodical.

ARTS, COMMUNITY

Il Centro Newsletter of Italian Canadian Community, Italian Cultural Centre Society, 3075 Slocan St., Vancouver, BC V5M 3E4. 604-430-3337. Editor: Anna Terrana. Newsletter of the Italian Canadian community published annually. Sub free with $30/yr membership. Circ. 4,000. Accepts no freelance mss. Sample free.

CANADA, COMMUNITY, MINORITIES/ETHNIC

Images, Lane County ESD, PO Box 2680, Eugene, OR 97402. 503-689-6500. Editor: Dr. Marilyn Olson. Publication of poetry and art by students in Lane County. Guidelines; sample $5.

ARTS, CHILDREN/TEEN, POETRY

Impact, OSPIRG, 1536 S.E. 11th Ave., Portland, OR 97214-4701. Periodical.

OREGON, PUBLIC AFFAIRS

In Common, Tsunami Publications, Box 104004, Anchorage, AK 99510. 907-337-0872. Editor/Ads: Jay Brause. Gay/lesbian monthly. Accepts freelance material. Byline given. Submit ms, SASE. Dot matrix, photocopies OK. Uses nonfiction, fiction, poetry, photos, cartoons. Only gay/lesbian oriented material, preferably with an Alaska or Pacific N.W. slant. Photos: B&W glossy news/documentation photos, as well as artistic photos suitable for a general public audience.

GAY/LESBIAN

In Context, The Context Institute, PO Box 11470, Bainbridge Is., WA 98110. Editor: Alan Atkisson. Quarterly journal. Sub $18/yr. Circ. 7,000. Uses freelance material. Byline given. Pays money, copies on publication. Submit complete ms, SASE. Accepts nonfiction, poetry, cartoons, photos (B&W), interviews. Guidelines; sample $5.

CULTURE, ENVIRONMENT/RESOURCES

In Stride Magazine, 12675 S.W. 1st, Portland, OR 97005. Periodical.

UNSPECIFIED

Incredible Idaho, Div. of Tourism & Industrial Development, Room 108 Capitol Bldg., Boise, ID 83720. Quarterly.

BUSINESS, IDAHO, TRAVEL

Independent Senior, 1268 W. Pender, Vancouver, BC V6E 2S8. Periodical.

SENIOR CITIZENS

Info, International Sled Dog Racing Assoc., PO Box 446, Nordman, ID 83848. Editor: Nancy Molburg. Bimonthly. Circ. 2,000.

ANIMALS, OUTDOOR, SPORTS

Infoletter, International Plant Protection Center, Oregon State University, Corvallis, OR 97331. 503-754-3541. Editor: A. E. Deutsch. Free quarterly. Circ. 8,600. Not a freelance market. Sample free.

AGRICULTURE/FARMING, COLLEGE/UNIVERSITY, GARDENING

Inky Trails Publications, Box 345, Middletown, ID 83644. Editor: Pearl Kirk. Literary magazine published 3 times a year. Circ. 300. 90% freelance poems. Non-subscribers must buy issue in which their efforts appear. Does not pay. Submit ms, SASE. Reports in 2-8 wks; publishes in 2-3 yrs. "Uses nonfiction, fiction, poetry, illustrations. Adventure, fantasy, historical, humorous, mystery, religious (not preachy), romance, western and animals....prefers unpublished material and do not want to receive: horror, make fun of, porno or gay/lesbian material." Offers periodic cash awards for best subscriber efforts. Guidelines w/SASE/44 cents; sample for 9x12 SASE with 70¢ postage.

FANTASY/SCI FI, FICTION, HUMOR

Inland, English Department, Boise State University, Boise, ID 83725. 208-385-1246. Editor: Driek Zirinsky. Semiannual magazine for English teachers. Sub $8/yr. Circ. 600. Uses freelance material. Byline given, pays copies. Acquires 1st rights. Submit query letter, complete ms, SASE, phone. Photocopy, disk/modem subs OK. Responds in 6 wks; publishes in 6 mos. Accepts fiction, nonfiction, cartoons, poetry, photos, interviews, op/ed, reviews, memoirs, art, student work. Sample $4.

EDUCATION, ENGLISH

Inland Country, Inland Power & Light Company, E. 320 Second Ave., Spokane, WA 99202. Editor: Yvonne C. Morton. Ads: Chris Aiken. Monthly magazine. Circ. 19,000. Sub/$3. Freelance material accepted, byline given, pays copies. Acquires no rights. Query by letter or phone, complete ms. Photocopy OK. Responds in 10 days; publishes in 1 month. Accepts fiction, cartoons, news items, biography, nonfiction, photos, interviews, articles. "In-house publication. Limited budget for freelance submissions."

COMMUNITY, HISTORY NW/REGIONAL, WASHINGTON

Inland Northwest, PO Box 574, Newman Lake, WA 99025. 509-633-0342; 509-484-5472. Editor: Jerry D. Vandervert. Ads: Bill Leaming. Quarterly. Sub $3/year; Circ. 15-7500. Does not accept unsolicited submissions. Uses freelance material. Byline given. Pays on acceptance, publication, or assignment. Some advances, royalties, and money. Acquires first rights. Query w/SASE, phone, clips, complete manuscript, simultaneous sub OK, photocopy OK, dot matrix OK, but not preferred. Replies in 6 weeks, publishes in 2-4 months, pays $350-$700. Accepts cartoons, news, biography, nonfiction, photos, interviews, op/ed, articles, reviews, memoirs. Photos: 35 mm & B&W transpar-

encies, caption, model releases & ID of subject required; $50-$100 B&W, $125-$175 color. Regional quarterly magazine covering people, places, and events both past and present which affect Eastern WA, Northern ID, and Western MT. Writers guidelines for No. 10 SASE.

AMERICANA, COMMUNITY, NORTHWEST

Inland Register, PO Box 48, Spokane, WA 99210-0048. 509-456-7140. Ads: Margaret Nevers. Regional Catholic news magazine published 17X/yr. founded in 1942. Sub $15. Circ. 8,500. Accepts freelance material. Byline given. Author qualification: Roman Catholic. Pays money (10/wd) on publication. Submit ms, SASE. Photocopies OK. Reports in 1 mo; publishes in 1 mo. Accepts nonfiction, photos, ($10 negotiable). Sample $1.

RELIGION

Inner Voice, AFSEEE, PO Box 11615, Eugene, OR 97440. Editor: Tom Ribe. Quarterly newsletter. Sub $20/yr. Circ. 50,000. Occasionally uses freelance material. Submit query, SASE. Responds in 3 wks; publishes in 6 mos. Accepts nonfiction, cartoons, photos (B&W), op/ed. Topics: current forest service policy or procedure issues. Sample $2.

ENVIRONMENT/RESOURCES

Innkeeping World, PO Box 84108, Seattle, WA 98124. Contact: Charles Nolte. Published 10 times per yr for the hotel industry worldwide. Uses nonfiction on marketing, managing, advertising, hospitality, trends, labor relations. SASE for ample and guidelines. Query w/SASE.

BUSINESS, TRADE/ASSOCIATIONS

Inscriptions, Department of English, GN-30, University of Washington, Seattle, WA 98195. Periodical.

COLLEGE/UNIVERSITY, WRITING

Inside Basic, Ariel Publishing Inc., Box 398, Pateros, WA 98846. 509-923-2249. Monthly magazine for Macintosh developers. Columns on programming skills, introductory programming and advanced development. Sub $36.95.

COMPUTERS, TECHNICAL

Insight Northwest, PO BOX 25450, Seattle, WA 98125-2330. Bimonthly on human potential. From statement of philosophy: We create our own reality. We can heal ourselves. Synergy works better. Query w/SASE. Sample/free.

HEALTH, PHILOSOPHY, PSYCHOLOGY

Insurance Adjuster, 1001 4th Ave. #3029, Seattle, WA 98154-1190. 206-624-6965. Monthly.

BUSINESS

Insurance Week, 1001 4th Ave. #3029, Seattle, WA 98154-1190. 206-624-6965.

BUSINESS

The Insurgent Sociologist, University of Oregon Sociology Dept., Eugene, OR 97403. Quarterly journal of radical analysis in sociology.

COLLEGE/UNIVERSITY, SOCIALIST/RADICAL, SOCIOLOGY

Interact, PO Box 1862, Lake Oswego, OR 97035. 503-649-2065; Fax 503-649-2309. Editor: Ed Forrest. Ads: Debra Palm. Published 3x/yr. Free. Founded 1983. Circ. 5,000. Articles, short synopses, and letters to the editor on all forms of interactive technology.

COLLEGE/UNIVERSITY, EDUCATION

Interface, 1910 Fairview Ave. E., Seattle, WA 98102-3699. Periodical.

UNSPECIFIED

Intermountain Logging News, Statesman-Examiner, Inc., Box 271, Colville, WA 99114. 509-684-4567. Monthly.

BUSINESS, LUMBER

International Art Post, Banana Productions, PO Box 3655, Vancouver, BC V6B 3YB. 604-876-6764. Editor: Anna Banana. Ongoing periodical of cooperatively published stamps by artists. Founded 1988. Subs/$50 for three editions.

ARTS

International Examiner, 622 S. Washington St., Seattle, WA 98104-2704. 206-624-3925. Editor: Danny Hovue, Ads: Emily Wong. Semi-monthly newsletter for Asian American communities of Seattle/King County. Circ. 20,000. Sub $18. Accepts freelance material. Payment: $15 on publication. Byline given. Query w/SASE or by phone. Dot matrix, photocopies OK. Topics of interest and significance to Asian Americans, particularly in the N.W. Historical articles, feature interviews, investigative journalism, straight news, analysis. Sample/50.
ASIA, ASIAN AMERICAN, MINORITIES/ETHNIC

IPEA News, Idaho Public Employees Association, 1434 W. Bannock, Boise, ID 83702. Editor: Jim Vineyard. Quarterly. Circ. 4,700.
IDAHO, LABOR/WORK

The Island Grower RR4, RR 4, Sooke, BC V02 1N0. 604-642-4129. Contact: Phyllis Kusch. Monthly (except Jan) magazine on living and garden on the N. Pacific coast. Buys 1st rights for how-to's, profiles, travel. Practical slant with emphasis on natural gardening and thorough research. Pay varies after publication. Byline given. Reports in 1 mo. Query w/clips & SASE. Sample and guidelines for SASE.
GARDENING, NORTHWEST

Island Men, 35 Cambridge St., Victoria, BC V8V 4A7. 604-383-6253. Contact: Jim Richardson. A quarterly magazine published by the Island Men's Network. Circ. 6000. Subs by donation. Freelance material accepted. Byline given. No payment, no rights acquired. Query by letter, phone, outline, send SASE. Simultaneous sub, photocopy OK. Responds in 4 weeks, publishes in 4 months. Accepts fiction, poetry, cartoons, news, nonfiction, photos, interviews, op/ed, articles, reviews, and memoirs. "Masculinity, gender roles, and the men's movement are our areas of interest." Some back issues available with donation.
MEN, PSYCHOLOGY, SEX

IWA Woodworker, International Woodworkers of America, 25 Cornell Ave., Gladstone, OR 97027-2547. Membership newsletter.
LABOR/WORK

IWUA Alert, Idaho Water Users Association, 410 S. Orchard, Ste. 144, Boise, ID 83705. Editor: Sherl L. Chapman. Quarterly devoted to water resource management issues. Circ. 1,250. Not a freelance market.
AGRICULTURE/FARMING, CONSERVATION, IDAHO

The Jason, Willamette University - D248, 900 State St., Salem, OR 97301. 503-370-6905. Editor: Margaret Jester. Annual for students writers only. No pay. Byline given. Submit ms. Dot matrix, photocopied OK. Accepts fiction, poetry, photos, plays, cartoons, other. Sample $2.
COLLEGE/UNIVERSITY, FICTION, POETRY

Jeopardy, Western Washington University, 350 Humanities Building, Bellingham, WA 98225. 206-676-3118. Editor: Lori L. Fox. Annual literary magazine. Sub $3. Circ. 4,000. Accepts unsolicited mss. Pays copies, on publication. Rights acquired: First. Byline given. Submit: ms, SASE. Dot matrix, photocopies, simultaneous OK. Accepts fiction, poetry, photos (slides if color or B&W prints), art work. No over-long stories or poems.
FICTION, POETRY, VISUAL ARTS

The Jewish Review, 6800 S.W. Beaverton-Hillsdale Hwy., Portland, OR 97225-1408. 503-292-4913. Editor: Paul Paul Haist. Ads: Jerry Neumann. Monthly. Sub/free. Circ. 5,000. Uses 13 mss per issue. Writers must have good writing, knowledge, or interest of Oregon Jewish community. Payment is 10 cents per word on publication. Byline given; 1st rights acquired. Query w/SASE. Reports in 1 month. News: 150-250 words; features to 1,000 words. Cartoons. Photos: $25, B&W. Sample with SASE.
CULTURE, OREGON, RELIGION

Jimmy Come Lately Gazette, PO Box 1750, Sequim, WA 98382. 206-683-7238. Editor: JoAnne Booth. Ads: Dianne Christensen. Weekly community newspaper. Circ. 10,500. Sub $15. Infrequently accepts freelance material. Writers must have very strong local emphasis. Payment: Usually $25. Byline given. Query w/SASE. Dot matrix, photocopies OK. Uses nonfiction, poetry, photos, cartoons. Emphasis on local people, events and issues. Our 3 person news staff provides about all the material we have space for, although we do work with some freelancers for historical pieces, etc. Sample/$1.
CALENDAR/EVENTS, COMMUNITY, PHOTOGRAPHY

Journal For Architecture & Design, 2318 Second Ave., Box 54, Seattle, WA 98121.
ARCHITECTURE, ARTS

Journal of B.C. English Teachers' Association, Port Coquitlam Secondary, 3550 Wellington St., Port Coquitlam, BC V3B 3Y5. Contact: Pat Curtis.
EDUCATION, ENGLISH

The Journal of Ethnic Studies, Western Washington University, Bellingham, WA 98225.
COLLEGE/UNIVERSITY, MINORITIES/ETHNIC, SOCIOLOGY

Journal of Everett & Snohomish Co. Hist., Everett Public Library, 2702 Hoyt, Everett, WA 98201. Biannual.
NW/REGIONAL HISTORY

Journal of Financial & Quantitative Analysis, UW, School of Business, 326 Lewis Hall, DJ-10, Seattle, WA 98195. 206-543-4598. Published quarterly. Circ. 3200; subs $40/$75.
BUSINESS, COLLEGE/UNIVERSITY, ECONOMICS

Journal of Health Physical Education, Recreation, Dance & Athletics, UI, Dept. of Health, Physical Ed, Moscow, ID 83843. Editors: Sharon Stoll/ Frank Pettigrew. Published semiannually.
DANCE, EDUCATION, HEALTH

Journal of Pesticide Reform, N.W. Coalition for Alternatives to Pesticide, PO Box 1393, Eugene, OR 97440. 503-344-5044. Editor: Caroline Cox. Quarterly journal. Sub $15/yr. Circ. 2,500. Occasionally uses freelance material. Pay negotiable, 1 copy or more. Byline given. Submit query letter, outline, sample chapters, synopsis, complete ms, SASE. Phone query OK. Dot matrix, photocopies, computer disk subs OK. Uses illustrations. Topics: scientific or public interest material on pesticides, pesticide reform, sustainable forestry & agriculture, pesticide policies & alternatives. Call first to get approval, guidelines. Prefer experienced specialists in field. Occasional research papers, interviews with specialists. Guidelines; sample $3.
AGRICULTURE/FARMING, ENVIRONMENT/RESOURCES, TECHNICAL

Journal of Seattle-King Co. Dental Soc., PO Box 10249, Bainbridge Island, WA 98110. 206-682-7813. Monthly.
BUSINESS, HEALTH

Journal of the Idaho Academy of Science, Idaho Academy of Science, Ricks College, Rexburg, ID 83460. 208-356-2022. Editor: Lawrence Pierson. Semiannual journal. Circ. 200. Uses freelance scientific research material. Byline given. Acquires 1st rights. Submit query letter, three photocopies of complete ms, SASE. Responds in 1 mo; publishes in 6 mos. Accepts nonfiction (original scientific research); book reviews; regional emphasis. Topics: biology, geology, physics, science education, chemistry, medicine, etc. Guidelines; sample $2.50.
SCHOLARLY/ACADEMIC, SCIENCE, TECHNICAL

The Journal of the Oregon Dental Assn, 17898 S.W. McEwan Rd., Portland, OR 97224. 503-620-3230. Editor: Howard F. Curtis, DMD. Quarterly.
BUSINESS, HEALTH

Just Dogs, PO Box 954, Auburn, WA 98071-0954. 206-852-0294. Editor: Bob Hughes. Bimonthly magazine. Circ. 8,000. Uses freelance material. Byline given, pays money/copies on publication, acquires 1st rights. Submit query/SASE. Disk/modem, dot matrix, simultaneous subs OK. Responds in 2 mos; publishes within 4 mos. Accepts fiction, poetry, nonfiction, articles, photos, cartoons, interviews, news items. "Material should be targeted to dog owners in the Puget Sound region." Guidelines; for back issues send 9x12 envelope with 45 cents postage.
ANIMALS, RECREATION

Just Out, PO Box 15117, Portland, OR 97215. 503-236-1252. Editor: Beth A. Allen. Ads: Yvonne Mammarelli. Monthly tabloid for the gay/lesbian community. Sub $17.50/yr. Circ. 15,000. Uses freelance material. Byline given, may pay money on publication. Submit query letter, clips, SASE. Dot matrix, simultaneous subs OK. Responds in 1 mo; publishes in 1 mo. Accepts news items, interviews, photos, articles. Sample $2.
GAY/LESBIAN, MINORITIES/ETHNIC, OREGON

KBOO Program Guide, 20 S.E. 8th, Portland, OR 97214. 503-231-8032. Editor/ads: Tony Hansen. Accepts freelance material. No pay. Byline given. Uses nonfiction, fiction, poetry.
CULTURE, MEDIA/COMMUNICATIONS, MUSIC

Ketch Pen, Washington Cattlemen's Association, Inc., PO Box 96, Ellensburg, WA 98926. Editor: Ann E. George. Monthly.
AGRICULTURE/FARMING

Key to Victoria, 1001 Wharf St., 3rd Floor, Victoria, BC V8W 1T6. 604-388-4342. Editor: Janice Strong. Monthly magazine about Vancouver Island and Victoria. Circ. 30,000. Acquires 1st or all rights to nonfiction of 500-2,500 wds with photos. Query w/SASE. Sample free.
BRITISH COLUMBIA, TRAVEL

Kid Care Magazine, P. O. Box 1058, Clackamas, OR 97015. 503-239-2334. Editor: Margaret Ramsom. Ads: Clay Sheldon. Quarterly. Sub $5. Circ. 10,000+. Uses freelance material. Writers must be knowledgeable about the topic. Pays copies. Acquires first rights. Byline given. Query w/clips, ms, SASE. Dot matrix, photocopied OK. Reports in 2-4 wks. Publishes within 1-2 mos. Accepts nonfiction, fiction, poetry, photos, cartoons, tips & ideas. Topics: infants through teens; adults taking care of/living with children; day care; how to. 100-650 wds length, short, easy to read. Photos: B&W, children & adults in everyday action. Guidelines. Sample $3.
CHILDREN (BY/ABOUT), CHILDREN/TEEN, HEALTH

KILSA News, Shoreline Community College Library, 16101 Greenwood Ave. N., Seattle, WA 98133. Periodical.
COLLEGE/UNIVERSITY

Kinesis, 301-1720 Grant St., Vancouver, BC V5L 2Y6. Periodical 10 times a yr. Query/SASE.
WOMEN

Kinesis, PO Box 4007, Whitefish, MT 59937. 406-862-3002. Editor: David Hipschman. Monthly magazine devoted to exposure of established and emerging writers. Besides fiction & poetry, emphasis is on essays of all kinds and political and investigative reporting. Accepts freelance material. Byline given. Pays money on publication. Query with SASE. Photocopies, simultaneous subs, disk/modem OK.
ARTS, LITERATURE, MEDIA/COMMUNICATIONS

Kinnikinnik, UC Bookstore, PO Box 5148, Missoula, MT 59806. 406-549-2560. Editor: Joe Friederich. Bimonthly. Free. Circ. 2,000. Accepts freelance material. Pays copies upon publication. Submit query with SASE, photocopy OK. Phone queries OK. Reports in 2 months; publishes in 2 months. Welcomes submissions of fiction, nonfiction, poetry, prose, and B&W photos on the theme of birth (metaphorical or actual) and parenthood. Back issues NC.
FICTION, POETRY

KSOR Guide to the Arts, 1250 Siskiyou Boulevard, Ashland, OR 97520. Periodical.
ARTS, MEDIA/COMMUNICATIONS

La Lucha Solidaria, 3558 S.E. Hawthorne Blvd., Portland, OR 97214-5142. 503-236-7916. Editor: Jenny Guyer. Quarterly newsletter. Founded 1979. Circ. 2000. Sub/$12. No freelance material accepted. Byline given. Pays nothing, acquires no rights. Send query letter. Accepts news items, op/ed, articles. Back issues $1 ea.
MINORITIES/ETHNIC, PEACE, POLITICS

La Posta: A Journal of American Postal History, PO Box 135, Lake Oswego, OR 97034. 503-657-5685. Editor: Richard W. Helbock. Ads: Cathy R. Clark. Bimonthly magazine. Sub $10. Circ. 1,200. Uses 5-6 freelance mss per issue. Byline given. Submit ms. Dot matrix, electronic subs OK. Accepts nonfiction. Sample $3.
CRAFTS/HOBBIES, NW/REGIONAL HISTORY

Land, Bill Anderson's Trap & Farm Journal, 4466 Ike Mooney Rd., Silverton, OR 97381. 503-873-8829. Editor: Bill Anderson. Magazine (AKA Living Among Nature Daringly) published 5X/yr. Sub $9/yr. Circ. 500. Accepts freelance material. Byline given, pays money on publication. Acquires 1st rights. Submit complete ms, SASE. Photocopy, dot matrix, disk/modem (Mac) OK. Responds in 3 wks; publishes in 10 wks. Seeks vernacular writing style, how-to's. Sample.
AGRICULTURE/FARMING, AMERICAN HISTORY, CANADIAN HISTORY

Landmark, 1000 Friends of Oregon, 534 S.W. 3rd Ave. #300, Portland, OR 97204. 503-223-4396. Editor: Kevin Kasowski. Quarterly on land use planning. Circ. 5,000. Sub w/membership in 1,000 Friends of Oregon/$3 single issue. Payment: Copies on publication. Byline given. Rights purchased: First. Submit ms, SASE. Phone queries, dot matrix, photocopies, simultaneous submissions OK. Reports in 2 wks. Nonfiction: 500-2,500 wds on farm/forest land conservation; efficient, environmentally sound development. For educated, professional readership, interested in concrete examples or research/economic facts. Photos: B&W glossy. Sample.
CONSERVATION, ECONOMICS

Landmarks, 835 Securities Building, Seattle, WA 98101. 206-622-3538. Editor: Barbara Krohn. Quarterly on N.W. history, archaeology, historic preservation. Circ. 12,000. Sub $10. Accepts freelance material. No pay; byline given. Acquires first rights. Query with ms, SASE. Phone queries, dot matrix, photocopies OK. Reports in 1-3 months. Uses nonfiction, photos (B&W, no preferred size). Guidelines, free sample.
ANTHROPOLOGY/ARCHAEOLOGY, NW/REGIONAL HISTORY, NORTHWEST

Lane Regional Air Pollution, 225 N. 5th #501, Springfield, OR 97477. Editor: Marty Douglass. Periodical.
ENVIRONMENT/RESOURCES

The Lariat, 12675 S.W. First St., Beaverton, OR 97005. 503-644-2233; Fax 503-644-2213. Editor: Barbara Zellner. Monthly devoted to horses and related subjects.
ANIMALS, RECREATION

Latah Co. Genealogical Soc. Newsletter 110 S. Adams, Moscow, ID 83843. 208-882-5943. Editor: Dorothy Viets Schell. Quarterly. Circ. 80. Sub with membership fee of $8. Not a freelance market. Sample: $2.
GENEALOGY, IDAHO

Latah Legacy, 110 S. Adams, Moscow, ID 83843. 208-882-1004. Quarterly on local historical subjects. Circ. 550. Sub w/membership in historical society. Sometimes accepts freelance material if of interest to audience. Payment: Copies. Byline given. Submit ms w/SASE. Phone queries, dot matrix, photocopies OK. Nonfiction and photos (related to article). Sample: $2.
NW/REGIONAL HISTORY, IDAHO

LaVoz de Idaho, Idaho Migrant Council, 104 N. Kimball, Caldwell, ID 83606-0490. 208-454-1652. Editor: Maria Salazar. Ads: Maria Salazar. Quarterly bilingual (English/

Spanish) newsletter. Sub $10/yr. Circ. 2,000. Uses freelance material. Query w/SASE. Accepts nonfiction, poetry, cartoons, news items, photos, interviews, op/ed. Sample.
BILINGUAL, IDAHO, MINORITIES/ETHNIC

LaVoz Newsmagazine, 157 Yesler Way #400, Seattle, WA 98104. 206-461-4891. Editor: Raquel Orbegoso. Ads: Ana Meekins. Bilingual/Spanish tabloid published 10X/yr. Sub $10. Circ. 15,000 statewide. Accepts freelance material. Payment on publication negotiable. Acquires 1st rights. Byline given. Submit phone query. Dot matrix, photocopied OK. Accepts nonfiction, cartoons. Topics: subjects of interest to Latinos. Sample.
BILINGUAL, CHICANO/CHICANA, COMMUNITY

LC Review, Lewis & Clark College, 0615 S.W. Palatine Hill Rd., Portland, OR 97219. 503-244-6161. Periodical.
COLLEGE/UNIVERSITY

Learning Etc., 1012 17th Ave., Lewiston, ID 83501-3759. Contact: John M. Gurgel.
EDUCATION

Left Bank, 24450 N.W. Hansen Rd., Hillsboro, OR 97124. 503-621-3911; Fax: 503-621-9862. Editor: Linny Stovall. Assoc. Ed: Steve Beard. Ads: John Johnson. A series of thematic collections (or a magazine in bookform) published semi-annually in June and December. Circ. 6000. Founded 1992, Subs/$14. Freelance material accepted. Pays money between acceptance and publication. Acquires first or second rights. Query by letter or phone. Send SASE, complete ms, disk. Simultaneous sub OK, "but inform us." Disk/modem or photocopy OK. Publishes in 2 to 3 months. Accepts mainly nonfiction, but also short fiction, poetry, cartoons, art. Accepts B&W photos, vertical. "Publish only N.W. writers/artists. Each issue based on a theme so send for guidelines. Looking for eclectic work from writers in science and history as well as 'literary' writers." Guidelines with SASE, catalog. Back issues $10.45 ea.
VISUAL ARTS, LITERATURE

Lesbian Contradiction:, A Journal of Irreverent Feminism, 1007 N. 47th, Seattle, WA 98103. Editor: Betty Johanna, Jane Meyerding. Quarterly newspaper format with journal content. Sub $6/yr. Circ. 2,000. Uses freelance material. Pays copies on publication. Byline given. Submit ms, SASE. Dot matrix, photocopies OK. Reports in 2-8 wks; publishes within 1 yr. Accepts nonfiction, photos (B&W), cartoons, line drawings; emphasis on non-academic material, with analysis or commentary based on personal experience. Uses essays, interviews, commentaries (10 pp. or less); book, movie, music reviews (3 pp. or less), queries, testimonies. Guidelines; sample $2.
FEMINISM, GAY/LESBIAN

Letter to Libraries, Oregon State Library, State Library Building, Salem, OR 97310. 503-378-4243. Editor: Jo Ann Sipple. Newsletter to libraries only. Uses freelance material. Byline given. Pays copies. Submit query letter, complete ms, SASE. Responds in 3 mos. Accepts nonfiction, news items, interviews, articles.
BOOK ARTS/BOOKS, REFERENCE/LIBRARY

Life Scribes, Box 848, Livingston, MT 59047. 406-222-7079. Quarterly magazine. Sub $17. Accepts freelance material. Pays copies. Rights acquired: First. Byline given. Submit ms; SASE. Dot matrix, photocopies, simultaneous, electronic OK. Reports in 6 mos. Publishes in 23 mos. We like short articles dealing with the journaling process or journal entries dealing with date and name. Guidelines, sample.
WRITING

Lifeprints, Blindskills, Inc., PO Box 5181, Salem, OR 97304. Editor: Carol M. McCarl. Ads: Robert McCarl. Quarterly newsletter for blind teens and adults. Sub $15/yr. Circ. 500. Uses freelance material. Byline given, pays money. Submit query letter, SASE, phone. Accepts nonfiction, poetry, interviews, articles. Sample.
DISABLED

The Light, PO Box 7534, Olympia, WA 98507. 206-456-3078. Contact: W. W. Koopman. Monthly periodical.
UNSPECIFIED

The Light Spectrum, Box 215-mp, Kootenai, ID 83840. Periodical.
UNSPECIFIED

Lighthouse, Lighthouse Publications, PO Box 1377, Auburn, WA 98001. Editor: Tim Clinton. Bimonthly magazine. Uses freelance material. Circ. 400. Sub $7.95/yr. Byline given, pays money, copies on publication. Acquires 1st/other rights. Submit complete ms, SASE. Photocopy OK. Responds in 4-8 wks; publishes in 1 1/2-2 yrs. Accepts fiction, poetry; children's stories and poetry. Guidelines; sample $3.
CHILDREN/TEEN, FICTION, POETRY

Line, c/o English Dept., Simon Fraser University, Burnaby, BC V5A 1S6. 604-291-3124. Editor: R. Miki. Ads: I. Niechoda. Semiannual journal. Sub $12. Circ. 300. Uses 5 freelance mss per issue. Pays money, copies on publication. Acquires all rights. Submit query w/clips. Dot matrix, photocopied OK. Reports in 3-4 mos. Publishes in 5-12 mos. Accepts nonfiction: literary criticism, reviews; Contemporary (Canadian & American) writing & its modernist sources; 30 pp. max; payment rate yet to be determined. Sample $8.
LITERARY, LITERATURE, WRITING

Line Rider, Idaho Cattle Association, PO Box 15397, Boise, ID 83705. Editor: Carol Reynolds. Published 10 times a year. Circ. 1,600.
AGRICULTURE/FARMING, ANIMALS, IDAHO

Listen: Promoting Positive Choices, Pacific Press Publishing Association, PO Box 7000, Boise, ID 83707. 208-465-2500. Editor: Lincoln Steed. Monthly magazine of the Seventh-day Adventist Church. Circ. 75,000; sub $17.95. Accepts freelance material. Byline given. Pays money, copies on acceptance. Submit query letter, complete manuscript, SASE. Photocopies, dot matrix, disk submissions OK. Responds 2 mos; publishes 6-9 mos. Accepts fiction, poetry (teens only), cartoons, news items (drug related), interviews, photos, articles. Guideline; sample $1.
FAMILY, RELIGION

Listen To Your Beer, Box 546, Portland, OR 97207. Periodical.
CONSUMER, CRAFTS/HOBBIES

Listening Post - KUOW FM, Box 9595, Seattle, WA 98195. 206-543-9595. Editor: Anna Manildi. Monthly of public radio station. Circ. 12,000. Sub w/membership. Uses 1 mss per issue. Byline given. Phone queries OK. Nonfiction, fiction, photos, cartoons. Short articles of interest to KUOW listener supported radio. Classical music, news and info, arts, theater.
ARTS, MEDIA/COMMUNICATIONS, PUBLIC AFFAIRS

Literary Creations, PO Box 1339, Albany, OR 97321. 503-451-1372. Editor: Margaret L. Ingram. Monthly newsletter. Sub $10/yr. Freelance material accepted; byline given. Pays in copies upon publication. No rights acquired. Submit with SASE, complete manuscript, simultaneous subs OK. Reports in 2 weeks. Publishes in 3 months. Accepts fiction, poetry, cartoons, nonfiction, articles, reviews, memoirs. Sample $2.
LITERARY, WRITING

Literary Markets, PO Drawer 1310, Point Roberts, WA 98281-1310. 604-277-4829. Editor: Bill Marles. Bimonthly newsletter. Sub $15/yr. Circ. 1,000. Uses freelance material. Pays in copies on publication. Submit ms, SASE. Photocopied OK. Reports in 2 mos; publishes immediately after acceptance. Topics: about writing & the writing life. Accepts fiction, nonfiction. Length limit: 250 wds or 30 lines. Guidelines, sample.
POETRY, WRITING

Lithiagraph Classifieds, 507 Clay St. #B-1, Ashland, OR 97520-1395. Periodical.
COMMUNITY

Livestock Express, 4346 S.E. Division, Portland, OR 97206. Monthly.
AGRICULTURE/FARMING, ANIMALS, BUSINESS

Loggers World, 4206 Jackson Hwy., Chehalis, WA 98532. 206-262-3376. Monthly magazine. Circ. 16,000. Sub $10/year. Freelance material accepted. Pays nothing. Acquires no rights. Query by phone. Dot matrix, disk/modem OK. Accepts poetry, cartoons, news items, biography, nonfiction, photos (continuous tone/neg.), interviews. Back issues $2.
BUSINESS, LABOR/WORK, LUMBER

Logging & Sawmill Journal, 1111 Melville St., Ste. 700, Vancouver, BC V6E 3V6. 604-683-8254. Editor: Norm Poole. Ads: Robert Stanhope. Monthly trade magazine. Sub $33/yr. Circ. 19,000. Uses freelance material. Byline given, payment on publication. Assignment only, query by phone, letter. Responds in 1 mo; publishes in 1-3 mos. Accepts news items, interviews, geared to small-medium independent contractors and mills. Sample.
FORESTRY, LUMBER, TRADE/ASSOCIATIONS

Logistics & Transportation Review, University of British Columbia, 1924 West Mall, Vancouver, BC V6T 1W5. 604-228-5922. Editor: W. G. Waters, II. Periodical.
BRITISH COLUMBIA, BUSINESS, COLLEGE/UNIVERSITY

Loud Pedal, Oregon Region, S.C.C.A., 154 Idylwood Dr. S.E., Salem, OR 97302. Editor: Margie Swanson. Monthly.
UNSPECIFIED

LUNO: Learning Unlimited Network of Oregon, 31960 S.E. Chin St., Boring, OR 97009. 503-663-5153. Newsletter published 9 times a yr. Sub $10. Circ. 180. Accepts unsolicited mss. Pays copies. Byline given. Submit w/SASE. Photocopies OK. Accepts nonfiction, poetry, cartoons. Topics: "Education, especially family/home schooling, education alternatives, learning styles, related politics."
CHILDREN/TEEN, EDUCATION

Lynx, PO Box 169, Toutle, WA 98649. 206-274-6661. Editor: Terri Lee Grell. Quarterly journal of renga. Sub $15/yr. US. Circ. 1,000. Accepts freelance material. Byline given. Pays money, copies on publication. Acquires 1st rights. Submit query letter, complete ms, SASE. Photocopy OK. Responds in 1-2 mos; publishes in 3-6 mos. Accepts poetry: renga. Guideline; sample $4.
ASIA, AVANT-GARDE/EXPERIMENTAL, POETRY

Madisonian, 122 W. Wallace, PO Box 367, Virginia City, MT 59755. Periodical.
UNSPECIFIED

The Malahat Review, University of Victoria, PO Box 3045, Victoria, BC V8W 3P4. 604-721-8524. Editor: Derk Wynand. Quarterly magazine of fiction/poetry. Sub $20/yr. Circ. 1,800. Uses freelance material. Pays fiction: $40 per 1,000 wds + 1 yr sub on acceptance; poetry: $20 per pg + 1 yr sub. Reports in 3 mos; publishes in 6 mos. Accepts fiction, poetry, plays. No restrictions on topic, slant or length. Send one story at a time, or 6-10 pgs of poetry. Guidelines; sample $6.
FICTION, LITERARY, POETRY

Marketing Index International Pub, PO Box 19031, Portland, OR 97219. Bimonthly.
BUSINESS

Marketing Reports & Trade Leads, USA Dry Pea & Lentil Council, PO Box 8566, Moscow, ID 83843. Editor: Don Walker. Published 18 times a year.
AGRICULTURE/FARMING, BUSINESS

Marple's Business Newsletter, 117 W. Mercer St., Ste. 200, Seattle, WA 98119-3960. 206-281-9609; Fax 206-281-8035. Contact: Michael J. Parks. Newsletter published 26 times a year. Circ. 4000. Sub/$72. No freelance material accepted.
BUSINESS, NORTHWEST

The Martlet, University of Victoria, Box 1700, Victoria, BC V8W 2Y2. 604-721-8359. Editors: Mike O'Brian/Kim Balfour. Periodical.
COLLEGE/UNIVERSITY

Master Gardener Notes, OSU Extension Service, 211 S.E. 80th Ave., Portland, OR 97215. Monthly.
GARDENING

Masterstream, PO Box 1523, Longview, WA 98632. Periodical.
UNSPECIFIED

Matrix, 132 Communications DS/20, University of Washington, Seattle, WA 98195. 206-543-2700. Monthly literary supplement of poetry and short fiction in the UW paper, The Daily. Circ. 25,000. No pay. Byline given. Simultaneous submissions OK. Publishes submissions in 1-2 mos. Fiction: 1,500 wds, any subject. Poetry: Varies. Photos: B&W. "We prefer to print the work of UW students, but on occasion have published non-student works. We receive about 100 submissions a month but have space for about 20-25."
COLLEGE/UNIVERSITY, FICTION, POETRY

Mazama, 909 N.W. 19th, Portland, OR 97209. Periodical on rock and mountain climbing and related subjects for club w/members. Sub w/membership.
OUTDOOR, RECREATION, SPORTS

McKenzie River Reflections, PO Box 12, McKenzie Bridge, OR 97413. 503-822-3358. Editors/ads: Ken & Louise Engelman. Weekly of local tourist, recreation news. Sub $12/yr. Circ. 1,100. Uses freelance material. Pays copies. Byline given. Query w/SASE. Dot matrix, photocopies OK. Accepts nonfiction, fiction, poetry, photos (B&W), plays, cartoons. Sample free.
COMMUNITY, NORTHWEST, RECREATION

Media Inc., Media Index Publishing Inc., PO Box 24365, Seattle, WA 98124. 206-382-9220; Fax 206-822-9372. Editor: Paul Gargaro. Ads: James Baker. Monthly. Sub $25/yr. Circ. 12,000. Founded 1987. Uses freelance material. Byline given. Pays money on publication. Acquires all rights. Query by phone. Responds in 1 wk; publishes in 1 mo. Accepts news items, articles, reviews, photos (B&W or color glossy, rates negotiable). Topics: hard news-oriented, in-depth articles about advertising and advertising crafts such as photography, film/video, design, printing, etc. Sample $3.
FILM/VIDEO, MEDIA/COMMUNICATIONS, PHOTOGRAPHY

Mentor, The Oregon Resource for Men, PO Box 10863, Portland, OR 97210. 503-621-3612; 503-645-6147. Editor: Dick Gilkeson. Ads: Jim Sleeper. Bimonthly newsletter. Circ. 15,000. Sub/$10. Uses freelance material. Byline given. No rights acquired. Query by phone. Pays in copies. Mac disk sub preferred. Responds in 1 wk; publishes in 2 mos. Accepts fiction, poetry, nonfiction, cartoons, photos, interviews, reviews, memoirs. Topics: men's issues, redefining masculinity, freedom from racism, classism, sexism. Sample $1.
MEN, PSYCHOLOGY, NEW AGE

Mercury Services Inc., P. O. Box 1523, Longview, WA 98632-0144. 206-577-8598. Ads: Bruce Grimm. Bimonthly newsletter. Sub $6/yr. Circ. 2,500. Uses 1 freelance ms per issue. Pays on publication in copies. Acquires 1st rights. Byline given. Submit query w/clips, SASE. Dot matrix, photocopies, simultaneous, computer disk subs OK. Reports in 4-6 wks. Publishes 45-50 days. Accepts nonfiction: transportation related; safety issues. B&W photos.
GOVERNMENT, LAW

Message, Montana Info, Box 229, Condon, MT 59826. Quarterly.
UNSPECIFIED

METAlink, Rt. 4 Box 4155, Hermiston, OR 97838. 503-567-7618. Editor: Chris Cromer. A newsletter for Earth People of the Columbia Basin Plateau. Query w/SASE.
NEW AGE

Metrocenter YMCA, PO Box 85334, Seattle, WA 98145. 206-547-4003. Editor: Jack C. Thompson. Quarterly on pop culture, music, politics. Circ. 500. Accepts freelance material. Byline given. Query w/SASE. Phone queries, simultaneous submissions, electronic OK. Nonfiction, cartoons, essays, analysis. Guidelines, sample.
CULTURE, MUSIC, POLITICS

Metropolis, 2207 S.W. Iowa, Portland, OR 97201. 503-244-0535. Editor: Mary Catherine Koroloff. Free in Portland area. Monthly magazine of literature and arts. Interested in all types of short fiction (7,000 wds max), poetry, and experimental writing forms (concrete poetry, graphic short stories, etc.). Submit ms w/SASE. It is the avowed policy to treat writers with respect and dignity, for that is something that professional writers see all too infrequently.
ARTS, LITERARY, POETRY

Metropolis Monthly, 2173 N.W. Irving #6, Portland, OR 97210. Publisher: Robert C. Kenneth. Monthly publication. Sub $15/yr. Accepts unsolicited manuscripts and artwork.
LITERARY

Micro Cornucopia, 155 N.W. Hawthorne, Bend, OR 97701. 503-382-8048. Editors: Cary Gattan, Larry Fogg, Dave Thompson. Bimonthly magazine. Sub/$18. Circ. 30,000. Uses avg 6 freelance mss per issue. Pays $100-150 plus copies on publication. Acquires 1st rights. Byline given. Submit ms/SASE. Dot matrix, photocopied, electronic, computer disk OK. Reports in 1 mo, publishes in 4 mos. Accepts nonfiction, fiction. Topics: Low level (hacker) hardware and software projects for MS-DOS machines; columns for start-up companies and silly computer stories. Technical, but also personal & humorous; 10-20,000 character length; also interested in the nature of thought, creativity, and problem-solving. Guidelines; sample $3.95.
COMPUTERS, SATIRE, TECHNICAL

Microaccess, PO Box 5182, Bellingham, WA 98227. 206-671-1155. Contact: Mitch Lesoing/Carol Anderson. Computer newsletter. No unsolicited mss. Query with clips, SASE. Topics: computer education materials.
COMPUTERS, EDUCATION

Mid-Valley Arts Council, 265 Court St. N.E., Salem, OR 97301. 503-364-7474. Contact: Mark McCrary. Monthly newsletter. Circ. 10,000. Uses freelance material. Byline given. Submit query letter, SASE. Photocopy, dot matrix subs OK. Responds in 1 wk; publishing varies. Accepts poetry, news items, interviews, photos (B&W glossy), articles, reviews. Sample 50.
ARTS

Midwifery Today, PO Box 2672, Eugene, OR 97402. 503-345-1979; 503-343-2408. Editor: Jan Tritten. Ads: Bobbi Corcoran. Quarterly for midwifery practitioners and consumers. Sub $18. Uses 1-3 mss per issue. Payment: Copies on publication. Byline given. Rights purchased: First. Query w/ms, SASE. Phone queries, dot matrix, photocopies, simultaneous submissions OK. Reports in 6 wks. Nonfiction, fiction, poetry, photos, cartoons. Articles to help birth practitioners do their work well. We have 20 different columns and take a variety of articles, both scientific and spiritual. We always need good research articles. Biographical sketch of writer included. Guidelines; sample: $5.
HEALTH, WOMEN

Mining Review, 124 W. 8th St., North Vancouver, BC V7M 3H2. 604-985-8711. Periodical.
BUSINESS, SCIENCE

Minutes Magazine, 141 N. State St. #208, Lake Oswego, OR 97034. 503-243-2616. Editor: Len Rothbaum. Periodical.
UNSPECIFIED

The Mirror, 1015 Republican St., Seattle, WA 98109. 206-464-2125; 206-464-8493. Contact: Lynn Jacobson, Managing Editor. Manager: Debbie Frol. Monthly by and for teens. Free. 50% written by freelance teen writers. Byline given; pays money on publication. Send query. Covers sports, movies, music, local issues, current events. Features should be about 4 pages typed; news, reviews, opinion should be about 2 pages. "Read publication first. We're not looking for dry, formal journalese, but for lively, personal writing that sparks interest and debate." Guidelines.
CHILDREN/TEEN

The Mirror, Marylhurst College, for Lifetime Learning, Marylhurst, OR 97036. Editor: Courtney Rojas. Periodical.
COLLEGE/UNIVERSITY

The Missing Link, Daffodil Press, 6426 198th St. E., Spanaway, WA 98387. 206-847-4892. Contact: Sandra Van Orman. Sub $12/yr. Bimonthly newsletter. Accepts freelance material. Pays copies. Acquires 1st rights. Byline given. Submit ms/SASE. Dot matrix, photocopied OK. Reports in 2-3 wks. Publishes quickly. Accepts poetry. Guidelines; sample $2.50.
POETRY

Mississippi Mud, 1336 S.E. Marion St., Portland, OR 97202. 503-236-9962. Editor: Joel Weinstein. Literary/arts magazine published 2-3x/yr. Sub $19/4 issues. Circ. 1,500. Uses freelance material. Pays money, copies on publication. Byline given. Acquires 1st rights. Submit ms, SASE. Dot matrix, simultaneous subs OK. Reports in 2-4 mos; publishes in 3-12 mos. Accepts fiction (2,500-5,000 wds); poetry (no restrictions). Guidelines; sample $6.
FICTION, POETRY

The Missoula Independent, 115 S. 4th W., Missoula, MT 59801. 406-543-6609. Weekly literary magazine. Circ. 8,000; sub $25-$50. Accepts freelance material. Byline given. Pays money, copies on publication. Query by phone or send complete manuscript w/SASE. Photocopies OK. Responds 2-8 wks; publishes 1-4 wks. Accepts fiction, poetry, nonfiction, reviews, interviews, biography/memoirs. Sample $3.
LITERARY, MONTANA

Modern & Contemporary Poetry of the West, BSU, Department of English, 1910 University Dr., Boise, ID 83725. Editor: Tom Trusky. Periodical 3 times a year. Circ. 500.
LITERARY, POETRY

Modern Language Quarterly, 4045 Brooklyn Ave. N.E., Seattle, WA 98105. Quarterly.
ENGLISH, LANGUAGE(S)

Monday Magazine, 1609 Blanshard St., Victoria, BC V8W 2J5. 604-382-6188. Editor: Sid Tafler. Ads: Adrian Andrew. Weekly alternate news magazine. Sub $30/yr Cdn, $46/outside. Circ. 40,000. Uses freelance material. Byline given. Pays on publication. Acquires 1st rights. Submit query letter, ms, SASE. Photocopy, disk/modem subs OK. Reports in 4 wks; publishing time varies. Accepts nonfiction, news items, biography, photos, humor, interviews, op/ed, reviews. Topics: features of local or regional interest about politics, government, social issues, arts & entertainment. Guidelines.
CANADA, ENTERTAINMENT

Montana Agricultural Statistics Service, PO Box 4369, Helena, MT 59604. 406-449-5303. Editor: Lyle H. Pratt. Semimonthly newsletter. Sub $12/yr. Circ. 1,800. Not a freelance market.
AGRICULTURE/FARMING, ANIMALS, MONTANA

Montana Author, PO Box 20839, Billings, MT 59104. Editor: Richard Wheeler. Quarterly publication of Montana Authors Coalition. Submit to R. Wheeler, PO Box 1449, Big Timber, MT 59011. Articles and news on Montana authors and their work.
MONTANA, WRITING

Montana Business Quarterly, Bureau of Business & Economic Research, University of Montana, Missoula, MT 59812. 406-243-5113. Editor: Marlene Nesary. Quarterly journal founded in 1947. Circ. 1700, sub/$20. Freelance material accepted, byline given, pays in copies. Query letter, SASE, phone query, complete ms. Simultaneous subs OK. Responds in 2-4 weeks; publishes in 1-8 months. Accepts articles. "Our focus is Montana's business & economic climate. Sometimes we publish how-to articles on business management. Call to pitch an idea." Guidelines; back issues $6.
BUSINESS, ECONOMICS, MONTANA

The Montana Catholic, PO Box 1729, Helena, MT 59624. 406-442-5820. Editor: Gerald M. Korson. Journal published 16X/yr. Sub $10. Circ. 8,500. Uses freelance material. Submit query letter, complete ms, SASE. Dot matrix, simultaneous subs OK. Responds in 3 wks; publishes in 16 mos. Accepts news items, photos, interviews, articles. Catholic angle necessary. Sample $3 for 3 issues.
RELIGION

Montana English Journal, Montana State University, Department of English, Bozeman, MT 59717. 406-586-2686. Editor: Sharon Beehler. Periodical.
EDUCATION, ENGLISH

Montana Farmer-Stockman, N.W. Unit Farms Magazines, PO Box 2160, Spokane, WA 99210. 509-459-5361. Semimonthly farm magazine. Also see listing for OR, WA, ID editions.
AGRICULTURE/FARMING, BUSINESS, MONTANA

The Montana Journal, PO Box 4087, Missoula, MT 59804. 406-728-5520. Editor: Jamie Kay. Semimonthly magazine, focus on Montana history. Sub $15/yr. Circ. 20,000. Uses freelance material. Byline given. Pays money, copies on publication. Acquires 1st rights. Submit ms, SASE. Responds in 1 mo, publishes in 1 mo. Accepts nonfiction, articles, memoirs, photos ($5). Guidelines, sample.
HISTORY, MONTANA, UNSPECIFIED

Montana Library Association Focus, Renne Library, Montana State University, Bozeman, MT 59717. 406-994-3162. Editor: Gregg Sapp. May be reached at internet address SAPP/LIB@RENNE.LIB.MONTANA.EDU Quarterly newsletter. Sub $12/yr. Circ. 650. Uses freelance material. Byline given, pays copies, acquires 1st rights. Submit query, synopsis, outline, disk copy and/or complete ms, SASE, phone. Dot matrix, photocopy, simultaneous subs OK. Responds in 1 mo; publishes in 4-6 mos. Accepts news items, interviews, photos, articles. Topics: libraries, education, regional publishing trade. Guidelines; sample.
BOOK ARTS/BOOKS, MONTANA, PUBLISHING/PRINTING

Montana Magazine, American Geographic Publishing, 3020 Bozeman Ave, Helena, MT 59601. 406-443-2842. Editor: Carolyn Cunningham. Bimonthly magazine. Circ. 60,000; sub $18/yr. Accepts some freelance material — Montana subjects only. Pays money on publication. Byline given. Submit query w/ms, SASE. Dot matrix, disk/modem, simultaneous subs OK. Reports in 6-8 wks, publishes in 6-18 mos. Accepts nonfiction, photos (write for guidelines; $75 cover, $50 center section, $25 B&W). Topics: Montana outdoor, history, places to go, geology, hunting, wildlife, personality profiles, etc. Guidelines.
MONTANA

Montana Newsletter, Montana State Library, 1515 E. 6th Ave., Helena, MT 59620. Periodical.
REFERENCE/LIBRARY, SCHOLARLY/ACADEMIC

The Montana Poet, PO Box 100, Three Forks, MT 59752. 406-284-6655. Editor: Don Akerlow. Bimonthly newspaper. Sub $10/yr. Circ. 5,000. Uses freelance material. Pays copies on publication, acquires 1st rights, byline given. Submit ms w/SASE. Dot matrix, photocopied, simultaneous subs OK. Reports in 8 wks; publishes in 2-6 mos. Accepts: poetry about Montana or by a Montanan, cartoons, photos

(of author). Submissions must be neatly printed or typed. Guidelines; sample $2.
POETRY, PUBLISHING/PRINTING, WOMEN

Montana Review, 1620 N. 45th St., Seattle, WA 98103. 206-633-5929. Editor: Rich Ives. Ads: Rich Ives. Semiannual literary periodical. Circ. 500. Sub $9. Accepts freelance material. Payment: Money, copies on publication. Byline given. Rights purchased: First. Submit ms w/SASE. Dot matrix, photocopies OK. Reports in 2-8 wks. Nonfiction, fiction, poetry, translations, book reviews. Any length, subject. Literary quality is our only criteria. Pay varies according to current grant status.
FICTION, LITERARY, POETRY

Montana Senior Citizen News, PO Box 3363, Great Falls, MT 59403. 406-761-0305; 1-800 672-8477 (in Montana). Editor: Jack W. Love, Jr. Ads: Susan Colvin. Bimonthly tabloid. Founded 1984. Sub $8. Circ. 23,000. Uses 1 freelance mss per issue. Pays 4 cents/word on publication. Acquires 1st rights. Byline given. Submit ms w/SASE, phone query. Dot matrix, photocopied, electronic/modem OK. Reports in 3 months. Accepts nonfiction, fiction, poetry, photos, cartoons. Topics: stories and articles of interest to seniors, particularly colorful, unique biographical sketches. Photos required with personality profiles; submit contact sheet, negatives, pay $5. Length generally 500-1,000 wds; positive, upbeat, focus on the value of life experiences; humor/satire preferred for political topics. Sample $3.
MONTANA, SENIOR CITIZENS, TRAVEL

Montana Snowmobile Association, PO Box 367, Virginia City, MT 59755. 843-5341; 843-5484. Editor: Daryl Tichenor. Published 4 times/season.
RECREATION, SPORTS

Montana The Magazine of Western History, PO Box 210201, 225 N. Roberts St., Helena, MT 59620. 406-444-4708. Editor: Charles Rankin. Quarterly newsletter. Sub $20/yr. Circ. 9,000. Uses freelance material. Pays copies on publication. Submit query letter, complete ms, SASE. Dot matrix, disk/modem subs OK. Responds in 3 mos; publishes in 6-12 mos. Accepts biography, interviews, reviews, articles. Topics: authentic history, footnotes and bibliography required. Guidelines, sample.
NW/REGIONAL HISTORY, MONTANA, SCHOLARLY/ACADEMIC

Montana Wildlife, PO Box 6537, Bozeman, MT 59771-6537. 406-587-1713. Editor: Rich Day. Bi-monthly. Sub $10/yr.
ANIMALS

Motes, PO Box 40043, Portland, OR 97240. Poetry journal — send up to three poems with SASE.
POETRY

(m)Other Tongues, R.R. 2 Alders C-14, Ganges, BC VOS 1E0. Contact: Mona Fertig. Sub $14 per year US; $12 in Canada. Circ. 200-300. Accepts freelance material and unsolicited submissions. Byline given. Pays copies on publication. Acquires no rights. Query by letter w/ SASE, photocopy and simultaneous sub OK. Responds in 3-5 months; publishes in 12 months. Accepts fiction, poetry, nonfiction, interviews, articles, plays, reviews, memoirs, dreams, journals, and worksheets of poetry and prose. Guidelines; ad rates on request. Back issues; $7. "International literary biannual. Translations of poetry from mother tongue into English very welcome."
FICTION, POETRY

The Motorist, 330 Sixth Ave. N., Seattle, WA 98109. 206-448-5353; Fax 206-448-8627. Editor: Janet Ray. Ads: Brian Rounds. Circ. 307,000. Free to AAA members. Monthly tabloid of travel and transportation news & features.
CONSUMERS

The Mountain Guide, Blue Mountain Community College, Box 100, Pendleton, OR 97801. 503-276-1260. Periodical.
COLLEGE/UNIVERSITY

Mountain Light, Idaho Historical Society, 450 N. 4th St., Boise, ID 83702. 208-334-3428. Editor: Judith Austin. Quarterly newsletter. Sub w/membership. Circ. 2,000. Submit query letter, complete ms, SASE, phone.
NW/REGIONAL HISTORY, IDAHO

Mr. Cogito, Pacific University, Humanities PO Box 627, Forest Grove, OR 97116. 503-226-4135. Editors: Robert Davies, John Gogol. Irregularly published magazine. Sub $9/3 issues. Circ. 500. Submit ms, SASE. Dot matrix OK. Reports in 2-8 wks. Infrequently pays. Acquires 1st anthology and publishing rights. Accepts poetry: 1 pg; image and sound and diction important; line drawings & photos (up to 3.5" wide x 10" long). Topics: poems in English and translated into English, various themes, leans toward social and political poetry, Central America. Sample $3.
POETRY

Mukluks Hemcunga, PO Box 1257, Klamath Falls, OR 97601. Monthly.
UNSPECIFIED

Musher Monthly, PO Box 305, Bethel, AK 99559. 907-543-2845. Contact: Mike Murray. A publication for and by children of Bethel, AK.
ALASKA, CHILDREN (BY/ABOUT)

Mushing, PO Box 149, Ester, AK 99725. Contact: Todd Hoener. International periodical for recreational and competitive dog sledders. Uses freelance interviews, features (1,500-2,000 wds), profiles, and shorter departmental reports. Pays money on acceptance. Query w/SASE. Guidelines.
OUTDOOR, RECREATION, SPORTS

Mushroom, The Journal, Box 3156, Moscow, ID 83843. 208-882-8720. Editors Don Coombs & Maggie Rogers. Quarterly. Sub $16. Circ. 2,000. Uses 4 freelance mss per issue. Pays copies on publication. Acquires 1st rights. Byline given. Submit query w/clips, ms. Dot matrix, photocopied, computer disk (DOS/ASCII) OK. Reports in 1 mo. Publishes in 2-6 mos. Accepts nonfiction, poetry, photos, cartoons. Material should be relevant in some way to what's going on outdoors with plants, animals and insects. Personal experience okay if it includes valuable learning for the reader. B&W and color prints or slides. Guidelines; sample $4 (3 or more $3 ea).
HOW-TO, NATURAL HISTORY, OUTDOOR

Musings, Campbell River Museum, 1235 Island Hwy., Campbell River, BC V9W 2C7. 604-287-3103. Contact: Thelma Silkens. Newsletter published 3 times a year on local history, Museum activities. Sub $10/yr. Circ. 375. Not a freelance market. Sample: $1.25, SASE.
NW/REGIONAL HISTORY

Mustard Seed Faith Inc., Seed Faith Printing, PO Box 3, St. Helens, OR 97051. 503-397-3735. Editor: Diane Barrick. Quarterly Christian newspaper. Circ. 10,000 Free. Uses freelance material. Byline given. Query w/SASE. Responds in 2-3 wks; publishes in 2-3 mos. Accepts fiction, nonfiction, poetry, cartoons, news items, biography, photos ($10). Topics: religious, Christian, testimonies. Sample $1.
RELIGION

My Little Salesman, PO Box 70208, Eugene, OR 97401. Monthly.
UNSPECIFIED

Mystery News, PO Box 1201, Port Townsend, WA 98368. 206-385-6116. Contact: Larry & Harriet Stay. Bimonthly tabloid. Circ. 1,200. Sub $13.95/yr. Previews and reviews of current mystery novels. No freelance submissions. Sample free.
MYSTERY

NAPRA Trade Journal, New Age Publishers & Retailers Alliance, PO Box 9, Eastsound, WA 98245. 206-376-2702. Editor: Marilyn McGuire. Circ. 10,000. Bimonthly features new age book reviews, audio/video, author tours, and bookseller events.
PUBLISHING/PRINTING, NEW AGE

National Boycott Newsletter, 6506 28th Ave. N.E., Seattle, WA 98115. 206-523-0421. Editor: Todd Putnam. Quarterly on consumer action in the market place, boycotts and socially responsible investing. Circ. 4,000-5,000. Sub $3. Uses 1-2 mss per issue. Payment: Money, copies on publication. Byline given. Query w/ms, SASE. Phone queries, dot matrix, photocopies, electronic OK. Nonfiction, photos, cartoons. Corporations/multinationals and their environmental, social, economic impacts; boycotts and consumer action; boycotts called by human rights, peace, labor, environmental, and civil, women's and animal rights organizations. Sample.
CONSUMER, LABOR/WORK, PEACE

National Fisherman Magazine, 4215 21st W., Seattle, WA 98199. 206-283-1150. Periodical.
FISHING

The National Hemlock Society, PO BOX 11830, Eugene, OR 97440. 503-342-5748. Contact: Derek Humphry. Quarterly periodical.
MEDICAL, PHILOSOPHY

National Percent for Art Newsletter, 1120 S. Elm St., Spokane, WA 99204-4244. Editor: Richard Twedt. Quarterly of news on state, regional and local public art commissions and % for art programs. Sub $24.
ARTS

National Radio Guide, 240 1075 W. Georgia, Vancouver, BC V6E 3C9. 604-688-0382. Editor: C. Robertson. Ads: J. Knight. Monthly magazine. Sub $23.95/yr. Circ. 20,000. Accepts freelance submissions. Pays money on publication for 1st rights. Gives byline. Query first. Responds in 1 mo; publishes in 2 mos. Canada's only complete guide to CBC radio programming. publishes articles that refer to on air programming that month.
MEDIA/COMMUNICATIONS

Natural Living, 611 Market St., Kirkland, WA 98033.
HEALTH

Network News, E. 1419 Marietta Ave., Spokane, WA 99207-5026. 509-487-3383. Editor: Elinor Nuxoll. Quarterly newsletter. Sub $8. Circ. 300+. Uses freelance material from writers age 50+. Byline given; pays copies/prizes. Acquires 1st rights. Submit ms, SASE. Dot matrix, photocopied, simultaneous subs OK. Reports in 1-2 weeks; publishes in 2 months. Accepts nonfiction, memoirs, and personal profiles. "For seniors 50 or older who write for fun or profit." Guidelines, back issues $1.
MEDIA/COMMUNICATIONS, SENIOR CITIZENS, WRITING

Network News, OR Coalition Against Domestic & Sexual Violence, 2336 S.E. Belmont, Portland, OR 97214. Contact: Holly Pruitt. Quarterly newsletter. Query w/SASE.
FEMINISM, POLITICS, WOMEN

New Age Retailer, Continuity Publishing, Inc., 114 W. Magnolia St., #204, Bellingham, WA 98225-4354. Contact: Duane Sweeney. Ads: Pat Brown. Magazine published 7x/yr. Sub $15/yr. Circ. 3,200. Uses 1 freelance ms per issue. Pays copies/ad credit on publication. Byline given. Submit by phone query. Dot matrix, photocopies, computer disk subs OK. Publishes in 1-4 mos. Accepts nonfiction. Topics: info of use or interest to owners of new age bookstores. 1,500-3,000 words. Sample $2.50.
BUSINESS, NEW AGE

New River Times, 201 1st Ave., Fairbanks, AK 99701-4848. Periodical.
UNSPECIFIED

News & Reports, Idaho Department of Education, 650 W. State St., Boise, ID 83720. 208-334-3300. Editor: Helen J. Williams. Monthly newsletter. Circ. 20,000. Not a freelance market.
EDUCATION, IDAHO

News Bulletin, Salem Area Seniors, Inc., 1055 Erixon N.E., Salem, OR 97303. Monthly.
SENIOR CITIZENS

The Newspoke, Anchorage School District, 1800 Hillcrest, Anchorage, AK 99503. Periodical.
EDUCATION

News-Standard, PO Box 488, Coulee City, WA 99115. 509-632-5402. Editor/ads: Sue Poe. Weekly newspaper focusing on local agriculture and schools. Circ. 700. Sub $12-15. Not a freelance market.
AGRICULTURE/FARMING, COMMUNITY, EDUCATION

Nexus, 30 Ridgemond Dr., Fernie, BC V0B 1M2. Contact: Bev Delyea.
UNSPECIFIED

Nike Times, Nike, Inc., 3900 S.W. Murray Rd., Beaverton, OR 97005. Editor: Chris Van Dyke. Company publication.
BUSINESS

Nomadic Newsletter, Nomadic Books, 1911 N. 45th St., Seattle, WA 98103-6804. Periodical.
UNSPECIFIED

Nordic West, PO Box 7077, Bend, OR 97708. Editor: Richard Coons. Monthly magazine devoted to cross-country skiing in the western USA. Query w/SASE.
OUTDOOR, RECREATION, SPORTS

North American Post, 662-1/2 S. Jackson St., PO Box 3173, Seattle, WA 98114. 206-623-0100. Editor: Akiko Kusunose. Japanese language newspaper, published 3 times a week, with an English section once a week. Sub $60/yr. Circ. 2,000. Accepts freelance material very infrequently. No pay. Byline given. Submit ms, SASE. Accepts nonfiction, poetry, photos. Sample.
ASIAN AMERICAN, LANGUAGE(S), MINORITIES/ETHNIC

North Seattle Press/Lake Union Review, 4128 Fremont N., Seattle, WA 98103. 206-547-9660. Editor: Clayton Park, James Bush. Ads: Karina Erickson, Terry Denton. Biweekly newspapers. Sub $12/both. Circ. 20,000. Uses freelance material. Byline given. Pays money on publication. Submit query letter, clips, SASE, phone. Responds in 1 wk; publishes in 12 wks. Accepts news items, photos!, articles. Assignments readily given! Sample.
COMMUNITY

Northern Aquaculture Magazine, 4652 William Head Rd., Victoria, BC V9B 5T7. 604-478-9209. Editor: Peter Chettleburgh. Bimonthly magazine. Circ. 4,500; sub $20/yr. Uses 1-5 mss per issue. Payment: 15 cents/wd on publication. Byline given. Acquires first rights. Query w/SASE. Phone query, dot matrix, photocopies, electronic OK. Accepts nonfiction, photos, drawings. Topics: Readable profiles on fish farmers, processors and research facilities; technical, how-to articles; in-depth analysis of political and resource issues with a bearing on Canadian aquaculture industry. Guidelines, sample ($3.50).
AGRICULTURE/FARMING, BUSINESS, CONSERVATION

Northern Lights, PO Box 8084, Missoula, MT 59807-8084. 406-721-7415. Editor/Ads: Deborah Clow. Quarterly about ID, WY, MT, and the N.W., public policy issues. Circ. 4,000. Sub minimum donation $15. Uses 5-10 freelance mss per issue. Payment 10 cents/wd and copies on publication. Byline given; acquires first rights. Query with clips, ms, SASE. Dot matrix, photocopies OK. Responds in 6-8 weeks; publishes in 3-6 months. Accepts nonfiction, photos, cartoons. Encourage writers & artists to send SASE for guidelines. We want articles that capture not only the facts, but also the mood, landscape, humor, and personalities of the subject in question. We are interested in problems in the West that need solutions, but we are also interested in writing about the things in the West that make it such a wonderful place to live. Sample $5.
ENVIRONMENT/RESOURCES, HUMOR, NORTHWEST

Northern Star, PO Box 811, Great Falls, MT 59403-0811. 406-453-3035. Editor/Publisher: William Marsik. Monthly magazine. Sub $10/yr. Circ. 5,000. Freelance material accepted. Bylines given. Pays money, copies upon publication. First rights acquired. Query by phone. Report time varies. Accepts fiction, poetry, cartoons, news items, nonfiction, B&W, 8X10 photos. Presently statewide publication; outdoor oriented; must know Montana.
OUTDOOR, MONTANA

Northwest Anthropological Research Notes, University of Idaho, Laboratory of Anthropology, Moscow, ID 83843. 208-885-6123. Editor: Roderick Sprague. Semiannual. Circ. 300. Query w/SASE, disk submission preferred. Guidelines.
ANTHROPOLOGY/ARCHAEOLOGY, SCHOLARLY/ACADEMIC, NATIVE AMERICAN

Northwest Arctic NUNA, Maniilaq Assoc., PO Box 256, Kotzebue, AK 99752. 907-442-3311. Free monthly. Circ. 3,000. Uses 2 freelance mss per issue. Pays copies. Byline given. Submit by phone, SASE. Dot matrix, photocopied OK. Report and publishing time varies. Accepts nonfiction, fiction, poetry, photos. Sample free.
ALASKA, NATIVE AMERICAN

Northwest Boat Travel, PO Box 220, Anacortes, WA 98221. Editor: Gwen Cole. Quarterly magazine on boat travel from Olympia, WA to Skagway, AK: sites, resorts, cruises, anchorages. Uses 6 mss for the May and June issues only. Payment: $75-100 on publication. Byline given. Submit ms, SASE. Photocopies OK. Nonfiction: 24 pgs; cruises, history of boating sites, anchorages, towns, sea life. Photos: B&W 3 1/2x5 or larger; parks, landmarks, city scenes; $510; color slides for cover/$100.
BOATING, TRAVEL

Northwest Chess, PO Box 84746, Seattle, WA 98124-6046. 206-935-7186. Monthly magazine. Sub $116.00/yr. Circ. 700. Query w/SASE. Accepts news items, poetry, cartoons, photos, interviews. Topics: chess.
ENTERTAINMENT, RECREATION

Northwest Computing, PO Box 75061, Seattle, WA 98125. 206-547-3620. Contact: T. Kathleen Lynn. Circ. 30,000 Publication of the Northwest Computer Society.
COMPUTERS

Northwest Construction News, 3000 Northrup Way #200, Bellevue, WA 98004. 206-827-9900. Trade periodical.
BUSINESS, ECONOMICS

Northwest Cyclist Magazine, PO Box 9272, Seattle, WA 98109. 206-286-8566. Editor: Thomas G. Braman. Ads: Vicki Bliss. Monthly magazine. Sub rate $12/yr. Freelance material accepted. Byline given. Pays money, copies on publication. Submit query letter, SASE or by phone. Dot matrix, disk OK. Responds, publishes 1 mo. Accepts cartoons, news items, photos (B&W, color slide cover), interviews, op/ed, and travel articles. Read magazine and follow style. (Available free at N.W. bike shops.)
SPORTS, RECREATION, TRAVEL

Northwest Discovery, Journal of Northwest & Natural History, 1439 E. Prospect, Seattle, WA 98112. Editor: Harry Majors. Not accepting mss.
NW/REGIONAL HISTORY, NATURAL HISTORY

The Northwest Dispatch, 913 S. 11th St., Box 5637, Tacoma, WA 98405. 206-272-7587. Periodical.
COMMUNITY

Northwest Energy News, 851 S.W. 6th, Portland, OR 97204. 503-222-5161. Editor: Carlotta Collette. Bimonthly magazine reporting on power planning, fish, wildlife restoration activities in OR, WA, ID, MT. Published by N.W. Power Planning Council. Circ. 15,000 to electric energy professionals, fisheries managers, N.W. Indian tribes. Generally does not accept freelance, but will entertain story ideas. Photos: B&W, salmon (live, not on hooks) and other N.W.

wildlife; pay varies. Not responsible for unsolicited photos or mss. "We have in-house writers, but an occasional story idea, w/clips, may make it." SASE.
CONSERVATION, NORTHWEST, OUTDOOR

The Northwest Environmental Journal, FM-12, University of Washington, Seattle, WA 98195. 206-543-1812. Semiannual of N.W. environmental research and policy. Sub $16. Uses 1-2 freelance mss per issue. Payment: Reprints; no pay. Byline given. Submit ms, SASE. Phone queries OK. Scholarly articles written for a broad audience, sans jargon. All N.W. environmental topics may be relevant (NW= AK, BC, WA, OR, ID, Western MT). Usual length 20-25 pgs (top length of 50). Ours is a refereed journal; 3 scholarly reviewers read each ms. Photos: as needed to make a point. Guidelines; sample $9.
ENVIRONMENT/RESOURCES, NORTHWEST, PUBLIC AFFAIRS

Northwest Ethnic News, 3123 Eastlake Ave. E., Seattle, WA 98102-3875. 206-522-2188. Editor: Kent Chadwick. Monthly newspaper. Sub $12/yr. Circ. 12,000. Uses freelance material. Byline given. Pays copies. Acquires 1st rights. Submit query letter, complete ms, SASE, phone. Simultaneous subs OK. Responds in 1 mo; publishes in 1 mo. Accepts nonfiction, news items, photos (B&W, $5), poetry, interviews, op/ed, reviews. Topics: an ethnic angle. Guidelines; sample $2.50.
CULTURE, MINORITIES/ETHNIC

Northwest Gay and Lesbian Reader, 1501 Belmont Ave., Seattle, WA 98122. 206-322-4609. Editor: Ron Whiteaker. Bimonthly magazine founded 1989. Sub $2/yr. Circ. 4,000. Uses freelance material. Byline given. No pay, acquires no rights. Submit complete ms, SASE. Dot matrix, photocopy, disk/modem subs OK. Responds in 2 wks; publishes in 6 wks. Accepts fiction, poetry, essays, cartoons, interviews, op/ed, articles, book reviews, photos (half-tone, credit but no pay). Topics: reflecting the lesbian/gay experience. Guidelines w/SASE. No simultaneous submissions.
FEMINISM, GAY/LESBIAN, SEX

Northwest Golf Magazine, 5206 Ballard N.W., Seattle, WA 98107. 206-781-1554. Editor: Dick Stevens. Ads: Stein Svenson. Monthly magazine. Sub $18/yr. Circ. 10,000. Uses freelance material. Byline given. Pays money on publication. Submit query letter, SASE. Sample.
SPORTS

Northwest Golfer, PO Box 992, Bellevue, WA 98009-0992. 206-455-5545. Periodical.
NORTHWEST, RECREATION

Northwest Indian Fisheries Commission, 6730 Martin Way E., Olympia, WA 98506. 206-438-1180. Contact: Steve Robinson. Quarterly newsletter. Free. Circ. 10,000. Uses some freelance material. Pay varies. Submit complete ms, SASE. Dot matrix, photocopy, simultaneous, disk/modem subs OK. Responds only on request. Publishes in 1-3 mos. Accepts nonfiction, cartoons, news items, photos.
FISHING, MINORITIES/ETHNIC

Northwest Inland Writing Project Newsletter, c/o Elinor Michel, U of I College of Education, Moscow, ID 83843. 208-885-6586. Submissions editor: Duane Pitts, Box 385, Odessa, WA 99159. 509-982-0171. Quarterly. Sub $5/$10/$25. Circ. 300. Uses freelance material. Pays copies on publication. Byline given. Submit query w/clips, ms, SASE. Dot matrix, photocopied, simultaneous OK. Reports in 3 wks. Publishes in next issue usually. Accepts nonfiction, fiction, poetry, cartoons, other (student/teacher work). Topics: elementary, jr/sr high, college writing; reading-writing connections; teaching ideas/techniques about writing; classroom research in reading/writing. Tips: length may vary: 50-300+ wds, depends on subject. Practical ideas for use in classroom stressed; limited amounts of student work produced in writing workshops accepted. Sample $1.
EDUCATION, ENGLISH, WRITING

Northwest Living, 20629 S.E. 281, Kent, WA 98042-8564. 206-672-6716; Fax 206-672-2824. Editor: Terry W. Sheely. Ads: Bonnie Kostic. Monthly of N.W. people doing N.W. things. Sub $19.95/yr. Circ. 20,000. Uses freelance material. Pays money on publication. Acquires 1st rights. Byline given. Query letter, SASE. Photocopies OK. Reports in 6 wks; publishes in 6-12 mos. Accepts nonfiction, photos, interviews, articles. Topics: suburban and rural subjects; natural science, natural history, homes, foods, gardening, outdoor recreation, regional travel, cottage industries, crops and related subjects. Guidelines; sample $3.95.
NATURAL HISTORY, OUTDOOR, TRAVEL

Northwest Lookout, PO Box 3366, Salem, OR 97302. 503-364-2942. Contact: Dennis L. Tomkins. Trade publication of Northwest Christmas Tree Association published 3 times a year. Circ. 2,000 to Christmas tree growers, wholesalers, retailers, related product mfgs and sellers. Byline given. Query w/SASE to editor at 324 Sumner Ave, Sumner, WA 98390. Guidelines.
AGRICULTURE/FARMING, BUSINESS, NORTHWEST

Northwest Motor: Journal for Automotive Ind., Northwest Motor Publishing Co., PO Box 25, Port Gamble, WA 98364-0025. 206-697-6200. Editor: Peter DuPre. Ads: Ed Swanzey. Monthly for the automotive parts and service industry. Circ. 5,000. Sub $12. Accepts freelance material. Byline given. Writers must have industry documentation. Pays copies on publication. Byline given. Acquires all rights. Query w/SASE. Accepts news items, interviews, articles, reviews. N.W. Automotive Aftermarket trade news and features only. Sample: $2.
BUSINESS, TRADE/ASSOCIATIONS

Northwest Nikkei, PO Box 3173, Seattle, WA 98114. 206-624-4169. Fax: 206-625-1424. Editor: Sandee Taniguchi. Ads: Steve Uyeno. Monthly English language newspaper serving the Japanese-American community. Sub $15/yr. Circ. 10,000. Uses freelance material. Byline given. Pays money, copies on publication. Submit query letter, SASE, phone. Accepts nonfiction, photos, interviews, articles, reviews.
ASIAN AMERICAN, MINORITIES/ETHNIC

Northwest Notes, St. Peter Hospital Library, 415 Lilly Rd., Olympia, WA 98506. Periodical.
HEALTH, REFERENCE/LIBRARY

Northwest Nurserystock Report, 10830 E. Riverside Dr., #B101, Bothell, WA 98011-1557. 206-821-2535. Editor: John Bjork. Periodical.
AGRICULTURE/FARMING, BUSINESS

Northwest Oil Report, 4204 S.W. Condor Ave., Portland, OR 97201. Editor: C. J. Newhouse. Periodical.
BUSINESS

Northwest Outpost, Paralyzed Veterans of America, 213 S.W. 152nd St., Seattle, WA 98166-2307. Periodical.
MILITARY/VETS, NORTHWEST, DISABLED

Northwest Pace, RR 6 Box 247, Astoria, OR 97103-9806. 503-826-7700. Editor: Mark Flint. Periodical.
UNSPECIFIED

The Northwest Palate, PO Box 10860, Portland, OR 97210. 503-538-0317; 503-228-4897. Contact: Judy Peterson-Nedry. Ads: Bruce Watkins. Bimonthly magazine. Circ. 15,000. Sub/$21. Byline given; pays money and copies on publication. Acquires 1st/2nd rights. Submit query, ms SASE. Phone queries OK. Accepts nonfiction, interviews, articles, photos. Topics: food & wine, breweries, distilleries, travel, restaurants, lodging, lifestyles by N.W. writers. "Study magazine, must have N.W. perspective." Sample $3.50.
FOOD/COOKING, NORTHWEST, TRAVEL

Northwest Parent Publishing, 2107 Elliott Ave., #303, Seattle, WA 98121-2159. Contact: Ann Bergman. Publisher magazine for/by children. Sub/$15. Circ. 80,000. Pays money, royalties on publication. Submit query w/SASE, ms, outline, sample chapters. Dot matrix, photocopies OK. Reports in 3 months; publishes in 6-12 months. Accepts nonfiction, interviews, and reviews. Concentrates on issues relevant to parents, educators, professionals working with children 12 or under. Guidelines; sample $1.50.

CHILDREN/TEEN

Northwest Passage, Western Oregon State College/ English Dept., 345 N. Monmouth Ave., Monmouth, OR 97361. 503-838-8599. Editor: Leslie Murray

COLLEGE/UNIVERSITY, FICTION, OREGON

Northwest Passages Hist. Newsletter, c/o Calapooia Publications, PO Box 160, Brownsville, OR 97327. 503-926-0350; 503-369-2835. Editors: Patricia Hainline, Margaret Carey. Bimonthly newsletter. Sub $13. Uses freelance material. Byline given. Pays copies on publication. Acquires 1st rights. Submit complete ms, SASE. Reports in 4-6 wks; publishes in 4-12 mos. Accepts nonfiction, photos. Topics: historical articles about the Northwest, 250-750 wds, well-researched and historically accurate, reminiscences within word limit; also accepts obscure but interesting material from old newspapers and out-of-print books. Guidelines; sample $2.50.

NW/REGIONAL HISTORY, NORTHWEST

Northwest Photonetwork, 16300 Mill Creek Blvd., #205, Mill Creek, WA 98012. 206-745-9069. Publisher: Dave Rambock. Ads: Gary Halpern. Sub free. Circ. 12,000+. Uses 2-3 freelance mss per issue. Pays money/copies on publication. Acquires 1st rights. Byline given. Submit query/SASE, phone. Photocopied, computer disk OK. Reports in 2 wks. Publishing time variable. Accepts nonfiction, photos, cartoons. Prefers writers knowledgeable in Northwest photography. We are in need of writers whose ties to the photo community will help generate stories beyond those that we assign. Guidelines.

PHOTOGRAPHY

Northwest Poets & Artists Calendar, 261 Madison South, Bainbridge Island, WA 98110. 206-842-4855. Contact: Nancy Rekow. Annual calendar of art and poetry selected from competition open to residents of AK, ID, MT, OR, WA and BC, deadline late January each year. Accepts poetry, original artwork. See also listing under Contests. Write for purchase or competition guidelines. Sample $5.

ARTS, POETRY

Northwest Prime Times, 10829 N.E. 68th St., Kirkland, WA 98033-7100. 206-827-9737. Editor: Neil Strother. Monthly for seniors. Sub $5/yr. Circ. 30,000. Uses freelance material. Pays money on publication. Byline given. Submit query letter, SASE. Accepts nonfiction, articles, photos.

LITERARY, SENIOR CITIZENS

Northwest Public Power Bulletin, PO Box 4576, Vancouver, WA 98662. 206-254-0109. Editor: Rick Kellogg. Ads: Tina Nelson. Monthly periodical on public power issues in the N.W. Circ. 4,000. Sub $18. Accepts freelance material. Payment: Generally $100-300 for major articles with photos, on publication. Byline given. Rights purchased: First. Query w/SASE. Phone queries OK. Reports in 1 month. Nonfiction: People, issues, activities relating to public power entities, regional electrical issues. Area covered: OR, WA, ID, Western MT, Northern CA, BC and AK. Photos: B&W glossies. Rates negotiable. "Not interested in investor owned utilities, counter-culture energy schemes, anti-nuke propaganda." Sample.

NORTHWEST, PUBLIC AFFAIRS

Northwest Report, 101 S.W. Main St. #500, Portland, OR 97204. 503-275-9516. Monthly newsletter founded in 1966. Editor: Lee Sherman Candell. Circ. 9,000. Not a freelance market.

EDUCATION

Northwest Review, 369 PLC, University of Oregon, Eugene, OR 97403. 503-686-3957. Editor: John Witte, po-

etry; Cecelia Hagen, fiction. Ads: Rachel Barton-Russell. Literary triannual published 3X/yr (Jan, May, Sept). Sub $14. Circ. 1,100. Accepts unsolicited submissions. Pays in copies on publication. Acquires 1st rights. Byline given. Submit complete mss, SASE. Dot matrix, photocopies OK. No simultaneous submissions. Reports in 5-10 wks; publishes in 1-4 mos. Accepts nonfiction, fiction, poetry, plays, interviews, essays, artwork. Receives approx 4,000 submissions annually, publishes 90. Guidelines; sample $3.

FICTION, LITERARY, LITERATURE

The Northwest Review of Books, 535 N.E. 95th St., Seattle, WA 98115. 206-323-3597. Editor: Jane Friedman. Quarterly magazine focusing on N.W. authors and publishers. Circ. 5,000. Uses 16-20 mss a year. Payment: Money on publication. Byline given. Submit ms, SASE. Phone queries, dot matrix, simultaneous submissions OK. Reports in 1 month. Publishes in 1-3 mos. Nonfiction: 600-900 wds; history, biography, photography, science; $15. Columns: 100 wds; brief review section, $5. Photos: 85 line screen. "Lively writing for our wide audience."

BOOK ARTS/BOOKS, LITERARY, PUBLISHING/PRINTING

Northwest Roadapple Newspaper for Horsemen, 4346 S.E. Division, Portland, OR 97206. 503-238-7071. Editor: John Jangula. Monthly tabloid for horse people. Circ. 24,000. Submit ms, SASE. Phone queries, dot matrix, simultaneous submissions OK. Publishes in 2 mos. Nonfiction, poetry, photos (80 lines, 3x5).

ANIMALS, RECREATION

Northwest Runner, 1231 N.E. 94th, Seattle, WA 98115. 206-526-9000. Editor/ads: Jim Whiting. Monthly. Sub $15.97/yr. Circ. 7,000. Uses freelance material. Byline given. Pays money on publication. Acquires 1st rights. Query by phone. Reports in 2-4 wks. Accepts: short articles (300-1,000 wds, $25-50); features (1,000 wds up, $35-75); photos (B&W glossy, $15). "Readers range from beginners to veterans, most have been running for at least a couple of yrs. We like training articles, how-to, personal experiences, and especially humor." Sample: $3.

SPORTS

Northwest Sailboard, PO Box 918, Hood River, OR 97031. 503-386-7440. Periodical.

RECREATION, SPORTS

Northwest Science, Washington State University Press, Pullman, WA 99164-5910. 509-335-3518. Quarterly. Sub $25.

COLLEGE/UNIVERSITY, NORTHWEST, SCIENCE

Northwest Seasonal Worker, Northwest Seasonal Workers Association, 203 N. Oakdale St., Medford, OR 97501. Editor: Jana Clark

AGRICULTURE/FARMING, CHICANO/CHICANA, MINORITIES/ETHNIC

Northwest Skier & Northwest Sports, PO Box 95229, Seattle, WA 98145. 206-547-6229. Editor: Jenny Petersen. Ads: Trish Drew. Monthly magazine. Sub $7.95/yr. Circ. 30,000. Uses freelance material. Byline given. Pays money, copies, other on publication. Acquires all rights. Query w/ SASE, phone. Responds 1-60 days, publishes in 3-6 mos. Accepts fiction, poetry, cartoons, interviews, articles, op/ ed. Topics: N.W. skiing, all kinds, areas, etc. Sample 2.

OUTDOOR, SPORTS

Northwest Travel, Northwest Regional Magazines, PO Box 18000, Florence, OR 97439. 503-997-8401. Editors: Rob & Alicia Spooner, Dave Peden, Judy Fleagle. Ads: Glenda Ryall. Bimonthly magazine. Circ. 25,000; sub $12.95. Uses freelance material, byline given, pays money, copies on publication, acquires 1st rights. Responds in 1-3 mos; publishes in 3-12 mos. Submit query letter, clips, SASE. Topics: travel in Oregon, Washington, Idaho, and British Columbia. Well-researched historical pieces welcome, ms with photos preferred. List resources used.

NORTHWEST, RECREATION, TRAVEL

Northword: Alaska State Writing Consortium Newsletter, c/o Alaska Dept of Education, 801 W. 10th, Ste. 200, Juneau, AK 99801-1894. 907-465-2841. Editor: Judith Entwife. Quarterly. Circ. 1400. Uses freelance material. Pays copies on publication. Byline given. Submit ms. Photocopies OK. Reports in 1-2 wks; publishes in 1-2 mos. Accepts nonfiction, fiction, poetry, interviews, news items, cartoons. Topics: Writing across the curriculum, writer's residencies with children and adolescents, computers and writing, ties between oral language and writing and reading.

EDUCATION, WRITING

Nor'westing, PO BOX 1027, Edmonds, WA 98020. 206-776-3138. Editor: Thomas F. Kincaid. Ads: Wendelborg Hansen. Monthly for N.W. boaters. Circ. 11,000. Sub $15. Uses freelance material. Pays $100 on publication. Byline given. Acquires 1st rights. Query w/SASE. Phone queries, dot matrix, photocopies, simultaneous submissions, electronic subs OK. Reports in 1 mo. Accepts nonfiction, 1,500-3,000 wds; photos (covers $75). Guidelines.

BOATING, OUTDOOR, RECREATION

Noted, 919 N.W. 63rd St., Seattle, WA 98107. Periodical.

UNSPECIFIED

NRG Magazine, 6735 S.E. 78th, Portland, OR 97206. Editor: Dan Raphael. Biannual magazine of nonfiction, fiction, poetry, photos and graphics. Sub $4/yr. Circ. 600. Any form or genre, but it should be work with energy, work that doesn't end up open ended. Byline given. Pays copies. Acquires no rights. Reports in 1 month. Submit ms, SASE. Dot matrix, photocopied and simultaneous subs OK. Sample: $1.50.

AVANT-GARDE/EXPERIMENTAL, FICTION, POETRY

Nuclear News Bureau, CALS, 454 Willamette, Eugene, OR 97401. Periodical.

BUSINESS

The Nurse Practitioner, 3000 Northrup Way #200, Bellevue, WA 98004-1407. 206-285-2050. Editor: Linda J. Pearson. Ads: Barton Vernon. Monthly for nurses in advanced primary care practice. Circ. 11,600. Sub. $27. Accepts freelance material. Writers must be nurse practitioners. No pay. Byline given. Query w/SASE. Phone queries, dot matrix, photocopies OK. Clinical articles; reports of appropriate research; role, legal and political issues. Guidelines; sample $3.

HEALTH, MEDICAL

Nursery Trades BC, Hortwest, Ste. 107, 14914-104th Ave., Surrey, BC V3R 1M7. 604-585-2225. Contact: Phil Pearsall. Bimonthly periodical. Accepts articles; no pay. Anything on horticulture industry.

AGRICULTURE/FARMING, BUSINESS

Nutrition Notebook, Idaho Dairy Council, 1365 N. Orchard, Boise, ID 83706. Editor: Mary Pittam. Semiannual. Circ. 3,000.

AGRICULTURE/FARMING, ANIMALS, HEALTH

NW Gallery Art Magazine, 7276 S.W. Beaverton-Hillsdale Hwy., #126, Portland, OR 97225. 503-293-3067. Editor: Jane Talisman

ARTS, NORTHWEST

NW Stylist and Salon, PO Box 1117, Portland, OR 97207. 503-226-2461. Editor: David Porter. Monthly trade magazine. Sub $10/free to salons. Circ. 26,000. Accepts freelance material. Pays money, when assigned. Byline given. Query w/SASE, phone. Accepts news items, interviews, articles (500-750 wds with photo), photos (B&W; $5 or $15-20 for cover). Query first. "I prefer to give a writer the slant I want, and I would like to talk to people to give them hints on things I'd like covered in their area." Topics: hair and beauty for the industry, professional beauty salons, schools and supply houses. Sample $2.

BUSINESS, FASHION

Observer, Oregon State Council on Alcoholism, 2560 Center St. N.E., Salem, OR 97310. Monthly.
HEALTH

OCLC PAC-News, PO Box 03376, Portland, OR 97203. 503-283-4794. Periodical.
UNSPECIFIED

OCTE Chalkboard Newsletter, Sutherlin High School, PO Box 1068, Sutherlin, OR 97479. Editor: Bill Mull. Educational newsletter of the Oregon Council of Teachers of English. No submission info (also see Oregon English Journal)
EDUCATION, ENGLISH

ODOT News, Via Oregon Department of Transportation, 519 Transportation Building, Salem, OR 97310. 503-378-6546. Editor: Andy Booz. Monthly magazine featuring news items, nonfiction, photos (in-house). Freelance material accepted. Query. Reports 1 wk, publishes 1 month from acceptance. Guidelines.
GOVERNMENT, PUBLIC AFFAIRS

Old Bottle Magazine/Popular Archaeology, Drawer 5007, Bend, OR 97708. 503-382-6978. Editor: Shirley Asher. Monthly. Circ. 3,000. Sub $12. Uses 10 mss per issue. Payment: $10 published pg. on publication. Byline given. Rights purchased: All. Query w/ms, SASE. Dot matrix, photocopies, simultaneous submissions, eléctric OK. Reports in 6 wks. Nonfiction: "Dedicated to the discovery, research and preservation of relics of the industrial age in general and the establishment of specialized, representative collection by individuals." Photos: $50 color cover. Sample/$1.
ANTIQUES, ARCHITECTURE, COLLECTING

Old Oregon, 101 Chapman, University of Oregon, Eugene, OR 97403. 503-686-5047. Editor: Tom Hager. Quarterly. No unsolicited submissions. Uses 6 freelance mss per issue. Pays 10 cents/wd on acceptance + 2 copies. Byline given. Query w/clips, SASE. Photocopies, electronic, computer disk OK. Reports in 3 wks. Publishes in 3-6 mos. Nonfiction: features 2,500-3,000 wds; columns 1,500 wds. Photos: 8x10 B&W glossy. All topics relate to UO issues, people, ideas. Sample, guidelines.
COLLEGE/UNIVERSITY, OREGON, PUBLIC AFFAIRS

Old Stuff, The Paddlewheel Press, PO Box 230220, Tigard, OR 97223. 503-639-5637. Editor: Marge Davenport.
GENERAL HISTORY

Older Kid News, PO Box 1602, Pendleton, OR 97801. 503-276-9035. Editor: John Brenne. Periodical.
COMMUNITY, ENTERTAINMENT, SENIOR CITIZENS

OMGA Northwest Newsletter, Oregon Master Gardener Association, PO Box 765, Albany, OR 97321. Periodical devoted to home gardening for graduates of the Master Gardener program of the OSU Agricultural Extension Program. Includes news of the programs and the local MG chapters. No payment. Query w/SASE.
AGRICULTURE/FARMING, EDUCATION, GARDENING

One Cook to Another, Sumner House Press, 2527 W. Kennewick Ave, Ste. 190, Kennewick, WA 99336. 509-783-7800. Contact: Barbara Hill. Quarterly cooking newsletter.
FOOD/COOKING

Onion World, Columbia Publishing, PO Box 1467, Yakima, WA 98907-1467. 509-248-2452. Editor: D. Brent Clement. Circ. 5,500. Monthly magazine of onion production and marketing for the industry. Uses nonfiction with photos. Query w/SASE.
AGRICULTURE/FARMING, BUSINESS

Ontario, PO Box 130, Ontario, OR 97914. Editor: Fran McLean. Quarterly.
UNSPECIFIED

Opinion Rag, PO Box 20307, Seattle, WA 98102. Contact: Debbie Lester. Periodical.
UNSPECIFIED

Optical Engineering, PO Box 10, Bellingham, WA 98227. 206-676-3290. Editor: L. Palagi. Bimonthly technical journal. Not a freelance market.
TECHNICAL

The Optimist, Idaho State School for the Deaf & Blind, 202 14th Ave. E., Gooding, ID 83330. Editor: Edward Born. Monthly.
DISABLED

Oregon Arts News, Oregon Arts Commission, 550 Airport Rd. S.E., Salem, OR 97301-1300. 503-378-3625. Quarterly newsletter founded in 1967. Circ. 6,500. Uses freelance material. Byline given. Pays copies. Assignment only. Accepts news items, interviews, op/ed, articles, reviews, photos (B&W). Sample.
ARTS, CULTURE, OREGON

Oregon Assn of Christian Writers Newsletter, 2495 Maple Ave. N.E., Salem, OR 97303. 503-364-9570. Published 3 times a year. Sub $5. Not a freelance market.
RELIGION, WRITING

Oregon Authors, c/o Oregon State Library, Salem, OR 97310. 503-387-4198. Editors: Jey Wann/Deanna Iltis. Sub $5 + $1 S&H. Circ. 350. Annual bibliography produced by the Oregon Authors Committee of the Oregon Library Association, listing works published during the preceding year by authors residing in Oregon. Excluded are works by corporate authors/editors and textbooks, unless timely or of regional interest. Authors wishing to be included should submit bibliographic information to the State Library at the address above.
LITERATURE, OREGON, REFERENCE/LIBRARY

Oregon Birds, S. Willamette Ornithological Society, PO Box 3082, Eugene, OR 97403. Quarterly devoted to the study and enjoyment of Oregon's birds.
ANIMALS, OREGON, RECREATION

Oregon Birds, Oregon Field Ornithologists, PO Box 10373, Eugene, OR 97440. 503-282-9403. Contact: Owen Schmidt. Quarterly journal. Sub $18/year. Circ. 440. Freelance material accepted. Byline given. No pay. First rights acquired. Query by letter, SASE, photocopy, disk/modem, dot matrix, simultaneous sub all OK. Responds in one month; publishes in 3 months. Accepts cartoons, news items, biography, nonfiction, photos, interviews, op/ed, articles, reviews, and memoirs. Slides preferred for photos. Back issues $4 ea. "Wild birds only."
CONSERVATION, ENVIRONMENT/RESOURCES, SCHOLARLY/ACADEMIC

Oregon Business Magazine, 921 S.W. Morrison St. #407, Portland, OR 97205-2722. 503-223-0304. Editor: Kathy Dimond. Monthly on the business and economy in Oregon. Circ. 23,000 business owners, executives. Uses freelance material. Pays 10 cents/wd on publication, byline given, acquires 1st rights. Query w/ms, SASE. Simultaneous submissions OK. Reports in 1-2 mos. Publishes in 1-8 mos. Accepts nonfiction: 1,000-2,000 wds on business topics; departments, 500-1,000 wds. Guidelines; sample send SASE with $1.05 postage.
BUSINESS, OREGON

Oregon Business Review, 264 Gilbert Hall, University of Oregon, Eugene, OR 97403. Periodical on Oregon business issues.
BUSINESS, COLLEGE/UNIVERSITY

Oregon Central News, Oregon Central Credit Union, 336 N.E. 20th, Portland, OR 97232. Editor: Arleen Payne.
BUSINESS

Oregon Chinese News, The Chinese Cons. Benevolent Association, 1941 S.E. 31st Ave., Portland, OR 97214. Periodical.
ASIAN AMERICAN, MINORITIES/ETHNIC, OREGON

Oregon Coast Magazine, PO Box 18000, Florence, OR 97439. 800-727-8401. Editors: Rob Spooner, Alicia

Spooner. Ads: Glenda Ryall. Bimonthly covering the entire Oregon coast. Founded 1982. Sub $12.95/yr. Circ. 65,000. Accepts freelance material. Byline given. Pays money on publication. Acquires 1st rights. Query letter, clips, SASE. Dot matrix OK. Reports in 1 mo; publishes in 6-12 mos. Accepts nonfiction on Oregon coast topics. Photos: Transparencies 35mm or larger, B&W prints or color slides with article. "Study an issue and understand our style before submitting an article." Guidelines. Sample $3.
OREGON, TRAVEL

Oregon Commentator, Box 30128, Eugene, OR 97403. 503-686-3721.
OUTDOOR

Oregon Conifer, Sierra Club, 1413 S.E. Hawthorne Blvd., Portland, OR 97214-3640. Editor: Teresa A. Kennedy. Bimonthly journal for the OR chapter of the Sierra Club; covers local wildernesses, current legislation on the environment, chapter club outings. Circ. 6,000. Sub w/membership. Accepts freelance material. Payment: Copies. Byline given. Rights purchased: First. Query w/ms, SASE. Phone queries, photocopies OK. Nonfiction, fiction, poetry, cartoons. Pro-environmental reports, essays, book reviews, map reviews. Articles of outdoor activity interests. Photos: B&W and color prints; no slides; 4x5 prints preferred; screened photos must be 85 lines.
ENVIRONMENT/RESOURCES, OREGON, OUTDOOR

Oregon Contractor, Oregon PHCC Contractors, 8755 S.W. Citizens Dr. #202, Wilsonville, OR 97070. 503-399-7344. Bimonthly trade journal for member contractors.
BUSINESS, TRADE/ASSOCIATIONS

Oregon Council on Alcoholism & Drug Abuse Newsletter, 4506 S.E. Belmont St., Ste. 220, Portland, OR 97215. 503-232-8083. Executive Director: Jacque Wallace. Bimonthly providing info on alcoholism and drug abuse, issues pertaining to families. Query w/ms, SASE. Phone query OK. No pay. Nonfiction. Interested in current topics on alcoholism and drug treatment, legislative issues, and family therapy. Sample.
FAMILY, HEALTH, PUBLIC AFFAIRS

Oregon Cycling, 23750 S.W. Gage Rd., Wilsonville, OR 97070. 503-638-6306. Published 8 times a year. Circ. 8,000. Sub $4.50. Accepts freelance material. Byline given. Dot matrix, photocopies, simultaneous submissions, electronic OK. Nonfiction, poetry, photos, cartoons. O.C. appeals mainly to well-heeled middle class. Health, fitness, personal experiences, personal opinions, anything related to cycling. Sample/free.
BICYCLING, RECREATION, SPORTS

Oregon East Magazine, Eastern Oregon State College, Hoke Hall, La Grande, OR 97850. 503-962-3787. Editor: Christian Reiten. Annual of creative literature and visual art. Circ. 1,000. Sub $5. 50% of each issue freelance material. Payment: Copies on publication. Byline given. "We reserve the right to print piece in specified issue and maybe again in future anthology, nothing more." Query w/ms, SASE. Dot matrix, photocopies, simultaneous submissions, electronic OK. Deadline: March. Reports by June. Publication: Sept. Fiction: short stories, max of 3,000 wds. Poetry: no line max; accepts haiku. Photos, plays, essays, criticism, interviews, any art medium. Guidelines; sample $5.
DRAMA, POETRY, VISUAL ARTS

Oregon Education, Oregon Education Association, 6900 S.W. Haines Rd., Tigard, OR 97223. 503-684-3300. Editor: Shari Forbes Thomas. Monthly newsletter. Circ. 38,000; sub $10. Does not accept freelance material.
EDUCATION

Oregon English Journal, Portland State University, PO Box 751, Portland, OR 97207. 503-725-4677. Contact: Ulrich H. Hardt. Semiannual journal of the Oregon Council of Teachers of English. Sub $10/yr. Circ. 1,500. Accepts freelance submissions; byline given. Pays copies on pub-

lication; acquires first rights. Send complete ms, simultaneous subs OK. Responds in 1-2 months; publishes in 2 weeks. Accepts fiction, poetry, nonfiction, interviews, articles, and reviews. "Our audience is primarily language arts teachers who love good teaching ideas, poetry, and fiction." Back issues $5.
EDUCATION, FICTION, POETRY

Oregon Episcopal Churchman, PO Box 467, Lake Oswego, OR 97034. 503-636-5613. Editor: Annette Ross. Monthly. Sub $2.
RELIGION

Oregon Farm Bureau News, 1701 Liberty St. S.E., Salem, OR 97302-5158. Monthly.
AGRICULTURE/FARMING

Oregon Farmer-Stockman, PO Box 2160, Spokane, WA 99210-2160. Editor: Dick Yost. Ads: Eric Bosler. Semimonthly periodical of farming, ranching. Circ. 20,000. Sub $9. Uses 1 ms per issue. Writer must have intimate knowledge of agriculture. Payment: Up to $50 on acceptance. Byline given. Rights purchased: First. Query w/ms, SASE. Dot matrix OK. Reports in 1 month. Nonfiction; photos: color prints with negatives. Will consider all submissions, but majority of copy is staff produced. Sample.
AGRICULTURE/FARMING

Oregon Focus, City of Roses Publ. Co. for OPB, 7140 S.W. Macadam Ave., Portland, OR 97219. 503-293-1904. Editor: Marjorie Columbus. Ads: Ann Romano. Monthly magazine for membership. Sub $35/yr. Circ. 90,000. Rarely accepts freelance material, very specific to TV & radio programs. Accepts nonfiction on assignment only, esp. background material on a new public TV or radio series or a personality connected to public TV and radio.
BIOGRAPHY, FILM/VIDEO, MEDIA/COMMUNICATIONS

Oregon Freemason, 709 S.W. 15th Ave., Portland, OR 97205. 503-228-3446. Editor: Sally Spohn. Monthly.
TRADE/ASSOCIATIONS

Oregon Future Farmer, Agricultural Education, OBE, 700 Pringle Parkway S.E., Salem, OR 97310. Quarterly.
AGRICULTURE/FARMING

Oregon Gay News, PO Box 2206, Portland, OR 97208. 503-222-0017. Editor: Christopher L. Smith. Weekly.
GAY/LESBIAN

Oregon Geographic Alliance, Portland State University, PO Box 751, Portland, OR 97207-0751. 503-725-3916. Dr. Gil Latz, Coordinator.
GEOLOGY/GEOGRAPHY

Oregon Geology, Oregon Dept. Geology/Mineral Industries, Ste. 965, 800 N.E. Oregon St. #28, Portland, OR 97232-2109. 503-731-4100. Editor: Beverly F. Vogt. Bimonthly for audience ranging from professional geologists to amateur geologists to planners and politicians. Sub $8. Circ. 2,000-3,000. Accepts freelance material from writers qualified to write about geology. No pay. Rights acquired: All. Byline given. Submit ms, SASE. Dot matrix, photocopies, computer disk OK. Reports in 1 month. Accepts nonfiction: geology, mining, mining history, field trip guides, anything related to geology in OR; 40 ds typed pages max length. Also: cartoons; photos: B&W glossy. Guidelines, sample.
GEOLOGY/GEOGRAPHY, OREGON

Oregon Golfer, PO Box 604, Bend, OR 97709. 503-389-6890; FAX 389-7022. Editor: Jeff Chase. 10 times monthly tabloid. Accepts freelance material. Response varies. Pays on publication. Query with SASE.
OREGON, RECREATION, SPORTS

Oregon Grange Bulletin, Oregon State Grange, 1313 S.E. 12th, Portland, OR 97214. Semimonthly publication of Oregon State Grange, concerning news and issues of importance to agriculture.
AGRICULTURE/FARMING

Oregon Historical Quarterly, Oregon Historical Society, 1230 S.W. Park Ave., Portland, OR 97205. 503-222-1741. Editor: Rick Harmon. Quarterly. Sub $25/yr. Circ. 8,600. Uses 3-4 freelance mss per issue. Pays copies. Acquires all rights. Byline given. Phone queries OK. Reports in 8 wks. Publishes in 2 1/2 yrs. Accepts nonfiction history and culture of Pacific Northwest. Photos used. Sample $2.50.
GENERAL HISTORY, NORTHWEST, OREGON

Oregon Historical Society News, 1230 S.W. Park Ave., Portland, OR 97205. 503-222-1741. Editor: Elizabeth Buehler. OHS newsletter.
NW/REGIONAL HISTORY, NORTHWEST, OREGON

The Oregon Horse, PO Box 17248, Portland, OR 97217. 503-285-0658. Editor: Jim Burnett. Ads: Rich Weinstein. Bimonthly trade magazine on thoroughbred racing and breeding industry. Circ. 3,000. Sub $12. Uses 1-3 mss per issue. Payment: $75-150 (for feature) on publication. Byline given. Rights purchased: First. Query w/ms, SASE. Phone query, photocopies OK. Reports in 2 wks. Particularly need profiles of Oregon breeders, owners, trainers. Sample.
ANIMALS, OREGON, SPORTS

Oregon Humanities, Oregon Council for the Humanities, 812 S.W. Washington St. #225, Portland, OR 97205-3210. 503-241-0543. Editor: Richard Lewis. Semiannual magazine. Circ. 10,500. Accepts freelance material. Pays money on publication. Byline given. Acquires 1st rights. Query letter, complete ms, SASE. Dot matrix, photocopies, disk subs OK. Reports in 2 wks; publishes in 3 mos. Accepts nonfiction & essays on topics relevant to the humanities, 1,000-3,000 wds. Oregon writers and scholars preferred. Guidelines, sample.
CULTURE, ENGLISH, GENERAL HISTORY

Oregon Independent Grocer, Oregon Independent Retail Grocers Assoc., 310 S.W. 4th, Portland, OR 97204. Bimonthly trade.
BUSINESS, FOOD/COOKING, OREGON

Oregon Ink, Oregon Institute of Literary Arts, PO Box 10608, Portland, OR 97210. 503-223-3604. Editor: Kay Reid. Free annual tabloid on Oregon books, distributed to libraries and bookstores throughout the state.
BOOK ARTS/BOOKS, LITERATURE, OREGON

The Oregon Insider, Oregon Environmental Foundation, 2637 S.W. Water, Portland, OR 97201. 503-222-2252. Contact: Peter Ravalla. Twice-monthly environmental newsletter for lawyers, businesses, political groups, and public agencies. Sub $175/yr.
CONSERVATION, ENVIRONMENT/RESOURCES, OREGON

Oregon Law Journal, PO Box 25067, Portland, OR 97225. 503-371-6469. Editor: Michael A. Campbell. Sub $132. Circ. 5,000. Weekly journal for lawyers. Uses freelance material. Pays by arrangement on publication. Byline given. Acquires 1st rights. Submit query w/clips, ms, phone, SASE. Dot matrix, photocopied, simultaneous, electronic/modem, computer disk OK. Accepts nonfiction, cartoons. Topics: current issues and news of interest to practicing attorneys in Oregon. Photos and graphics welcome, but not necessary. Sample for 9x12 SASE.
LAW, POLITICS, PUBLIC AFFAIRS

Oregon Law Review, School of Law, University of Oregon, Eugene, OR 97403. Quarterly.
LAW, OREGON

Oregon Legionnaire, 7420 S.W. Hunziker Rd. #A, Tigard, OR 97223-8242. Bimonthly.
MILITARY/VETS

Oregon Libertarian, P. O. Box 40471, Portland, OR 97240-0471. Editor/Ads: Jo McIntyre. Monthly newsletter. Sub $12. Circ. 200/250. Accepts unsolicited freelance material. Uses 1-5 mss per issue. Pays money ($5-10 per 250-500 wds) or copies on publication. Acquires first rights.

Byline given. Submit query w/SASE, phone query. Dot matrix, photocopies OK. Reports in 1-6 wks. Publishes in 1-2 mos. Accepts nonfiction, photos, cartoons. Topics: victims of government, beating city hall, grassroots freedom fighting, benefits of freedom, how personal liberty stimulates creativity, Would like articles from Greens, bioregionalists, decentralists, anarchists, feminists, tax protesters and others interested in networking with fellow freedom lovers. B&W prints only, pays $10 if screened, $5 if not. Free sample.
GOVERNMENT, OREGON, POLITICS

Oregon Library News, Hood River County Library, 502 State St., Hood River, OR 97031. Editor: June Knudson. Periodical.
EDUCATION, REFERENCE/LIBRARY

Oregon Masonic News, PO Box 96, Forest Grove, OR 97116. Periodical.
TRADE/ASSOCIATIONS

Oregon Motorist, 600 S.W. Market, Portland, OR 97201. Editor: Doug Peeples. Monthly for members of Oregon AAA. Circ. 225,000. Accepts freelance material on limited basis. Query w/ms, SASE. Dot matrix, simultaneous submissions OK. Pay and rights purchased are negotiable. Nonfiction: 2 ds pages. Fillers: no pay. Guidelines, sample.
OREGON, TRAVEL

Oregon Music Educator, 337 W. Riverside Dr., Roseburg, OR 97470. Quarterly.
EDUCATION, MUSIC

Oregon Newsletter, CH2M Hill, Inc., PO Box 428, Corvallis, OR 97339. 503-752-4271. Contact: Mary O'Brien. Newsletter published 5 times a yr by engineering firm.
BUSINESS, TECHNICAL

Oregon Optometry, College of Optometry, Pacific University, Forest Grove, OR 97116. Quarterly.
COLLEGE/UNIVERSITY, HEALTH

Oregon Outlook, State School for the Deaf, 999 Locust N.E., Salem, OR 97310. 503-378-3825. Editors: Shermalee Roake, Fred Farrior. Newsletter published 8 times a year. Sub $1.50/yr. No submission info, query w/SASE.
EDUCATION, DISABLED

The Oregon Peaceworker, 333 State St., Salem, OR 97301. 503-371-8002. Editor: Peter Bergel. Monthly newspaper. Circ. 11,000; sub $15/yr. Uses some freelance material. Byline given. Accepts cartoons, news items, photos, op/ed, articles. Disk/modem and simultaneous subs OK. Sample $1.
ENVIRONMENT/RESOURCES, PEACE, POLITICS

Oregon Public Employee, PO Box 12159, Salem, OR 97309-0159. Monthly.
LABOR/WORK, OREGON, PUBLIC AFFAIRS

Oregon Public Employees Retirement System, 200 S.W. Market, Portland, OR 97207-0073. 503-229-5643. Contact: David Bailey. Monthly, free to members.
TRADE/ASSOCIATIONS

Oregon Publisher, Oregon Newspaper Publishers Association, 7150 S.W. Hampton St., Ste. 111, Portland, OR 97223. 503-624-6397. Editor: Shelly Sanderlin. Quarterly trade newspaper. Circ. 2,000. Submit query letter, SASE. Photocopy, disk/modem subs OK. Responds immediately. Accepts news items, articles. Sample.
COMPUTERS, MEDIA/COMMUNICATIONS, TRADE/ASSOCIATIONS

Oregon Realtor, Oregon Association of Realtors, PO Box 351, Salem, OR 97308. Editor: Max Chapman. Monthly.
BUSINESS, OREGON, TRADE/ASSOCIATIONS

Oregon Restaurateur, 50 S.W. 2nd Ave., Ste. 410-AZ, Portland, OR 97204. 503-223-9091. Editor: Sally Cumming. Ads: Brian Dunleavy. Founded 1985. Circ. 15,000. Sub/$3.95 per issue. Bimonthly trade magazine for Northwest restaurateurs and food service industry operations.

All editorial content is commissioned on a work-for-hire basis; writing and photography guidelines are given with each assignment. The editor is not responsible for unsolicited contributions which must include a SASE if return is requested. Back issues $3.95.

BUSINESS, TRADE/ASSOCIATIONS, FOOD/COOKING

Oregon School Study Council Bulletin, 1787 Agate St., University of Oregon, Eugene, OR 97403. 503-686-5045. Monthly publication offers an in depth description of effective programs in the state's schools. Each issue focuses on topics of significance to administrators and lay board members. Sub with membership.

EDUCATION, OREGON

Oregon Science Teacher, Rt. 1 Box 148, Hillsboro, OR 97123. Quarterly.

EDUCATION, OREGON, SCIENCE

Oregon Snowmobile News, PO Box 6328, Bend, OR 97708. Monthly of the Oregon State Snowmobiling Assoc.

OREGON, OUTDOOR, RECREATION

Oregon Sport & Recreation Magazine, Sportland Publishing, 733 N.W. Everett St. #26, Portland, OR 97209-3517. 503-287-5408. Editor: Mike Fazzolari. Ads: Gary Dunsworth. Annual magazine. Circ. 30,000. Uses freelance material. Byline given, pays money on publication. Submit query, ms, SASE. Photocopy, disk/modem, dot matrix subs OK. Responds in 1-2 wks. Uses fiction, cartoons, nonfiction, photos, interviews, articles. Photos: color slides or B&W glossy. "Editorial directed at winter recreation preferred." Sample free for 9x12" SASE.

OREGON, RECREATION, SPORTS

Oregon Sports & Recreation Magazine, 733 N.W. Everett St. #26, Portland, OR 97209-3517. 503-287-5408. Contact: Mike Fazzolari, editor. Ads: Gary Dunsworth. Bi-annual. Sub $4/yr. Circ. 25,000. Uses 5 freelance mss per issue. Pays money ($40/article) on publication. Byline given. Submit query w/clips, or phone. Computer disk OK. Accepts nonfiction, fiction, photos, cartoons. Topics: outdoor recreation and all sports. 500-2,000 wds. Photos: B&W 5x7 or 8x10 glossy, color-chrome, $10 B&W, $15 color. Sample $1.

NORTHWEST, RECREATION, SPORTS

Oregon State Parks Quarterly, 525 Trade Street N.E., Salem, OR 97310. 503-378-2796.

OREGON, OUTDOOR, RECREATION

Oregon State Trooper, PO Box 717, Tualatin, OR 97062. 503-639-9651. Editor: Ralph Springer. Magazine published 3 times a yr. Sub $8/4 issues. Circ. 2,000. Accepts freelance material. Pays money or copies. Byline given. Submit query w/clips. Dot matrix OK. Reports in 4 wks. Publishing time varies. Accepts nonfiction, photos. Seeking photos, mss covering OSP officers at work, off-duty, etc.; accident scenes w/OSP slant, etc.; features on OSP troopers, hobbies, etc. B&W photos preferred, usually pays $7.50 per photo.

LABOR/WORK, OREGON, TRADE/ASSOCIATIONS

The Oregon Stater, OSU Alumni Association, 104 Memorial Union Bldg., OSU, Corvallis, OR 97331. 503-754-4611. Editor: Ellen Saunders. Published 7 times a year. Circ. 96,000. Uses 4 freelance mss per issue. Pays money on publication. Rights acquired: first. Byline given. Submit query w/clips. Dot matrix, photocopies, computer disk OK.

COLLEGE/UNIVERSITY, EDUCATION, OREGON

Oregon Teamster, 1872 N.E. 162nd Ave., Portland, OR 97230-5642. Semimonthly union publication.

LABOR/WORK, OREGON

Oregon Vintage Motorcyclist Newsletter, PO Box 14645, Portland, OR 97124. Editor: Wally Skyman.

LABOR/WORK, TRADE/ASSOCIATIONS

Oregon Wheat, 305 S.W. 10th, PO Box 400, Pendleton, OR 97801. 503-276-7330. Editor: Scott Duff. Bimonthly

magazine dedicated to the improvement of wheat farming in OR. Circ. 9,000. Interested in general trade mss by industry professionals only. Byline given. Query w/SASE. Dot matrix, simultaneous submissions OK. Reports in 1 mo. Publishes in 2 mos. Nonfiction: 3 typewritten, ds pgs on issues pertaining to wheat farming. Rarely print anything outside of technical wheat farming subjects. Guidelines; free sample.

AGRICULTURE/FARMING, BUSINESS, OREGON

Oregon Wine Press, 644 S.E. 20th Ave., Portland, OR 97214. 503-232-7607. Fax: 503-233-6746. Editor: Richard Hopkins. Ads: Bryan Hopkins. Monthly tabloid newspaper founded in 1984. Sub $9/yr. Circ. 20,000. Uses freelance material. Byline given. Pays money on publication. Acquires all rights. Submit query letter, SASE, phone. Photocopy, simultaneous subs OK. Responds in 2-3 wks; publishes in 1 mo. Accepts news items, interviews, articles, photos (B&W). Topics: Oregon wine, the wine industry, Oregon hospitality industry, wine education. Sample $2.

CALENDAR/EVENTS, FOOD/COOKING, TRAVEL

The Oregon Witness, The Coalition for Human Dignity, PO Box 40344, Portland, OR 97240. 503-232-5070. Editors: Jason McGraw, Pat McGuire. Tabloid published 6 times a yr.

MINORITIES/ETHNIC, PUBLIC AFFAIRS

Oregon/Washington Labor Press, 4313 N.E. Tillamook, Portland, OR 97213. 503-231-4990. Editor: Mary Lyons. Monthly newspaper of the Oregon & Washington AFL-CIO organizations. Sub $10/yr.

LABOR/WORK, OREGON

Ornamentals Northwest, Department of Horticulture, Oregon State University, Corvallis, OR 97331. Editor: James L. Green. Quarterly.

AGRICULTURE/FARMING, COLLEGE/UNIVERSITY, GARDENING

Orpheus, 65267 Hull Ln., Imbler, OR 97841-8111. Editor: Christopher Hatten. Science fiction and fantasy tabloid seeking undiscovered talent. Accepts stories, poems, art, cartoon. Max 1,500 wds, B&W artwork. Pays copies. Query w/SASE.

FANTASY/SCI FI, POETRY

Orphic Lute, 1713 14th Ave., Seattle, WA 98122. 206-323-2115. Editor: David Sparenberg. Poetry quarterly. Founded 1950. Sub/$12. Accepts lyric verse of 40 lines or less. Include SASE with all submissions. Special interests include pathos of human condition, experiences of love and beauty, healing, mythic, dream, maintaining bio and cultural diversity, Native American, and ecological themes. Sample $3.50.

POETRY

Other Press, Douglas College, PO Box 2503, New Westminster, BC V3L 5B2. 604-525-3830. Periodical.

COLLEGE/UNIVERSITY

Our Little Friend, PO Box 7000, Boise, ID 83707. Editor: Louis Schutter. Weekly magazine for children published by Seventh-Day Adventist Church. Circ. 65,785.

CHILDREN/TEEN, RELIGION

Outdoors West, 512 Boylston Ave. E., #106, Seattle, WA 98102. Editor: Hazel A. Wolf. Semiannual tabloid concerning use and protection of wilderness and recreation resources.

CONSERVATION, ENVIRONMENT/RESOURCES, OUTDOOR

Outlaw Newsletter, PO Box 4466, Bozeman, MT 59772. 406-586-7248. Editor: Jeri Walton. Quarterly newsletter of Western happenings, cowboy poetry & book reviews. Sub $7. Does not accept unsolicited submissions. Submit query w/clips.

FICTION, NORTHWEST, POETRY

Outlook, Canadian Jewish Outlook Society, #3 - 6184 Ash St., Vancouver, BC V5Z 3G9. 604-324-5101. Editor:

Henry Rosenthal. Monthly magazine founded in 1962. Sub $25, US $31. Freelance material accepted. Pays in copies. Byline given. Submit ms. Photocopy, dot matrix OK. Reports in 3 wks; publishes in 3 mos. Accepts poetry, cartoons, interviews, op/ed, articles, reviews, memoirs.

MINORITIES/ETHNIC, PEACE, PUBLIC AFFAIRS

Overlook, Sierra Club, 1413 S.E. Hawthorne Blvd., Portland, OR 97214-3640. Periodical.

CONSERVATION, ENVIRONMENT/RESOURCES

The Overseas Times, PO Box 442, Surrey, BC V3T 5B6. 604-588-8666. Contact: Ben P. Sharma. Periodical.

UNSPECIFIED

The Ovulation Method Newsletter, Ovulation Method Teachers Association, PO Box 10-1780, Anchorage, AK 99501. Quarterly. Sub $10. Circ. 500. Uses freelance material. Pays in copies. Byline given. Submit ms, SASE. Dot matrix, photocopied OK. Accepts nonfiction, cartoons. Sample.

FAMILY, HEALTH, WOMEN

Owyhee Outpost, Owyhee County Museum, PO Box 67, Murphy, ID 83650. 208-495-2319. Annual. Circ. 500. Sub $10.25. Uses 2-4 mss per issue. Payment: Copies on publication. Byline given. Rights purchased: First. Query w/ms, SASE. Dot matrix, photocopies OK. Reports in January. Nonfiction: only articles on Owyhee County history, 3-10 typed, ds pgs. Photos: 5x7 or 8x10 B&W. Tip: Articles must include bibliography or source of information. Sample/$10.25

AMERICAN HISTORY, NW/REGIONAL HISTORY, IDAHO

Oyate Wo'wapi, Tahana Whitecrow Foundation, PO Box 18181, Salem, OR 97305. 503-585-0564. Contact: Melanie Smith. Self-publisher & quarterly newsletter founded in 1987. Sub/$5. Uses freelance material; byline given. Pays copies; acquires 1st rights. Submit query letter, SASE. Simultaneous subs OK. Responds in 2-4 weeks; publishing time varies. Accepts news items, poetry. Guidelines. See Resources for annual poetry contest.

NATIVE AMERICAN, POETRY

Pacific, The Seattle Times, PO Box 70, Seattle, WA 98111. 206-464-2283. Weekly Sunday supplement to the Seattle Times. Accepts very little freelance material. Query w/SASE.

CULTURE, NORTHWEST, WASHINGTON

Pacific Affairs, University of British Columbia, 2029 West Mall, Vancouver, BC V6T 1Z2. 604-822-6508; Fax 604-822-9452. Quarterly scholarly journal of UBC. Sub $35/indiv. $50/inst. Circ. 4,000. Uses freelance material. Byline given. Submit query letter. Responds in 3 wks; publishes in 6 mos. Accepts solicited book reviews. Guidelines.

ASIA, POLITICS, SCHOLARLY/ACADEMIC

Pacific Builder & Engineer, 3000 Northup Way #200, Bellevue, WA 98004-1407. 206-827-9900. Contact: Richard C. Bachus. Trade journal. Accepts freelance material. Pays money on publication. Acquires first rights. Byline given. Submit query w/clips, SASE. Dot matrix, photocopied, computer disk OK. Reports in 1 mo. Accepts nonfiction stories on non-residential construction in Washington, Oregon, Alaska, Montana, and Idaho. Length about 1,500-2,000 wds, must include art. Photos: color transparencies or B&W negatives & contact sheet.

BUSINESS, NORTHWEST, TRADE/ASSOCIATIONS

Pacific Coast Nurseryman Magazine, 303 N.W. Murray Rd., Ste. 6A, Portland, OR 97229. 503-643-9380. Editor: John Humes. Monthly trade magazine of the nursery, horticulture industry. Circ. 10,000. Byline given. Seldom purchase because we have more info than can usually use. Minimal fee of $25. Query w/ms, SASE. Phone query, dot matrix, simultaneous submissions OK. Publishes in 2-12 mos. Nonfiction: 300-1,200 wds. Photos: B&W glossies; reimburse cost. All submissions subject to editing. Small business retailing, new horticulture research, new agricultural breakthroughs. Not interested in articles aimed at home gardener. Sample/$2.

AGRICULTURE/FARMING, BUSINESS, TRADE/ASSOCIATIONS

Pacific Fisheries Enhancement, PO Box 5829, Charleston, OR 97420. Periodical.

BUSINESS, FISHING

Pacific Fishing, 1515 N.W. 51st, Seattle, WA 98107. 206-789-5333. Contact: Steve Shapiro. Monthly magazine for the commercial fishing industry on the West Coast. Acquires 1st rights to nonfiction on all aspects of the business and the people, especially features with quality photos. Query w/SASE. Query w/SASE.

BUSINESS, FISHING

Pacific Marketer, Northwest Furniture Retailer, 121 Borea N., Seattle, WA 98109. Monthly.

BUSINESS

Pacific Network News, PO Box 1224, Portland, OR 97207. 503-788-6920. Contact: Brent Vaughters, Editor. Sub $12/yr or free at drop-off points. Circ. 20,000. Topics: Portland-Vancouver business, financial, real estate networking. Welcomes freelance submissions. SASE for guidelines.

BUSINESS, ECONOMICS

Pacific Northwest Executive, UW, Grad. School of Bus. Admin., 336 Lewis Hall, DJ-10, Seattle, WA 98195. 206-543-1819. Editor: Jerry Sullivan. Quarterly of business management/economics. Circ. 25,000. Sub free. Uses 1-2 mss per issue. Payment: $250500 on acceptance. Byline given. Rights purchased: First. Query w/SASE. Dot matrix, photocopies, simultaneous submissions, electronic OK. Nonfiction: 1,500-3,000 wds. Our typical issue will be read at the workplace by people who are keeping themselves informed as part of their jobs. Thus, we serve an educational, not an entertainment function. In recent issues we have featured a debate on comparable worth, a series on Japanese business, a story on the implications for managers of an employee with a life-threatening illness, and an overview on wheat in a changing marketplace. Guidelines/sample.

BUSINESS, ECONOMICS, NORTHWEST

Pacific Northwest Forum, M.S. 27, Eastern Washington University, Cheney, WA 99004. Contact: J. William, T. Young. Quarterly journal. Sub $5/yr. Circ. 500. Uses 3 freelance mss per issue. Pays $20 & 10 copies on publication. Byline given. Submit query w/clips, ms, SASE, phone. Dot matrix, photocopied, Mac disk OK. Reports in 3 mos. Publishes in 6-12 mos. Accepts nonfiction, fiction. Topics: history, literature, environmental issues in the N.W.; for scholars and the general reader.

COLLEGE/UNIVERSITY, NW/REGIONAL HISTORY, LITERATURE

Pacific Northwest Magazine, 701 Dexter Ave. N. #101, Seattle, WA 98109-4339. 206-284-1750. Editor: Ann Nauman. Ads: Peggy Bilous. Magazine published 9X/yr. Sub $24.95/yr. Circ. 80,000. Uses freelance material. Pays money, copies on publication. Acquires 1st rights. Submit query letter, clips, SASE. Responds in 3 wks; publishes in 4 mos. Accepts articles, photos. Guidelines; sample $4.

NORTHWEST, RECREATION, TRAVEL

Pacific Northwest Quarterly, University of Washington, 4045 Brooklyn N.E., JA-15, Seattle, WA 98105. 206-543-2992.

COLLEGE/UNIVERSITY

The Pacific Review, Pacific University, U.C. Box 607, Forest Grove, OR 97116. 503-357-61512406. College literary magazine. Circ. 500; sub $2. Accepts unsolicited material. Pays in copies. Accepts fiction, poetry, cartoons, nonfiction, photos, plays, memoirs. SASE for guidelines. Sample $3.50 + shipping.

COLLEGE/UNIVERSITY, FICTION, OREGON

Pacific Yachting, 1132 Hamilton St., #202, Vancouver,

BC V6B 2S2. 604-687-1581. Mday be reached at E-Mail address: A32@MINDLINK.UUCP. Fax: 604-687-1925. Monthly magazine founded in 1968. Editor: John Shinnick. Sub $30/yr. Circ. 25,000. Uses freelance material. Byline given. Pays money on publication. Acquires 1st, 2nd rights. Submit query letter, complete ms, SASE (Cdn postage or international coupons). Dot matrix, photocopy, disk/modem subs OK. Accepts news items, interviews, op/ed, reviews, photos (prints or slides, color, $25-300). Topics: industry news and features on boating people, places and events. High level of expertise required. Guidelines.

BOATING, BUSINESS, RECREATION

Palouse Journal, 112 W. 4th, Moscow, ID 83843. 208-882-6704. Editors: Ed Hughes. Ads: Patty Dimmitt. Tabloid journal published 5/yr. Sub $12/yr. Circ. 15,000. Uses freelance material (5-8 mss per issue). Pays money on publication. Acquires 1st rights. Byline given. Query w/clips & SASE or phone. Dot matrix, photocopied, or disk submissions OK. Reports in 1 mo; publishing time varies. Accepts biography, photos (on request), interviews, op/ed, articles, cartoons, photos, reviews, short fiction (1,000 wds). Topics: local history, natural history, politics, environment issues, sports, food, science, business, regional travel, arts, people, must be of interest to interior Northwest readers. Study sample before querying. Guidelines; sample $2.

COMMUNITY, IDAHO, TRAVEL

Panegyria, Aquarian Tabernacle Church, PO Box 85507, Seattle, WA 98145. 206-793-1945. Contact: Pete Pathfinder. Newsletter published 8x/yr. Founded 1983. Circ. 500-1,000, subs. $12/yr. Uses freelance material. Byline given, pays copies on publication, acquires some rights. Submit query, complete ms; SASE, phone. Disk/modem subs OK. Responds in 2-4 wks; publishes in 4 mos. Accepts fiction, cartoons, news, nonfiction, interviews, reviews. Topics: related to ancient cultures of Europe, magic, self-mastery, goddess-oriented religion (not Satanist). Sample $3.

FEMINISM, RELIGION, NEW AGE

Paper Radio, PO Box 4646, Seattle, WA 98104. 206-830-5356. Publisher & Fiction editor: Neil S. Kvern. Three issues annually. Sub $9/yr. Circ. 2000. Fully freelance written. Pays in copies on publication. No rights acquired. Byline given. Submit ms, SASE. Dot matrix, photocopied, simultaneous OK. Reports in 1-2 months; publishes in 1-6 mos. Accepts nonfiction, fiction, poetry, photos, plays, cartoons, B&W art. Topics: short stories (under 3,000 wds), poetry (under 20 lines), visual art (8x11" or smaller). Prefers things which are radical, experimental, political (that which is oblique rather than direct). We have published humor, erotica & essays. See an issue before sending anything. Send poetry submissions to Serge Lecomte, PO Box 82052, Fairbanks, AK 99708. Sample $3.

AVANT-GARDE/EXPERIMENTAL, LITERATURE, VISUAL ARTS

Parallel DisCourse, A Magazine of Graphic & Written Arts, PO Box 2473, Seattle, WA 98111. 206-323-6779. Contact: Phoebe Bosche/James Maloney. Tabloid published whenever the time is ripe. Query w/SASE. Sample $2.

ARTS, LITERARY

Paralog, OPVA Newsletter, 16079 S.E. McLoughlin Blvd., Portland, OR 97267-4649. 503-775-0938. Periodical. Circ. 600. Sub free to members. Payment: Copies on publication if requested. Byline given. Query w/ms, SASE. Phone query, dot matrix, photocopies, simultaneous submissions OK. Reports in 2 mos. Nonfiction: subjects of interest to paralyzed veterans. Sample.

MILITARY/VETS, DISABLED

Parsley Sage &. Time, Pike Market Senior Center, 1931 1st Ave., Seattle, WA 98101. Periodical.

SENIOR CITIZENS

Passage, Seattle Arts Commission, 312 First Ave N., 2nd Floor, Seattle, WA 98109. 206-648-7171. Contact: Diane

Shamash. Self-publisher only. All materials published are in promotion of agency's own programs, generated in-house or contracted according to Agency's needs.

ARTS, CULTURE, VISUAL ARTS

Passages, Reed College, PO Box 219, Portland, OR 97202.

LITERARY

Patchwork, 1615 N.W. Hillcrest Dr., Corvallis, OR 97330. Quarterly welcomes submissions from writers 55 or older. No pay. 500 word maximum. Images of today and memories of yesterday, stored in the fabric of our minds, now pieced together for your reading enjoyment.

BIOGRAPHY, GENERAL HISTORY, SENIOR CITIZENS

Pathways, Inky Trails Publications, PO Box 345, Middleton, ID 83644. Editor: Pearl Kirk. Published 3 times a year. Circ. 300. Query w/ms, SASE. Reports in 2-8 wks. Publishes in 2-3 yrs. Nonfiction, fiction, poetry. Fantasy, animals, essays, humor, travels, historical and childrens own ideas. 500-1,200 wds. Encourage new writers, especially children. Do not want horror or porn. Guidelines: SASE/44 cents post. Sample: $7 w/9x12 SASE.

CHILDREN (BY/ABOUT), FANTASY/SCI FI, HUMOR

PAWS, Progressive Animal Welfare Society, PO Box 1037, Lynnwood, WA 98046. Periodical.

ANTHROPOLOGY/ARCHAEOLOGY

PDXS, 2305 N.W. Kearny, Portland, OR 97210. 503-224-7316. Editor/Ads: Jim Redden. Biweekly tabloid of news and arts coverage for Portland metro area. Seeks freelance submissions of political commentary, arts reviews (rock and roll), profiles, coverage of anything local and outrageous. Uses photos with news stories. Query by phone on news or ms w/SASE. Byline given. Payment varies. Reports in 1 wk; publishing time varies.

AVANT-GARDE/EXPERIMENTAL, POLITICS

Pea & Lentil News, PO Box 8566, Moscow, ID 83843. 208-882-3023. Contact: Tracy Bier. Quarterly trade publication. Circ. 4,500. Not a freelance market.

AGRICULTURE/FARMING, BUSINESS

Peak Media Inc., Box 925, Hailey, ID 83333-0925. 208-726-9494. Publishes magazines with a focus on the region. Owner of The Valley Magazine and Idaho Grain.

FOOD/COOKING, OUTDOOR, RECREATION

Pen Names, 1480 Birchwood Ave #306, Bellingham, WA 98225-1388. 206-676-9974. Editor: David Eldred. Published annually.

COLLEGE/UNIVERSITY, FICTION

Pen Pals Northwest, E. 1419 Marietta Ave, Spokane, WA 99207-5026. 509-487-3383. Editor: Elinor Nuxoll. Quarterly newsletter. Sub $5. Circ. 200+. Uses freelance material. Byline given. Pays copies on publication. Acquires first rights. Submit query letter, ms, SASE. Dot matrix, photocopies, simultaneous subs OK. Accepts nonfiction travel articles, memoirs. Reports in 2 mos. Sample $1.

FAMILY, NORTHWEST, TRAVEL

People's Food Store Newsletter, 3029 S.E. 21st, Portland, OR 97202. 503-244-9133. Contact: Dave Kehoe. Bimonthly. Circ. 500. Seeking freelance material. No pay. Topics: Natural foods and wellness. Length: 425 wds is ideal. Wants food-oriented graphics, MacPaint or similar. Sample for SASE.

CONSUMER, ENVIRONMENT/RESOURCES, FOOD/COOKING

Perceptions, 1317 S. Johnson St., Missoula, MT 59801-4805. 406-543-5875. Editor: Temi Rose. Chapbook journal of mostly women's poetry published 3 times a year. Uses 30 freelance mss per issue. Sub $3/yr. Pays copies on publication. Byline given. Submit query letter, SASE. Responds in 1 mo; publishing time varies. Accepts nonfiction, fiction, poetry, photos (B&W), cartoons. Guidelines; sample $3.

FICTION, POETRY, WOMEN

Perceptions, Mt. Hood Community College, 26000 S.E. Stark, Gresham, OR 97030. Annual magazine. Circ. 500. Uses freelance material. Byline given, pays copies, acquires 1st rights. Submit complete ms./SASE. Responds in 3 mos; publishes in early December. Accepts fiction, poetry, nonfiction, photos, fine art drawings. Send SASE for submission form and special announcements. Sample $3.
COLLEGE/UNIVERSITY, LITERARY

Permaculture With Native Plants, Box 38, Lorane, OR 97451. Editor: Curtin Mitchell.
AGRICULTURE/FARMING, ENVIRONMENT/RESOURCES, GARDENING

Permafrost, University of Alaska-Fairbanks, Department of English, Fairbanks, AK 99775-0640. 907-474-5237. Periodical. Sub $7. Circ. 500. Uses freelance material. Pays copies. Submit ms, SASE. Dot matrix, photocopied OK. Reports in 1-3 mos. Accepts nonfiction, fiction, poetry, photos, other. Guidelines; sample $4.
COLLEGE/UNIVERSITY, FICTION, POETRY

Pet Owners' Tribune, PO Box 2807, Portland, OR 97208. 503-297-7530. Editor: Joan Dahlberg. Bimonthly magazine. Circ. 3500; subs $6/yr. Very limited acceptance of freelance material, assignment only. Byline given. Pays money on acceptance. Accepts cartoons, articles. Retail management articles wanted. Catalog. Sample $2.
ANIMALS, BUSINESS, TRADE/ASSOCIATIONS

Phinney Ridge Review, Phinney Neighborhood Association, 6532 Phinney Ave. N., Seattle, WA 98103. Editor: Ed Medeiros. Quarterly.
COMMUNITY, FAMILY, HEALTH

Pioneer Square Gazette, Pioneer Square Association, PO Box 4006, Seattle, WA 98104. Editor: Lori Kinnear. Periodical, 3 times per yr.
UNSPECIFIED

Pioneer Trails, Umatilla County Historical Society, PO Box 253, Pendleton, OR 97801. 503-276-0012. Contact: Julie Reese. Published 3X/yr. Sub $10/yr. Circ. 800. Uses freelance material; byline given. Submit query letter, complete ms, SASE. Photocopy, dot matrix OK. Responds in 2 mos; publishes in 6-12 mos. Accepts Umatilla County history: biography, photos, articles, memoirs. Sample $2.
NW/REGIONAL HISTORY, OREGON

Plant's Review of Books, PO Box 14081, Portland, OR 97214-0081. 503-234-6345. Contact: Darrel Plant or Barbara Moshofsky. Quarterly literary magazine. Circ. 5,000. Founded 1992. Accepts freelance material; byline given. Pays money on publication; acquires 1st rights. Query by phone or w/SASE, assignment only. Photocopies, electronic, dot matrix OK. Responds in 2 wks; publishes within 3 mos. Accepts fiction, poetry, cartoons, news items, biography, nonfiction, photos, interviews, op/ed, articles, and reviews. Contact editors for photo requirements. Guidelines.
BOOK ARTS/BOOKS, FICTION, PUBLISHING/PRINTING

Playboard Magazine, 7560 Lawrence Dr., Burnaby, BC V5A 1T6. 604-738-5287. Contact: Mick Maloney. Mass circulation monthly magazine of entertainment and arts.
ARTS, ENTERTAINMENT

Plazm, 1101 S.W. Washington, Ste. 104, Portland, OR 97205. 503-727-2613. Contact: Nan Kinett. "Published 3 times a year by a non-profit collective dedicated to freedom of expression. Our open submissions format and editorial policy, 'quality over all,' allow creative genius to flourish. The result is a progressive blend of visual art, literature, ideas. Works are diverse and readership runs the gamut. Content includes staff work as well as pieces from anywhere on the planet. Each issue is completely different...."
AVANT-GARDE/EXPERIMENTAL, LITERARY

Plugging In, Columbia Education Center, 11325 S.E. Lexington, Portland, OR 97266. 503-760-2346. Editor: Dr. Ralph Nelsen. Periodical.
EDUCATION

PMUG Mousetracks, PO Box 8895, Portland, OR 97207. 503-254-2111; 503-641-1587. Editor: Michael Pearce. Ads: Jim Lyle. Monthly. Sub $24. Circ. 900. Uses 710 freelance mss per issue. Written by Mac users. No pay. Acquires 1st rights. Byline given. Submit ms, SASE, phone. Electronic sub OK. Accepts nonfiction, cartoons. Guidelines; sample $4.
COMPUTERS

PNLA Quarterly, 1631 E. 24th Ave., Eugene, OR 97403. 503-344-2027. Editor: Katherine G. Eaton. Quarterly. Sub $15. Circ. 1,100. Uses freelance material. Byline given. Phone query. Photocopied OK. Accepts nonfiction, cartoons. Sample. $6.50.
BOOK ARTS/BOOKS, LANGUAGE(S), PUBLISHING/PRINTING

Poe Studies, Washington State University Press, Pullman, WA 99164-5910. 509-335-3518. Semiannual. Sub $8. Nonfiction.
COLLEGE/UNIVERSITY, SCHOLARLY/ACADEMIC, LITERARY

Poetic Space, PO Box 11157, Eugene, OR 97440. 503-485-2278. Editor: Don Hildenbrand. Magazine irregularly published 2/yr. Sub $10/yr. Circ. 800+. Uses freelance material. Pays copies on publication. Byline given. Acquires 1st rights. Submit ms, SASE. Dot matrix, photocopied subs OK. Reports in 1-3 mos. publishes in 2-3 mos. Accepts nonfiction, fiction, contemporary poetry, literary essays (1,200-1,500 wds), line drawings, simple graphics, book reviews (600-1,000 wds). Theater reviews, short 1-act plays, film reviews. Guidelines; sample $4.
AVANT-GARDE/EXPERIMENTAL, FICTION, POETRY

Poetry Exchange, PO Box 85477, Seattle, WA 98145-1477. Editor: Staff. Monthly community newsletter. Circ. 1,400. Sub $10/yr. Assignment only. The Poetry Exchange includes a calendar of literary readings, announcements about small press books, workshops, and a mss wanted column. Also contains reviews and articles (query 1st, unsolicited material is not accepted.)
FICTION, POETRY, PUBLISHING/PRINTING

Poetry Northwest, 4045 Brooklyn Ave. N.E., University of Washington, Ja-15, Seattle, WA 98105. Periodical.
COLLEGE/UNIVERSITY, NORTHWEST, POETRY

Poetry Today, 5136 N.E. Glisan St., Portland, OR 97213. Periodical.
LITERARY, POETRY

Point of View, Aperture Northwest, Inc., PO Box 24365, Seattle, WA 98124-0365. 206-382-9220. Editor: Richard K. Woltjer. Monthly.
MEDIA/COMMUNICATIONS, NATURAL HISTORY, VISUAL ARTS

The Pointed Circle, Portland C.C., Cascade Campus, 705 N. Killingsworth, Portland, OR 97217. 503-244-6111x5230. Editor/contact: M. McNeill, M. Dembrow, D. Averill. Annual literary magazine. Pays copies, acquires 1st rights. Submit ms w/SASE Dec 1-Mar 1. Dot matrix, photocopied OK. Simultaneous subs OK with notice. Accepts previously unpublished nonfiction, fiction, poetry, photos, plays, cartoons. Guidelines; back issues; sample $2.50.
COLLEGE/UNIVERSITY, FICTION, POETRY

Points Northwest, Washington State University, Owen Science & Engineering Lib, Pullman, WA 99164-3200. Periodical.
COLLEGE/UNIVERSITY

Pome News, Home Orchard Society, PO Box 776, Clackamas, OR 97015. 506-630-3392. Editors: Winnifred and Ken Fisher. Quarterly newsletter. Sub $10. Circ. 1,200. Uses freelance material. Byline given. Phone query. Photocopied, computer disk OK. Reports in 8 wks. Publishes in 1 yr. Accepts nonfiction articles on home-growing of fruits and nuts and recipes. Sample.
AGRICULTURE/FARMING, FOOD/COOKING, GARDENING

Poptart, 3505 Commercial Dr., Vancouver, BC V5N 4E8. Accepts fiction, poetry, drawings.
FICTION, POETRY

Port Side: The Port of Portland Magazine, PO Box 3529, Portland, OR 97208. Quarterly with news and economic facts relating to shipping and cargo handling.
BUSINESS

The Portable Wall/Basement Press, c/o Dan Struckman, 215 Burlington, Billings, MT 59101. 406-256-3588. Editor: Gray Harris. Journal published 1 or 2 times a yr. Sub $5. Circ. 200-500. Accepts freelance material. Pays copies on acceptance. Byline given. Submit ms, SASE. Dot matrix, photocopied OK. Publishes in 6-12 mos. Accepts nonfiction, fiction, poetry, cartoons. "This magazine is highest quality hand-set type on fine paper articles and stories must be short, terse. Can reproduce almost any line drawing." Sample $5.
HUMOR, MONTANA, VISUAL ARTS

Portfolio, College of Business, Boise State University, Boise, ID 83725. Semiannual. Circ. 2,500.
BUSINESS, COLLEGE/UNIVERSITY

The Portland Alliance, 2807 S.E. Stark, Portland, OR 97214. 503-239-4991 (Editorial); 503-239-0087 (Ads). Contact: Benjamin Dawson. Ads: Dianne Alyn & Andrea Skufca. Monthly magazine. Circ. 8,000, subs. $20/yr. Uses freelance material. Byline given, pays copies, acquires all rights. Query w/SASE. Simultaneous, disk/modem subs OK. Responds in 1 wk; publishes in 1 mo. Accepts nonfiction, photos, news items, photos, cartoons, op/ed, reviews. Topics: news and views by and for progressive activists in Portland and the Northwest. Sample 50 cents.
NW/REGIONAL HISTORY, POLITICS, SOCIALIST/RADICAL

Portland and Area Events, Three World Trade Center, 26 S.W. Salmon St., Portland, OR 97204-3299. 503-275-9787. Jacquie R. Smith. Monthly newspaper. Query letter, SASE, phone. Accepts news items.
CALENDAR/EVENTS, ENTERTAINMENT

Portland Atari Club Computer News, PO Box 1692, Beaverton, OR 97005. 503-667-3306. Editor: Teri Williams. Monthly.
COMPUTERS

Portland Family Calendar, Pry Publishing Co., 600 N.W. 14th Ave., Portland, OR 97209. 503-226-8335. Editor: Victoria Hyde. Ads: Doug Martel. Monthly tabloid, founded 1980. Sub $10/yr. Circ. 13,500. Uses freelance material. Byline given. Pays money, copies on publication. Submit query letter, clips, SASE, phone. Responds in 1 mo; publishes in 2 mos. Accepts news items, photos (B&W $5/ea.), interviews, op/ed, articles, reviews. Topics: prefer factual articles related to local parenting issues, resources, products. Focus on Portland metro area is desirable, though not absolutely essential. Guidelines, sample.
CALENDAR/EVENTS, CHILDREN (BY/ABOUT), FAMILY

Portland Gray Panther Pulse, 1819 N.W. Everett, Portland, OR 97209. 503-224-5190. Monthly on issues of importance to older citizens.
SENIOR CITIZENS

The Portland Guide, 4475 S.W. Scholls Ferry Rd., Ste. 256, Portland, OR 97225. Monthly visitor's guide for Portland. Focuses on events and directories.
CALENDAR/EVENTS, ENTERTAINMENT, TRAVEL

Portland Live Music Guide, PO Box 12072, Portland, OR 97212. 503-288-5846. Editor: Boyd Martin. Monthly magazine, directory. Sub $20/yr. Circ. 8,000. Uses freelance material. Byline given. Pays copies on publication. Acquires 1st, 2nd rights. Assignment only, submit query. Photocopy, dot matrix, simultaneous subs OK. Responds in 2 wks; publishes in 1 mo. Accepts interviews, cartoons, Photos (8x10 glossy). "Most acceptable submissions are interviews with Portland musical artists." Sample $1.
CALENDAR/EVENTS, ENTERTAINMENT, MUSIC

Portland Magazine, University of Portland, 5000 N. Willamette Blvd., Portland, OR 97203. 503-283-7202. Quarterly magazine. Circ. 25,000. Accepts freelance material. Byline given. Pays money, copies on publication. Submit query letter, clips, outline, or complete manuscript, SASE. Responds 1-2 mos; publishes 3-4 mos. Accepts nonfiction, articles, interviews. "We are a quarterly university magazine and so grind slow and fine; but twice in recent years we were rated best in U.S." Guidelines, sample.
EDUCATION, OREGON, RELIGION

Portland News of the Portland Chamber of Commerce, 221 N.W. 2nd, Portland, OR 97209. 503-228-9411. Monthly Newsletter of the Portland Chamber of Commerce. Editor: Vanessa E. Blake. Sub $25/yr. Circ. 4,500.
TRADE/ASSOCIATIONS

Portland Observer, 2201 N. Killingsworth, Box 3137, Portland, OR 97208. Weekly.
COMMUNITY

Portland Parent, PO Box 19864, Portland, OR 97280. 503-245-8036; 503-684-4419. Contact Ilana Hoffman. Monthly news-magazine. Sub. $12/yr. Circ. 20,000. Byline given. Pays money upon publication. Acquires first rights. Submit query with letter or by phone, assignment only. Reports in 2-3 weeks. Publishing time varies. Accepts articles. Back issues free.
FAMILY, CALENDAR/EVENTS, CHILDREN

Portland Pen, c/o National League of American Pen Women Inc., 2039 S.E. 45th Ave., Portland, OR 97215. Co-Editor: Dorothy Clery. Features information valuable to League members.
WRITING, WOMEN

Portland Review, PO Box 751, Portland, OR 97207. 503-725-4531. Triannual magazine. Sub $12. Circ. 1,000. Uses freelance material. Pays copies on publication. Submit ms, SASE. Dot matrix, photocopied, simultaneous OK. Accepts nonfiction, fiction (under 6,000 wds), poetry, photos, plays, cartoons. Photos: B&W only. "We're a city publication with an urban look and perspective encourage cultural variety and political overtones. We'd like to hear from more Black, American Indian, Hispanic, and Asian writers, or works dealing with other subcultural groups. Don't be afraid to be radical." Guidelines; sample $3.
AVANT-GARDE/EXPERIMENTAL, LITERATURE, PHOTOGRAPHY

Portland Scribe, Multnomah County Medical Society, 4540 S.W. Kelly Ave., Portland, OR 97201. 503-222-9977. Editor: Rob Delf. Biweekly trade publication, founded 1983. Sub $30/yr. Circ. 3,000. Uses freelance material. Byline given. Pays money on publication. Acquires 1st rights. Submit query letter, complete ms, phone. Photocopy subs OK. Responds in 1 day, publishes in 2 wks. Accepts news items, photos, interviews, articles. Topics: health and the politics, economics and business of health care. Sample.
GOVERNMENT, HEALTH, PUBLIC AFFAIRS

Positively Entertainment & Dining, PO Box 16009, Portland, OR 97233. 503-253-0513. Editor: Bonnie Carter. Monthly. Sub $14. Circ. 10,000. Uses freelance material. Byline given. Submit query w/clips, phone. Photocopied OK. Accepts nonfiction, photos, plays, cartoons. Sample.
ENTERTAINMENT, FOOD/COOKING, SPORTS

Postcard/Paper Club Newsletter, Box 814, E. Helena, MT 59635. Editor: Tom Mulvaney. Quarterly.
CRAFTS/HOBBIES

Potato Country, Box 1467, Yakima, WA 98907. 509-248-2452. Editor: D. Brent Clement. Published 9 times a year featuring potato industry of OR, WA, ID. Circ. 6,000. Payment: $100 on publication. Byline given. Rights purchased: All. Query w/ms, SASE. Dot matrix OK. Reports immediately. Nonfiction: 5-6 ds pages on features and news. Photos: W/mss, B&W. Guidelines.
AGRICULTURE/FARMING, BUSINESS

Potato Grower of Idaho, PO Box 949, 1010 W. Bridge St., Blackfoot, ID 83221. Editor: Steve Janes. Monthly.
AGRICULTURE/FARMING, BUSINESS, IDAHO

Potboiler Magazine, Richards Rd., Roberts Creek, BC V0N 2W0. 604-885-3985. Editor/ads: L. R. Davidson. Semiannual. Circ. 250-300. Sub $5. Uses 7-12 mss per issue. Payment: Copies on publication. Byline given. Rights purchased: First. Query w/ms, SASE. Photocopies OK. Reports in 6-8 wks. Fiction, cartoons, comics. Science fiction, fantasy, horror, weird, unusual, mainstream, graphic stories, fumetti, comics, collage pieces. Guidelines, sample.
AVANT-GARDE/EXPERIMENTAL, FANTASY/SCI FI, SATIRE

Potlatch Times, Potlatch Corporation, Western Division, PO Box 1016, Lewiston, ID 83501. Editor: Bea Davis. Monthly for employees and business community. Circ. 6,500.
BUSINESS

Primary Treasure, PO Box 7000, Boise, ID 83707. Editor: Louis Schutter. Periodical.
CHILDREN (BY/ABOUT), RELIGION

The Printer's Devil, P. O. Box 66, Harrison, ID 83833-0066. 208-689-3738. Contact: Joe M. Singer. Quarterly journal founded 1986. Sub $5 yr. Circ. 200. Uses freelance material. Byline given. Pays copies on publication. Acquires no rights. Submit query letter, complete ms, SASE. Photocopies OK. Reports in 1 mo; publishes in 6 mos. Accepts news items, interviews, nonfiction, reviews, photos (B&W glossy, query on color), cartoons. Topics: graphic arts for the small press, best formalized and illustrated. This is a technical magazine. Guidelines, catalog; back issues $2.50.
HOW-TO, PUBLISHING/PRINTING, TECHNICAL

The Printer's Northwest Trader, PO Box 450, Woodburn, OR 97071-0450. 503-982-6333; 800-426-2416. Editor: Sandy Hubbard. Ads: Rod Stollery. Monthly for graphic arts industry. Sub $10. Circ. 5200. Uses freelance material. Byline given. Query by phone. Dot matrix, photocopied subs OK. Responds in 1 wk; publishes in 1-2 mos. Accepts nonfiction, news items, photos (B&W glossy), interviews, reviews. Topics: new products, printing news, trade activity highlights. Guidelines; sample $2.50.
ARTS, PUBLISHING/PRINTING, TRADE/ASSOCIATIONS

Prism, University Student Media Committee, Oregon State University, Corvallis, OR 97331. Editor: Linda Anderson. Annual literary/arts magazine.
ARTS, LITERATURE, COLLEGE/UNIVERSITY

PRISM International, Department of Creative Writing, University of British Columbia, Vancouver, BC V6T 1W5. 604-255-9332. Editor: Blair Rosser. Quarterly magazine. Sub $12/yr. Circ. 1,200. Uses freelance material. Pays $30/page on publication. Acquires 1st rights. Byline given. Submit ms, SASE. Dot matrix, photocopied OK. Reports & publishes up to 3 mos. Accepts fiction, poetry, plays, cover art, imaginative nonfiction (as opposed to reviews, articles). We like to see imaginative, fresh & new work. US contributors use SASE w/IRCs. "Read one or two back issues before submitting. Always looking for new and exciting writers." Guidelines. Sample $4.
DRAMA, FICTION, POETRY

P.R.O. Newsletter of Oregon PO Box 86781, Portland, OR 97286. 503-775-2974. Editor: S. Alexander. Ads: Michelle Tennesen. Bimonthly. Sub $15/yr. Circ. 500. Uses freelance material. Pays copies. Acquires 1st rights. Byline given. Submit query w/clips, ms, phone, SASE. Dot matrix, photocopied, simultaneous OK. Reports in 1 mo. Accepts nonfiction. Topics: children, family. Sample, SASE.
CHILDREN (BY/ABOUT), FAMILY

The Progress, 910 Marion, Seattle, WA 98104. Editor: Bill Dodds. Monthly.
UNSPECIFIED

Progressive Woman, 8835 S.W. Canyon Ln., #304, Portland, OR 97225-3453. Editor: Dianne Perry. Ads:

Brenda Fay. Monthly newspaper. Sub $12. Circ. 20,000+. Uses freelance material. Pays on publication. Acquires 1st rights. Byline given. Unsolicited submissions accepted. Submit query w/clips, SASE; phone query, dot matrix, photocopied. Reports in 4-6 weeks. Publishes in 1-3 months. Accepts fiction, nonfiction, poetry, cartoons, photos, news items, biographies, interviews, op/ed, reviews, memoirs. Topics: articles of interest to Oregon women. Back issues $3 each.
WOMEN, FEMINISM, CALENDAR/EVENTS

Property Tax Charges, Associated Taxpayers of Idaho, PO Box 1665, Boise, ID 83701. Editor: Holly Cawley. Annual.
CONSUMER, IDAHO, PUBLIC AFFAIRS

The Province, 2250 Granville St., Vancouver, BC V6H 3G2. Query w/SASE.
UNSPECIFIED

PSU Magazine, Portland State University Alumni News, PO Box 751, Portland, OR 97207. 503-725-4451. Contact: Office of Publications. Magazine published 3x/yr. Circ. 49,000. Uses assigned freelance material. Byline given. First rights acquired. Pays 18 cents/wd on publication. Submit query letter. Responds in 2 wks; publishes in 1 mo. Accepts nonfiction. Sample.
COLLEGE/UNIVERSITY, EDUCATION, ENTERTAINMENT

Puget Sound Business Journal, 101 Yesler Way #200, Seattle, WA 98104. 206-583-0701; Fax 206-447-8510. Editor: Don Nelson. Ads: Tim Jones. Weekly of local and regional business news and business features. Circ. 20,000. Sub $26. Uses 1 ms per issue. Pays $75-100 on acceptance; byline given. Acquires first rights. Phone queries, dot matrix OK. Reports in 1 week. Nonfiction pieces can be up to 4 ds pages. Cartoons. Photos by assignment only. Sample with SASE.
BUSINESS, ECONOMICS, WASHINGTON

Pulphouse: A Fiction Magazine, Box 1227, Eugene, OR 97440. 503-935-6322. Editor: Dean Wesley Smith. Science fiction and fantasy magazine. Uses freelance material. Byline given. Pays money, advance, royalties. Acquires 1st rights. Submit complete ms. Responds in 2 mos; publishes in 1-8 mos. Accepts fiction, cartoons, photos. Guidelines.
FANTASY/SCI FI, FICTION, WRITING

Puncture, PO Box 14806, Portland, OR 97214. 503-236-8270. Editor: Katherine Spielmann. Ads: Steve Connell. Quarterly magazine. Circ. 9,000. Uses freelance material. Quary w/SASE and samples. Alternative rock. Uses interviews/profiles. 100 recosrd reviews per issue. Reviews related books. Caters to independent music more likely to be on smaller labels. Sample $2.50.
CULTURE, MUSIC

Puzzle Mystery Magazine, Huckleberry Mtn Press, 2903 Fernan Terrace, Coeur d'Alene, ID 83814. 208-664-9476. Contact: Laurie Carlson. Quarterly magazine. Accepts freelance material. Byline given. Pays copies on publication. Query w/SASE, complete manuscript, synopsis. Photocopy, dot matrix, simultaneous subs OK. Guidelines.
MYSTERY, FICTION, IDAHO

QNC!, 85000 Laughlin Rd., Eugene, OR 97405. 503-343-0406. Editor: Scott Laughlin. Quarterly journal. Sub $7.75 per year US, $13.45 International. Circ. 250. Freelance material accepted. Byline given. Payment on publication. Pays in copies. First rights acquired. Send complete ms. Responds in 4 weeks, publishes in 1-2 weeks. Accepts articles, nonfiction, interviews, memoirs. "Must be related to Morse code in some manner; international or American." Guidelines; back issues $2.50 each.
TECHNICAL, MEDIA/COMMUNICATIONS

The Quarterdeck Review, Columbia River Maritime Museum, 1792 Marine Dr., Astoria, OR 97103. 503-325-2323. Editor: Hobe Kytr. Quarterly for museum members on museum news and maritime history. Circ. 2,000. Not a freelance market. Sample $1.

NW/REGIONAL HISTORY

Queen Anne's Lace Quarterly, Doorway Publishers, 703 N.E. Hostmark St. #13, Poulsbo, WA 98370-8709. 206-297-7952. Editors: Doris Moore, Connie Lord. Quarterly magazine. Circ. 500; subs $20/yr. Uses freelance material. Byline given, pays copies on publication. Query w/SASE. Responds in 2 wks; publishes in 3 mos. Accepts poetry, nonfiction, articles, memoirs. Topics: natural history, environment/resources, philosophy. Guidelines; sample $5.

ENVIRONMENT/RESOURCES, NATURAL HISTORY, PHILOSOPHY

Quest for Excellence, St. Luke's Regional Medical Center, 190 E. Bannock, Boise, ID 83712. Editor: Rita Ryan. Quarterly magazine for patients, staff and friends of the hospital. Circ. 17,000.

HEALTH

Racing Wheels, 7502 N.E. 133rd Ave., Vancouver, WA 98662. 206-892-5590. Periodical.

CRAFTS/HOBBIES

Raddle Moon, 9060 Ardmore Dr., Sidney, BC V8L 3S1. 604-656-4045. Editor: Susan Clark. Semiannual literary magazine. Sub $12. Circ. 700. Uses freelance material. Submit ms with SASE. Photocopies OK. Reports in 3-4 months; publishes in 3-6 months. Acquires 1st rights; pays with 1-year sub. Accepts nonfiction, poetry, photos, poetics. Publishing language-centered and new lyric poetry, essays, fiction, photographs, graphics. Back issues $5.

LITERARY, POETRY

Radiance Herbs & Massage Newsletter, 113 E. Fifth, Olympia, WA 98501. 206-357-9470. Editor: Barbara Park. Ads: Carolyn McIntyre. Bimonthly periodical. Sub free/$5. Circ. 10,000. Uses 1-2 freelance mss per issue. Byline given. Phone assignment, SASE. Accepts nonfiction, poetry, photos, cartoons. Sample 50.

GARDENING, HEALTH, POETRY

Rain, Clatsop Community College, Astoria, OR 97103. College literary magazine. SASE for guidelines.

COLLEGE/UNIVERSITY, FICTION, LITERARY

Rain, Box 30097, Eugene, OR 97403. Contact: Danielle Janes. Quarterly magazine on alternative communities, environment, economies, self-help, technology. Circ. 3,000-4,000; sub $20/yr. Accepts unsolicited material: cartoons, nonfiction, photos, articles, reviews. Byline given. Pays money on publication. Tip: query editor before sending or researching articles. We have to like the idea before spending time reading whole articles. SASE for guidelines. Sample $5.

COMMUNITY, ENVIRONMENT/RESOURCES, 035

Rain, Tristen, RR 2, Alders Box 2, Ganges, BC V0S 1E0. Circ. 300, 6 issues per year. Sub/$12, sample $1.50. Pays in small gifts. "We lean toward mysticism and gothic images, yet have no biases. Anyone unique will be welcomed."

UNSPECIFIED

Rain City Review, 7215 S.W. LaView Dr., Portland, OR 97219. 503-771-1907. Editor: Brian Christopher Hamilton. Literary magazine published 3x yearly. Founded 1992. Freelance material accepted. Pays copies on publication; acquires 1st rights. "No specific length, thematic, or stylistic guidelines. Our tastes are very diverse. We prefer to see cover letters accompanying submissions." SASE. Photocopy, simultaneous subs OK. Responds in 4-12 wks; publishes in 3-6 mos. Accepts fiction, poetry, interviews, reviews, essays.

POETRY, FICTION, LITERARY

Rainbow News, Oregon Rainbow Coalition, PO Box 6797, Portland, OR 97228-6797. Periodical of political news.

LAW, MINORITIES/ETHNIC, POLITICS

Rancher-Stockman-Farmer, PO Box 714, Meridian, ID 83642. 208-888-1165. Contact: Frank Thomason. Quarterly newspaper.

AGRICULTURE/FARMING

Random Lengths, PO Box 867, Eugene, OR 97440. 503-686-9925. Weekly periodical with reports on North American forest products marketing. Print run: 12,300. Sub rate: $145. Not a freelance market. Sample/$2.50.

BUSINESS, LUMBER

The Raven Chronicles, PO Box 95918, Seattle, WA 98145. 206 543-0249. Editors: Kathleen Alcala, Phoebe Bosche, and Philip H. Red Eagle. Magazine dedicated to quality multicultural arts and writing. Seeks fiction, poetry, essays, interviews and B&W art by multi-ethnic artists and writers. Circ. 3,500; sub $12/yr. Accepts freelance material. Pays money, copies on publication. Acquires first rights. Submit ms w/SASE. Photocopies, dot matrix, disk OK. Responds 3 mos. Publishes 3-6 mos. Sample $2.

LITERATURE, MINORITIES/ETHNIC, POETRY

The Reader, 1701 W. Third Ave., Vancouver, BC V6J 1K7. 604-732-7631. Contact: Celia Duthie. Bimonthly magazine of book reviews. Sub free. In-house publication of Duthie Books.

BOOK ARTS/BOOKS, LITERARY

Realms, Black Matrix Press, PO Box 5737, Grants Pass, OR 97527. Contact: Guy Kenyon, editor. Bimonthly journal. Sub $8/yr. Pays 3 copies for first rights. Submit ms. Dot matrix, photocopied OK. No simultaneous subs. Topics: traditional fantasy fiction sorcery, elves, dragons, castles, etc. Max 12-15,000 words, possible serialization. Also seeking cover and interior artwork. Sample $1.50.

FANTASY/SCI FI, FICTION,

The Record, Ste. 4 EMU, University of Oregon, Eugene, OR 97403. Periodical.

COLLEGE/UNIVERSITY

Recovery Life, Alcoholism & Addiction Magazine, PO Box 31329, Seattle, WA 98103. 206-527-8999. Editor: Neil Scott. Bi-monthly inserted into Alcoholism & Addiction Magazine. Uses freelance material. Pays in copies. Byline given. Submit ms, SASE. Dot matrix, photocopied OK. Accepts nonfiction, fiction, poetry. Topics: principles of addiction recovery, first-person stories, physical fitness, nutrition, humor, tips, recipes. Upbeat poetry, tips on planning a sober vacation, holiday season, etc. Guidelines. Sample $5.

HEALTH, PSYCHOLOGY

Reed The Quarterly Mag of Reed College, Reed College, 3203 S.E. Woodstock, Portland, OR 97202. Editor: S. Eugene Thompson.

COLLEGE/UNIVERSITY, EDUCATION

Reference & Research Book News, Book News, Inc., 5600 N.E. Hassalo, Portland, OR 97213. 503-281-9230. Editor/ads: Jane Erskine. Publishes 8 times/yr. reviews reference books. Sub $40 (indiv)/$58 (institutions). Circ. 2,100. Assigned only. Will consider assigning reviews to specially qualified librarians. Pays money on acceptance. Possible byline. Lists and reviews 500-600 newly published reference books each issue for the benefit of librarians who buy books. Reviews are 80-150 wds. Payment varies with the qualifications of the reviewer. Sample $5.

REFERENCE/LIBRARY

Reflections Directory, PO Box 13070, Portland, OR 97213. 503-281-4486. Resource Directory published by Portland Reflections. Editor: Patrick Mazza. Ads: John Nosek. Quarterly. Circ. 38,000. Sub $10. Accepts freelance material. Byline given. Rights purchased: First. Phone query, dot matrix, photocopies, electronic OK. Nonfiction (max 700 wds), poetry, photos (B&W glossy), cartoons. Topics: holistic health, conscious living, environmental issues, new paradigm thinking/approach to business/living. Guidelines, sample.

HEALTH, COMMUNITY, ENVIRONMENT/RESOURCES

Rendezvous, Idaho State University, Dept of English, PO Box 8113, Pocatello, ID 83209. Annual. Accepts article, prose, poetry and photo essay submissions.

COLLEGE/UNIVERSITY, EDUCATION, ENGLISH

Renewal, PO Box 1314, Ashland, OR 97520. 503-488-1645. Contact: Richard & Maraji Gwynallen. Bimonthly. Mail sub $10/yr. Free regional retail distribution. Circ. 20,000. Uses freelance material. Pays in copies. Query or ms w/SASE. Mac disk OK. Accepts fiction, nonfiction, poetry. Topics: health, environment, metaphysical, occult, innovative psychology, book & music reviews, anything related to natural/holistic lifeways. Guidelines; sample $2.

ENVIRONMENT/RESOURCES, NEW AGE

Resource Recycling Inc., PO Box 10540, Portland, OR 97210. 503-227-1319. Editor: Jerry Powell. Ads: Rick Downing. Monthly trade journal. Sub $42/yr. Circ. 6,500. Uses freelance material. Pays money, copies on publication. Acquires first rights. Byline given. Submit query w/clips. Photocopied, electronic, computer disk OK. Reports in 6-8 wks; publishes 6+ mos. Accepts nonfiction articles on multi-material recycling topics. B&W glossy photos preferred, rates variable. Guidelines, sample.

CONSERVATION, ENVIRONMENT/RESOURCES

Retirement Life News, 10211 S.W. Barbur Blvd., Ste. 109 A, Portland, OR 97219. 503-245-6442. Editor: Carl Olson. Monthly. Sub $7.50.

COMMUNITY, SENIOR CITIZENS

The Retort, Idaho Academy of Science, BSU, Department of Chemistry, Boise, ID 83725. Editors: Edward Matjeka & Richard Banks. Published 3 times a year.

COLLEGE/UNIVERSITY, EDUCATION, SCIENCE

Review, Seattle Community College, 1718 Broadway Ave., Seattle, WA 98122. Periodical.

COLLEGE/UNIVERSITY

Review of Social & Economic Conditions, Institute of Social & Economic Research, Univ. of AK, 3211 Providence Dr., Anchorage, AK 99508. 907-786-7710. Editor: Linda Leask. Irregularly published magazine. Sub free except Canada & foreign. Circ. 1,800-2,500. Not a freelance market. Catalog, sample.

ALASKA, ECONOMICS

Rhapsody!, Clackamas Community College, 19600 S. Molalla, Oregon City, OR 97045. 503-657-8400x309. Semiannual literary magazine. Circ. 500. Query w/ms, SASE. Phone query, dot matrix OK. Fiction: 3-5 ds typed pages on any subject. Fillers: 3-4 ds typed pages on people in the arts (writing, photo, art, music, etc.). Poetry: 4-25 lines. Photos: good, creative photographs. "We accept submissions from Clackamas County residents or students of Clackamas CC only."

FICTION, LITERARY, PHOTOGRAPHY

Riffs, Washington Jazz Society, PO Box 2813, Seattle, WA 98111. 206-324-2794. Contact: Ed Foulks.

MUSIC

R.N. Idaho Idaho State Nurses Association, 200 N. 4th St. #20, Boise, ID 83702-6001. Periodical 6 times a year. Circ. 750.

BUSINESS, HEALTH, LABOR/WORK

RNABC News, Registered Nurses' Association, 2855 Arbutus St., Vancouver, BC V6J 3Y8. 604-736-7331. Contact: Bruce Wells.

BRITISH COLUMBIA, HEALTH, LABOR/WORK

Rock Rag, 13879 S.E. Foster Rd., Dayton, OR 97114. Editors Toby & Troy. Ads: Bryce Van Patten.

MUSIC

The Rocket/Murder Inc., 2028 5th Ave., Seattle, WA 98121. 206-728-7625. Editor: Charles R. Cross. Ads: Courtney Miller. Monthly magazine. Sub $12. Circ. 65,000. Accepts freelance material, usage varies. Freelance quali-

fications require knowledge of popular music. Pays money on publication. Byline given. Submit query w/clips, ms w/ SASE. Dot matrix, photocopies OK. Reports in 1 mo. Accepts nonfiction, photos, cartoons. Record review 12 paragraphs; features 500-1,000 wds. B&W photos preferred. Guidelines; sample cost varies.
MUSIC

Rockhound Rumblings, 6775 River Rd. N., Salem, OR 97303. Editor: Les Puffer. Monthly.
COLLECTING, CRAFTS/HOBBIES, RECREATION

Rocking Chair Studio, SS2 S12 C36, Fort St. John, BC V1J 4M7. 604-827-3515. Contact: Ann Simmons.
BRITISH COLUMBIA, FISHING, CANADIAN HISTORY

Rocky Mountain Poetry Magazine, PO Box 269, Gallitan-Gateway, MT 59730. Accepts poetry, essays, and short stories. Focus is on cowboy poetry, poetry from the Rocky Mountain region, and other walks of life. Pays in copies. Byline given. Query w/SASE.
FICTION, POETRY

Room of One's Own, PO Box 46160, Station G, Vancouver, BC V6R 4G5. 604-327-1423. Feminist literary quarterly. Sub $25. Circ. 1,000. Uses freelance material. Pays money on publication. Acquires 1st rights. Byline given. Submit ms. Photocopies OK, but no simultaneous submissions. Reports in 10 mos. Publishes in 3-6 mos. Accepts fiction, poetry, some artwork. Sample $7.
LITERATURE, FICTION, POETRY

The Rose, Publication of the Portland Jaycees, PO Box 622, University Station, Portland, OR 97207. 503-231-2800. Editor: Keeya Prowell.
BUSINESS, TRADE/ASSOCIATIONS

Roseburg Woodsman, c/o Chevalier Advertising, 1 Centerpointe Dr. #300, Lake Oswego, OR 97035-8613. Monthly on wood & wood products to customers and friends of Roseburg Forest Products Co. Circ. 7,500. Sub free. Uses 2-3 mss per issue. Payment: $50-100 on publication. Rights acquired: One time. Query with ms, SASE. Photocopies OK. Reports in 2 wks. Nonfiction: with photos; must be wood-related; 500-1,000 wds. Photos: Color transparencies only (35mm OK) accompanying ms only. No single photos. $25 per printed photo, $125 cover. Only buy mss & photos together. Assignments occasionally available at higher rate. Guidelines; free sample.
ANIMALS, ARCHITECTURE, LUMBER

Ruah, Sacred Art Society, 0245 S.W. Bancroft, Portland, OR 97201. 503-236-2145. Editor: LaVaun Maier. Quarterly. Sub $12.
UNSPECIFIED

The Rude Girl Press, Reed College, Box 331, 3203 S.E. Woodstock Boulevard, Portland, OR 97202. Periodical.
COLLEGE/UNIVERSITY, FEMINISM

Rumors & Raggs, 19924 Aurora Ave. N. #57, Seattle, WA 98133. 206-742-4FUN. Editor: Seaun Richards. Monthly.
UNSPECIFIED

Ruralite, Box 558, Forest Grove, OR 97116. 503-357-2105. Feature editor: Walt Wentz. Ads: Reva Bassler. Monthly. Sub $6. Circ. 260,000. Accepts freelance material. Payment: $50-$400 on acceptance. Byline given. Purchases first rights. Query first, SASE. Dot matrix, photocopies, simultaneous submissions OK. Accepts nonfiction: Northwest focus; general family interest stories slanted to Pacific N.W.; oddities in history, admirable or unusual characters, humor, community improvement, self-help, rural electrification, unusual events or interesting places, etc. (max length 1,000 wds). Photos add greatly to chances of acceptance: B&W, preferably with 35 or 120 mm negatives, pay included with story. Guidelines; sample: $1.
FAMILY, HUMOR

RV Life Magazine, PO Box 55998, Seattle, WA 98155. 206-745-5665. Editor: Gayle Harrison. Monthly magazine.

Sub $12/yr. Circ. 25,000. Uses freelance material. Byline given. Submit query letter, SASE, phone. Responds in 1 mo, publishes in 1-4 mos. Accepts articles, photos (prefers B&W prints). Topics: anything related to the RV life-style buying RVs, campgrounds, historic sites, pets, travel with kids, recipes, outdoor cooking, etc. Guidelines; sample 50¢.
OUTDOOR, SCHOLARLY/ACADEMIC, TRAVEL

Salmon Trout Steelheader, Frank Amato Publications, PO Box 82112, Portland, OR 97282. 503-653-8108. Asst. editor: Nick Amato. Ads: Joyce Sherman. Bimonthly magazine. Sub $12.95. Circ. 37,000. Uses freelance material. Pays money on publication. Acquires 1st rights. Byline given. Submit query letter, complete ms, SASE. Dot matrix, disk subs OK. Reports in 2 wks. Accepts nonfiction related to fishing and conservation. Topics: how-to salmon, steelhead, trout fishing. Articles should be accompanied by B&W or color (35 mm or 5x7 prints). Guidelines; sample $2.50.
FISHING

Salud de la Familia News, PO Box 66, Woodburn, OR 97071. Quarterly.
MINORITIES/ETHNIC

Satellite Guide, CommTek, 9440 Fairview Ave., Boise, ID 83704. Editor: Fran Fuller. Monthly satellite reception guide. Circ. 10,000.
REFERENCE/LIBRARY

Saving Energy, 5411 117 Ave. S.E., Bellevue, WA 98006.
CONSUMER

Saxifrage, Pacific Lutheran University, Tacoma, WA 98447. 206-535-7387. Annual student creative arts magazine.
COLLEGE/UNIVERSITY

School Media Services, Dept. of Education, Public Office Bldg., Salem, OR 97310. Periodical for school media specialists.
EDUCATION

The School Paper, Eugene Public Schools, 200 N. Monroe, Eugene, OR 97402.
EDUCATION

Science Fiction Review, PO Box 11408, Portland, OR 97211. Editor: Richard E. Geis. Quarterly.
FANTASY/SCI FI

Scitech Book News, Book News, Inc., 5600 N.E. Hassalo, Portland, OR 97213-3640. 503-281-9230. Editor: Jane Erskine. Monthly list, reviews 500-600 newly published scientific, medical, technical books for librarians primarily. Sub $60. Circ. 2,200. Not a freelance market. Assignment only. We will consider assigning book reviews to specially qualified scientific and technical people. Pays money on acceptance. Sample $3.
REFERENCE/LIBRARY, SCIENCE

Screef, MPO Box 3352, Vancouver, BC V6B 3Y3. 604-681-5295. Contact: Jerome Cranston, editor. Sub $12/yr. Quarterly publication of the Pacific Reforestation Workers Association. Uses freelance material. Query w/SASE.
FORESTRY, LABOR/WORK

Screenings, Oregon Archaeological Society, PO Box 13293, Portland, OR 97213. Monthly.
ANTHROPOLOGY/ARCHAEOLOGY, NATURAL HISTORY, SCIENCE

Sea Kayaker, 6327 Seaview Ave. N.W., Seattle, WA 98107. 206-789-1326; 789-6413 (Ads). Editor: Christopher Cunningham. Quarterly magazine, founded 1984. Sub $13 (US). Circ. 10,000. Uses freelance material. Requires sea kayaking expertise. Pays 10¢/wd on publication. Acquires 1st rights. Byline given. Submit query letter, clips, outline, SASE. Dot matrix OK. Reports in 2-3 mos; publishes in 6-9 mos. Accepts nonfiction, fiction, photos (B&W, $15-35), cartoons. Topics: sea kayaking. Best guidelines contained in our back issues. Guidelines; sample $4.85 (US).
ADVENTURE, BOATING, TRAVEL

Seafood Leader, 1115 N.W. 45th St., Seattle, WA 98107. 206-283-8848. Contact: Peter Redmayne. Bimonthly trade journal of the seafood industry. Uses nonfiction on the business and the people, including historical pieces, profiles of individuals and companies, op/ed, news, etc. Uses color photos. Issues have themes. No sport or recreational. Query w/clips, or ms. Pay varies.
BUSINESS, FISHING

Seattle, 2107 Elliott Ave., #303, Seattle, WA 98121-2159. Monthly.
COMMUNITY

Seattle Art Museum Program Guide, PO Box 22000, Seattle, WA 98122-9700. 206-654-3100. Contact: Paula Thurman. Quarterly newsletter. Circ. 50,000. Free with museum membership. Does not accept freelance material.
ARTS, CULTURE

Seattle Arts, Seattle Arts Commission, 305 Harrison, Seattle, WA 98109. 206-625-4223. Contact: Steve Munzenmaier. Monthly relating to SAC concerns. Circ. 5,000. Accepts freelance material relevant to arts in Seattle by competent author. Guest editor program. Pay depends on budget. Byline given. Phone queries OK. Assignments only. "We have a literary supplement to the newsletter 2 times per year. Authors are accepted only if they respond to the call for submissions (published in the newsletter). Those accepted are selected by jury process." Sample.
ARTS

Seattle Audubon Society Newsletter, 8028 35th Ave. N.E., Seattle, WA 98115. 206-523-4483. Monthly newsletter. Circ. 5500; sub $15/yr. Uses freelance material. Byline given. Pays in copies. Query w/SASE, outline. Photocopies, simultaneous subs OK. Responds 15 days. Publishes 30-45 days. Accepts fiction, poetry, cartoons, news items, nonfiction, photos, interviews, articles and reviews. "This is an active environmental organization. It helps to understand the audience." Guidelines; sample $1.75.
WASHINGTON, NORTHWEST, CONSERVATION

Seattle Gay News, 704 E. Pike St., Seattle, WA 98122. 206-324-4297. Editor: George Bakan. Weekly for gay/lesbian audience. Circ. 20,000. Sub $35/yr. Accepts freelance material. Payment: Money, copies, on publication. Dot matrix OK. Nonfiction, fiction, photos ($5), cartoons. Sample.
GAY/LESBIAN

Seattle Post Intelligencer, 101 Elliott Ave. W., Seattle, WA 98119. 206-448-8000. Editor: John Reistrup. Features editor: Janet Grimley. Managing editor: Kerry Slagel. Book editor: Michael Conant. Daily. Accepts a little freelance material. Byline given; pays money on publication. Acquires 1st rights. Query letter, sample. OK to make follow-up calls. Response time varies. Accepts travel, reviews of local arts. Accepts photos, rates vary.
COMMUNITY

The Seattle Review, Department of English, GN-30, University of Washington, Seattle, WA 98195. 206-543-9865. Editor: Colleen J. McElroy. Semiannual literary magazine. Sub $8/yr. Circ. 800. Uses freelance material. Pays money, copies, 1 year sub on publication. Byline given. Acquires 1st rights, revert to author. Submit ms, SASE. Dot matrix, photocopies OK. Reports in 3-6 mos. Accepts fiction, poetry, essays on the craft of writing. Will consider most topics and length varies, limited only by issue requirements. No photos. Guidelines; sample 1/2 price.
COLLEGE/UNIVERSITY, FICTION, POETRY

Seattle Star, PO Box 30044, Seattle, WA 98103. 206-633-4701. Editor: Michael Dowers. Bi-monthly cartoon tabloid. Accepts freelance material. Pays copies/advertising trade. Submit w/SASE. Photocopied OK. Looking for humorous cartoons. Sample $1.
HUMOR

Seattle's Child/Eastside Project, 2107 Elliott Ave., #303, Seattle, WA 98121-2159. Editor: Ann Bergman. Ads: Alzyne Sulkin. Monthly magazine. Sub $15. Circ. 20,000. Uses 3 freelance mss per issue. Pays 10¢ word on publication. Acquires 1st rights. Byline given. Submit query w/ clips, ms, SASE. Dot matrix, photocopied, simultaneous OK. Reports in 3 mos. Publishes in 6-24 mos. Accepts nonfiction. Directed to parents and professionals working with kids. Audience well-read, sophisticated. Tips: 400-2,500 wds. Guidelines.
CHILDREN/TEEN, COMMUNITY, FAMILY

The Senior Messenger, PO Box 1995, Vancouver, WA 98668. 206-696-8171. Editor: Marilyn Westlake. Ads: Barbara Nylander, Denny Faulkner. Monthly for senior citizens. Circ. 14,000. Founded 1972. Sub $7. Uses 1-2 mss per issue. Payment: Free sub. Byline given. Rights purchased: First. Phone queries, PC disk, photocopies OK. Responds in 1-2 mos; publishes in 1-3 mos. Nonfiction, photos (B&W glossy, any size, not prescreened), cartoons. All material must relate directly to seniors. Strong preference for upbeat informational or feature articles from N.W. writers. 500-1,000 words max. Deadline, 12th of each month for following month's issue. "All material for this nonprofit publication must be non-promotional. I encourage novice freelancers to submit pieces." Sample: Free.
CONSUMER, NW/REGIONAL HISTORY, SENIOR CITIZENS

Senior News of Island County, 2845 E. Hwy 525, Langley, WA 98260. 206-321-1600. Editor: Claudia Fuller. Monthly, free. Circ. 3,600. Uses freelance material. No pay. Submit ms, SASE. Dot matrix, photocopied OK. Accepts nonfiction, poetry, photos, cartoons.
PHOTOGRAPHY, POETRY, SENIOR CITIZENS

Senior Scene, 223 N. Yakima, Tacoma, WA 98403. 206-622-5427. Contact: Kathleen Pfeifle. Uses freelance material. Byline given. Pays money, copies on publication. Submit query letter, ms, SASE. Photocopy, simultaneous subs OK. Responds in 2 wks; publishes in 3 mos. Accepts cartoons, news items, biography, photos, interviews, op/ed, articles, reviews. Sample $2.
SENIOR CITIZENS

Senior Times, 7802 E. Mission, Spokane, WA 99212.
SENIOR CITIZENS

Senior Tribune & Northwest Advocate, 6420 S.W. Macadam Ave. #210, Portland, OR 97201-3518. 503-777-5436. Editor: Jill Warren. Monthly tabloid serving those 55 and older in Multnomah, Clackamas and Washington counties. Distributed free to banks, savings and loans, senior and community centers, retirement complexes, medical clinics, Social Security offices. "Individuals and organizations are encouraged to submit articles of interest to older persons." Deadline for all copy is the 15th of each month.
SENIOR CITIZENS

The Senior Voice, 325 E. 3rd Ave., Anchorage, AK 99501. 907-277-0787. Editor: Liz Lauzen. Ads: Pat Bressett. Monthly, senior advocate for legislative, health, consumer affairs. Sub $10 for Alaskans over 55/others $20. Seldom accepts freelance material. Source should be well versed in Alaskan concerns. Byline given.
AMERICANA, SENIOR CITIZENS

Sesame, Windyridge Press, PO Box 327, Medford, OR 97501. 503-772-5399. Editor: Gene Olson. Monthly newsletter for writers. Sub $26.
LITERARY, WRITING

Shalom Oregon, c/o NCCJ, PO Box 8094, Portland, OR 97207. Quarterly of the Oregon chapter of the National Council of Christians and Jews.
RELIGION

Shaping the Landscape, Dept. of Education, 801 W. 10th, Ste. 200, Juneau, AK 99801-1984. 907-465-2841. Contact: Judith Entwife. Annual journal. Accepts fiction, nonfiction, and poetry from Alaskan educators only for re-

view and selection by an editorial board. Pieces are limited to 4000 words. "Supports teachers of writing as writers themselves."
EDUCATION, WRITING

Sherman County For The Record, PO Box 173, Moro, OR 97039-0173. Editor: Sherry Kaseberg & Patty Moore. Semiannual magazine of local history. Prints 1,000 copies, mainly for residents of Sherman County. No pay. Submit ms, SASE. Phone queries OK. Nonfiction: "Our authors are mostly local people. No one is paid. Profit is for the historical society." Sample.
NW/REGIONAL HISTORY

Shoban News, Box 427, Fort Hall, ID 83203. Weekly. Circ. 1,500.
COMMUNITY

Sign of the Times-a Chronicle of Decadence, PO Box 70672, Seattle, WA 98107-0672. 206-323-6779. Editor: Mark Souder. Biannual. Sub $15/2 yrs. Circ. 750. Uses 11 freelance mss per issue. Pays copies on publication. Byline given. Submit ms w/SASE. Dot matrix, photocopied, electronic OK. Reports in 6 wks. Accepts fiction, photographs, drama, cartoons. Guidelines.
FICTION, HUMOR, PHOTOGRAPHY

The Signal, Network International, PO Box 67, Emmett, ID 83617. 208-365-5812. Editor: Joan Silva. Semiannual magazine founded in 1987. Sub $10/yr. Circ. 500. Uses freelance material. Byline given. Pays copies. Submit query letter, complete ms, SASE, phone. Photocopy, dot matrix, simultaneous subs OK. Responds in 2-6 wks; publishes in 1 yr. Accepts fiction, poetry, cartoons, nonfiction, photos, interviews, op/ed, articles, reviews. Topics: worldwide issues, human and planetary issues; no religious material. Guidelines; sample $5.
ARTS, LITERATURE, POETRY

Signatures from Big Sky, 928 4th Ave., Laurel, MT 59044. 406-628-7911; 406-628-7063. Contact: Shirley Olson. Annual. Publishes only Montana student work (K-12). Sub $5/year. Circ. 1000. Freelance MT material accepted. No payment. Sketches, art, fiction, poetry, and cartoons accepted. Back issues $5 ea. Guidelines.
CHILDREN/TEEN, WRITING, CHILDREN (BY/ABOUT)

Signpost for Northwest Trails, 1305 4th Ave. #512, Seattle, WA 98101. 206-625-1367. Editor: Dan Nelson. Ads: Barbara Allen. Monthly magazine founded in 1966. Sub $25/yr. Circ. 3,000. Uses freelance material. Pays money, copies on publication. Byline given. Acquires 1st rights. Submit complete ms, SASE. Dot matrix, photocopies, disk/modem, simultaneous subs OK. Reports in 2-8 wks. Publishing time varies. Accepts nonfiction, photos (B&W glossy, 5x7 minimum, $25, must show a scene from WA or OR, and include a person or people), illustrations. Topics: non-motorized backcountry recreation, primarily backpacking, hiking X-C skiing; including climbing, paddling. Guidelines; sample $2.50.
ENVIRONMENT/RESOURCES, OUTDOOR, RECREATION

Signs of the Times, PO Box 7000, Boise, ID 83707. 208-465-2577. Editor: Greg Brothers. Monthly magazine "shows how Bible principles are relevant in today's world." Circ. 265,000; sub $11.95/yr. Pays money on acceptance. Byline given. First rights acquired. Submit ms, SASE. Phone queries, simultaneous submissions OK. Reports in 1 mo. Publishes in 1 yr. Nonfiction: 500-3,000 wds on "home, marriage, health, inspirational human interest articles that highlight a Biblical principle, and personal experiences solving problems with God's help." Photos: B&W contact sheets, 5x7 & 8x10 prints, 35mm color transparencies. Buys photos with or without articles. Guidelines; sample.
RELIGION

The Silver Apple Branch, 1036 Hampshire Rd., Victoria, BC V8S 4S9. Editor: Janet P. Reedman. Periodical of Irish myths and legends. Accepts freelance material. Pay-

ment: Copies. Byline given. Query w/SASE. Reports in 3-6 wks. Fiction, poetry. Max story length 1,500. Original fiction featuring Irish heroes.
CULTURE, FICTION, POETRY

Silverfish Review, PO Box 3541, Eugene, OR 97403. 503-344-5060. Editor: Rodger Moody. Literary review published irregularly. Sub $12/3 issues, indiv; $15 for inst. Circ. 750. Uses freelance material. Sponsors a poetry chapbook competition. Query w/SASE. Reports in 6 wks; time to publication varies. Accepts fiction, poetry, photos, interviews, reviews. Guidelines; sample.
FICTION, POETRY

Single Scene, PO Box 5027, Salem, OR 97304. Monthly.
ENTERTAINMENT, UNSPECIFIED

Skagit Art Magazine, Freedom Press, PO Box 762, Sedro-Woolley, WA 98284-0762. 206-856-2290. Editor: Diane Freethy. Freelance material accepted.
ARTS

Ski Canada Magazine, 202-1132 Hamilton, Vancouver, BC V6V 2S8. Magazine devoted to Canadian skiing.
CANADA, RECREATION, SPORTS

Skies America, 7730 S.W. Mohawk, Tualatin, OR 97062. 503-691-1955. Contact: Robert Patterson. In-flight magazine. Accepts freelance material. Payment: $100-300 for feature articles, on publication. Query w/SASE. Nonfiction: features 1200-1500 wds; departments 500-700 words, $50-100. Prefer photos with article, B&W prints and color transparencies. Timely, original material in the fields of business, investing, travel, humor, health/medicine, sports, city features, geographical features. Guidelines; sample $3.
BUSINESS, TRAVEL

Skipping Stones, PO Box 3939, Eugene, OR 97403-0939. 503-342-4956. Editors: Arun N. Toke, Amy Klauke. Quarterly magazine by and for children (multicultural childrens forum). Circ. 2,500, subs $15/yr indiv; $20 inst. Uses freelance mss; pays in copies. Submit query, ms w/ SASE. Responds in 3 mos; published in 4-6 mos. Accepts nonfiction, fiction, poetry, photos, cartoons. Topics: "Environmental awareness, cultural diversity, multi-ethnic literature." Pen-pal letters, childrens activities, project reports welcome. Shorter items preferred (1-2 ds pages). If writing is other than English, submit translation if possible. Guidelines. Sample $5.
CHILDREN/TEEN, CULTURE, MINORITIES/ETHNIC

Skyviews, PO Box 2473, Seattle, WA 98111. 206-323-6779. Editor: Jim Maloney.
UNSPECIFIED

Skyword, 610-1200 W. 73rd Ave., Vancouver, BC V6P 6G5. 604-264-7311. Editor: Gabriele Walkou. Publishes tourism magazines such as British Columbia Skiing and BC Outdoor Adventure Guide. Both are annual. Query by phone. Accepts nonfiction and photos.
TRAVEL

Slightly West, The Evergreen State College, CAB 320, Olympia, WA 98505. 206-866-6000 x6879. Editors: Brian Almquist & Sharon Romeo. Biannual. Sub $5. Circ. 1,500. Uses freelance material. Pays in copies. Byline given. Submit ms, SASE. Dot matrix, photocopied OK. Reports in 1 mo. Accepts nonfiction, fiction, poetry, literary essays, photos, cartoons, plays, reviews, memoirs. Aims for diverse cultures and ideas. Photo submissions should reproduce well in black & white. Guidelines, sample.
COLLEGE/UNIVERSITY, FICTION, POETRY

Small Farmer's Journal, PO Box 1627, Sisters, OR 97759. 503-683-6486. Contact: Lynn R. Miller. Farmers' literary quarterly, including poetry.
AGRICULTURE/FARMING, LITERATURE

Small Town, Small Towns Institute, PO Box 517, Ellensburg, WA 98926. 509-925-1830. Bi-monthly concerning small town health in the US, provides original re-

search into local problem-solving. Sub. $30.
COMMUNITY

The Smallholder Publishing Collective, Argenta, BC V0G 1B0. 604-366-4283. Editor: Betty Tillotson. Magazine published approx. 4 times a year. Sub $14/6 issues. Circ. 750. Nonprofit. Uses freelance material. No pay. Acquires all rights. Byline given. Query w/SASE. Photocopies OK. "We're a group of volunteers putting together a magazine for country people regarding rural living (all aspects) & our copy is largely made up of letters and articles from readers."
COMMUNITY, GARDENING

Smoke Signals, Pacific Press Publishing Association, 1350 Kings Rd., Nampa, ID 83651. Editor: Francis A. Soper. Monthly of the Seventh-Day Adventist Church.
RELIGION

SmokeRoot, University of Montana, Department of English, Missoula, MT 59812. University literary publication.
COLLEGE/UNIVERSITY, LITERARY

Smurfs in Hell, PO Box 2761, Boise, ID 83701-2761.
UNSPECIFIED

Snake River Alliance Newsletter, PO Box 1731, Boise, ID 83701. 208-344-9161. Contact: Deanah Messenger. Monthly newsletter. Circ. 1,200. Accepts some freelance material. Submit query letter or query by phone. Responds 1-2 wks; publishes 3 wks. Accepts cartoons, nonfiction articles and photos (B&W, camera ready). The group works for peace and sane nuclear policies.
ENVIRONMENT/RESOURCES, PEACE

Snake River Echoes, PO Box 244, Rexburg, ID 83440. 208-356-9101. Editors: Louis Clements/Ralph Thompson. Quarterly on Snake River history. Circ. 700. Sub $10. Uses 6 mss per issue. Byline given. Submit ms, SASE. Photocopies OK. Nonfiction, photos (B&W). We print history of Snake River area of Eastern Idaho, Eastern Wyoming. Sample/$1.
NW/REGIONAL HISTORY, IDAHO, NORTHWEST

Snake River Reflections, 1863 Bitterroot Dr., Twin Falls, ID 83301. 208-734-0746. Newsletter, 10X/yr. Sub $5.50. Uses freelance material. Pays copies. Byline given. Query, SASE. Dot matrix, photocopied OK. Reports in 2 wks; publishes in 1-2 mos. Accepts nonfiction, short-short stories, poetry, cartoons. Guidelines; sample 25 cents & #10 SASE.
FICTION, POETRY, WRITING

The Sneak Preview, PO Box 639, Grants Pass, OR 97526. 503-474-3044. Editor: Curtis Hayden. Ads: John Kochis. Biweekly. Sub $34/yr. Circ. 11,000. Uses freelance material. Pays money on publication. Byline given. Submit ms. Photocopied OK. Accepts nonfiction, fiction, poetry. Humor and satire appreciated. Guidelines; sample 65¢.
COMMUNITY, CULTURE, ENTERTAINMENT

Snow Action, 520 Park Ave., Idaho Falls, ID 83402. 208-524-7000. Contact: Steve Janes
BUSINESS

Snow West Magazine, 520 Park Ave., Idaho Falls, ID 83402. 208-524-7000. Contact: Steve Janes.
SPORTS

Snowmobile West, Motor Media, 520 park Ave., Idaho Falls, ID 83402. 208-524-7000. Editor: Darryl Harris. Bimonthly. Circ. 95,000.
CRAFTS/HOBBIES, OUTDOOR, RECREATION

Society for Industrial Archeology, Dept. of History/ Social Sciences, Northern Montana College, Havre, MT 59501. Quarterly.
ANTHROPOLOGY/ARCHAEOLOGY, COLLEGE/UNIVERSITY

SONCAP News, PO Box 402, Grants Pass, OR 97526. 503-474-6034. Editor: Louise Nicholson. Quarterly newsletter. Sub $10. Circ. 700. Accepts freelance material. Submit ms. Dot matrix, photocopied, simultaneous, electronic/ modem OK. Accepts nonfiction, poetry, cartoons. Topics:

forestry & environmental ecology, pesticides & herbicides alternatives; air, soil, water, visual quality; worker right-to-know; roadside vegetation management, organic gardening, clearcutting, etc. Sample.
ENVIRONMENT/RESOURCES, FORESTRY, GARDENING

Soul Town Review, 510 S.W. 3rd St., Ste. 100, Portland, OR 97204. Editor: Connie Cameron. Periodical on the local music scene.
CULTURE, MUSIC

The Sourdough, Fairbanks Law Library, 604 Barnette St., Fairbanks, AK 99701.
LAW, REFERENCE/LIBRARY

Southeastern Log, Box 7900, Ketchikan, AK 99901. 907-225-3157. Editor: Nikki Murray Jones.
UNSPECIFIED

Southern Oregon Arts, The Arts Council of Southern Oregon Newsletter, 33 N. Central Ave. #308, Medford, OR 97501. 503-779-2820. Editor: Jill Whalley. Quarterly. Membership $15/yr. Circ. 1,600. Uses freelance material. Byline given, pays copies. Submit ms, query/SASE. Photocopied, disk, dot matrix subs OK. Responds in 1 wk; publishes in 1 mo. Accepts poetry, news items, biographies, nonfiction, photos, interviews, reviews. Photos: B&W any size, no payment, photos returned. Sample $1.
ARTS, COMMUNITY, CULTURE

Southern Oregon Currents, PO Box 1468, Grants Pass, OR 97526. 800-525-2624. Editor: Cathy Noah. Ads: Michele Thomas. Weekly magazine founded in 1989. Sub $24/yr. Circ. 19,300. Uses freelance material. Byline given. Pays money, copies on publication. Submit query, clips, complete ms, SASE, or phone. Responds in 12 mos; publishes in 12 mos. Accepts nonfiction, poetry, articles, photos (B&W prints, $15; color slides, $25). Topics: entertainment, primarily things to do and places to go; the arts, local personalities and current trends. Guidelines; sample 75¢.
ARTS, ENTERTAINMENT, RECREATION

The Spectator, Seattle University, Seattle, WA 98122.
COLLEGE/UNIVERSITY, EDUCATION

Spindrift, Shoreline Community College, 16101 Greenwood Ave. N., Seattle, WA 98133. 206-546-4789. Annual literary magazine. Sub $6.50/yr. Circ. 500. Accepts freelance material. Pays copies on publication. Byline given. Submit ms, SASE. Acquires first rights. Dot matrix, photocopied OK. Reports in 3 mos. Accepts nonfiction, fiction, poetry, photos, plays, cartoons, B&W drawings. 4,500 wds on prose, 6 poems, 1-5 pages dialogue. Photos & art: B&W, 24x24 max. Audience includes essay, fiction & poetry lovers, art enthusiasts. Genuine work that avoids greeting card sentiment. Sample $4.
COLLEGE/UNIVERSITY, FICTION, POETRY

Spokes, Rotary Club of Portland, 1119 S.W. Park Ave., Portland, OR 97205. Weekly.
TRADE/ASSOCIATIONS

Spokes, Canadian Poetry Association, Box 46658, Sta. G, Vancouver, BC V6R 4K8. 604-266-0396. Editor: Katie Eliot. Quarterly newsletter. Circ. 150; sub $10/yr. Uses freelance material. Byline given, pays copies, no rights. Submit query/SASE, phone, photocopy OK. Responds in 1 mo; publishes within 4 mos. Accepts poetry, cartoons, interviews, reviews, news of past or future poetry events. "We publish modern poetry that reflects the involvement and intricacies of contemporary living." Sample $2.
BRITISH COLUMBIA, POETRY, WRITING

Sports Etc Magazine, PO Box 9272, Seattle, WA 98109. 206-286-8566. Publisher/Ads: Carolyn Price. Editor: Jody Brannon. Published 10X/yr. Sub $12. Circ. 35,000. Freelance material accepted. Pays money, copies on publication. Byline given. Query w/SASE. Disk/modem OK. Reports in 1 mo. Accepts cartoons, news, photos, interviews, op/ed, articles. Color negs for cover; B&W inside. Guidelines with SASE. Sample $2. "Seeking tidbits and

profiles in the world of outdoor, participant and recreational sports and fitness for readers in Washington and Oregon."
SPORTS, RECREATION, ADVENTURE

Sports Northwest Magazine, 4556 University Way N.E. #203, Seattle, WA 98105-4511. 206-547-9709. Editor: John Erben. Monthly tabloid on participant sports: running, bicycling, hiking, skiing, triathletics, and lesser known sports such as ultimate Frisbee, lacrosse, etc. Circ. 25,000. Payment: $1.50 column inch, on publication. Byline given. Query w/SASE. Phone queries, simultaneous submissions OK, modem preferred. Nonfiction: up to 2,000 wds. Fiction: up to 2,000 wds (humor, a personal account or satire. Photos: color slide for cover pays $85, interior B&W action shots, pay varies. Guideline; sample with SASE.
PHOTOGRAPHY, RECREATION, SPORTS

Sports Vue, 112-2465 Beta Ave., Burnaby, BC V5C 5N1. 604-291-1320. Editor: Mike Condon. Weekly (45x/yr) mag. Uses some freelance material. Payment negotiable with each article. Primarily regional coverage. Focus is professional and amateur sports in Vancouver.
SPORTS

The Sproutletter, Sprouting Publications, Box 62, Ashland, OR 97520. 503-488-2326. Editor: Michael Linden. Bimonthly newsletter. Sub $14/yr. Circ. 3,000. Uses freelance material. Pays on publication for 1st & 2nd serial rights. Byline given. Submit query letter, SASE. Photocopy, dot matrix, disk/modem, simultaneous subs OK. Responds in 4-8 wks; publishes in 3-4 mos. Accepts nonfiction, cartoons, news items, photos, interviews, reviews. Topics: holistic health through live and raw foods, sprouting and indoor gardens. Sample $3.
FOOD/COOKING, GARDENING, HEALTH

St. Alphonsus Today, St. Alphonsus Regional Medical Center, 1055 N. Curtis Rd., Boise, ID 83706. 208-378-2121. Editor: Bob Hieronymus. Quarterly. Circ. 12,500. Not a freelance market.
HEALTH, MEDICAL

Star Film & Video News, 909 N.W. 19th Ave, Portland, OR 97209-1403. Editor: Don Smith
FILM/VIDEO

Stat, Oregon Medical Association, 5210 S.W. Corbett, Portland, OR 97201. 503-226-1555. Contact: Quita Terill. Monthly. $25/yr sub. Circ. 5,200. No unsolicited submissions. Query by phone.
HEALTH, MEDICAL, TRADE/ASSOCIATIONS

SteppingOut Arts Magazine, 510 S.W. 3rd Ave., Ste. #1, Portland, OR 97204. 503-241-ARTS. Editor: James Bash. Ads: Rex Ruckert. Semiannual magazine of creative endeavors in the fine arts. Sub $14/2 yrs. Circ. 180,000. Accepts freelance material. Pays money, varies upon article requirements, on publication. Byline given. Acquires all rights. Submit query letter, SASE, phone for assignment. Photocopies, dot matrix, disk/modem subs OK. Accepts nonfiction. Topics: the arts and artists; creative undertakings. Guidelines; sample $2.50.
ARTS, BUSINESS, TRAVEL

The Steward, Erb Memorial Union, University of Oregon, Eugene, OR 97403.
COLLEGE/UNIVERSITY

The Stranger, 4739 University Way N.E., Ste. 1516, Seattle, WA 98105-4412. 206-547-7968. Contact: Christine Wenc. Weekly mag. Circ. 25,000; sub $15/12 issues. Uses freelance material. No poetry or phone calls, please. Byline given. Pays in money, copies on publication. Acquires 1st rights. Submit query letter, clips or complete ms w/SASE. Dot matrix, photocopies, disk/modem or Fax OK. Responds 2-6 wks. Accepts essays, articles and interviews, short fiction plus reviews and articles for arts and entertainment section. "Read some recent issues before submitting, keep submission short (500-1800 wds)."
ARTS, CULTURE, ENTERTAINMENT

Strawberry Fields, PO Box 33786, Seattle, WA 98133-0786. Contact: Ken Boisse. Bimonthly.
UNSPECIFIED

Street Times, 1236 S.W. Salmon, Portland, OR 97205. 503-223-4121. Editor: Louis Folkman. Bimonthly. Circ. 1,500. Uses freelance material. Query w/SASE. Accepts nonfiction, fiction, poetry, photos, cartoons. Sample.
CHILDREN/TEEN

Stylus, PO Box 1716, Portland, OR 97207. Contact: Michael Olson, editor; Michael Palmer, book review editor. Bimonthly newsletter. An eclectic review of music & books. Not a freelance market.
BOOK ARTS/BOOKS, CULTURE, MUSIC

sub-TERRAIN, Anvil Press, #15 - 2414 Main St., Vancouver, BC V5T 3E3. 604-876-8700. Contact: B. Kaufman. Magazine published 3 times yearly, founded in 1988. Sub 4 issues $10 Cdn, $12 US, $15/Institution. Circ. 2000. Uses freelance material. Pays copies. Acquires 1st rights. Byline given. Submit ms/SASE. Dot matrix, photocopied OK. Reports in 2-3 mos; publishes in 3 mos. Accepts fiction (any subject/style, 200-2000 wds), nonfiction (social commentary/literary criticism, 500-2,000 wds), poetry (any subjects/style, 1-2 pg), photos (B&W, max 7x10, experimental/arty), line art (Pen & ink, woodcut, linocut), rants/polemic, plays, cartoons, op/ed. Topics: opinions, questions and alternatives for the underprivileged, the disenfranchised, the silent many below the surface of Canadian/North American society. Read an issue before submitting. Guidelines; sample $3.
FICTION, LITERARY, SOCIALIST/RADICAL

Sugar Producer, Harris & Smith Communication, 520 Park Ave., Idaho Falls, ID 83402. Editor: Darryl Harris. Semiannual. Circ. 20,000.
AGRICULTURE/FARMING, BUSINESS

Sun Valley Magazine, PO Box 2950, Ketchum, ID 83340. Editor: Mike Riedel. Published 3 times a year. Circ. 2,600.
ENTERTAINMENT, IDAHO, RECREATION

The Suspicious Humanist, 549 B St., #3, Ashland, OR 97520. Contact: Steve Weiner. Founded in 1972. Circ. 350. Sub/$5 or sliding scale. Published 1-3 times yearly. Literary journal of the arts and opinion. Freelance material accepted. Byline given; pays copies on publication. Rights acquired vary. SASE, complete ms. Response time "at least six months." Accepts fiction, poetry, cartoons, news items, biography, nonfiction, photos, interviews, op/ed, articles, plays, reviews, memoirs. "Extremely inclusive. Special interests: non-dogmatic philosophy (esp. political); disability; medical; Jewish-interfaith; humor; mental illness/health; west coast history." A few back issues; cost is negotiable.
PHILOSOPHY

Sustainable Farming Quarterly, 44 N. Last Chance Gulch, Helena, MT 59601. 406-442-8396. Editor: Sally K. Hilander. Founded 1989. Quarterly free newsletter. Freelance material accepted; byline given. Pays copies on publication; acquires no rights. Query letter, complete ms, synopsis, query by phone. Photocopy, dot matrix OK. Responds in 3 months; publishes in 3 months. Accepts news items, interviews, articles, and reviews. For photos, send B&W film or negatives, or B&W prints. "Material is strictly limited to sustainable agriculture in the inland Pacific Northwest (MT, ID, WY, UT, OR, WA, western Canada)." Guidelines, back issues. Free.
AGRICULTURE/FARMING, CALENDAR/EVENTS, TECHNICAL

Swedish Press, 1294 W. 7th Ave., Vancouver, BC V6H 1B6. 604-731-6381. Editor/ads: Anders Neumueller. Monthly of Swedish interest, founded 1929. Sub $19. Uses 2 mss per issue. Pays copies. Byline given. Acquires 1st rights. Submit ms, SASE. Photocopies OK. Accepts nonfiction. Topics: Swedes, Swedish descendants, Swedish slants on general stories. Photos: B&W and color land-scapes for cover, B&W on inside. Sample $2.
MINORITIES/ETHNIC, PHOTOGRAPHY

The Table Rock Sentinel, Southern Oregon Historical Society, 106 N. Central Ave., Medford, OR 97501. 503-899-1847. Editor: Cathy Noah. Ads: Stacy Williams. Self-publisher of membership magazine & newsletter. Circ. 2,000. Sub $30/year membership. Uses one freelance ms per issue. Requires historical accuracy & expertise. Pays money ($75-200) on acceptance (30-60 days). Byline given. Submit query letter, SASE. Dot matrix, photocopied OK. Reports in 30 days. Publishing time varies. Accepts nonfiction feature articles and interviews, biography and book reviews. Topics: relating to the history of the southern Oregon region. Photos 8X10 glossy, professional ($5-50). Guidelines; sample $3.95.
NW/REGIONAL HISTORY, OREGON, US HISTORY

Tacoma Arts Commission Newsletter, Tacoma Municipal Bldg., 747 Market St., Rm. 900, Tacoma, WA 98402-3768. 206-591-5191. Contact: Dorothy McCuistion. Bimonthly newsletter. Free. Circ. 4,000. Freelance material accepted. Byline given. No pay. Acquires no rights. Query letter, SASE, query by phone. Responds in 2 weeks; publishes in 2 months. Accepts poetry, cartoons, announcements of interest to writers in this area. Back issues free.
ARTS

Take Five, PO Box 5027, Salem, OR 97304. Contact: Tim Hinshaw.
ENTERTAINMENT

Talking Leaves, 1430 Willamette, Ste. 367, Eugene, OR 97401. 503-342-2974. Editor: Carolyn Moran. Ads: Richard Bredsteen. Sub $15/yr. Circ. 8,000. Monthly journal. Uses freelance material. Byline given. Pays copies. Acquires 1st rights. Query w/SASE. Photocopied, dot matrix subs OK, disk/modem preferred. Publishes in 2 mos. Accepts fiction, poetry, articles, news items, biography, photos, interviews, op/ed, articles, plays, reviews, memoirs. Topics: bioregional; deep ecology and spiritual activism. Sample $1.50.
CONSERVATION, ENVIRONMENT/RESOURCES, FEMINISM

Teaching Home, PO Box 20219, Portland, OR 97220-0219. Editor: Sue Welch. Sub $15/yr. Bimonthly magazine for Christian home educators. No submission information.
CHILDREN (BY/ABOUT), EDUCATION, RELIGION

Teaching Research Infant and Child Center News, Monmouth, OR 97361.
CHILDREN (BY/ABOUT), CHILDREN/TEEN, EDUCATION

TECHbooks Journal, 12600 S.W. First, Beaverton, OR 97005. 503-223-4245. Editor: Jim Deibele. Monthly newsletter. Circ. 5,000; sub $15/yr. Freelance material accepted. Byline given. Payment in copies on acceptance. All rights acquired. Query by phone. Disk/modem, photocopies OK. Responds 24 hours; publishes 60 days. Accepts nonfiction. Topics: "...interested only in technical books and documentation. Articles about publishers and authors are secondary to our reviews of books & magazines, but we do run some articles."
BOOK ARTS/BOOKS, COMPUTERS, SCIENCE

Technical Analysis of Stocks & Commodities, Technical Analysis, Inc., 3517 S.W. Alaska St., Seattle, WA 98126-2730. 206-938-0570. Editor: Thom Hartle. Ads: Lou Knoll Kemper. Monthly magazine. Sub $64.95/yr. Circ. 25,000. Uses freelance material. Writers should be knowledgeable about trading. Pays $3/col inch, $50 min on publication; cartoons, small items, flat $15. Acquires 1st rights. Byline given. Submit ms, SASE. Dot matrix, photocopied, electronic, disk-modem OK. Reports in 1 day; publishes in 3-6 mos. Accepts nonfiction, fiction, how-to articles on trading. Topics-theme blocks: psychology of trading, technical vs fundamental, using statistics, chart work & technical analysis, new technical methods (charting, computer use), trading techniques,

basics, reviews (books, articles, software, hardware), humor (incidents, cartoons, photos). Guidelines; sample $5.
COMPUTERS, HOW-TO

Technocracy Digest, 3642 Kingsway, Vancouver, BC V2V 4H9. 604-434-1134. Editor: Bette Hiebert. Quarterly magazine, founded 1934. Sub $6/yr for digest only. $12/yr includes Northwest Technocrat, 7513 Greenwood Ave N, Seattle, WA 98103. Editor: John Berge.
EDUCATION, PHILOSOPHY

Technology Edge, 215 W. Harrison, Seattle, WA 98119. 206-282-8111. Contact: Heather Evans. Quarterly magazine. Reprints of articles from professional and trade publications and academic journals, job prospects, book reviews, and profiles.
TECHNICAL

Testmarketed Downpour, Linfield College, Box 414, McMinnville, OR 97128. 503-472-4121. Editor: Barbara Drake. College literary magazine. Editor could change yearly. SASE for guidelines.
COLLEGE/UNIVERSITY, FICTION, OREGON

These Exist Times, PO Box 86646, Portland, OR 97286. Editor: Les U. Knight
UNSPECIFIED

These Homeless Times, Burnside Community Council, 313 E. Burnside St., Portland, OR 97214. 503-231-7158. Editor: Susan Elwood. Quarterly. Sub $10. Uses freelance material.
COMMUNITY

This Is Alaska, 8600 Hartzell Rd., Anchorage, AK 99507-3417. 907-349-7506. Editor: Frank Martone.
ALASKA

This Is Just to Say, Assembly on American Literature (NCTE), PO Box 1305, Lake Oswego, OR 97035. 503-245-4526. Editor: Sandi Brinkman. Quarterly newsletter on American authors. Circ. 300. Accepts freelance material. Byline given. Query w/ms, SASE. Dot matrix, simultaneous submissions OK. Reports in 1-3 mos. Nonfiction: 1,000 words on authors, literature. Photos. Sample.
EDUCATION, AMERICAN HISTORY, LITERATURE

Thurston County Senior News, 529 W. 4th Ave., Olympia, WA 98501. 206-786-5595. Editor: Rick Crawford. Ads: Don Hellum. Monthly tabloid free to senior citizens. Circ. 15,000. Uses freelance material. May pay copies on publication. Byline given. Submit ms, SASE. Dot matrix, photocopied OK. Accepts nonfiction, cartoons. Topics: local news, health, nutrition, leisure, travel, finance, legislation for retirees. Sample for postage.
COMMUNITY, SENIOR CITIZENS

Tickled by Thunder, 7385 129th St., Surrey, BC V3W 7B8. 604-591-6095. Contact: Larry Lindner. Quarterly newsletter. Circ. 100. 100% freelance written. Copies sent upon publication (cash as Circ. increases). Acquires 1st rights, byline given. Submit w/SASE. Dot matrix, photocopies, simultaneous, electronic/modem submission OK. Reports in 1 month, publishes on acceptance. Accepts nonfiction, fiction, poetry, and cartoons. Articles: 2,000 words max on writing, personal experience, etc. Fiction: 2,000 words max, anything goes. Poems, 60 lines max. Guidelines and sample issues with $2 and SASE.
FICTION, LITERARY, POETRY

Tidepools, Peninsula College, Port Angeles, WA 98362. 206-452-9277. Editor: Alice Derry.
COLLEGE/UNIVERSITY

Tidewater, 2210 N.W. Everett St., #402, Portland, OR 97210-5511. Contact: Scott Hartwich, editor. Irregular journal of fiction and poetry). No preachy or sexist material. Try not to offend. Cover letter w/SASE. Be professional. Payment in copies, usually. All subjects welcome.
FICTION, LITERARY, POETRY

Timber!, Willamette Timbermen Association, Inc., 589 S. 72nd St., Springfield, OR 97478. 503-726-7918. Editor: Ted Ferrioli. Monthly.

FORESTRY, LUMBER

Timberbeast, PO Box 3695, Eugene, OR 97403. 503-686-8416. Editor/Ads: Bill Roy. Journal. Sub $14/4 issues. Circ. 1,200+. Uses freelance material. Pays copies. Byline given. Submit query w/clips, ms, SASE, phone. Dot matrix, photocopied, computer disk OK. Reports in 3 wks; publishes in 6 mos. Accepts nonfiction, photos, cartoons. Topics: Pacific N.W. historical logging — individuals, companies, equipment, methods. "Reviews of relevant materials, 'great loggers I have known.'" Sample $3.50.

FORESTRY, NW/REGIONAL HISTORY, LUMBER

Timberline, 6150 Indian Tree Lane, Pocatello, ID 83204. 208-236-2470. Editor: Kathleen King. Literary magazine published three times yearly. Sub/$15. Emphasis on writers of the Rocky Mountain region. Pays copies on publication. Accepts poetry, short fiction, personal essays (12 pgs max). Submit ms, SASE. Reports 1 mo of pub deadline. Submissions should include a 100-wd biographical sketch. Deadlines: 1 December, 1 February, 1 August.

LITERARY

Timber/West Magazine, PO Box 610, Edmonds, WA 98020. 206-778-3388. Editor: Dennis Stuhaug, Ads: Don Pravitz. Specialized logging industry publication. Monthly. Circ. 10,000+. Uses 23 freelance mss. per issue, by assignment only. Byline given. Pays money on publication. Acquires all rights. Query w/SASE. Disk/modem, dot matrix OK. Responds immediately, publication in 1-3 months. Topics: logging, heaving on techniques, equipment. Guidelines.

LUMBER, BUSINESS

Time Designs, 29722 Hult Rd., Colton, OR 97017. Editor: T. Woods.

UNSPECIFIED

Time to Pause, Inky Trails Publications, PO Box 345, Middleton, ID 83644. Editor: Pearl Kirk. Semiannual literary magazine featuring poetry, fiction, nonfiction, and art. Circ. 200. Submit ms, SASE. Reports in 28 wks. Nonfiction: 3,500-5,500 wds on book reviews, essays, historical or nostalgic humor, inspirational, personal experience and travel. Fiction: 3,500-5,500 wds on fantasy, historical, humorous, mystery, romance, suspense, and western. Poetry: 4-70 lines of verse, free verse, light verse, or traditional. "Do not want horror, porno, etc." Sample: SASE.

FANTASY/SCI FI, HUMOR, TRAVEL

T.I.P.S. Employment Guide, PO Box 2548, Redmond, WA 98073-2548. Editor: Jim Massey.

BUSINESS, CONSUMER, LABOR/WORK

Totline, 11625-G Airport Rd., Everett, WA 98204. 206-353-3100. Editor: Jean Warren. Ads: David Warren. Publisher of hard- & softcover books, bimonthly newsletter. Sub $24/yr. Circ. 10,000. Uses freelance material from writers with early childhood educational experience. Pays money on acceptance. Acquires all rights. Byline given. Submit sample chapters, SASE. Dot matrix, photocopied OK. Reports in 10-12 wks. Accepts nonfiction poetry. Topics: activity ideas, i.e., craft, art, educational, games, cultural diversity; activities around a central theme, inspirational poetry for adults. Sketches encouraged for clarification. Guidelines, back issues.

CHILDREN/TEEN, EDUCATION

TOWERS Club USA Newsletter, Box 2038, Vancouver, WA 98668. 206-574-3084. Contact: Jerry Buchanan. Monthly covers the field of selling info in printed or taped format directly to the consumer. Advertising tips, sources, news of the industry. Sub $60/yr. Not a freelance market.

BUSINESS, PUBLISHING/PRINTING

Trail Breakers, Clark Co. Genealogical Soc. & Library, PO Box 2728, Vancouver, WA 98668. 206-256-0977. Editor: Rose Marie Harshman. Quarterly newsletter. Sub $12. Circ. 500. Accepts freelance material. Byline given. Submit query, ms, SASE. Nonfiction, photos: how-to articles, research articles, Clark County genealogy. Sample $3.

GENEALOGY, NW/REGIONAL HISTORY

Training & Culture Newsletter, Gildane Group, 13751 Lake City Way N.E. #105, Seattle, WA 98125-8612. Sub $59/yr org, $39/yr individual. Bimonthly newsletter with monthly bulletins.

UNSPECIFIED

The Trainmaster, PNC-National Railway Historical Society, 800 N.W. 6th Ave., Portland, OR 97209. 503-226-6747. Contact: Kristopher Lundt. Monthly newsletter. Sub $37/yr. Circ. 600. Freelance material accepted. Byline given. Acquires all rights. Query w/clips, sample chapters. Accepts nonfiction, news items, photos (B&W prints), any railroad-related items. Tip: news and stories must be related to RR (past or present) that operate in the N.W. Stories from Chapter members get first priority.

GENERAL HISTORY, TRAVEL

Trainsheet, c/o Tacoma Chapter NRHS Inc., PO Box 340, Tacoma, WA 98401-0340. 206-537-2169. Editor: Art Hamilton. 206-537-2169. Published 10 times a year. Circ. 300. Sub $17. Uses 1 ms per issue. No pay. Submit ms, SASE. Phone queries, dot matrix, photocopies OK. Nonfiction: railroad history; max 2 pgs (1,000 + wds) typed 3 1/2 wide max. Photos: 5x7, B&W; no pay.

GENERAL HISTORY, TRAVEL

Transformation Times, PO Box 425, Beavercreek, OR 97004. 503-632-7141. Editor: Connie L. Faubel. Ads: E. James Faubel. Published 10X/yr. Sub $8. Circ. 8,000. Uses freelance material. Pays money, copies on publication. Acquires 1st rights. Byline given. Submit ms, SASE. Dot matrix, photocopies, simultaneous subs, disk/modem OK. Reports in 1-2 mo; publishes in 1-6 mos. Accepts nonfiction, fiction, cartoons, interviews, photos (85 line screen & sized), articles. Topics: metaphysical, holistic, human potential, occult sciences, environmental quality, socially responsible issues, book and video reviews. No longer than 1,500 wds. Guidelines; sample $2.

ASTROLOGY/SPIRITUAL, CALENDAR/EVENTS, NEW AGE

Transonic Hacker, 1402 S.W. Upland Dr., Portland, OR 97221-2649. Editor: Eric Geislinger.

COMPUTERS, UNSPECIFIED

Transport Electronic News, 3-1610 Kebet Way, Port Coquitlam, BC V3C 5W9. 604-942-4312. Contact: Rob Robertson. Canadian trucking industry quarterly on electronics advances and uses. Query w/clips.

BUSINESS, CANADA

Travelin' Magazine, PO Box 23005, Eugene, OR 97402. 503-689-1116. Fax: 503-689-4993. Editor: Russ Heggen. Sub $17.95/yr. Circ. 10,000. Bimonthly mag using 10-20 freelance mss per issue. Reports 2-4 wks, publishes 90 days. Pays money, copies on publication. Byline given. Query w/clips. Topics: traveling in the eleven western states for adults (45-65 yrs) who travel mostly by car or RV, emphasis on backroads, unusual places. "Please read magazine and follow our style." Guidelines; sample $3.

NORTHWEST, RECREATION, TRAVEL

Trestle Creek Review, North Idaho College, 1000 W. Garden Ave., Coeur d'Alene, ID 83814. 208-769-3384. Contact: Chad Klinger.

FICTION, POETRY

The Trolley Park News, 1836 N. Emerson, Portland, OR 97217. 503-285-7936. Editor/ads: Richard Thompson. 503-285-7936. Semimonthly on historic electric railway preservation. Circ. 200. Sub w/membership $10-25. Uses 1 ms per issue. Payment: negotiable; on publication. Byline given. Rights purchased: First. Phone queries, dot matrix, photocopies, simultaneous submission, electronic OK. Reports in 1-2 mos. Nonfiction: Historic articles on

N.W., particularly OR, street and interurban railways (including where vehicles are now, tracing abandoned rights-of-way; how to restore streetcars; and memories of lines ridden). Photos: 8x10, 5x7, 3x5; B&W glossy preferred. Maps & car body plans also useful. Sample/SASE.

COLLECTING, NW/REGIONAL HISTORY, TRAVEL

Trout, PO Box 6255, Bend, OR 97708. 503-382-2327; 503-382-9177. Editor: Thomas R. Pero.

AGRICULTURE/FARMING, CONSERVATION, OUTDOOR

Truck Logger, 124 W. 8th St., North Vancouver, BC V7M 3H2. 604-985-7811. Contact: Vivian Rudd.

BUSINESS, LABOR/WORK, LUMBER

Truck World, 3 1610 Kebet Way, Port Coquitlam, BC V3C 5W9. 604-942-4312. Contact: Rob Robertson. Monthly Canadian trucking industry trade journal. Pays on publication and gives byline for 1st right on nonfiction of 200-2,000 words. Subjects: product news, photo features, truck financing and maintenance, new technologies, profiles, industry news. Uses photos. Query w/clips. Reports in 2 wks. Pay varies.

BUSINESS, CANADA

Truth on Fire (Hallelujah), PO Box 223, Postal Sta. A, Vancouver, BC V6C 2M3. 604-498-3895. Editor: Wesley H. Wakefield. Bimonthly evangelical magazine. Sub $5. Circ. 1,000-10,000. Uses freelance material. Pays $15 & up on acceptance. Byline given. Submit query w/clips. Dot matrix, photocopied, simultaneous OK. Reports in 6 wks. Publishing time varies. Accepts nonfiction, photos. Biblically oriented to evangelical & Wesleyan viewpoint. Topics: peace, anti-nuclear, racial equality & justice, religious liberty, etc. "Prefer action or solution-oriented articles; must understand evangelical viewpoint & lifestyle." Guidelines/sample.

RELIGION

Tumwater Action Committee Newsletter, 500 Tyee Dr., Tumwater, WA 98502.

PUBLIC AFFAIRS, WASHINGTON

TV Week, 401-4180 Lougheed Hwy., Burnaby, BC V5C 6A7. 604-299-2116. Weekly.

ENTERTAINMENT, LITERATURE

Two Louies Magazine, 2745 N.E. 34th Ave., Portland, OR 97212. 503-284-5391. Editor: Buck Munger. Monthly. Circ. 10,000. Accepts freelance material, news items, photos (B&W), interviews and articles. All rights acquired. Pays money on publication. Responds 2 wks; pub 6 wks. Two Louies is a music trade publication covering the original music community in Oregon. Sample.

MUSIC

Umatilla County Historical Society News, PO Box 253, Pendleton, OR 97801. Quarterly.

NW/REGIONAL HISTORY, OREGON

Umpqua Trapper, Douglas County Historical Society, 759 S.E. Kane, Roseburg, OR 97470. 503-673-4572. Contact: Jane Clarke. Quarterly historical journal for county. Sub/$10. Circ. 300. Accepts freelance material. No pay. Byline given. Nonfiction: historical relating to Douglas County or family stories. Query w/SASE. Write for back issues.

NW/REGIONAL HISTORY

Uncommon Sense, c/o The Portland Pataphysical Clinic, PO Box 40710, Portland, OR 97240-0710. Editor: Eric Blair. Ads: Jeff Dahmer. Irregularly published magazine. Circ. 250. Sub/$250/yr. No freelance material accepted. Also publishes softcover books. Back issues $2.50

HOW-TO

Universal Entity, PO Box 728, Milton, WA 98354. 206-941-0833. Editor: Ginny Huseland. Monthly newsletter.

ASTROLOGY/SPIRITUAL

Universe, Washington State University, Pullman, WA 99163-9986. Contact: Tim Steury. Glossy magazine of research and scholarship conducted at WSU. Audience is well-educated, but magazine is not solemn. Written queries are welcome, but mostly written in-house and on assignment. Payment negotiable.

SCHOLARLY/ACADEMIC, WASHINGTON

University of Portland Review, 5000 N. Portland Blvd., Portland, OR 97203. 503-283-7144. Contact: Dr. Thompson Faller. Semiannual magazine for college educated laymen. Circ. 1,000. Accepts 200 mss per year. Payment: 5 copies. Byline given. Phone queries OK. Reports in 6 mos. Publishes in 1 year. Nonfiction: to 2,000 wds on any subject. Fiction: to 2,000 wds on any subject. Poetry: any length and style. "Its purpose is to comment on the human condition and to present information on expanding knowledge in different fields. With regard to fiction, only that which makes a significant statement about the contemporary scene will be employed." Sample 50 cents.

CULTURE, EDUCATION, FICTION

University of Portland Writers, English Department, U. of Portland, 5000 N. Willamette Boulevard, Portland, OR 97203-5798.

COLLEGE/UNIVERSITY, WRITING

Upper Snake River Valley Historical Society, Box 244, Rexburg, ID 83440. 208-356-9101. Editor: Louis Clements.

NW/REGIONAL HISTORY, IDAHO

Upstream, The Literary Center, PO Box 85116, Seattle, WA 98145-1116. Editor: Ken Smith. Quarterly literary magazine. Free sub to Literary Center members, others $15. Circ. 2,000. Accepts freelance material. Byline given. Pays copies on publication. Submit query letter w/SASE. Responds 1-3 mos; publishes 3-5 mos. Accepts fiction, poetry, nonfiction articles, interviews, op/ed, plays, reviews.

LITERARY, LITERATURE, WRITING

The Urban Naturalist, Audubon Soc. of Portland, 5151 N.W. Cornell Rd., Portland, OR 97210. 503-292-6855. Editor/Ads: Mike Houck. Quarterly journal. Sub $20/yr. Circ. 1,500. Uses 46 freelance mss per issue. No pay. Byline given. Submit by assignment only. Publishes in 2 mos. Topics: Volunteer only, articles & illustrations on Portland area natural history topics. Volunteer authors and artists, decisions by entire group. Guidelines; sample $5.

CONSERVATION, ENVIRONMENT/RESOURCES, NATURAL HISTORY

Valley Magazine, Peak Media, Inc., PO Box 925, Hailey, ID 83333. 208-788-4500. Quarterly magazine. Uses freelance material. Pay starts at 10/wd on publication. Written queries preferred, mss possibly considered. SASE a must. Computer printouts must be legible. Computer disk okay (WordPerfect or ASCII only). Articles should be timeless, upscale and positive. The subject matter should focus to the Wood River Valley and surrounding areas. Feature article (about 2,000 wds) must lend itself to spectacular photography. Guidelines; sample $3 + 8.5x11 SASE.

IDAHO

The Valley Magazine, PO Box 1469, Ketchum, ID 83340. 208-788-0057. Contact: Celeste H. Earls. Ads: Kelly D. Coles. Quarterly magazine. Uses freelance material. Pay starts at 10 cents; pays on publication. Written queries preferred, mss possibly considered. SASE a must. Computer printouts must be legible. Computer disk OK (WordPerfect or ASCII only). Articles should be timeless, upscale, and positive. The subject matter should be focused on the Wood River Valley and surrounding areas. Feature articles (about 2,000 wds) must lend themselves to spectacular photography. Guidelines; sample $3 + 8.5x11 SASE.

FICTION, POETRY

The Vancouver Child, 757 Union St., Vancouver, BC V6A 2C3. 604-251-1760. Editor: Wendy Wilkins. Ads: Stephen Linley. Monthly magazine founded in 1988. Sub/ $5. Circ. 30,000. Uses freelance material. Byline given. Pays money on publication. Acquires 1st rights. Submit query letter, complete ms, SASE. Photocopy, dot matrix, disk/modem, simultaneous subs OK. Responds in 2 wks; publishes in 2 mos. Accepts fiction, cartoons, news items, nonfiction, photos (B&W, custom print, $25-35), interviews, reviews. Topics: performing arts, literature, music, etc. available to families; also educational alternatives and innovations; upbeat, purpose is to empower parents. Guidelines.

CHILDREN (BY/ABOUT), EDUCATION, FAMILY

The Vancouver Courier, 2094 W. 43rd Ave., Vancouver, BC V6M 2C9. Daily.

UNSPECIFIED

Vancouver History, Vancouver Historical Society, PO Box 3071, Vancouver, BC V6B 3X6. Quarterly.

BRITISH COLUMBIA, CANADIAN HISTORY, NW/REGIONAL HISTORY

Vancouver Magazine, Ste 300 Southeast Tower, 555 W. 12th, Vancouver, BC V5Z 4L4. 604-877-7732. Editor: Malcolm F. Parry. Mass market monthly of local entertainment & culture.

CULTURE, ENTERTAINMENT

VCC, Vancouver Community College, 100 W. 49th Ave., Vancouver, BC V5Y 2Z6. 604-324-5415.

COLLEGE/UNIVERSITY

Veda News, PO Box 802, Bandon, OR 97411. Editor: Mildred Robinson. Bimonthly.

UNSPECIFIED

Vernon Publications, 3000 Northrup Way, Ste. 200, Bellevue, WA 98004. 206-827-9900. Various business and trade periodicals.

BUSINESS, ECONOMICS

Vet's Newsletter, 700 Summer St., N.E., Salem, OR 97310-1201. 503-373-2000. Editor: Barb Nobles. Bimonthly.

MILITARY/VETS

Victory Music Review, PO Box 7515, Bonney Lake, WA 98390. 206-863-6617. Editor: Judy Grantham. Ads: Chris Lunn. Monthly. Sub/$20. Circ. 6,000. Uses freelance material. Pays copies. Phone query. Dot matrix OK. Publishes in 15-90 days. Topics: folk, jazz record reviews 100 wds; local concert reviews 150 wds. Sample $2.

CALENDAR/EVENTS, ENTERTAINMENT, MUSIC

The Video Librarian, PO Box 2725, Bremerton, WA 98310. 206-377-2231. Editor/Ads: Randy Pitman. Monthly. Sub $35. Circ. 350. Uses 1 freelance ms per issue. Pays copies on publication. Byline given. Dot matrix, photocopied OK. Reports in 2 wks. Accepts nonfiction. Free sample.

FILM/VIDEO, MEDIA/COMMUNICATIONS

Videosat News, CommTek, 5257 Fairview Ave. #110, Boise, ID 83706-1700. Editor: Tom Woolf. Monthly. Circ. 24,500.

CONSUMER, ENTERTAINMENT, FILM/VIDEO

The Village Idiot, Mother of Ashes Press, PO Box 66, Harrison, ID 83833-0066. 208-689-3738. Editor: Joe M. Singer. Magazine 3X/yr. Founded 1970. Sub/$7.50. Circ. 100. Uses freelance material. Pays in copies on publication. Acquires 1st rights. Byline given. Submit ms, SASE. Reports in 14 mos. Publishes in 4 mos. Accepts fiction, poetry, cartoons, news items, biography, nonfiction, interviews, op/ed plays, reviews, memoirs, photos (query on color), art. "This magazine is as personal an expression as any poem you will ever hope to write."

FICTION, POETRY

The Villager, PO Box 516, Wilsonville, OR 97070-0516. Editor: K. C. Swan. Monthly.

UNSPECIFIED

Vincentury, St. Vincent Hospital & Medical Center, 9205 S.W. Barnes Rd., Portland, OR 97225. Periodical for patients, relatives, employees and community.

HEALTH

Vintage Northwest, PO Box 193, Bothell, WA 98041. 206-821-2411. Editor: Lawrence T. Campbell. Ads: Jean and George Immerwahr. Semiannual magazine founded in 1980. No sub. Circ. 550 at local senior centers. Accepts freelance only from age 50+. Pays in copies on publication. Submit ms, SASE, no more than 1,000 wds. Photocopies OK. Reports in 1 wk; publishes 6-12 mos. Accepts nonfiction, fiction, poetry, illustrations, photos (returned after use). Topics: variety, seniors experiences, humorous stories or poems; no sexist language, sermonic, or political. Guidelines with SASE; sample $2.75.

FICTION, POETRY, SENIOR CITIZENS

Virtue, PO Box 850, Sisters, OR 97759. 503-549-8261. Editor: Marlee Alex. Ads: Debbie Mitchell. Bimonthly non-denominational Christian women's magazine. Circ. 150,000; sub $16.95. Uses freelance material. Byline given. Acquires 1st rights. Query w/SASE. Dot matrix, photocopies OK. Responds in 6-8 wks. Accepts fiction, poetry, cartoons, nonfiction, interviews, articles. Guidelines; for sample send 9x12 SASE, 5 1st Class stamps.

RELIGION, WOMEN

Visions, Oregon Graduate Center, 19600 N.W. Von Neumann Dr., Beaverton, OR 97006. 503-690-1121. FAX 503-690-1029. Editor: Steve Dodge. Ads: Norman Elder. Quarterly magazine. Free. Circ. 15,000. Uses 2 freelance mss per issue. Pays money on acceptance. Acquires at least 1st rights. Byline given. Submit query w/clips, 9x12 SASE. Dot matrix, photocopied, simultaneous, computer disk OK. Reports in 2-4 wks. Publishes 1-4 mos. Accepts nonfiction, photos, cartoons. Topics: science and technology, from computer advances and high technology to biology and environment. Length: 1,000-3,000 wds. Science briefs (250 wds) with emphasis on the unusual. Personality profiles of scientists (1,000 wds). Photos: photomicrographs, B&W and color, needed; photos that reveal the unusual or relatively unseen, $50-350. "Science with an emphasis on people and non-technical explanations of technology especially welcome. Would like to see clips from experienced N.W. writers willing to work on assignment." Guidelines & free sample for 9x12 SASE.

COMPUTERS, ENVIRONMENT/RESOURCES, SCIENCE

The Voice, Oregon Advocates for the Arts, 707 13th St. S.E. #275, Salem, OR 97301-4027. Contact: Elaine K. Young. Irregular newsletter. Accepts freelance material.

ARTS

The Voice, Ore-Ida Foods, PO Box 10, Boise, ID 83707. Editor: Susan C. Gerhart. Company journal published 3 x per year for employees, management and business contacts. Circ. 6,000.

ARTS, CULTURE, OREGON

WAPITI, PO Box 8249, Missoula, MT 59807-8249. 406-523-4565. Newsletter. Accepts material from members only.

ANIMALS, CONSERVATION, OUTDOOR

Warner Pacific College Art & Literature Magazine, Warner Pacific College, 2219 S.E. 68th Ave., Portland, OR 97215. College literary magazine. SASE for guidelines.

COLLEGE/UNIVERSITY, FICTION, OREGON

Warren Publishing House, Totline Books, PO Box 2250, Everett, WA 98203. 206-355-7007. Editor: Gayle Bittinger. Ads: Susan Sexton. Bimonthly newsletter, founded 1980. Sub $24/yr. Circ. 8,500. Uses freelance material. Byline given. Pays money on acceptance. Acquires all rights. Query w/SASE. Responds in 6 wks; publishes in 1 yr. Accepts nonfiction, poetry, articles, activity ideas. Topics: pre-school children songs, activity ideas; sketches for clarification encouraged. Guidelines, catalog.

CHILDREN (BY/ABOUT), EDUCATION, MUSIC

The Washboard, Washington State Folklife Council, 11507 N.E. 104th St., Kirkland, WA 98033. 206-586-8252.

CRAFTS/HOBBIES, CULTURE, AMERICAN HISTORY

Washington Business, PO Box 658, 1414 S. Cherr St., Olympia, WA 98507. 206-943-1600. Contact: Bill Carter. Newsletter published semi-monthly. Circ. 3,800. Available only to members. Founded 1962. News of state government and the legislature which may impact the Washington business community.
BUSINESS, GOVERNMENT

Washington Cattleman, Box 2027, Wenatchee, WA 98801. 509-662-5167. Monthly.
AGRICULTURE/FARMING, ANIMALS, BUSINESS

Washington CEO, 2505 2nd Ave., 602, Seattle, WA 98121-1426. 206-441-8415; Fax 206-441-8325. Editor: Kevin Dwyer. Founded 1989. Deals with the major personalities, trends, events, and ideas shaping the current and future direction of the state's economy. Sub/$20. Copy $3. Circ. 18,500.
BUSINESS

Washington Clubwoman, 11404 N.E. 97th St., Vancouver, WA 98662. Monthly.
WOMEN

Washington Farmer Stockman, 211 Review Building, Spokane, WA 99210. 509-455-7057. Semimonthly ag business publication.
AGRICULTURE/FARMING, BUSINESS, WASHINGTON

Washington Fishing Holes, PO Box 32, Sedro Woolley, WA 98284. Editor/Ads: Brad Stracener. Monthly. Sub $15/yr. Circ. 10,000. Uses 45 freelance mss per issue. Pays money on publication. Acquires 1st rights. Byline given. Submit query w/clips, SASE. Photocopied, electronic subs OK. Accepts nonfiction, photos. Guidelines, sample.
OUTDOOR, RECREATION, SPORTS

Washington Food Dealer Magazine, 480 E. 19th St., Tacoma, WA 98421-1501. 206-522-4474. Editor/Ads: Arden D. Gremmert. Grocery trade magazine published 11 times per year. Sub $20/yr. Circ. 4,000. Accepts freelance material. Pays in copies. Acquires 1st rights. Byline given. Query w/clips, SASE, phone query on ideas. Dot matrix, photocopies, simultaneous, computer disk OK. Reports in 1 mo. Publishing time varies. Accepts nonfiction, grocery related only, particularly focusing on Northwest. Length variable. Photos B&W or color, originals, (no-pre-screened), no payment. Sample free.
BUSINESS, FOOD/COOKING, TRADE/ASSOCIATIONS

The Washington Horse, PO Box 88258, Seattle, WA 98188. 206-226-2620. Editor: Joe LaDuca/Bruce Batson. Ads: Joe LaDuca at 206-772-2381. Monthly periodical on thoroughbred horse racing & breeding. Circ. 3,400. Sub $30/yr. Uses 2 mss per issue. Pays money on publication. Byline given. Assignment only. Photocopies OK. Nonfiction, B&W photos. Sample/free.
ANIMALS, BUSINESS, SPORTS

Washington Library News, Washington State Library AJ-11, Olympia, WA 98504.
REFERENCE/LIBRARY

Washington Newspaper, 3838 Stone Way North, Seattle, WA 98103. 206-643-3838. Monthly.
BUSINESS, PUBLISHING/PRINTING

Washington State Bar News, 500 Westin Building, 2001 Sixth Ave., Seattle, WA 98121-2599. 206-727-8215. Contact: Managing Editor. Ads: Jack Young. Monthly magazine, founded 1947. Sub/$24. Circ. 18,000. Uses freelance material from attorneys only. Byline given. Acquires all rights. Submit outline, synopsis. Disk required if accepted. Accepts news items, photos (contact managing editor), articles, reviews.
LAW

Washington State Migrant Ed News, c/o Heritage College, 3240 Fort Rd., Toppenish, WA 98948. Editor: Larry Ashby. Monthly.
CHICANO/CHICANA, EDUCATION, WASHINGTON

Washington Stylist and Salon, PO Box 1117, Portland, OR 97207. 503-226-2461. Editor: David Porter. Monthly trade magazine. Circ. 36,000. Free to licensed salons, others $10. Accepts freelance material. Pays only when assigned, on publication. Byline given. Query w/SASE. Accepts nonfiction, 500750 wds w/photos. Topics: anything to do with hair and beauty for the industry, professional beauty salons, schools and supply houses. Photos: B&W, $5, or $15-20 for cover. Needs stringers in OR/WA. Query first. "I prefer to give a writer the slant I want, and I would like to talk to people to give them hints on things Id like covered in their area."
BUSINESS, FASHION

Washington Thoroughbred, P. O. Box 88258, Seattle, WA 98138. 206-226-2620. Editor: Sue Van Dyke. Ads: Joe LaDuca. Monthly. Sub $40/yr. Uses one freelance article per issue. Assignment only. Pays money on publication. Byline given. Photocopy OK. Reports in 1 wk. Publishes in 2-4 mos. Accepts nonfiction, fiction: thoroughbred horse racing and breeding, local angle preferred. Photos: B&W, color acceptable with good lighting.
ANIMALS, SPORTS

The Washington Trooper, Grimm Press & Publishing Co., PO Box 1523, Longview, WA 98632-0144. 206-577-8598. Editor: Bruce Grimm. Quarterly. Accepts freelance material. Payment: $5-75 on publication. Query w/SASE. Nonfiction: Wants mss on legislation, traffic and highway safety for members of WA State Patrol Troopers Association as well as for state legislators, educators, court officials and like-minded folks in the state of WA. 500-3,500 wds. "Contributors must be familiar with goals and objectives of the WA State Patrol and with law enforcement in general in the Pacific N.W."
PUBLIC AFFAIRS, WASHINGTON

Washington Water News, Washington State University, Pullman, WA 99164.
AGRICULTURE/FARMING, ENVIRONMENT/RESOURCES, PUBLIC AFFAIRS

Washington Wildfire, PO Box 45187, Seattle, WA 98145-0187. 206-633-1992. Editor: Nancy Boulton.
UNSPECIFIED

WashPIRG Reports, 340 15th Ave. E. #350, Seattle, WA 98112. 206-322-9064. Editor: Kathleen Krushas. Published quarterly on environmental and consumer issues. Circ. 30,000. Sub $15/mbr. Uses freelance material. Query letter, SASE, phone. Dot matrix, photocopies, simultaneous subs OK. Accepts nonfiction. Topics: hazardous waste, environment, consumer issues, accountable government. Sample free.
CONSUMER, ENVIRONMENT/RESOURCES, PUBLIC AFFAIRS

Waterlines Magazine, 4111 Stone Way N., Seattle, WA 98103-8013. Contact: Kay Walsh.
UNSPECIFIED

Watermark, Oregon State Library, State Library Building, Salem, OR 97310. Monthly.
BOOK ARTS/BOOKS, REFERENCE/LIBRARY

The Watershed Sentinel, Box 105, Whaletown, BC VOP 1Z0. 604-935-6992. Contact: Delores Broten. Environmental news for Georgia Strait from Cortes Island. Circ. 1000. Published 6 times per year. Sub $10. Submissions welcome "on controversial environmental matters, but reserves the right to edit for clarity, brevity, legality, and taste." Pays copies on publication. Byline given. Query by phone. Disk/modem OK. Responds 1 mo; publishes 1 mo. Accepts fiction, poetry, cartoons, news items, photos (B&W), interviews, and articles. Sample $10.
ENVIRONMENT/RESOURCES, BRITISH COLUMBIA, FORESTRY

Waves, PO Box 47111, c/o Eridani Prod, Seattle, WA 98146-7111. 206-325-8037.
UNSPECIFIED

Wayside Journal, Longfellow's, PO Box 269, Goldendale, WA 98620-0269. 206-773-4750. Editors: John & Patricia Longfellow. Monthly, $10/12 issues.
UNSPECIFIED

WCCF World Chess, 8530 Steilacoom Rd. S.E. #99, Lacey, WA 98503-1793. Editor: Robert A. Karch. Chess correspondence directory; $15.
ENTERTAINMENT

We Alaskans, The Anchorage Daily News, 1001 Northway Dr., Anchorage, AK 99514-9001. 907-257-4318. Editor: George Bryson. Ads: Bill Megivern. Weekly newspaper magazine, founded 1980. Circ. 105,000. Uses freelance material. Byline given. Pays money on publication. Acquires 1st rights. Submit complete ms, phone. Responds in 1 mo; publishes in 1 mo. Interested in dramatic nonfiction, biography, interviews, op/ed articles, memoirs, fiction. Photos: $100 cover, $50 color slides, $25 B&W. Topics: Alaska and Alaskans. Guidelines.
ALASKA

We Proceeded On, Lewis/Clark Trail Heritage Foundation, 5054 S.W. 26th Pl., Portland, OR 97201. Editor: Robert E. Lange. Quarterly.
AMERICAN HISTORY

Welcome to Planet Earth, Great Bear Publishers, PO Box 5164, Eugene, OR 97405. Editor: Mark Lerner. Monthly.
ENVIRONMENT/RESOURCES, UNSPECIFIED

West Coast Review, Department of English, Simon Fraser University, Burnaby, BC V5A 1S6. 604-291-4287. Editor: Tom Martin. Quarterly. Sub/$12. Circ. 700. Uses 20 mss per issue. Payment: $10-15/pg for unsolicited mss, on acceptance. Byline given. Rights purchased: First. Submit ms, SASE. Dot matrix OK. Reports in 2 mos. Nonfiction, fiction, and poetry. No restriction on theme, style. Read at least 1 issue before submitting (sample copy of current issue available for $3.50). American contributors enclose sufficient Canadian postage or IRC. Guidelines; sample $2.50.
COLLEGE/UNIVERSITY, FICTION, POETRY

West Side, Box 5027, Salem, OR 97304. 503-362-8987. Editor/Ads: Tim Hinshaw. Monthly. Sub $6. Circ. 7,500. Uses 3 freelance mss per issue. Requires journalism/photo experience. Pays money, copies on publication. Acquires 1st rights. Byline given. Phone query. Dot matrix, photocopied OK. Reports in 1 wk. Accepts nonfiction, photos. Free sample.
PHOTOGRAPHY

West Wind Review, English Department, Southern Oregon State College, Ashland, OR 97520. 503-552-6518. Annual journal/contest. Subs $10-12. Uses freelance material. Byline given. Pays copies. Submit ms, SASE. Photocopy, dot matrix subs OK. Responds in 2 wks., publishes in 6 mos. Accepts fiction, poetry, photos (B&W, suited for small reproduction), plays. Guidelines.
COLLEGE/UNIVERSITY, FICTION, POETRY

Western Banker Magazine, Western Banker Publications, 1100 N. Cole Rd., Boise, ID 83704-8644. Monthly. Circ. 5,500.
BUSINESS

Western Business, PO Box 31678, Billings, MT 59107-1678. 406-252-4788. Editor: James Strauss. Monthly. In-depth analysis and reporting of business news in the intermountain north. Circ. 26,000. Founded 1983. Sub/$18, $2 copy.
BUSINESS

Western Cascade Tree Fruit Association Quarterly, 9210 131st N.E., Lake Stevens, WA 98258.
AGRICULTURE/FARMING, BUSINESS

Western Engines, PO Box 192, Woodburn, OR 97071. Monthly.
UNSPECIFIED

Western Farmer-Stockman Magazines, PO Box 2160, Spokane, WA 99210-1615. 509-459-5377. Contact: E.W. Ramsey. Monthly magazines. Sub/$9. Circ. 79,200. Infrequently uses freelance material. Byline given. Query w/SASE. Responds in 1 mo. Topics: agriculture-related.
AGRICULTURE/FARMING

Western Fisheries, Ste. 202-1132 Hamilton St., Vancouver, BC V6B 2S2. 604-687-1581. Attn: Henry L. Frew.
BUSINESS, CONSERVATION, FISHING

Western Genesis, Cascade County Historical Society, 1400 First Ave. N., Great Falls, MT 59401-3299. 406-452-3462. Contact: Cindy Kittredge. Quarterly newsletter. Sub/$15. Circ. 700. Occasionally uses freelance material. Byline given. No pay. Acquires all rights. Submit query, SASE. Response and publication time vary. Accepts poetry, cartoons, news items, biography, nonfiction, photos, interviews, articles, reviews, memoirs. Sample $1.50.
NW/REGIONAL HISTORY, MONTANA

Western Investor, Willamette Publishing, Inc., 400 S.W. 6th, Ste. 1115, Portland, OR 97204. Contact: Shannon P. Pratt. Quarterly.
BUSINESS

Western Journal of Black Studies, Washington State University Press, Pullman, WA 99164-5910. 509-335-3518. Quarterly. Sub $15.
BLACK, HISTORY, SOCIOLOGY

Western Living, 504 Davie St., Vancouver, BC V6B 2G4. 604-669-7525. Editor: Andrew Scott. Monthly of western Canadian living, with emphasis on home design. Sub free. Accepts freelance material. Pay averages 30 cents/wd on acceptance. Acquires 1st rights. Query first with outline, SASE. Accepts nonfiction, fiction, poetry. Topics: cuisine, fashion, recreation, the arts, foreign and local travel, architecture and interior design; prefers a regional Western angle. Photos with story: $25-200, B&W 8x10 glossies preferred; prefer 2 1/4 or 4x5 slides. Guidelines.
ARCHITECTURE, BRITISH COLUMBIA, RECREATION

Western Mills Today, PO Box 610, Edmonds, WA 98020. 206-778-3388. Contact: John Nederlee. Highly specialized trade publication. Monthly. Circ. 10,000. Uses freelance material by assignment only. Byline given. Pays money on publication. Acquires all rights. Query w/SASE. Disk/modem, dot matrix OK. Responds almost immediately, publishes in 1-3 months. Topics: mill operations profiles, heavy technical emphasis. Guidelines.
BUSINESS, LUMBER

Western Newsletter, The Book Shop, 908 Main St., Boise, ID 83702. Editors: Jean Wilson & Susan Matthews. Published 3 times a year. Circ. 350.
LITERARY, LITERATURE

Western Remodeler Magazine, PO Box 2022, Lake Oswego, OR 97035. 503-635-7642. Contact: Clark Schenkenberger. A monthly magazine targeted to the remodeling construction industry and related professions and trades. Circ. 11,500. Accepts freelance material. Byline given. Pays money on publication. Acquires first rights. Submit query letter w/SASE or query by phone. Responds 30 days. Publishes 60 days. Accepts photos (B&W), articles aimed at remodeling and residential construction industry.
BUSINESS, TRADE/ASSOCIATIONS

Westgate Press, 15050 S.W. Koll Pkwy #G-2, Beaverton, OR 97006. 503-646-0820. Editor: Dr. Pam Munter. Quarterly newsletter. Sub/$10. Circ. 250. Not a freelance market. Sample $2.50.
PSYCHOLOGY

Westwind, Northwest Science Fiction Society, PO Box

24207, Seattle, WA 98124. Editor: Jodi Scanlon. Publishes a monthly newsletter. Circ. 350. Sub/$15. Freelance material accepted. Byline given; pays copies on publication. Acquires first or second rights. SASE, query by phone, complete ms. Photocopy, disk/modem, dot matrix OK. Responds in 3 months; publishes in 3 months. Publishes fiction, poetry, interviews, articles, science illustrations and articles. "Fresh and new is our guidelines. Quality fiction with a science bent is preferred." Back issues $1.
FANTASY/SCI FI, FICTION, SCIENCE

Westworld Magazine, Canada Wide Magazines, 401-4180 Lougheed Hwy., Burnaby, BC V5C 6A7. 604-299-7311. Editor: Robin Roberts. Ads: Pat Meyers. Periodicals published quarterly. Circ. 420,000. Not a freelance market.
CANADA

Whalesong Journal, PO Box 39, Cannon Beach, OR 97110.
UNSPECIFIED

What's Happening, 1251 Lincoln, Eugene, OR 97401. 503-484-0519. Editor: Lois Wadsworth. Weekly tabloid, founded 1982. Sub $35/6 mos. Circ. 25,000. Uses freelance material. Byline given. Pays 37 cents wd, on publication. Acquires 1st rights. Submit query letter, clips, complete ms, phone. Dot matrix, photocopy, simultaneous, disk/modem subs OK. Accepts fiction, poetry, cartoons, news items, interviews, op/ed, articles, reviews, photos (B&W prints). Topics: arts, politics, environment, social, cultural with alternative/progressive focus. Guidelines; sample $1.
ARTS, ENVIRONMENT/RESOURCES, PUBLIC AFFAIRS

Wheat Life, 109 East First, Ritzville, WA 99169. 509-659-0610. Editor/Ads: Sherrye Wyatt Phillips. Publishes 11 issues per year. Sub $12/yr. Circ. 14,000. Uses 2 freelance mss per year. Pays in copies. Acquires 1st rights. Byline given. Submit ms, SASE. Nonfiction only: agriculture wheat & barley, but with warmth. Recipes/cooking profiles, or features using barley or wheat in a unique way. B&W prints. Sample 50 cents.
AGRICULTURE/FARMING, FOOD/COOKING

White Ribbon Review, Oregon Women Temperance Union, 4557 Sean St., Eugene, OR 97402. 503-688-2152. Bimonthly newsletter. Circ. 350; sub $5/yr. Not a freelance market.
RELIGION, WOMEN

Whitefish, PO Box 152, Whitefish, MT 59937. 800-554-5257. Magazine.
UNSPECIFIED

Whitehall Ledger, 15 W. Legion, Whitehall, MT 59759.
UNSPECIFIED

Whole Air, PO Box 98786, Tacoma, WA 98498-0786. 206-588-1743. Editor: Bruce Williams. Periodical on hang gliding. Uses 2-3 freelance mss per issue. Payment: $3 an inch, 1 month after publication. Byline given. Rights purchased: First. Submit ms, SASE. Phone queries, dot matrix, simultaneous subs OK. Reports in 2-3 wks. Publishes in 1-3 mos. Nonfiction: 1,500-3,500 wds. Query on fiction, poetry, columns. Photos: B&W prints, color slides, prints. Guidelines; sample $2.
AVIATION, RECREATION, SPORTS

Whole Self, PO Box 513, Grants Pass, OR 97526-0043. 503-474-7700. Contact: Michael Mirdad, editor. Bimonthly magazine of holistic living.
HEALTH, NEW AGE

Wild Oregon, Oregon Natural Resources Council, 522 S.W. Fifth, Ste. 1050, Portland, OR 97214. 503-223-9001. Editor: Scott Greacen. Quarterly journal. Founded 1975. Sub $15. Circ. 6,500. Seldom uses freelance material. Byline given. Pays copies, acquires all rights. Query w/SASE. Accepts nonfiction, photos (B&W, no payment).
CONSERVATION, ENVIRONMENT/RESOURCES, OREGON

Wildfire, PO Box 148-mp, Tum Tum, WA 99034. Magazine.
UNSPECIFIED

Wildfire, Bear Tribe Medicine Society, PO Box 9167, Spokane, WA 99209. 509-326-6561. Editor: Matthew Ryan. Ads: Joseph LaZenka. Quarterly magazine. Sub $10. Circ. 10,000. Uses freelance material. Pays money. Acquires 1st rights. Submit ms/SASE. Photocopied Apple/Mac computer disk OK. Accepts nonfiction, fiction, poetry, photos, cartoons. Topics: New Age, permaculture, Native American, philosophy, UFOs. Tip: No sensationalism. Guidelines; sample $2.95.
ASTROLOGY/SPIRITUAL, ENVIRONMENT/RESOURCES, NATIVE AMERICAN

Wildlife Safari Game Search Newsletter, Safari Game Search Foundation, PO Box 1600, Winston, OR 97496. 503-679-6761. Editor: Sally Lawson.
ANIMALS

The Willamette Jrl of the Liberal Arts, Willamette University D-180, 900 State St., Salem, OR 97301. 503-370-6272. Editor: Lane McGaughy. Ads: Elsa Struble. Sub $5/issue. Circ. 700. Journal published 1-2 times a year. Uses freelance material. Pays in copies. Acquires all rights. Byline given. Submit ms, SASE. Photocopied, computer disk OK. Accepts nonfiction, fiction, poetry, photos. Topics: any scholarly essays in the liberal arts. Guidelines; sample $3.75.
COLLEGE/UNIVERSITY, SCHOLARLY/ACADEMIC

Willamette Law Review, College of Law, Willamette University, Salem, OR 97301. 503-370-6300. Quarterly journal. Sub $22/yr. Circ. 850.
LAW

The Willamette Writer, 9045 S.W. Barbur Blvd. #5A, Portland, OR 97219. 503-452-1592. Editor: Linda Stirling-Wanner. Monthly newsletter for the membership of Willamette Writers. Circ. 1500. Sub w/membership. Not a freelance market.
TRADE/ASSOCIATIONS, PUBLISHING/PRINTING, WRITING

Willow Springs, Eastern Washington University, MS #25, Cheney, WA 99004. 509-458-6429. Editor: Nance Van Winckel. Sub $8. Circ. 1,000. Uses freelance material. Pays money, copies on publication. Acquires all rights. Byline given. Submit ms, SASE. Photocopied OK. Does not accept mss May 15-Sept 15. Reports in 1-2 mos. Publishes in 1 yr. Accepts nonfiction, fiction, fine poetry, photos (B&W or slides), interviews, reviews. Guidelines; sample $4.50.
FICTION, LITERARY, POETRY

Wind Row, English Dept., Washington State University, Pullman, WA 99164. 509-335-4832. Annual magazine. Sub $3.50. Circ. 500. Uses freelance material only from current students or alumni. Byline given. Pays copies. Submit complete ms. Dot matrix, photocopy subs OK. Responds in 4 mos; publishes in 6-12 mos. Accepts fiction, poetry, cartoons, articles, photos, reviews, memoirs. ID number must accompany submission. Sample $3.50.
COLLEGE/UNIVERSITY

The Wire Harp - SFCC, Communications Bldg. 5, MS 3050, W. 3410 Fort George Wright Dr., Spokane, WA 99204. 509-459-3594. Contact: Almut McAuley. Annual magazine. Circ. 1500. Pays copies. Submit query, complete ms, SASE. Photocopies, phone queries OK. Responds in 4 wks. Accepts fiction, poetry, cartoons, nonfiction, photos, interviews, articles, B&W art. For guidelines or sample, send postage.
ARTS, LITERARY, PHOTOGRAPHY

Wise Buys, 511 N.W. 74th St., Vancouver, WA 98665-8414. Editor: Pat Stenback.
CONSUMER

WLA Highlights, Washington Library Association, 1232-143rd Ave. S.E., Bellevue, WA 98007.
REFERENCE/LIBRARY

Woman To Woman Magazine, 704 Clarkson St., New Westminster, BC V3M 1E2. 604-540-8448. Editor: Anne Brennan. Ads: Rosemarie Aiken. Monthly tabloid. Circ. 40,000. Sub $27/GST. 100% freelance. Byline given. Pays a flat fee (negotiable, based on length, complexity, skill) 30 days after publication. Acquires 1st North American rights in English and French. Copyright reverts to author in 60 days. Query w/SASE; response time varies. Accepts news items, biography, interviews, articles. Interested in issues of importance to B.C. women: business, health, economics, beauty, food. Some columns generated in-house. "Readers like profiles, whether the subject is well-known or not."
FASHION, FOOD/COOKING, WOMEN

Women's Work, 603 Avenue A, Snohomish, WA 98290. 206-249-6993. Editor & Ads: Andrea Damm. Monthly journal. Sub $5/6 months, $9 per year. Circ. 500 Freelance material accepted. Byline given. Payment on publication. Pays in copies. First rights acquired. Query by letter, SASE. Responds in 6-8 weeks, publishes in 2-3 issues. Accepts fiction, poetry, biography, nonfiction, interviews, op/ed, articles, news items and reviews. Guidelines. Back issues $1.50 ea. Sample issues: $2. "Serves as a conduit for the exploration of the traditional and modern definitions and expressions of 'women's work.'"
CULTURE, LABOR/WORK, WOMEN

Women's Yellow Pages, 8835 S.W. Canyon Ln., #304, Portland, OR 97225-3453. 503-297-8040. Editor: Dianne Perry. Ads: Brenda Fay. Annual business and professional women's directory with edition for Portland. Circ. 25,000. $5/copy. Uses 10 mss per issue. Payment: Copies on publication. Byline given. Query w/SASE. Phone queries, photocopies OK. Reports in 4-6 wks. Publishes in up to a year. Nonfiction, 1-6 pgs, typed ds. Women in bus. or professions, and related women's issues. For guidelines and back issues, send SASE.
COMMUNITY, WOMEN, TRADE/ASSOCIATIONS

Wood Design Focus, World Forestry Center, 4033 S.W. Canyon Rd., Portland, OR 97221. 503-737-4212; 503-228-1367. Contact: Robert Leichti, Editor. Ad contact: Jennifer McBlaine. Quarterly newsletter. Sub/$25 year US, $40 International sub. per year. Circ. 1200. Uses freelance material. Byline given. Pays cash. Acquires no rights. Query by phone or letter, dot matrix, photocopies OK. Reports in 1 week. Publishes in 4-6 months. "Engineering design of wooden structures." Guidelines; sample $7.00.
TECHNICAL

Woodburn Drag Script, 7730 State Hwy. 214 N.E., Woodburn, OR 97071.
RECREATION, SPORTS

Word Works, PO Box 2206 MPO, Vancouver, BC V6B 3W2. Quarterly writers group newsletter. Circ. 900, subs. $35/yr. Uses freelance material. Byline given, pays copies. Submit query, synopsis, outline, SASE. Photocopy, dot matrix, simultaneous subs OK. Responds in 3 mos; publishes in 3-6 mos. Accepts cartoons, nonfiction, photos, interviews, articles. Articles on computers, writers' organizations, political issues affecting writers. "We prefer to publish member-written material, but will consider other submissions." Free sample.
WRITING

Wordworks, Federation of BC Writers, PO Box 2206, Main PO, Vancouver, BC V6B 3W2. 604-683-2057. Contact: Corey Van't Haff. Quarterly newsletter, free with membership. Circ. 500+. No unsolicited submissions. Accepts freelance material; byline given. Pays money on acceptance. Acquires 1st rights. Query letter, assignment only. Photocopies, disks, phone queries OK. Responds in 3 months; publishes in 6 weeks. Accepts nonfiction, interviews, and articles.
WRITING

Writers, Oregon Association of Christian Writers, 1625 S.W. 87th Ave, Portland, OR 97225. 503-297-2987. Contact: Tom Luther, Managing Editor. Quarterly newsletter for the members of Oregon Association of Christian Writers. Sub $25 w/annual membership. Circ. 400. Articles by assignment only.
WRITING

Writers Information Network, Professional Assn for Christian Writers, PO Box 11337, Bainbridge Island, WA 98110. 206-842-9103. Contact: Elaine Wright Colvin. Bimonthly newsletter of The Professional Association for Christian Writers. Founded 1983. Sub/$15. Circ. 600+. Uses freelance material. Byline given. Query letter, complete ms, SASE. Accepts news items, articles, reviews. Topics: writing helps, tips, connections, how-to advice, announcements, info on religious publishers. Sample free w/ SASE.
BOOK ARTS/BOOKS, RELIGION, WRITING

Writers' Open Forum, PO Box 516, Tracyton, WA 98393. Contact: Sandra E. Haven. Bimonthly designed as an idea and critique exchange for writers. Sub $14/yr. Pays $5 plus 2 copies on acceptance for 1st rights for short stories and articles. Byline given. No poetry. Readers requested to send in critiques on those mss published. Critiques are collected (some published) and redirected to authors. Also pays in copies for tips on writing (up to 300 wds). Submit ms w/ SASE (2,000 wds max) and brief bio. Photocopies OK. Accepts material on any subject or genre (except no slice of life, violence, graphic sex, or experimental formats). No simultaneous subs. Guidelines w/SASE; sample issue $3.
FICTION, WRITING

Writing Magazine, Box 69609, Sta. K, Vancouver, BC V5K 4W7. 604-738-2032. Editor: Colin Browne. Published 3 times a yr. Circ. 650. Accepts freelance submissions. Pays money and subscription. Submit several poems, a long poem, 1-2 stories, a chapter, SASE. Photocopied OK. Reports in 2 mos. Accepts fiction, poetry. Sample $3.
FICTION, POETRY, WRITING

The Written ARTS, 506 2nd Ave. #1115, Seattle, WA 98104-2322. 206-344-7580. Editor: Deborah Moulton. Bi-annual literary magazine of the King County Arts Commission. Open to King County residents. Uses 30 mss per issue. Byline given. Pays modest honorarium. Rights revert to author on publication. Query w/SASE. Nonfiction, fiction, poetry. Submit up to 5 poems and/or 3,000 wds, unbound, without covers. Do not include name or acknowledgments on samples; cover letter to include titles and first lines of submission and short author's bio. Write for current deadlines. Guidelines, sample.
FICTION, LITERARY, POETRY

WSEO Dispatch, Washington State Energy Office, 400 E. Union, 1st Floor, ER-11, Olympia, WA 98504. Editor: Linda Waring. Bimonthly.
GOVERNMENT, WASHINGTON

Yakima Valley Genealogical Soc. Bulletin, PO Box 445, Yakima, WA 98907. 509-248-1328. Editor: Ellen Brzoska. Quarterly journal. Sub $11/yr. Uses freelance material. No pay. Submit ms, SASE. Photocopied, computer disk OK. Accepts articles related to family history. Sample.
GENEALOGY, WASHINGTON

Yinka Dene Language Institute, PO Bag 7000, Vanderhoof, BC V0J 3A0. 604-567-9236. Contact: Linden A. Pinay. Publishes a newsletter and distributes board games and audio-visual materials. Educational organization. Newsletter published semi-monthly. Sub $20/year. Circ. 3000. Freelance material and unsolicited submissions not accepted. Query by letter or phone. Responds in 7 days. Accepts fiction, news items, biography, nonfiction, photos, interviews, op/ed, articles, reviews, and memoirs. Catalog; back issues free.
LANGUAGE(S)

YIPE, Washington Poets Association, Box 71213, Rainier, OR 97048. Editor: Carolyn Norred.
POETRY

Yokoi A. Quarterly Journal of the Arts, PO Box 726, Bozeman, MT 59771. 406-587-8947. Contact: Marjorie Smith. Quarterly magazine. Sub $20/yr. Circ. 600+. Uses freelance material. Byline given. Pays copies on publication. Acquires 1st or 2nd rights. Submit complete ms, SASE. Photocopy, dot matrix, simultaneous subs OK. Accepts fiction, poetry, cartoons, op/ed, reviews, essays on the Montana arts scene. Guidelines; sample $6.
ARTS, LITERARY, MONTANA

Young Voices, PO Box 2321, Olympia, WA 98507. 206-357-4683. Editor: Steve Charak. Bimonthly magazine. Founded 1988. Sub $15/yr. Circ. 1,000. Uses freelance material from elementary and middle school age children. Byline given. Acquires 1st rights. Submit complete ms, SASE. Responds in 3 mos; publishes in 3 mos. Accepts fiction, poetry, cartoons, nonfiction, interviews, articles, plays, reviews. Guidelines; sample $3.
CHILDREN (BY/ABOUT), FICTION, POETRY

Your Public Schools, Superintendent of Public Instruction, Old Capitol Bldg. FG-11, Olympia, WA 98504. Periodical news of/for Washington public schools.
EDUCATION

Zap News, Box 1994, Eugene, OR 97440.
UNSPECIFIED

Zeitgeist Magazine, PO Box 1006, Kalispell, MT 59903. 406-257-2663. Editor & ads: Steve Slack. Quarterly magazine. Sub $10/4 issues. Circ. 70. Accepts freelance material. Byline given. Pays copies on publication. First rights acquired. Send complete ms, SASE. Photocopy, dot matrix, simultaneous subs all OK. Replies in 6-10 weeks; publishes in 3-9 months. Accepts poetry, cartoons, nonfiction, photos (B&W, 8x10 max), op/ed, articles, reviews, open to other categories. "We tend toward provocative 'in your face' work. We favor strong imagery and material that makes one think." Guidelines; back issues $3.
POETRY, MONTANA, ENTERTAINMENT

Newspapers

Aberdeen Daily World, 315 S. Michigan, PO Box 269, Aberdeen, WA 98520. 206-532-4000. Daily. Also publishes Harbor Country.
COMMUNITY

Advance, 7267 Pioneer Ave., Agassiz, BC V0M 1A0. Contact: Helen Parker. Weekly.
COMMUNITY

Advocate, PO Box 327, Sprague, WA 99032. 509-257-2311. Weekly.
COMMUNITY

Advocate, Mt. Hood Community College, 26000 S.E. Stark, Gresham, OR 97030. 503-667-7253. Student newspaper.
COLLEGE/UNIVERSITY

Agri-Times Northwest, Box 189, Pendleton, OR 97801. 503-276-7845. Editor: Virgil Rupp. Weekly, Eastern WA, OR, ID. Uses freelance material. Pays 75 cents/col inch on publication. Photos $5-10. Submit phone query. Responds in 1 wk; publishes in 1 mo. Topics: farmers and agribusiness, ag-related community fairs and festivals in eastern OR, WA, & ID. Accepts cartoons, nonfiction, and photos. Newspaper style, max. 3 ds pages. Guidelines; sample 50 cents.
AGRICULTURE/FARMING

Alaska Highway Daily News, 9916 98th St., Fort St. John, BC V1J 3T8. 604-785-5631. Contact: Lee Brdish. Ads: Cindy Noble. Daily.
COMMUNITY

Alaska Journal of Commerce, 3710 Woodland Dr., #2100, Anchorage, AK 99517. 907-272-7500. Editor: S J. Suddock. Ads: L. Brown. Weekly business newspaper. Sub $49. Circ. 5,000. Uses 1-3 freelance mss per issue. Payment on publication, rates vary. Acquires 1st rights. Byline given. Submit ms by assignment only; query w/SASE. Photocopied, computer disk w/hard copy OK. Reports in 2 wks. Publishing time varies. Accepts nonfiction, cartoons. Photos: B&W or color print. Some travel features. "Press releases welcome." Sample.
ALASKA, BUSINESS, ECONOMICS

Albany Democrat-Herald, 138 Sixth Ave. S.W., Albany, OR 97321. 503-926-2211; Fax 503-926-5298. Editor: Hasso Hering. Ads: Clark Gallagher. Circ. 22,500. Sub/ $7.50. Founded 1865. Daily.
COMMUNITY

Albany Democratic-Herald, Box 130, Albany, OR 97321. 503-926-2211. Daily.
COMMUNITY

Alberni Valley Times, Box 400, 4918 Napier St., Port Alberni, BC V9Y 7N1. 604-723-8171.
COMMUNITY

The Aldergrove Star, PO Box 220, 3089-272 St., Aldergrove, BC V0X 1A0. 604-856-8303. Weekly.
COMMUNITY

Aleutian Eagle, PO Box 406, Dutch Harbor, AK 99692. 907-562-4684. Weekly.
COMMUNITY

Aloha Breeze, PO Box 588, Hillsboro, OR 97123. Weekly.
COMMUNITY

Anaconda Leader, 121 Main St., Anaconda, MT 59711. 406-563-5283. BiWeekly.
COMMUNITY

Anacortes American, PO Box 39, Anacortes, WA 98221. 206-293-3122. Weekly.
COMMUNITY

Anchorage Daily News, 1001 Northway Dr., Anchorage, AK 99508. 907-257-4200. Contact: Features Editor, Kathleen McCoy. Daily.
COMMUNITY

Argus Observer, 1160 S.W. Fourth St., Box 130, Ontario, OR 97914. 503-889-5387. Daily.
COMMUNITY

Arlington Times, PO Box 67, Arlington, WA 98223. 206-435-5757. Editor: Audrey Black. Weekly. Subs. $26/yr. Circ. 3,000. Uses freelance material. Byline given, pays on publication. Query w/SASE. Responds in 4 wks; publishes in 6 wks. Accepts news items, interviews that specifically apply to the local area. Sample $1.50.
COMMUNITY

Armstrong Advertiser, Box 610, Armstrong, BC V0E 1B0. 604-546-3121. Weekly.
COMMUNITY

Associated Press, 1320 S.W. Broadway, Portland, OR 97201. 503-228-2169. News bureau.
UNSPECIFIED

The Asterisk, Oregon Press Women, Inc., PO Box 25354, Portland, OR 97225. 503-639-6578. Editor: Serena Lesley. Quarterly for prize-winning high school journalists & photographers. Sample $2.
CHILDREN (BY/ABOUT), CHILDREN/TEEN

Athena Press, 431 E. Main, Box 597, Athena, OR 97813. 503-566-3452. Weekly.
COMMUNITY

Axis, Western States Chiropractic College, 2900 N.E. 132nd, Portland, OR 97230. 503-256-3180.
HEALTH, MEDICAL

Bainbridge Review, PO Box 10817, Bainbridge Island, WA 98110. 206-842-6613. Weekly.
COMMUNITY

Baker Democrat-Herald, PO Box 807, Baker City, OR 97814. 503-523-3673. Editor: Dean Brickey. Ads: Lynette Perry. Daily. Circ. 3,500. Founded 1870. Uses freelance material. Byline given, pays money on publication. Submit query letter w/SASE. Responds in 2-4 wks; publishes in 1-2 weeks. Accepts: news items, articles, op/ed. Photos $5.50 ea. Sample 35 cents.
COMMUNITY, NW/REGIONAL HISTORY, RECREATION

Ballard News-Tribune, 2208 N.W. Market, Seattle, WA 98017. 206-783-1244. Weekly.
COMMUNITY

Bandon Western World, Box 248, Bandon, OR 97411. 503-347-2423. Weekly.
COMMUNITY

BC BookWorld, 3516 W. 13th Ave, Vancouver, BC V6R 2S3. 604-736-4011. Publisher: Alan Twigg. Circ. 40,000. Sub $2/issue. A quarterly tabloid, with new stories about books and authors related to BC. Accepts unsolicited/freelance mss. Pays money on publication. Rights purchased: None. Byline given. Submit: ms w/SASE. Photocopy OK. Accepts nonfiction, photos (photos necessary). Hints: Keep it educational & brief & true.
BOOK ARTS/BOOKS, BRITISH COLUMBIA, WRITING

BCIT Link, BC Institute of Technology, 3700 Willingdon Ave., Burnaby, BC V5G 3H2. 604-434-5734.
COLLEGE/UNIVERSITY

Beacon, University of Portland, 5000 N. Willamette Blvd., Portland, OR 97203. 503-283-7376. Student newspaper. No pay. Byline given. Opinion pieces for editorial page and articles on entertainment in the Portland area considered. Preference given to students and faculty. Query w/SASE.
COLLEGE/UNIVERSITY, EDUCATION, ENTERTAINMENT

Beacon Hill News, 2314 3rd Ave., Seattle, WA 98121-1789. Weekly.
COMMUNITY

Bellingham Herald, 1155 N. State St., Bellingham, WA 98225. 206-676-2600; Fax 206-676-7113. Editor: Jack Keith. Ads: Gerry Rhea. Founded 1891. Circ. 26,300. Daily. Sub/$10.25
COMMUNITY

The Bengal, Idaho State University, PO Box 8009, Pocatello, ID 83209. 208-236-3990. Student newspaper.
COLLEGE/UNIVERSITY

Benton Bulletin, Box 351, Philomath, OR 97370. 503-929-3043. Weekly.
COMMUNITY

Big Horn County News, 204 N. Center Ave., Hardin, MT 59034. 406-665-1008. Contact: Richard Bowler. Weekly.
COMMUNITY

Big Sky Business Journal, PO Box 3263, Billings, MT 59103. Editor: Evelyn Pyburn. Sub/$22. Accepts freelance material, byline given, pays money on publication. Accepts cartoons, news items, nonfiction, and photos. B&W or color photos. Guidelines, back issues ($1.50).
BUSINESS

The Big Timber Pioneer, PO Box 190, Big Timber, MT 59011. Editor: Becky Oberly.
COMMUNITY, UNSPECIFIED

Bigfork Eagle, PO BOX 406, Bigfork, MT 59911. 406-837-5131.
COMMUNITY

Billings Gazette, 401 N. Broadway, Billings, MT 59101. 406-657-1200. Editor: Richard J. Wesnick.
COMMUNITY

The Billings Times, 2919 Montana Ave., Billings, MT 59101.
COMMUNITY

Blackfoot Morning News, PO Box 70, Blackfoot, ID 83221. 208-529-4919. Newspaper.
COMMUNITY

Blue Mountain Eagle, 741 W. Main St., Box 69, John Day, OR 97845. 503-575-0710. Weekly.
COMMUNITY

Blue Stocking, PO Box 4525, Portland, OR 97208. 503-283-9621. Editor: Judy Smith. Monthly radical feminist newspaper "open to all writing with a feminist bent." Circ. 8,000; sub $10. Accepts freelance material. Byline given. Pays money, copies on publication. Query w/SASE. Responds 1-2 months. Publication time varies. Accepts fiction, poetry, cartoons, news items, biography, nonfiction, photos, interviews, op/ed. Guidelines.
FEMINISM, WOMEN

Bluesnotes, PO Box 14493, Portland, OR 97214-0493. 503-285-3470. Editor: Ardis Hedrick. Ads: Dave Clingan. Monthly newspaper. Sub $12/yr. Circ. 4,000. Uses 2-3 freelance mss per issue. Byline given. Submit ms. Dot matrix, photocopied OK. Reports in 2 wks. Publishes in 2-6 wks. Accepts nonfiction, photos. Topics: blues music, legends, performers, interviews, reviews. Sample $1.
CULTURE, ENTERTAINMENT, MUSIC

Boise Idaho Register, PO Box 2835, Boise, ID 83701.
COMMUNITY

The Boulder Monitor, PO Box 66, 103 W. Center, Boulder, MT 59632. 406-225-3821. Weekly.
COMMUNITY

Bozeman Daily Chronicle, 32 S. Rouse, Bozeman, MT 59715. 406-587-4491. Bill Wilke, Editor. Daily.
COMMUNITY

Bremerton Sun, 545 Fifth St., PO Box 259, Bremerton, WA 98310. 206-377-3711. Daily. Circ. 39,000. Sub $8.50 per month. Freelance material accepted. Byline given; pays on publication. Query letter w/SASE. Responds in 2 weeks; publication time varies. Accepts new items, nonfiction,

food/travel, lifestyle/home.
COMMUNITY

Brewster Quad-City Herald, PO Box 37, Brewster, WA 98812. 509-689-2507. Weekly.
COMMUNITY

The Bridge, Portland Community College, 12000 S.W. 49th, Portland, OR 97219. 503-244-6111. Editor: Po Smith. Ads: Chris Mootham. Published 32 times a yr. Uses freelance material. Pays 50¢ column inch on publication. Acquires 1st rights. Byline given. Query w/clips, SASE. Dot matrix OK. Accepts nonfiction, photos. Topics: consumerism, entertainment, computers. Photos: B&W only, $10 on publication. Sample for postage.
COLLEGE/UNIVERSITY, COMPUTERS, CONSUMER

The Broadside, Central Oregon Community College, College Way, Bend, OR 97701. 503-382-2743. Editor: Todd Pittman. Ads: Paula Brown. Biweekly. Circ. 2,000.
COLLEGE/UNIVERSITY

The Bulletin, 1526 N.W. Hill St., Bend, OR 97701. 503-382-1811; 503-385-5802. Editor: Robert W. Chandler. Ads: Michael Thorpe. Daily. Circ. 25,000. Sub/$8.00. Founded 1903. Freelance material accepted. Byline given; payment on publication. Pays in money; acquires 1st rights. Query w/letter, by phone, send complete ms. Photocopy, dot matrix, simultaneous subs OK. Accepts news items, articles, photos, op-ed.
COMMUNITY, UNSPECIFIED

Burley South Idaho Press, 230 E. Main, Burley, ID 83318. 208-678-2202.
COMMUNITY

Burns Times-Herald, 355 N. Broadway Ave., Burns, OR 97720-1704. 503-573-2022. Weekly. Subs $20/yr in county, $25 out of county. Circ. 3,400. Uses freelance material. Byline given, pays copies, acquires 1st rights. Submit query letter, ms, SASE, phone. Accepts: news items.
COMMUNITY

Business Opportunities Journal, PO Box 990, Olalla, WA 98359. 206-857-7444; 604-521-9711. Published monthly, this tabloid sized newspaper contains business opportunities from around the world. Canadian address: PO Box 82008, Burnaby, BC V5C 5P2.
BUSINESS

Byline, Rogue Community College, 3345 Redwoods Hwy., Grants Pass, OR 97526. 503-479-5541. College newspaper.
COLLEGE/UNIVERSITY

Camas-Washougal Post-Record, PO Box 1013, Camas, WA 98607. 206-834-2141. Weekly.
COMMUNITY

The Campbell River Courier, Box 310, 1040 Cedar St., Campbell River, BC V9W 5B5. 604-287-7464. Editor: Neil Cameron. Weekly.
COMMUNITY

The Campbell River Mirror, 104-250 Dogwood St., Box 459, Campbell River, BC V9W 5C1. 604-287-9227. Editor: Alistair Taylor. Weekly.
COMMUNITY

The Campbell River Upper Islander, 1040 Cedar St., Box 310, Campbell River, BC V9W 5A7. 604-287-7464. Editor: Neil Cameron. Weekly.
COMMUNITY

Canby Herald/North Willamette News, 241 N. Grant St., PO Box 1108, Canby, OR 97013. 503-266-6831. Weekly.
COMMUNITY

Cannon Beach Gazette, 132 W. Second, Box 888, Cannon Beach, OR 97110. 503-436-2812. BiWeekly.
COMMUNITY

Capital City Weekly, 8365 Old Daird Rd., Juneau, AK 99801. 907-789-4144. Weekly.
COMMUNITY

Capital Press, Box 2048, Salem, OR 97308. 503-364-4431; Fax 503-370-4383. Editors: Donna Henderson, Mike Forrester. Ads: Dick Schultz. Weekly. Sub $30/yr. Circ. 33,500. Pays $1.25/inch on publication. Byline given, acquires all rights. Query by phone. Photocopy, disk/modem, Fax subs OK. Reports in 1-2 wk; publishes in 1-2 mos. Accepts nonfiction: 10-20 column inches. Topics: agriculture, livestock and small woodlands in Oregon, Washington, Idaho, western Montana, northern California. Photos: B&W glossies ($15) or color slides ($20).
AGRICULTURE/FARMING, FORESTRY

Capitol Hill Times, 2314 Third Ave., Seattle, WA 98121. 206-461-1308. Weekly.
COMMUNITY

Carbon County News, PO Box 970, 202 S. Hauser, Red Lodge, MT 59068. 406-446-2222. Editor: James Moore. Weekly.
COMMUNITY

Cascade Courier, PO Box 8, 17 N. Front, Cascade, MT 59421. 406-468-9231. Editor: Dean Brown. Weekly.
COMMUNITY

Cashmere Record, PO Box N., Cashmere, WA 98815. 509-782-3781. Weekly.
COMMUNITY

Catholic Sentinel, 5536 N.E. Hassalo, Portland, OR 97213.
RELIGION

Central Idaho Star News, PO Box 985, McCall, ID 83638. 208-634-2123. Contact: Tom Grote.
COMMUNITY

Central Oregonian, 558 N. Main, Prineville, OR 97754. 503-447-6205. SemiWeekly.
COMMUNITY

Channel Town Press, PO Box 575, LaConner, WA 98257. 206-466-3315. Weekly.
COMMUNITY

Chelan Valley Mirror, PO Box 249, Chelan, WA 98816. 509-682-2213. Weekly.
COMMUNITY

The Chetwynd Echo, Box 750, Chetwynd, BC V0C 1J0. 604-788-2466. Editor: Maureen Gammon. Weekly.
COMMUNITY

The Chetwynd Pioneer, 5021 49th Ave., Box 600, Chetwynd, BC V0C 1J0. 604-788-3255. Editor: Ruth Torgerson. Weekly.
COMMUNITY

The Chewalah Independent, PO Box 5, Chewalah, WA 99109. 509-935-8422. Weekly.
COMMUNITY

Chilliwack Progress Advertiser, 45860 Spadina Ave., Chilliwack, BC V2P 6H9. 604-792-1931. Editor: Andrew Holota. Weekly.
COMMUNITY

Chilliwack Progress Market Place, 45860 Spadina Ave., Chilliwack, BC V2P 6H9. 604-792-1931. Editor: Duane Geddes. Weekly.
COMMUNITY

Chinook Observer, PO Box 427, Long Beach, WA 98631. 206-642-3131. Weekly.
COMMUNITY

Chinook Opinion, PO Box 97, 217 Indiana, Chinook, MT 59523. 406-357-2680. Editor: Michael Perry. Weekly.
COMMUNITY

Choteau Acantha, PO Drawer O, 119 1st N.W., Choteau,

MT 406-466-2403. 406-466-2403. Editors: Jeff & Melody Martinsen. Weekly.
COMMUNITY

The Chronicle, PO Box 88, Aberdeen, WA 98520.
UNSPECIFIED

The Chronicle, PO Box 1115, Port Angeles, WA 98362. Query w/SASE.
COMMUNITY

Chronicle, 195 S. 15th St., Box 1153, St. Helens, OR 97051. 503-397-0116. SemiWeekly.
COMMUNITY

The Chronicle/The Guide, 244 W. Oregon Ave., P. O. Box 428, Creswell, OR 97426. 503-895-2197. Editor/Ads: Gerri Hawkins. Sub $12. Circ. 3,400. Weekly. Accepts freelance material relating to Creswell only. Byline given. Pays money, copies, on publication. Acquires 1st rights. Assignment only, phone. Dot matrix OK. Responds immediately, publishes in a few wks. Accepts nonfiction, photos (B&W). Sample $2.
COMMUNITY

Chugiak/Eagle River Star, 16941 N. Eagle River Loop Rd., Eagle River, AK 99577. 907-694-2727. Editor: Lee B. Jordan. Weekly.
COMMUNITY

The City Collegian, Seattle Central Community College, 1718 Broadway Ave., Seattle, WA 98122. Student newspaper.
COLLEGE/UNIVERSITY

Clackamas County News, 224 S.W. Zobrist, Box 549, Estacada, OR 97023. 503-630-3241. Weekly.
COMMUNITY

Clatskanie Chief, 90 Artsteele St., Box 8, Clatskanie, OR 97016. 503-728-3350. Weekly.
COMMUNITY

The Clatsop Common Sense, Clatsop Community College, Astoria, OR 97103. 503-325-0910x311. Quarterly newspaper.
COLLEGE/UNIVERSITY

Clearwater Tribune, PO Box 71, Orofino, ID 83544. 208-476-4571.
COMMUNITY

Coeur d'Alene Press, 2nd & Lakeside Ave., Coeur d'Alene, ID 83814. 208-664-8176.
COMMUNITY

Coffee Break, Box 248, Bandon, OR 97411. 503-347-2423.
UNSPECIFIED

Columbia Basin Herald, PO Box 910, Moses Lake, WA 98837. 509-765-4561. Daily. Query/SASE.
COMMUNITY

The Columbia Press, 926 E. Harbor, Box 130, Warrenton, OR 97146. 503-861-3331. Weekly community newspaper. Sub/$21.50. Circ. 1,450. Uses freelance material. Byline given. Pays money on publication, acquires 1st rights. Query w/SASE. Responds in 1 week; publishing time varies. Accepts cartoons, news items, articles, B&W photos.
COMMUNITY

The Columbian, 701 W. Eighth St., PO Box 180, Vancouver, WA 98666. 206-694-3391; Fax 206-699-6029. Editor: Tom Koenninger. Ads: John McDonagh. Daily. Founded 1890. Circ. 52,000. Sub/$8.50. Tuesday food section to three community zones.
COMMUNITY

Community Style, PO Box 2588, Bremerton, WA 98310. 206-373-7969. Editor: Yvonne Beasley. Ads: Stephanie Cordall. Weekly. Founded 1992. Circ. 23,600. Sub $20 delivery; $50 mail. Only local freelance material is accepted. Pays on publication.
COMMUNITY

Commuter, Linn-Benton Community College, 6500 S.W. Pacific Blvd., Albany, OR 97321. 503-928-236113.
COLLEGE/UNIVERSITY

The Compass, Concordia Lutheran College, 2811 N.E. Holman, Portland, OR 97211. 503-288-9371.
COLLEGE/UNIVERSITY

Cooper Point Journal, Evergreen State College, Campus Activities Bldg., Rm 306A, Olympia, WA 98505. Weekly.
COLLEGE/UNIVERSITY

Coos Bay World, 350 Commercial, Coos Bay, OR 97420. 503-269-1222. Editor: Charles Kocher. Daily. Circ. 17,500. Uses freelance material. Byline given. Pays money on publication, acquires 1st rights. Query by phone, letter, complete ms w/SASE. Dot matrix, photocopied subs OK. Responds in 1 wk; publishing time varies. Accepts news items, poetry, interviews, photos (B&W negatives). Sample $1.
COMMUNITY

Coquille Valley Sentinel, Box 519, Coquille, OR 97423. 503-396-3191; 503-572-2717. Weekly.
COMMUNITY

The Cordova Times, PO Box 200, Cordova, AK 99574-0200. 907-424-7181. Editor: Don Adams. Weekly.
COMMUNITY

Corvallis Gazette Times, 600 S.W. Jefferson Ave., Box 368, Corvallis, OR 97339. 503-753-2641. Daily.
COMMUNITY

The Costco Connection, 10809 120th Ave. N.W., Kirkland, WA 98033. 206-828-8100; Fax 206-828-8106. Editor: David Fuller. Ads: Jane Klein. Circ. 470,540. Founded 1987. Monthly 4-color tabloid with articles of interest to owners/operators of small businesses and others.
BUSINESS

Cottage Grove Sentinel, Box 31, Cottage Grove, OR 97424. 503-942-3325. Weekly.
COMMUNITY

The Courier, 174 N. 16th St., Box 268, Reedsport, OR 97467. 503-271-3633. Weekly.
COMMUNITY

Courier 004, Chemeketa Community College, PO Box 14007, Salem, OR 97309. 503-399-5134.
COLLEGE/UNIVERSITY

Courier-Herald, PO Box 157, Enumclaw, WA 98022. 206-825-2555. Weekly.
COMMUNITY

Courier-Pioneer-Advertiser, PO Box 1091, Polson, MT 59860.
UNSPECIFIED

Courier-Times, PO Box 32, Sedro Woolley, WA 98284. 206-855-1641. Weekly.
COMMUNITY

Cowlitz County Advocate, PO Box 368, Castle Rock, WA 98611. 206-274-6663. Weekly. Editor: Terri Lee Grell. Ads: Barbara Thompson. Sub $20. Circ. 5,000. Uses freelance material. Byline given. Pays copies on publication. Acquires 1st rights. Submit: query w/clips, ms, SASE, phone. Dot matrix, photocopies, electronic, computer disk OK. Accepts nonfiction, photos, news, features, columns. A weekly column called Ad-libs is written by anyone with a unique story to tell; topics preferably local area or Mt. St. Helens, but all submissions considered. No more than 4 typed pgs. Sample $1.
CALENDAR/EVENTS, COMMUNITY, NW/REGIONAL HISTORY

The Coyote, College of Idaho, 2112 Cleveland Blvd., Caldwell, ID 83605. 459-5509. Student newspaper.
COLLEGE/UNIVERSITY

The Crescent, George Fox College, Box A, Newberg, OR 97132. 503-538-8383.
COLLEGE/UNIVERSITY

Creston Valley Advance, PO Box 1279, Creston, BC V0B 1G0. 604-428-2266. Editor: Ross Hunter. Ads: Lorne Eckersley. Fax: 604-428-3320. Published semi-weekly on Thursday. Founded 1948. Circ. 3,950. US sub/$45; CDN sub/$32. Freelance material accepted. Byline given. Pays money on publication. Acquires first rights. Query by letter. Responds in 2 wks; publication time varies. Accepts news items. Back issues 75¢.
BRITISH COLUMBIA, COMMUNITY

Crosswind, PO Box 10, Oak Harbor, WA 98277. 206-675-6611. Weekly.
COMMUNITY

The Crusader, Northwest Nazarene College, Nampa, ID 83651. 208-467-8556. BiWeekly. Query w/SASE.
COLLEGE/UNIVERSITY

Curry Coastal Pilot, 507 Chetco Ave., Box 700, Brookings, OR 97415. 503-469-3123. Weekly.
COMMUNITY

Curry County Reporter, 510 N. Ellensburg Ave., Box 766, Gold Beach, OR 97444. 503-247-6643. Weekly. Query with/SASE.
COMMUNITY

Cut Bank Pioneer Press, PO Box 478, 217 W. Main, Cut Bank, MT 59427. 406-873-2201. Editor: John Barber. Weekly.
COMMUNITY

The Daily, 144 Communications, DS-20, University of Washington, Seattle, WA 98195. 206-543-2335. Query with SASE.
COLLEGE/UNIVERSITY

The Daily Astorian, Box 210, Astoria, OR 97103. 503-325-3211.
COMMUNITY

Daily Barometer, Oregon State University, Memorial Union East 106, Corvallis, OR 97331. 503-754-2231.
COLLEGE/UNIVERSITY

Daily Bulletin, PO Box 770, Colfax, WA 99111. 509-397-4333.
COMMUNITY

The Daily Bulletin, 335 Spokane St., Kimberley, BC V1A 1Y9. 604-427-5333. Contact: Gary Waters. Ads: Diane Maletta. Daily.
COMMUNITY

The Daily Chronicle, 321 N. Pearl, PO Box 580, Centralia, WA 98531. 206-736-3311.
COMMUNITY

The Daily Courier, 550 Doyle Ave., Kelowna, BC V1Y 7V1. 604-762-4445. Contact: Bob Boxall. Ads: Don Herron. Book editor: Scott Inniss. Daily. Scott Inniss wishes to remind publishers of this paper's interest in Canadian material, especially from western Canada. Books should be sent to him at the Courier.
COMMUNITY

Daily Emerald, University of Oregon, Box 3159, Eugene, OR 97403. 503-686-5511.
COLLEGE/UNIVERSITY

Daily Evergreen, Room 113, Edward R. Murrow Cntr., PO Box 2008 C.S., Pullman, WA 99165-9986. 335-4573. Editor: Michael Strand.
COLLEGE/UNIVERSITY

Daily Journal American, 1705 - 132nd N.E., Bellevue, WA 98005. 206-455-2222; Fax 206-453-4273. Editor: Jack Mayne. Ads: Hallie Olson. Founded 1930. Circ. 33,500. Daily. Sub/$8.50.
COMMUNITY

Daily Journal of Commerce, PO Box 10127, Portland, OR 97210. 503-226-1311. Editor: Jeff McIvor. Ads: Bob Smith. Daily, general business with emphasis on local news.

Circ. 4,000. Uses 1 mss per issue. Payment: Negotiable; on publication. Byline given. Query w/ms, SASE. Makes assignments. Phone query, dot matrix, photocopies, simultaneous submissions (if noncompeting) OK. Reports in 12 wks. Nonfiction: 600-700 wds. Photos: B&W 5x7 or larger.
BUSINESS, ECONOMICS

The Daily News, PO Box 580, Prince Rupert, BC V8J 3R9. 604-624-6781. Editor: Scott Crowson. Daily.
COMMUNITY

The Daily News, PO Box 189, Longview, WA 98632. 206-577-2500; Fax 206-577-2536. Editor: Ted Natt. Ads: William Marcum. Founded 1923. Circ. 24,900. Published weekdays and Saturday afternoons. Sub/$8.00
COMMUNITY

The Daily News Port Angeles, PO Box 1330, Port Angeles, WA 98362. 206-452-2345; 800-826-7714. Editor: Tony Wishik. Ads: Bob Blumhagen. Serving Clallam/Jefferson counties. Circ. 12,500. Sub $6.75. Accepts freelance material. Payment: Money on publication. Byline given. Rights purchased: First. Query w/SASE. Dot matrix, photocopies, electronic OK. Nonfiction: up to 1,000 wds; $20-25. Photos: $5-35 per assignment. Must be directly related to Clallam/Jefferson counties. Sample.
COMMUNITY

The Daily Olympian, 1268 East Fourth Ave., PO Box 407, Olympia, WA 98507. 206-754-5400.
COMMUNITY

The Daily Sitka Sentinel, PO Box 799, 112 Barracks St., Sitka, AK 99835. 907-747-3219. Thad or Sandy Poulson. Daily.
COMMUNITY

The Daily Tidings, 1661 Siskiyou Blvd., Box 7, Ashland, OR 97520. 503-482-3456.
COMMUNITY

The Daily Townsman, 822 Cranbrook St. N., Cranbrook, BC V1C 3R9. 604-426-5201. Editor: Drew Drinan. Daily.
COMMUNITY

Daily Vanguard, PO Box 751 V6, Portland, OR 97207. 503-725-4531. Editor: Greg Smiley. Circ. 7000, sub/$36. No freelance material accepted. "You must be an enrolled student at PSU to work at the Vanguard." Back issues, send postage.
COLLEGE/UNIVERSITY, COMMUNITY

The Dalles Chronicle, 414 Federal St., The Dalles, OR 97058. 503-296-2141. Daily.
COMMUNITY, UNSPECIFIED

The Dalles Weekly Reminder, PO Box 984, The Dalles, OR 97058. 503-298-4725. Editor: Gerald Ericksen. 503-298-4725. Ads: Saundra Bernards. Weekly. Circ. 4,000. Sub $18. Almost never accepts freelance material, but I'll look at anything of local interest. Byline given. No pay: If something were exclusive and really good, we could possibly negotiate a small payment. Submit ms, SASE. Phone queries, dot matrix, photocopies, simultaneous submission OK. Reports immediately. Local means Wasco or Sherman counties only. Photos: B&W photos or negatives preferred.
AGRICULTURE/FARMING, NW/REGIONAL HISTORY, PUBLIC AFFAIRS

Davenport Times, PO Box 66, Davenport, WA 99122. 509-725-0101. Weekly.
COMMUNITY

Dayton Chronicle, PO Box 6, Dayton, WA 99328. 509-382-2221. Weekly.
COMMUNITY

Dayton Tribune, 408 4th, Box 68, Dayton, OR 97114. 503-864-2310. Weekly.
COMMUNITY

Dead Mountain Echo, P. O. Box 900, Oakridge, OR 97463. 503-782-4241. Editor: Christy Roberts-Truelove. Ads: Larry Roberts. Weekly. Sub $25/20. Circ. 1,500. Uses freelance material. Byline given. Pays copies. Query letter, SASE. Responds in 1-2 wks; publishing time varies. Accepts nonfiction, cartoons, news items, op/ed, photos (B&W screened). Sample $1.
COMMUNITY

Delta Wind, PO Box 986, Delta Junction, AK 99737. 907-895-4310. Editor: Loretta Nistler. Weekly.
COMMUNITY

Dillon Tribune-Examiner, 22 S. Montana, Dillon, MT 59725.
COMMUNITY

The Direct Express, 928 Broadwater, Billings, MT 59101.
UNSPECIFIED

Dispatch, PO Box 248, Eatonville, WA 98328. 206-832-4411. Weekly.
COMMUNITY

The Drain Enterprise, PO Box 26, Drain, OR 97435-0026.
COMMUNITY

East Oregonian, 211 S.E. Byers, Box 1089, Pendleton, OR 97801. 503-276-2211. Daily.
COMMUNITY

East Washingtonian, PO Box 70, Pomeroy, WA 99347. 509-843-1313. Weekly.
COMMUNITY

Eastbank Focus, Pry Publishing, 600 N.W. 14th, Portland, OR 97209. 503-226-8335. Editors: Tom or Marcia Pry. Ads: Greg Hudson. Monthly tabloid, founded 1988. Circ. 10,000. Uses freelance material. Byline given. Pays money on publication. Acquires 1st rights. Submit query letter, clips, SASE. Dot matrix OK. Responds in 12 wks. Accepts new items, nonfiction, photos, articles. Topics: events and people of inner N.E. and S.E. Portland, Albina, Lloyd Center, Hawthorne. Guidelines.
COMMUNITY

Eastside Courier-Review, PO Box 716, Redmond, WA 98052. 206-885-4178. Weekly.
COMMUNITY

Echo, PO Box 39, Leavenworth, WA 98826. 509-548-7911. Weekly.
COMMUNITY

The Edge, 3201 Campus Dr., Oregon Institute of Technology, Klamath Falls, OR 97601. 503-885-1835.
MEDIA/COMMUNICATIONS, COLLEGE/UNIVERSITY

The Edmonds View, 1827 160th Ave. N.E., Bellevue, WA 98008-2506. Weekly.
COMMUNITY

The Ekalaka Eagle, PO Box 66, Ekalaka, MT 59324. 406-775-6275. Editor: Jim Anderson. Weekly.
COMMUNITY

The Elder Statesman, 301 - 1201 West Pender, Vancouver, BC V6E 2V2.
UNSPECIFIED

Ellensburg Daily Record, Fourth & Main, PO Box 248, Ellensburg, WA 98926. 509-925-1414. Daily.
COMMUNITY

EMC Retort, Eastern Montana College, Billings, MT 59101. Editor: Angela Enger.
COLLEGE/UNIVERSITY

Emmett Messenger Index, PO Box 577, Emmett, ID 83617. Weekly.
COMMUNITY, UNSPECIFIED

Empire Press, PO Box 430, Waterville, WA 98858. 509-745-8782. Weekly.
COMMUNITY

Endeavor, Treasure Valley Community College, 650 College Blvd., Ontario, OR 97914. 503-889-6493. Biweekly carrying campus news and nonfiction articles. Circ. 1,400. Payment: Copies. Byline given. Query w/ms. Simultaneous submission OK. Nonfiction: 300-500 wds on experiences, problems of Eastern Oregon college students. Query before submitting lengthy feature. Sample free.
COLLEGE/UNIVERSITY

Enterprise, PO Box 977, Lynnwood, WA 98046. 206-775-7521. Weekly.
COMMUNITY

Equinews, Whitehouse Publishing, PO Box 1778, Vernon, BC V1T 8C3. 604-545-9896. Editor: Dr. B. J. White. Monthly. Sub $15/CDN, $20/US. Circ. 16,792. Uses freelance material. Pays $30-100/article on publication. Byline given. Submit ms, SASE. Dot matrix, photocopied OK. Reports in 2 mos. Publishes in 1-2 mos. Accepts nonfiction, photos, cartoons. Topics: all equine aspects. Photos, $5. Sample $2.
ANIMALS, RECREATION

Facts Newspaper, 2765 East Cherry, Seattle, WA 98122. 206-324-0552. Weekly.
UNSPECIFIED

Fairbanks Daily News-Miner, PO Box 70710, 200 N. Cushman St., Fairbanks, AK 99701. 907-452-5054. Editor: Dan Joling. Daily.
COMMUNITY

Fairbanks News-Miner, Box 710, Fairbanks, AK 99707. 907-456-6661. Daily.
COMMUNITY

Fairchild Times, PO Box 218, Cheney, WA 99004. Weekly.
COMMUNITY

Fairfield Times, Box 578, Fairfield, MT 59436. 406-467-2334. Editor: Jim Anderson. Weekly.
COMMUNITY

Fallon County Times, PO Box 679, 115 South Main, Baker, MT 59313. 406-778-3344. Editor: Nancy Schillinger. Weekly.
COMMUNITY

Federal Way News, 1634 South 312th, Federal Way, WA 98003. 206-839-0700. Weekly.
COMMUNITY

Forks Forum & Penninsula Herald, PO Box 300, Forks, WA 98331. 206-374-2281. Weekly.
COMMUNITY

Fort Lewis Ranger, PO Box 98801, Tacoma, WA 98499. 206-584-1212. Army base Weekly.
MILITARY/VETS

Franklin County Graphic, PO Box 160, Connell, WA 99326. 509-234-3181. Weekly.
COMMUNITY

Free Press, PO Box 218, Cheney, WA 99004-0218. 509-235-6184. Weekly.
COMMUNITY

The Frontiersman, 1261 Seward Meridian Rd., Wasilla, AK 99654. 907-376-5225. Contact: Susan Morgan Howk. Ads: Barb Stephl. Biweekly. Uses freelance material. Pays money on publication. Acquires 1st rights. Byline given. Submit query w/clips, SASE. Photocopied OK. Reports in 2 wks. Publishes in 2 wks. Accepts nonfiction about rural Alaska.
ALASKA, ENVIRONMENT/RESOURCES, NW/REGIONAL HISTORY

Gazette, PO Box 770, Colfax, WA 99111. 509-397-4333. Weekly.
COMMUNITY

Gazette-tribune, PO Box 250, Oroville, WA 98844. 509-476-3602. Weekly.
COMMUNITY

Glacier Reporter, PO Box R, Browning, MT 59417. 406-338-2090. Weekly.
COMMUNITY

Glasgow Courier, 341 3rd Ave. South, Glasgow, MT 59230. 406-228-9301. Editor: Doris Vallard. Ads: Stanley D. Sonsteng. Weekly. Sub $18/yr. Circ. 4,200. Does not accept unsolicited submissions. Query letter, SASE. Accepts news items, photos.
COMMUNITY

Glendive Ranger-Review, PO Box 61, 119 W. Bell St., Glendive, MT 59330. 406-365-3303. Editor: Tana Reinhardt. Weekly.
COMMUNITY

Goal Lines, The Oregon Youth Soccer Association, 1750 Skyline Blvd., #25, Portland, OR 97221. 503-292-5542. Editor: Judy Davidson. Ads: Don Patch. Published 5 times/yr. Sub $6. Circ. 25,000. Uses freelance material. Byline given. Query w/clips, SASE. Dot matrix, computer disk OK. Reports in 2 wks. Publishes in next issue. Accepts nonfiction, photos. Guidelines available; sample $1.
CALENDAR/EVENTS, SPORTS

Golden Star News, Missoula Aging Services, 227 West Front, Missoula, MT 59802. 406-728-7682; 406-251-2243. Editor: Duane Gimbel. Free sub.
SENIOR CITIZENS

Goldendale Sentinel, 117 W. Main St., Goldendale, WA 98620. 509-773-4212. Local newspaper.
COMMUNITY, UNSPECIFIED

Gooding County Leader, PO Box 56, Gooding, ID 83330-0056. 208-934-4449.
COMMUNITY

Grant County Journal, PO Box 998, Ephrata, WA 98823. 509-754-4636. Weekly.
COMMUNITY

Grants Pass Daily Courier, 409 S.E. Seventh St., Grants Pass, OR 97526. 503-474-3700; Fax 503-474-3814. Editor: Dennis Roler. Ads: Michele Thomas. Founded 1885. Circ. 18,900. Sub/$9.75. Daily.
COMMUNITY

Grays Harbor County Vidette, PO Box 671, Montesano, WA 98563. 206-249-3311. Weekly.
COMMUNITY

Great Falls Montana Catholic Register, PO Box 1399, Great Falls, MT 59403.
RELIGION

Great Falls Tribune, 205 River Dr. S., PO Box 5468, Great Falls, MT 59403. 406-791-1444. Gary Moseman, Editor. Daily. Accepts freelance material. Byline given; pays money on publication. Acquires first rights. Query by letter or phone. Responds in 60 days. Accepts outdoor features; places to go, things to do, yard work stories, etc. Also accepts photos.
COMMUNITY

Gresham Outlook, 1190 N.E. Division St., PO Box 880, Gresham, OR 97030. 503-665-2181. Semiweekly.
COMMUNITY

Guide, One in Ten Publishing Co., PO Box 23070, Seattle, WA 98102. 206-323-7374. Editor: Bill Swigart. Ads: Lee Johnson. Monthly, gay-lesbian oriented issues, social info. Sub $12.95. Circ. 12,000. Uses 3 freelance mss per issue. Pays money on publication, $5 for photos. Rights acquired: First. Byline given. Submit query w/clips, SASE. Dot matrix, photocopies, simultaneous, computer disk OK. Reports in 4 wks. Publishes in 2 mos. Accepts nonfiction, fiction, photos, cartoons. Sample $1.
GAY/LESBIAN, GOVERNMENT, MINORITIES/ETHNIC

Hardball Northwest Baseball, PO Box 31541, Seattle, WA 98103. Editor: Sean Kimball. Sub $18/yr, Circ. 150+.

Uses freelance material. Byline given. Pays copies on publication. Submit complete ms, SASE. Photocopied OK. Accepts nonfiction, fiction, poetry, photos, cartoons, news items, biography, interviews, reviews. Topics: baseball historical, personal interest, statistical, opinions, etc.; focus is Northwest. Sample.
COLLECTING, NW/REGIONAL HISTORY, SPORTS

Hardin Herald, Box R, Hardin, MT 59034. 307-665-1008.
COMMUNITY

Harlem News, PO Box 278, Harlem, MT 59526. 406-353-2441. Editor: Michael Perry. Weekly.
COMMUNITY

Havre Daily News, 119 2nd St., Havre, MT 59501. 406-265-6798. Elizabeth Kannberg, Editor. Daily.
COMMUNITY

Headlight Herald, Pacific Coast Newspapers, Inc., 1908 Second St., Tillamook, OR 97141. 503-842-7535. Editor: Mark H. Dickson.
UNSPECIFIED

Heppner Gazette-times, 147 W. Willow, Box 337, Heppner, OR 97836. 503-676-9228. Weekly.
COMMUNITY

The Herald, PO Box 930, Everett, WA 98206. 206-339-3000; Fax 206-339-3049. Editor: Stan Strick. Ads: Ann Reed. Founded 1891. Circ. 53,180. Daily. Sub $9-10. Has a food section zoned by zip code.
COMMUNITY

Herald, 107 Division, Grandview, WA 98930. 509-882-3712. Weekly.
COMMUNITY

Herald & News, PO Box 788, Klamath Falls, OR 97601. 503-883-4410; Fax 503-883-4007. Editor: Dwight Tracy. Ads: Ken Larsen. Circ. 17,900. Founded 1906. Sub/$7.50. Daily.
COMMUNITY

Herald News, PO Box 639, Wolf Point, MT 59201. 406-653-2222.
COMMUNITY

The Hermiston Herald, 158 E. Main, Box 46, Hermiston, OR 97838. 503-567-6457. Weekly.
COMMUNITY

Hi Prep, PO Box 714, Meridian, ID 83642. 208-888-1165. Editor: Frank Thomason.
UNSPECIFIED

High Country Ind. Press, 220 S. Broadway, Belgrade, MT 59714. 406-388-6762. Editor: Devon Hubbard Sorlie. Weekly.
COMMUNITY

Highline Times & Des Moines News, PO Box 518, Burien, WA 98166. 206-242-0100. Weekly.
COMMUNITY

Hillsboro Argus, 150 S.E. Third, Hillsboro, OR 97123. 503-684-1131. Semiweekly.
COMMUNITY

The Hispanic News, 2318 Second Ave., Seattle, WA 98121. 206-768-0421. Editor: Tony Badillo. Sub $30/yr. Circ. 10,000. Weekly dedicated to serving the more than 127,000 Hispanics in Washington State. Accepts freelance submissions of news items, nonfiction, photos, interviews, and articles. Query w/SASE.
BILINGUAL, CHICANO/CHICANA, MINORITIES/ETHNIC

The Hispanic News, PO Box 22526, Portland, OR 97222. 503-777-6759. Contact: Juan Prats. Weekly. Sub $25/yr. Bilingual news and features (local, national, and international) for both Hispanic and non-Hispanic communities. Accepts freelance submissions. For news, query by phone. For features, typed query w/SASE.
BILINGUAL, CHICANO/CHICANA, MINORITIES/ETHNIC

The Hollywood Star, Pry Publishing Co., 600 N.W. 14th, Portland, OR 97209. 503-226-8335. Editors: Tom or Marcia Pry. Ads: Greg Hudson. Monthly tabloid, founded 1984. Circ. 15,000. Uses freelance material. Byline given. Pays money on publication. Acquires 1st rights. Submit query letter, clips, SASE. Dot matrix OK. Responds in 1-2 wks. Accepts new items, nonfiction, photos, articles. Topics: events and people of central N.E. Portland including Hollywood, Alameda, Grant Park, Rose City Park, Madison neighborhoods. Guidelines.
COMMUNITY

Homer News, 3482 Landing St., Homer, AK 99603-7948. 907-235-7767. Editor: Mark Tunner. Weekly.
COMMUNITY

Hood River News, 409 Oak St., Box 390, Hood River, OR 97031. 503-386-1234. Weekly.
COMMUNITY

Hungry Horse News, 926 Nucleus Ave., PO Box 189, Columbia Falls, MT 59912. 406-862-2151.
COMMUNITY

The Idaho Argonaut, Student Union Building, University of Idaho, Moscow, ID 83843. 208-885-7825. Semiweekly newspaper written & published by students. Sub $18/yr. Circ. 7,000. Not a freelance market.
COLLEGE/UNIVERSITY, IDAHO

Idaho County Free Press, PO Box 690, Grangeville, ID 83530. 208-983-1070.
UNSPECIFIED

Idaho Falls Post-Register, 333 Northgate Mile, Idaho Falls, ID 83401. 208-522-1800.
COMMUNITY

Idaho Farm Bureau News, Idaho Farm Bureau Federation, PO Box 167, Boise, ID 83701-0167. Editor: Mike Tracy. Monthly . Circ. 29,000. Does not accept freelance material.
AGRICULTURE/FARMING, IDAHO

Idaho Fish & Game News, PO Box 25, Boise, ID 83807. Editor: Jack Trueblood. Bimonthly newspaper.
FISHING, OUTDOOR

Idaho Press-Tribune, PO Box 9399, Nampa, ID 83652-9399. 208-467-9251. Editor: Richard Coffman. Daily.
COMMUNITY

Idaho Register, Box 2835, Boise, ID 83701. 208-342-2997. Editor: Colette Cowman. Weekly. Circ. 14,300.
COMMUNITY

Idaho State Journal, 305 S. Arthur, Pocatello, ID 83204. 208-232-4161.
IDAHO

The Idaho Statesman, Box 40, Boise, ID 83707. 208-377-6200. Contact: Judy McConnell Steele. Daily.
COMMUNITY

Idahonian/Palouse Empire News, PO Box 8197, Moscow, ID 83843. 208-882-5561. Daily.
COMMUNITY

Illinois Valley News, 319 Redwood Hwy., Box M, Cave Junction, OR 97523. 503-592-2541. Editor/ads: Robert R Rodriquez. Weekly. Circ. 3,300. Sub $9. Uses 2 mss per issue. Payment: Average 20 per column inch on publication. $3 per photo. Byline given. Photocopies, simultaneous submissions OK. Reports in 2 wks. Nonfiction, photos (B&W). News & general interest for Illinois Valley. Sample: 35/SASE.
COMMUNITY

In Focus, 5000 Deer Park Dr., S.E., Salem, OR 97301. 503-581-8600.
UNSPECIFIED

Independent, PO Box 27, Port Orchard, WA 98366. 206-876-4414. Weekly.
COMMUNITY

Independent, PO Box D, Tenino, WA 98589. 206-264-2500. Weekly.
COMMUNITY

Independent, PO Box 67, Wapato, WA 98951. 509-879-2262. Weekly.
COMMUNITY

Independent Observer, PO Box 966, 7 3rd Ave., Conrad, MT 59425. 406-278-5561. Contact: Buck Traxler. Weekly.
COMMUNITY

The Independent Record, 317 Cruse Ave, PO Box 4249, Helena, MT 59604. 406-442-7190. Editor: Charles Wood. Daily.
COMMUNITY

Inland Farmer-Stockman, PO Box 2160, Spokane, WA 99210. 509-459-5361; 509-459-5102. Editor: E. W. Ramsey. Ads: Barry Roach. Founded 1884. Circ. 17,700. Sub/$15. Tabloid published 11 times per year covering agricultural news.
AGRICULTURE/FARMING

Issaquah Press, PO Box 1328, Issaquah, WA 98027. 206-392-6434. Weekly.
COMMUNITY

Jefferson Review, 145 S. Main St., Box 330, Jefferson, OR 97352. 503-327-2241. Weekly.
COMMUNITY

Jefferson Star, 134 W. Main, Rigby, ID 83442. 208-745-8701.
COMMUNITY

Jewish Transcript, 2031 3rd Ave. #200, Seattle, WA 98121-2418. 206-624-0136. Weekly.
COMMUNITY, RELIGION

The Journal Leader, Box 190, Ashcroft, BC V0K 1A0. 604-453-2261. Editor: Barry Tait. Weekly.
COMMUNITY

Journal of Business, Northwest Business Press, Inc., S. 104 Division, Spokane, WA 99202. 509-456-5257. Editor: Norman Thorpe. Ads: Scott Crytser. Biweekly. Sub $18/yr. Circ. 15,000. Uses freelance material. Byline given. Pays $2075 per piece, depending on quality, work put into it, and amount of work we have to do on it. Pays on publication. Acquires 1st rights. Phone query. Dot matrix OK. Reports in 23 wks; publishes in 23 mos. Accepts business news about the Spokane-Coeur d'Alene market and surrounding area. Sample $2.
BUSINESS

Journal of the San Juans, PO Box 519, Friday Harbor, WA 98250. 206-378-4191.
COMMUNITY

Journey Press, 116 North 78th St., Seattle, WA 98103. 206-783-4554. Contact: Mary LeLoo. Monthly aimed at individuals in recovery from dysfunctional families. Seeking poetry, articles, photos. SASE for guidelines.
HEALTH, POETRY, PSYCHOLOGY

Judith Basin Press, Box 507, 117 Central, Stanford, MT 59479. 406-566-2471. Contact: Lance Davis. Weekly.
COMMUNITY

Juneau Empire, 3100 Channel Dr., Juneau, AK 99801. 907-586-3740. Contact: Carl Sampson.
COMMUNITY

Kalispell Daily Interlake, 727 E. Idaho, Kalispell, MT 59901. 406-755-7000. Contact: Dan Black. Newspaper
COMMUNITY

Kalispell News, PO Box 669, Kalispell, MT 59901. 406-755-6767. Editor: JoAnn Speelman. Weekly.
COMMUNITY

The Kamloops Daily News, 106-63 West Victoria St., Kamloops, BC V2C 6J6. 604-372-2331. Editor: M.G.

Rothenberger. Daily.
COMMUNITY

Keizertimes, 142 Chemawa Rd. N., Keizer, OR 97303-5356. 503-390-1051. Weekly.
COMMUNITY

Kellogg Evening News, 401 Main St., Kellogg, ID 83837. 208-783-1107.
COMMUNITY

Kenmore Northlake News, PO Box 587, Woodinville, WA 98072. 206-483-0606. Weekly.
COMMUNITY

Kent News Journal, 600 S. Washington, Kent, WA 98032. Contact: Diane Glamser.
COMMUNITY

Ketchikan Daily News, PO Box 7900, Ketchikan, AK 99901. 907-225-3157. Biweekly.
COMMUNITY

Kitsap County Herald, PO Box 278, Poulsbo, WA 98370. 206-779-4464. Weekly.
COMMUNITY

Kodiak Daily Mirror, 1419 Selio St., Kodiak, AK 99615-6450. 907-486-3227. Daily.
COMMUNITY

Lake County Examiner, 101 N. F St., Box 271, Lakeview, OR 97630. 503-947-3370. Weekly.
COMMUNITY

Lake Oswego Review, 111 A St., PO Box 548, Lake Oswego, OR 97034. 503-635-8811. Weekly.
COMMUNITY

Lakes District News, Box 309, Burns Lake, BC V0J 1E0. Editor: Bruce Finley. Weekly.
COMMUNITY

The Lamron, Western Oregon State College, WOSC College Center, Monmouth, OR 97361. 503-838-1171.
COLLEGE/UNIVERSITY

Laurel Outlook, PO Box 278, 415 E. Main St., Laurel, MT 59044. 406-628-4412. Editor: Milton Wester. Weekly.
COMMUNITY

Leader, c/o Port Townsend Publishing, PO Box 552, Port Townsend, WA 98368-0552. 206-385-2900. Weekly.
COMMUNITY

Leader Bldg., PO Box 850, Scobey, MT 59263. 406-487-5303. Editor: Larry Bowler. Weekly.
COMMUNITY

Lebanon Express, 90 E. Grant St., Box 459, Lebanon, OR 97355. 503-258-3151. Semiweekly.
COMMUNITY

Lewis County News, PO Box 10, Winlock, WA 98596. 206-785-3151. Weekly.
COMMUNITY

Lewis River News & Kalama Bulletin, PO Box 39, Woodland, WA 98674. 206-225-8287. Weekly.
COMMUNITY

Lewiston Morning Tribune, Box 957, Lewiston, ID 83501. 208-743-9411. Arts editor: John McCarthy. Daily, art section once a wk. Circ. 25,000. Accepts freelance book reviews. Pays in copies. Byline given. Submit ms. Dot matrix, photocopied, simultaneous OK. Publishes within 1 mo. Book reviews on Northwest writers, fiction or nonfiction with subjects centered in the N.W. & Rocky Mountains (Washington, Oregon, Idaho & Montana).
COMMUNITY, LITERARY, NORTHWEST

Lewistown News-Argus, PO Box 900, Lewistown, MT 59457. Editor: Vonnie Jacobson.
COMMUNITY

Liberty County Times, PO Box 689, Chester, MT 59522.

406-759-5355. Editor: Jeanne Larson. Weekly.
COMMUNITY

The Linfield Review, Linfield College, PO Box 395, McMinnville, OR 97128. 503-472-0585. Weekly campus newspaper. Sub $7.50. Circ. 1,600.
COLLEGE/UNIVERSITY

Livingston Enterprise, 401 S. Main, PO Box 665, Livingston, MT 59047. 406-222-2000. Editor: John Sullivan. Daily.
COMMUNITY

The Log, Rogue Community College, 3345 Redwood Hwy., Grants Pass, OR 97526. 503-479-554x1201. Weekly.
COLLEGE/UNIVERSITY

The Madras Pioneer, 452 Sixth St., Box W., Madras, OR 97741. 503-475-2275. Weekly.
COMMUNITY

Magnolia News, 225 West Galer, Seattle, WA 98119. 206-282-0900. Weekly.
COMMUNITY

The Mail Tribune, 33 N. Fir St., Box 1108, Medford, OR 97501. 503-776-4411; 503-776-4369. Editor: Bob Hunter. Ads: Grady Singletary. Lifestyles Editor: Cleve Twitchell. Daily. Founded 1906. Circ. 28,000. Sub/$8.75. Only accepts occasional travel articles from freelance writers in Medford. Query by phone, ask for Richard Sept.
COMMUNITY

Malheur Enterprise, 263 A Street W., Box 310, Vale, OR 97918. 503-473-3377. Weekly.
COMMUNITY

Marysville Globe, 8213 State St., Marysville, WA 98270. 206-659-1300. Editor: Brent Anderson. Ads: Dan Berentson. Weekly. Sub $16/yr. Uses freelance material. Byline given. Pays on publication. Submit query letter, SASE, phone. Accepts nonfiction, cartoons, interviews, articles, photos.
COMMUNITY

Mason County Journal & Belfair Herald, PO Box 430, Shelton, WA 98584. 206-426-4412. Weekly.
COMMUNITY

Masonic Tribune, Murray Publishing Company, 2314 Third Ave., Seattle, WA 98121. 206-285-1505. Editor: Ruth Todahl. Ads: Sid Worbass. Weekly. Sub $15. Circ. 5,500. Material supplied by fraternal members. No pay. Byline given. Uses B&W glossy photos. Guidelines; sample 50 cents.
DISABLED

The Mast, Pacific Lutheran University, Tacoma, WA 98447. 206-535-7387. Weekly student newspaper.
COLLEGE/UNIVERSITY

The Meagher County News, PO Box 349, 13 E. Main, White Sulphur Spring, MT 59645. 406-547-3831. Editor: Verle Rademacher. Weekly.
COMMUNITY

Medium, PO Box 22047, Seattle, WA 98122. 206-323-3070. Weekly.
COMMUNITY

Methow Valley News, PO Box 97, Twisp, WA 98856. 509-997-7011. Weekly. Sub $15-30/yr. Circ. 3,000. Uses freelance material. Byline given. Pays money on publication. Query w/SASE. Responds in 2 wks; publishes in 2 wks. Accepts news items, nonfiction, photos (B&W), interviews, op/ed.
COMMUNITY

Mid-County Memo, 4052 N.E. 22nd Ave., Portland, OR 97212-1503. Editors: Rich Riegel. Ads: Tim Curran. Monthly tabloid, founded 1985. Circ. 15,000. Sub/$11. Uses freelance material. Byline given. Pays nothing. Acquires all rights. Query by phone. Responds immediately; publishes in 1-3 months. Accepts news items, photos, in-

terviews. "We are a community newspaper serving the area between 82nd Ave. and 155th Ave., with Stark as the southern boundary, Sandy Blvd. as the north." Verbal guidelines. Back issues free.
COMMUNITY

Miles City Star, 13 N. 6th St., PO Box 1216, Miles City, MT 59301. 406-232-1216. Editor: Zack Jennings.
COMMUNITY

The Mill City Enterprise, 117 N.E. Wall, Box 348, Mill City, OR 97360. 503-897-2772. Weekly.
COMMUNITY

Miner & Gem State Miner, PO Box 349, Newport, WA 99156. 509-447-2433. Weekly.
CRAFTS/HOBBIES, GEOLOGY/GEOGRAPHY, RECREATION

Mineral Independent, PO Box 98, 106 Second Ave. W., Superior, MT 59872. 406-822-3329. Editor: Joe Rapier. Weekly.
COMMUNITY

Missoulian, PO Box 8029, Missoula, MT 59807. 406-523-5200. Editor: Brad Hurd. Daily. Features editor: Teresa Jordan. Accepts a small amount of freelance material, mainly from Missoula writers. Pays money on publication; acquires first rights. Query letter, clips, sample. Responds in one month. Accepts general material. Sometimes accepts photos.
COMMUNITY

Molalla Pioneer, 217 E. Main St., Box 168, Molalla, OR 97038. 503-829-2301. Weekly.
COMMUNITY

Monroe Monitor/Valley News, PO Box 399, Monroe, WA 98272. 206-794-7116. Editor: Fred Willenbrock. 206-794-7116. Ads: Pat Oliffeer. Weekly. Circ. 3,500. Sub $17 out of county. Not a freelance market.
COMMUNITY

Montana Kaimin, University of Montana, Missoula, MT 59812. Student newspaper.
COLLEGE/UNIVERSITY

Montana Standard, 25 W. Granite St., PO Box 627, Butte, MT 59703. 406-782-8301. Contact: Rick Foote, Editor. Daily.
COMMUNITY

Morton Journal, PO Drawer M, Morton, WA 98356. 206-496-5993. Weekly.
COMMUNITY

Mountain Home News, PO Box 1330, Mountain Home AFB, ID 83647. 208-587-3331.
COMMUNITY, MILITARY/VETS

The Mountaineer, PO Box 529, Johames Ave., Big Sandy, MT 55920. 406-378-2176. Editor: James Rettig. Weekly.
COMMUNITY

MSU Exponent, Montana State University, 330 Strand Union Building, Bozeman, MT 59717-0001. 406-994-2611. Semiweekly Student newspaper.
COLLEGE/UNIVERSITY

Mt. Tabor Bulletin, 12311 N.E. Glisan #103, Portland, OR 97230. 503-256-2833. Contact: Quentin Smith.
COMMUNITY

Myrtle Point Herald, PO Box 128, Myrtle Point, OR 97458-0128. 503-572-2717. Weekly.
COMMUNITY

Nanaimo Daily Free Press, Box 69, 225 Commercial St., Nanaimo, BC V9R 5K5. 604-753-3451. Editor: Wayne Campbell. Daily.
COMMUNITY

The Neighbor, Pry Publishing Co., 600 N.W. 14th Ave., Portland, OR 97209. 503-226-8335. Editor: Bill Morgan. Ads: Kimberly Myers. Semimonthly tabloid, founded 1975. Circ. 16,500. Uses freelance material. Byline given. Pays

money on publication. Acquires 1st rights. Submit query letter, clips, SASE. Dot matrix OK. Responds in 1-2 wks. Accepts new items, nonfiction, photos, articles. Topics: events and people of N.W. Portland and surrounding neighborhoods.
COMMUNITY

Nelson Daily News, 226 Baker St., Nelson, BC V1L 4H3. 604-352-3552. Editor: Morrie Zaitlin. Daily.
COMMUNITY

The New Era Newspaper, 1200 Long St., Box 38, Sweet Home, OR 97386. 503-367-2135. Weekly.
COMMUNITY

The New Times, PO Box 51186, Seattle, WA 98115-1186. 206-524-9071. Editor: Krysta Gibson. Monthly. Sub $12/ yr. Circ. 17,000. Uses freelance material. Pays on acceptance in subs. Acquires 1st rights. Byline given. Submit photocopied ms, SASE. Reports in 3 mos; publishes in 6 mos. Accepts nonfiction, cartoons, interviews. Topics: New Age, spirituality, human potential, holistic health, interviews. Photos B&W, 5x7 or larger, nature or human interest; 1 yr. subs for payment. Tip: looking for positive information which will help our readers grow spiritually, emotionally & physically. Guidelines SASE. Sample $2.
ASTROLOGY/SPIRITUAL, HEALTH, NEW AGE

Newberg Graphic, 109 N. School, Box 110, Newberg, OR 97132. 503-538-2181. Weekly.
COMMUNITY

Newberg Times, PO Box 370, Beaverton, OR 97075-0370. Weekly.
COMMUNITY

Newport News-Times/Lincoln County Leader, 831 N.E. Avery, Box 965, Newport, OR 97365. 503-265-8571. Weekly.
COMMUNITY

News, Box 3007, Castlegar, BC V1N 3H4. 604-365-7266. Editor: Simon Birch. BiWeekly.
COMMUNITY

The News Guard, 930 S.E. Highway 101, Box 848, Lincoln City, OR 97367. 503-994-2178. Weekly.
COMMUNITY

News Register, 611 E. Third, Box 727, McMinnville, OR 97128. 503-472-5114. Daily.
COMMUNITY

News Tribune, PO Box 499, Snohomish, WA 98290. 206-258-9396. Weekly.
COMMUNITY

Newsbrief, 320 S. Kimball Ave., Caldwell, ID 83605. 454-9300. Contact: Larry Blackburn.
UNSPECIFIED

Newscast, PO Box 998, Ephrata, WA 98823. 509-754-4636. Weekly.
COMMUNITY

The News-Examiner, PO Box 278, Montpelier, ID 83254. 208-847-0552. Editor: Rosa Moosman. Weekly. Uses freelance material by assignment only. Byline given. Accepts news items, photos (B&W). Topics: Bear Lake area.
COMMUNITY

News-Journal, 600 South Washington, Kent, WA 98031. 206-872-6600. Daily.
COMMUNITY

News-Miner, PO Box 438, Republic, WA 99166. 509-775-3558. Weekly.
COMMUNITY

The News-Review, 345 N.E. Winchester, Roseburg, OR 97470. 503-672-3321; Fax 503-673-5994. Editor: Faith Leith. Ads: Kelly Gant. Circ. 28,000. Founded 1867. Sub/ $6.50. Daily.
COMMUNITY

News-Times, PO 408, Forest Grove, OR 97116. 503-357-3181. Weekly.
COMMUNITY

NIC Sentinel, North Idaho College, 1000 West Garden, Couer d'Alene, ID 83814. 769-3388. Student newspaper. Not a freelance market.
COMMUNITY, COLLEGE/UNIVERSITY

Nisqually Valley News, PO Box 597, Yelm, WA 98597. 206-458-2681. Weekly.
COMMUNITY

North Beach Beacon, PO Box 1207, Ocean Shores, WA 98569. 206-289-3359. Weekly.
COMMUNITY

North Side News, PO Box 468, Jerome, ID 83338. 208-324-3391.
COMMUNITY, UNSPECIFIED

Northern Kittitas County Tribune, PO Box 308, Cle Elum, WA 98922. 509-674-2511. Weekly.
COMMUNITY

Northshore Citizen, PO Box 647, Bothell, WA 98041. 206-486-1231. Weekly.
COMMUNITY

Northwest Airlifter, PO Box 98801, Tacoma, WA 98499. 206-584-1212. Weekly.
AVIATION

Northwest Comic News, PO Box 11825, Eugene, OR 97440. 503-344-1922. Editor: Taft Chatham. Biweekly founded in 1989. Sub $15/yr. Circ. 25,000. Uses freelance material. Pays money, copies on publication. Submit complete ms, query letter, SASE. Responds in 2 wks; publishes in 2 mos. Accepts cartoons, political satire (1,000 wds). Sample.
HUMOR

Northwest Computer News, 7904 S.W. 14th Ave., Portland, OR 97219. 503-245-3381. Contact: Ed Reid. Monthly newspaper.
BUSINESS, COMPUTERS

Northwest Labor Press, 4313 N.E. Tillamook, #206, Portland, OR 97213. 503-288-3311; Fax 503-288-3320. Editor: Michael Gutwig. Biweekly tabloid newspaper covering labor-related issues. Circ. 52,000. Founded 1900. Mailed to union members for $10 yearly.
LABOR/WORK

Northwest Yachting, 5206 Ballard N.W., Seattle, WA 98107. 206-789-8116. Editor: Daniel Schworer. Monthly tabloid. Pays money. Submit phone query. Accepts nonfiction, photos. Topics: news, activities and information related to boating in the Northwest and southwest Canada.
BOATING, SPORTS

Nugget, Box 610, Nome, AK 99762. 907-443-5235. Weekly.
COMMUNITY

NW Examiner, 2066 N.W. Irving, Portland, OR 97209. 503-241-2353. Contact: Allan Classen. Monthly tabloid. Circ. 15,000. Accepts submissions w/SASE. Payment negotiable. Byline given. Topics: issues of interest to N.W. Portland community.
COMMUNITY

The Observer, 1710 6th St., Box 3170, La Grande, OR 97850. 503-963-3161. Daily.
COMMUNITY

Oceanedge, 8423 South 19th, Tacoma, WA 98466. 206-564-5515. Contact: Tom Heidlebaugh. Irregularly published. Focus is on storytelling. Accepts freelance material. Write for more information.
ENTERTAINMENT

Olympia News, PO Box 366, Olympia, WA 98507. 206-943-2950. Weekly.
COMMUNITY

Omak Chronicle, PO Box 553, Omak, WA 98841. 509-826-1110. Weekly.
COMMUNITY

The Oregon Scientist, P. O. Box 230220, Tigard, OR 97223. 503-639-5637; 503-292-8460. Editor: Marge Davenport. Ads: L. B. Cady. Quarterly founded in 1988. Sub $8/yr. Circ. 32,000. Uses freelance material. Requires research/science or technology expertise. Pays money on publication. Acquires 1st rights. Byline given. Submit phone query. Accepts news items, photos, interviews, op/ed, articles. Sample $2.
SCIENCE, TECHNICAL

The Oregonian, 1320 S.W. Broadway, Portland, OR 97201. 503-221-8279; Fax 503-294-4199. Editor: William A. Hilliard. Daily. Founded 1850. Sub/$11 per month. Circ. 343,000. Regional coverage of Portland appears in Thursday's paper. Areas: Metro West, Mid-county/Metro East, Metro South, Metro Portland. No guidelines.
COMMUNITY, ENTERTAINMENT

Osoyoos Times Ltd, 8712-76th St., Boa 359, Osoyoos, BC V0H 1V0. 604-495-7225. Contact: Patrick Turner. Weekly community newspaper. Accepts some freelance material of local impact. Submit query letter or query by phone. Photocopies OK. Responds in 1 week. Accepts news items, photos, articles, interviews, op/ed.
COMMUNITY

Othello Outlook, PO Box O, Othello, WA 99344. 509-488-3342. Weekly.
COMMUNITY

Outlook, PO Box 455, Sedro Woolley, WA 98284. 206-855-1306. Weekly.
COMMUNITY

Pacific Index, Pacific University, U.C. Box 695, Forest Grove, OR 97116. 503-357-6151.
COLLEGE/UNIVERSITY

Palouse Empire Daily News, S. 107 Grand, Pullman, WA 99163. 509-334-6397.
COMMUNITY

The Pathfinder, Lewis-Clark State College, 6th St. & 8th Ave., Lewiston, ID 83501. 799-2470. Student newspaper.
COLLEGE/UNIVERSITY

Peace River Block News, 901-100 Ave., Dawson River, BC V1G 1W2. 604-782-4888. Editor: Stan Wieczorek. Ads: Kathleen Block. Daily.
COMMUNITY

The Peak, Peak Trailers, Simon Fraser University, Burnaby, BC V5A 1S6. 604-291-3598. Student newspaper published 39 times a year. Circ. 8,000. Sub $28. Accepts freelance material typed ds. Byline given. No pay. Nonfiction, student issues.
COLLEGE/UNIVERSITY, CULTURE, EDUCATION

Pendleton Record, 809 S.E. Court, Box 69, Pendleton, OR 97801. 503-276-2853. Weekly.
COMMUNITY

The Peninsula Clarion, PO Box 3009, Trading Bay & Granite Point Aves., Kenai, AK 99611. 907-283-7551. Contact: Lori Evans. Daily.
COMMUNITY

Peninsula Gateway, PO Box 407, Gig Harbor, WA 98335. 206-858-9921. Weekly.
COMMUNITY

Penticton Herald, 186 Nanaimo Ave. W., Penticton, BC V2A 1N4. 604-492-4002. Contact: Michael Ingraham. Daily.
COMMUNITY

Petersburg Pilot, PO Box 930, 214 Harborway, Petersburg, AK 99654. 907-772-9393. Contact: Ronald J. Loesch. Weekly.
COMMUNITY

The Philipsburg Mail, PO Box 160, Philipsburg, MT 59858. 406-859-3223. Contact: Dean & Trilby Neitz. Weekly.
COMMUNITY

The Phillips County News, PO Box 850, 18 S. 1st St., Malta, MT 59538. 406-654-2020. Editor: Curtis Starr. Weekly.
COMMUNITY

Pierce County Business Examiner, 5007 Pacific Hwy East, Ste. 22, Tacoma, WA 98424. 206-922-1522. Editor: Jeff Rhodes. Ads: Jeff Rounce. Biweekly of business news for Tacoma-Pierce County. Circ. 17,000. Sub $15. Uses 4 freelance mss per issue. Payment: $2/column inch and copies on publication. Byline given. Purchases 1st rights. Query w/SASE. Phone query, dot matrix, photocopies OK. Nonfiction: 2.5 pages ds. Articles on business topics primarily for Pierce Co, but applicable to all of WA considered. Photos: B&W 5x7 or larger. $2/inch. Sample, SASE.
BUSINESS, WASHINGTON

Pike Place Market News, 93 Pike St. #312, Seattle, WA 98101. 206-587-0351. Contact: Clayton Park. Monthly. Sub $12. Circ. 20,000. Uses freelance material; pays copies, occasionally up to $25. Byline given. Assignment only. Phone queries, photocopies, dot matrix, OK. Accepts nonfiction, fiction, photos. Topics: articles about Pike Place Market or other public markets in the US, personal memoirs, or direct experience. Sample with SASE.
COMMUNITY, ARTS, ENTERTAINMENT

Pioneer Log, Lewis and Clark College, LC Box 21, Portland, OR 97219. 503-244-6161. Student newspaper.
COLLEGE/UNIVERSITY, EDUCATION, ENTERTAINMENT

Plentywood Herald, 111 W. 2nd Ave., PO Box 297, Plentywood, MT 59254. 406-765-1150. Contact: J. Stuart Polk. Weekly.
COMMUNITY

Polk County Itemizer-Observer, 147 S.E. Court St., Box 108, Dallas, OR 97338. 503-623-6364. Weekly.
COMMUNITY

Polson Flathead Courier, PO Box 1091, Polson, MT 59860. 406-883-4343.
COMMUNITY

Port Orford News, 519 W. 10th, Box 5, Port Orford, OR 97465. 503-332-2361. Weekly.
COMMUNITY

Post Register, 333 Northgate Mile, Idaho Falls, ID 83401.
COMMUNITY

Prime Time, North Bend Publishing Co., PO Box 248, Bandon, OR 97411-0248. Editor: Gail Snyder. Ads: Bruce Root. Monthly. Free to seniors. Circ. 9,000. Uses freelance material. Pays $25 on publication. Byline given. Submit query for assignment only, SASE. Simultaneous OK. Reports in 2-3 mos; publishes in 1-2 mos. Accepts nonfiction, photos (B&W negatives), senior issues and features with a local slant (Coos County), 500-600 wds. Guidelines; sample 75 cents.
SENIOR CITIZENS

The Prince George Citizen, PO Box 5700, 150 Brunswick St., Prince George, BC V2L 5K9. 604-562-2441. Contact: R. Nagel. Daily.
COMMUNITY

Prince Rupert Daily News, Box 580, Prince Rupert, BC V8J 3R9. 604-624-6781. Contact: Lois Armas. Ads: Bonnie Roberts. Daily. Circ. 3500, sub $84. Freelance material accepted by assignment only. Byline given. Pays money on publication. Acquires first rights.
COMMUNITY

The Print, Clackamas Community College, 19600 S. Molalla Ave., Oregon City, OR 97045. 503-657-8400x309.
COLLEGE/UNIVERSITY

Progress, Clark College, 1800 E. McLoughlin, Vancouver, WA 98663. 206-699-0159. Weekly.
COLLEGE/UNIVERSITY

Prosser Record-Bulletin, PO Box 750, Prosser, WA 99350. 509-786-1711. Weekly.
COMMUNITY

Puget Sound Computer User, 3530 Bagley Ave. N.', Seattle, WA 98103. 206-547-4950; Fax 206-547-5355. Editor: Terry Hansen. Ads: Ray Kehl. Circ. 85,000. Founded 1985. Monthly tabloid providing advice on computer purchases, installation, and uses. Free to qualified subscribers or $12/year.
COMPUTERS

Queen Anne News, 225 West Galer, Seattle, WA 98119. 206-282-0900. Weekly.
COMMUNITY

Quest, Reed College, 3203 S.W. Woodstock Blvd., Portland, OR 97202. 503-771-111x2373. Weekly.
COLLEGE/UNIVERSITY

Quincy Valley Post-Register, PO Box 217, Quincy, WA 98848. 509-787-4511. Weekly.
COMMUNITY

Ravalli Republic, 232 Main St., Hamilton, MT 59840. 406-363-3300. Editor: John McConnaghey. Daily.
COMMUNITY

Record, PO Box 458, Odessa, WA 99159. 509-982-2632. Weekly.
COMMUNITY

The Record-Courier, 1718 Main, Box 70, Baker, OR 97814. 503-523-5353. Weekly.
COMMUNITY

Redmond Spokesman, 226 N.W. Sixth, Box 788, Redmond, OR 97756. 503-548-2184. Weekly.
COMMUNITY

Reflector, PO Box 2020, Battle Ground, WA 98604. 206-687-5151. Weekly.
COMMUNITY

Register, 610 Ash, Othello, WA 99344. Weekly.
COMMUNITY

The Register-Guard, 975 High St., Box 10188, Eugene, OR 97401. 503-485-1234; Fax 503-683-7622. Editor: Patrick Yack. Ads: Michael Raz. Daily. Founded 1867. Sub/ $9. Circ. 73,000.
COMMUNITY

Reporter, PO Box 38, Mercer Island, WA 98040. 206-232-1215. Weekly.
COMMUNITY

Review, PO Box 511, Toppenish, WA 98948. 509-865-4055. Weekly.
COMMUNITY

Richland Free Press, PO Box 1939, Sidney, MT 59270. 406-482-5885. Weekly.
COMMUNITY

Richmond Review, 507-13231 Delf Pl., Richmond, BC V6V 2A2. 604-273-7744. Occasionally uses freelance material, mainly coverage of local events.
COMMUNITY

The Ritzville Adams County Journal, PO Box 288, Ritzville, WA 99169. 509-659-1020. Weekly.
COMMUNITY

The River Press, PO Box 69, 1212 Front St., Fort Benton, MT 59442. Contact: Joan Stewart. Weekly.
COMMUNITY

Ronan Pioneer, 123 Main St. S.W., Ronan, MT 59864. 406-676-3800.
COMMUNITY

Roseburg News-Review, 345 N.E. Winchester, Roseburg, OR 97470. 503-672-3321. Daily.
COMMUNITY

Rotund World, 1336 S.E. Marion St., Portland, OR 97202. 503-236-9962. Editor: Joel Weinstein. Quarterly. Sub/$10. Freelance material is accepted by commission only. Pays money on publication; acquires 1st rights. Query letter, clips, idea. Responds in 4-6 wks; publishes in 6 mos. Accepts nonfiction and travel. Request sample copy.
LITERARY

The Roundup Record-Tribune, PO Box 747, 24 Main St., Roundup, MT 59072. 406-323-1105. Contact: Louise Rasmussen. Weekly.
COMMUNITY

Salmon Recorder-Herald, PO Box 310, Salmon, ID 83467. 208-756-2221.
COMMUNITY, UNSPECIFIED

Sammamish Valley News, PO Box 716, Redmond, WA 98052. 206-885-4178. Weekly, founded in 1945. Editor: Rick Beasley. Ads: Phyllis Neimeyer. Sub $15. Circ. 18,400. Uses freelance material. Byline given. Pays money on publication. Submit query letter, complete ms, SASE, phone. Responds in 1 wk; publishes in 1 wk. Accepts news items, cartoons, photos (B&W film or print), interviews, op/ed, articles. Topics: local to reader area.
COMMUNITY

Sanders County Ledger, PO Box 219, 604 Main St., Thompson Falls, MT 59873. 406-827-3421. Contact: Bina Eggensperger. Weekly.
COMMUNITY

Sandpoint Daily Bee (News Bulletin), PO Box 159, Sandpoint, ID 83864. 208-263-9534. Daily.
COMMUNITY, UNSPECIFIED

The Sandy Post, 17270 Bluff Rd., Box 68, Sandy, OR 97055. 503-668-5548. Editor: Scott Newton. Weekly.
COMMUNITY

The Scroll, Ricks College, Spori Building, Rexburg, ID 83460. 208-356-2903. Student newspaper.
COLLEGE/UNIVERSITY

The Searchlight, Wold Point c/o Herald-News, Culbertson, MT 59218. 406-787-5821. Contact: Ila Mae Forbregd. Weekly.
COMMUNITY

Seaside Signal, 113 N. Holladay, Box 848, Seaside, OR 97138. 503-738-5561. Weekly.
COMMUNITY

Seattle Chinese Post, 414 8th Ave S., Seattle, WA 98104. 206-223-0623. Contact: Susan L. Cassidy, Editor. Weekly.
ASIAN AMERICAN, COMMUNITY, CULTURE

The Seattle Medium, 2600 S. Jackson, Seattle, WA 98144. 206-632-3307. Editor: Connie Bennett Cameron. "Pacific Northwest's largest Black-owned newspaper."
BLACK

Seattle Times, Fairview Ave. N. & John St., PO Box 70, Seattle, WA 98111. 206-464-2111; Fax 206-464-2131. Contact: Kathy Andrisevic. Ads: Marji Ruiz. Daily. Founded 1896. Sub/$8.50. Circ. 238,000. Accepts freelance material; byline given. Pays money on publication; acquires 1st rights. Query w/SASE, complete ms. Photocopy OK. Responds in 2 wks; publishes in 6 wks. Fiction, cartoons, nonfiction, articles, humor, home features. 3,000-4,000 words; regional writers and topics preferred. Guidelines.
COMMUNITY

Seattle Weekly, 1931 Second Ave., Seattle, WA 98101. Editor: David Brewster. Weekly tabloid. Circ. 30,000. Payment: Money on publication. Byline given. Query, outline w/SASE. Nonfiction. Guidelines; sample 75¢.
CULTURE, LITERARY

Seeley Swan Pathfinder, PO Box 702, Seeley Lake, MT 59686-0702. 406-677-2022. Editor: Gary Noland. Published weekly. Sub $15-18/yr.
COMMUNITY

The Sellwood Bee, Pry Publishing Co., 600 N.W. 14th Ave., Portland, OR 97209. 503-226-8335. Editor: Marcia Pry. Ads: Greg Hudson. Weekly tabloid, founded 1904. Circ. 2,500. Uses freelance material. Byline given. Pays money on publication. Acquires 1st rights. Query with clips, SASE. Dot matrix OK. Responds in 1-2 wks. Accepts news items, nonfiction, photos, articles. Topics: S.E. Portland neighborhoods, Sellwood-Moreland. Guidelines.
COMMUNITY

Sentinel, Box 799, Sitka, AK 99835. 907-747-3219. Daily.
COMMUNITY

Sequim Sun, PO Box 2049, Sequim, WA 98382.
COMMUNITY

The Seward Phoenix Log, PO Box 89, Seward, AK 99664. 907-224-8070. Contact: Edgar Blatchford. Weekly.
COMMUNITY

The Shelby Promoter, PO Box 610, 119 Maple Ave., Shelby, MT 59474. 406-434-5171. Contact: John Kavanagh. Weekly.
COMMUNITY

Sherman County Journal, 107 W. 1st, Box 284, Moro, OR 97039. 503-565-3515. Weekly.
COMMUNITY

Shoshone News-Press, 401 Main St., Kellogg, ID 83837. 208-783-1107.
COMMUNITY

Sidney Herald, PO Box 1033, Sidney, MT 59270. 406-482-2706.
COMMUNITY

Silver State Post, PO Box 271, 312 Missouri Ave., Deer Lodge, MT 59722. 406-846-2424. Contact: Aubrey Larson. Weekly.
COMMUNITY

Silverdale Reporter - Kitsap Newspaper Group, 2817 Wheaton Way #104, PO Box 2588, Bremerton, WA 98310. 206-373-7969. Editor: Julie Seibert. Ads: David Bird. Sub $16/yr. Circ. 17,000. Weekly. Uses freelance material. Pays $5-$10 per story, depending; $5-10 per B&W glossy, any size, on acceptance. Byline given. Submit clips, ms, SASE, phone. Reports ASAP, publishes in 1-2 wks. Accepts nonfiction, photos, news items, interviews.
COMMUNITY

The Silverton Appeal-Tribune, 399 S. Water, Box 35, Silverton, OR 97381. 503-873-8385. Weekly.
COMMUNITY

Siskiyou, Southern Oregon State College, Stevenson Union, Ashland, OR 97520. 503-482-6306.
COLLEGE/UNIVERSITY, CULTURE, EDUCATION

The Siuslaw News, PO Box 10, 148 Maple St., Florence, OR 97439. 503-997-3441. Fax 503-997-7979. Editor: Robert Serra. Ads: Pamela Girard. Weekly, founded in 1890. Circ. 6,000. Sub Lane County $18/$26 out of county/$45 out of state/$90 out of country. Accepts freelance material. Byline given. Query with ms, SASE. Phone queries, dot matrix, photocopies OK. Accepts news, articles, op/ed, reviews photos.
COMMUNITY

Skagit Argus, PO Box 739, Mount Vernon, WA 98273. 206-336-6555. Weekly.
COMMUNITY

Skagit Farmer and Tribune, PO Box 153, Lynden, WA 98264. 206-354-4444. Weekly.
COMMUNITY

Skagit Valley Herald, PO Box 578, Mount Vernon, WA 98273-0739. 206-336-5751. Daily.
COMMUNITY

Skamania County Pioneer, PO Box 250, Stevenson, WA 98648. 509-427-8444. Weekly.
COMMUNITY

The Skanner, 2337 N. Williams, PO Box 5455, Portland, OR 97228. Weekly tabloid of the Portland Black community.
BLACK, COMMUNITY

Snohomish County Tribune, PO Box 499, Snohomish, WA 98290. 206-776-7546. Weekly.
COMMUNITY

South County Citizen, c/o Northshore Citizen, PO Box 647, Bothell, WA 98041. 206-486-1231. Weekly.
COMMUNITY

South District Journal, 2314 3rd Ave., Seattle, WA 98121-1789. Weekly.
COMMUNITY

South Pierce County Dispatch, PO Box 248, Eatonville, WA. 98328. 206-832-4411.
COMMUNITY

South Whidbey Record, Box 10, Oak Harbor, WA 98277. 206-321-5300. Weekly.
COMMUNITY

Southern Willamette Alliance, 454 Willamette, Eugene, OR 97401. 503-342-0565. Editor: Peter Holden. Ads: Dave Zupan. Monthly. Sub $10-25/yr. Circ. 7,000. Uses freelance material. Pay varies. Byline given. Submit query letter, complete ms, SASE, phone. Simultaneous, disk/modem subs OK. Accepts nonfiction, photos, cartoons, poetry, news items, interviews, op/ed, reviews; art work for cover. Topics: particularly interested in investigative pieces focusing on current environmental and human rights issues. Guidelines; sample $1.
ENVIRONMENT/RESOURCES, POLITICS

The Southwestern, Southwestern Oregon Community College, Coos Bay, OR 97420. 503-888-2525x333. Biweekly.
COLLEGE/UNIVERSITY, CULTURE, EDUCATION

Spectrum, 6420 S.W. Macadam Ave #210, Portland, OR 97201. 503-244-2227. Monthly. Contact: Lynda Leary. Circ. 150,000; sub $12/yr. Rarely accepts freelance material. Query by phone. Accepts cartoons, memoirs, nonfiction. No payment for memoirs but byline. Spectrum insert "Yester Year" accepts memoirs/nostalgia pieces (short). Byline, no pay. submit to 1385 S Colorado Blvd. #218, Denver, CO 80222. Sample.
BIOGRAPHY, SENIOR CITIZENS

Spilyay Tymoo, PO Box 870, Warm Springs, OR 97761. 503-553-1644. Editor: Sid Miller. Sub $9. Biweekly for tribal membership. Uses local news, Native American issues. Sample $1.
COMMUNITY, MINORITIES/ETHNIC, NATIVE AMERICAN

Spokane Chronicle, PO Box 2160, Spokane, WA 99210. 509-455-7010. Daily.
COMMUNITY

The Spokesman-Review, PO Box 2160, Spokane, WA 99210. 509-455-7010. Daily. No submission information. Query w/SASE.
COMMUNITY

The Spotlight, 52644 N.E. First, Box C, Scappoose, OR 97056. 503-543-6387. Publisher: Kathy Erickson. Second office: 145 N 18th, St. Helens, OR 97056.
COMMUNITY

The Sprague Advocate, PO Box 327, Sprague, WA 99032. 509-257-2311. Editor/Ads: Kim Nolt. Weekly founded in 1888. Sub $20/yr. Circ. 600. Does not accept freelance material. Accepts news items, biography, op/ed, memoirs, photos (B&W). Topics: must be relevant to area, used on space-available basis. No payment for unsolicited copy. Sample $1.50.
AGRICULTURE/FARMING, COMMUNITY, WASHINGTON

The Springfield News, 1887 Laura St., Box 139, Springfield, OR 97477. 503-746-1671. Editor: Steve Collier. Ads: Tom Chastain (retail)/Carol Roberts (classified). Semi-Weekly. Circ. 10,000; sub $27/yr. Accepts some freelance material (occasional travel or specialty work only). Byline given. Pays money, copies on publication. First rights acquired. Query w/SASE.
TRAVEL, COMMUNITY

St. Helens Chronicle, 195 S. 15th St., St. Helens, OR 97051. 503-397-0116.
COMMUNITY

St. Johns Review, 600 N.W. 14th Ave., Portland, OR 97209-2203. 503-226-8335. Editors: Tom or Marcia Pry. Weekly tabloid. Uses freelance material. Byline given. Pays money on publication. Acquires 1st rights. Query with clips, SASE. Dot matrix OK. Responds in 1-2 wks. Accepts new items, nonfiction, photos, articles. Topics: St. Johns neighborhood of Portland. Guidelines.
COMMUNITY

St. Maries Gazette Record, 127 S. 7th, St. Maries, ID 83861. 208-245-4538.
COMMUNITY

Stamp Collector, PO Box 10, Albany, OR 97321-0006. 503-928-3569. Editor: Ken Palke. Ads: Mary Mansfield. Weekly. Sub $29.90. Circ. 22,000. Uses 8 freelance mss per issue. Pays $25+ on publication. Acquires 1st rights. Byline given. Submit query w/SASE, phone query. Dot matrix OK. Reports in 14 days. Publishing time variable. Accepts nonfiction geared toward stamp collectors, including beginner and advanced collectors and their interests. B&W photos preferred. Sample $1.
COLLECTING, CRAFTS/HOBBIES

The Stamp Wholesaler, 520 E. First Ave, Albany, OR 97321. 503-928-4484. Editor: Dane Claussen. Published 28 times a yr. Sub $20. Circ. 5,000. Uses 4 freelance mss per issue (experienced stamp collectors and/or dealers only). Pays money on publication. Acquires all rights. Byline given. Submit phone query, SASE. Dot matrix OK. Accepts nonfiction. Topics: How to run a retail stamp shop, how to buy and sell stamps through the mail and at stamp shows, developments at U.S. Postal Service, ways dealers can use computers, handle inventory, save on taxes. Sample.
BUSINESS, COLLECTING, CRAFTS/HOBBIES

The Standard-Register, PO Box 988, Tekoa, WA 99033. 509-284-5782. Editor: Bonita Lawhead. Ads: Sandra Nicholson. Weekly. Sub $19/yr. in-county. Circ. 1,800. Uses freelance material. Pays 50¢/col. inch on publication. Byline given. Submit query w/clips, SASE, phone. Dot matrix, photocopied subs OK. Reports in 2 wks; publishes in 1-2 mos. Accepts nonfiction of local human interest, recreation, agriculture. B&W photos or negatives, color photos, $3 on publication. Sample.
AGRICULTURE/FARMING, COMMUNITY, RECREATION

Stanwood/Camano News, PO Box 999, Stanwood, WA 98292. 206-629-2155. Weekly.
COMMUNITY

The Star, PO Box 150, Grand Coulee, WA 99133. 509-633-1350. Weekly.
COMMUNITY

Star-News, PO Box 985, McCall, ID 83638. Editor: Tom Grote.
COMMUNITY, UNSPECIFIED

The Statesman Journal, 280 Church Street N.E., Box 13009, Salem, OR 97309. 503-399-6611; Fax 503-399-6706. Editor: William Florence. Ads: Gary Husman. Daily.

Founded 1851. Sub/$10.50. Circ. 62,000.
COMMUNITY

Statesman-Examiner, PO Box 271, Colville, WA 99114. 509-684-4567. Weekly.
COMMUNITY

Stayton Mail, PO Box 400, Stayton, OR 97383. 503-769-6338. Weekly.
COMMUNITY

The Stillwater County News, PO Box 659, Columbus, MT 59019. 406-322-5212. Contact: Larry Tanglen. Weekly.
COMMUNITY

Sun, PO Box 689, Sunnyside, WA 98944. 509-837-3701. Weekly.
COMMUNITY

The Sun, 248 S. Bridge, Box 68, Sheridan, OR 97378. 503-843-2312. Weekly.
COMMUNITY

Sun Enterprise, 258 Monmouth St., Independence, OR 97351-2424. 503-838-3467. Weekly.
COMMUNITY

The Sun Tribune, 104 E. Central, Box 430, Sutherlin, OR 97479. 503-459-2261. Weekly.
COMMUNITY

Sunnyside Daily News, PO Box 878, Sunnyside, WA 98944. 509-837-4500. Daily.
COMMUNITY

Sunriver SUN, PO Box 3589, Sunriver, OR 97707. 503-593-4285. Contact: Marti Cheshire. Ads: Susan Williamson. Monthly. Circ. 10,000. Sub $15/year. Freelance material accepted. Byline given. Pays on publication, no rights acquired. Query by letter w/ SASE, dot matrix OK. Responds in 15 days, publishes in 2 months. Interviews and news items accepted. "We are looking for stories to fill our 'Lookback' section. They must be written in first person, be based in truth and take the reader back in time." Guidelines; back issues; $1 each.
COMMUNITY

Sweet Home New Era, 1200 Long St., Sweet Home, OR 97386. 503-367-2135.
COMMUNITY

Tacoma Daily Index, PO Box 1303, Tacoma, WA 98401. 206-627-4853. Daily.
COMMUNITY

Tacoma News Tribune, PO Box 11000, Tacoma, WA 98411-0008. 206-597-8551. Editor: Al Gibbs. Daily. "The only freelance writing currently being accepted by our newspaper is for the travel section." Query w/SASE.
COMMUNITY, TRAVEL

Teaching Today, U of I Off-Campus Programs, College of Education, Moscow, ID 83843. Contact: Sid Eder. Published in November & April each year provides a communication link between the U of I and the education community of Idaho and the Inland Northwest. Guest editorials solicited; pay $25.
EDUCATION, IDAHO, NORTHWEST

The Terry Tribune, PO Box 127, 203 Logan Ave., Terry, MT 59349. 406-637-5513. Contact: Fred Roach. Weekly.
COMMUNITY

The Third Age Newspaper, 8221 44th Ave. W., Ste. E., Mukilteo, WA 98275. 206-290-1277. Monthly.
UNSPECIFIED

This Week, RFD Publications Inc., 9600 S.W. Boeckman Rd., Wilsonville, OR 97070. 503-682-1881; Fax 682-2133. Editor: Don Campbell. Ads: 503-682-1223. Weekly. Free Circ. 500,000 mailed to homes. Uses freelance material. Nonfiction, articles, interviews, profiles. Reports 1 mo. Pays money on publication. Byline given. Query w/SASE. Accepts nonfiction: 600-1,800 wds.; dot matrix, simultaneous

sub., photocopy OK. "Most is local by assignment. If writers' clips show a lot of style, might give assignments." Guidelines.
COMMUNITY, CONSUMER, FOOD/COOKING, ENTERTAINMENT, ARTS, CALENDAR/EVENTS

Three Forks Herald, Box 586, Three Forks, MT 59752. 406-285-3414. Contact: R.W. Knauber. Weekly.
COMMUNITY

Tillamook Headlight-Herald, 1908 2ND St., Tillamook, OR 97141. 503-842-7535.
COMMUNITY, UNSPECIFIED

Timberman Times, Umpqua Community College, PO Box 967, Roseburg, OR 97470. 503-440-4600x697.
COLLEGE/UNIVERSITY

Times, PO Box 97, Waitsburg, WA 99361. 509-337-6631. Weekly.
COMMUNITY

The Times, 109 Spalding Ave., Box 278, Brownsville, OR 97327. 503-466-5311. Weekly.
COMMUNITY

The Times Clarion, 111 S. Central, Harlowton, MT 59036-0307. 406-632-5633. Editor: Gerald H. Miller. Ads: Julie Killorn. Weekly. Circ. 1625, subs $20. Accepts freelance material. Byline given. Pays money on publication. No rights acquired. Query w/SASE. Topics: news items.
COMMUNITY

The Times News, 132 3rd St. W., Twin Falls, ID 83301.
COMMUNITY

Times-Colonist, 2621 Douglas St., Victoria, BC V8W 2N4. 604-380-5211. Contact: John Wells. Daily.
COMMUNITY

The Times-Journal, 319 S. Main, Box 746, Condon, OR 97823. 503-384-2421. Weekly.
COMMUNITY

Tobacco Valley News, Box 307, Eureka, MT 59917. 406-296-2514. Contact: Mark Svoboda. Weekly.
COMMUNITY

The Torch, Lane Community College, 205 Center Bldg., 4000 E. 30th Ave., Eugene, OR 97405. 503-747-450x1265. Weekly.
COLLEGE/UNIVERSITY

Townsend Star, PO Box 1011, 417 Broadway, Townsend, MT 59644. 406-266-3333. Contact: Esther Tichenor. Weekly.
COMMUNITY

Trail Daily Times, 1163 Cedar Ave., Trail, BC V1R 4B8. 604-368-8551. Contact: Lloyd Mack. Ads: Ray Picco. Daily.
COMMUNITY

Tribune, PO Box 400, Deer Park, WA 99006. 509-276-5043. Weekly.
COMMUNITY

Tri-city Herald, P. O. Box 2608, Tri-Cities, WA 99302-2608. 509-582-1512. Editor: Matt Taylor. Daily, founded 1947. Sub/$8.50. Circ. 40,000. Not a freelance market.
COMMUNITY

Tundra Drums, PO Box 868, Bethel, AK 99559. 9907-543-3500. Contact: James MacPherson. Weekly.
COMMUNITY

Tundra Times, PO Box 92241, Anchorage, AK 99509-2247. 907-274-2512; Fax 907-277-7217. Contact: Marilyn Richards. Weekly of Eskimo, Indian, and Aleut news. Sub/$20. Circ. 7000. Accepts freelance material. Byline given; pays money on publication. Acquires 1st rights. Query letter, SASE, complete ms. Electronic subs, phone queries OK. Responds in less than 10 days; publishes in less than 10 days. Poetry, news items, op/ed, features. Accepts B&W glossy photos or slides; pays $25-$200.
ALASKA, NATIVE AMERICAN

Twin Falls Times-News, 132 3rd St. W., Twin Falls, ID 83301. 208-733-0931.
COMMUNITY

Umpqua Free Press, 425 N.W. Second Ave., Box 729, Myrtle Creek, OR 97457. 503-863-5233. Weekly.
COMMUNITY

Union-Bulletin, PO Box 1358, Walla Walla, WA 99362. 509-525-3300. Daily.
COMMUNITY

United Press International, 1320 S.W. Broadway, Portland, OR 97201. 503-226-2644. News Bureau.
UNSPECIFIED

University Herald, 2314 3rd Ave, Seattle, WA 98121-1712. 206-522-9505. Weekly.
COMMUNITY

The University News, Boise State University, 1910 University Dr., Boise, ID 83725. 208-385-1464. Weekly. Circ. 15,000.
COLLEGE/UNIVERSITY

Valdez Vanguard, PO Box 98, 339 Fairbanks, Valdez, AK 99686. 907-835-2211. Contact: Stephen Dunson. Weekly.
COMMUNITY

Valley Herald, PO Box 141268, Spokane, WA 99214. 509-924-2440. Weekly.
COMMUNITY

Valley Herald, 205 N. Main, Box 230, Milton-Freewater, OR 97862. 503-938-3361. Weekly.
COMMUNITY

Valley News, 77 E. Idaho, PO Box 365, Meridian, ID 83642. 208-888-1941. Editor: Marty Waters. Ads: Jayne Dachlet. Weekly newspaper, founded 1900. Sub $12/yr. Circ. 2,500. Uses freelance material. Pays copies on publication. Submit query letter, SASE, phone. Responds in 1 wk; publishes in 2 wks. Accepts nonfiction, cartoons, news items, photos (B&W $10), interviews, articles. Topics: Western Ada County; former Meridian/Eagle residents. Sample.
COMMUNITY

Valley Optimist, 111 W. Naches Ave., Selah, WA 98942. 509-697-8505. Weekly.
COMMUNITY

Valley Record & North Bend Record, PO Box 300, Snoqualmie, WA 98065. 206-888-2311. Weekly.
COMMUNITY

The Valley Sun, 1261 Seward Meridian, Ste F, Wasilla, AK 99654. 907-376-5525. Contact: Sandra Medearis.
COMMUNITY

Valley Times, 9730 S.W. Cascade Blvd., PO Box 370, Beaverton, OR 97075. 503-684-036-. Weekly.
COMMUNITY

The Vancouver Sun, 2250 Granville St., Vancouver, BC V6H 3G2. 604-732-2319. Editor: Ian Haysom. Ads: Ron Clark. Daily. Circ. 230,000. Byline given. Pays money on publication. Query letter. Material accepted: articles, photos, interviews, news items, op/ed.
COMMUNITY

Vashon-Maury Island Beachcomber, PO Box 447, Vashon, WA 98070. 206-463-9195. Editor: Jay Becker. Ads: Randy Pendergrass. Weekly. Circ. 4,200. Sub $14-22.50. Uses some freelance material. Pays money on publication. Byline given. Acquires 1st rights. Assignment only, query letter, SASE, phone. Disk/modem subs OK. Responds in 1 mo; publishes in 1-2 mos. Accepts nonfiction. Topics: relating to the Island and Islanders; nothing else. $50 for package of 450 wds about interesting Islander with picture (send 35mm negs and we'll develop). Does not need to live on Island now. Guidelines; sample 50¢.
COMMUNITY

Vernon Daily News, 3309 31st Ave., Vernon, BC V1T 6N8. 604-545-0671. Contact: John Clarke. Ads: George Solomonides. Daily.
COMMUNITY

The Voice, Multnomah School of the Bible, 8435 N.E. Glisan, Portland, OR 97220. 503-251-5325. Editor: Shelley Sonnenberg. Ads: Shelley Lockwood. Monthly. Sub/$10. Circ. 1,000. Accepts freelance from MSB staff, students, alumni only. Byline given, pays copies on publication. Query w/SASE. Disk (IBM) OK. Responds in 4 wks; publishing time varies. Accepts fiction, poetry, cartoons, news, biography, nonfiction, photos, interviews, op/ed, articles, reviews, memoirs. Guidelines; sample $2.
COLLEGE/UNIVERSITY, RELIGION

Wahkiakum County Eagle, PO Box 368, Cathlamet, WA 98612. 206-795-3391. Weekly.
COMMUNITY

Wallowa County Chieftan, 106 N.W. First St., Box 338, Enterprise, OR 97828. 503-426-4567. Weekly.
COMMUNITY

Warner World, Warner Pacific College, 2219 S.E. 68th, Portland, OR 97215. 503-775-4366.
COLLEGE/UNIVERSITY

Washington Grange News, PO Box 1186, Olympia, WA 98507. Official publication of the Washington State Grange. Semimonthly.
AGRICULTURE/FARMING, PUBLIC AFFAIRS, WASHINGTON

Washington Teamster Newspaper, 552 Denny Way, Seattle, WA 98109. 206-622-0483. Union weekly.
LABOR/WORK, WASHINGTON

Wednesday Magazine, 1748 N.E. Riddell Rd., Bremerton, WA 98310. 206-377-7464. Editor: Paul Goheen. Weekly community newspaper. Sub/$18. Circ. 25,000. Accepts freelance material. Byline given. Query, complete ms w/SASE. Photocopies, simultaneous subs OK. Responds 6 wks; publishes 2-4 wks. Accepts nonfiction articles, photos, interviews, op/ed, reviews, memoirs, cartoons, news items.
COMMUNITY

Weekly, PO Box 587, Woodinville, WA 98072. 206-483-0606. Weekly.
COMMUNITY

The Wenatchee World, PO Box 1511, Wenatchee, WA 98801. 509-663-5161; Fax 509-662-5413. Editor: Rufus Woods. Ads: Jay White. Daily. Founded 1905. Sub/$8.50. Circ. 28,300.
COMMUNITY

West Hills Bulletin, 12311 N.E. Glisan #103, Portland, OR 97230. 503-256-2833. Editor: Shelli Smith. Ads: Quentin Smith. Monthly. Sub $5/yr. Circ. 31,000. Uses 8-15 freelance mss per issue. Pays on publication. Byline given. Submit ms, SASE, phone query. Dot matrix, photocopied, simultaneous, electronic, computer disk OK. Reports in 3-4 wks. Accepts nonfiction, local human interest, cartoons. Sample for postage.
CALENDAR/EVENTS, COMMUNITY, PUBLIC AFFAIRS

West Lane News, 25027 Dunham, Box 188, Veneta, OR 97487. 503-935-1882. Weekly.
COMMUNITY

Western Livestock Reporter, PO Box 30758, Billings, MT 59107. 406-259-4589. Editor: Marcia Krings. Ads: Bonnie Zieske. Weekly, founded 1940. Annual "Breeders Book." Sub/$23. Circ. 12,000. Occasionally uses freelance material. Byline given. Pays money on publication. Acquires all rights. Submit query letter, SASE, phone. Assignment only. Disk/modem subs OK. Responds in 2 wks; publishing time varies. Accepts news items, interviews, photos (B&W). Topics: agricultural features, cattle, people who raise them. Sample.
AGRICULTURE/FARMING, ANIMALS

Western News, PO Box M, Libby, MT 59923. 406-293-4124. Editor: June McMahon. Weekly.
COMMUNITY

Western RV News, 1350 S.W. Upland Dr., Ste. B, Portland, OR 97221. 503-222-1255. Editor: Elsie Hathaway. Ads: Jim Hathaway. Monthly. Sub/$8. Circ. 22,000. Uses freelance material. Byline given. Pays money on publication, acquires 1st, 2nd rights. Submit query letter, complete ms, SASE, phone. Simultaneous subs OK. Responds in 2-3 wks; publishes in 3-6 months. Accepts news items, cartoons, articles, op/ed, photos (B&W, 3X5 glossy preferred). Topics: must have RV slant. Guidelines; free sample.
NORTHWEST, RECREATION, TECHNICAL

Western Viking, PO Box 70408, Seattle, WA 98107. 206-784-4617. Weekly.
COMMUNITY

Westside Record Inc., PO Box 38, Ferndale, WA. 98248-0038. 206-384-1411. Weekly.
COMMUNITY

Wheat Center News, Box 578, Fairfield, MT 59436. 406-467-2334. Contact: Jim Anderson. Weekly.
COMMUNITY

Whidbey News Times & Whidbey Today, PO Box 10, Oak Harbor, WA 98277. 206-675-6611. Weekly.
COMMUNITY

White Salmon Enterprise, PO Box 218, White Salmon, WA 98672. 206-493-2112. Weekly.
COMMUNITY

Whitefish Pilot, 312 2nd St., Whitefish, MT 59937. 406-862-3505.
COMMUNITY

The Wibaux Pioneer-Gazette, PO Box 218, 118 S. Wibaux St., Wibaux, MT 59353. 406-795-2218. Contact: Louise Sherman. Weekly.
COMMUNITY

Wilbur Register, PO Box 186, Wilbur, WA 99185. 509-647-5551. Weekly.
COMMUNITY

Willamette Collegian, 900 State St., Salem, OR 97301. 503-370-6053. Weekly student newspaper of Willamette University.
COLLEGE/UNIVERSITY

Willamette Week, 2 N.W. 2nd Ave., Portland, OR 97209. 503-243-2122. Editor: Mark Zusman. Weekly alternative news, art and regional living magazine. Circ. 50,000. Uses 60% freelance mss per copy. Pays 10-15 cents/wd. Query w/ms, SASE. Dot matrix, simultaneous subs (if informed) OK. Publishes in 1 mo. Nonfiction: to 5,000 wds; art, entertainment, politics, Portland-based subjects. Guidelines and sample w/SASE.
ARTS, ENTERTAINMENT, POLITICS

The Willapa Harbor Herald, PO Box 706, Raymond, WA 98577. 206-942-3466. Weekly.
COMMUNITY

Winnett Times, PO Box 747, 24 Main St., Roundup, MT 59072. 406-323-1105. Contact: Eric Rasmussen. Weekly.
COMMUNITY

Womyn's Press, PO Box 562, Eugene, OR 97440. 503-689-3974. Editors: J. R. David, Jonni Erickson. Ads: J. R. David. Bimonthly. Sub $8/individual, $18/institution. Circ. 1,000. Uses freelance material from women only. Pays in copies. Byline given. Query, SASE. Dot matrix, photocopied OK. Reports 6-8 mos. Publishes 2-3 mos. Accepts nonfiction, fiction, poetry, photos, cartoons. Poetry, not more than a page; articles 2,000 wds. Sample $2.
FEMINISM, GAY/LESBIAN, WOMEN

Wood River Journal, 112 S. Main, Hailey, ID 83333. 208-788-3444.
COMMUNITY

Woodburn Independent, 650 N. 1st St., Box 96, Woodburn, OR 97071. 503-981-3441. Weekly.
COMMUNITY

Woodstock Independent News, PO Box 02354, Portland, OR 97202. 503-233-1797. Editor: Jerry Schmidt. 503-233-1797. Ads: same. Monthly. Circ. 20,000. Sub free.
COMMUNITY

The World, Box 1840, Coos Bay, OR 97420. 503-269-1222; Fax 503-267-0294. Editor: Charlie Kocher. Ads: Julie Goebel. Daily. Founded 1878. Sub/$6.75. Circ. 15,300.
COMMUNITY

Wrangell Sentinel, PO Box 798, Wrangell, AK 99929. 907-874-2301. Contact: Ann Kirkwood or Alvin Bunch. Weekly.
COMMUNITY

Writer's NW, Media Weavers, 24450 N.W. Hansen Rd., Hillsboro, OR 97124. 503-621-3911. Editors: Linny Stovall, Dennis Stovall. Ads: Darlene Fesler, John Johnson. Quarterly tabloid from Media Weavers (imprint of Blue Heron Publishing Inc.) for writers, teachers, publishers, librarians, students. Uses freelance material. Query w/SASE first. Pays in copies. 500-1,000 wd articles on all aspects of writing and publishing; regular columns include book reviews, profiles of publishers, and technical reviews (software, how-to). Welcomes news from writers, teachers, publishers, and librarians for items in Calendar and News & Notes sections. Sub $10/yr US, $12/yr CDN. Single copy $2.50.
NORTHWEST, PUBLISHING/PRINTING, WRITING

Yakima Herald-Republic, 114 North Fourth St., PO Box 9668, Yakima, WA 98909. 509-248-1251. Daily.
COMMUNITY

Yakima Nation Review, PO Box 310, Toppenish, WA 98948. 509-865-5121x716.
NATIVE AMERICAN, NORTHWEST

The Yellowstone County News, Box 101, 1348 Main, Billings Heights, MT 59105. 406-245-1624. Contact: Beccy Oberly. Weekly.
COMMUNITY

SECTION VII

R
E
S
O
U
R
C
E
S

Arts Organizations

Classes

Contests

Distributors

Events

Writers' Organizations

Photographers' Organizations

Publishers' Organizations

Other/Miscellaneous

Arts Organizations

Alaska

Alaska Arts Southeast, Box 2133, Sitka, AK 99835. Contact: Director.

Alaska State Council on the Arts, 411 W. 4th Ave. #1-E, Anchorage, AK 99501. 907-279-1558. Contact: Christine D'Arcy. Offers a biennial fellowship for resident writers. Travel grants are also available to Alaskan writers. Write for guidelines & application deadlines.

Institute of Alaska Native Arts, Box 80583, Fairbanks, AK 99708.

Juneau Arts & Humanities Council, PO Box 020562, Juneau, AK 99802. 907-586-ARTS. Exec. Director: Natalee Rothaus. Projects Coordinator: Marie Popovich. Official arts agency of Juneau. Publishes newsletter, circ. 300.

Ketchikan Area Arts & Humanities Council, 338 Main St., Ketchikan, AK 99901.

100 Mile & District Arts Council, Box 2262, 100 Mile House, BC V0K 2E0. 604-395-4077. Contact: James Scott.

British Columbia

Abbotsford - Matsqui Arts Council, Box 336, Abbotsford, BC V2S 4N9. 604-852-9358. Contact: Freddy Latham.

Alberni Valley Community Arts Council, c/o Rollin Art Centre, 3061 - 8th Ave., Port Alberni, BC V9Y 2K5. 604-724-3412. Contact: Rob Dom

The Alcuin Society, PO Box 3216, Vancouver, BC V6B 3X8. Contact: Doreen Eddy. Formed in the mid-sixties, supports book arts and fine printing with publications and events. Sponsors the Alcuin Society's Canadian Book Design awards annually. For more information, check in the listings for their publication, Amphora.

Arrow Lakes Arts Council, Box 895, Nakusp, BC V0G 1R0. 604-265-3086. Contact: Terry Taylor.

Bella Coola Valley Arts Council, Box 591, Bella Coola, BC V0T 1C0. 604-982-2453. Contact: Barbara Gilbert.

Bulkley Valley Community Arts Council, Box 3971, Smithers, BC V0J 2N0. 604-847-2986. Contact: Todd Glover.

Burnaby Arts Council, 6528 Deer Lake Ave., Burnaby, BC V5G 2J3. 604-298-7322. Contact: Linda Cunningham.

Burns Lake & District Arts Council, Box 202, Francois Lake, BC V0J 1R0. 604-695-6389. Contact: Julia Fortin.

Campbell River Community Arts Council, Box 927, Campbell River, BC V9W 6Y4. 604-287-7899. Contact: Michael Utgaard.

Castlegar Arts Council, Box 3352, Castlegar, BC V1N 3H6. 604-365-3553. Contact: Donna Moyer.

Chetwynd Community Arts Council, Box 1795, Chetwynd, BC V0C 1J0. 604-788-2267. Contact: Yvonne Elden.

Chilliwack Community Arts Council, 45899 Henderson Ave., Chilliwack, BC V2P 2X6. 604-792-2069. Contact: Bradley Whittaker.

Comox Valley Community Arts Council, Box 3053, Courtenay, BC V9N 5N3. 604-334-2983. Contact: Kathleen Kerr.

Coquitlam Area Fine Arts Council, PO Box 217, Port Coquitlam, BC V3C 3V7. 604-931-8255. Contact: Guy Risebrough.

Cowichan Valley Arts Council, Box 703, Duncan, BC V9L 3Y1. 604-746-1611. Contact: Allison Callihoo.

Cranbrook & District Arts Council, Box 861, Cranbrook, BC V1C 4J6. 604-426-8324. Contact: Deanne Perreault.

Creston Community Arts Council, Box 2236, Creston, BC V0B 1G0. 604-428-5186. Contact: Glenna Fay Taylor.

Cultural Services Branch, Ministry of Tourism & Culture, Parliament Buildings, 800 Johnson St., Victoria, BC V8V 1X4. 604-356-1727. Contact: Dawn Wallace, Coordinator of Literary & Publishing Programs. 604-356-1727. Funding programs for BC books publishers and writers.

Delta Community Arts Council, Box 287, Delta, BC V4K 3N7. 604-946-0525.

District 69 Community Arts Council, Box 1662, Parksville, BC V0R 2S0. 604-248-8185. Contact: Jennifer Tindall.

Eagle Valley Arts Council, Box 686, Sicamous, BC V0E 2V0. 604-836-2570. Contact: Betty Tehonchuk.

Fernie & District Arts Council, Box 1453, Fernie, BC V0B 1M0. 604-423-6133. Contact: Beth Gregg.

Fort Nelson Arts Council, Box 1829, Fort Nelson, BC V0C 1R0. 604-774-2357. Contact: John Barry.

Fort St. John Community Arts Council, 10003 - 100th St., Fort St. John, BC V1J 3Y5. 604-785-1990. Contact: Kevin Truscott.

Golden District Arts Council, Box 228, Golden, BC V0A 1H0. 604-344-6365. Contact: Catherine Green.

Grand Forks Area Art Council, Box 2636, Grand Forks, BC V0H 1H0. 604-442-8233. Contact: John Nilsen.

Greater Victoria Comm. Arts Council, #511 - 620 View St., Victoria, BC V8W 1J6. 604-381-2787. Contact: Bruce Stanley.

Hope & District Arts Council, Box 2, Hope, BC V0X 1L0. 604-869-9971. Contact: William H. Scott.

Kamloops Community Arts Council, Box 467, Kamloops, BC V2C 5L2. 604-374-2704. Contact: Dita Aronowski.

Kaslo Arts Council, Box 1000, Kaslo, BC V0G 1M0. 604-353-2372. Contact: Barbara Bavington.

Kent Harrison Arts Council, Box 502, Agassiz, BC V0M 1A0. 604-796-9851. Contact: Carye Osmack.

Kimberley Arts Council, Box 102, Kimberley, BC V1A 2Y5. 604-427-3209. Contact: Veronica Paauw.

Kitimat Community Arts Council, Box 342, Kitimat, BC V8C 2G8. 604-632-6225. Contact: Steffan Wegner.

Kootenay Cultural Network - Rockies, Box 1043, Sparwood, BC V0B 2G0. 604-425-7117. Contact: Geri Rothel.

Langley Arts Council, Box 3101, Langley, BC V3A 4R3. 604-534-0781. Contact: Iris Preston.

Logan Lake Arts Council, Box 299, Logan Lake, BC V0K 1V0. 604-523-9532. Contact: Janet Kohar.

Mackenzie Arts Council, Box 301, Mackenzie, BC V0J 2C0. 604-997-5818. Contact: June Golding.

Maple Ridge Arts Council, Box 331, Maple Ridge, BC V2X 7G2. 604-467-3825. Contact: Candace Gordon.

Mission District Arts Council, Box 3352, Mission, BC V2V 4J5. 604-826-6717. Contact: Peggy Staber.

Nanaimo District Arts Council, Box 557, Nanaimo, BC V9R 5L5. 604-758-5412. Contact: Faye Luchyk.

Nechako Community Arts Council, Box 2288, Vanderhoof, BC V0J 3A0. 604-567-2653. Contact: Joyce Reid.

Nelson & District Arts Council, Box 422, Nelson, BC V1L 5R2. 604-352-2402. Contact: Dennis Zomerschoe.

New Westminster Arts Council, Box 722, New Westminster, BC V3L 4Z3. 604-524-0514. Contact: Alex Webber.

Nicola Valley Community Arts Council, Box 1711, Merritt, BC V0K 2B0. 604-378-5686. Contact: Brian Dodd.

Normal Art Society, 3505 Commercial St., Vancouver, BC V5N 4E8. 604-873-3129. Nonprofit society established in 1988 to encourage art and the creative process. Publishes pop-tart Magazine (see Listings), organizes the Small Press Festival, performances, exhibitions.

North Vancouver Community Arts Council, 333 Chesterfield Ave., N. Vancouver, BC V7M 3G9. 604-988-6844. Contact: Donna Oseen.

Oceola Arts Council, Box 535, Winfield, BC V0H 2C0. 604-766-4205. Contact: Doug Middleton.

Okanagan Mainline R.A.C., Box 134, Kelowna, BC V0H 1G0. 640-766-2644. Contact: Gordon Harris.

Oliver Community Arts Council, Box 1711, Oliver, BC V0H 1T0. 604-498-6319. Contact: Mona Meredith.

Osoyoos Community Arts Council, Box 256, Osoyoos, BC V0H 1V0. 604-495-6939. Contact: Ruth Schiller.

Pacific Rim Arts Society, Box 468, Ucluelet, BC V0R 3A0. 604-726-7448. Contact: Donna Fitzpatrick.

Penticton & District Community Arts Council, 220 Manor Park Ave., Penticton, BC V2A 2R2. 604-492-7997. Contact: Laura McCartney.

Powell River Community Arts Council, Box 406, Powell River, BC V8A 5C2. 604-487-9287. Contact: Don Reid.

Prince George & District Arts Council, 2880 - 15th Ave., Prince George, BC V2M 1T1. 604-563-1702. Contact: Mary Pfeiffer.

Prince Rupert Community Arts Council, Box 341, Prince Rupert, BC V8J 3P9. 604-627-1274. Contact: Ralph Troschke.

Queen Charlotte Islands Arts Council, Box 35, Q. Charlotte City, BC V0T 1S0. 604-559-4533. Contact: Paul Sametz. Publishes a quarterly newsletter which is free with annual membership.

Quesnel & District Community Arts Council, Box 4069, Quesnel, BC V2J 3J2. 604-992-8885. Contact: Don Hendry.

Revelstoke & District C.A.C., Box 1931, Revelstoke, BC V0E 2S0. 604-837-2557. Contact: Vern Enyedy.

Richmond Community Arts Center, 7671 Minoru Gate, Richmond, BC V6Y 1R8. 604-276-4012. Contact: Ron Jeffels.

Robson Valley Community Arts Council, Box 638, McBride, BC V0J 2E0. 604-569-2265. Contact: Dave Marchant.

Shuswap District Arts Council, Box 1181, Salmon Arm, BC V1E 4R3. 604-832-2663. Contact: Mary Landers.

Slocan Lake Gallery Society, Box 123, Silverton, BC V0G 2B0. 604-358-7788. Contact: Donna Jean Wright.

Slocan Valley Community Arts Council, Box 18, Winlaw, BC V0G 2J0. 604-226-7708. Contact: Bridley Morrison Morgan.

South Cariboo Community Arts Council, Box 1441, Lillooet, BC V0K 1V0. 604-256-4346. Contact: Merle P. Elesko.

South Coast Community Arts Council, Box 46, Snooke, BC V0S 1N0. 604-642-5211. Contact: Kathy Kirk.

South Peace Community Arts Council, Box 2314, Dawson Creek, BC V1G 4P2. 604-782-1838. Contact: Anne Matheson Exner.

Sparwood Arts Council, Box 1043, Sparwood, BC V0B 2G0. 604-425-7117. Contact: Sherry Benko.

Squamish Arts Council, Box 193, Garibaldi Highlands, BC V0N 1T0. 604-892-5482. Contact: Maureen Brown.

Summerland Community Arts Council, Box 1217, Summerland, BC V0H 1Z0. 604-494-4494. Contact: Sherrill Foster.

Sunshine Coast Arts Council, Box 1565, Sechelt, BC V0N 3A0. 604-885-2986. Contact: Therese Egan.

Surrey & District Arts Council, 13750 - 88th Ave., Surrey, BC V3W 3L1. 604-596-7461. Contact: Rey Ortmann.

Terrace & District Arts Council, Box 35, Terrace, BC V8G 4A3. 604-635-9960. Contact: Barbara Kenney.

Thompson Valley North Arts Council, Box 75, McNab Rd., Little Fort, BC V0E 2C0. 604-677-4379. Contact: Darlene Jennings.

Trail & District Community Arts Council, Box 326, Trail, BC V1R 4L6. 604-368-6922. Contact: Muriel Griffith.

Tumbler Ridge Community Arts Council, Box 240, Tumbler Ridge, BC V0L 2W0. 604-242-4754. Contact: Colleen Doylend.

Vancouver Community Arts Council, 837 Davie St., Vancouver, BC V6Z 1B7. 604-683-4358. Contact: Anthony Norfolk.

Vernon Community Arts Council, 3300 - 37th Ave., Vernon, BC V2T 2Y5. 604-542-6243. Contact: Marianne Morrison.

West Vancouver Community Arts Council, 200 Keith Rd., West Vancouver, BC V7T 1L3. 604-922-1110. Contact: Lynne Flipse.

Western Communities Arts Council, Box 468, Ucluelet, BC V9B 4Z3. 604-479-6085. Contact: Lois Klages.

Whistler Community Arts Council, Box 383, Whistler, BC V0N 1B0. 604-932-5378. Contact: Joan Richoz.

White Rock Community Arts Council, Station Art Centre, 14970 Marine Dr., White Rock, BC V4B 1C4. 604-536-2432. Contact: Corlin Bordeaux.

Williams Lake Community Arts Council, Box 4537, Williams Lake, BC V2G 2V5. 604-398-6323. Contact: Sidney Gooch.

Idaho

Citizen's Council for the Arts, 307 S. 19th St., Coeur d'Alene, ID 83814.

Coeur d'Alene City Arts Commission, 710 E Mullan Ave., Coeur d'Alene, ID 83814.

El-Wyhee Arts Council, 1520 E. 8th N., Mt. Home, ID 83647.

Idaho City Arts Council, PO Box 219, Idaho City, ID 83631.

Idaho Commission on the Arts, 304 W State St., Boise, ID 83720. 208-334-2119. Contact: Betty J. Rudolph, Asst. Director. Grants, fellowships, apprenticeships, artists-in-education program residencies.

Lost River Community Arts Council, Box B, Arco, ID 83213.

Magic Valley Arts Council, PO Box 1158, Twin Falls, ID 83301.

McCall Arts Council, McCall Area Chamber of Commerce, Box D, McCall, ID 83638. 208-634-7631. Contact: Eileen McCabe.

Moscow City Arts Commission, 122 E. 4th St., Moscow, ID 83843.

Oakley Valley Arts Council, PO Box 176, Oakley, ID 83346.

Pend Oreille Arts Council, c/o Eve's Leaves, 326 N. 1st Ave., Sandpoint, ID 83864.

Salmon Arts Council, PO Box 2500, 200 MAIN St., Salmon, ID 83467. 208-756-2987. Contact: Pat Hauff.

Montana

Beall Park Art Center, 409 N. Bozeman, Bozeman, MT 59715. 406-586-3970. Contact: Bonnie Lain-Malcomson, Director

Montana Arts Council, The City/County Bldg., 316 Park Ave., Helena, MT 59620. 406-444-6430. Contact: Arlyn Fishbaugh. State arts organization, publishes Artistsearch, a monthly newsletter. Also publishes 1 book annually as part of their First Book Award for MT residents. Send for guidelines for grant/fellowship applications, and to get on mailing list for newsletter.

Valley Community Arts Council, PO Box 744, Hamilton, MT 59840. Contact: Carlotta Grandstaff, Editor.

Yellowstone Art Center's Regional Writers Project, 401 N. 27th St., Billings, MT 59101. 406-656-1238. Contact: Adrea Sukin, Pat Palagi. Promotes Western literature through a retail outlet and mail order catalog and lecture series featuring authors and small press publishers.

Oregon

Artists-In-Education Oregon, Oregon Arts Commission, 550 Airport Rd., Salem, OR 97310. 503-378-3625.

Arts & Crafts Guild of Oregon, PO Box 601, Oakridge, OR 97463. 503-782-4431. Contact: Clara Bailey.

Arts Council of Pendleton, PO Box 573, Pendleton, OR 97801. 503-276-9177. Contact: Carolyn Wallace.

Arts Council of Southern Oregon, 33 N. Central Ave. #308, Medford, OR 97501. 503-482-5594. Contact: Donovan Gray.

Bay Area Arts Council/South Coast Tourism Assn., 886 S. 4th St., Coos Bay, OR 97420. 503-267-6500. Contact: Lionel Youst.

Beaverton Arts Commission, Beaverton City Hall, PO Box 4755, Beaverton, OR 97076. 503-526-2222. Contact: Jayne Bruno Scott.

Cannon Beach Arts Association, PO Box 684, Cannon Beach, OR 97110. 503-436-1204. Contact: Rainmar Bartle.

Central Curry Council for the Arts & Humanities, PO Box 374, Gold Beach, OR 97444. 503-247-6854. Contact: Robert E Simons.

Clackamas County Arts Council, Clackamas Community College, 19600 S. Molalla Ave., Oregon City, OR 97045. 503-656-9543. Contact: Harriet Jorgenson.

Columbia Gorge Arts Council of Washington/Oregon, 1107 Lewis St., The Dalles, OR 97058. 503-298-1585; 503-773-3733. Contact: Ed Bonham.

Coos Arts Council & Tourism Assn., PO Box 1641, Coos Bay, OR 97420. Members are museums, local theater groups, galleries. We publish a monthly planning calendar, which is included with $15 annual membership dues.

Coquille Valley Art Association, HC 83, Box 625, Coquille, OR 97423. 503-396-2866. Contact: Yvonne Marineau.

Corvallis Arts Center, 700 S.W. Madison, Corvallis, OR 97330. 503-754-1551. Contact: Susan Johnson.

Crossroads Arts Center, PO Box 235, Baker, OR 97814. 503-523-3704. Contact: Peter Decius.

Dallas Arts Association, PO Box 192, Dallas, OR 97338. 503-623-5700; 503-623-5567. Contact: LaVonne Wilson or Janet Burton.

Desert Arts Council/Blue Mountain CC, 405 N. 1st, Ste. 107, Hermiston, OR 97838. 503-567-1800. Contact: Karen Bounds.

Eastern Oregon Regional Arts Council, EOSC - Loso Hall, #220, 1410 "L" Ave., La Grande, OR 97850. 503-962-3624; 800-452-8639 x2-3624. Contact: Anne Bell.

Elgin Arts Council, Rt. 1, Box 1A, Elgin, OR 97827. 503-437-7772. Contact: Pamela Davis or Christine McLaughlin.

Florence Arts & Crafts Assoc., PO Box 305, Florence, OR 97349.

Grants Pass Arts Council, 201 Barbara Dr., Grants Pass, OR 97526. 503-479-5541. Contact: Doug Norby.

Greater Condon Arts Association, Box 165, Condon, OR 97823. 503-384-5114. Contact: Darla Ceale.

Hillsboro Community Arts, PO Box 1026, Hillsboro, OR 97123. 503-648-1169. Contact: Bill Baldwin.

Keizer Art Association, PO Box 8900, Keizer, OR 97303. 503-390-3010. Contact: Lois Graham.

Klamath Arts Council, PO Box 1706, Klamath Falls, OR 97601. Contact: Anita Ward.

Klamath Falls Arts Association, 2310 Marina Dr., Klamath Falls, OR 97601.

La Grande Arts Commission, 1605 Walnut, La Grande, OR 97850. 503-963-6963. Contact: Michael Frasier.

Lake Arts Council, 307 S. E, Lakeview, OR 97630. 503-947-2931. Contact: Stanley Wonderly.

Lane Arts Council, 411 High St., Eugene, OR 97401. 503-485-2278; FAX: 503-485-2478. Contact: Douglas Beauchamp. Provides education, information, and services to the professional arts community. Newsletter, Artists Notes, is a monthly publication listing professional opportunities for writers & artists; consulting for projects.

Lebanon Arts Council, 54 W. Sherman, Lebanon, OR 97355. 503-451-3934.

Medford Arts Commission, 2950 Barnett Rd., Medford, OR 97504. 503-664-5681. Contact: Peter Schmitz.

Metropolitan Arts Commission, 1120 S.W. 5th, Room 518, Portland, OR 97204. 503-796-5111. Grants to artists and arts organizations (including small presses) for public, non-profit projects (no fellowship program). Bimonthly newsletter listing MAC programs, other deadlines, competitions.

Mid-Valley Arts Council, 265 Court N.E., Salem, OR 97301. 503-364-7474.

Monmouth/Independence Community Arts Association, PO Box 114, Monmouth, OR 97361. 503-838-4141. Contact: Deb Curtis.

North Santiam Arts League Inc., 383 N. 3rd Ave., Stayton, OR 97383-1725.

Nyssa Fine Arts Council, PO Box 2356, Nyssa, OR 97913. 503-372-2981. Contact: Marie Wilson.

Oregon Arts Commission, 550 Airport Rd., Salem, OR 97310. 503-378-3625. Individual, non-repeating literary fellowships given biennially. A writer can suggest any project to a non-profit organization (including a non-profit small press), and the organization can apply to OAC for a annual project grant. If the organization has a budget of less than $50,000, they should seek funding from a regional arts council. Those with budgets over $50,000 should apply to the OAC. Staff (paid or unpaid)of writing and publishing organizations may apply for professional development funding (up to $200) for a workshop, conference, or other training. If interested, inquire early in the year. These funds are quickly exhausted. Write for guidelines or check with local arts councils in Oregon.

Oregon Business Committee for the Arts, 221 N.W. 2nd Ave., Portland, OR 97209. 503-228-9411.

Oregon Coast Council for the Arts, PO Box 1315, Newport, OR 97365. 503-265-9231. Contact: Sharon Morgan. "We are a regional arts council with a strong history of literary programs and support for emerging writers."

Oregon Institute of Literary Arts, PO Box 10608, Portland, OR 97210. 503-223-3604. Annual Oregon book awards ceremony; awards for young readers literature, creative nonfiction, poetry, fiction, playwrights; fellowships for writers and publishers; book exhibits; publication of tabloid on Oregon books, Oregon Ink and a newsletter.

Port Orford Arts Council, PO Box 771, Port Orford, OR 97465.

Portland Society for Calligraphy, PO Box 4621, Portland, OR 97208. Contacts: Patricia Grass, Ann Mueller. Newsletter, circ. 400.

Reedsport Arts Council, PO Box 7, Reedsport, OR 97467. Contact: Donna Fulhart.

Regional Arts Council of Central Oregon, 63085 N. Hwy. 97, Ste. 103, Bend, OR 97701. 503-382-5055.

Seaside Guild of Artists Inc., PO Box 1122, Seaside, OR 97138.

Springfield Arts Commission, City of Springfield, Office of Community & Economic Development, 225 N. 5th St., Springfield, OR 97477. 503-726-3783. Contact: Bruce Newhouse.

Tiimutla Arts Council, Rt. 3, Box 71, Pendleton, OR 97801. 503-276-1881. Contact: Leah Conner.

Tillamook Arts Association, PO BOX 634, Tillamook, OR 97141. Contact: Ed Sharples.

Umpqua Valley Arts Association, PO Box 1105, Roseburg, OR 97470. 503-672-2532. Contact: Heidi Land.

Valley Art Association, PO Box 333, Forest Grove, OR 97116. 503-357-3703. Contact: Merrie French. Free newsletter, circ. 3,000.

Wallowa Valley Arts Council, PO Box 306, Enterprise, OR 97828. 503-426-4775. Contact: Michael Kurtz or Terri Barnett.

Willamette Arts Council, 456 S.W. Monroe, Ste. 102, Corvallis, OR 97333. 503-757-6800. Contact: Barbara Ross.

Washington

Allied Arts Association, 89 Lee Blvd., Richland, WA 99352. 509-943-9815. Contact: Rosemary Merckx.

Allied Arts Council Yakima Valley, 5000 W. Lincoln. Ave., Yakima, WA 98908. 509-966-0930. Contact: Ann Byerrum

Allied Arts Council of the Mid-Columbia Region, PO Box 730, Richland, WA 99352. 509-943-0524. Contact: Jackie Geiler

Allied Arts Council N. Central Washington, PO Box 573, Wenatchee, WA 98807. 509-662-1213. Contact: Kathleen Gilstrap.

Allied Arts Literary Guild, PO Box 5182, Bellingham, WA 98227. 206-672-1155. Contact: Carol Anderson

Allied Arts of Renton, 400 S. 3rd St., Renton, WA 98055. 206-255-2590. Contact: Annette McCully, President.

Allied Arts of Seattle, 107 S. Main St., Seattle, WA 98104. 206-624-0432. Contact: Francis Van Ausdal.

Arts Council Clark County, PO Box 1995, Vancouver, WA 98668. 206-694-1835. Contact: Carolyn Neubauer.

Arts Council Mid-Columbia Region, PO Box 730, Richland, WA 99352. 509-735-4612. Contact: Program Manager.

Arts Council of Snohomish County, PO Box 5038, Everett, WA 98206. 206-252-7469. Contact: Laura McNally.

Associated Arts of Ocean Shores, PO Box 241, Ocean Shores, WA 98569. Contact: Margie McBride.

Auburn Arts Commission, 25 W. Main, Auburn, WA 98001. 206-931-3043. Contact: Josie Emmons Vine. Writers Conference last weekend in October.

Bainbridge Island Arts Council, 261 Madison S., Bainbridge Island, WA 98110. 206-842-7901. Contact: Janis Shaw. In addition to other activities, including writing workshops, they publish a Poets & Artists Calendar from their annual Poets & Artists Competition.

Bellevue Allied Arts Council, 9509 N.E. 30th, Bellevue, WA 98004. 206-455-2589. Contact: Gigi Mauritzen.

Bellevue Arts Commission, PO Box 90012, Bellevue, WA 98009. 206-453-8259. Contact: Carol Cullivan.

Bellingham Arts Commission, City Hall, 121 Prospect St., Bellingham, WA 98225. 206-676-6981. Contact: John Keppelman.

Centrum Foundation, PO Box 1158, Port Townsend, WA 98368. 206-385-3102. Contact: Carol Jane Bangs. Activities include: The Port Townsend Writers' Conference, held annually in July; A residency program for 3-4 writers each year; a press-in-residence, Copper Canyon Press; special workshops featuring writers and experts in other fields convened to address major societal issues; writing workshops for high school students from Washington State.

Columbia Basin Allied Arts, 28th & Chanute, Moses Lake, WA 98837. 509-762-5351. Contact: Brenda Teals.

Coop Arts Council Clark County, 4900 Wintler Dr., Vancouver, WA 98661. 206-693-5557. Contact: Barbara Bray Hart.

Des Moines Arts Commission, 22513 Marine View Dr., Des Moines, WA 98188. Contact: Jack Kniskern.

Edmonds Arts Commission, 700 Main St., Edmonds, WA 98020. 206-771-0228. Contact: Christine Sidwell. Sponsors Write-on-the Sound writers conference each fall.

Ellensburg Arts Commission, 420 N. Pearl, Ellensburg, WA 98926. 509-986-3065. Contact: Phyllis Stamm. 509-986-3065.

Enumclaw Arts Commission, 1339 Griffin, Enumclaw, WA 98022. 206-825-1038. Contact: Evelyn Lercher.

Everett Cultural Commission, 3002 Wetmore, Everett, WA 98201. 206-259-8701. Contact: Lynda Vanderberg.

Interurban Center for the Arts, 12401 S.E. 320th St., Auburn, WA 98002. 206-833-9111. Contact: Helen S. Smith.

Island County Arts Council, PO Box 173, Langley, WA 98260. 206-321-6439. Contact: Frank Rose. 206-321-6439. $25/per family, newsletter.

Kent Arts Commission, 220 S. 4th Ave., Kent, WA 98031. 206-872-3350. Contact: Patrice Thorell.

King County Arts Commission, 1115 Smith Tower Bldg., 506 2nd Ave., Seattle, WA 98104. 206-296-7580. The Commission publishes The Written Arts, a literary magazine and The Arts, a newsletter; it funds grants for small press publications of juried manuscripts. Contact them to get guidelines for submissions and for grants, or to get on their mailing list for publications.

Lake Chelan Arts Council, PO Box 627, Chelan, WA 98816. 509-687-3171. Contact: Karen Koch.

Lynnwood Arts Commission, City Hall, PO Box 5008, Lynnwood, WA 98046. 206-775-1971. Contact: Alice Taylor.

Marysville Advisory Committee, City of Marysville, 514 Delta Ave., Marysville, WA 98270. Contact: Steve Dinwiddie.

Classes

Mercer Island Arts Council, Community Center at Mercer View, 8236 S.E. 24th St., Mercer Island, WA 98040. 206-233-3545. Contact: Judith Clibborn.

Mountlake Terrace Arts Commission, Parks & Recreation Department, 228th St. S.W., Mountlake Terrace, WA 98043. 206-776-9173. Contact: David Fair.

Olympia Arts Commission, Olympia Parks & Recreation Dept., 222 N. Columbia, Olympia, WA 98507. 206-753-8380. Contact: Linda Oestreich, Program Manager.

Peninsula Cultural Arts Center, 533 N. Sequim Ave., Sequim, WA 98382. 206-683-8364. Contact: Patricia Gallup.

Pierce County Arts Commission, 3711 Center St., Tacoma, WA 98400.

Port Townsend Arts Commission, City Hall, 607 Water St., Port Townsend, WA 98368.

Renton Municipal Arts Commission, 200 Mill Ave. S., Renton, WA 98055. 206-235-2580. Contact: Harriette Hilder

Sea-Tac Arts Council, 1809 S. 140th, Seattle, WA 98168. 206-241-5960. Contact: Dorothy Harper.

Seattle Arts Commission, 312 1st Ave. N., Seattle, WA 98109. 206-684-7171. Contact: Barbara Thomas. Send for their guidelines for grants, and get on their newsletter mailing list for information on area events.

Snohomish Arts Commission, 116 Union Ave., Snohomish, WA 98290. 206-568-3115. Contact: Volkert Volkersz.

Spokane Arts Commission, City Hall - 4th Floor, W. 808 Spokane Falls Blvd., Spokane, WA 99201. 509-456-3857. Contact: Sue Ellen Heflin. Free newsletter, circ. 2,500.

Tacoma Arts Commission, Tacoma Municipal Bldg., 747 Market St., Rm 900, Tacoma, WA 98402. 206-591-5191. Contact: Dorothy McCuiston.

Upper Valley Arts, 321 9th St., Leavenworth, WA 98826. 509-548-5202. Contact: R. J. Ritz.

Vashon Allied Arts Inc., PO Box 576, Vashon, WA 98070. 206-463-5131. Contact: Jeffery Basom.

Washington State Arts Commission, PO Box 42675, 234 E. 8th Ave., Olympia, WA 98504-2675. 206-753-3860. Send for guidelines for grants and get on mailing list for their newsletter of information on the arts.

Wenatchee Arts Commission, PO Box 519, Wenatchee, WA 98801. Contact: Peggy Mead.

Yakima Arts Council, 5000 W. Lincoln, Yakima, WA 98908. 509-966-0930. Contact: Anne Byerrun.

Alaska

Eagle River Fine Arts Academy, Box 773989, Eagle River, AK 99577.

Sitka Summer Writers Symposium, Box 2420, Sitka, AK 99835. 907-747-3794. Contact: Carolyn Servid.

British Columbia

En'Owkin Centre, 257 Brunswick St., Penticton, BC V2A 5P9. Writing classes.

The Federation of BC Writers, PO Box 2206, Vancouver, BC V6B 3W2. 604-683-2057; Fax 604-683-8269. Contact: Corey Van't Haaff, Manager. "As the voice of BC writers, the Federation, a non-profit society, acts or comments on a variety of issues affecting writers of all genres. We work cooperatively with other writing organizations to ensure wider funding and support for writers. Our services include a quarterly newsletter, literary competition, employment referral, information and networking, advocacy and government lobbying.

Kootenay School of Writing, #306-152 W. Hastings St., Vancouver, BC V6B 3A0.

Writing and Publishing Program, Simon Fraser University, Harbour Centre, 515 W Hastings, Vancouver, BC V6B 5K3. 604-291-5100. Contact: Christine Hearn. Offers writing and publishing programs to adult learners, courses in fall and spring. Also Canadian Centre for studies in publishing.

Idaho

Confluence Press Inc., 8th Ave. & 6th St., LCSC, Lewiston, ID 83501. 208-799-2336. Contact: James R Hepworth. Courses in the publishing arts at Lewis Clark State College are available through Confluence Press. Offers on-the-job training to student interns at the Press; and occasional half-day workshops in publishing for junior high, high school and college editors. Sponsor of Writers-in-the-Schools Projects. Also sponsors The Visiting Writers Series, offering 5 residencies to writers a year. They regularly meet with classes.

Moscow Moffia, 621 E. "F" St., Moscow, ID 83843. 208-882-3672. Contact: Jon Gustafson. Weekly writer's discussion groups. Sponsors workshops throughout the Northwest.

Montana

Montana Writing Project, English Department, University of Montana, Missoula, MT 59812. 406-243-5231. Contact: Dr. Beverly Ann Chin.

The Writer's Voice of the Billings Family YMCA, 402 No. 32nd St., Billings, MT 59101. 406-248-1685; Fax 406-248-3450. Contact: Corby Skinner. Offers a variety of services including readings, workshops, after school programs for elementary grades, a writers exchange program, and a rural outreach project that sends one of six writers to rural jr & sr high schools to offer a half day workshop.

Oregon

Arts at Menucha, PO Box 4958, Portland, OR 97208. Contact: Barbara Davis

Fishtrap Gathering, PO Box 457, Enterprise, OR 97828. 503-426-3623. Contact: Rich Wandschneider. Annual summer conference with presentations from Northwest and East Coast authors, editors, and publishers; followed by writing workshops. Also conducts an annual midwinter conference.

Lane Literary Guild, c/o Lane Arts Council, 411 High St., Eugene, OR 97401. 503-485-2278. Contact: Erik Muller, Alice Evans. Membership $10/indiv. Newsletter, circ 20,000. Nonprofit organization representing the professional interests of poets, fiction writers and dramatists living in Lane County.

Northwest Writing Institute, Campus Box 100, Lewis & Clark College, Portland, OR 97219. 503-768-7745; 503-768-7960. Contact: Kim Stafford, Director. The Northwest Writing Institute at Lewis & Clark College supports campus writing courses and seeks to assist writers and the literary community in the region through workshops and other programs. Coordinates Oregon Writing Project; Writer to Writer (a seminar for high school students); the Imaginative Writing Seminars; and a wide variety of workshops for teachers and writers.

Oregon Association of Christian Writers, 17768 S.W. Pointe, Forest Ct, Aloha, OR 97006. Contact: Sally Stuart, Exec Editor. Organized for the purpose of promoting higher standards of craftsmanship in the field of Christian journalism and encouraging a greater sense of spiritual responsibility in the Christian writer. The group holds writers seminars 3 times a year in Salem, Eugene and Portland and a 3-day summer conference in July.

Oregon Writers' Workshop, 1219 S.W. Park, Portland, OR 97205. 503-239-0504. Contact: Kathleen Culligan. Graduate level workshops in poetry, fiction, nonfiction.

Oregon Writing Project, Department of English, University of Oregon, Eugene, OR 97403. 503-346-3911. Nathaniel Teich, Project Director. Affiliated with the National Writing Project network. Includes more than 140 projects in 44 states and abroad which have adopted the successful model of the University of California, Berkeley/Bay Area Writing Project. This model has achieved national recognition for improving students writing by increasing teachers' knowledge and instructional skills in composition. Experienced teachers are eligible for the 4-week summer institute.

O-Ya-Ka Story League, Multnomah County Central Library, 801 S.W. 10th Ave., Portland, OR 97205. 503-244-9415. Meets monthly. Affiliated with National Story League, Western District. Story workshop sponsored by Western District held at Marylhurst alternate summers.

Willamette Writers, 9045 S.W. Barbur Blvd. #5A, Portland, OR 97219. 503-452-1592. Monthly programs, newsletter, annual conference and contest, small critique groups, and ongoing workshops. Newsletter circ 900.

Washington

Centrum Foundation, PO Box 1158, Port Townsend, WA 98368. 206-385-3102. Contact: Carol Jane Bangs. Activities include: The Port Townsend Writers' Conference, held annually in July; A residency program for 3-4 writers each year; a press-in-residence, Copper Canyon Press; special workshops featuring writers and experts in other fields convened to address major societal issues; writing workshops for high school students from Washington State.

Clarion West, 340 15th Ave. E., Ste. 350, Seattle, WA 98112. 206-322-9083. Contact: Richard Terra. Intensive program in fantasy and science fiction.

Clark College Open Contest & Workshop, 4312 N.E. 40th St., Vancouver, WA 98661. 206-695-2777. Contact: Arlene Paul. Spring poetry contest (reading fee required), poetry workshop, and writing craft lectures.

King County Arts Commission, 1115 Smith Tower Bldg., 506 2nd Ave., Seattle, WA 98104. 206-296-7580. The Commission publishes The Written Arts, a literary magazine and The Arts, a newsletter; it funds grants for small press publications of juried manuscripts. Contact them to get guidelines for submissions and for grants, or to get on their mailing list for publications.

The Literary Center, PO Box 85116, Seattle, WA 98145. 206-524-5514. Contact: Sarah Sarai. The Literary Center, 1716 N 45th St., is a writers' resource organization to help writers help themselves. It includes: a small press gallery (containing small press books, magazines, broadsides, tapes, etc.); a resource library (containing foundation directories, information about local readings and workshops, national markets, etc. is located at the Seattle Public Schools Teacher Resource Center at Marshall School, 520 NE Ravenna Blvd., Seattle); Literary Hotline (524-5514), a 24-hour pre-recorded listing of local literary events. Newsletter, $15/yr; circ 2,000.

National Writers Club - Seattle Chapter, PO Box 55522, Seattle, WA 98155. 206-783-3401. Contact: Leon Billig. Monthly programs, special workshops and symposia, social events, critique groups, networking, special interest activities, professional visibility.

Northwest Playwrights Guild, PO Box 95259, Seattle, WA 98145. 206-545-7955. Contact: Barbara Callander. The organization's goal is to satisfy needs of NW playwrights and organizations interested in supporting the new works of Northwest playwrights. Initial membership fee of $25, $15 per year renewal dues. Services include quarterly and monthly newsletters, seminars and workshops with visiting playwrights and play readings.

Pacific Northwest Writers Conference, 2033 6th Ave. #804, Seattle, WA 98121-2586. 206-443-3807. Membership organization sponsoring conferences and contests for adult and young writers. Summer conference includes workshops, appointments with editors/agents, etc.

Playwrights-in-Progress, 5048 44th Ave. N.E. #1, Seattle, WA 98105-2910. Contact: Nikki Louis. Weekly meetings for readings of members plays. PIP also sponsors workshops.

Rattlesnake Mountain Writers' Workshop, 5124 Grosscup, Richland, WA 99352. 509-967-9324. Contact: Nancy Girvin. 509-967-9324.

Summer Writing Workshop, c/o James McAuley, Creative Writing Program, Cheney, WA 99004. 509-359-2829. Program is held in Ireland.

Tacoma Writer's Club, 14710 30th St. Ct. E., Sumner, WA 98390. 206-473-9632. Weekly/monthly workshops including poetry, articles, and fiction. Members study marketing their work, and discuss ideas about illustrating, query letters, etc. The group publishes a monthly newsletter. Meets at the South Hill branch of the Tacoma Public Library.

Washington Poets Association, 6002 S. Fife St., Tacoma, WA 98409. Contact: Amelia Haller. Organization to raise awareness and appreciation of poetry; publishes a newsletter 4 times a year, holds an annual meeting/banquet in May, and workshops/events across the state. Refer to Poetry in Vancouver USA, A Poetry Event at Longview, and Rattlesnake Mountain.

Notes

Contests

Alaska

Explorations, UAS, 11120 Glacier Hwy., Juneau, AK 99801. Contact: Art Petersen or Ron Silva. Annual poetry and short fiction contest. Prizes, publication, write for guidelines.

British Columbia

BC Book Prizes, 3516 W. 13th Ave., Vancouver, BC V6R 2S3. 604-736-4011. Contact: Alan Twigg. Annual event.

B.C. Historical Federation Writing Competition, PO Box 933, Nanaimo, BC V9R 5N2. Contact: Pamela Mar. Annual competition of books or articles for Writers of British Columbia History. Book deadline early January each year. Articles are selected from submissions published in the BC Historical News magazine. Guidelines available.

B.C. Historical Writing Competition Box 105, Wasa, BC V0B 2K0. Contact: Mrs. Naomi Miller.

The Canadian Writers' Journal Short Fiction Contest, Box 6618, Depot 1, Victoria, BC V8P 5N7. Accepts entries of original, unpublished stories, any genre or style, with a maximum of 1200 words. $5 entry fee, SASE, and short author bio must accompany entry. Cash prizes and subscriptions.

Cecilia Lamont Literary Contest, c/o 405-4955 River Rd., Delta, BC V4K 4V9. 604-946-3773. Contact: Michael Bennett. Annual contest sponsored by the White Rock & Surrey Writers' Club. Open to poets and writers of prose. Trophy, cash prizes, certificates. Guidelines available.

Event, Douglas College, PO Box 2503, New Westminster, BC V3L 1X1. 604-527-5293. Contact: Dale Zieroth. Creative nonfiction contest. Query for details.

F.G. Bressani Literary Contest, Italian Cultural Centre Society, 3075 Slocan St., Vancouver, BC V5N 3E4.

Great Expeditions, PO Box 46499, Station G, Vancouver, BC V6R 4G7. Contact: Marilyn Marshall.

International 3-Day Novel Contest, Anvil Press, PO Box 1575, Station A, Vancouver, BC V6C 2P7. 604-876-8710. Contact: Brian Kaufman. Held Labor Day weekend. Guidelines for SASE.

PRISM International Short Fiction Contest, Department of Creative Writing, University of British Columbia, Vancouver, BC V6T 1W5. 604-228-2514. Contact: Heidi Neufeld Raine. Annual short fiction contest. Deadline each year on Dec. 1. Prizes: $2,000 first, five $200 honorary mention prizes. Send an SASE for entry form and rules.

Tickled by Thunder Poetry Contests, 7385 129th St., Surrey, BC V3W 7B8. Entry fee is $2 for three poems, $4 for extras. Prize is $10 plus publication. Write for more information.

Vernon Writers Group, 3503 18th St., Vernon, BC V1T 4A9. Contact: Francis Hill. Local organization. Also holds contests.

Montana

AAUW Essay Contest, c/o Margaret Murphy, 1301 Rimrock Rd., Billings, MT 59102.

Ag in Montana Schools, c/o Pauline Webb, 10 Parker Loop, Toston, MT 59643. Contact: Pauline Webb. Essay contest for young Montana writers, grades 7-10. Winners attend expense paid workshop on Agri-science and Ag Related Careers available in today's job market.

The American Association of University Women Montana Division, 2200 W. Dickerson #58, Bozeman, MT 59715. Essay contest.

CutBank Competition, c/o English Department, University of Montana, Missoula, MT 59812. 406-243-5231. A B Guthrie, Jr. Short Fiction Award & Richard Hugo Memorial Poetry Award. CutBank holds an annual competition for the best short story and best poem published each year in CutBank.

Montana Arts Council, The City/County Bldg., 316 Park Ave., Helena, MT 59620. 406-444-6430. Contact: Bill Pratt. State arts organization, publishes Artistsearch, a monthly newsletter. Also publishes 1 book annually as part of their First Book Award for MT residents. Send for guidelines for grant/fellowship applications, and to get on mailing list for newsletter.

Oregon

Benton County Fair Poetry Contest for Youngsters, 471 N.W. Hemlock, Corvallis, OR 97330. 503-753-3335. Contact: Linda Smith. Poetry contest for children; also exhibits adult poems at the fair. Entrants must be Benton County residents. Guidelines available.

The Eighth Mountain Poetry Prize, 624 S.E. 29th Ave., Portland, OR 97214. 503-233-3936. Contact: Ruth Gundle. Biennial prize for a book-length poetry manuscript by a woman writer. Winner will receive $1000 prize and have her ms published by Eighth Mountain Press. Send SASE for guidelines.

Evelyn Sibley Lampman Award, Oregon Library Assoc. - Salem Library, 1270 Chemeketa St. N.E., Salem, OR 97301.

Nicholas Roerich Poetry Contest, Storyline Press, 3 Oaks Farm, Brownsville, OR 97327-9718. 503-466-5352. Contact: Joseph Bednarik. Annual contest for poets who have not had a book published. Deadline for submissions is Oct. 15. Send SASE for guidelines. Prizes include publication of the winner's ms and a scholarship to a writers conference.

Oregon Council of Teachers of English, Crescent Valley High, Corvallis, OR 97330. Contact: Kay Stephens. For teachers of English, language arts, literature and creative writing at all levels. Publishes Oregon English and Chalkboard. Sponsors Teachers-as-Writers, regular conferences, and sponsors the Oregon Writing Festival for young writers.

Oregon Institute of Literary Arts, PO Box 10608, Portland, OR 97210. 503-223-3604. Annual Oregon book awards ceremony; awards for young readers literature, creative nonfiction, poetry, fiction, playwrights; fellowships for writers and publishers; book exhibits; publication of tabloid on Oregon books, Oregon Ink and a newsletter.

Oregon Press Women, PO Box 25354, Portland, OR 97225. 503-292-4945. Contact: Glennis McNeal. Professional group for broadcasters, journalists, public relations practitioners, freelancers, photographers, journalism educators. Meets twice yearly. Sponsors contests for members, high school students.

Oregon State Poetry Association, 1645 S.E. Spokane, Portland, OR 97206. 503-283-3682. Contact: Wilma Erwin. Contact for information on local groups and meetings. OSPA contests are held spring and fall and offer cash prizes in several categories ($300 total, April 1986). The number and theme of categories vary from year to year. Guidelines are published in the spring and fall issues of the OSPA Newsletter. Non-members may request them in March and August by sending SASE to above address. No entry fee to members.

Oregon Student Magazine Contest, Eastern Oregon State College, English Dept., La Grande, OR 97850. Contact: David Axelrod. Contest cosponsored by the Oregon Council of Teachers of English. Open to students and teachers publishing student writing in a magazine format. Awards six prizes of $100 each.

Oregon Students Writing & Art Foundation, PO Box 2100, Portland, OR 97208. 503-232-7737. Contact: Chris Weber. An organization of students and teachers involved in publishing an anthology of student writing compiled from the winners of the Starfire Contest. Students are involved in all aspects of the book, editing, design, publicity, etc.

Oregon Writers Colony, PO Box 15200, Portland, OR 97215. 503-284-8604. Contact: Rae Richen. Membership organization for writers in all genres. Publishes newsletter, Colonygram. Operates writers' retreat (Colony House) on Oregon coast. Holds 6 weekend workshops annually at the coast and in Portland, also one week-long workshop per year. Sponsors readings at the Heathman Hotel (LiteraTea).

Pacific Northwest Booksellers Assoc., 5903 S.E. 19th, Portland, OR 97202. 503-232-7515. Contact Bonny McKenney. Sponsors semiannual trade shows and annual book awards.

Physicians for Social Responsibility, 921 S.W. Morrison, Ste 500, Portland, OR 97205. Sponsors an annual writing contest for Oregon students grades 7-12. Prizes. Send for guidelines.

Silverfish Review Poetry Chapbook Competition, PO Box 3541, Eugene, OR 97403. 503-344-5060. Editor: Rodger Moody. Literary review sponsors a poetry chapbook competition. Query w/SASE. Guidelines available.

Society of Professional Journalists, Willamette Valley Chapter, 1320 S.W. Broadway, Portland, OR 97201. 503-244-6111. Contact. Carol Riha. Assn representing all areas of journalism and all levels of experience. Meets monthly September through May, annual contest, monthly newsletter.

Tahana Whitecrow Foundation, PO Box 18181, Salem, OR 97305. 503-585-0564. Contact: Melanie Smith. Annual spring/summer poetry contest. Closing date May 31. Native theme only, limit 30 lines. Winners published in anthology. Publishes Oyate Wo'wapi, quarterly newsletter (see Listings). Guidelines available for SASE.

Teachers as Writers Competition, Chemeketa Community College, PO Box 14007, Salem, OR 97309. Contact: Paul Suter. Sponsored by the Oregon Council of Teachers of English. Prose and poetry contest open to Oregon teachers of kindergarten through college and to any OCTE member. (See OCTE, Organizations.)

Valentine Poetry Contest, Washington Park Zoo, 4001 S.W. Canyon Rd., Portland, OR 97221. 503-226-1561. Contact: Anne Brown. Annual contest for preschool through high school age students. Submit entry on wild animals that live in a zoo. Each winner receives a copy of the anthology of winning poems.

Willamette Writers, 9045 S.W. Barbur Blvd. #5A, Portland, OR 97219. 503-452-1592. Monthly programs, newsletter, annual conference and contest, small critique groups, and ongoing workshops. Newsletter circ 900.

Washington

Bainbridge Island Arts Council, 261 Madison S., Bainbridge Island, WA 98110. 206-842-7901. Contact: Janis Shaw. In addition to other activities, including writing workshops, they publish a Poets & Artists Calendar from their annual Poets & Artists Competition.

Bumbershoot, PO Box 9750, Seattle, WA 98109. 206-622-5123. Contact: Judith Roche. Major book and literary fair as part of Seattle's Labor Day arts festival. Includes small press displays and sales, book arts exhibits, readings, roundtables, lectures, Writers-in-Performance program, publishing and book arts contests, The Bumbershoot Literary Magazine, and the Bumbershoot/Weyerhaeuser Publication Award.

Bumbershoot/Weyerhaeuser Publication Award, PO Box 9750, Seattle, WA 98109. 206-622-5123. Contact: Judith Roche. Open competition award for a collection of previously unpublished fiction or poetry (alternate years; poetry in 1992) to be published by a press from Washington, Oregon, Alaska, Montana, Idaho, or British Columbia. The publisher will be awarded $5,000 toward production; the author will receive an honorarium of $2,000 and will be asked to read in the Bumbershoot program. Bumbershoot will also promote the winning book, press, and author. Write for award criteria.

Clark College Open Contest & Workshop, 4312 N.E. 40th St., Vancouver, WA 98661. 206-695-2777. Contact: Arlene Paul. Spring poetry contest (reading fee required), poetry workshop, and writing craft lectures.

Composers Authors &. Artists of Am., Rt. 1, Box 53, Reardan, WA 99029. 509-796-5876. Contact: David Chester. Sponsors a state poetry contest. Write for info.

Governor's Writers Awards, Washington Authors Collection, State Library, PO Box 42475, Olympia, WA 98504-2475. 206-586-7010; 206-682-1770. Contact: Grace Eubanks, Hidde Van Duym, or Gayle Palmer. Awards certificates to 10 Washington authors annually. Guidelines available.

Northwest Poets & Artists Calendar, Bainbridge Island Arts Council, 261 Madison S., Bainbridge Island, WA 98110. 206-842-6374. Contact: Linda Wakefield. Material for the annual Calendar is jury selected from entries in Annual Poets & Artists Competition, which is open to residents of AK, ID, MT, OR, WA, BC, and northern California. (Deadline late January each year). The calendar is a full-color, 12 month wall calendar, 12 x 12. Each month features a full color reproduction of an original artwork with a poem. For info on calendar or competition, write to the above address.

Owl Creek Press, 1620 N. 45th St., Seattle, WA 98103. 206-633-5929. Contact: Rich Ives. Poetry Chapbook contest: under 40 pgs, $8 entry fee, Aug 15 deadline. Poetry Book Contest: over 50 pgs, $9 entry fee, Feb 15 deadline. Prize: publication with 10% payment in copies of the first printing and additional pay in cash or copies for additional printing.

Pacific Northwest Writers Conference, 2033 6th Ave. #804, Seattle, WA 98121-2586. 206-443-3807. Membership organization sponsoring conferences and contests for adult and young writers. Summer conference includes workshops, appointments with editors/agents, etc.

Pacific Northwest Young Reader's Choice Award, Pacific Northwest Library Association, UW, 133 Suzzallo Library, FM-30, Seattle, WA 98195. 206-543-1794. Contact: Carol Doll. Children vote for their favorite title from a list of 15 selected from works nominated by teachers, librarians, children, or other interested persons. Titles published three years prior to contest year. Guidelines available for SASE.

Playwright's Contest, C/O Northwest Asian American Theatre, 409 Seventh Ave. S., Seattle, WA 98104.

Puget Sound Literary Arts Competition, PO Box 215, Langley, WA 98260.

The Signpost Press Inc., 1007 Queen St., Bellingham, WA 98225. 206-734-9781. Contact: Susan Hilton. Cash awards poetry contest, entry fee, submissions must be postmarked between October 1, 1988 and January 3, 1989. Write for guidelines.

Tacoma Writer's Club, 14710 30th St. Ct. E., Sumner, WA 98390. 206-473-9632. Weekly/monthly workshops including poetry, articles, and fiction. Members study marketing their work, and discuss ideas about illustrating, query letters, etc. The group publishes a monthly newsletter. Meets at the South Hill branch of the Tacoma Public Library.

Washington Poets Association, 6002 S. Fife St., Tacoma, WA 98409. Contact: Amelia Haller. Organization to raise awareness and appreciation of poetry; publishes a newsletter 4 times a year, holds an annual meeting/banquet in May, and workshops/events across the state. Refer to Poetry in Vancouver USA, A Poetry Event at Longview, and Rattlesnake Mountain.

Writers' Open Forum Magazine Contest, PO Box 516, Tracyton, WA 98393. Contact: Sandra Haven. Annual Contest for fiction and nonfiction. Send SASE for rules.

Other

Western States Book Awards, Western States Art Federation, 236 Montezuma Ave., Santa Fe, NM 87501. 505-988-1166. Contact: Sandra Bigley. Awards presented to publishers & authors in three categories: fiction, nonfiction, poetry. Cash award to publisher and author, technical assistance, and promotional aid.

Notes

Distributors

Alaska

Alaska News Agency, Inc., 325 W. Potter Dr., Anchorage, AK 99518. 907-563-3251. Fax: 907-562-0827.

Rainforest Publishing, PO Box 101251, Anchorage, AK 99510. 907-274-8687.

British Columbia

ABZ Books, PO Box 1404, Station A, Vancouver, BC V6C 2P7. 604-263-0014. Contact: Jackson House.

Milestone Publications Ltd., 3284 Heather St., Vancouver, BC V5Z 3K5. 604-875-0611. Contact: Anne Werry. Adv: Helen Werry. Distributor/wholesaler.

Raincoast Books, 112 E. 3rd Ave., Vancouver, BC V5T 1C8.

Sandhill Book Marketing, PO Box 197, Sta A, Kelowna, BC V1Y 7N5. 604-763-1406. Contact: Nancy Wise.

Idaho

Highway Milemarker Guide Co. (HMG Co), 525 E. Bridge St., Blackfoot, ID 83221. 208-785-5125. Contact: John Aulik. Wholesaler of nonfiction about Idaho and the northern Rocky Mountains with some titles reflecting things to do in Idaho, i.e., hiking, skiing, hunting, prospecting, fishing, archaeology. Sells in all of Idaho: bookstores, but mostly small gift, gas, and sports shops.

Montana

Billings News Inc., 711 Fourth Ave. N, Billings, MT 59101. Contact: Jim Maddox. Distributes to central and eastern Montana. Does a Montana shelf in selected locales. Authors and publishers with appropriate titles should contact him with citations.

Northwest News, 101 S. California, Missoula, MT 59802. Contact: Ken Grinsteiner. Pocketbook distributor. Promotes Montana authors' sections in bookstores.

Silverbow News Distributing Co Inc., 219 E. Park, Butte, MT 59701. Contact: Joe Floreen. Paperback distributor, interested in Montana authors.

Yellowstone Art Center's Regional Writers Project, 401 N. 27th St., Billings, MT 59101. 406-656-1238. Contact: Adrea Sukin, Pat Palagi. Distributes Western literature through a retail outlet, a mail order catalog, and sales displays at other Montana museums.

Oregon

Blackwell North America Inc., 6024 S.W. Jean Rd., Bldg. G, Lake Oswego, OR 97034. 503-684-1140. Contact: John Walsdorf.

Drift Creek Press, PO Box 511, Philomath, OR 97370. 503-929-5637; 800-338-0136. Contact: Craig J Battrick. Distributing cookbooks, regional NW, poetry.

Eclectic Press Inc., PO Box 14462, Portland, OR 97214. 503-286-4018. Contact: Barbara Cogan Neidig. Wholesale distributor of imported floral craft books and gift books.

Far West Book Service, 3515 N.E. Hassalo, Portland, OR 97232. 503-234-7664. Contact: Katherine McCanna/Larry Burns. Distributor of general NW Americana.

Himber's Books, 1380 W. Second Ave., Eugene, OR 97402.

International Specialized Book Services Inc., 5602 N.E. Hassalo St., Ste. F5, Portland, OR 97213.

Pacific Northwest Books, PO Box 314, Medford, OR 97501. 503-664-5205; 503-664-4442, order desk. Contact: Bert Webber. Distributes only books about the Pacific Northwest and the Oregon Trail. Books must have ISBN, CIP desired.

Spring Arbor Distributors, 5600 N.E. Hassalo, Portland, OR 97213. 800-521-3690.

T.M.S. Book Service, PO Box 1504, Beaverton, OR 97075. 503-646-8081.

Washington

Adams News Co. Inc., 1555 W. Galer St., Seattle, WA 98119. 800-533-7617. Fax: 206-284-7599.

Creative Communications, 322 Queen Anne Ave. N., Seattle, WA 98109.

MacRae's Indian Book Distributors, PO Box 652, 1605 Cole St., Enumclaw, WA 98002.

Moving Books Inc., PO Box 20037, Seattle, WA 98102. 206-762-1750; Fax 206-762-1896. Contact: Frank Kroger. Book distributor specializing in health, alcoholism/addiction, new age, self-help, and metaphysical.

Pacific Periodical Services Inc., 4630 95th S.W., Lakewood Industrial Park Bldg. 6, Tacoma, WA 98499. 206-581-1940. Distributes childrens' books.

Pacific Pipeline Inc., 19215 66th Ave. S., Kent, WA 98032-1171. 206-872-5523. Wholesale book distributor of all categories, one specialty being NW & regional books.

Paragon Publications, 7311 69th Ave. N.E., Marysville, WA 98270. 206-659-8350. Contact: Bob Graef. Distributor of specialty collections for schools and libraries.

Rainier News, 18825 67th Ave. N.E., Arlington, WA 98223-8941.

Robert Hale & Co., 1803 132nd Ave. N.E. #4, Bellevue, WA 98005. 206-881-5212. Distributor of nautical books.

Servatius News Agency, 601 Second St., Clarkston, WA 99403. 509-758-7592.

Small Changes, 3443 12th Ave. W., Seattle, WA 98119. 206-282-3665. Contact: Shari Basom. Distributor of magazines and calendars. Catalog available.

Spilled Ink, Studio 403, PO Box 70672, Seattle, WA 98107. 206-323-6779.

Townson Publishing Co Ltd, Box 8023, Blaine, WA 98230. 604-263-0014. Contact: Jackson House.

Events

Alaska

Sitka Summer Writers Symposium, Box 2420, Sitka, AK 99835. 907-747-3794. Contact: Carolyn Servid.

British Columbia

Canadian Authors Association, Okanagan Branch, PO Box 1436 - Station A, Kelowna, BC V1X 7V8. 604-762-3021. Contact: Chloe Yeats. National association for writers and those who seek to become writers. Sponsors annual conference, quarterly journal, awards.

The Federation of BC Writers, PO Box 2206, Vancouver, BC V6B 3W2. 604-683-2057; Fax 604-683-8269. Contact: Corey Van't Haaff, Manager. "As the voice of BC writers, the Federation, a non-profit society, acts or comments on a variety of issues affecting writers of all genres. We work cooperatively with other writing organizations to ensure wider funding and support for writers. Our services include a quarterly newsletter, literary competition, employment referral, information and networking, advocacy and government lobbying.

Festival of the Written Arts, Box 2299, Sechelt, BC V0N 3A0. 603-885-9631. Contact: Betty Keller. Annual 3-day program of readings and discussions by Canadian writers. Writers-in-Residence programs, small workshop groups with professional instruction. Write for information.

Kootenay School of Writing, #306-152 W. Hastings St., Vancouver, BC V6B 3A0.

Normal Art Society, 3505 Commercial St., Vancouver, BC V5N 4E8. 604-873-3129. Nonprofit society established in 1988 to encourage art and the creative process. Publishes pop-tart Magazine (see Listings), organizes the Small Press Festival, performances, exhibitions.

Vancouver International Writers Festival, 1243 Cartwright St., Vancouver, BC V6H 4B7. 604-681-6330. Contact: Alma Lee, Producer. Festival brings writers from around the world each year for an exchange of culture and ideas with readers.

Idaho

Idaho Council of Teachers of English, c/o Judy Decime, Caldwell High School, Caldwell, ID 83605. Organization with newsletter, sponsors annual conference.

Montana

Authors of the Flathead, c/o Debbie Burke, 52 Wellington Place, Kalispell, MT 59901. Writer's group meets regularly and holds annual conference.

Bozeman Readings, c/o Bob Garner, 916 S. Willson Ave., Bozeman, MT 59715.

Cowboy Poetry Committee, c/o Lewistown Chamber of Commerce, PO Box 818, Lewistown, MT 59457. 406-538-5436. Contact Kathy Thompson or Webb Brown. Yearly Montana Cowboy Poetry Gathering.

Western Montana Writers Conference, Office of Continuing Education, Western Montana College, Dillon, MT 59725. 406-683-7537. Contact: Sally Garrett-Dingley or Susan K. Jones. Annual conference featuring a writer-in-residence with expertise in a specific writing genre.

The Writer's Voice of the Billings Family YMCA, 402 No. 32nd St., Billings, MT 59101. 406-248-1685; Fax 406-248-3450. Contact: Corby Skinner. Offers a variety of services including readings, workshops, after school programs for elementary grades, a writers exchange program, and a rural outreach project that sends one of six writers to rural junior & senior high schools to offer a half day workshop.

Yellow Bay Writers Conference, Ctr. for Continuing Ed & Summer Programs, University of Montana, Missoula, MT 59812. 406-243-2900. Contact: Judy L Jones, Program Mgr. Annual, usually in August, for one week with nationally known writers. Classes included 2 fiction, 1 poetry, 1 creative nonfiction or personal essay.

Yellowstone Art Center's Regional Writers Project, 401 N. 27th St., Billings, MT 59101. 406-656-1238. Contact: Adrea Sukin, Pat Palagi. Promotes Western literature through a lecture series featuring authors and small press publishers.

Oregon

Ars Poetica, Eastern Oregon State College, La Grande, OR 97850. Contact: Tom Madden. Poetry and fiction readings series.

Authors' & Artisans' Fair, Allegory Bookshop, PO Box 249, Gleneden Beach, OR 97388. 503-764-2020. Contact: Veronica Johnson.

Columbia Gorge Writers Group, 2470 Lichens Dr., Hood River, OR 97031. 503-386-3112. Contact: Lana Fox. Organized to share and promote the development of good writing habits and to encourage the submission of materials for publication. Regular meetings, 3rd Monday at 7 pm; critiquing, 1st Thursday at 7 pm. Summer conference.

Fishtrap Gathering, PO Box 457, Enterprise, OR 97828. 503-426-3623. Contact: Rich Wandschneider. Annual summer conference with presentations from Northwest and East Coast authors, editors, and publishers; followed by writing workshops. Also conducts an annual midwinter conference.

Keizer Artfair, 4748 Lowell Ave. N.E., Keizer, OR 97303. 503-393-2457. Third weekend in September each year. Writers can contact Keizer Art Assn for an application.

Lane Literary Guild, c/o Lane Arts Council, 411 High St., Eugene, OR 97401. 503-485-2278. Contact: Erik Muller, Alice Evans. Membership $10/indiv. Newsletter, circ 20,000. Nonprofit organization representing the professional interests of poets, fiction writers and dramatists living in Lane County.

LitEruption, 8650 S.W. White Ct., Portland, OR 97225. 503-292-8902. Contact: Lorie Topinka. A 2-day book fair and celebration in March in Portland with readings by well known Northwest authors; exhibits from book stores, publishers, writers and artists groups; children's literary room; films; and book art exhibits.

Mountain Writers Series, Mt. Hood Community College, 26000 S.E. Stark, Gresham, OR 97030. 503-232-7337. Contact: Sandra Williams. The Mountain Writers Series presents regular literary readings, each preceded by a brief musical performance, featuring artists of local, regional and national reputation, at noon on scheduled Fridays during the academic year (Oct.-June) on the MHCC campus. The public is welcome at all performances, and those wishing to receive announcements of events should write to be included on the mailing list. Artists wishing to perform in the Series should apply by August 15 with a sample of their work, phone number, and brief statement of biographical/publication/performance history.

Northwest Writers Inc., PO Box 3437, Portland, OR 97208. 503-234-2507. President: Anndee Hochman. Organization of professional writers intended to offer support, pool resources, and share information and job opportunities. Meets the 3rd Thursday of each month, Northwest Service Center, NW 18th & Everett, Portland, 7:30 pm.

Oregon Authors' Table, Mission Mill Museum Association, 1313 S.E. Mill St., Salem, OR 97301. Contact: Betty Reilly, Chairman.

Oregon Book Awards, Oregon Institute of Literary Arts, PO Box 10608, Portland, OR 97210. 503-223-3604. Contact: Kay Reid. Recognizes and promotes Oregon writers and publishers. Write for information.

Oregon Coast Council for the Arts, PO Box 1315, Newport, OR 97365. 503-265-9231. Contact: Sharon Morgan. "We are a regional arts council with a strong history of literary programs and support for emerging writers."

Oregon Council of Teachers of English, Crescent Valley High, Corvallis, OR 97330. Contact: Kay Stephens. For teachers of English, language arts, literature and creative writing at all levels. Publishes Oregon English and Chalkboard. Sponsors Teachers-as-Writers, regular conferences, and sponsors the Oregon Writing Festival for young writers.

Oregon Institute of Literary Arts, PO Box 10608, Portland, OR 97210. 503-223-3604. Annual Oregon book awards ceremony; awards for young readers literature, creative nonfiction, poetry, fiction, playwrights; fellowships for writers and publishers; book exhibits; publication of tabloid on Oregon books, Oregon Ink and a newsletter.

Oregon State Poetry Association, 1645 S.E. Spokane, Portland, OR 97206. 503-283-3682. Contact: Wilma Erwin. Contact for information on local groups and meetings. OSPA contests are held spring and fall and offer cash prizes in several categories ($300 total, April 1986). The number and theme of categories vary from year to year. Guidelines are published in the spring and fall issues of the OSPA Newsletter. Non-members may request them in March and August by sending SASE to above address. No entry fee to members.

Oregon Writers Colony, PO Box 15200, Portland, OR 97215. 503-284-8604. Contact: Rae Richen. Membership organization for writers in all genres. Publishes newsletter, Colonygram. Operates writers' retreat (Colony House) on Oregon coast. Holds 6 weekend workshops annually at the coast and in Portland, also one week-long workshop per year. Sponsors readings at the Heathman Hotel (LiteraTea).

Pacific Northwest Booksellers Assoc., 5903 S.E. 19th, Portland, OR 97202. 503-232-7515. Contact Bonny McKenney. Sponsors semiannual trade shows and annual book awards.

Poet Tree, P O BOX 2585, Portland, OR 97208. 503-235-0157. Educational organization gives performance seminar/workshops.

Poetry Plus, Lake Oswego Festival of the Arts, PO Box 368, Lake Oswego, OR 97034. 503-636-3634. Joan Sappington, Dir. An interactive literary, visual, and acoustic program. Contact for dates and program information.

Portland Poetry Festival, PO Box 8452, Portland, OR 97207. Sponsors statewide and nationwide contests for adults & children. For information on upcoming events, call 503-236-4893. Yearly festival in August, co-sponsored with the student literary committee at PSU. Quarterly newsletter, dues $10 year.

Rogue Valley Writers Conference, c/o Continuing Education/SOSC, 1250 Siskiyou Blvd., Ashland, OR 97520.

Salem Art Fair, Mission Mill Museum Assn., 1313 Mill St. S.E., Salem, OR 97301. 503-585-7012. Contact: Patti Wilbrecht. Oregon Authors' Table at annual July art fair.

Valley Writers Series, Linn-Benton Community College, 6500 S.W. Pacific Blvd., Albany, OR 97321-3779. 503-928-2361. Contact: Jane White, Liberal Arts Div. Provides readings and workshops sponsored by the Linn-Benton Council for the Arts and the LBCC English Department.

Willamette Writers, 9045 S.W. Barbur Blvd. #5A, Portland, OR 97219. 503-452-1592. Monthly programs, newsletter, annual conference and contest, small critique groups, and ongoing workshops. Newsletter circ 900.

Young Audiences of Oregon Inc., 418 S.W. Washington, Rm. 202, Portland, OR 97204. 503-224-1412. Nonprofit educational organization sponsors professional literary artists (e.g., storytelling, poetry) and performing artists in schools in Oregon and Washington. Artists work in both assembly and classroom settings, with performances, workshops, and residencies.

Young Writers Competition, Oregon Arts Commission, 835 Summer St. N.E., Salem, OR 97301. A program of the Oregon Arts Commission, this writing workshop takes various forms. Offered to middle schools only in 1991, teams of students and teachers work together in a week-end residency.

Washington

Bainbridge Island Arts Council, 261 Madison S., Bainbridge Island, WA 98110. 206-842-7901. Contact: Janis Shaw. In addition to other activities, including writing workshops, they publish a Poets & Artists Calendar from their annual Poets & Artists Competition.

Bumbershoot, PO Box 9750, Seattle, WA 98109. 206-622-5123. Contact: Judith Roche. Major book and literary fair as part of Seattle's Labor Day arts festival. Includes small press displays and sales, book arts exhibits, readings, roundtables, lectures, Writers-in-Performance program, publishing and book arts contests, The Bumbershoot Literary Magazine, and the Bumbershoot/Weyerhaeuser Publication Award.

Castalia Series, 239 Savery, University of Washington, Seattle, WA 98105.

Centrum Foundation, PO Box 1158, Port Townsend, WA 98368. 206-385-3102. Contact: Carol Jane Bangs. Activities include: The Port Townsend Writers' Conference, held annually in July; A residency program for 3-4 writers each year; a press-in-residence, Copper Canyon Press; special workshops featuring writers and experts in other fields convened to address major societal issues; writing workshops for high school students from Washington State.

Christian Writers Conference (SPU), Humanities Dept., Seattle Pacific University, Seattle, WA 98119. 206-281-2109. Contact: Linda Wagner. Offers information, inspiration, and instruction for writers for both inspirational markets and secular with major focus on the inspirational markets. Conference is held Monday through Wednesday of the last week of June each year. Includes opportunity for appointments with editors.

Edmonds Arts Commission, 700 Main St., Edmonds, WA 98020. 206-771-0228. Contact: Christine Sidwell. Sponsors Write-on-the Sound writers conference each fall.

Foothills Poetry Series, Peninsula College, Port Angeles, WA 98362. 206-452-9277. Contact: Alice Derry or Jack Estes.

The Literary Center, PO Box 85116, Seattle, WA 98145. 206-524-5514. Contact: Sarah Sarai. The Literary Center, 1716 N 45th St., is a writers' resource organization to help writers help themselves. It includes: a small press gallery (containing small press books, magazines, broadsides, tapes, etc.); a resource library (containing foundation directories, information about local readings and workshops, national markets, etc. is located at the Seattle Public Schools Teacher Resource Center at Marshall School, 520 NE Ravenna Blvd., Seattle); Literary Hotline (524-5514), a 24-hour pre-recorded listing of local literary events. Newsletter, $15/yr; circ 2,000.

Meet the Author Program Series, Rainier Beach Library, 9125 Rainier Ave. S., Seattle, WA 98118. 206-386-1906. Fall & winter scheduling.

Puget Sound Writing Program for Young Writers, English Department, GN-30, University of Washington, Seattle, WA 98195. 206-543-0141. Contact: Linda Clifton. Week-long workshop held in summer for students entering grades 5-11.

Rattlesnake Mountain Writers' Workshop, 5124 Grosscup, Richland, WA 99352. 509-967-9324. Contact: Nancy Girvin. 509-967-9324.

Red Sky Poetry Theatre, Five-O Tavern, 507 15th Ave. E., Seattle, WA 98112. 206-322-9693.

Washington Poets Association, 6002 S. Fife St., Tacoma, WA 98409. Contact: Amelia Haller. Organization to raise awareness and appreciation of poetry; publishes a newsletter 4 times a year, holds an annual meeting/banquet in May, and workshops/events across the state. Refer to Poetry in Vancouver USA, A Poetry Event at Longview, and Rattlesnake Mountain.

Young Authors Conference, School of Education, Seattle Pacific University, Seattle, WA 98119. Contact: Nancy Johnson. For young writers grades 1-8 in Western Washington and Oregon. Workshops, critiques.

Young Writers' Conference, English Dept., MS-25, Eastern Washington University, Cheney, WA 99004. 509-359-6032. Contact: Mary Ann Nelson.

Writers' Organizations

Alaska

Alaska Council of Teachers of English, PO Box 3184, Kodiak, AK 99615. Contact: Kate O'Dell.

Alaska Historical Society, PO Box 101251, Anchorage, AK 99510.

Alaska Press Women, PO Box 104056, Anchorage, AK 99510. 907-753-2622. Contact: Carolyn Rinehart

Amniote Egg Writers Group, 1123 F St., Anchorage, AK 99501.

Romance Writers of America, c/o Sally Fozoft, 1065 Cherry, Anchorage, AK 99504.

The Alaska State Writing Consortium, Department of Education, PO Box F, Juneau, AK 99811. This is known as the Writing Project in other states and publishes a quarterly newsletter and an annual journal of Alaskan educators' writing.

British Columbia

Argenta Writers' Group, Nowick Gray, Argenta, BC V0G 1B0. Contact: Nowick Gray

BC Book Promotion Council, Box 2206 MPO, Vancouver, BC V6B 3W2. 604-683-2057. Contact: Robert Webster. Acts as a clearing house for information of importance to all sectors of the book industry.

BC Writers Guild, Box 1717, Hope, BC V0X 1L0. 604-869-9848. Contact: Estelle McLachlan.

Burnaby Writers Society, 6450 Deerlake Ave., Burnaby, BC V5G 2J3.

CAA Vancouver Lower Mainland Branch, Canadian Authors Association, 24750 58A Ave., RR #3, Aldergrove, BC V0X-1A0.

Campbell River Scribes, 881 Thulin, Campbell River, BC V9W 2L4.

Canadian Authors Association (B.C. Branch/Vancouver), 726 Parkside Rd., W. Vancouver, BC V7S 1P3. Contact: Frank Wade.

Canadian Authors Association, Okanagan Branch, PO Box 1436 - Station A, Kelowna, BC V1X 7V8. 604-762-3021. Contact: Chloe Yeats. National association for writers and those who seek to become writers. Sponsors annual conference, quarterly journal, awards.

Canadian Poetry Assn. Eastwing, Eastwing, 1850 Charles St., Vancouver, BC V5L 2T7. Contact: David Bouvier.

Canadian Poetry Association Vancouver, PO Box 46658 Sta. G, Vancouver, BC V6G 4K8. 604-266-0396. Contact: Katie Eliot. Network of local poets, meets last Friday of alternate months. Publisher of SPOKES Newsletter.

Caribou Writers Group, c/o Williams Lake Library, 110 Oliver St., Williams Lake, BC V2G 1G0.

Castlegar Writer's Guild, 3012-4th Ave., Castlegar, BC V1N 2S2.

Comox Writers Group, 319 Church St., Comox, BC V9N 5G6.

Courtney-Comox Writers Group, C12 Site 170 RR1, Comox, BC V0N 5N1.

Downtown Eastside Poets, Carnegie Centre, 401 Main St., Vancouver, BC V6A 2T7. Contact: Sheila Baxter.

Esquimalt Writers Group, 527 Fraser St., Victoria, BC V9A 6H6.

The Federation of BC Writers, PO Box 2206, Vancouver, BC V6B 3W2. 604-683-2057; Fax 604-683-8269. Contact: Corey Van't Haaff, Manager. "As the voice of BC writers, the Federation, a non-profit society, acts or comments on a variety of issues affecting writers of all genres. We work cooperatively with other writing organizations to ensure wider funding and support for writers. Our services include a quarterly newsletter, literary competition, employment referral, information and networking, advocacy and government lobbying.

Gold River Writers Group, Box 985, Gold River, BC V0P 1G0.

Langley Literary Guild, 9582 - 132A St., Surrey, BC V3V 5R2.

The League of Canadian Poets/Vancouver, 2588-124B St., Surrey, BC V4A 3N7. 604-538-8214. Contact: Tom Konyves.

Nanaimo Writers, 3693 Oakridge Dr., Nanaimo, BC V9T 1M3.

Okanagan Writers' League, Room 10, Leir House, 220 Manor Park Ave., Penticton, BC V2A 2R2. 604-493-6035.

Playwrights Union of Canada, 746 E. Pender St., Vancouver, BC V5A 1V7. 604-251-3496. Contact: Peter Anderson.

Port Alberni Writers, #38 4467 Wallace St., Port Alberni, BC V9Y 3Y4.

Prince Rupert Writers' Group, Box 1080, Prince Rupert, BC V8J 4H6. Writer's group with annual newsletter.

Quadra Island Writers' Group, Support Group, Box 167, Quathiaski Cove, Quadra Island, BC V0P 1N0. 604-285-3570.

Romance Writer's Assn., Greater Vancouver Chapter, c/o 12548 - 216th St., Maple Ridge, BC V2X 5K7.

Sointula Writers, Box 1479, Port McNeil, BC V0N 2R0.

Spindrift Writers, 349 Poplar Ln, Qualicum Beach, BC V9K 1J7. 604-752-9723. Contact: Eswyn Lyster.

Vancouver Industrial Writers' Union, #203 1160 Burrard St., Vancouver, BC V6Z 2E8. 604-687-1330. Contact: Dr. Kirsten Emmott. Group meets regularly for support and criticism; interest in work writing committed to promoting the new fiction, poetry, and drama written by people about their daily work. Membership is by invitation.

Vancouver Island Literary Society, 2610 Lynburn Crescent, Nanaimo, BC V9S 3T6.

Vernon Writers Group, 3503 18th St., Vernon, BC V1T 4A9. Contact: Francis Hill. Local organization. Also holds contests.

The West Coast Book Prize Society, 107 - 100 W. Pender, Vancouver, BC V6B 1R8. 604-734-1611. Annual $1,500 book award.

West Coast Women and Words, Box 65563 - Station F, Vancouver, BC V5N 5K5. 604-872-8014. An organization of women dedicated to furthering the work of women writers. A major annual project is a summer school/writing retreat for women, WEST WORD. Brochure/application upon request in February.

West End Writers' Group, c/o W. End Community Centre, 870 Denman St., Vancouver, BC V6G 2L8.

White Rock & Surrey Writers Club, c/o 405-4955 River Rd., Delta, BC V4K 4V9. 604-946-3773. Contact: Michael Bennett. We are a group of professional and non-professional writers. Meeting every third Wednesday of each month at Centennial Arena, White Rock, BC. Criticizing and exchanging ideas and markets available for manuscripts in process. Also see listing for Cecilia Lamont Literary Contest.

Writers' Support Group, 411 Winger Rd., Williams Lake, BC V2G 3S6. Contact: Ann Walsh.

The Writers' Union of Canada, 3102 Main St., 3rd Fl., Vancouver, BC V5T 3G7. 604-874-1611.

Idaho

Boise Poets, c/o Jack Hoffman, 2401 Apple St. #J-204, Boise, ID 83706-5197.

Clearwater Writers Guild, Rt. 2 Box 159, Grangeville, ID 83530.

Gem State Writers Guild, PO Box 13, Homedale, ID 83628. 208-337-3613. Contact: Janet Leep.

Idaho Council of Teachers of English, c/o Judy Decime, Caldwell High School, Caldwell, ID 83605. Organization with newsletter, sponsors annual conference.

Idaho Falls Advanced Fiction Workshop, c/o Sharon Bowman, 692 Lomax, Idaho Falls, ID 83401. 208-529-9803. Writers' group.

Idaho Falls Fiction Workshop, c/o Sharon Bowman, 692 Lomax, Idaho Falls, ID 83401. 208-529-9803.

Idaho Press Women, N. 9103 Cuff Rd., Hayden, ID 83835. 208-664-8176. Contact: Susan Cuff.

Idaho Writers' League, PO Box 1234, Pocatello, ID 83204-1234. President: Barbara Larsen. Has many local chapters throughout Idaho; regular meetings, newsletter, workshops, a conference, and occasionally book publishing.

Moscow Moffia, 621 E. "F" St., Moscow, ID 83843. 208-882-3672. Contact: Jon Gustafson. Weekly writer's discussion groups. Sponsors workshops throughout the Northwest.

Pilot Knobs Writers Group, Rt. 1 Box 591, Victor, ID 83455. 208-354-8522. Contact: Christina Adams. One year old non-membership group in rural SE corner of Idaho. It sponsors a visiting writers series, and plans to have a mentorship program for students enabling them to work with writers through the mail.

Pocatello Poetry Workshop, c/o Pocatello Public Library, 812 E. Clark St., Pocatello, ID 83201. 208-232-8496. Contact: Jenny Lewis.

Montana

Authors of the Flathead, c/o Debbie Burke, 52 Wellington Place, Kalispell, MT 59901. Writer's group meets regularly and holds annual conference.

Beaverhead Writers Workshop, Library, Western Montana College, Dillon, MT 59725. 406-683-6794. Contact: Ron Fischer. A critique group for fiction and poetry writers; meets in the Western Montana College Library, 3rd Fridays, 7 pm.

Billings Arts Association Writers, 3706 Duck Creek Rd., Billings, MT 59101. 406-656-2524. Contact: Alice Madsen.

Great Falls Writers Group, c/o Eileen Brandt, PO Box 429, Power, MT 59468.

Hellgate Writers, PO Box 7131, 210 N. Higgins, Missoula, MT 59807. 406-721-3620. Contact: Kristin Bloomer. Writers' group with newsletter, workshops; brings in writers from out of state, puts on events in the community.

Montana Assoc. of Teachers of English, c/o Rebecca Stiff, Helena High School, Helena, MT 59601.

Montana Sagebrush Writers, PO Box 414, Dillon, MT 59725-0414. 406-683-4539; 406-932-5242. Newsletter & meetings: Sally Garrett Dingley. Workshop coordinator: Gwen Petersen. Workshop info: PO Box 1255, Big Timber, MT 59011-1255. Meetings are the 2nd Tuesday of each month from Sept. through May in Dillon, MT, Sherrif"s Annex.

Montana Writing Project, English Department, University of Montana, Missoula, MT 59812. 406-243-5231. Contact: Dr. Beverly Ann Chin.

Romance Writers of America, c/o Sally Garret Dingley, PO Box 212, Dillon, MT 59725.

Seely Lake Writers Club, c/o Vernon Printing & Publishing, 1701 Hwy 83 N, Seely Lake, MT 59868. Informal group of writers and history buffs. No bylaws, rules or dues.

Oregon

Adventist Composers Arrangers and Poets, Inc, PO Box 11, Days Creek, OR 97429. Contact: Eleanor B. Davis.

Bend-in-the-River Writers Guild, c/o Doris M. Hall, 62340 Powell Butte Rd., Bend, OR 97701. 503-389-5845. ORG

Cascade Poets, 6123 N. Commercial, Portland, OR 97217. 503-283-3682. Contact: Wilma Erwin. We meet on the last Monday of the month at Cascade Center, 705 N. Killingsworth, Portland, OR 97217. We welcome all poets. Poets should bring 12 copies of a poem they'd like to have critiqued. Free. We're looking forward to seeing you.

Central Oregon Coast Writers, Rt. 1, Box 59X, Otis, OR 97368. 503-994-5476. Contact: Mary Esther Miller

Christian Scribes, 9340 S.E. Morrison, Portland, OR 97216. Contact: Shirley Cody.

Coastal Fellowship of Christian Writers, PO Box 186, Toledo, OR 97391. 503-336-3410. Contact: Beth Dickinson. Coastal Fellowship of Christian Writers meets at the Toledo Public Library. group focus: encouragement and critique.

Columbia Gorge Writers Group, 2470 Lichens Dr., Hood River, OR 97031. 503-386-3112. Contact: Lana Fox. Organized to share and promote the development of good writing habits and to encourage the submission of materials for publication. Regular meetings, 3rd Monday at 7 pm; critiquing, 1st Thursday at 7 pm. Summer conference.

Coos Head Writers, 950 Spaulding Rd., Coos Bay, OR 97420. 503-267-7236. Contact: Mary Scheirman. Support group.

Creative Arts Guild, 520 S.W. 5th, Albany, OR 97321. 503-926-2211. Contact: Connie Petty.

Entheos, PO Box 1509, Philomath, OR 97370. 503-830-4758. Contact: Karen C. Hayden. Writers and photographers organization.

Friends of the Library, c/o Dianne Sichel, 3057 S.W. Fairview, Portland, OR 97201. 503-228-0841. Organizes readings by nationally known writers.

Grants Pass Writers Workshop, 114 Espey Rd., Grants Pass, OR 97526. 503-476-2038. Contact: Dorothy Francis

Lane Literary Guild, c/o Lane Arts Council, 411 High St., Eugene, OR 97401. 503-485-2278. Contact: Erik Muller, Alice Evans. Membership $10/indiv. Newsletter, circ 20,000. Nonprofit organization representing the professional interests of poets, fiction writers and dramatists living in Lane County.

Northwest Native American Writers, PO Box 6403, Portland, OR 97228. 503-232-3513. Contact: Elizabeth Woody.

Northwest Playwrights Guild, Oregon Chapter, 8959 S.W. 40th Ave., Portland, OR 97219. Contact: Michael Whelan. Annual dues $15. Support group for regional playwrights, provides both regional and state newsletters, occasionally cosponsors workshops, readings, and productions.

Northwest Writers Inc., PO Box 3437, Portland, OR 97208. 503-234-2507. President: Anndee Hochman. Organization of professional writers intended to offer support, pool resources, and share information and job opportunities. Meets the 3rd Thursday of each month, Northwest Service Center, NW 18th & Everett, Portland, 7:30 pm.

Oregon Association of Christian Writers, 17768 S.W. Pointe, Forest Ct, Aloha, OR 97006. Contact: Sally Stuart, Exec Editor. Organized for the purpose of promoting higher standards of craftsmanship in the field of Christian journalism and encouraging a greater sense of spiritual responsibility in the Christian writer. The group holds writers seminars 3 times a year in Salem, Eugene and Portland and a 3-day summer conference in July.

Oregon Council of Teachers of English, Crescent Valley High, Corvallis, OR 97330. Contact: Kay Stephens. For teachers of English, language arts, literature and creative writing at all levels. Publishes Oregon English and Chalkboard. Sponsors Teachers-as-Writers, regular conferences, and sponsors the Oregon Writing Festival for young writers.

Oregon Journalists Coalition, Oregonian, 1320 S.W. Broadway, Portland, OR 97201. 503-221-8134. Contact: Stan Chen/Copy Desk.

Oregon Newspaper Publishers Association, 7150 S.W. Hampton, Ste. 111, Portland, OR 97223. President: Marcia Pry.

Oregon Press Women, PO Box 25354, Portland, OR 97225. 503-292-4945. Contact: Glennis McNeal. Professional group for broadcasters, journalists, public relations practitioners, freelancers, photographers, journalism educators. Meets twice yearly. Sponsors contests for members, high school students.

Oregon State Poetry Association, 1645 S.E. Spokane, Portland, OR 97206. 503-283-3682. Contact: Wilma Erwin. Contact for information on local groups and meetings. OSPA contests are held spring and fall and offer cash prizes in several categories ($300 total, April 1986). The number and theme of categories vary from year to year. Guidelines are published in the spring and fall issues of the OSPA Newsletter. Non-members may request them in March and August by sending SASE to above address. No entry fee to members.

Oregon Students Writing & Art Foundation, PO Box 2100, Portland, OR 97208. 503-232-7737. Contact: Chris Weber. An organization of students and teachers involved in publishing an anthology of student writing compiled from the winners of the Starfire Contest. Students are involved in all aspects of the book, editing, design, publicity, etc.

Oregon Writers Alliance, 4950 S.W. Hall Blvd., Beaverton, OR 97005. Writers' support group meets twice a month.

Oregon Writers Colony, PO Box 15200, Portland, OR 97215. 503-284-8604. Contact: Rae Richen. Membership organization for writers in all genres. Publishes newsletter, Colonygram. Operates writers' retreat (Colony House) on Oregon coast. Holds 6 weekend workshops annually at the coast and in Portland, also one week-long workshop per year. Sponsors readings at the Heathman Hotel (LiteraTea).

O-Ya-Ka Story League, Multnomah County Central Library, 801 S.W. 10th Ave., Portland, OR 97205. 503-244-9415. Meets monthly. Affiliated with National Story League, Western District. Story workshop sponsored by Western District held at Marylhurst alternate summers.

Pacific Northwest Booksellers Assoc., 5903 S.E. 19th, Portland, OR 97202. 503-232-7515. Contact Bonny McKenney. Sponsors semiannual trade shows and annual book awards.

Pacific Poets, Rt. 1 Box 4099, Coquille, OR 97423. Contact: Miriam Roady.

Portland Science Fiction Society, PO Box 4602, Portland, OR 97208. 503-655-6189.

Regional Arts Council of Central Oregon, 63085 N. Hwy. 97, Ste. 103, Bend, OR 97701. 503-382-5055.

Romance Writers of America Cascade, c/o Elly Ibarra, 4825 N.E. 17th, Portland, OR 97211. 503-284-4200.

Romance Writers of America Portland/Vancouver Chapter, c/o Clackamas Book Exchange, 7000 S.E. Thiessen Rd., Milwaukie, OR 97267. 503-659-2559. Contact: Iona Lockwood. To give encouragement and support to writers, published and unpublished, who are interested in the romance genre via monthly meetings, newsletters, workshops, etc. Meets monthly.

Roseburg Writers Group, c/o Pat Banta, Rt. I Box 4010, Coquille, OR 97423. 503-673-6486.

Salem Writers and Publishers, PO Box 575, Dayton, OR 97114. 503-868-7345. Sue Henry, President. Monthly meeting and newsletter, Fishwrap; focusing on marketing. Dues $10/yr.

Society of Children's Book Writers, 2513 S.E. Taylor St., Portland, OR 97214. 503-235-6210. Contact: Liz Vaughan.

Society of Children's Book Writers NW Chapter, c/o Robert Rubinstein, 90 E. 49th St., Eugene, OR 97405.

Society of Professional Journalists, Willamette Valley Chapter, 1320 S.W. Broadway, Portland, OR 97201. 503-244-6111. Contact: Carol Riha. Assn representing all areas of journalism and all levels of experience. Meets monthly September through May, annual contest, monthly newsletter.

Valley Poets of Medford, c/o Leona Williams, 725 Royal Ave. #74, Medford, OR 97504. 503-773-8329.

Willamette Literary Guild, 835 S.W. 11th St., Corvallis, OR 97333. Provides community support for writers interested in literary arts in the mid-Willamette area. Publishes a newsletter 3 or 4 times each year, holds 3 Literary Cabarets per year, and supports other literary events. Dues $10/yr.

Willamette Writers, 9045 S.W. Barbur Blvd. #5A, Portland, OR 97219. 503-452-1592. Monthly programs, newsletter, annual conference and contest, small critique groups, and ongoing workshops. Newsletter circ 900.

Women in Communications Inc., PO Box 3924, Portland, OR 97208. 503-292-1324.

Young Audiences of Oregon Inc., 418 S.W. Washington, Rm. 202, Portland, OR 97204. 503-224-1412. Nonprofit educational organization sponsors professional literary artists (e.g., storytelling, poetry) and performing artists in schools in Oregon and Washington. Artists work in both assembly and classroom settings, with performances, workshops, and residencies.

Washington

Adventist Writer's Assoc. of Western Washington, 18115 116th Ave. S.E., Renton, WA 98058. 206-235-1435. Contact: Marian Forschler

Adventist Writers' Assn. of WA, 17529-26th Dr. S.E., Bothell, WA 98102. 206-486-6836. Contact: Maylan Schurch. Publishes a newsletter for members, $10 per year.

American Penwomen, Rt. 1, Box 53, Reardan, WA 99029. 509-796-5872. Contact: Charlotte Chester

American Penwomen Seattle, 7584 Meadowmeer Lane N.E., Bainbridge Island, WA 98110. 206-842-4269. Contact: Kay Stewart. Monthly newsletter, 8 meetings a year.

Bainbridge Writer's Guild, c/o Nancy Rekow, 8489 Fletcher Bay Rd. N.E., Bainbridge, WA 98110. 206-842-4855.

Before Columbus Foundation, American Ethnic Studies, GN-80, University of Washington, Seattle, WA 98195. 206-543-4264. Contact: Shawn Wong. Promotes the efforts of minority and multicultural writers and topics; awards, journal.

Children's Book Writers of the Eastside, c/o Carol Krefting Youngberg, 6133 111th Ave. N.E., Kirkland, WA 98033. 206-822-1170.

Christian Writers, c/o Mrs. Carl T. Jones, 207 N.E. A St., College Place, WA 99324. 509-525-4350.

Composers Authors &. Artists of Am., Rt. 1, Box 53, Reardan, WA 99029. 509-796-5876. Contact: David Chester. Sponsors a state poetry contest. Write for info.

Creative People Support Group, Supportletter, 2905 Mayfair Ave. N., Seattle, WA 98109. 206-283-0505. Contact: Beth Bauer. Informal pot luck dinner; encouragement, emotional support, positive critique of works in progress to promote creativity; writers, artists, musicians, song writers, poets, needle workers, cooks, photographers, craftpersons we encourage and enjoy creativity and creative people. Supportletter mailed to those showing continuing interest in group (by attendance, or by verbal contact with editor).

Ferndale Writers Group, c/o Ferndale Library, PO Box 1209, Ferndale, WA 98248.

Fictioneers, 3648 Burke Ave. N., Seattle, WA 98103-8337. Contact: Beth Casey. Monthly meetings for writers, held at Seattle Downtown Public Library, 3rd Saturday of the month at 10:30 am. Group has been in existence for over 40 years, and is not sponsored by the Library. Meetings include manuscript reading, critiques, discussions.

Kitsap County Christian Writers Support Group, PO Box 11337, Bainbridge Island, WA 98110. Contact: Elaine Wright Colvin at 206-842-9103 or Kay Stewart at 206-842-4269. Monthly meetings, retreats, workshops, etc.

Kitsap Writers Club, c/o Phil Kirschner, 916 Hull Ave., Port Orchard, WA 98366. 206-876-3622.

The Literary Center, PO Box 85116, Seattle, WA 98145. 206-524-5514. Contact: Sarah Sarai. The Literary Center, 1716 N 45th St., is a writers' resource organization to help writers help themselves. It includes: a small press gallery (containing small press books, magazines, broadsides, tapes, etc.); a resource library (containing foundation directories, information about local readings and workshops, national markets, etc. is located at the Seattle Public Schools Teacher Resource Center at Marshall School, 520 NE Ravenna Blvd., Seattle); Literary Hotline (524-5514), a 24-hour pre-recorded listing of local literary events. Newsletter, $15/yr; circ 2,000.

Literary Lights, 6918 Spada Rd., Snohomish, WA 98290.

Mystery Writers of America - Northwest, c/o Frank Denton, 14654 8th Ave. S.W., Seattle, WA 98166.

N by NW Writers, 655 Main St. #305, Edmonds, WA 98020. 206-776-4365. Contact: R. Kermit Fisher. Monthly meetings on 3rd Wednesday in Edmonds; publishes monthly newsletter to benefit members. Dues $12/yr.

National League Am. Pen Women Spokane, E. 1020 Bedivere Dr., Spokane, WA 99218. Contact: Thalia Kleinoeder.

National League of American Pen Women/ Tacoma, 7606 37th W., Unit 3d, Tacoma, WA 98466. 206-564-5542. Contact: Jane Keffler.

National Writers Club - Seattle Chapter, PO Box 55522, Seattle, WA 98155. 206-783-3401. Contact: Leon Billig. Monthly programs, special workshops and symposia, social events, critique groups, networking, special interest activities, professional visibility.

Nightwriters, 10941 Pt. Vashon Dr. S.W., Vashon, WA 98070. 206-567-4829. Contact: Joyce Delbridge. Regular meetings at Vashon Library, open invitation, small fee, critique group.

No Frills Writer's Workshop, 1118 Hoyt Ave., Everett, WA 98201. 206-259-0804. Contact: Ron Fleshman. Active working writers meet Tuesdays for critiques. Share brags, moans, and dues for space rental. Meets weekly.

Northwest Christian Writers Association, 17462 N.E. 11th St., Bellevue, WA 98008. 206-644-5012. Contacts: Agnes Lawless, Pauline Sheehan.

Northwest Outdoor Writers Assoc., 3421 E. Mercer St., Seattle, WA 98112. 206-323-3970. Contact: Stan Jones. Assn of professional outdoor writers, editors, artists and photographers in Western US and Canada.

Northwest Playwrights Guild, PO Box 95259, Seattle, WA 98145. 206-545-7955. Contact: Barbara Callander. The organization's goal is to satisfy needs of NW playwrights and organizations interested in supporting the new works of Northwest playwrights. Initial membership fee of $25, $15 per year renewal dues. Services include quarterly and monthly newsletters, seminars and workshops with visiting playwrights and play readings.

Northwest Renaissance, 214 N St. N.E., Auburn, WA 98002. 206-833-4798. Contact: Marjorie Rommel. Poetry workshop with approximately 50 members, Bellingham to Olympia. Meets monthly in members' homes. Membership by application and election, dues $20/yr, includes newsletter. Occasional publication of member anthology, etc. Literature available.

Ocean Shores Writers, c/o Marlene Thomason, PO Box 1262, Ocean Shores, WA 98569. 206-289-2165.

Pacific Northwest Writers Conference, 2033 6th Ave. #804, Seattle, WA 98121-2586. 206-443-3807. Membership organization sponsoring conferences and contests for adult and young writers. Summer conference includes workshops, appointments with editors/agents, etc.

Playwrights-in-Progress, 5048 44th Ave. N.E. #1, Seattle, WA 98105-2910. Contact: Nikki Louis. Weekly meetings for readings of members plays. PIP also sponsors workshops.

Poetry Scribes, 3328 E. 36th, Spokane, WA 99223. 509-448-8292. Contact: Betty Egbert. Poetry critique group, meets monthly. Publishes Turquoise Lanterns, an annual anthology.

Poets & Writers Inc., 4045 Brooklyn Ave. N.E., Seattle, WA 98105. 206-543-4050.

Red-Wood Writers Workshop, 12031 Pleasant Pl. N.E., Bainbridge Island, WA 98110-1316. 206-481-3240. Contact: Linda Foss. Support group for area writers. Meetings include readings, creative exercises, sharing ideas, and information.

Renton Writers Workshop, c/o Beth Cole, 18618 S.E. 128th St., Renton, WA 98056. 206-255-5711. Contact: Beth Cole/Marilyn Kamcheff. Meets in the Administrative Center of the Renton School District, 435 Main Ave. South, Renton. We try to improve our craft by pursuing regular writing habits, giving constructive criticism, and sharing publishing information. Meets twice a month from 9:30 am. to 12:30 pm.

Romance Writers of America, c/o Selwyn Young, 620 N. 202, Seattle, WA 98133.

Romance Writers of America, c/o Darlene Layman, 7270 Thasof Ave. N.E., Bremerton, WA 98310.

Romance Writers of America, c/o Margo MacIntosh, 1206 E. Pike St. #1004, Seattle, WA 98122.

Romance Writers of America Tacoma Chapter, c/o Lutheran Church of Christ the King, 1710 85th St. E., Tacoma, WA 98445. 206-847-7351. Contact: Arlene Dubacker.

Scribe's Forum, 1206 E Pike St. #1004, Seattle, WA 98122. Contact: Margo MacIntosh. Group to improve skills, share market info.

Scribes of Ellensburg, PO Box 1392, Ronald, WA 98940. 509-649-2236. Contact: Judith Parker. Writers' group offers magazine, Scribbles, and short story and poetry contest. Deadline 12/31 each yr. "No 'slice of life.' Looking for well plotted stories with good characterization. No erotica. All types of poetry." SASE for details.

Seahurst Writers, 13404 Military Rd. S., Seattle, WA 98168. Contact: Barbara Benepe. Writers' group meets twice a month at Burien Library. All writers welcome.

Seattle Freelances, c/o Patricia Mauser, 20021 Hollyhills Dr. N.E., Bothell, WA 98011. 206-863-2656.

Skagit Valley Writers League, PO Box 762, Sedro Woolley, WA 98284-0762. Contact: Diane Freethy. Informal group of writers (all genres) meets 2nd and 4th Wed at Washington Federal Savings & Loan in Burlington, WA at 1 pm. Format includes critiquing, guest speakers, annual contest (regional).

Society of Children's Book Writers, 1215 N.E. 168th, Seattle, WA 98155. 206-362-6442. Contact: Shellen Reid.

Society of Children's Book Writers, Eastside, 6133 111th Pl. N.E., Kirkland, WA 98033. 206-822-1170. Contact: Carol A Youngberg.

Southwest Washington Writers, 15007 N.E. 25 A St., Vancouver, WA 98684. 206-254-2458. Contact: Trish Covington.

Spokane Christian Writers, Beautiful Savior Lutheran Church, S. 4320 Conklin St., Spokane, WA 99203. 509-448-6622. Contact: Niki Anderson. Christian writers' critique group. Meets monthly.

Tacoma Writer's Club, 14710 30th St. Ct. E., Sumner, WA 98390. 206-473-9632. Weekly/monthly workshops including poetry, articles, and fiction. Members study marketing their work, and discuss ideas about illustrating, query letters, etc. The group publishes a monthly newsletter. Meets at the South Hill branch of the Tacoma Public Library.

Them Dam Writers Club, c/o Jean Nicholson, Box 307, Electric City, WA 99123. Meets twice a month in members' homes.

Washington Christian Writers Fellowship, PO Box 11337, Bainbridge Island, WA 98110. 206-842-9103. Contact: Elaine Wright Colvin. Writers' group sharing networking, inspiration, marketing how-to, and critiquing. Sponsors annual conference.

Washington Library Media Assn., PO Box 1413, Bothell, WA 98041. Contact: Carol Mackey.

Washington Poets Association, 6002 S. Fife St., Tacoma, WA 98409. Contact: Amelia Haller. Organization to raise awareness and appreciation of poetry; publishes a newsletter 4 times a year, holds an annual meeting/banquet in May, and workshops/events across the state. Refer to Poetry in Vancouver USA, A Poetry Event at Longview, and Rattlesnake Mountain.

Washington State Council of Teachers of Eng., c/o Port Angeles High School, 304 E. Park Ave., Port Angeles, WA 98362.

Wenatchee Christian Writers Fellowship, 24216 104th Pl. W., Edmonds, WA 98020. 509-884-3279. Contact: Millie Hynes.

Whatcom Writers, c/o Margot Rowe, 1237 W. Racine St., Bellingham, WA 98226. 206-734-9818. A group of published and unpublished writers of adult age. Members manuscripts are read aloud followed by constructive criticism aimed at helping the author to produce a salable piece of work. Market news, contests, workshops, etc. are brought to the attention of members. We share success and failure with equal interest. Meetings held the 3rd Tuesday of each month.

Wordsmiths of Battle Ground, 13210 N.E. 199th St., Battle Ground, WA 98604. 206-687-3767. Contact: Pat Redjou. Writer support group.

Writers Information Network, PO Box 11337, Bainbridge Island, WA 98110. 206-842-9103. Director: Elaine Wright Colvin. Professional association for Christian writers founded in 1983. Includes a variety of services, including a bimonthly newsletter, marketing information, speaker referral system, and more.

Photographers' Organizations

American Society of Magazine Photographers, Aperture PhotoBank, Inc., 1530 Westlake Ave. N., Seattle, WA 98109. 206-282-8166. Contact: Marty Lokins.

American Society of Magazine Photographers/ Oregon, 431 N.W. Flanders, Portland, OR 97209. Contact: Bruce Forester.

Association for the Multi-Image/Idaho Chapter, Custom Recording & Sound, 3907 Custer Dr., Boise, ID 83705.

Association for the Multi-Image/Montana Chapter, c/o Doug Brekke, PO Box 1295, Big Timber, MT 59011. Photographers organization.

Association for the Multi-Image/Washington, Pacific Northwest Bell, 1600 7th Ave. #2604, Seattle, WA 98101. Contact: Tony Beck

Publishers' Organizations

Association of Book Publishers of British Columbia, 100 W. Pender St., Ste 107, Vancouver, BC V6B 1R8. 604-684-0228. Contact: Margaret Reynolds. Organization to support and promote book publishers in B.C. Displays members books in office and at fairs. Publishes EndPaper quarterly.

Book Publishers Northwest, PO Box 22048, Seattle, WA 98122.

International Association of Scholarly Publishers, c/o University of Washington Press, PO Box C50096, Seattle, WA 98195. 206-543-8870. Contact: Dorothy Anthony.

Northwest Association of Book Publishers, PO Box 663, Marylhurst, OR 97036. 503-236-7359. Contact: William Kotke. Meets on the last Thursday of the month (except Dec) at Clackamas Community College from 10 am to 12 am. Membership open to all publishers; associate memberships open to individuals and businesses related to publishing. Serves as a production and marketing resource for members. Publishes a monthly newsletter (*Publisher's Focus*), an annual membership directory, and a catalog of books by member publishers.

Small Press Action Network (SPAN), c/o Petarade Press, Box 65746 Station F, Vancouver, BC V5N 5N7. 604-873-2703. Nonprofit coalition of small and/or independent publishers. Publishes quarterly newsletter and a catalog. Holds small press festivals, etc. Membership $25/yr (CDN). Literature available.

Other/ Miscellaneous

Alaska

Alaska Media Directory, 6200 Bubbling Brook Circle, Anchorage, AK 99516. 907-346-1001. Contact: Alissa Crandall. Annual directory with listings of media related companies in Alaska; includes publications, radio, television, ad and marketing agencies, artists, photographers, writers, printers, typesetters, etc. Cost: $68 for current edition; $34 for past edition.

Alaska Theatre of Youth, Box 104036, Anchorage, AK 99510. Contact: Director.

Young & Associates, Artists in Schools, 715 L St. #6, Anchorage, AK 99501.

British Columbia

Canadian Centre for Studies in Publishing, English Department, Simon Fraser University, Burnaby, BC V5A 1S6. 604-291-3689. Contact: Rolly Lorimer, Director. Among other work, published a survey on BC publishers which resulted in increased government arts support.

Eastwing, 3389 William St., Vancouver, BC V5K 2Z4. Contact: Gail D Whitter.

Freelance Editors' Association of Canada, PO Box 1688, Stn. A, Vancouver, BC V6C 2P7. 604-681-7184. A support and networking organization for professional editors, offering a job hotline, seminars, books sales, and evening programs. Also publishes a newsletter for members.

North Pacific Women Writers Retreat, 3091 W. 15th Ave., Vancouver, BC V6K 3A5. 604-734-9816. Contact: Joni Miller. Ads: Karen Grant. "We run an untutored writing retreat. We're a non-profit organization of writers." Last retreat was May 22-June 1 in Sechelt, BC.

Idaho

Idaho State Library, 325 W. State St., Boise, ID 83720.

Idaho Writers' Archive, Hemingway Western Studies Center, 1910 University Dr., Boise, ID 83725. Contact: Chuck Guilford. Recently developed project to archive Idaho's literary output; includes a newsletter "intended to help make Idaho writers more aware of the many contests, grants, workshops, and publishing opportunities available to them."

Montana

Montana Books and Authors, c/o Sue Hart, English Department, Eastern Montana College, Billings, MT 59101. 406-657-2011. Cable Channel 21 program produced by Montana Author's Coalition. Half-hour program interviews published authors, as well as people in allied fields such as bookselling, agenting, book editing, library work.

Montana Office of Public Instruction, State Capitol, Helena, MT . 406-444-3095. Contact: Jean Cladouhos

Oregon

Oregon Book Artists Guild, PO Box 994, Beaverton, OR 97075. 503-324-8081. Contact: Patricia Grass. A group of diverse people whose interests include papermaking, marbling, bookbinding, fine printing. Newsletter $15/yr; circ 200.

Oregon Center for the Book, Oregon State Library, State Library Building, Salem, OR 97310. 503-378-4367. A statewide program including exhibits, special collections and speakers all designed to increase awareness and appreciation of books and reading. The Center is supported with contributions by the public. It is affiliated with The Center for the Book in the Library of Congress. Writer's Northwest Handbook is an official resource of the Oregon Center for the Book.

Oregon Committee for the Humanities, 812 S.W. Washington St. #225, Portland, OR 97205. 503-241-0543. Contact: Robert W Keeler. Grantmaking philanthropic organization. Grants available for public programs involving humanities scholars; consultation grants for organizations needing humanities expertise, research grants to humanities scholars.

Oregon State Archives, 1005 Broadway N.E., Salem, OR 97310. 503-378-4241. Contact: John Lazud. Publishes high school curriculum packet, historical resources, informational guides, source records on genealogy, Oregon history, law.

Walden Residency for Oregon Writers, Northwest Writing Institute of Lewis & Clark College, Campus Box 100, Lewis & Clark College, Portland, OR 97219. 503-768-7745; 503-768-7960. Contact: Kim Stafford. Three residencies awarded annually on the basis of a project proposal and a writing sample. Six and twelve week residencies take place at a mountain farm in Southern Oregon, partial board, utilities, no phone.

Washington

The Adamant Program, 7055 N.E. Crawford Dr., Kingston, WA 948346. 206-297-7220. Contact: Magdalena Herreshoff, Resident Manager. Residencies for playwrights, artists, writers, poets, ceramacists, and composers. Write for application and information.

Center for Pacific Northwest Studies, Western Washington University, Bellingham, WA 98225. 206-647-4776; 206-676-3125. Contact: James W Scott, Director. Collections include manuscript materials, business records, maps, photographs, etc. on the PNW, especially NW Washington. Phone ahead of visit.

Clark County Genealogical Society & Library, PO Box 2728, Vancouver, WA 98668. Contact: Rose Marie Harshman.

Cottages at Hedgebrook, 2197 E. Millman Rd., Langley, WA 98260. 206-321-4786. Two application deadlines, April 1 and October 1. Residencies from 1 week to 3 months. Guidelines available. Applicants must be women.

Guild of Natural Science Illustrators, Box 95721, Seattle, WA 98145.

KSER 90.7 FM, 14920 Highway 99 #150, Lynnwood, WA 98037. 206-742-4541. Joan & David Blacker produce a combination book review and author-interview segment. One segment is telephone interviews with NW authors or books with a NW emphasis.

National Endowment for the Arts, Literature Program, 1100 Pennsylvania Ave., Washington, DC 20506. 202-682-5451. Grants to individual writers and small presses.

Spruce Street School, 411 Yale Ave. N., Seattle, WA 98109. 206-621-9211. Contact: Harvey Sadis. A private school with a book arts program for K-4.

Storytelling Workshop, Graduate School of Library Science, University of Washington FM-30, Seattle, WA 98195. Contact: Spencer G Shaw.

Washington Coalition Against Censorship, 5503 17th N.W. #604, Seattle, WA 98107. 206-624-2184. Contact: Barbara Dority. Coalition of organizations joined to fight the attack on First Amendment rights. Acts as an information clearinghouse for Washington state, and puts out newsletter; sells books, videos, T-shirts.

Washington State Library, Northwest Room, WSL AJ-11, Olympia, WA 98504. Contact: Jeanne Engermann, Librarian.

Western States Arts Federation, 236 Montezuma Ave., Santa Fe, NM 87501. 505-988-1166. Contact: Sandra Gibley. Literary activities include the Annual Western States Book Awards, a quarterly literature newsletter, technical assistance workshops, and literature presenting initiatives.

SECTION VIII

Art

Binding

Books

Classes

Consulting

Design

Editing

Indexing

Legal advice

Literary agents

Magazines

Mailing Lists

Newspapers

Organizations

Photo services

Printing

Recreation

Recycled paper

Software

Typesetting

Typing

Workshop

Writing

GOODS & SERVICES

Introduction to the Advertisers

The following section displays the services and wares of vendors who serve the writing and publishing community. Their support of *Writer's Northwest Handbook* is of considerable help in covering daily expenses, paying writers, properly promoting the book, and keeping it affordable. Of course, they're not buying space simply out of the goodness of their hearts. They expect that many readers will look here first when they need something related to their writing, publishing, or reading.

We have had good experiences with some of the folks listed here, but there are many we don't know. While we hope that all of them will consistently deliver what they promise, an advertisement or listing in this section does not represent an endorsement by Blue Heron Publsihing, Inc. We recommend that our reader consider these businesses on their own merits.

Please tell our advertisers that you found them in *Writer's Northwest Handbook*.

Classified Ads

BOOKS BY MODEM?? INKLINK (sm) connects Book Collectors, Dealers and Writers Nationwide. Modem Line (Data-8N1): 617/923-4990. Voice Line: 617/923-4991.

EDITING, SCANNING: Typed manuscripts scanned to common wp formats. Manuscripts edited, proofed, or evaluated. **Fiction** a specialty. Paul Blanding, Associated Agent, Golden West Literary Agency 503/236-9942.

Expert WORD PROCESSING. Fast/accurate. Easy parking. Alpine Secretarial, 738 E. Burnside 503/233-7756.

HERMES: Editorial Services for Mortals! Call for brochure. Jonika Mountainfire, 509/485-2702.

Mailing Lists compiled from the newspaper *Writer's NW*: 2700 NW publishers; also NW writers' resources, writers, teachers, librarians, bookstores. $60 per thou. *Writer's NW*, 24450 NW Hansen Rd, Hillsboro, OR 97124. 503/621-3911.

Manuscript Consulting by Nancy Henderson: New York experience at Oregon prices. Plus workshops that rejunenate your writing at its source. See essay p. 18. For info: PO Box 1472, Coos Bay, OR 97420.

Publish your book your way — save money. Low cost from camera-ready copy or disc (Mac-IBM). For price list write: Artex Publishing, Inc., 1924A N. 7th St., Sheboygan, WI 53081.

RECYCLED PAPER — Many colors and weights for your printing project. We'll help you find **real** recycled paper that fits your needs. Household and office products, too! Peacetree Recycled Paper. 503/233-5821.

WORD PROCESSING. Manuscripts, Theses, Resumes, Letters. IBM compatible with HP LazerJet. Reasonable rates. Call Beth at 503/257-9732.

WORD WOMAN transforms manuscripts, newsletters, special projects into professional presentations. Word 5.1. PageMaker. Editing available. Linette True 503/282-6308.

Desktop Publishing
Dollars & Sense

A nuts & bolts approach to successfully operating a small desktop publishing service business. Specifically designed for wordsmiths, graphic artists, and typographers who want to roll up their sleeves and expand their businesses sanely. This isn't about boardrooms and fancy offices. It's about succeeding — and enjoying it.

by Scott Anderson

"Interviews with dozens of publishers are the best part..."
– Home Office Computing

Only $14.95 plus $2.50 s&h.
From Blue Heron Publishing,
24450 NW Hansen Road,
Hillsboro, Oregon 97124
For credit card order:
503.621.3911.

New 1993 Edition!

THE WRITER'S HANDBOOK

Edited by Sylvia K. Burack

Widely hailed as the best and most authoritative guide on writing for publication, this indispensable volume belongs on every writer's bookshelf. The new, revised edition of **THE WRITER'S HANDBOOK** has been greatly expanded to include **110** chapters by the world's most successful writers, editors, and literary agents. Market lists, also updated and enlarged, include names and addresses of more than **3,000** magazines and book publishers; the type of material editors are looking for; and payment rates.

The distinguished writers who share their experience and discuss approaches that will help you achieve publication include—

JAMES APPLEWHITE ◆ SIDNEY SHELDON ◆ LaVYRLE SPENCER ◆ DICK FRANCIS
EVAN HUNTER ◆ JOHN IRVING ◆ URSULA K. LE GUIN ◆ KATHERINE PATERSON
ELIZABETH FORSYTHE HAILEY ◆ BARBARA TAYLOR BRADFORD ◆ T. ALAN BROUGHTON
PHYLLIS A. WHITNEY ◆ BARNABY CONRAD ◆ THOMAS FLEMING ◆ PATRICIA D. CORNWELL
JOHN LUTZ ◆ RICK DeMARINIS ◆ MARY HIGGINS CLARK ◆ MARCIA MULLER
MARSHA NORMAN ◆ EDWARD NOVAK ◆ RANDALL SILVIS ◆ HERBERT GOLD
ROGER ZELAZNY ◆ RICHARD MARTIN STERN ◆ ANN HARLEMAN ◆ LOIS LOWRY
MADELEINE L'ENGLE ◆ SAMM SINCLAIR BAKER ◆ DAVID KIRBY ◆ PATRICIA A. McKILLIP
JAMES CROSS GIBLIN ◆ EVE BUNTING ◆ GRAHAM MASTERTON ◆ ROSAMUNDE PILCHER
DONALD M. MURRAY ◆ LINDA PASTAN ◆ JAMES MELVILLE ◆ PETER MEINKE
JOAN LOWERY NIXON ◆ JOAN AIKEN ◆ JACK PRELUTSKY ◆ KATHERINE RAMSLAND

Part I of the 1993 edition covers background essentials for a successful writing career: the creative process, inspiration, persistence, journals, courses, reaching your reader, and how to respond to criticism. **Part II** covers writing techniques— the nuts and bolts used to create all types of material. **Part III**— Where to Sell— includes more than 3,000 up-to-date markets for a wide spectrum of magazines and publishers. **THE WRITER'S HANDBOOK** also includes lists of representative literary agents, writers' organizations, contests, awards, and grants.

An Alternate of the Book-of-the-Month Club   *Clothbound*   873 pages $29.95 *

❀   ❀   ❀   ❀   ❀   ❀   ❀

THE WRITER, INC., *Publishers*
120 Boylston Street, Boston, MA 02116-4615

* *Plus $2.75 for shipping and handling.*

Join America's most successful and soon-to-be-successful writers who read PUBLISHERS WEEKLY for profit and pleasure

Today, a serious author has to get up from the typewriter and get down to business. *The business of books.*

PUBLISHERS WEEKLY has been keeping authors informed about the business of books for over 100 years. Each issue gives you a broad and colorful overview of all that's new and newsworthy in the field...

Who's writing what. What kinds of books are selling now-and what kinds will sell best a year from now. Rights and permissions-for paperbacks, movies, TV. Author tours and publicity. Industry trends and prospects-and how they affect writers, agents, publishers and booksellers...

Book design and manufacturing. News of people in the field. Bookselling and marketing. The international scene. Media tie-ins. Calendars of upcoming events. Convention reports...

Of particular interest to you are the regular, in-depth interviews with writers who are making news today or will be making news tomorrow. They're men and women writing in all fields-from fiction to finance, poetry to politics and they all have valuable thoughts, experiences, ideas and working tips to share with you.

Each issue also brings you advance reviews-by PW's own expert critics-of approximately 100 hardcover and paperback books. These reviews appear *five or ten weeks before publication dates.* So you'll always know which books will be worth looking for-long before they're on bookstore library shelves.

Then there are the advertisements in PUBLISHERS WEEKLY-some 2800 pages a year. Surveys indicate that these book ads are particularly valuable to writers.

If you're serious about writing, the best thing to write today is your name and address on the PW subscription coupon below.

We can free the writer in you

I'm often asked when it was that I first knew I wanted to be a writer. I laugh and tell people it was the day I sold my first short story and I went out and bought a chandelier. But the truth is, as far back as I can remember, I believed there was a writer in me.

Of course, I didn't become a writer overnight. For the longest time, I didn't write at all. I did other things. I told myself I didn't have time to write. I had a family to raise, and besides, what could an everyday person like me have to write about that anyone would want to read?

I guess you could say that's when fate stepped in. I met an experienced writer, a pro, who listened to me and believed me when I said I wanted to write. She got me writing. She read what I wrote, encouraged me when it was good, gave me pointers when it wasn't so good. She freed the writer in me.

Today, I'm living my dream. I'm a professional writer and Director of NRI's School of Writing. I owe so much to my old friend. That's why I feel privileged now to be able to offer you the same kind of help she gave me.

One-on-one, professional guidance

Together with my colleagues at NRI, I've developed a new and complete at-home writing course to give you professional guidance from our team of successful writers.

As my friend was to me, these writers will be your instructors…even more,

Carol Bennett brings a remarkable range of writing and teaching skills to NRI. She has lectured on writing at two colleges and has published her short stories, poems, and feature articles in newspapers and business, trade, travel, and general interest magazines.

your mentors. They'll guide you, advise you, and help you believe in yourself as a writer.

In personal letters to you and in the margins of the work you send in, they'll give you specific, thoughtful recommendations on improving your technique. Word for word, line for line, they'll help you master the basics of good writing, then dare you to take risks and encourage you to excel. Soon, you'll be doing the kind of clean, clear, strong writing today's publishers pay well for — and readers love to read.

But that's not all. Your mentors will teach you something I learned only long after I'd been writing professionally: how to use a computer not only to write efficiently, but to write freely and with abandon, and to perfect and polish your work for publication.

IBM-compatible computer and software included

I love my computer — and so does every writer I know who uses one. That's why I'm happy to tell you that NRI, unlike any other writing school, includes an IBM-compatible computer and software in your at-home writing course.

Your computer won't do the writing for you, but take it from me, it will take the drudgery out of writing, allowing you to edit and reorganize your work at the touch of a button. Even better, it will free you to experiment; to play with words, sentences, phrases; to write off the top of your head; to be as creative as you truly can be.

I admit, I was a little bit nervous about using a computer in the beginning, but I soon discovered how easy it was. Now, I wouldn't be without one. I truly believe my computer has helped me be a faster, more creative, better writer. I know yours will do the same for you.

Free NRI School of Writing catalog

I'd like to tell you everything about NRI's new at-home writing course, but there's just not enough room here. So I invite you to send for your free NRI catalog. In it you'll find all the details about NRI's at-home writing course, including complete descriptions of your computer, lessons, and writing projects.

One final thought: as a professional writer, I know the thrill of seeing my name in print and being paid for what I love to do. I can tell you, there's no more rewarding life than the writing life. So if something deep down inside of you says "I want to be a writer," I urge you to send for your free NRI catalog today.

Just fill out and mail the coupon or write to us at NRI School of Writing, McGraw-Hill Continuing Education Center, 4401 Connecticut Avenue, NW, Washington, DC 20008.

Sincerely,

Carol Bennett

Carol Bennett
Director, NRI School of Writing

NRI *School of Writing*
McGraw-Hill Continuing Education Center
4401 Connecticut Avenue, NW
Washington, DC 20008

YES! Please rush me my free catalog describing NRI's new at-home writing course. I'm interested in writing (check one):

❑ FICTION   ❑ NONFICTION

NAME	(please print)	AGE

ADDRESS

CITY

| STATE | ZIP | 3201-0293 |

PORTLAND STATE UNIVERSITY

Haystack

PROGRAM ┃ IN THE ARTS & SCIENCES

The PSU Haystack Program in the Arts & Sciences is one of the most outstanding programs of its kind in the nation.

One-week and weekend workshops from the end of June through the first week of August provide exciting writing opportunities at the inspired setting of the north Oregon Coast.

Haystack's success is based on sound academic quality; most courses are available for optional credit at the undergraduate and graduate level. A dazzling corps of instructors, well-known to the writing world of the Pacific Northwest and beyond, provide consistently high instruction. Writing instructors have included: Molly Gloss, Ursula Le Guin, Craig Lesley, Tom Spanbauer, William Stafford, and many others.

For a brochure or further information, please call or write:

Haystack Program in the Arts & Sciences
PSU Summer Session
PO Box 751
Portland, OR 97207

(503)725-4081

Toll-free: 1-800-547-8887

Northwest Writing Institute
of Lewis & Clark College

Please join us for the following programs:
☐ Courses in Imaginative Writing
☐ Magazine Article Writing
☐ Oregon Writing Project
☐ Bard Workshops in Writing and Thinking
☐ Workshops for Young Writers
☐ Oregon Folk Arts
— *Kim R. Stafford, Director*

For information contact:
Northwest Writing Institute
Campus Box 100
Lewis & Clark College
Portland, Oregon 97219
503-768-7745

Portland & Eugene
Desktop Publishing Certificate Program

The University of Oregon Continuation Center has developed an exciting program to meet the needs of graphic designers, production managers and people involved in the desktop publishing field.

The desktop publisher of the 90's needs to have a solid background in design concepts and traditional publication techniques, project management and be current with leading edge applications.

Nowhere can you acquire the blending of these seemingly disparate skills. . . until now.

Write now for more information:
Desktop Publishing Certificate
UO Continuation Center
1553 Moss Street
Eugene, OR 97403

Call Kassia Dellabough for information:
toll-free inside Oregon 1-800-824-2714,
or 503-346-3537 outside Oregon.

University of Oregon
CONTINUATION CENTER

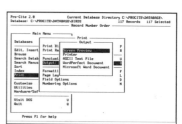

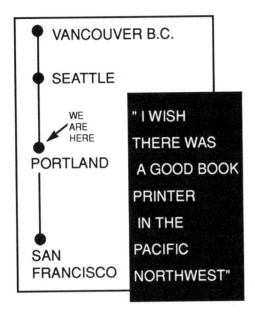

VANCOUVER B.C.

SEATTLE

WE ARE HERE

PORTLAND

SAN FRANCISCO

" I WISH THERE WAS A GOOD BOOK PRINTER IN THE PACIFIC NORTHWEST"

906 NW 14th PORTLAND, OR 97209

WISHES DO COME TRUE! QUALITY, DEPENDABLE DELIVERY, AND COMPETITIVE PRICING ARE NOW YOURS.

NETWORK GRAPHICS

503-223-5226

FAX 503-294-0228

If you haven't been able to find the phone number of the

Sylvia Beach Hotel,

it's (503) 265-5428. It's probably the only hotel for book lovers in the world.

SUNG IN PRINTING AMERICA

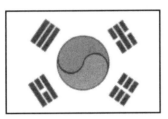

Where Quality And Service Are The Languages Of Our Seoul

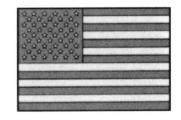

The partnership between an American customer service team and Korean craftsmen translates into quality results that speak for themselves.

Your American service representative communicates your needs to our parent company, Sung In Printing Co. Ltd. of Seoul, Korea. Your entire project — from pre-press to final binding — is handled in-house by our team of dedicated technicians, using the most advanced equipment in the world.

SUNG IN PRINTING AMERICA, INC.
901 Mariner's Island Blvd. #525
San Mateo, CA 94404
(Headquarters)
(415) 578-0206; Fax (415) 578-0805

1939 S.E. Hawthorne
Portland, OR 97214
(503) 238-2556; Fax (503) 239-5734
Contact: Ron Wilks

Your American team oversees all details – quotes, delivery of proofs, customs clearance and final delivery to your requested destination.

By combining quality with local service, Sung In Printing Company has become Korea's largest supplier of full color printing to the U.S. and Canadian publishing industry.

For some straight talk on your next multi-color book or calendar, call or write Ron Wilks today.

THE FINE ART OF TECHNICAL WRITING

KEY POINTS TO HELP YOU THINK YOUR
WAY THROUGH WRITING
SCIENTIFIC OR TECHNICAL PUBLICATIONS,
THESES, TERM PAPERS, & BUSINESS
REPORTS

"Concise and useful. This will be to technical writers what Strunk and White has been to all — always close at hand."
— *John Gordon, Dean,*
Yale School of Forestry and
Environmental Studies

"A wealth of facts packed into a compact presentation…concise, connected, and an interesting read. It is also very human."
—*Journal of the Society for*
Technical Communication

"An outspoken enemy of long-winded, pretentious writing…a friendly little paperback that will hold your hand as you contemplate starting [to write]."
—*Editorial Workshop*

The book's premise — that technical writing is a creative act — is meant to explode the prevailing myth that the process of writing about "dry" subject matter is itself mechanical. To write well, one must think, not only about content but about form, and thinking is never mechanical. Through this book, rich with examples, writers will recognize both the structural pitfalls that weaken technical writing and the misguided attitudes that deaden it.

$7.95 + $2.50 S&H, paper, 112 pages, 5 ½ x 8 ½
Blue Heron Publishing, Inc., 24450 NW Hansen Rd., Hillsboro, Oregon 97124 § 503.621-3911

Writing & Fishing   Extinction   Sex, Family, Tribe

URSULA Le GUIN, WALLACE STEGNER, WILLIAM STAFFORD, BARRY LOPEZ, WILLIAM GIBSON, KEN KESEY, COLLEEN McELROY, CHARLES JOHNSON, TESS GALLAGHER, CRAIG LESLEY, and others...

LEFT BANK

Semiannual collections of thematic writing. At your favorite bookstore, or send $7.95 each (add $2.50 S&H for the 1st book and 75¢ for each add'l) to Blue Heron Publishing, 24450 NW Hansen Road, Hillsboro, OR 97124 or by credit card at 503/621-3911.

WRITER'S N.W.

Supplement *Writer's Northwest Handbook* with this quarterly tabloid (75,000 readership) and keep up with:

• Issues, resources, news, and tips covering topics such as censorship, new magazines, technical writing, cover design, sexist language, working with printers
• Articles by and interviews with leading authors such as James Welch, Marilynne Robinson, Larry Colton, Tom Spanbauer
• Updated market listings and resources
• Reviews of Northwest books; software reviews
• Calendar of events

Build the community of the printed word.
Subscribe now!

I read **WRITER'S NW**; I support it; and I'd love to keep it coming to my door.

☐ Yes! Enter my 1-year subscription. My $10 ($12 US in Canada) is enclosed.

☐ I'd like to help even more; here's my contribution of

name

address

city/state/zip

phone

Pay by check, MO, VISA, or MC in US$ to Media Weavers.

CC Type   *CC #*   *Exp. Date*